Tense and Aspect in Second Language Acquisition: Form, Meaning, and Use

Language Learning Monograph Series

Richard Young, Editor
Alexander Z. Guiora, General Editor

Schumann:
The Neurobiology of Affect in Language

Bardovi-Harlig:
Tense and Aspect in Second Language Acquisition: Form, Meaning, and Use

Tense and Aspect in Second Language Acquisition: Form, Meaning, and Use

Kathleen Bardovi-Harlig
Indiana University

BLACKWELL
Publishers

© 2000 Language Learning Research Club, University of Michigan

Blackwell Publishers, Inc.
350 Main Street
Malden, MA 02148 USA

Blackwell Publishers, Ltd.
108 Cowley Road
Oxford OX4 1JF
United Kingdom

0-63122-149-2
A CIP catalog record for this book is available
from the Library of Congress

To Jeff
husband and friend

To Regina and Alexandra
queens and muses,
and makers of crowns

Contents

Foreword

If we trace the beginning of the systematic study of second language acquisition to Werner Leopold's 10-year diary study of the simultaneous acquisition of English and German by his daughter Hildegard, then the field is just over 50 years old. The knowledge that scholars have accreted over this half century—particularly since the 1970s—has given us a panoramic picture of the linguistic and psychological processes that learners experience on the path to bilingualism. The big picture, however, is in fact more like a collage of several smaller ones: detailed studies of specific learners and of particular areas of language. This volume in the *Language Learning* Monograph Series presents one part of the picture in depth and in detail: learners' talk about time.

Because all activity takes place in time, all languages have ways in which speakers talk about time. Speakers make distinctions between the moment of utterance and the time of an event. The event may, for example, occur before, after, or at the same time as the utterance that references it. And speakers have ways of distinguishing among different temporal organizations of an event—whether, for example, they view the event as a bounded whole or whether they choose to focus inside the temporal boundaries of the event. Most scholars have referred to these two kinds of time talk as tense and aspect, and have looked inside the verb phrase, in particular at verbal morphology, for their realization in linguistic form.

While the study of European languages has focused on verbal morphology as the principal means of time talk, the study of interlanguage reveals that second language learners, as indeed all speakers, have a varied repertoire for talk about time that extends beyond verbal morphology. The speech and writing of second language learners evidence lexical resources for referencing time, such as time adverbials, as well as discourse resources, such as sequencing verbs to reflect the chronological order of the events they reference.

Thanks to the work that Kathleen Bardovi-Harlig and her colleagues have done over the past two decades, we now know more about second language learners' time talk than about any other area of interlanguage. There is no other area of SLA where the total picture of acquisition has been described as comprehensively as Bardovi-Harlig has done in this volume. She does so by describing the linguistic phenomena in depth and by placing those phenomena in a broad social context.

There are two approaches to the in-depth study of time talk, each associated with different linguistic traditions. In the tradition of European studies, the researcher starts with temporal semantics and then investigates the linguistic means that learners use to express temporal concepts. In the North American tradition, researchers look first at verbal morphology and then go on to investigate the patterns of emergent and developing verbal morphology. Bardovi-Harlig reviews both research traditions in her book and shows how different research methods and research findings are inextricably connected.

The volume is also broad in scope. Time talk occurs in a sociocultural context, and Bardovi-Harlig investigates the relation between time talk and the contexts in which it is elicited. She shows that discourse context—in particular learners' creation of narrative—is important in accounting for interindividual variation in time talk. And she conducts an important analysis of the role of instruction in the acquisition of verbal morphology based on her own longitudinal data. This investigation confirms two pedagogical principles: the teachability hypothesis, according to which the effects of instruction on the developing interlanguage are constrained by the learner's current stage of acquisition; and the quality of interaction hypothesis, according to which intensity of interaction in the target language is more important in aiding interlanguage development than is the length of the learner's stay in the host language community.

Bardovi-Harlig's "Tense and Aspect in Second Language Acquisition: Form, Meaning, and Use" is the second volume in the *Language Learning* Monograph Series. The volumes in the series review recent findings and current theoretical positions, present new data and interpretations, and sketch interdisciplinary research programs. Each volume is an authoritative statement by a scholar who has led in the development of a particular line of interdisciplinary research and is intended to serve as a benchmark for interdisciplinary research in the years to come. Bardovi-Harlig's book provides a rich resource for current and future researchers in the acquisition of temporality in a second language.

Richard Young
University of Wisconsin–Madison

Acknowledgments

The present book is the culmination of a decade of research carried out with learners at the Intensive English Program, Center for English Language Training, at Indiana University. Many learners, language teachers, graduate students, and colleagues at Indiana University and in the wider academic community contributed to the research that is reported here. First, I would like to thank all the learners who participated in the various studies, particularly the students who participated in the longitudinal study and whose progress is reported in several chapters. I would also like to thank the numerous teachers for their cooperation in completing the teaching logs, bringing their classes for the interviews and films, and contributing to the data collection. The directors of the Intensive English Program, Marlin Howard and Susan Greer, were invaluable to all my studies, facilitating the data collection and keeping track of learners and teachers for almost 3 full years for the longitudinal study alone. The director of the Center for English Language Training and chair of TESOL and Applied Linguistics, Harry L. Gradman, was a valuable consultant and sounding board through every stage of the project, from the grant proposal to the completion of this book. His support means more than I can say.

I would like thank to the National Science Foundation, who supported my dream to carry out a large-scale longitudinal study through Grant DBS-8919616 from 1989–1992. I am also grateful to the College of Arts and Sciences, Small Grants Program, at Indiana University, for funding the narrative project reported in Chapter 5, and to the Center for English Language Training for support, research assistants and research assistance, and access to their students over many years.

I am indebted to Roger Andersen for his many appraisals of my work in various stages over the years, for valuable prepublication manuscripts, and for his friendship, and to Yas Shirai for his good-natured intellectual challenges ever since we met. I thank my colleague Beverly Hartford for many discussions about tense and aspect in second language acquisition.

Several of my present and former graduate students contributed to my work in important ways. I thank my research assistants who helped in innumerable ways, Dudley Reynolds, my head research assistant during the longitudinal study, and Tom Salsbury, my research assistant during the preparation of the book, responsible for the technical production of the numerous tables and figures herein. I also thank Anna Bergström, Leyla Hasbún, and John Moses, graduate students whose interest in tense and aspect has infused life into the intellectual inquiry.

Several people read the manuscript and gave me valuable feedback: my colleagues Roger Andersen and Yas Shirai, my graduate students Llorenç Comajoan and Deborah Burleson, and three anonymous reviewers. There could be no better series editor than Richard Young, whose enthusiasm never failed. My thanks finally to Alexander Z. Guiora, the general editor of *Language Learning*, for his commitment to this book from the proposal stage to the very end.

My interest in tense and aspect in second language acquisition was sparked by the work on tense and aspect in Hungarian of my husband and fellow student at the University of Chicago, Jeff Harlig. Last and most of all, I thank my family for the love and support that sees me through all of my work.

CHAPTER ONE

The Study of Time Talk in Second Language Acquisition

This book is about the acquisition of temporal expression in second language. Temporal expression, or what C. Smith (1980) has called "time talk," has come into its own as an area of research in adult second language acquisition. The investigation of temporal expression includes all linguistic means of reference to time, although it will be most familiar to the reader in its morphological instantiation. The study of tense-aspect morphology has been the focus of many descriptive and pedagogical accounts of language. In fact, tense-aspect morphology occupies a central place in the curricula of many language programs. It is not uncommon for language teaching programs to include mastery of certain tense-aspect forms in their criteria for advancement from one course to another, and tense and aspect clearly play an important role in grammatically focused pedagogical materials. Although the pedagogy of tense and aspect has received a great deal of attention, the acquisition of tense-aspect systems has received relatively little attention in comparison. However, momentum has been growing for the investigation of the acquisition of tense and aspect, beginning with seminal studies by American and European researchers in the mid-1980s. This has gradually begun to include investigations of the relationship between instruction and the acquisition of tense-aspect, increasing the prospects of an acquisitionally informed pedagogy.

However, it is not just its familiarity that makes the temporal system, and particularly tense-aspect, a viable target of second language acquisition research. Temporal expression is at once both varied and limited. The definable area of time talk proscribes the area of investigation, and is thus limited, but means of time talk are varied. Lexical means of referring to time, such as adverbs, and discourse principles, such as chronological order, interact with tense-aspect morphology. The set of tense-aspect morphemes in any one target language is finite, forming a closed set, and is therefore limited. The acquisition of any one part of the system has an effect on the other parts of the system. For example, the emergence of a new tense-aspect morpheme and the ensuing form-meaning association may have an effect not only on other form-meaning associations but also on other means of temporal expression such as time adverbials or dependence on chronological order. Thus, within the expression of temporal semantics we find a subsystem of language with many of the characteristics of the larger linguistic system, which at the same time is limited enough to study closely. This monograph draws together the research on the acquisition of temporal expression of which tense and aspect form a part.

In many ways the development of research on the acquisition of systems of temporal expression reflects the development of research in second language acquisition in general: from early inquiry that investigated acquisition and accuracy orders across grammatical subsystems to recent, domain-specific inquiries that have developed largely independently of research into other areas of the interlanguage grammar. After the investigations of accuracy orders that characterized much of the work involving tense-aspect through the 1970s, the published work of the 1980s reflected a shift in interest to the semantics that structure the tense-aspect system. Temporal semantics became the focus of investigation on two distinct fronts. On the North American front, research into the distribution of verbal morphology in emergent second language temporal systems was fueled by the identification of a semantically determined acquisition sequence in child language acquisition. On the European front, investigation into the expression of meaning took precedence over the investigation of the distribution of form. Both lines of inquiry have been extremely fruitful and have been pursued by researchers from both the North American and European traditions.

This book can be read from three perspectives, each of which develops across chapters. First, the book is about the acquisition of temporal expression. A reader will find descriptions of acquisitional stages for a number of European languages, discussions of principles of acquisition, and proposed universals. Second, the book is about how we study the acquisition of temporal expression. Each chapter presents a distinct theoretical or analytic framework that informs inquiry into temporal expression. On one hand, examining multiple approaches leads to a fuller description of time talk (the first perspective). On the other hand, the approaches themselves contribute a view of acquisition not available from the other approaches, including, for example, what facets of language should be investigated. The book is also about the research methods used to collect data on time talk and the analyses used to interpret those data. Although certain frameworks may favor certain methods and analyses, researchers still employ a significant range of methods in any area of investigation. Finally, the book is as much as an invitation to do research in second language temporal expression as it is a summary and synthesis of the research that has been conducted thus far. Although far more is known about the acquisition of temporality in second language than at any previous time, inquiry has by no means been exhausted. I hope readers will find many interesting questions for research in each of the perspectives presented in this book.

This chapter provides an introduction to the study of the acquisition of time talk in second language research. It begins with the first studies of tense-aspect morphology, which were concerned with the occurrence of the grammatical morphemes in interlanguage. It then introduces later inquiries that investigated form-meaning associations within the developing system of temporal expression. Lastly, it outlines the presentation of the following chapters.

Early Studies of Verbal Morphology

The first studies to include tense-aspect morphology did so incidentally. These approaches to the study of tense-aspect morphology are important not only for their historical value, but also for their continuing influence in the field. There were essentially two types of studies that investigated tense-aspect morphology as part of other questions: studies of morpheme order and studies of phonetic constraints. The following sections review each of these in turn.

The Morpheme Order Studies

Morpheme order studies did not investigate the emergent tense-aspect system in its own right, but included verbal morphology as examples of grammatical morphemes that also included the plural and possessive, prepositions, articles, auxiliaries, and the copula. Modeled on the morpheme studies of child language acquisition (e.g., Brown, 1973; de Villiers & de Villiers, 1973), large cross-sectional studies of L2 learners of English as a second language investigated a similar range of morphemes. Separating the verbal morphology from the other morphemes included in the early studies revealed a single order of verbal morphemes for both children and adults: -*ing*, irregular past, and third person singular -*s* (Andersen, 1978; Bailey, Madden, & Krashen, 1974; Dulay & Burt, 1973; VanPatten, 1984).[1] Later studies of second language acquisition investigated the order of the regular and irregular past, revealing some variation: Rank order studies found that the regular past preceded the irregular past for children and adults (Dulay & Burt, 1974; Larsen-Freeman, 1975). In contrast, hierarchical ordering of morphemes (e.g., Krashen, 1977) placed irregular past before regular past. Andersen's (1978) implicational model, which tested individual scores against group scores, found that although group scores place irregular past before regular past in accuracy, a test for individual fit to this order determined that irregular and regular past are unordered with respect to each other in his data. He argued that grouping data from different learners obscures important individual variation. Longitudinal studies of individual child learners suggested other orders: irregular before regular (Hakuta, 1974) and simultaneous acquisition (Rosansky, 1976). Interest in the acquisition of regular and irregular past has continued beyond the morpheme order studies: Longitudinal studies have supported the irregular-before-regular order originally identified in the rank order studies.[2]

Pursuing the study of accuracy orders from a variationist viewpoint, Ellis (1987) investigated style-shifting of three realizations of English past tense: regular and irregular past, and the past copula. Ellis found different accuracy orders for planned written narratives, planned oral narratives, and unplanned oral narratives; however, the irregular past itself showed little variation in the rate of appropriate use across conditions. In contrast, the regular past and past copula showed greater variation in rates of appropriate use as well as in rank order. The relation of tense-aspect morphology to styles arose again in a slightly different form as researchers compared findings across elicitation tasks and more subtly across variations of the same discourse types (Bardovi-Harlig, 1994a, 1999a; Comajoan, 1998; Noyau, 1990; Wiberg, 1996).

The chief flaw of morpheme studies lay in their focus on the end point of acquisition (Andersen, 1977, 1978; Hatch & Wagner-Gough, 1975). Dittmar (1981) observed that "the criterion approach" (used in the morpheme order studies) treats a feature of acquisition as if the morpheme and its meaning were "indissolubly wedded; or at least, shows no interest in either form or meaning until they reach 80% or 90% appropriate use" (p. 146). From the point of view of understanding the emerging temporal system, studies that focus on high rates of both accuracy (well-formedness) and appropriate use of tense-aspect morphology focus on the endpoint of acquisition and not the arguably more interesting process of acquisition. Moreover, focusing on the endpoint of acquisition, especially in the acquisition of tense and aspect, ignores most of a learner's developmental history.

Later studies lent quantitative support to Dittmar's claim that form and meaning should be considered separately in acquisition. An error analysis of composition exams written by advanced learners of English found 7.5 times more errors in the use of tense-aspect morphology than in the form (Bardovi-Harlig & Bofman, 1989). Accuracy rates (or form) were also significantly higher than rates of appropriate use (meaning) of tense-aspect morphology in cloze passages and compositions matched for topic (Bardovi-Harlig, 1992a). Similarly, Klein (1993, 1994a) identified a stage in the acquisition of temporal expression in which verbal morphology appears without targetlike functions, a stage that he sums up as "form precedes function" (1994a, p. 244).

Thus, a review of morpheme order studies shows that the early studies examined the order of acquisition of the morphemes themselves, but did not investigate the acquisition of verbal morphology as representing a tense-aspect system in its own right. Furthermore, the investigation of emergent temporal semantics could only begin once accuracy and appropriate use—or form and meaning—had been disentangled.

Phonetic Constraints

The studies of phonetic constraints on past-tense use maintained the focus on the morpheme. These studies attempted to account for the frequency with which verbs occurred with past morphology. The analyses went beyond the simple investigation of irregular and regular past morphology begun by the morpheme order studies to investigate differences in the realization of the simple past tense within the categories of regular and irregular past. These studies showed that the phonetic realization of the past tense was dependent on phonological environments. This is of particular significance in English where the regular past creates word-final consonant clusters.

Wolfram (1984, 1985, 1989; Wolfram & Hatfield, 1986) hypothesized that phonological salience determines the distribution of simple past morphology across phonetic environments. The principle of saliency has two main claims: (a) that irregular verbs will show greater tense marking than regular verbs; and (b) that the phonetic shape of the past tense of the verb and the following phonological environment will further determine the likelihood of its exhibiting past tense. (In his work Wolfram refers to "tense unmarking." For ease of comparison with other studies, I will discuss his work in terms of presence of marking.)

Working with conversational interviews of 16 Vietnamese learners of English, Wolfram (1985) showed that for regular verbs, the most likely verbs to be marked are those with syllabic past [ɪd], followed by [d], then clusters (all [t] forms). Clusters are more likely to surface before a vowel (e.g., *missed it*) than before a consonant (e.g., *missed me*; Wolfram 1985, p. 235). In a study of 32 Vietnamese ESL learners, Wolfram (1989) showed that among the irregular verbs, marking is the most likely when the past is least like the nonpast form. Marking is most likely with suppletives (*be*), then internal vowel change with suffix (*sleep/slept*), internal vowel change (*come/came*), and modal (*will/would*); it is least likely with replacives (*have/had*). Word-final consonants and consonant clusters are less likely to surface when they result from the past tense than when they are part of a lexical stem.

Bayley (1991, 1994) showed that both phonetic saliency (Wolfram, 1985, 1989) and the semantics of verbs are relevant to the distribution of interlanguage tense marking. In this section I focus on the phonetic constraints. Bayley collected oral personal narratives from 20 Mandarin-speaking learners of English as a second language. The learners were divided into two broad levels of proficiency: 10 learners with TOEFL scores of 550 and higher and 10 with TOEFL scores of 510 or lower (pre-TOEFL). Bayley found that "the more salient the phonetic difference between the past and present tense forms of the verb, the more likely a past-reference verb is to be marked for tense" (1994, p. 170). Bayley posited the following hierarchy, from the most likely to be marked to the least: suppletive (*be*), doubly marked (*sleep/slept*), internal vowel (*sing/sang*), change in final segment (*send/sent*), weak syllabic (*pat/patted*), and modal. Although the hierarchy posited by

Wolfram and colleagues and later by Bayley is specific to English, work by Lafford (1996) suggests that phonological salience (in the form of ultimate stress) may be relevant to the formation of the preterite by adult learners of Spanish as a second language.

Phonological constraints also interact with a learner's L1 phonological structure. Wolfram's work on American Indian English suggested that the first language may influence the phonological realization of verbal morphology. Wolfram (1984) compared the use of the regular past tense by two Pueblos: Pueblo A, whose ancestral language lacks word-final consonant clusters, and Pueblo B, whose ancestral language allows them. The use of past tense in past time contexts for regular verbs ending in clusters (e.g., *walked* [kt], or *bobbed* [bd]) was consistently higher for Pueblo B than Pueblo A.

In a longitudinal study, Sato (1986, 1990) found that two Vietnamese-speaking children learning English as a second language used the irregular past more frequently as they had more contact with English. However, neither child exhibited any use of the regular past, with the exception of one token in the eighth month of the study. Because Vietnamese does not permit word-final consonant clusters (Nguyen, 1987; Sato, 1984), Sato concluded that Vietnamese syllable structure constrained the production of syllable-final consonant clusters created by the English past tense. However, not all regular past verbs end in consonant clusters, as verbs such as *allowed* and *voted* show. Because Vietnamese has a tendency toward syllables that end in consonants (Sato, 1984), L1 syllable constraints should not operate on the pronunciation of all past-tense verbs, just the ones that end in consonant clusters. Thus, pronunciation cannot be entirely responsible for the lack of production of regular past.[3]

The influence of a learner's L2 phonology may also confound task effects. Ellis's (1987) study of variation showed clear task effects: Learners of English as a second language from mixed language backgrounds (German, French, Spanish, Portuguese, Polish, Farsi, Japanese, and Korean) showed the highest use of regular past in planned writing, less in planned oral narratives, and still less in unplanned oral narratives (77%, 57%, and 43% use respectively). Ellis found much more modest differences in the use of regular past in written and oral narratives than those found by Bardovi-Harlig (1992b). In the latter study, two intermediate learners of English as a second language, one a native speaker of Korean and one a native speaker of Chinese, showed 87% and 88% appropriate use of past tense in past time contexts in the written narratives but only 23% and 15% respectively in the elicited oral narratives. This greater distance between oral and written production suggests that phonological constraints may be operating in addition to other task effects. Neither Chinese nor Korean allows consonant clusters word finally, and neither has voiced stops in word-final position (Kim, 1987; Li & Thompson, 1987).[4] L1 phonology could influence the pronunciation of the allomorphs of simple past.[5] However, a learner's stage of interlanguage phonological development must also be taken into account because other Chinese and Korean learners in the study showed much less difference between oral and written tasks, more like the learners in the study by Ellis. Although these data are anecdotal in that the study did not attempt to test the development of interlanguage phonology and its influence on the pronunciation of simple past in English, my point here is that oral production may reflect a learner's pronunciation as much as his or her morphological development, and that pronunciation may interact with other task effects.

Like the morpheme order studies, the investigation of the phonetic realization of the past focused on the morphology itself rather than on the emerging system of tense and aspect. The phonetic characteristics of the past are independent of its meaning. In the remainder of this chapter I focus on studies that hold meaning to be central in the investigation of the acquisition of tense and aspect. Nevertheless, even as we focus on meaning, it is important to keep in mind, that, as Sato (1986, 1990) cautioned, a learner's interlanguage phonology is likely to be relevant whenever an oral sample is collected. For researchers who study the acquisition of English, the phonological issue is particularly important because of the syllable structures (closed syllables and consonant clusters) created by the regular past. However, every analyst must deal with the interlanguage phonology of learners, no matter what language is investigated (see for example Harley & Swain, 1978, on the acquisition of French).

Investigating the Expression of Temporality

The shift in focus in the 1980s from the acquisition of morphology as form to a focus on morphology as the surface realization of an underlying semantic system derived from an interest in the semantics of interlanguage in general and temporal semantics in particular. Advances in theories of temporal semantics and cross-linguistic studies of primary languages in the 1970s and 1980s laid a further foundation for the study of emergent temporal semantics in second language acquisition. In the study of the acquisition of systems of temporal expression three concepts are crucial: tense, grammatical aspect, and lexical aspect. *Tense* locates an event or situation on the time line. In English, *John loves Mary* (present) and *John loved Mary* (past) show a difference in tense. *Grammatical aspect* provides a means of expressing one's view of a situation or event. For example, we may view a event as completed or continuing. *John sang* (simple past) and *John was singing* (past progressive) show a contrast in grammatical aspect, although both are in the past tense. *Lexical aspect* deals with the semantics of a predicate. For example, a predicate may express a state or an action (compare *John seems happy* and *John swims*), or an action with duration or one that has no duration (*John changed the tire* and *John recognized Mary*). Within second language acquisition research, two main strands of inquiry can be distinguished: the meaning-oriented approach, which investigates the expression of semantic concepts through various linguistic devices; and the form-oriented approach, which investigates the distribution of verbal morphology as an indicator of the underlying semantic system of interlanguage. Unlike the phonological and morpheme order studies, research in both traditions suggests that semantic features may be applicable to a range of languages, if not universal. Both the meaning-oriented and the form-oriented approaches take an interlanguage perspective, describing the interlanguage as a system independent of the target language. Both strands of research have been fruitful, not only in yielding important findings, but also in drawing new researchers into the area of inquiry.

The functional form-oriented studies (also known as form-to-function studies, e.g., Long & Sato, 1984; Sato, 1990) and the formal form-oriented perspective (Berretta, 1995) follow a particular form and ask how and where it is used by learners, thus determining what it means in the system. In the study of temporal expression, the forms that are investigated include tense-aspect morphemes such as the simple past in English, the preterite and imperfect in Spanish, and the passé composé and imparfait in French. The meaning-oriented studies (also known as the concept-oriented approach, von Stutterheim & Klein, 1987, the semantically oriented approach, Giacalone Ramat, 1992, the functional-grammatical perspective, Skiba & Dittmar, 1992, the notional perspective, Berretta, 1995, and function-to-form studies, Long & Sato, 1984; Sato, 1990; see also Trévise & Porquier, 1986) investigate a particular concept and ask how it is expressed. In the meaning-oriented studies it is as though the researcher sets up a window on interlanguage and looks through it to see the range of linguistic devices used to express a particular concept. Meaning-oriented approaches have been used successfully to study the acquisition of expressions of spatial relations (Becker & Carroll, 1997), reference (Broeder, 1995), and—of particular interest to this review—temporality (Dietrich, Klein, & Noyau, 1995).

In the study of temporal expression, an investigation might follow how learners express the concept of the past or of the future. This means that a study following the meaning-oriented approach will investigate different types of linguistic devices, which not only cross grammatical categories, but which mix grammatical devices with pragmatic ones. For example, we might find that to express past a learner would draw on chronological order of a text, time adverbials, and/or past morphology.

The meaning-oriented approach is a functional approach and may seem at first blush to be antithetical to the grammar-focused inquiry that has dominated American second language acquisition research. Nevertheless, the approaches can be viewed in relation to one another as in Figure 1.1.

The meaning-oriented approach has identified three main stages of development in the acquisition of temporal expression: the pragmatic stage, the lexical stage, and the morphological

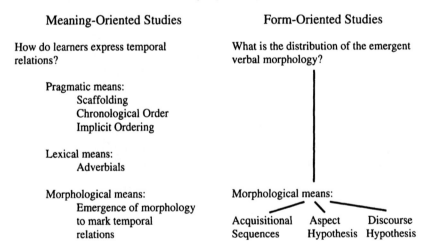

Figure 1.1. Overview of studies of temporal expression in second language acquisition

stage. By stage of acquisition I mean a developmental period that can be characterized by the use of a particular feature. The concept of stage is used widely in the study of the acquisition of temporal semantics by a range of researchers from different theoretical backgrounds (e.g., Andersen 1986a, 1986b, 1989, 1991; Dietrich et al., 1995). For example, the meaning-oriented approach may characterize a stage by the use of adverbials and connectives to make temporal reference, and by the absence of verbal morphology. That means that the dominant means of temporal reference is lexical, but it does not mean that features from an earlier stage or a later stage are entirely absent. Likewise, a form-oriented study may describe a stage as being characterized by the use of simple past with a certain category of verbs. That means that the dominant tense-aspect morpheme is the simple past, but it does not mean that other tense-aspect morphology is never used, or that the past is not used elsewhere. The boundaries of stages are not abrupt because the acquisition of temporal expression is gradual. Nevertheless, it is possible to identify stages in the development of interlanguage temporality by identifying the characteristic means of expression of each stage. As Figure 1.1 shows, the meaning-oriented approach identifies three stages of which the morphological stage is only one and, in fact, the last one.

The meaning-oriented approach represents the inquiry of larger scope. It investigates all means of temporal expression for a particular concept, including pragmatic devices (such as use of chronological order or building on an interlocutor's discourse that provides temporal reference), lexical means (such as the use of temporal adverbials), and verbal morphology. Form-oriented inquiry concentrates only the third means, namely verbal morphology. Form-oriented inquiry, in turn, has investigated three main areas: acquisitional sequences, the influence of lexical aspect, and the influence of discourse structure. Studies of acquisitional sequences describe the order of emergence of tense-aspect morphology, the meaning associated with each form, and the contrasts between form-meaning associations. These studies are reviewed in Chapter 3. Studies of the influence of lexical aspect (labelled as the aspect hypothesis in Figure 1.1) investigate the emergence and distribution of tense-aspect morphology relative to the inherent temporal semantics of the verb and its arguments. Chapter 4 contains a discussion of these studies. Studies of the influence of narrative structure (labelled the discourse hypothesis in Figure 1.1) examine the influence of narrative structure and the informational function of predicates on the emergence and distribution of tense-aspect morphology. The dual influences of lexical aspect and narrative structure are discussed in Chapter 5. Finally, the investigation of the influence of instruction cuts across the other approaches to understanding temporal expression. Researchers working within each approach have collected language samples from both instructed and uninstructed learners. This issue is addressed in Chapter 6.

Methods of Research and Analysis

Although concerns of research methodology are not unique to the study of tense and aspect, I review particular facets of research method and analysis throughout this book to highlight the interplay of research design and subsequent findings. Many of the suggestions for future research rest on recommendations of changes, expansions, or comparisons of different research designs. On the one hand, the breadth of the research designs shows the extent to which the findings are supported. Many studies come to the same conclusions even though they draw from different learner populations, study different target languages, or elicit data by different means. On the other hand, differences in research design and analysis can also introduce subtle differences in the findings.

Studies of the acquisition of temporality have included both second (host environment) and foreign language learners. Learners in the host environment have included both instructed and uninstructed learners. A range of target languages has also been investigated, among them English, French, German, Italian, Spanish, Swedish, and, recently, Japanese. Studies have also been conducted with different designs, ranging from case studies of single learners to longitudinal studies of both small and large groups to small and large cross-sectional studies. Researchers have met the challenge of describing and comparing learners according to their interlanguage development in a variety of ways: by stage along the basi-meso-acro-lang continuum (Robison, 1990; Schumann, 1987), time (in the case of longitudinal studies; Bardovi-Harlig, 1994b, 1997a; Dietrich et al., 1995; Housen, 1993, 1994; Sato, 1990), features of their emergent systems (Bardovi-Harlig, 1994b, 1997a, 1998; Bardovi-Harlig & Bergström, 1996; Bhardwaj, Dietrich, & Noyau, 1988; Collins, 1997; Dietrich et al., 1995), multitest placement in language programs (Bardovi-Harlig & Reynolds, 1995), placement in university language courses (Bergström, 1995; Hasbún, 1995; Martínez Baztán, 1994; Ramsay, 1990), length of study (Buczowska & Weist, 1991), and oral proficiency interview (OPI) ratings (Lafford, 1996; Liskin-Gasparro, 1997). Describing the proficiency of learners presents a continuing challenge to researchers in all areas of second language acquisition research (Thomas, 1994).

The analysis of the use of temporal expression has been based on language samples that have been elicited in a variety of ways: by observation of talk on a daily basis (Rohde, 1996, based on the data of Wode, 1981) or conversational interviews (Bardovi-Harlig, 1997b; Bayley, 1994; Kumpf, 1984b; Robison, 1990). Personal narratives have also been collected, as part of a conversational interview or elicited directly (Liskin-Gasparro, 1997). Impersonal narratives may also be elicited by means of a film retell task (Bardovi-Harlig, 1995a, 1998; Bhardwaj et al. 1988; Dietrich et al., 1995; Lafford, 1996; cf. Chafe, 1980, on the use of film for cross-linguistic investigations) or a story retell task (Bardovi-Harlig, 1992b). Film clips may favor action or description (e.g., Lafford, 1996). More directed samples may be collected via elicitation tasks such as cloze passages that form complete texts (Bardovi-Harlig, 1992a; Bergström, 1995), short contextualized passages (Bardovi-Harlig & Reynolds, 1995; Collins, 1997), or short contextualized passages which when taken together form a narrative (Collins,

1999a). All of these may be oral or written. The influence of task and discourse conventions is discussed at greater length in Chapter 5.

In general, free production, whether in the form of conversational interview or film retell task, has dominated the type of data collected. This is true of both the descriptive studies and the hypothesis-testing studies. Due to the concern for balancing different tokens across different verbal categories, hypothesis-testing studies also use the more controlled tasks mentioned in the previous paragraph. Analyses have also varied: some descriptive studies have presented qualitative analyses of their results, while others have used quantified analyses. The hypothesis-testing inquiries generally present their findings quantitatively, although, as I will show in Chapter 4, even studies that test the same hypothesis do not necessarily use the same analysis. Special issues in analysis will be pointed out in the relevant sections of the following chapters.

Overview of the Book

Like most of the research in L2 temporal semantics, this book focuses on the expression of past time in acquisition. Research in second language temporal semantics has concentrated on the past because in making reference to the past, the event or situation is displaced from the time of speaking and thus requires a marker of some sort in primary language as well as interlanguage. In Reichenbach's (1947) schema (to which I will return in some detail later), in the past, the event (E) precedes the time of speaking (S).[6] In contrast, in references to the present, when the event and the time of speaking are simultaneous and talk refers to the here-and-now, no special marking is required. A variety of linguistic devices may serve to mark displaced temporal reference, most common among which are adverbials and verbal morphology. Even more important than the acquisition of verbal morphology itself is the development of contrast between markers in interlanguage. In the acquisition of the past, the first contrast in interlanguage is between simple past morphology and zero (∅), rather than between past and present morphology. Only after the simple past is well established does morphological marking for the present appear, as in the case of English for example. From the point of view of the amount of information supplied by "present tense" morphology in interlanguage, present morphology functions more to indicate person and number than tense, since only one morphological tense (past) is needed to establish a contrast between the here-and-now and events occurring prior to the time of speaking, or, more generally between past events—events occurring prior to the time of speaking, and nonpast events—events occurring at the same time as the time of speaking or following it.

For English, the verbal morphology for referring to past includes the simple past, present perfect, pluperfect, and perfect progressives (Leech, 1971). For the purposes of this analysis, past progressive is also included. It differs from the simple past by aspect (progressive versus nonprogressive) but shares the same tense (past). All of these tense-aspect forms share the feature of referring to events which are prior to the time of speaking (E before S) in Reichenbachian analysis. Like the English simple past and past progressive, the Romance preterite (such as the Spanish preterite and the French passé composé) and the imperfective (the Spanish imperfect and the French imparfait) are past tenses, sharing the feature E before S but differing with respect to aspect. Of the tense-aspect morphology related to expressions of the past, the emergence of simple past form (or the perfective past in Romance languages) has been the most widely investigated due to the fact that it occurs early enough in interlanguage development that it can be studied for most learners.

Each chapter of this book surveys a single framework of analysis and includes research on a number of target languages. Although European languages have dominated the research as target languages, the first languages of learners are quite varied. Relevant issues in research design and analysis are discussed for each approach. Following the cross-linguistic reviews, each chapter presents a study of the acquisition of temporal expression in English as a second language within the framework discussed in the chapter. Throughout the book, corpora are examined from more than one research perspective to show how the frameworks that one adopts influence the results concerning acquisition processes.

In the following chapters I examine the meaning-oriented and the form-oriented approaches in detail. Although the form-oriented approach which identifies specific morphemes and traces their development is likely to be a more familiar starting point for many readers, I begin the review with the semantic-oriented approach to emphasize that learners have means available to them other than morphology to express temporality. Moreover, the emergence of tense-aspect morphology represents a relatively later stage not achieved by all learners. Thus, I will begin with the approach that allows us to understand the stages of acquisition which seem to be in evidence in all learners.

Chapter 2 presents studies that employ the meaning-oriented approach. Studies of a range of target languages emphasize the fact that the emergence of tense-aspect morphology is only one stage—the last stage—of the acquisition of temporal expression. Chapter 2 also investigates the early stages of acquisition of time talk, the pragmatic and lexical stages. This is followed by an illustration of the approach with two studies of the acquisition of English, one in early acquisition that examines the expression of past and the other in more advanced stages that investigates the expression of reverse-order reports (cases in which chronological sequencing of events is not observed).

Chapters 3 to 5 are devoted to the form-oriented approach. The form-oriented approach has enjoyed different manifestations as descriptive studies and hypothesis-testing studies. In Chapter 3 I present a longitudinal study of the expression of past which examines the sequence of emergence of temporal morphology, namely, simple past, past progressive, present perfect, and pluperfect. The morphology is traced throughout the developing interlanguage systems of 16 learners and is examined for its form-to-meaning mapping in the emergent tense-aspect system.

In Chapters 4 and 5 I examine hypothesis-testing studies of tense-aspect acquisition. Chapter 4 surveys the cross-linguistic literature on the aspect hypothesis and presents a cross-sectional study of English as a second language. Research design and analysis are examined extensively to show the effect of different quantitative analyses on the interpretation of the results. Chapter 5 examines the research on the relation of discourse structure and the distribution of tense-aspect morphology in second languages. Beginning with the discourse (or narrative) hypothesis, the chapter surveys the research on narrative structure. The cross-sectional data analyzed in Chapter 4 to test the aspect hypothesis are reanalyzed in Chapter 5 to test the discourse hypothesis. The influences of both aspect and discourse are compared, and an integration of the findings is presented. The chapter also examines ways in which research on the influence of discourse structure can be expanded to include nonnarrative texts.

Chapter 6 explores the influence of instruction on the acquisition of temporal expression. Experimental studies are reviewed, and instructed and uninstructed learners are compared for eventual attainment. The sequences of acquisition that were observed for the 16 learners of the longitudinal study that were reported in Chapter 3 are revisited in light of the instruction that they received during the observation period. Finally, Chapter 7 provides a summary of the research in the acquisition of second language time talk. I also look ahead to research questions for the future that are consistent with the different research programs reviewed in the preceding chapters.

In this book I review many approaches to the study of temporality in second language acquisition. The studies in L2 temporal semantics take into account form, meaning, use and distribution, and discourse structure. The approaches vary in terms of their main focus of inquiry. I try to present the advantages of each of the research approaches. I think that each one has much to offer and that by pursuing the acquisition of L2 temporality from a range of perspectives in research—collectively as a field, if not individually as researchers—we will arrive at a better understanding of time talk and acquisitional processes.

Notes

[1]Even more interesting than similar orders is the fact that, for the adults, temporal development lags behind general linguistic development such as sentence complexity and size of vocabulary when compared to childrens' acquisition (Schlyter, 1990).

[2]The irregular-before-regular order was generally confirmed in a longitudinal study of (largely untutored) adult learners of five target languages (English, German, Dutch, French, and Swedish) by all but one group, Turkish learners of German (Dietrich, Klein, & Noyau, 1995). Klein (1993, 1994a) argued that this process characterizes the learning of individual lexical items rather than the learning of rules. The focus on irregular and regular forms is also seen in later work such as that of Bailey (1987, 1989), Bayley (1991, 1994), E. Lee (1997), Rohde (1996, 1997), Salaberry (1999a), and Wolfram (1984, 1985, 1989).

[3]I owe this observation to Yas Shirai (personal communication, November 1999).

[4]Some dialects of Chinese, such as Mandarin, are more restrictive; where Mandarin allows only nasals in word final position, Cantonese also allows unreleased stops [p, t, k] (Li & Thompson, 1987).

[5]See Young (1988) for a fuller discussion of the influence of L1 and interlanguage phonology in the realization of the plural morpheme.

[6]There are many available (and competing) theoretical frameworks for the analysis of tense and aspect. It is my goal in this book to present the clearest possible picture of the study of the acquisition of the expression of temporality in second languages, rather than to review the rich literature on the theory and representation of tense-aspect systems. To that end, I have employed theoretical frameworks that are well known to most researchers in the area of tense and aspect and that have influenced research in second language acquisition. I have reviewed individual studies within the frameworks that they have employed, and I have selected analyses, such as Reichenbach's time lines, that are familiar to teachers from their use in English language textbooks. Where there is a debate regarding the analysis of tense and aspect, I have provided alternative sources for interested readers. Readers who would like to read about alternatives to Reichenbach's analysis might consult Klein (1994b) or Schopf (1987). Binnick (1991) provides an excellent history and analysis of the study of tense and aspect from multiple perspectives.

CHAPTER TWO

Meaning-Oriented Studies of Temporality

Meaning-oriented approaches to second language acquisition are not widely used by American researchers, and thus not well known to students of American second language acquisition research. However, meaning-oriented research is widely practiced and well known in the European second language acquisition research community. With its emphasis on the expression of semantic concepts, the meaning-oriented approach may seem to the reader not only new, but unfamiliar as it trades the familiar emphasis on form for the less familiar emphasis on meaning. The focus on the expression of temporal concepts results in the study of a range of unrelated linguistic devices. The linguistic devices used by learners to express temporality include pragmatic, lexical, and morphological devices, a wide range to anyone accustomed to a form-focused inquiry.

This chapter introduces the meaning-oriented approach and describes its basic principles with respect to the study of the expression of temporality in second language acquisition. The first half of the chapter reviews the findings of the studies of six languages (English, German, French, Italian, Dutch, and Swedish). Particular attention is paid to the work of the European Science Foundation scholars whose cross-linguistic study has defined research in this area. Using the meaning-oriented approach, three main stages of development in the acquisition of temporal expression in adult second language have been identified. The review is organized according to the order in which these stages are attested in acquisition: pragmatic, lexical, and morphological. The second half of the chapter presents two longitudinal studies that employ the meaning-oriented approach. The first study examines the interplay of lexical and morphological means used for signalling the past by learners of English as a second language at the onset of the morphological stage. The second study shows that even learners who are reasonably advanced in their use of verbal morphology may depend on lexical devices when new tense-aspect morphology emerges in the interlanguage temporal system.

Expressing Temporality

Meaning-oriented studies examine the range of linguistic devices that speakers use to express a particular concept (von Stutterheim & Klein, 1987). The meaning-oriented studies are known by a variety of names including the concept-oriented approach (von Stutterheim & Klein, 1987), the semantically oriented approach (Giacalone Ramat, 1992), the functional-grammatical perspective (Skiba & Dittmar, 1992), the notional perspective (Berretta, 1995), and function-to-form studies (Long & Sato, 1984; Sato, 1990; see also Trévise & Porquier, 1986). A basic tenet of the approach is that adult learners of second or foreign languages have access to the full range of semantic concepts from their previous linguistic and cognitive experience.[1] Von Stutterheim and Klein argue that "a second language learner—in contrast to a child learning his first language—does not have to acquire the underlying concepts. What he has to acquire is a specific way and a specific means of expressing them" (1987, p. 194).

A significant contribution of the meaning-oriented approach has been to broaden the concept of temporality in SLA research from the emphasis on the morphological system found in much SLA work (which Dietrich et al. attribute to the "inflexional paradigm bias," 1995, p. 18) to include other linguistic and pragmatic means. This results in a rich description of the role of time adverbials, discourse organization, and morphology and of their interaction. A number of target languages have been investigated in this framework, due in large measure to the cross-linguistic study sponsored by the European Science Foundation (ESF) under the guidance of Clive Perdue and Wolfgang Klein, which investigated the acquisition of English, German, Dutch, French, and Swedish. Italian has also been investigated within the meaning-oriented approach (e.g., Giacalone Ramat, 1992), as has English independently of the ESF study (Bardovi-Harlig, 1992c, 1994b; Schumann, 1987). The studies employing this approach are largely longitudinal, deal mostly with learners in the host environment, and have elicited interlanguage samples through both conversational interviews and oral film retell tasks, resulting in personal and impersonal narratives (Dietrich et al., 1995). Written narratives have also been collected from essentially parallel sources, journal entries and film retell tasks (Bardovi-Harlig, 1992c, 1994b). The investigations have largely focused on reference to the past, which involves displacement from the time of speaking (and thus requires marking) and occurs early enough in interlanguage development that it can be studied for most learners.

The focus on meaning in acquisition leads to research questions in which the linguistic forms used by the learners to express temporality are not assumed. The three main questions posed by the ESF inquiry illustrate the type of questions that a meaning-oriented study might ask: (a) How do learners express temporality at a given stage of their acquisitional process? (b) How does temporal reference change over time? (i.e., "what developmental patterns emerge?" Dietrich et al., 1995, p. 261); and (c) what are the explanatory factors that can account for the development from one stage to another, including targetlike usage?

The longitudinal design employed by the ESF researchers followed 40 adult learners over a period of 2½ years. The observation time was divided into three main periods, or cycles, of approximately 10 months each. Samples of learner language were collected through conversational interviews and film retell tasks; all data were oral.[2] Narrative discourse collected in this manner forms the corpus for the analysis of temporality. The study was also set up to answer questions regarding the influence of the first language and of the target languages. Dietrich et al. (1995) investigated the acquisition of five target languages by speakers of two languages each (speakers of Punjabi and Italian learning English, speakers of Italian and Turkish learning German, speakers of Turkish and Arabic learning Dutch, speakers of Arabic and Spanish learning French, and speakers of Spanish and Finnish learning Swedish). The main report for the study on temporality (Dietrich et al., 1995) reports on 23 learners, 4 for each target language of Dutch, French, and Swedish, 5 for German, and 6 for English.

In addition to the ESF study's obvious contribution of providing a consistent analysis of five different target languages, another significant contribution is that it studied the development of temporal expression against the background of the developing interlanguage as a whole (Klein & Perdue, 1992), illustrating the fact that no subsystem develops independently of the larger grammar. In the earliest stage of interlanguage development (the nominal stage), learners do not yet use verbs (Dietrich et al., 1995; Klein, 1993, 1994a), as illustrated in (1) (L2 German, L1 Turkish) from von Stutterheim & Klein (1987). (The examples in this chapter come from a variety of sources that employed several different presentation styles. I have regularized them here, and have attempted to retain all the information presented in the original examples. I indicate where I have added information not included in the original source. The gloss and the interpretation in the following example is original, von Stutterheim & Klein, 1987, p. 202).

1. *Türkei grosse Haus, Deutschland Wohnung ganz kleine.*
    TURKEY BIG HOUSE, GERMANY FLAT VERY SMALL.
    "In Turkey my house was big, but in Germany I have a small flat."

Following the nominal stage, verbs appear, which in itself can take some time (Klein & Perdue, 1992; Noyau, Houdaïfa, Vasseur, & Véronique, 1995). Targetlike expression of temporality through verbal morphology naturally requires the acquisition of verbs. Studies of at least six different target languages basically agree as to the linguistic devices employed in the expression of temporality and the order in which they appear: The expression of temporality exhibits a sequence from pragmatic to lexical to grammatical devices (e.g., Dietrich et al., 1995; Giacalone Ramat & Banfi, 1990; Meisel, 1987). This progression corresponds to the use of (a) discourse principles such as chronological order and scaffolding, (b) lexical means such as adverbials and connectives, and (c) verbal morphology.[3] Giacalone Ramat and Banfi (1990) suggested that the acquisitional sequence is probably universal and independent of the languages involved. The following section reviews the findings of meaning-oriented research and is organized according to the linguistic devices that characterize the three main stages of the development of L2 temporal expression. See Table 2.1 for an overview of meaning-oriented studies.

Pragmatic Means for Expressing Temporality

In the earliest stage of temporal expression, there is no systematic use of tense-aspect morphology. Without tense-aspect morphology, learners establish temporal reference in four ways: by relying on the contribution of their fellow speakers (scaffolded discourse), through reference inferred from a particular context (implicit reference), by contrasting events, and by following chronological order in narration (Meisel, 1987; Schumann, 1987). The relating of events in chronological order is widely recognized as a characteristic of learner narratives, although learners may also take advantage of the ordering conventions of other types of discourse (von Stutterheim, 1991). The phenomenon of iconic discourse ordering in which the order of mention parallels the order of occurrence has been given many names in the study of first and second language acquisition: the order of mention contract (Clark, 1971), the principle of natural order (PNO; Klein, 1986), serialization (Schumann, 1987),[4] and the principle of chronological order (von Stutterheim & Klein, 1987). The term

Table 2.1

Studies of Temporality Using the Meaning-Oriented Approach

Target language	Author	L1 / # of learners	Design	Instruction	Focus	Discourse type/ elicitation
Dutch	Klein, Coenen, van Helvert & Hendricks (1995; from DKN)	2 Turkish 2 Moroccan Arabic	Longitudinal, 3 years	No class, 8 months No class, 2 hr/week for 1 year	Temporality	Personal narratives, film retell tasks, guided conversations
English	Schumann (1987)	1 Chinese 1 Japanese 3 Spanish	Interviews of learners living in the US for at least 10 years, fossilized at basilang	None	Temporality	Conversational interview
	Sato (1990)	2 Vietnamese children (10 & 12)	Longitudinal, 10 months	No ESL courses, attended public school	Past	Wide range of oral tasks in a variety of settings
	Bardovi-Harlig (1992c)	8, Arabic, Korean, Japanese, Spanish	Longitudinal, 0–6 months ESL instruction	Intensive program	Past	Oral and written personal narratives
	Bardovi-Harlig (1994b)	16, Arabic, Korean, Japanese, Spanish	Longitudinal, up to 15.5 month ESL instruction	Intensive program	Reverse-order reports	Written personal narratives, some retell

Table 2.1 (continued)

Studies of Temporality Using the Meaning-Oriented Approach

Target language	Author	L1 / # of learners	Design	Instruction	Focus	Discourse type/ elicitation
	Klein (1995; from DKN)	2 Italian (+ 2 supplemental) 2 Punjabi	Longitudinal, 3 years	4–10 months, none	Temporality	Personal narratives, film retell tasks, guided conversations
	Salsbury (1997)	17 mixed	Longitudinal, 6 months	Intensive English	Hypotheticals	Essays
French	Noyau (1984)	2 Spanish	Longitudinal, 1 year	French for refugees	Past	Personal narratives, film retell tasks, guided conversations
	Véronique (1987)	5 Arabic 2 Berber	Cross-sectional, 3 levels	Illiterate in L1 and L2	Past	Past-time passages from conversational interviews, three narratives each where possible
	Trévise (1987)	2 Spanish	Single interviews	3 months or less	Past	Narratives from conversational interviews

Table 2.1 (continued)

Studies of Temporality Using the Meaning-Oriented Approach

Target language	Author	L1 / # of learners	Design	Instruction	Focus	Discourse type/ elicitation
	Schlyter (1990)	2 Swedish adults, 3 bilingual French-German children	Single taping at 9 and 11 months	None	Temporality and general acquisition	Conversational interviews (adults); conversations during play (children)
	Noyau (1990)	3 Spanish	Longitudinal, 18 months (selected from ESF project)	Not specified	Past	Personal narratives from free conversation
	Noyau, Houdaïfa, Vasseur, & Véronique (1995; from DKN)	2 Moroccan Arabic, 2 Spanish	3 years	None	Temporality	Personal narratives, film retell tasks, guided conversations
	Moses (1997)	74 English	Cross-sectional: 20 1st year, 22 2nd year, 14 3rd year; 18 4th year	University foreign language courses	Future	Written accounts of future plans

Table 2.1 (continued)

Studies of Temporality Using the Meaning-Oriented Approach

Target language	Author	L1 / # of learners	Design	Instruction	Focus	Discourse type/ elicitation
German	Meisel (1987)	45, Italian, Spanish, Portuguese 12 longitudinal subjects	Cross-sectional (45), longitudinal (7), 57–80 weeks	Not specified	Past	Conversational interviews, some formal tasks, oral proficiency tasks
	von Stutterheim (1991)	20 Turkish	Sampling from larger study	None	Past	Spontaneous conversational data, narratives and descriptions
	Dittmar & Terborg (1991)	16 Polish (1 learner selected)	Longitudinally, 2.5 years	Not specified	Modality	Narratives, reports, instruction-giving
	Skiba & Dittmar (1992)	3 Polish	Longitudinal, 3 years	1 learner occasional attendance at German class	Modality	Not specified
	Dietrich (1995; from DKN)	3 Italian 2 Turkish	Longitudinal, 3 years	Italians, none Turks up to 10 hrs/week	Temporality	Personal narratives, film retell tasks, guided conversations

Table 2.1 (continued)

Studies of Temporality Using the Meaning-Oriented Approach

Target language	Author	L1 / # of learners	Design	Instruction	Focus	Discourse type/elicitation
Italian	Giacalone Ramat (1995a)	2 Moroccan Arabic 2 Chichewa	Cross-sectional	Not specified	Modality	Oral directive tasks
Swedish	Noyau, Dorrots, Sjöström, & Voionmaa (1995; from DKN)	2 Spanish 2 Finnish	Longitudinal, 3 years	Classes in Swedish and trade courses	Temporality	Personal narratives, film retell tasks, guided conversations

Note. DKN = Dietrich, Klein, and Noyau (1995). From "From Morpheme Studies to Temporal Semantics: Tense-Aspect Research in SLA," by K. Bardovi-Harlig, 1999, *Studies in Second Language Acquisition, 21*, pp. 348–349. Copyright 1999 by Cambridge University Press. Adapted with permission.

principle of chronological order will be adopted here because of its transparency.

Learners may use more than one of the pragmatic means at a time. For example, the learner (M1) in (2) scaffolds his utterance on that of his wife (F2) and continues in chronological order. In the excerpt, M1 (L2 French, L1 Spanish) narrates the story of how he and his wife left Argentina (Trévise, 1987, p. 237). (The gloss is original, Trévise, 1987, p. 237 and p. 242; the interpretation is mine. Spanish L1 is indicated by asterisks.)

2. M1: *la chose toutes réfugiés comme R. et sa femme. . .*
    THE THING ALL THE REFUGEE LIKE R. AND HIS
    WIFE. . .
    "The thing is that all the refugees like R and his wife"
    va à la autorité française donne un foyer. . .
    GO TO THE FRENCH AUTHORITY GIVES A
    HOSTEL. . .
    "go to the French authority that gives them a hostel/
    lodging"
    mais nous. . .*nos salvamos?*
    BUT WE. . . **NOS SALVAMOS*?*
    "But we escaped that. . ."

    F2: *nous nous sommes sauvés parce—*
    WE HAVE ESCAPED BEC—
    "We escaped that bec—"

    M1: *parcé qué nous trouvons un Brasilien. . . ici. . .*
    BECAUSE WE FIND A BRAZILIAN. . . HERE. . .
    "because we found a Brazilian here"
    qué il est aussi refugié et qué il sortie de Brasil
    WHO/THAT HE IS ALSO A REFUGEE AND
    WHO/THAT HE GOES OUT OF BRAZIL. . .
    "who is also a refugee, who left Brazil,"
    et il va à Buenos Aires
    AND HE GOES TO BUENOS AIRES
    "and he went to Buenos Aires"

nous connaissons de Buenos Aires
WE KNOW FROM BUENOS AIRES
"who we know from Buenos Aires"
et dans cette époque il est. . . ensemble
AND IN THIS PERIOD HE IS. . . TOGETHER
"in this period we were together."

Example (2) also provides an example of implicit reference of the type von Stutterheim and Klein (1987) term "associative temporal reference" (pp. 200–201). The listener will know from the fact that Brazilians come from Brazil that "goes out of Brazil" precedes "goes to Buenos Aires." An example of implicit reference with contrast from an even lower-level learner (L2 German, L1 Spanish) is found in (1), presented earlier, in which no verb was used by the learner. Given the context, von Stutterheim and Klein interpreted this utterance to mean "in Turkey I *had* a big house, in Germany, I *have* a small flat" (p. 202). The use of implicit reference taxes listeners, challenging them to draw on world knowledge, situational knowledge, and contextual knowledge (von Stutterheim & Klein, 1987). A second case of contrast without verbs was identified by von Stutterheim and Klein (1987): in (3), the speaker relies on the mutual knowledge that he is working at the time of speaking and thus uses "pension" to signal reference to the future. (The gloss is original, von Stutterheim & Klein, 1987, p. 200; the interpretation is mine.)

3. *Türkei Rente, meine Wohnung schön*
    TURKEY PENSION, MY HOUSE NICE
    "I will take my pension to/in Turkey, and my house will be nice"

The listener's situational knowledge leads to a very different temporal interpretation for (1) and (3), even though on the surface, they appear rather similar. A second type of implicit reference, inherent temporal reference, is dependent on the aspectual category of the predicates (i.e., whether they are expressed by verb phrases or noun phrases). Von Stutterheim and Klein illustrate this with the pair of sentences in (4). (The gloss and translation are original, von Stutterheim & Klein, 1987, p. 201.)

4a. *Türkei Urlaub, meine Mann krank.*
TURKEY VACATION, MY HUSBAND ILL.
"When he was on vacation my husband was ill"

4b. *Türkei Urlaub zurückkomm, meine Mann krank.*
TURKEY VACATION, COMEBACK MY HUSBAND ILL.
"After he came back from vacation in Turkey, my husband was ill."

Although no explicit temporal reference is made in either (4a) or (4b), they are interpreted differently because of the semantics of the predicates. The sentence in (4a) is interpreted as "when he was on vacation my husband was ill" because *Türkei Urlaub* is interpreted as a state, "be on vacation in Turkey." In contrast, the first clause of (4b) establishes a temporal boundary with *zurückkomm* "come back," and thus the clauses are understood as being sequenced, as in "after he came back from vacation in Turkey, my husband was ill."[5]

The contrasting of events (Meisel, 1987) seems to be closely related to implicit reference, and specifically to associative temporal reference (von Stutterheim & Klein, 1987) as the following example from Meisel (1987) shows. In (5) the interviewer had asked the learner (L2 German, L1 Spanish) whether he plays soccer. (The gloss is original, Meisel, 1987, p. 216; the interpretation is mine.)

5. *hier in Deutschland nis, in Spain ja aber hier nis*
HERE IN GERMANY NOT, IN SPAIN YES BUT NOT HERE
"Here in Germany I don't [play soccer]. In Spain I did, but not here."

In (6), an Arabic learner of French relates a short story about an incident at work in which a plate was broken (Noyau, Houdaïfa et al., 1995, p. 158). The learner uses chronological order to structure her narrative and direct speech to convey three parts of the sequence. With only chronological order to work with, she uses what Dietrich et al. (1995, p. 265) call a "pre-basic variety" of interlanguage. (The gloss and translation are original, Noyau, Houdaïfa, et al., 1995, pp. 158–159.)

6.   *[jãna] [le kase] l'assiette (. . .)*
     THERE-IS HE BREAKS THE DISH
     "A dish was broken."
     "et toi [le kase]"
     AND YOU HE BREAK
     "The lady asked me whether I had broken it."
     "oui madame [e] moi"
     YES MADAM IS ME
     "I said, 'Yes, Madam I did.'"
     "[eskyz] moi [le kase]"
     EXCUSE ME HE BREAK
     "Excuse me for breaking it."
     et après [saje]
     AND THEN FINISHED
     "It was OK."
     [la želete] la poubelle
     HE THROW THE DUSTBIN
     "The plate was thrown away."

In (7) the learner (L2 English, L1 Punjabi) anchors his narrative with the adverbials *before, after, seventy-five* and *punjab* (see the next section), but the relative order of the events is indicated only by chronological order (Klein, 1995, p. 53). (The use of "+" indicates an unfilled pause.)

7.   punjab + I do agriculture farm
     before I go + seventy-five + in the arab country
     afghanistan [. . .]
     afghanistan to turkey
     to antakia
     to syria
     to lebanon
     after there go to syria
     yeah + jordan go india
     I work in indian house

This narrative may be understood as follows: "In Punjab I was a farmer. Then in 1975 I went to Arab countries. To Afghanistan, and from Afghanistan, to Turkey. To Antakia in Syria. To Lebanon. Then I went to Syria. Yeah. From Jordan I went to India. I worked in an Indian house."

Von Stutterheim and Klein emphasize the importance of the chronological order: "That this principle should not be violated is shown by the fact that the speaker [in (8)] has to repair those cases where the principle was not obeyed" (1987, pp. 198). (The gloss is original, von Stutterheim & Klein, 1987, pp. 198–199; the interpretation is mine.)

8a. *diese Kinder 3 Jahre komm immer deutsche Schule gehen*
   THESE CHILDREN 3 YEAR COME ALWAYS GERMAN SCHOOL GO
   "These children came three years [ago], they always go/went to German school"
   türkische Schule gehen inglische nicht verstehen
   TURKISH SCHOOL GO ENGLISH NOT UNDERSTAND
   "They went to Turkish school, they don't understand English"

8b. [self-repair] *7 Jahre Türkei Schule gehen*
   7 YEARS TURKEY SCHOOL GO
   "[These children] went to school in Turkey for 7 years"
   und dann Berlin komm 3 Jahre
   AND THEN BERLIN COME 3 YEARS
   "and then [they] came to Berlin 3 years ago"
   Schule gehen aber nicht verstehen inglische
   SCHOOL GO BUT NOT UNDERSTAND ENGLISH
   "They go/went to school, but they don't understand English."

Because chronological order is the distinguishing characteristic of all narrative (Dahl, 1984; Schiffrin, 1981; see also Chapter 5 of this book), chronological order is not restricted to learner language. As Schumann (1987) observed, "in standard language, verb morphology interacts with, supports, and often duplicates the work done by pragmatic devices in expressing temporality" (p. 38). Thus, the distinction between interlanguage and native language narratives lies not in the use of chronological order, but in recourse to other means of signaling temporal reference that emerge later. These means are discussed in the following sections.

Lexical Means for Expressing Temporality

Lexical means for expressing temporality include temporal and locative adverbials (*in the morning, now, then, here, there*), connectives (*and, and then, und dann*), calendric references (*May 19*), nouns (*Saturday*), and verbs (*start* and *finish*). Linguists have long recognized the complex interaction of the linguistic devices employed in the expression of temporality. The verbal categories of tense, aspect, and lexical aspect interact with each other and with adverbials, the type of text, and the order of mention. For example, the interplay of tense (the location of situations in time, Comrie, 1976) and adverbials has been discussed by Comrie (1985) and C. Smith (1978); the relation of aspect (the internal temporal constituency of events, Comrie, 1976) and adverbials by Dowty (1979) and Vendler (1957/1967); tense and aspect with narrative structure by Hopper (1979); and verbal categories with time adverbials, text type, and sentence structure by Nehls (1988) and Schopf (1984). However, it is linguists investigating adult second language acquisition who have identified the primacy of non-morphological means of expressing temporality (e.g. Dittmar, 1981; Meisel, 1987; Schumann, 1987; Trévise, 1987; Véronique, 1987). The primacy of lexical means of temporal expression characterizes the second stage of acquisition.

At the lexical stage, reference to the past is expressed explicitly through the use of lexical expressions. The most frequently used lexical expressions are connectives (e.g., *and, because,* and *so*) (Meisel, 1987) and adverbials, both locative (e.g., *here,* and *in my country*) and temporal (e.g., *yesterday, then,* and *after*; Trévise, 1987; Véronique, 1987).[6] Following Thompson and Longacre (1985), time adverbials include time adverbs such as *yesterday,* time adverbial phrases such as *at 11:45* and *in the morning,* and time adverbial clauses such as *when the sun rises*. Dittmar (1981) called interlanguage use of adverbials such as *schon* "already" "suggestive tense markers" (p. 146). Van Holk (1990) sees time adverbials so closely related to tense that he calls them "tense adverbials" (p. 370) completely independently of acquisitional studies, and yet this characterization is certainly consistent with the lexical stage of temporal expression. Research in other approaches to second language acquisition has noted the role of adverbials in temporal expression (e.g., Brindley, 1987; Wolfram, 1984), but the meaning-oriented approach has clarified how central a role they play (Dietrich et al., 1995; Giacalone Ramat, 1995a; Klein, 1993, 1994a; Meisel, 1987; Schumann, 1987).

At the lexical stage verbs occur in morphologically unmarked forms, often referred to as "base" forms or "default" forms. In a study of German, Meisel (1980, 1987) observed that an invariant form is chosen at the lexical stage: It is either a standard form that is generalized or an interlanguage form that does not exist in the target language. This seems to hold for a variety of languages thus far studied. For example, in English the default form is the base form, such as *go* and *say* (Bardovi-Harlig, 1995a; Bardovi-Harlig & Reynolds, 1995). In Spanish (Andersen, 1991; Hasbún, 1995), French (Bergström, 1995), and Italian (Giacalone Ramat & Banfi, 1990) it seems to be the third person singular present.[7]

Temporal adverbs can be further divided into four semantic types: adverbs of position (*now, then, yesterday at six*), duration (*for many days, all week*), frequency (*twice, quite often*), and contrast (*already, yet*) (Klein, 1993, 1994a). Adverbials are also acquired in stages (Klein, 1993; Noor, 1993; Starren & van Hout, 1996).[8] Adverbials of position, duration, and frequency appear early in interlanguage and gradually add members; adverbs of contrast appear later (Klein, 1993; for English: Klein, 1993, 1995; German: Dietrich, 1995; Dutch: Klein, Coenen, van Helvert & Hendriks, 1995; French: Noyau, Houdaïfa, et al., 1995; Swedish: Noyau, Dorriots, Sjöström & Voionmaa, 1995). There is also some evidence that L2 learners of Italian may mark aspect with adverbials (such as *appena* "hardly," "just," and *sempre* "always"; Giacalone Ramat, 1992).

The use of lexical markers to establish temporal reference is illustrated in (9). The speaker (L2 Swedish, L1 Spanish) also relies on chronological order to establish the sequence of events, but the spacing of the events in this narrative about the birth of his daughter is established by lexical means (Noyau, Dorriots, et al., 1995).[9] The narrator occasionally uses Spanish lexical items (marked off by asterisks in both Swedish and English), presumably when he cannot access the Swedish equivalent. (Note, however, that he uses both the Swedish and Spanish words for "hospital.") (The gloss is original, Noyau, Dorriots, et al., 1995, pp. 229–230; the interpretation is mine.)

9.   *arton eh oktober eh alicia hade mycke [ond]*
     EIGHTEEN . . . OCTOBER . . . ALICIA HAD MUCH PAIN
     "On the eighteenth of October Alicia had a lot of pain."
     kanske klockan + tolv + natt + åka till östrahaus
     MAYBE O'CLOCK TWELVE NIGHT GO TO HOSPITAL
     "Around midnight we went to the hospital."
     y sen eh titta + en doktor
     AND THEN LOOK DOCTOR
     "And the doctor looked at/examined Alicia"
     "varsågod + gå + inne *hospital*"
     PLEASE GO IN HOSPITAL
     "and he admitted her to the hospital"
     a klockan + *no se* klockan ett + ett + på tisda
     AH O'CLOCK *I DON'T KNOW* AT ONE O'CLOCK ON TUESDAY
     "At about one o'clock on Tuesday"
     será + en nittonde (. . .) hon har + hade mycke [ond] + (kontraktion)
     IT WOULD BE SHE HAS HAD SO MUCH PAIN CONTRACTION
     "She had so much pain with the contractions."
     eh ja hjälpa + hon *con* + med eh [o'sixen]

I HELP SHE *WITH* OXYGEN
"I helped her with the oxygen."
y + *klochan* + *tio* + *i sex* + *eh född* + *susan*
AND AT TEN TO SIX BORN SUSAN
"And at ten to six Susan was born."
[Interviewer: *på kvällen?* 'In the evening?']
på / på / kväll
IN THE EVENING
"In the evening."

Verbs are unmarked in (9) with the exception of one token of "have" which is corrected from unmarked *har* to the preterite *hade*. Birth narratives by native speakers[10] are similarly marked for temporal reference by adverbials, especially for the duration and spacing of events; the difference between learners' narratives at the early lexical stage and native speakers' is that there is no verbal morphology to support the learner's narrative.

The use of connectives also characterizes the lexical stage, with *and* and *and then* and their equivalents in the respective target languages being the most common. In the following excerpt, an L2 speaker of German (L1 Turkish) links all of the foreground clauses except the first with a connective. Note that although the speaker in (10) uses a single past form, *gesag* "said," other verbs are uninflected and some clauses lack verbs altogether. Clauses 1 and 2 fulfill the orientation or scene-setting function. The action of the narrative, or foreground, begins with the third clause. Clauses that are simultaneous with each other are bracketed following the analysis of von Stutterheim and Klein (1987). The narrative begins in response to a question posed by the interviewer. (The gloss is original, von Stutterheim & Klein, 1987, p. 202; the interpretation is mine.)

10. I: *du hast gekündigt?*
    I: Did you hand in your notice?

1.   *das ist Firma kündigen—das Krankenhaus*
    IT WAS THE FIRM THAT DISMISSED ME—THE HOSPITAL
    "It was the firm that dismissed me, the hospital"

2. *aber ich liebe Arbeit*
   BUT I LIKE THE WORK
   "But I like(d) the work."

3. *Schwester gesag, das ist bei mir helfen arbeiten*
   NURSE SAID, SHE HELP ME WORK
   "The nurse said that she would help me work"

4. **dann** *Leute gesag, das ist Türkin, Ausländer, komm warum Schwester helfen arbeiten,*
   THEN PEOPLE SAID, THAT IS TURK, FOREIGNER, COME, WHY NURSE HELP,
   "Then people said, 'Why is the nurse helping that Turk, a foreigner?'"
   muss deutsche Frau oder Fraulein arbeiten helfen
   GERMAN WOMAN OR GIRL SHOULD HELP TO WORK
   "'she should help a German woman or girl.'"

5. **dann** *alles Ärger Ärger*
   THEN EVERYTHING TROUBLE, TROUBLE
   "Then there was trouble."

6. **und dann** *gehen, das ist Chef sagen, warum Türkin Schwester helfen*
   AND THEN GO, TO TELL BOSS, WHY TURKISH WOMAN HELP NURSE
   "And then [people] went and asked the boss, why does the Turkish woman help the nurse."

7. **und dann** *was ist / was gesag*
   AND THEN, WHAT SAID
   "And then, what was said?"

[8. **und dann** *weiss nicht*]
   AND THEN (I) DON'T KNOW
   "I don't know"

[9. *schlechte gesag, gute gesag*]
   BAD SAID, GOOD SAID
   "some said bad, some said good"

10. **und dann** *gleich meine Kündigung komm*
AND THEN IMMEDIATELY MY DISMISSAL COME
"And then I was dismissed immediately."

[11. *und Schwester ganz weinen*]
AND NURSE ALL CRY
"And the nurses all cried,"

[12. *warum gehen, warum kündigen?*]
WHY GO, WHY HAND IN THE NOTICE
"'Why [were you] dismissed?'"

[13. *weiss nich, keine Ahnung*]
I DON'T KNOW, NO IDEA
"'I don't know, [I have] no idea.'"

14. **dann nachher** *ich gehen andere Firma*
THEN AFTERWARD I GO ANOTHER FIRM
"then afterward I went to another firm."

[15. **nachher** *bei mir Brief komm*]
AFTERWARD I GET A LETTER
"afterward I got a letter"

[16. *und bitte bitte komm nochmal Arbeit*]
AND PLEASE, PLEASE COME BACK TO WORK
"[asking me] 'please come back to work.'"

Although the corpora from which the preceding examples were drawn were all oral, similar uses of connectives and adverbials are also seen in written narratives by learners (Bardovi-Harlig, 1992c). In (11) a learner of English (L1 Arabic) uses *Saturday* and *10:00 o'clock* to provide an anchor and a boundary for the narrative; *around 2 hours* provides a final boundary to the action described as "go around the mall." Connectives move the sequence of events along. In this written text, and in all others, spelling and punctuation are original. I have made no attempt to regularize the written presentation of the learners.

11. It was *Saturday* is the wecknd I welk up *at 10:00 o'clock morning* I tulk my shoer *and after* that I go to my frind *when*

> *I pe there* they sead they well go to the mool [shopping mall]
> and I go with they we go around in the mool *around 2 hours*
> *than* we go to the movei in the Selima [cinema] in the mool
> to waching a good movei *after* the movei we go Back to our
> Dorms we seat to gather in our Friend room we talking to
> gather *and after that* every Budy go to he's room me too I go
> back to my room that all. [Hamad, L1 Arabic, journal entry]

The learner's awareness of his use of connectives and adverbials
is apparent in (12), a journal entry written 4 months later by the
author of (11), in which he responds to a comment made by his
teacher, apparently about his use of connectives (the teacher's
comment was not part of the corpus; Bardovi-Harlig, 1992c). By
this time, the learner has already begun to use verbal morphology,
but nevertheless relies heavily on connectives to sequence the
events of his narratives.[11]

12.   To my teacher you talled me about gernal you said I have to
       ching my way becaus I use *and, after than* toomuch what can
       I do I have to use these weard because if I want to write about
       what I do every day so I have to use these weard because they
       is many things I did it every day for exampel I went to my
       apartemnt *at 3:30 than* I cooked my dinner *after that* I went
       to my friends apartemant we sat together and we ate dinner
       that all any way nothing chnge every day same the other day
       [Hamad, L1 Arabic, journal entry]

There is general agreement about the importance of lexical
means of temporal expression. The studies reviewed here from a
range of languages demonstrate the functional load of lexical
devices, especially adverbials, in learner production. One factor
that contributes to this pattern may be the difficulty that learners
experience in comprehending verbal morphology (Brindley, 1987;
J. Lee, 1998, 1999). There is evidence from processing studies that
suggest that lexical cues in the input are more important to
learners than morphological cues.

Comprehension of Verbal Morphology

Experiments in input processing, an experimental and highly quantified inquiry that contrasts with the observational and qualitative nature of the meaning-oriented approach, also underscore the functional load carried by temporal adverbials. Studies of input processing suggest that (a) learners process for meaning before form, (b) learners process content words first, and (c) learners prefer to process lexical items over grammatical items for semantic information (VanPatten, 1996). A series of input processing studies reveal that learners of Spanish, French, and Italian as a foreign language scored higher in assigning temporal reference to sentences on a recall test when the stimulus sentence contained a time adverb plus verbal morphology than when it contained verbal morphology alone (Musumeci, 1989). When learners of Spanish as a foreign language were presented with sentences in which an adverb and tense conflicted, learners favored the time reference indicated by the adverb (Sanz & Fernández, 1992). And, on the discourse level, learners of Spanish as a foreign language who heard a passage with adverbials reconstructed significantly more of the events that had occurred with past reference than did the learners who heard the passage without adverbs (J. Lee, Cadierno, Glass, & VanPatten, 1997).

Boatwright (1999) reported a study of processing using reaction times rather than recall scores that yielded the same results. Learners heard isolated sentences with and without adverbials and judged them to be either true about the future, true now, or true about the past, pressing a button to indicate their responses. Both accuracy of interpretation and reaction times were recorded. The presence of a temporal adverbial facilitated more correct answers and faster reaction times. Additional evidence comes from J. Lee's (1999) study of comprehension and processing of the Spanish past tense (in this case the preterite), using a comprehension and processing task with learner retrospection. Lee found that in texts containing adverbials learners often use the adverbials, and not the verb forms, to construct the past reference. In texts without adverbials learners may use context in the same way. In fact, the comprehension strategies of some learners may focus their attention away from processing the information carried by the verbal morphology, even though processing the verbal morphology is necessary in the acquisition of the form-meaning association.

Production and processing studies agree on the importance of cues, lexical over morphological, and on the fact that lower-level learners rely more on adverbials than do advanced learners. Giacalone Ramat and Banfi (1990) suggest that tense marking may be less urgent because of the use of adverbs that indicate time reference (p. 421). In fact, many untutored learners may reach this stage and not go beyond it (Dietrich et al., 1995). Giacalone Ramat and Banfi (1990) also suggest that the strength of adverbial reference may free emergent verbal morphology for an aspectual function. (The aspectual functions of verbal morphology are addressed in Chapter 4.)

Limitations of Lexical Expression

In spite of the informational weight of adverbs and their importance in the lexical stage of temporal reference, there can also be miscommunication because a learner's repertoire of adverbials may not be fully developed or because the adverbials could be further supported by additional temporal reference provided by verbal morphology. Prior to (13) the learner, José (L2 German, L1 Spanish) and the interviewer were talking about José's former girlfriend, whom he no longer saw because they could not find the time to meet. The interviewer asked whether the real reason was because José had met another woman. His reply is presented in (13) (Meisel, 1987). (The gloss and the listener's interpretation and the learner's intended meaning are original, Meisel, 1987, p. 217).

13. *nächste montag isch andere frau auch, deutsche-italianisch-deustche*
    NEXT MONDAY I ALSO OTHER WOMAN, GERMAN-ITALO-GERMAN.
    Listener's Interpretation: "Next Monday, I also [meet] another woman, a German-Italian."
    Learner's Interpretation: "On the Monday after [I saw my former girlfriend], I met another woman, an Italian born in Germany"
    sprechen italianisch eh sprechen kein italianisch, nur sprechen deutsch
    SPEAK. . .ITALIAN EH SPEAK(S) NO ITALIAN, ONLY SPEAK(S) GERMAN"
    "who speaks no Italian and only speaks German."

The interviewer and the learner had different interpretations of the learner's turn. The interviewer interpreted *nächste montag* as the "next Monday" from the time of speaking and asked the learner "you already know that you are going to break up with her next Monday, this coming Monday, you know already?" (Meisel, 1987, p. 217). The learner, however, meant *nächste montag* to be interpreted as "the next Monday" or "the following Monday," that is, the Monday after which he had last seen his former girlfriend, thus locating the reference in the past. As Meisel observes, recourse to verbal morphology seems to be a necessary addition to the devices available up through the lexical stage of temporal expression. Naturally, such limitations on communication are also found when a learner must rely on an interlocutor to provide scaffolding in the predominantly pragmatic stage. Ease of communication may be one of the factors that spurs learners on to the next stage of development.[12]

Morphological Means for Expressing Temporality

Following the adverbial-only stage, verbal morphology appears. At first it is not used systematically (Meisel, 1987; Schumann,

1987), and learners continue to rely on time adverbials. As the use of tense morphology increases, the functional load of the adverbials decreases (Bardovi-Harlig, 1992c; Meisel, 1987) and the actual ratio of time adverbials to finite verbs may also decrease (Bardovi-Harlig, 1992c). The morphological stage can itself be viewed as a series of lesser stages as tense marking becomes an increasingly reliable indicator of temporal reference (Bardovi-Harlig, 1992c, 1994b; see also Chapter 3). Although the use of adverbials and tense morphology enhances a learner's linguistic repertoire, it does not replace the principle of chronological order. As Schumann observes, "in standard language, verb morphology interacts with, supports, and often duplicates work done by pragmatic devices in expressing temporality" (1987, p. 38).

High levels of appropriate use of verbal morphology seem to be more common in tutored learners than untutored learners, although appropriate use is by no means guaranteed by instruction (Bardovi-Harlig 1992c, 1994b; Bergström, 1995; Hasbún, 1995). Examples of high-achieving learners include Lavinia, an Italian learner of English, and Ayshe, a Turkish learner of German, both participants in the longitudinal ESF project. Lavinia had 10 months of ESL classes in England before she took prevocational and English language clerical skills courses (Bhardwaj et al., 1988; Klein, 1995). Dietrich (1995) reported that the instructed Turkish learners of German in the ESF study acquired productive use of past-tense morphology (i.e., the Präterium and the Plusquamperfekt), whereas the untutored Italian learners did not. However, Dietrich also points out that Ayshe, the Turkish learner who made the most progress, had the most positive attitude toward learning German of all the learners.[13]

The stabilization of past-tense verbal morphology apparently opens the way for (morphological) expression of other temporal relations in the past. As the expression of past tense stabilizes, learners begin to make references to anterior events (past events that occurred earlier than other past events), reporting events out of chronological order (Bardovi-Harlig, 1994b). Following the Principle of Natural Order (Klein, 1986)—that deviations from chronological order must be indicated—learners begin the cycle of dependency on adverbials again. (For example, English uses the pluperfect, adverbials, or both together to mark deviations from chronological order.) In interlanguage, adverbs are the most common marker of anteriority in the earliest examples of deviations from chronological order, or "reverse-order reports" (Bardovi-Harlig, 1994b). Nearly half of the reverse-order reports with no morphological contrast are marked by time adverbials; roughly half of those show a single adverbial and half employ two adverbials. When learners begin to use verbal morphology to signal the contrast between past and anterior events, roughly half of those also occur with time adverbials, although the number signalled by two adverbials drops dramatically. Learners may also take advantage of the simultaneous development of their interlanguage syntax (Klein & Perdue, 1992; von Stutterheim, 1991) and express the anterior event in subordinate clauses, especially those indicating causation. It is possible that this cycle of lexical to morphological marking occurs throughout the tense-aspect system whenever new forms—and meanings—are added to the system.

For example, in a pilot study of hypotheticals in English, Salsbury (1997) found that lower level learners of English as a second language mark hypothetical statements through the use of lexical markers such as *hope* and *wish*. Similarly, a cross-sectional study of narratives showed that learners used lexical markers such as *in the imagine/the imagine over* to indicate the boundaries of a future-oriented dream sequence occurring in an otherwise past-oriented narrative (Bardovi-Harlig, 1995a). The movement from pragmatic to lexical to grammatical devices is also found in the expression of epistemic modality (expectations based on a speaker's knowledge) by learners of Italian as a second language (Giacalone Ramat, 1992, 1995a, 1995b). Epistemic modality is expressed through lexical means, including adverbs such as *forse* and *magari* "perhaps" and modal adjectives such as *è possible che* "it is possible that," by first person verbs such as "I think" or "I believe," or by the use of verbs whose lexical meaning includes uncertainty (Giacalone Ramat, 1995a). Modal verbs appear next (Giacalone Ramat, 1995b); morphological means to express modality, such as the future, conditional, and subjunctive, appear only in the interlanguage of advanced learners.

The identification of the three main means of temporal expression is supported by research in a number of (inter-)languages. Although the characteristic use of pragmatic, lexical, and morphological devices can be associated with distinct stages of interlanguage development, characteristic use is not the same as exclusive use. As we saw, chronological order begins with the earliest learner narratives and persists (necessarily) through the narratives of advanced learners (and native speakers, as Schumann, 1987, explained). Base forms and inflected forms may occur one after another in the same interlanguage sample from a learner who has begun to use verbal morphology productively to indicate the past. Even learners who show high levels of appropriate use of past tense morphology may show use of base forms (e.g., the learner called Mohamed in Klein et al., 1995). As shown in linguistic research not related to acquisition, lexical devices—especially adverbials—co-exist and interact with tense-aspect morphology. In the next section of this chapter, I present two studies of the acquisition of English that investigate the interplay of pragmatic, lexical, and morphological means of expression in interlanguage.

Multiple Means for Expressing Temporality: Two Examples

What is the relation of pragmatic, lexical, and morphological means to each other as an interlanguage system develops and adds new means of expressing temporality? In this section I present two longitudinal studies designed to address that question. Study 1 investigates the interplay of adverbials and morphology in interlanguage that shows emergent use of the simple past. Study 2 investigates the relation of chronological order, deviations from chronological order, lexical means, and morphology in interlanguage that shows relatively stable use of the simple past. In addition to addressing the issue of interface among the means for addressing temporality, inclusion of these studies is intended to illustrate in some detail how one might conduct a study that employs a meaning-oriented approach. In contrast to some of the European studies that have utilized this research framework, these studies present quantitative results.

Study 1: Adverbials and the Acquisition of
Simple Past Morphology[14]

Introduction

In the lexical stage of temporal expression learners rely predominantly on adverbials. As L2 morphology develops adverbials become less important, although adverbials are part of the linguistic devices for temporal expression in all natural language (Meisel, 1987; Schumann, 1987). This study investigated the role of adverbials as temporal expressions as learners showed increasingly reliable use of verbal morphology. Specifically, it addressed the question of whether the use of adverbials would actually decline with the increased presence of tense-aspect morphology in the interlanguage system or whether the use of adverbials would remain the same, creating greater redundancy in the interlanguage.

Method

Participants. This study followed eight adult ESL learners during their first six months of residence in the United States. The learners were full-time students in the Intensive English Program (IEP), Center for English Language Training at Indiana University. Six of the learners—two speakers each of Arabic, Japanese, and Korean—were placed in the first level of instruction (low beginning) upon arrival. The remaining two learners (one Korean and one Japanese learner) joined the project eight weeks later in the second level. Students were placed in instructional levels independently of the study by the placement exams used by the program (which include composition, reading, grammar, and listening comprehension).

Data collection. The language samples that form the basis for the analysis were taken from accounts written by the learners. Of the 91 texts sampled, 87 report on events in which the learner participated. Eighty-five of those were taken from daily journal entries written by the learners, which included such student-determined topics as daily routines (e.g., going to class, meeting friends, studying, and thinking of family) and variations on the routine such as shopping, attending parties, traveling, and going on field trips or picnics arranged by the IEP. The remaining four texts (4.4% of the texts sampled) were narratives invented by the learners in response to a narrative prompt given in class. (See Bardovi-Harlig, 1992c, for a list of topics for each learner.) Journal entries and texts within the sample interval were selected for their reference to past time; multiple journal entries and other texts were included when available to yield a sample of at least 50 verbs. Past-time contexts were identified by the learners' own use of adverbials and serialized marking of past, the dates on the journal entries, and an IEP calendar listing some of the events described by the students. For the purpose of comparison, similar journal entries were collected from four native speakers (NSs) who also kept diaries.

Journal entries are an excellent source of connected narratives for beginning learners. Learners write without pressure and completely control the content of the texts. The topics in the journals may be emerging "discourse domains" (Selinker & Douglas, 1985, 1988; Douglas & Selinker, 1994). Selinker and Douglas (1988) describe discourse domains as "'slices of life' that directly involve the learner and are important or necessary for the learner to talk and/or write about" (p. 357). Written texts also have an additional advantage for the study of acquisition in literate learners: These learners were able to write connected narratives much earlier than they were able to produce them orally, permitting access to their early development. (I return to this point shortly.)

Finally, one oral interview for each of the learners was analyzed. The interviews were conducted by trained interviewers in a one-on-one format during the fifth month of the study. One passage of narration with past-time reference as indicated by either the interviewer or the learner was selected from each interview.

Results and Discussion

This section presents the linguistic analysis and quantification of the rates of use of verbal morphology and temporal adverbials. Group scores and individual rates of use are examined. The section concludes by comparing the rates of use for past morphology and temporal adverbials in written and oral samples and discussing potential reasons for the differences.

Analysis of verbal morphology. Verbs supplied in past-time contexts as defined by the learners were coded for their verbal morphology. Simple past-tense forms included regularized past-tense forms such as *telled*. The ratio of past-tense forms supplied to the number of past-time contexts multiplied by 100 gives a rate of appropriate use in percentage form (i.e., 16/24 × 100 = 66.7%). This analysis distinguishes between *tokens* of verbs, counting all the verbs in the learner texts, and *types* of verbs, counting only one instance of each verb form that occurred in the text. Types rather than tokens of verbs were counted; that is, each verb form was counted only once per sample. When multiple forms of the same verb occurred, such as *go, went,* and *have gone,* each form was counted as a single type regardless of the frequency of each of the forms (e.g., if *go* was used once, and *went* was used five times, each form was scored as one type). The use of types ensured that the rates of appropriate use were not inflated by multiple occurrences of common verbs like *was* and *went.* Thus, a type analysis provides a conservative view of the acquisition of tense-aspect morphology.[15]

The two most common verb forms supplied in past-time contexts were the simple past tense such as *stayed* and *called,* and the unmarked base form such as *stay* and *call*. There was some use of present tense, marked by the third person singular *-s,* such as *tells, stays,* and *is / are,* and emerging use of past progressive and to a lesser extent pluperfect. Since past progressive and pluperfect are formally (i.e., morphologically) past, the few instances of these forms were included in the accuracy rates for past-tense morphology.[16]

Analysis of time adverbials. The frequency of occurrence of adverbials used to make temporal reference was also calculated for each set of texts in the samples. Time adverbials include adverbs such as *yesterday,* and *then,* adverbial (or prepositional) phrases such as *at 9:00 in the morning* or *after dinner,* including calendric references, and adverbial clauses such as *when I was a child* or *before I came to Bloomington.* Time adverbials which function as subjects, such as *today* and *yesterday,* were also included.[17] Based on the findings of Meisel (1987), contrasting locatives such as *in Bloomington* and *in my country* were also included. For ease of reference, I will include this type of locative in the term "time adverbial." The conjunction *and* used alone was not counted because it can function as a general, non-temporal, cohesive device (Halliday & Hasan, 1976). Frequency adverbs such as *sometimes* and *always* and aspectual adverbs such as *again and again* were not counted because they do not help place an event on the time line. See Table 2.2 for an inventory of the time adverbials used by the learners and included in the analysis.[18]

The frequency of occurrence for time adverbials was calculated as the ratio of the number of time adverbials in a text to the number of finite verbs in the text. All finite verbs in the text samples were counted regardless of time reference, as in the following excerpt:

14. [I would like to write about Ramdhana.] I *went* every day to Islamic center in my country. I *visited* my friends when finished the prayed. . . . Ramdhana in Bloomington *is* more different because I *am studying* now. [Abdullah, L1 Arabic]

Finished is part of the adverbial clause *when finished the prayed,* and therefore was not included in the finite verb count. Verbs in tenseless *to*-clauses were not included (e.g., *to make* in *He wanted*

Table 2.2

Inventory of Time Adverbials from Sample Texts

(Listed alphabetically by preposition or adverb)	
after	in + locative (*in melitry school,*
after NP (*after dinner*)	*in my country*)
after S (*after I read it*)	just
after that/and after that	last N (*night, time*)
afterward	later
ago (*two years ago*)	long time
as soon as	next, next week/day
at (around) + time (at 1:00)	now
(also expressed with *in*)	on/in + day/date (*Monday, May 19*)
at/in that time, at the lunch	one day
before S (*before I went*)	recently
dates (*January 6, 1990; May 19*)	since S
days of the week (*Monday, Thursday*)	then/and then
duration ((*for*) *two hours*)	today
finally	until + time, day, "now"
first/second (also *the second day,*	when S
the first time)	while S (past prog)
in + time (*in the afternoon, in* 1988)	yesterday

Note. From "The Use of Adverbials and Natural Order in the Development of Temporal Expression," by K. Bardovi-Harlig, 1992, *IRAL, 30,* p. 318. Copyright 1992 by K. Bardovi-Harlig.

to make friends). Participle clauses (e.g., *He denied skipping class*) were not produced by the learners at this early stage, but would also not have been included. The adverb-to-verb ratio was calculated for learner and native-speaker samples.

The use of verbal morphology and time adverbials. Learners showed individual variation in development of verbal morphology, as shown in Table 2.3. The percentage of use for each learner across time is given for past-tense morphology and for base forms, the two most common forms. The adverb-to-verb ratio is given for each learner across time in the rows labelled "Adverb-to-verb ratio." Learners Sang Wook and Hiromi joined the study at the third sampling point, T3, and thus there are no data from them

Table 2.3

Past-Tense Morphology and Base Forms with Adverb-to-Verb Ratio by Learner and Sampling Time

Learner (L1)	Morphology	Written						Oral
		T1	T2	T3	T4	T5	T6	T5
Hamad (Arabic)	% Past	28.6	30.8	69.5	—	66.7	83.3	31.3
	% Base	71.4	69.2	26.1	—	25.9	16.7	37.5
	Adverb-to-verb ratio	0.70	0.55	0.65	—	0.30	0.47	0.10
Saleh (Arabic)	% Past	73.3	27.2	50.0	61.5	80.0	66.7	64.3
	% Base	26.7	18.2	33.3	30.8	11.4	25.0	35.7
	Adverb-to-verb ratio	0.35	0.29	0.30	0.13	0.30	0.27	0.14
Abdullah (Arabic)	% Past	no past contexts	no past contexts	no past contexts	83.3	100.0	no past contexts	33.3
	% Base				16.7	0.0		60.0
	Adverb-to-verb ratio	0.30	0.30	0.24	0.32	0.18	0.31	0.23
Ji-An (Korean)	% Past	75.0	81.3	95.5	100.0	88.9	92.3	71.5
	% Base	25.0	12.5	0.0	0.0	11.1	0.0	19.0
	Adverb-to-verb ratio	0.30	0.30	0.24	0.26	0.24	0.31	0.17

Table 2.3 (continued)

Past-Tense Morphology and Base Forms with Adverb-to-Verb Ratio by Learner and Sampling Time

Learner (L1)	Morphology	T1	T2	Written T3	T4	T5	T6	Oral T5
Sang Wook	% Past	—	—	94.7	85.0	97.1	100.0	38.9
(Korean)	% Base	—	—	0.0	10.0	2.9	0.0	55.6
	Adverb-to-verb ratio	—	—	0.29	0.26	0.25	0.20	0.18
Hiromi	% Past	—	—	100.0	91.7	85.7	81.1	90.0
(Japanese)	% Base	—	—	0.0	4.2	9.5	9.1	9.1
	Adverb-to-verb ratio	—	—	0.13	0.16	0.24	0.06	0.11
Toshihiro	% Past	89.7	81.5	88.8	95.5	95.4	—	76.9
(Japanese)	% Base	6.9	11.1	0.0	0.0	4.6	—	15.4
	Adverb-to-verb ratio	0.22	0.23	0.21	0.40	0.27	—	0.44
Noriko	% Past	66.7	68.8	71.4	90.9	91.6	100.0	33.3
(Japanese)	% Base	16.6	25.0	14.3	0.0	0.0	0.0	33.3
	Adverb-to-verb ratio	0.33	0.23	0.20	0.21	0.27	0.24	0.00

Table 2.3 (continued)

Past-Tense Morphology and Base Forms with Adverb-to-Verb Ratio by Learner and Sampling Time

Learner (L1)	Morphology	T1	T2	Written T3	T4	T5	T6	Oral T5
Group	% Past	70.3	63.9	85.4	88.6	87.3	86.3	55.3
	% Base	25.7	13.3	7.7	7.6	9.4	9.5	34.2
	Adverb-to-verb ratio	0.40	0.34	0.28	0.26	0.26	0.26	0.18
NS	% Past	100.0						
	% Base	0.0						
	Adverb-to-verb ratio	0.20						

Note. A dash indicates that no data were available for the sampling period. From "The Use of Adverbials and Natural Order in the Development of Temporal Expression," by K. Bardovi-Harlig, 1992, *IRAL, 30,* p. 318. Copyright 1992 by K. Bardovi-Harlig.

until T3. Abdullah never missed a journal entry, and yet did not make reference to events in the past until T4.

In cases where the use of past and base total 100%, as at T1 for Hamad, only past and base forms were used by the learner. Where the total is less than 100%, as at T3 for Hamad, other inflected nonpast forms were used in the past-time contexts.

Figure 2.1 shows that group scores for the use of adverbials appear to decrease over time. Group adverb-to-verb ratios decrease between T1 and T4, but show no further decrease between T4 and T6. The learners show higher usage as a group than the native speakers. The ratio of adverbials to finite verbs by learners at T1 is approximately two adverbials for every five verbs (.40), whereas the NS use approximately one adverbial for every five tensed verbs (or .20).[19] At T4 through T6 the learners use approximately one

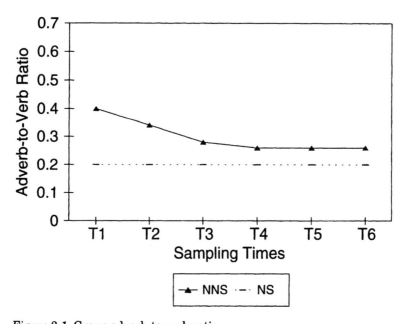

Figure 2.1. Group adverb-to-verb ratio
Note. The native speakers were sampled only once, but the line is drawn out for ease of comparison. Thus, a broken line is used. From "The Use of Adverbials and Natural Order in the Development of Temporal Expression," by K. Bardovi-Harlig, 1992, *IRAL*, 30, p. 306. Copyright 1992 by K. Bardovi-Harlig.

adverbial for every four tensed verbs (.26). Because the group is relatively small, individual ratios must be considered.

As was the case for verbal morphology, the learners showed individual variation in their use of time adverbials (Table 2.3). Learners began with higher adverb-to-verb ratios (in the range of one adverb to three verbs), but tended to move toward a lower, native-like usage. Two learners are particularly noteworthy: Hamad, who showed relatively high use of temporal expressions compared to the other learners, and Hiromi, who used relatively few adverbials, even fewer than the native speakers.

The use of time adverbials seems to decrease over time and the use of past-tense morphology increases over time (as time adverbials decrease; Figure 2.1). This can be illustrated by examining the use of time adverbials and the development of verbal morphology for three learners: the learner with the greatest use of adverbials (Hamad), the learner with the lowest use (Hiromi), and a learner representative of those in between (Ji-An) (Table 2.3). As might be expected, the language samples of the learner with the greatest use of adverbials (Hamad) shows the least use of past tense of all the learners sampled at T1 (28.6%). An example of Hamad's journal at T1 is presented in (11), repeated here as (15) for convenience.

15.   Deat [Date]: Jan 27

It was *Saturday* is the wecknd I welk up *at 10:00 o'clock morning* I tulk my shoer and *after that* I go to my frind *when I pe there* they sead they well go to the mool [shopping mall] and I go with they we go around in the mool around 2 hours *than* we go to the movei in the Selima [cinema] in the mool to waching a good movei *after* the movei we go Back to our Dorms we seat to gather in our Friend room we talking to gather *and after that* every Budy go to he's room me too I go back to my room that all. [Hamad, T1, L1 Arabic, journal]

Hamad must have been somewhat aware of his use of adverbials because he wrote about his use of adverbials and connectors in a journal entry addressed to his teacher, as shown in (12), presented earlier.

Hamad's sample at T5 in (16), just three days after the exchange with his teacher about his use of adverbials and connectives, shows the lowest use of adverbials in all of his samples. Whether the decrease was a direct result of the teacher's comments or the fact that the entries for T5 reported on different topics than Hamad's typical entries is not clear. Hamad typically reported his daily routines, but at T5 he wrote about a surprise party, his first day in the town in which he was living, and a picnic:

16. May 17, 1990

In these day I have many things I want to writ about it I want to write about Friday *in firday* I went to my frieds apartemnte I went there *at 3:30 in that time* they were mad a party for here fried but, they want to make a surprys for her so I help thim in these party I cooked the arabic food and I fixed the apartemnt with thim and *in 6:30* our friend came and she don't now about the party *when she got in her apartemnt* she is really surpryesed because she don't now about any thing so it was very nice party to her and really we like it so much. [Hamad, T5, L1 Arabic, journal]

Hamad's final entries, reporting more mundane occurrences, show a higher frequency of adverbials, but not as high as it had been previously.

Over time Hamad shows a decrease in the use of time adverbials and an increase in verbal morphology. There is not necessarily a corresponding decrease in the use of adverbials for each improvement in appropriate use of past tense. In fact, the most dramatic improvement in verbal morphology shown by any learner occurred in this learner's corpus, but it was not accompanied by a sharp drop in the use of adverbials at that time. The sharp drop, from .70 (at T1) to .55 (at T2) preceded the increase in verbal morphology from 30.8% at T2 to 69.5% at T3. The increase in verbal morphology at T6 was also preceded by a decrease in use of time adverbials at T5 (Table 2.3). (No data were available for this learner at T4.) Overall, the use of adverbials decreases as verbal morphology increases, but Hamad's production shows that adjustments in the system may proceed in a stepwise fashion rather than simultaneously. Shorter sampling intervals might help to interpret this learner's use of adverbials relative to the changes in his verbal morphology.

Learner Ji-An shows comparatively high use of verbal morphology, 75% at T1 and 92.3% at T6. Ji-An also shows a decrease in the use of adverbials between T1 and T5. At the same time there is an increase in her appropriate use of verbal morphology. The increase in the use of adverbials at T6 may be due to a topic effect: The text at T6 is an example of creative writing in response to a classroom prompt, rather than a personal account. Only a single text was available at T6.

Sang Wook shows a pattern similar to those of the other two learners (Table 2.3): high appropriate use of past-tense morphology in the four samples, T3–T6, ranging from 85% to 100% usage, and a corresponding decrease in the use of time adverbials. Learners Ji-An and Sang Wook began the study with relatively high rates of appropriate use of past-tense morphology, but the pattern of decreasing use of adverbials is shared by most of the learners. Saleh and Noriko also show overall decreases. Abdullah shows a decrease, but he produced past-oriented texts at only two sampling intervals. The apparent exception to this pattern is Hiromi, whose use of adverbials steadily increased over time. Toshihiro shows almost no change in T1–T3, but his adverb-to-verb ratio increased at T4 and decreased again at T5. For the majority of the learners in this study, the frequency of time adverbials seems to decrease as the appropriate use of verbal morphology increases. This is represented by the group scores in Table 2.3. The developing interlanguage seems to adjust the amount of redundancy in the system by decreasing the number of adverbials used.

Comparison of oral and written data. The communicative importance of the adverbials can be seen again in the data from the interviews. A passage from an oral interview at T5 was analyzed for each learner. These figures are given in the last column, labelled "Oral," in Table 2.3. Seven of the eight learners showed lower rates of appropriate use of past-tense morphology in the oral interviews than in the journal entries at T5. This may be related to task effect as reported by Ellis (1987), and, at least in part, to interlanguage phonology and the realization of the consonant clusters and closed syllables that result from the formation of the simple past with regular verbs (see Chapter 1). However, the rate of adverbial use also dropped, suggesting a second factor, namely scaffolding by the interlocutor. Five learners showed lower rates of use in both adverbials and verbal morphology (Hamad, Saleh, Ji-An, Sang Wook, Noriko), one used fewer adverbials only (Hiromi), and two showed lower use of verbal morphology only (Toshihiro and Abdullah). The decrease in the use of adverbials appears to be related to the scaffolding provided by the interlocutor's contributions. The use of adverbials by the learners to set the scene is preempted by the interviewers' use of adverbials to frame their questions as in (17) and (18).

17. I: So we came to class *last week* and you were gone. Your parents came?
    Ji-An: We went to trip.

18. I: So tell me what you did *this weekend.*
    Hiromi: Oh, I went to Chicago.

Where the interviewers supplied a temporal frame as in (17) and (18), the learners did not supply their own adverbials. In (19), however, when the interviewer supplied a frame that did not match what the learner wanted to say, he supplied his own (*last weekend*).

19. I: Do you guys, do you 'n' your friends go someplace *on the weekends?*
    Hamad: Yeah, *last weekend* I went to Ohio, King Island.

This points up the communicative value of the adverbials. When the same learners write, they must set the scene because a reader cannot contribute to the construction of the text in the same way as an interlocutor. Thus as writers, learners must fully specify the scene, including temporal reference. Compare the way in which Ji-An and Hiromi set the scene when telling about their trips in their journals.

20. Ji-An: I left Bloomington to Boston on May 19 because I have to visit my cousin. [Ji-An, T5; cf. (17)]

21. Hiromi: I got up at 5:00 am and we drove to Chicago this morning. [Hiromi, T5.5; cf. (18)]

Although the difference in appropriate use of verbal morphology under the oral and written conditions could be attributed to lack of monitor use in the oral condition (Krashen, 1985; see also Ellis, 1987) and to interlanguage phonology (Bayley, 1991, 1994; Sato, 1986, 1990; Wolfram, 1984, 1985, 1989; Wolfram & Hatfield, 1986), another possible explanation is that some learners may also treat tense, like adverbials, as essentially a communicative element rather than a required grammatical device and assume it is optional when the interviewer has supplied a temporal frame.

Another difference between oral and written production comes from the learners' ability to sustain continued production. From the beginning of the 6-month observation period learners were able to sustain written narratives, although they were some-times short. At the time learners were first interviewed (around T2), none were able to go beyond one turn (mostly phrasal) responses to the interviewers' prompts. The interviews discussed in this study that were conducted at T5 showed that learners could relate a narrative with some prompting from the interviewer. Interviews done at 7½ months show that most learners could sustain unprompted narratives of events in their lives. Thus, using the written journal entries as a source of data allows researchers to observe the emergence of temporal expression in the interlanguage of a given learner earlier than observation of the spoken interlanguage would allow.

Summary

The reduced reliance on time adverbials as verbal morphology becomes more systematic and more reliable seems to be manifested in an observable decrease in the frequency of the use of adverbials. As verbal morphology becomes more reliable, some of the information carried by the time adverbials (the basic past-nonpast distinction) is also carried by the verbal morphology. The decrease of the functional load of the adverbials in signalling the basic past-nonpast distinction may free adverbials to take on other functions, as will be shown in the following study.

Study 2: Adverbials and Morphology in Reverse-Order Reports

Introduction

Most of the research on the function of lexical devices in temporal expression has focussed on early stages of interlanguage development, either on the lexical stage, when verbal morphology has not emerged as a means of expressing temporality (Dietrich et al., 1995), or on early stages of morphological development (as in the previous study, Bardovi-Harlig, 1992c). In the following study (adapted from Bardovi-Harlig, 1994b) I investigate the relationship of lexical devices and temporal expression at a later stage, when the interlanguage system supports the systematic use of the simple past tense. This study shows that the use of lexical means of signalling temporal relations is not exclusively confined to the pre-morphological stages of temporal expression. Learners also use lexical devices to signal deviations from chronological order before they develop additional morphology to serve that function.

In narratives, events are typically presented in chronological order, as in (22). As we have seen, learners in the pragmatic stage of temporal expression rely on chronological order to indicate temporal reference. Although chronological order in narrative is the norm, and can be said to exemplify a basic principle of discourse organization, deviations from chronological order may also occur, as in (23).

22. John graduated from high school in 1975. He went to college five years later.

23. John entered college in 1980. He had graduated from high school five years earlier.

What changes take place in interlanguage that permit learners to successfully deviate from the principle of chronological order? To answer this question, I investigated the concept of deviations from chronological order—which I will call *reverse-order reports*—and asked how they are expressed in interlanguage. It is well known that low-level learners follow the principle of chronological order, but it is not known when learners begin to deviate from it or what might trigger that deviation.

The principle of chronological order. As discussed earlier in this chapter, the relating of events in chronological order is widely recognized as a characteristic of learner narratives. Chronological order is not restricted to learner language, however. It is such a central characteristic of narratives that some linguistic definitions of narrative rest on that fact alone. For example, Dahl defines a narrative as a text in which "the speaker relates a series of real or fictive events in the order in which they occurred" (1984, p. 116). Without evidence to the contrary, series of events are understood as sequential as in (24).

24. Arkady kicked out and Ali rocked. The fountain shifted, too. A hand grabbed Arkady's foot and dragged him down onto the bench, then to the floor. Ali took a handful of hair and pulled Arkady's hair back, but the motion made him slip on the slick floor and lose the knife. Arkady heard it rattle on the far side of the bath. They crawled over each other toward the sound. (M. Smith, 1992, p. 357)

The distinction between interlanguage and primary language lies not in the use of chronological order, which is common to all narratives, but in the recourse to other means of signalling temporal reference.

In spite of the fact that chronological order provides the basic principle of organization for narratives, narrators do in fact deviate from the principle of chronological order. Narrators may leave the sequence of events to predict a coming event, to evaluate an event in the sequence, or to supply an event that happened previously.[20] But as Klein (1986) observes in his formulation of the principle of natural order (PNO), deviations from chronological order must be marked: "PNO: Unless marked otherwise, the sequence of events mentioned in an utterance corresponds to their real sequence" (p. 127). English uses multiple means to signal reverse-order reports (RORs): tense (the pluperfect, as in 25), adverbials (26), or both (27).

25. The first one they met was a horse as thin as a stick, tied to an oak tree. He had eaten the leaves as far as he could reach, for he was famished. (Thompson, 1968, p. 2)

26. I ate my lunch after my wife came back from her shopping. (Leech, 1971, p. 43)

27. Once in Sibley's Enid lingered by herself after the other girls had left, moving along the aisles like a sleepwalker. (Oates, 1987, p. 41)

The meaning of the pluperfect and the function of reverse-order reports are well aligned in examples such as (25). The pluperfect, often called the past-in-the-past, is described by Comrie (1985): "[T]he meaning of the pluperfect is that there is a reference point in the past, and that the situation in question is located prior to that reference point" (p. 65). In (25), the reference point is established by *they met*. Before they met the horse, the first event had taken place, namely, *he ate the leaves*. Thus, the order of the events as indicated by the square brackets following the event in question is *he ate the leaves* [1], and *they met the horse* [2]. Although the pluperfect is a specialized marker of the ROR, it does not occur obligatorily in every English ROR. Note that in (26), the verbs are in the simple past, and it is the adverb *after* that signals the temporal order of the clauses *my wife came back* [1] and *I ate my lunch* [2]. In (27) the author uses both the adverb *after* and the pluperfect to convey the order of events: *the other girls left* [1] and *Enid lingered by herself* [2]. In each of these examples, the order of occurrence is in contrast to the order of presentation, which is [2], [1].

To achieve a targetlike system of temporality, a learner must be able not only to move forward but to look backward as well. At lower levels of interlanguage development, when learners lack sufficient linguistic devices to signal deviations from chronological order, they can be communicatively unsuccessful, as discussed earlier in light of (8) (von Stutterheim & Klein, 1987). Nevertheless, not all deviations from chronological order are disallowed in interlanguage, and certainly cannot be if a learner is to move toward the target language. What changes must take place to allow learners to move from unsuccessful deviations from chronological order to successful ones? This question has two parts: How are reverse-order reports expressed in interlanguage, and when do they emerge?

Method

This investigation was part of a larger longitudinal study of the acquisition of tense and aspect by adult learners of English as a second language. It began with the 8 learners introduced in Study 1 and grew to follow a total of 16 learners over the course of up to 15 months. Acquisition was monitored through a series of elicitation tasks including oral and written narrative retells, interviews, assigned compositions, and written daily journals.

Participants. Participation in the longitudinal study was determined solely by class enrollment. The learners were adult students in the IEP in the Center for English Language Training at Indiana University who were placed in the first level of instruction independently of this project in either the January or the August term. The first eight learners were included in Study 1 reported on earlier in this chapter. At the end of the data collection period eight additional learners were selected for the study on the basis of the length of enrollment in the program and the completeness of their portfolios, including journals. Because the daily journal was of primary importance in the data collection, any learner who did not keep a journal was not included in this phase of the analysis. On the basis of these criteria, 16 learners representing four language backgrounds were selected (Arabic, 5; Japanese, 6; Korean, 2; and Spanish, 3). Although they began the program at approximately the same level of proficiency as determined by program placement, they showed individual differences in rates of attainment, eventual proficiency, and length of enrollment in the program.[21]

At the time of the study, classes in the Intensive English Program met for 23 hours a week. Students received instruction in listening and speaking, reading, writing, and grammar. Because the learners received instruction in the host environment, all were potentially contact language learners as well as classroom language learners, although they differed individually in their patterns of contact with native speakers and with other nonnative speakers of different first language backgrounds. In other words, these learners were in what Ellis (1985, 1990) refers to as a mixed language environment.

Data collection. The data were collected in a variety of ways during the longitudinal study. This study focuses on the written language samples that were collected. The schedule of the data collection was determined in part by the schedule of the Intensive English Program. In a calendar year there are six 7-week terms, with the longest instructional breaks in the summer and at the year end, both 3 to 4 weeks in length.

For this study, journal entries were selected whenever available. If they were not available, narratives from the film retell tasks, essay exams, and finally class assignments in the absence of all other options were selected. The calendar year was divided into 24 half-month periods with the first sampling period of a month running from the 1st to the 15th of the month and the second sampling period from the 16th to the end of the month. This system was adopted because calendar dates, for example, January 10, fall in the first month for some learners and the sixth month for other learners. Half-month periods were used because learners often showed different patterns toward middle or the end of the month than at the beginning. Finally, the study also intended to examine learner responses to instruction and 1-month intervals were too broad for this purpose. (See Chapter 6.)

Three complete texts from each period were sampled wherever possible. (This sampling method is an improvement over the looser method used in the earlier study reported in Bardovi-Harlig, 1992c; see Study 1.) Each text that was selected recounted a past-time event. Wherever there were multiple past-time texts available, the first three were chosen. Past-time texts were identified by the use of time adverbials that provided time frames (Bardovi-Harlig, 1992a; Harkness, 1987; Thompson & Longacre, 1985) and by extra-linguistic information such as the program calendar that listed some of the events described by the students, the dates on the journal entries, and the knowledge that learners frequently wrote in their journals at the end of the day. This procedure yielded a total of 430 texts. Journal entries comprised 87% of the sample, 376 texts, and elicited narratives comprised the remaining 13% of the sample, 54 texts. Film retells accounted for 37 of the elicited texts (9% of the total sample) and class assignments and essay examinations accounted for the remaining 17 texts (4% of the sample).

The journal entries were generally about the students' daily routines (going to class, meeting friends, studying) and variations on the routine such as shopping, attending parties, traveling, and going on field trips or picnics arranged by the IEP. The journal topics, with the number and type of texts sampled for each learner, are provided in Table 2.4.

Table 2.4

Topics and Types of Learner Texts Sampled

Learner	Spontaneous	Elicited
Saleh [36 texts]	Daily (10), shopping, hospital, recovery, trip to Indianapolis, travel to US, marriage proposal, new car, high school, IEP picnic, airport, washing car, *Anansi*, bad day, weekend (2), junk mail, bad day, program director, meeting, sick, plans [31 texts]	Surprise Package (C), *Anansi* (F), *Modern Times* (F), *Tin Toy* (F), studying (C) [5 texts]
Hamad [41 texts]	Daily (25), trip to Indianapolis, weekend (7), conversation, party, first day in Bloomington, county fair, IEP picnic [38]	Childhood (C), *Modern Times* (F), ethnic groups (C) [3]
Abdullah [9 texts]	Holiday, uncle, Memorial Day, daily [4]	Squirrel (C), Saudi Arabia in 1940s (C), *Modern Times* (F), *Tin Toy* (F), *Pink Panther* (F) [5]
Khaled [25 texts]	Daily (5), travel (2), IEP picnics (2), Egypt, school days (2), Thanksgiving, party, spring break, weekend, King's Island [17]	*Anansi* (F), *Modern Times* (F), museum trip (C), education (C), *Thief of Baghdad* (F), *Red's Dream* (F), Life (C), *Superman* (F) [8]

Table 2.4 (continued)

Topics and Types of Learner Texts Sampled

Learner	Spontaneous	Elicited
Zayed [18 texts]	Vacation, Turkey (2), good days, coming to US, Thanksgiving, TOEFL, level 2, winter vacation, spring break, director, IEP picnic, deciding to come to the US [13]	*Modern Times* (F), *Tin Toy* (F), *Pink Panther* (F), *Thief of Baghdad* (F), *Red's Dream* (F) [5]
Guillermo [29 texts]	Daily (9), bike trip, opera, Nashville, concert (2), missing class, renovation, weekend (4), sick friend, competition, basketball, orchestra, music (2) [26]	*Modern Times* (F), *Pink Panther* (F), daily (C) [3]
Carlos [30 texts]	Daily (8), first day of school, weekend, IEP picnic, meeting w/sponsor, conversation hour, party, chess, aquariums, Thanksgiving, IEP party, library, Indianapolis, studying, phone call, work [23]	*Anansi* (F), *Modern Times* (F), museum trip (C), *Tin Toy* (F), *Pink Panther* (F), *Thief of Baghdad* (F) [7]
Eduardo [13 texts]	Daily (3), check, exercising, IEP picnic, sponsor, Thanksgiving, first snow, Indianapolis, high school [11]	*Anansi* (F), *Tin Toy* (F) [2]
Ji-An [24 texts]	Daily, coming to Bloomington, college, sales job (2), trip to Indianapolis, travel (Chicago), graduation, leaving home, Olympics, church, Indianapolis, mother, conversation hour, class, IEP picnic, party, travel, childhood swimming accident, new class, apology, airport, going home, piano recital [24]	

Table 2.4 (continued)

Topics and Types of Learner Texts Sampled

Learner	Spontaneous	Elicited
Sang Wook [14 texts]	Daily (7), weekend, phone call, conversation hour, friend, goodbye party [12]	Surprise Package (C), "A professor's life" (E) [2]
Idechi [23 texts]	Concert (5), daily (4), first day of classes (2), Kentucky, drinking, musical, opera (2), practice, trip to lake, audition, shopping, master (music) teacher [21]	*Anansi* (F), spare time (C) [2]
Kazuhiro [35 texts]	Daily (10), sports [tennis, golf, bowling, swimming] (8), conversation hour (3), being sick (2), IEP picnics (2), restaurant, TOEFL, concert, Indianapolis, dorm party, computers, friends [32]	*Anansi* (F), *Thief of Baghdad* (F), *Red's Dream* (F) [3]
Hiromi [37 texts]	Daily (6), letters (3), IEP picnics (2), Chicago (2), basketball, birthday party, news from home, video, vacuum, first day of class, pronunciation story, taking photos, cooking, package, JFL play, tapes, Japanese FL students, dorm meeting, dream, studying, driver's license, car accident, visiting, movie, *War of the Roses* [34]	Holiday (C), Surprise Package (C), *Elephant Child* (S) [3]
Tosihiro [30 texts]	Daily (20), weekend, IEP picnic, grammar, 4th of July, nightmare, Chicago, shooting, ski trip, military service, brother's visit [30]	

Table 2.4 (continued)

Topics and Types of Learner Texts Sampled

Learner	Spontaneous	Elicited
Satoru [20 texts]	Daily (7), coffee hour (2), dorm life, summer apartment, library, conversation partner, friend, sleep problems, playoffs [16]	Museum trip (C), *Anansi* (F), yesterday (C), *Thief of Baghdad* (F) [4]
Noriko [46 texts]	Daily (21), dinner w/friends (3), shopping (2), friends (2), Chicago, new class, 4th of July, birthday, restaurant, visiting, going home, IEP picnic, conversation partner, Canada, IEP party, problems, *A Chorus Line*, spring break, date, conversation partner party [44]	*Modern Times* (F), *Tin Toy* (F) [2]

Note. F = Narrative elicited by film retell task, C = class assignment, E = program-wide final examination. From "Reverse-Order Reports and the Acquisition of Tense: Beyond the Principle of Chronological Order," by K. Bardovi-Harlig, 1994, *Language Learning, 44*, pp. 280–282. Copyright 1994 by the Language Learning Research Club. Reprinted with permission.

Results and Discussion

Every verb supplied in past-time contexts was coded for its verbal morphology independently by two experienced coders (the researcher and her assistant) and all adverbials were identified and coded as time, duration, and frequency adverbials (Harkness, 1987). Once the verb tokens in each sampling period for each learner had been coded, they were sorted into types by a computer sorting program. Rates of appropriate use of past tense were calculated as the ratio of the number of past-tense forms (i.e., types) supplied to the number of obligatory environments. All rates of appropriate use are given as percentages (e.g., 16/24 × 100 = 66.7%).

All cases of reverse-order reports in the texts sampled were identified by the same two coders. There were 103 RORs in the 430 texts sampled. RORs were coded for verbal morphology and presence of other markers, namely adverbials, relative clauses, complements, and causal constructions.

The expression of reverse-order reports. Although a contrast in verb tense, usually between the past and pluperfect, is sufficient to signal a ROR, it is not the only marker that is used. Regardless of tense use, most RORs exhibit some marker that distinguishes them from the surrounding narrative. The markers fall into five categories: single uses of time adverbials, contrastive uses of time adverbials, relative clauses, complements, and *because.* Time adverbials comprise two categories: single adverbials in which a learner uses one time adverbial, such as *before,* and dual adverbials in which a learner contrasts two adverbials, as in *yesterday/two weeks ago.*[22] The 103 RORs identified in the corpus were classified into two main types according to their tense-aspect morphology: RORs that exhibit a tense-aspect contrast and those that do not. Of the 103 RORs, 40 showed no contrast in tense-aspect morphology, whereas 63 RORs showed a tense-aspect contrast.

Reverse-order reports without morphological contrast. RORs that show no contrast in verbal morphology typically employ other markers. Some exhibit only a single marker (25 RORs), but others

show two markers (12 RORs). Only three RORs without morphological contrast showed no overt markers (Table 2.5, left
column).

As may be expected from studies of earlier stages of temporal
expression (e.g., Bardovi-Harlig, 1992c; Dietrich et al., 1995;
Meisel, 1987), time adverbials play an important role in RORs. As
many as 46.2% of RORs with no morphological contrast are
marked by time adverbials; 25.0% show a single adverbial, as in
(28) and (29), and 21.2% employ two adverbials, as in (30), where
the contrast is between *Level 2* and *before [Level 2]*.

28. I went back to my apartment [2] *after* I finished washing [1].
     [Hamad, T9.5]

29. My sister played piano very well. *Before* she played [2], we
     were very nervous [1]. [Ji-An, T6.5]

30. *In level two* I studied many new things for me [2], I didn't
     study *befor* in the another school [1]. [Zayed, T3.5]

Table 2.5

Past-Time Reverse-Order Reports

No Morphological Contrast			Morphological Contrast		
Devices	Raw Scores	% of Total	Devices	Raw Scores	% of Total
No marking	3	5.8	Morphology only	14	20.6
Single adverb	13	25.0	Single adverb	23	33.8
Dual adverbs	11	21.2	Dual adverb	7	10.3
Relative clause	7	13.5	Relative clause	11	16.2
Because	12	23.1	Because	7	10.3
Complement	6	11.5	Complement	6	8.8
Total	52	100.1	Total	68	100.0

Note. From "Reverse-Order Reports and the Acquisition of Tense: Beyond the
Principle of Chronological Order," by K. Bardovi-Harlig, 1994, *Language
Learning, 44,* p. 253. Copyright 1994 by the Language Learning Research
Club. Reprinted with permission.

Causal constructions signalled by *because* form the next most common group of RORs, as illustrated in (31) and (32).

31. Yesterday was a pusy [busy] day because I had to go to Indiana bell [2] *because* I didn't biad [paid] my bell [1] so I did. [Hamad, T11]

32. I awake with a sore throat and temperature. Therefore I bought medicine and took it. But I didn't become to feel better [2], *because* I made big mistake [1]. [Kazuhiro, T7.5]

Relative clauses and complements form 25.0% of the RORs without morphological contrasts. Relative clauses and complements are typical (but not exclusive) environments for background information (Dry, 1981, 1983). A ROR reported with a relative clause is found in (33) and with a complement in (34) and (35). The complements often, though not always, report speech or thought, as in (35).

33. Then the bolice [police] but [put] the girl [2] which stole the bread [1] on the lory with Charlie. [Zayed, T5.5]

34. One of the women is cooking. He also stole foods from women, Then Some people were playing magic show. The thief was watching magic rope. And then, the women *found* [2] *that* thief man stole her food [1]. [Satoru, T9.0]

35. He *thought* [2] *that* I *said* "Coming" [1]. [Noriko, T6.0]

RORs that employ two markers include examples such as (36) in which the learner used dual adverbials and a relative clause as markers.

36. *at the moumint* I was so happy because I saw my old teachers [2] *who* tought me *befor* [1] [Hamad, T5.5]

Only three (5.8%) of the RORs used no overt marker. One of those, shown in (37), established event order through the lexical items *breakfast, lunch,* and *dinner.*

37. I told her I'm very hungry Can you eat *dinner*? She said to me "Yes." [2] She didn't eat *breakfast, lunch* [1] so also she

was hungry. After dinner, we took a walk Bloomington around. [Noriko, T7.5]

Failure to overtly signal a ROR may be a communicatively risky strategy since the learner does not alert the reader/listener to the deviation from chronological order. Such cases constitute violations of the principle of natural order for just the reason specified by Klein (1986): They do not signal the deviation.

Reverse-order reports with morphological contrast. Of the 103 RORs in the group corpus, 63 showed a contrast in verbal morphology. Although the target contrast is generally between past and pluperfect, learner RORs employed this contrast in only 66.7% of the cases showing morphological contrast. The remaining RORs are divided among other contrasts (Table 2.6). This suggests that learners recognize RORs as an environment for a morphological contrast before they are able to consistently produce the past-pluperfect contrast used by native speakers. The contrast between the simple past and pluperfect is illustrated in (38) and (39).

38. John and I *went* to her building [2]. She *had invited* her friends [1]. [Eduardo, T1.0]

Table 2.6

Type of Morphological Contrasts in Past-Time Reverse-Order Reports

Morphological Contrast	Raw Scores	Percent of Total
Past—Pluperfect	42	66.7
Past—Present Perfect	7	11.1
Past—Past Progressive	3	4.8
Present/Base—Past	7	11.1
Misc	4	6.3
Total	63	100

Note. From "Reverse-Order Reports and the Acquisition of Tense: Beyond the Principle of Chronological Order," by K. Bardovi-Harlig, 1994, *Language Learning, 44,* p. 255. Copyright 1994 by the Language Learning Research Club. Reprinted with permission.

39. There *were* many different shops' bagages [2] maybe she *had gone* shopping many times and different shops [1]. [Hiromi, T6.5]

The remaining 33.3% of the RORs with morphological contrasts are divided among other contrasts, such as past and present perfect, as in (40), and past and past progressive, as in (41). The latter represents a contrast in aspect rather than tense.

40. We went over to Steak and Shake for lunch. Then he *asked* me [2] if I *have been* in spring Mill Park [1]. [Guillermo, T8.0]

41. I *found* my conversation partner [2] and she was so happy because she *was trying* to find me from three weeks [1]. [Saleh, T10.0]

Another common contrast is the contrast between a base form and the simple past. These cases are particularly interesting because the learners generally begin their narratives in the past, then create a contrast by switching to the base form to relate the more recent event (event 2) and use the simple past for the anterior event (event 1) as in (42) and (43).

42. After that the policeman *caught* him. . . In the car, there *are* many people [2] who *did* bad things [1]. [Noriko, T11.0]

43. She met charlie the nice man who was trying to helpe her when he said "she didn't steel the bread I did that", No body *belive* that because [2] the lady *saw* the garil [1]. [Saleh, T13.0]

The presence of a contrast in tense-aspect morphology does not completely obviate the need for additional overt signals of deviations from chronological order. 79.4% of the RORs that exhibit morphological contrast also employ other markers. However, there are nearly four times as many RORs with morphological contrasts that do not utilize lexical markers (20.6%) than RORs with no morphological contrast (5.7%, Table 2.5) In addition, fewer RORs with a tense-aspect contrast employ two markers (only 5 out of 63) than those without a contrast (12 out of 40). Time adverbials continue to play an important role, with 44.1% of the markers falling into the adverbial category. There appears to be a shift from almost equal use of single and dual adverbials in the no-contrast RORs to a preference for a single adverbial in the presence of a morphological contrast. Single and dual adverbials with a morphological contrast are found in (44) and (45), respectively.

44. *By the time the baker caught her* [2] she had run into our hero [1]. [Carlos T5.5]

45. *Today morning* my father called us [2]. He told us [3] that grandmother has been sick *during two weeks* [1]. [Ji-An, T6.5]

In the RORs with a verbal contrast, the use of *because* (as in 46) falls to half its use compared to RORs without a morphological contrast, but the use of relative clauses (47) and complements (40 and 48) are similar in both environments.

46. I spent that time with my family [2] *because* I had been here since Ogust [1]. [Zayed, T7.5]

47. In order to avoid mistakes and misunderstanings I had to review severals time [2] *what I had done* [1]. [Eduardo, T7.5]

48. I thought about [2] *how she had bought them and packed them* [1]. [Hiromi, T6.5]

The emergence of reverse-order reports. To address the question of when RORs are first used, the study examines emergence in real time and with respect to other characteristics of interlanguage in order to determine the acquisitional sequence. Table 2.7 presents the time at which RORs and pluperfect emerge for each learner. In Table 2.7 times are given in half-month intervals. 10.0 indicates that the sample was taken in the first half of the 10th month; 5.5 indicates that the sample was taken in the second half of the 5th month. Thus, for learners who entered the program in January, T.5 represents the first 15 days and T1.0 represents days 16–31.

There is wide variation in the time at which RORs appear in the language samples. In Table 2.7, "ROR" gives the first sampling time that a ROR appears in a learner's language sample. Learners Eduardo, Carlos, and Guillermo (L1 Spanish) and Kazuhiro (L1 Japanese) show the earliest use of RORs. Among the other learners, the earliest instance appeared at 2.0 months (Idechi and Toshihiro). The mean for the group is 4.44 months (*SD* 3.52). The group mean is later still (6.19 months) if isolated use (a one-time use or use with only a single verb) and productive use (multiple uses in different environments) are distinguished. Kazuhiro and Satoru show early isolated uses of RORs that do not appear again for over six months; for example, Kazuhiro used one ROR at T1.0, but no RORs appeared in his samples again until T7.5. The time of the isolated and productive uses are given for Kazuhiro and Satoru in Table 2.7.[23] The variation in the emergence times illustrates the difficulty of approaching the expression of RORs in real time. (The same difficulty has been long recognized in child L1 acquisition research where real time is realized as a child's age; see, for example, Brown, 1973.)

Although the actual time of first use varies greatly across learners, there is a clear order of emergence when times of expression of RORs are compared to the rates of appropriate use of the simple past tense. The columns at the right of Table 2.7 provide the number of RORs produced by each learner. Column 1, labelled "Ror," gives the total number of RORs in the sample. Column 2, "Con," is a subset of column 1 indicating the number of RORs that employed a verb morphological contrast. Column 3, "Plu," is a subset of column 2 indicating how many of the contrasts employed the pluperfect. RORs generally appear before the pluperfect, showing that early RORs do not employ the pluperfect but employ other markers as discussed in the previous section. The number of RORs that exhibit the pluperfect is always less than the total number of RORs. Fourteen learners employed some form of morphological contrast in expressing RORs, but only 10 learners used the pluperfect. Six learners did not show a pluperfect ROR in their samples in this corpus.

If the emergence in real time is too varied to provide a clear picture of when RORs are expressed, examining the appropriate

Table 2.7

The Emergence of Reverse-Order Reports and Pluperfect

Subject	Month 1	1.5	2	2.5	3	3.5	4	4.5	5	5.5	6	6.5	7	7.5
Eduardo Spanish	ROR+PLU 78 (18)													
Carlos Spanish		ROR 96 (70)	PLU											
Hiromi Japanese					ROR+PLU 95 (79)									
Sang Wook Korean							97 (57)	ROR 96(56)		PLU 100 (24)				
Kazuhiro Japanese	ROR+PLU 89 (9)											84 (45)		ROR+PLU 83 (42)
Idechi Japanese			ROR 88 (68)								100 (16)			PLU 82 (22)
Zayed Arabic				84 (19)		ROR 64 (22)								PLU 81 (63)
Hamad Arabic										ROR 91 (22)				
Toshihiro Japanese	94 (34)		ROR 92 (52)				94 (53)							
Noriko Japanese							100 (26)				100 (16)	ROR 94 (31)		

Table 2.7 (continued)

The Emergence of Reverse-Order Reports and Pluperfect

Subject	Month 1	1.5	2	2.5	3	3.5	4	4.5	5	5.5	6	6.5	7	7.5
Guillermo Spanish	ROR 100 (14)													
Satoru Japanese				ROR 69 (26)										
Ji-An Korean												ROR 97 (35)		
Khaled Arabic													94 (16)	ROR 87 (37)
Saleh Arabic							82 (37)							
Abdullah Arabic							100 (12)							

ROR   Emergence of reverse-order reports
PLU   Emergence of pluperfect
numeral   Percentage of appropriate past tense use
(numeral)   number of verb types sampled in month 1
Ror   number of reverse-order reports sampled
Con   number of reverse-order reports showing a morphological contrast
Plu   number of reverse-order reports using pluperfect

Table 2.7 (continued)

The Emergence of Reverse-Order Reports and Pluperfect

Subject	Month 8	8.5	9	9.5	10	10.5	11	11.5	12	12.5	13	13.5	Ror raw	Con raw	Plu raw
Eduardo Spanish													7	7	5
Carlos Spanish													19	16	13
Hiromi Japanese													17	12	11
Sang Wook Korean													2	1	1
Kazuhiro Japanese													7	6	6
Idechi Japanese													4	3	2
Zayed Arabic													6	4	1
Hamad Arabic				PLU 85 (46)									10	1	1
Toshihiro Japanese							PLU 79 (65)						5	2	1
Noriko Japanese										PLU 86 (57)			9	3	1

Table 2.7 (continued)

The Emergence of Reverse-Order Reports and Pluperfect

Subject	Month 8	8.5	9	9.5	10	10.5	11	11.5	12	12.5	13	13.5	Ror raw	Con raw	Plu raw
Guillermo Spanish													7	4	0
Satoru Japanese			ROR 90 (10)										3	0	0
Ji-An Korean													2	1	0
Khaled Arabic													1	1	0
Saleh Arabic					ROR 71 (82)					.	ROR 37 (41)		3	2	0
Abdullah Arabic													1	0	0
TOTAL													103	63	42

Note. From "Reverse-Order Reports and the Acquisition of Tense: Beyond the Principle of Chronological Order," by K. Bardovi-Harlig, 1994, *Language Learning, 44*, pp. 260–263. Copyright 1994 by the Language Learning Research Club. Adapted with permission.

use of past tense in past-time contexts provides a clearer picture. Looking at the rate of appropriate use of past tense as a percentage of total verbs used in past-time contexts shows that RORs appear after the use of past tense has stabilized, that is, after tense reliably indicates time reference. For most learners, this means 80% or above. Two rates of appropriate use are given in Table 2.7. The number that appears under the label "Ror" is the rate of appropriate use of past tense in the sampling period during which the first ROR occurred. The first number gives the percentage of appropriate use, and the number in parentheses is the sum of distinct verb types sampled in the first and second half-month intervals.[24] One-month intervals were used to provide the largest possible samples for each learner. For example, Khaled showed his first ROR at 7.5 months, at which time he showed 87% appropriate use of past tense in a sample of 37 verbs. Because the rate of appropriate use drops for some learners when RORs first appear, an earlier figure is given that provides the highest rate of appropriate use of past in any sample prior to the emergence of RORs.[25] The rate appears in the table under the time at which it occurred. Khaled showed higher appropriate use of past at 94% in a sample of 16 verbs at T7.0, prior to the first ROR. For some learners, such as Zayed, the difference is more dramatic. In the sampling period in which his first ROR appeared, Zayed showed 64% appropriate use of past, but had reached 84% appropriate use in a previous sampling period. For the group as a whole, taking the sum of all the appropriate uses of past tense and dividing by the sum of all the environments for past tense (662 verbs) results in a group rate of 85% appropriate use at the appearance of the first ROR and a group rate of high use of 91%.

The emergence of pluperfect in reverse-order reports. Emerging still later, with slightly higher group accuracy rates for the use of past tense, is the pluperfect. Although all 16 learners eventually used RORs, only 10 learners used the pluperfect in this corpus. As Table 2.7 shows, for 7 of the 10 learners who used the pluperfect, RORs were expressed first. For the remaining 3 (Eduardo, Hiromi, and Kazuhiro), RORs and pluperfect appeared simultaneously. As

Hiromi's use of pluperfect in 11 out of 17 RORs indicates, even learners who can use the pluperfect do not use it invariably. The group rate of appropriate use of past tense at emergence of the pluperfect was 87%, and the group high was 92% for the 10 learners who attempted RORs with pluperfect. The lowest rate of appropriate use of past for any learner who used the pluperfect was 78% (Eduardo). Toshihiro showed his first use of pluperfect at 79% appropriate use of past in a sample of 65 verbs, but his highest rate of appropriate use reached 94% in a sample of 53 verbs.

This somewhat later use of pluperfect emphasizes its non-essential nature for learners (including instructed learners). The pluperfect is but one linguistic device that serves to signal a deviation from chronological order. In spite of the fact that the pluperfect seems to be the clearest and most readily accepted marker of RORs, it is not strictly necessary from a functional perspective. Early RORs are marked particularly successfully with time adverbials and *because,* which also serve other functions in interlanguage. Because not all learners who produced RORs used the pluperfect, the high rate of accuracy of past and the expression of RORs appear to be necessary but not sufficient conditions for the emergence of pluperfect.

Additional evidence for sequencing. Two learners, Carlos and Hiromi, produced more RORs than the other learners, with 19 and 17 RORs respectively. The robust presence of RORs in the texts of Carlos and Hiromi provides a further opportunity to examine how learners express RORs over time. Table 2.8 presents a chronology of RORs produced by Carlos and Hiromi. For each ROR, the sampling time, the morphological contrast, and the number of each type produced is given by learner.

At T1.5, Carlos produced a ROR that showed no contrast (both verbs occur in simple past). At T2.0 there is competition between three forms: no contrast (both verbs occur in the past), present perfect, and pluperfect as shown in (49)–(51).

Table 2.8

Type and Order of RORs Produced by Carlos and Hiromi

Carlos			Hiromi		
T1.5	No contrast	1	T3.0	No contrast	1
				Past/Pluperfect	1
T2.0	No contrast	1	T5.5	No contrast	1
	Past/Pres Perf	2		Past/Pluperfect	1
	Past/Pluperfect	1			
T2.5	No contrast	1	T6.0	No contrast	2
	Past/Pluperfect	2		Past/Pluperfect	1
T3.0	Past/Pluperfect	1	T6.5	Past/Pluperfect	3
T3.5	Past/Pluperfect	1	T7.5–9.5	Past/Pluperfect	5
				Past/Ø Perfect	1
				No contrast	1
T5.5	Past/Pres Perf	1			
	Past/Pluperfect	4			
T6.0–9.0	Past/Pluperfect	4			
Total		19	Total		17

Note. From "Reverse-Order Reports and the Acquisition of Tense: Beyond the Principle of Chronological Order," by K. Bardovi-Harlig, 1994, *Language Learning, 44,* p. 266. Copyright 1994 by the Language Learning Research Club. Reprinted with permission.

49. and we saw [2] that him was the man that gave us the real adress at the store [1].

50. . . . and he *was* very happy [2] because he *has seen* his father [1].

51. I went to take it, and after I *discovered* the person [2] that *had called* [1] me was fool.

From T3.0 on, the past-pluperfect contrast is dominant, with one case of present perfect at T5.5. No further occurrence of present perfect in RORs is seen in Carlos's texts after that.

Hiromi shows somewhat later use of RORs. For Hiromi, there is no apparent experimentation with the present perfect in the context created by the RORs. Her texts show that RORs with no tense-aspect contrasts remain a common alternative until T6.5. Hiromi's production at T5.5 is illustrated by (52) and (53).

52. Today was first day of Summer II program. I could be a level 4 student, and I had many new friends at new class. I was very happy [2] because most of my friends who studied at last and two before last [1] became my clase mate again.

53. I thought [2] that to sell my old books half price which *I'd bought* [1] was help me and a student.

For these learners, the pluperfect gradually replaces other tense-aspect forms over time. Although Carlos and Hiromi take slightly different routes, they arrive at the exclusive use of pluperfect in RORs within one sampling period of each other.[26]

Summary

As predicted by Klein's (1986) principle of natural order, deviations from chronological order must be signalled in interlanguage as well as in the target language. Only 3 of 103 RORs did not occur with markers, and one of those employed implicit marking through lexical items. The obligatory presence of a marker of deviation from chronological order, at least in part, determines when learners will express RORs. The expression of RORs is delayed until the learner can use a marker to distinguish them from the surrounding narrative.

The main distinction in marking seems to be between those RORs that mark the distinction with a morphological contrast plus an optional secondary marker and those that only use the secondary markers. Without a morphological contrast, and even with one, RORs are marked by time adverbials, causal adverbials, relative clauses, and complements. The latter markers are themselves available only in later stages of acquisition because of their inherent syntactic complexity. The emergence of the pluperfect provides a specialized morphological marker of RORs, but the longitudinal evidence shows that even with instruction the expression of

RORs precedes the acquisition of the pluperfect. Thus, it is not the emergence of pluperfect that allows the expression of RORs, but the expression of RORs that creates an environment for the pluperfect.

The finding that the acquisition of the pluperfect serves the expression of RORs but does not itself make RORs possible is an important result of employing a meaning-oriented approach to this inquiry. Both a form-focused approach (i.e., focusing on the acquisition of the pluperfect) and a meaning-oriented approach (focusing on the expression of RORs) could identify the acquisitional prerequisite of high appropriate use of past tense. However, focus on the form of the pluperfect alone would fail to capture the fact that the pluperfect moves into an established semantic environment. Through a meaning-oriented approach two prerequisites for the acquisition of pluperfect are revealed: high appropriate use of past tense and expression of RORs.

The study of interlanguage development from a meaning-oriented approach highlights the relationship of the various linguistic devices that learners may employ for temporal reference. It provides a functional view of pluperfect as only one marker of RORs, albeit an unambiguous one. In addition, studying the environment in which pluperfect occurs suggests why it is acquired relatively late: The environment itself—the expression of RORs—appears only after the use of past tense has reached moderate stability.

Chapter Summary

A meaning-oriented approach emphasizes the importance of pragmatic and lexical means in the expression of temporality. Production data, both oral and written, form the corpora examined by meaning-oriented studies. A meaning-oriented approach to the analysis of learner production reveals that learners develop a functional, and often rich, means of temporal expression before the acquisition of verbal morphology. A meaning-oriented approach also highlights the interplay of the pragmatic, lexical, and morphological devices that learners use. Much work emphasizes the central role played by time adverbials and lexical expressions in the second stage of temporal development, where the use of lexical devices to mark temporal expression is the defining characteristic of the stage.

The use of adverbials is not restricted only to the pre-morphological lexical stage, however. Lexical devices continue to be used well into the morphological stage, although they exhibit both an actual decrease in frequency of occurrence relative to the number of inflected verbs and a reduction in functional load as the use of past tense stabilizes. Research on the emergence of reverse-order reports shows that lexical devices, including adverbials, also play an important role in defining semantic environments well into the morphological stage, where learners show stable and reliable use of simple past morphology.

The next chapter investigates a form-oriented approach in which the tracking of the verbal morphology becomes central. Although form-meaning associations are still investigated, the investigations begin with the form rather than the meaning. Clearly, such an approach may not be suitable for the earliest stages of acquisition in which learners do not employ verbal morphology to express temporal reference, but it does allow for an alternative perspective on the acquisition process. Following the acquisition of verbal morphology reveals that learners may use it in innovative ways, developing interlanguage tense-aspect systems that share often prototypical features with the target language as they move toward the target norm.

Notes

[1]These concepts may differ cross-linguistically (Guiora, 1983), but in second language acquisition, language acquisition is distinct from cognitive development; these are often simultaneous in child language acquisition.

[2]Dietrich et al.'s study on temporality, *The Acquisition of Temporality in a Second Language* (1995), is only one of a number of important studies that resulted from the ESF's longitudinal study. Thus, the tasks and the corpus for this portion of the inquiry are but part of the tasks performed by the learners (e.g., the direction-giving re-enactment for the study on spatial relations in L2, reported by Becker & Carroll, 1997).

[3]The stages of acquisition which are characterized by the use of pragmatic, lexical, and morphological means correspond respectively to the general levels of interlanguage development labelled the pre-basic variety, the basic variety, and what is called "beyond the basic variety" (Dietrich et al., 1995). The latter analysis is part of a more comprehensive approach to the analysis of interlanguage adopted by the ESF researchers (e.g., Becker & Carroll, 1997; Dietrich et al., 1995; Klein & Perdue, 1992). I focus on the primary linguistic categories for expression of temporality because they can easily be adopted by researchers and teachers working in a range of theories of second language acquisition and pedagogy. It should also be noted that not all proponents of the meaning-oriented approach employ the "basic-variety" categorization (e.g., Meisel, 1987; Giacalone Ramat, 1992; Giacalone Ramat & Banfi, 1990).

[4]Serialization includes the concept of bracketing (von Stutterheim & Klein, 1987) as well as chronological order. Schumann (1987) defined serialization as "the fixing of a temporal reference point and allowing the sequence of events to reflect the actual order of reported events" (p. 21).

[5]The relationship of aspectual categories and the interpretation of sequentiality is taken up at length in Chapter 5.

[6]Adult second language acquisition differs from child language acquisition in the early stages of temporal acquisition in that children do not regularly use temporal adverbials (Slobin, 1993; Smith, 1980; Weist, Wysocka, & Lyytinen, 1991).

[7]Interestingly, Giacalone Ramat and Banfi (1990) note a difference between learner populations: Most learners use the third singular of present indicative for the base form, but learners who live in isolated groups and get poor input may choose infinitives (p. 424).

[8]Bhat (1999) offers a different analysis of adverbials, dividing temporal adverbials into (a) temporal adverbials proper, those that are associated directly with tense (i.e., locating an event on a time line, such as *at 3 o'clock*) and (b) aspectual adverbs, those that denote duration, frequency, or habituality, such as *for 3 hours* and *he went to the library every week*.

[9]This difference in the sequential and referential parallels the distinction that Erickson and Shultz (1982) made for discourse analysis (of academic interviews): sequential time and real time (1982, p. 72). *Kairos* time, or sequential time, refers to the ordering of the events in the narrative; the learner uses chronological order to establish sequence in the birth story. In contrast, *chronos* time refers to real time or time on the clock. Adverbs which specify how long certain episodes took (*15 minutes, two hours*) or when they began or ended (*3 p.m.*) mark chronos time.

[10]This chapter is dedicated to Maya Rachel Salsbury, whose arrival during the writing of the chapter occasioned birth narratives by my research assistant, Tom Salsbury, and his wife, Lysa Salsbury.

[11]In fact, this learner (Hamad) shows the greatest use of adverbials of all eight low-level learners studied by Bardovi-Harlig (1992c).

[12]Many researchers are likely to agree with the claim that learners' desires to communicate help propel them from the pragmatic to the lexical stage where they are less reliant on scaffolding and thus can independently build meaning. As Meisel (1987) argues, communication also improves between the lexical and morphological stages. Although the researchers who contributed to the studies in Dietrich et al. (1995) characterize the basic variety as a practical communicative system, they too acknowledge four main shortcomings to communicative efficiency: (a) absence of contrast adverbials such as *again* and *yet,* (b) lack of aspectual variation, (c) presence of many ambiguities, and (d) no easy way to distinguish between single case readings, and habitual or generic readings. However, in their conclusion to Dietrich et al. (1995), Klein, Dietrich, and Noyau (1995) cite social factors as an additional motivating factor: The basic variety "stigmatises the learner as an outsider" (p. 272). The desire to imitate the input and for social acceptance may be strong in some learners.

Offering a different interpretation of the communicative power of the lexical stage, Starren and van Hout (1996) suggest that the lexical stage (i.e., the basic variety), with its flexibility in communication, especially when there is an expanded inventory of adverbials, "compensate[s] for the functions of grammatical tense and aspect marking and therefore an optimalisation of this system has to be considered as a serious blocking factor in the grammaticalisation process" (pp. 48–49). Although they disagree on the communicative motivation for acquiring tense-aspect morphology, they agree with Klein et al. (1995) that the social motivation causes learners to embark on the "insecure grammaticalisation process" (p. 49).

[13]The influence of instruction is discussed in detail in Chapter 6.

[14]This study was originally reported in Bardovi-Harlig (1992c).

[15]Verbs such as *was* and *went* may occur several times in a text, giving an overall appearance of past tense use, when in fact the past is restricted to only a few verbs. Type analysis gives the same credit for the use of past with every verb (e.g., *was* used six times and *walked* used once are both counted as one type). Thus, type counts provide a conservative view of the acquisition of verb morphology once it begins to spread. This was the case with the learners investigated here. However, in the very earliest stages of morphological development, a type count could equalize a single use of a past form such as *went* and multiple uses of a base form such as *go* by counting each one as a type. This would inflate the importance of a single use of *went,* in our example. In this corpus, the use of a type count had the effect of depressing the rate of use scores for the past.

It should be noted that although the use of types provides a more conservative view of the emergence and control of tense-aspect morphology, it does not preserve the integrity of the text. A learner may achieve the feeling of a past-tense text by the use of multiple occurrences of a small number of verbs in past tense, but this effect is not captured in a type analysis. For this reason, any discourse analysis of tense-aspect must take tokens into account. (See Chapter 5; Bardovi-Harlig, 1992b, 1995a, 1998.)

[16]Past progressive and simple past (*was speaking/spoke*) are unequivocally past tense, differing in aspect. Pluperfect constitutes a separate tense (Comrie, 1985; Nehls, 1988), but nevertheless shares past-tense morphology.

[17]Quirk, Greenbaum, Leech, and Svartvik suggest that forms such as *today* and *yesterday* lie on a continuum from adverb to noun and that cases such as *Yesterday was my birthday* "illustrate blurring of nominal and adverbial functions" (1985, p. 736fn). In spite of the fact that these are not clearly adverbs—or perhaps not only adverbs—they are included here because their semantic, if not syntactic, function is adverbial.

[18]For readers who have followed the previously published accounts of these learners (Bardovi-Harlig, 1992c, 1994b, 1997a), I provide the following list of the codes that I used earlier and the pseudonyms that I have adopted here: SA=Saleh, MA=Hamad, AR=Abdullah, WA=Khaled, RZ=Zayed, IS=Idechi, JU=Kazuhiro, HK=Hiromi, TO=Noriko, TS=Toshihiro, ST=Satoru, YJ=Ji-An, WS=Sang Wook, OS=Carlos, ER=Eduardo, and LU=Guillermo. Only 8 learners were observed in the present study, but all 16 were observed in the study that immediately follows in this chapter.

[19]The native speakers show little variation in their individual adverb-to-verb ratios.

NS	Adverb-to-Verb Ratio
A	.22
B	.19
C	.20
D	.18
Group	.20

[20]All of these are background functions. Chronological order is essentially a characteristic of foreground, although it may also occur in the background, particularly in embedded sequences. See Chapter 5 for a discussion of narrative analysis as it relates to tense-aspect morphology.

[21]An academic history regarding enrollment in the IEP is provided for each learner in Chapter 3.

[22]The categories of markers were derived by analysis of the interlanguage RORs, but with the exception of dual adverbials can all be found in common (written) English.

[23]I am indebted to Shona Whyte for the design of Table 2.7.

[24]Types were calculated separately for half-month intervals, then totalled.

[25]The drop in rates of appropriate use may be due in part to the contrasts which learners employ to signal early RORs, which include base, present, and present perfect forms. It may also be due to a general U-shaped curve as the tense-aspect system expands to include morphology not under investigation here.

[26]The potential relation of instruction on the emergence of RORs is discussed in Chapter 6.

CHAPTER THREE

The Emergence of Verbal Morphology

As seen in Chapter 2, adult learners of second languages are able to express temporal relations long before the emergence of tense-aspect morphology. The first two stages of temporal expression, the pragmatic and the lexical, together establish a communicatively viable system. This chapter focuses on the third stage of the acquisition of temporal expression, the morphological stage, and is the first of three chapters devoted to form-oriented studies. American research into tense-aspect has been particularly concerned with the acquisition of morphology. European researchers have characterized the American interest in morphology as the "inflexional paradigm bias" (Dietrich, 1995, p. 18), suggesting that American research has been overly concerned with form to the exclusion of meaning. Nevertheless, I believe that the meaning-oriented approach and the form-oriented approach together afford a better opportunity for understanding the acquisition of tense-aspect than either approach alone. This chapter, as well as Chapters 4 and 5, describes the research that has been devoted to studying the emergence of verbal morphology in the tense-aspect system. In this chapter I focus primarily on studies of the emergence of verbal morphology and the acquisitional sequences that characterize this stage of development.

The first half of the chapter reviews the research on acquisition sequences in the acquisition of tense-aspect morphology in English, Dutch, German, French, Italian, Spanish, and Swedish. A brief grammatical sketch is provided for each target language.

The studies in this area are predominantly longitudinal in design, as in the case of the meaning-oriented studies, and have collected either oral production data alone or both oral and written production data. The longitudinal design distinguishes this body of research from accuracy order studies conducted earlier. (See Chapter 1.) The second half of the chapter presents a longitudinal study of the development of morphology related to the expression of past in English: the simple past, past progressive, present perfect, and pluperfect. This study follows the progress of the 16 learners introduced in Chapter 2 from the perspective of a form-oriented rather than meaning-oriented inquiry. A comparison illustrates the difference between the two approaches to the same corpus.

The early morpheme order studies reflected the interest in second language acquisition research in determining acquisition orders. As demonstrated in Chapter 1, these early studies included verbal morphology along with articles, prepositions, and nominal morphology. However, as Ellis (1994), Larsen-Freeman and Long (1991), and many others have argued, early studies focused more on accuracy orders than on acquisition. As argued by reviews of research method, longitudinal studies are a more reliable means of determining acquisition order than cross-sectional studies are. Because of the methodological difficulties inherent in longitudinal design and a shift in the theoretical agenda of second language acquisition, interest in morpheme order studies ceased to be a big part of SLA research in general in the late 1970s. However, SLA researchers maintained an interest in tense-aspect studies because this is a closed and reasonably well-defined subsystem of grammar. Investigation of tense-aspect was facilitated by the adoption of the longitudinal design. These longitudinal studies not only provide information about the emergent tense-aspect system, but also offer a model for longitudinal research in other areas of interlanguage development.

Studies of the acquisition of tense-aspect morphology and its related temporal semantics contrast with earlier studies of accuracy or acquisition orders in at least two ways: they focus on *emergence* rather than *acquisition* and they focus on *sequences* rather than *orders*. Following Ellis (1994), accuracy or acquisition orders are obtained when a researcher compares "different morphological features" (p. 20). In contrast, sequences are stages of development in the acquisition of a single linguistic feature. Thinking in terms of sequences in studying the acquisition of tense and aspect emphasizes that a single grammatical subsystem is being investigated and that the parts of the systems are intrinsically related to the other parts and will have an impact on each other as the system develops. (See VanPatten, 1984, for an early division of morpheme order studies into grammatical categories.) The focus on emergence contrasts with studies of acquisition that attempted to establish when learners reach targetlike accuracy or appropriate use, or both, as in obligatory occasion analysis (e.g., Dulay & Burt, 1974; Larsen-Freeman, 1975) and targetlike use measures (Pica, 1984). Studies that focus on emergence as part of acquisition attempt to document when certain tense-aspect forms establish themselves in the learner's repertoire for expressing temporality. This maintains the focus on the process of acquisition rather than on the end product of acquisition. This is particularly important when investigating related components of a single subsystem. Because learners revise their form-meaning associations for any given tense-aspect morpheme as new morphemes are added to the system, we will see that we cannot think of any single form-meaning association as being acquired until the entire tense-aspect system has been acquired.

Although European researchers have a meaning-oriented focus and have objected to the American emphasis on morphology, it is nevertheless the case that the European Science Foundation longitudinal studies have dominated the morphological emergence studies. It should be noted that their dominance in the research of sequences in the acquisition of morphology is a result of the comprehensive study of the expression of temporality which culminates in the acquisition of morphology, rather than the result of an exclusive focus on morphology. These studies are quite different from those which focus exclusively on verbal morphology, such as those reviewed in the section on cross-sectional studies.

The European Science Foundation longitudinal studies have included the target languages of English, Dutch, French, German, and Swedish. Additional longitudinal studies have been carried out by Bardovi-Harlig (English, 1992c, 1997a), Schlyter (French, 1990), and Giacalone Ramat (Italian, 1995d, 1997; Giacalone Ramat & Banfi, 1990). See Table 3.1 for a summary of these studies.

Tense-Aspect Morphology in European Languages

In studies of the acquisition of Romance languages—namely French, Italian, and Spanish, as second languages—both tense and grammatical aspect have been investigated. Tense is a deictic category that locates an event on the time line, usually with reference to the time of speaking (Comrie, 1976; Dahl, 1985). In contrast, grammatical aspect does not locate an event or situation on the time line, nor does it relate the time of one situation to another. Rather, it is concerned with "the internal temporal constituency of one situation; one could state the difference as one between situation-internal time ([grammatical] aspect) and situation-external time (tense)" (Comrie, 1976, p. 5). Grammatical aspect contrasts with lexical, or inherent, aspect, which is not morphologically marked and resides in the semantics of verbs and their arguments. Lexical aspect is the focus of Chapter 4. Grammatical aspects provide different ways of viewing situations (Comrie, 1976; Dahl, 1985; C. Smith, 1983). In Romance languages there are two past tense forms—the perfective and the imperfective. The perfective forms—the preterite in Spanish, the passé composé in French, and the passato prossimo in Italian—encode the view of a situation or event as a whole and as completed. In contrast, the imperfective past—the imperfect in Spanish, the imparfait in French, and the imperfetto in Italian—encode explicit reference to the internal temporal structure of a situation, "viewing a situation from within" (Comrie, 1976, p. 24). According to Comrie, the characteristics of the imperfective in all languages tend to be habituality and continuousness (also known as durativity).

Table 3.1

Studies of Sequences in Morphological Development

Target language	Author	L1 / # of learners	Design	Instruction	Morphology	Discourse type
Catalan	Comajoan (1998)	1 English	Longitudinal, 9 months	CFL, also Spanish FL, French FL	Preterite and imperfect	Conversational interviews, oral film retell tasks
Dutch	Klein, Coenen, van Helvert & Hendricks (1995; from DKN)	2 Turkish 2 Moroccan Arabic	Longitudinal, 3 years	No class, 8 months, no class, 2 hrs/wk for 1 year	Infinitive, present, compound past (Perfectum)	Personal narratives, film retell tasks, guided conversations
English	Bailey (1987, 1989)	26 mixed L1	Cross-sectional, tested 6 weeks apart	Intensive program	Past, past progressive	Pictures prompted "tell about" and "ask about" tasks, oral & written personal narrative, oral & written story retell task
	Bardovi-Harlig (1994b)	16, Arabic, Korean, Japanese, Spanish	Longitudinal, up to 15.5 months ESL instruction	Intensive program	Pluperfect, past	Written personal narratives, some retell / reverse-order reports
	Bardovi-Harlig (1997a)	16, Arabic, Korean, Japanese, Spanish	Longitudinal, up to 15.5 months ESL instruction	Intensive program	Present perfect, past	Written personal narratives, some retell

Table 3.1 (continued)

Studies of Sequences in Morphological Development

Target language	Author	L1 / # of learners	Design	Instruction	Morphology	Discourse type
	Klein (1995; from DKN)	2 Italian (+ 2 supplemental) 2 Punjabi	Longitudinal, 3 years	4 months– 10 months, none	Past, present perfect, pluperfect	Personal narratives, film retell tasks, guided conversations
	Stanley & Mellow (1998)	8, Chinese, Greek, Korean, Spanish, Vietnamese	Longitudinal, 4 months	Low-intermediate composition course at community college; intermediate composition in intensive ESL program	Present, past, present perfect	4 free written narratives, 1 written film retell, 1 cloze passage
French	Harley & Swain (1978)	5 L1 English immersion children	Single taping at 5½ years of immersion education	Immersion, 5½ years	Compound past (passé composé) and imperfect (imparfait)	Conversational interviews with personal narrative, explanation of activities, future plans
	Kaplan (1987)	16 English	Cross-sectional	FFL	Passé composé and imparfait	Semi-structured, 10-min interviews

Table 3.1 (continued)

Studies of Sequences in Morphological Development

Target language	Author	L1 / # of learners	Design	Instruction	Morphology	Discourse type
	Schlyter (1990)	2 Swedish adults, 3 bilingual French-German children	Single taping at 9 & 11 months	None	Passé composé, imparfait, future, pluperfect, conditional, subjunctive	Conversational interviews (adults), conversations during play (children)
	Noyau, Houdaïfa, Vasseur, & Véronique (1995; from DKN)	2 Moroccan Arabic, 2 Spanish	3 years	None	Emergent participle and base forms	Personal narratives, film retell tasks, guided conversations
German	Dietrich (1995; from DKN)	3 Italian, 2 Turkish	Longitudinal, 3 years	Italians, no instruction; Turks, up to 10 hrs/week	Present, Perfekt, Prateritum, Plusquamperfekt	Personal narratives, film retell tasks, guided conversations
Italian	Giacalone Ramat & Banfi (1990)	4 Chinese	Longitudinal, 7 months	ISL, municipal course for beginners	Present, past participle, compound past (passato prossimo), infinitive	Oral narration of picture stories and film retell task

Table 3.1 (continued)

Studies of Sequences in Morphological Development

Target language	Author	L1 / # of learners	Design	Instruction	Morphology	Discourse type
	Giacalone Ramat (1995c, 1997)	20 mixed L1	Longitudinal	4 learners, some instruction; 16, none	Progressive	Conversational interview
	Wiberg (1996)	24 Italian-Swedish heritage learners of Italian, 8–17 years old	Cross-sectional	Yes, in Sweden	Passato prossimo & imperfect (imperfetto)	Guided conversations
Spanish	Andersen (1986a, 1986b, 1991)	2 English children, 6–14 years old	Longitudinal	No	Preterite & imperfect	Conversational sample
	Hasbún (1995)	80 English	Cross-sectional	SFL	Preterite & imperfect	Written narrative film retell task
	Salaberry (1999b)	16 English	Cross-sectional	SFL	Preterite & imperfect	Oral narrative retell tasks
Swedish	Noyau, Dorriots, Sjöström, & Voionmaa (1995; from DKN)	2 Spanish, 2 Finnish	Longitudinal, 3 years	Classes in Swedish and trade courses	Present, preterite, future, perfect	Oral narration of picture stories and film retell task

Note. DKN = Dietrich, Klein, & Noyau (1995). C = Catalan, E = English, I = Italian, S = Spanish, FL = Foreign Language, SL = Second Language.

In the remainder of this section, I present a brief overview of the morphology of tense and grammatical aspect in the languages that have been studied in second language acquisition research. In introducing the tense-aspect forms I give what is traditionally considered to be their English equivalent, but in referring to the terms I will use the grammatical term used by the researchers whose work I review here to avoid the appearance that everything can be reduced to the English grammatical equivalent. Researchers who investigate Spanish, for example, generally refer to the preterite and imperfect, whereas researchers writing about French in English generally refer to the passé composé and the imparfait.

In Spanish, the contrast between perfective and imperfective grammatical aspect is found between the preterite *Juan bailó* "Juan danced" and the imperfect *Juan bailaba* "Juan was dancing, Juan used to dance."[1] Examples of the Spanish preterite and imperfect are found in (1) and (2). French and Italian share the formal feature of a compound past, formed by the use of a past participle preceded by an auxiliary (*have* or *be*), in French *être* or *avoir* as in (3), in Italian *essere* and *avere* as in (5). The selection of the auxiliary is determined by the semantics of the verb. Examples of the French and Italian imperfects, the imparfait and the imperfetto, are presented in (4) and (6), respectively. Italian has a second imperfective form, namely the progressive, which is formed by *stare* + gerund as in (7).[2] The acquisition of the progressive in Italian has been investigated by Giacalone Ramat (1995c, 1997).

Spanish (Andersen, 1989, 1991)

(1) *Nadie bailó tan bien como él.*
    NOBODY DANCE-PRETERITE AS WELL AS HE
    "Nobody danced as well as he did (in the dance contest that we just saw)."

(2) *Nadie bailaba tan bien como él.*
    NOBODY DANCE-IMPERFECT AS WELL AS HE
    "Nobody danced as well as he did (when we were young/while everyone was watching him dance)."

French (Bergström, 1995)

(3) *Jean a chanté.*
JEAN AUXILIARY SING-PAST PARTICIPLE
"Jean sang/has sung."

(4) *Jean chantait.*
JEAN SING-IMPERFECT
"Jean sang/was singing/would (used to) sing."

Italian (Giacalone Ramat, 1997)

(5) *Mio fratello ha giocato a scacchi tutta la sera.*
MY BROTHER AUXILIARY PLAYED-PAST PARTICI-
PLE CHESS ALL EVENING
"My brother played/has played chess all evening."

(6) *Mentre mio fratello giocava a scacchi, ho finito i com-
piti.*
WHILE MY BROTHER PLAY-IMPERFECT CHESS I
FINISHED MY HOMEWORK
"While my brother was playing chess, I finished my
homework."

(7) *Giovanni sta vedendo la partita alla televisione.*
GIOVANNI AUXILIARY SEE-PROGRESSIVE THE
MATCH ON TELEVISION
"Giovanni is watching the match on television."

The Germanic languages lack the morphological distinction
of preterite and imperfect found in the Romance languages (Comrie, 1976; Klein, 1995; C. Smith, 1986). In Germanic languages,
such as English, German, Dutch, and Swedish, acquisition studies have recorded the emergence of past, perfect, and pluperfect. In
English, the acquisition of the past progressive has also been observed. English exhibits contrast in all these tense-aspect categories (discussed in detail shortly), whereas neither German nor Dutch
marks grammatical aspect as English does in the opposition
between the progressive and the simple. In the past, German
distinguishes a preterite, perfect, and pluperfect. Like all Germanic

languages, German has strong verbs which undergo vowel alternation in the stem (called ablaut) and weak verbs which do not. *Sagen* is a weak verb whose preterite form is *sagt* (third person singular), and *tragen* is a strong form whose preterite form is *trug* (third person singular). The present perfect is formed with the present of the auxiliaries *haben* or *sein* and the past participle, as in *ich habe gesagt* "I have said" and *ich bin gegangen* "I have gone"; the pluperfect is formed with the past of the auxiliary, as in *ich hatte gesagt* "I had said" (Hawkins, 1987). In Dutch the compound past, known as the Perfectum (formed by *hebben* "have" or *zijn* "be" plus the participle), is used for unmarked reference to the past (Housen, 1994; Klein et al., 1995). The selection of the auxiliary in German and Dutch is lexically determined as in French and Italian.[3] The English and German perfects belong to the same category, but the German perfect can express the notion of simple past time, whereas the English perfect cannot (Binnick, 1991). Thus *Goethe hat* "Hermann und Dorothea" *geschrieben* is understood as a simple past "Goethe wrote *Hermann and Dorothea*," whereas the English perfect equivalent, *Goethe has written* Hermann and Dorothea, is not. The Dutch perfect works the same way as the German perfect. In French and some varieties of German, the perfect has replaced the preterite as the narrative tense (Binnick, 1991), which also appears to be the case for Italian and Dutch.

Swedish morphology distinguishes between a preterite (known in Swedish as the Imperfektum, a term I will not adopt here because Swedish lacks a grammatical distinction between perfective and imperfective past) and the Perfekt. The Perfekt is formed by the use of *har* + V-*t*, *har sett* "have seen" and the Plusqvamperfektum (pluperfect) with the preterite of *har,* as in *hade sett* "had seen" (Haugen, 1987). (Verbs of motion require the auxiliary 'be.') Swedish verbal morphology is transparent: According to Haugen (1987) and Noyau, Dorriots, et al. (1995), there is no person agreement, and no change of stress in the lexical base upon inflection. However, Noyau, Dorriots, et al. (1995) observed that learners of Swedish face difficulty in the input because in colloquial Swedish the preterite, V-*de,* can be reduced to V-*a,* which is the same form as the infinitive in the most productive verb class. This rule is subject to sociolinguistic variation, but potentially poses a problem for learners. Classroom learners, however, get clear input of the preterite V-*de* forms.

Tense-Aspect Morphology Related to Past in English

Semantics of the Past Progressive[4]

As in the case of the contrast between the functional preterites (including the compound past) and the imperfect of the Romance languages, the contrast between the simple past (*walked*) and the past progressive (*was walking*) is one of grammatical aspect, also known as viewpoint aspect (Comrie, 1985, p. 32; Dahl, 1985; Leech, 1971; C. Smith, 1983, 1986). Reichenbach called the past progressive the "simple past, extended" (1947, p. 290) and diagrammed the arrangement of E, R, and S in the same way as the simple past, but with an interval over E and R as shown in (8) and (9).

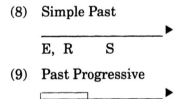

    (8)   Simple Past

        E, R   S

    (9)   Past Progressive

        E, R   S

The progressive is often described as being continuous (Comrie, 1985; Gass & Ard, 1984), hence the alternative label "present/past continuous" used by some authors (Bybee, 1985; Dietrich et al., 1995). Binnick (1991) identifies four theories of the progressive which include durative aspect, action in process or progress, incompletion, and progressive of the frame (p. 284).[5] Many accounts combine more than one feature of the progressive. For example, Leech (1971) identifies three features of the progressive: duration, limited duration, and incompletion. Leech argues that duration is played out in the past progressive as temporal framing, that is, the establishing of a time frame around an action denoted by a nonprogressive (an interpretation that Binnick, 1991, also attributes to Jespersen, 1924). Leech also identifies temporal framing as a function of the past progressive, as in (10), but argues that the framing derives from the basic concept of limited duration. He contends that the relationship between two simple past forms as in (10a) is usually one of time-sequence, whereas the relationship between the progressive and the simple past is usually one of time inclusion as in (10b).

(10) a. When we arrived she made some fresh coffee.

b. When we arrived she was making some fresh coffee.

In the first example, making the coffee followed the arrival, whereas in the second the arrival took place during the coffee-making.

Leech (1971) also argues that the feature of lack of completion is particularly noticeable in the past progressive (as opposed to the present progressive), as in (11).

(11) a. The man was drowning.

b. The man drowned.

In the case of (11a) one could add *But I jumped into the water and saved him;* this phrase cannot be added to (11b), which implies that the man actually died.

Bybee and Dahl (1989) describe the progressive as a situation in progress at reference time, and Shirai and Andersen (1995) also identify "action-in-progress" as the prototype of the progressive category, proposing the features [−telic] (not completed) and [+durative] for the progressive, thus capturing three of the characteristics of the progressive. Comrie (1985) identifies the core features of the progressive universally as a combination of continuous meaning and nonstativity. Bybee, Perkins, and Pagliuca (1994) state that the progressive either explicitly or implicitly includes the following elements of meaning: "(a) an agent (b) is located spatially (c) in the midst of (d) an activity (e) at a reference time" (p. 136). Both Comrie (1985) and Dahl (1985) agree that the English progressive has a meaning that extends beyond the progressive in other languages. Comrie classifies the progressive as a type of imperfect that does not fundamentally include habituality (compared to the Romance imperfect, which strongly implies habituality). Comrie argues that a situation can be progressive without being habitual.

(12) John was writing a poem at five o'clock on the fifth of June 1975.

Examples such as (12) in which the past progressive appears with an adverbial that specifies a specific time argue that habituality is not part of the invariant meaning of the past progressive. Leech (1971) showed that habitual interpretations of the progressive are possible, but because I am primarily concerned with the prototypical meaning of the past progressive, I will not pursue those cases here.[6]

Semantics of the Present Perfect

The present perfect in English, exemplified by sentences such as *Einstein has visited Princeton* and *John has lived here since August,* has also inspired many semantic analyses, but the most common interpretation of the present perfect is that it expresses what is known as "current relevance" (Inoue, 1979; McCoard, 1978).[7] The notion of current relevance has been formulated by Comrie (1976) as "the continuing relevance of a past situation" (p. 52).[8] Likewise, Dowty (1979) states that "the perfect serves to locate an event within a period of time that began in the past and extends up to the present moment" (p. 341). Inoue (1979) further defines "current" or "present" relevance as a condition of repeatability on the situation described in the topic proposition. Taking the well-known example "Einstein has visited Princeton," and keeping in mind that Einstein is presupposed to be dead, Inoue shows that this sentence can occur with some topics (c–d) but not others (a–b, indicated with an asterisk) (Inoue, 1979, p. 577).

(13) Einstein has visited Princeton.
a. *Talking about Einstein engaging in various activities.
b. *Talking about Einstein visiting American universities.
c. Talking about Princeton University having memorable occasions.
d. Talking about the Nobel Prize winners visiting Princeton.

Regarding (13a) and (13b), since Einstein is no longer living, he cannot engage in activities or visit American universities, that is, these events are not considered to be repeatable if the discourse topic is "Einstein." However, the acceptability of (13) changes if the topic is Princeton's memorable events, as in (13c). Since Princeton can be expected to have many memorable events in its future, (13) can serve as an example of a memorable event in the history of the university or of the visits of Nobel Prize winners.

The meaning of the present perfect (and current relevance) can be broken down into its past and present components. Leech (1971) has glossed the present perfect as "past-time-related-to-present-time" (p. 30). Suh (1992) observed that by using the present perfect the "speaker brings what happened in the past to the realm of the present" (p. 82). McCawley (1971) saw the present perfect as "an interval stretching from the past into the present" (p. 105). McCoard (1978) described the invariant meaning of the present perfect as "an identification of prior events with the 'extended now'" (p. 19), distinguishing it from the simple past defined as "then time which is conceived of as separate from the present" (p. 19). Suh has suggested that the present perfect and the simple past share the feature [+anterior], but differ on the feature [current relevance], with the present perfect carrying [+current relevance] and the simple past [–current relevance].

The shared feature of anterior, or past, has led many to argue that the simple past and present perfect are truth-functionally identical, that is, that they share the same truth value (Haegeman, 1989; Inoue, 1979; N. Smith, 1981). As an illustration, consider the pair of sentences *Max has met the President* and *Max met the President;* if the first is true, the second is also true, and vice versa. Smith (1981) summarizes this position as follows: "there is no good evidence that the past and the perfect are ever truth-conditionally distinct . . . they can never be consistently asserted and denied at the same time" (1981, p. 259).

Also considered part of the present perfect is the present perfect progressive (hereafter the "perfect progressive" following Johnson, 1985), as in *She has been practicing law for five years.* In general, the perfect progressive is regarded as combining the meaning of the present perfect with that of a continuous event or process (Comrie, 1976; Johnson, 1985; Quirk et al., 1985).

The semantics of the present perfect also determine the adverbials with which it may occur. Anomalous combinations of present perfect with various adverbials are well known. The present perfect occurs with temporal adverbials which include a sense of the present, such as *at present, up till now, so far,* and *lately* (Leech, 1971; Suh, 1992).[9] *Recently, already,* and *yet* also have an element of present, as do *since*-phrases. In fact, the present perfect occurs felicitously with *since*-phrases, whereas the simple past in English cannot (Harkness, 1987; Inoue, 1979).

(14) a. Jack has taught at MIT since 1969.

b. *Jack taught at MIT since 1969.

On the other hand, the present perfect does not occur with time adverbials that indicate a specific time in the past, but the simple past does (Comrie, 1985; Harkness, 1987; Klein, 1992; McCoard, 1978).

(15) a. *I have arrived yesterday.

b. I arrived yesterday.

(16) a. *John has been to Canada when he was a child.

b. John went to Canada when he was a child.

This is due to the fact that specific time adverbials are incompatible with the semantics of the present perfect, which allows the encoding of a situation as obtaining at an unspecified time (Inoue, 1979; Suh, 1992). That is, the choice of the present perfect allows the timing of an event to go unmentioned, whereas the purpose of the adverbial is to identify a specific time, and the two are thus semantically and functionally inconsistent in their purpose.

The present perfect is used to show the orientation of the speaker towards past events. Just such a use is what C. Smith (1983) has called "viewpoint" (p. 480).[10] Viewpoint is as much a pragmatic consideration as it is a semantic one, according to Binnick (1991) and Givón (1984). The point of view involved in the choice of the present perfect or the simple past is particularly evident where both allow the same time adverbial, as is the case with *for*-phrases. For example, whether speakers report (17a) or (17b) depends on their interpretation of the relevance of their English study to the topic at hand.

(17) a. I have studied English for six years.

b. I studied English for six years.

Following Inoue (1979), the present perfect in (17a) is allowable if the speaker sees him- or herself as able to repeat or re-engage in the study of English, whereas (17b) is used if the speaker does not. The same holds true for the negative with the present perfect. In (18a), the use of the present perfect suggests that the speaker sees him- or herself as being able to complete whatever is being discussed, whereas the use of simple past in (18b) does not.

(18) a. I haven't finished it.

b. I didn't finish it.

A final difference between the simple past and the present perfect (for the purposes of this discussion) is the interpretation of sequentiality, or chronological order. In general, a series of events reported in the simple past is understood as sequential unless there is an indication to the contrary (Klein, 1986), whereas events reported in the present perfect receive no such interpretation.

Semantics of the Pluperfect

The pluperfect, often called the past-in-the-past, is described by Comrie (1985) in these words: "[T]he meaning of the pluperfect is that there is a reference point in the past, and that the situation in question is located prior to that reference point" (p. 65). Leech (1971) also calls it "a time further in the past, seen from the viewpoint of a definite point of time already in the past" (p. 42). The reference point (R) in (19) is the finding of the horse; prior to that the event (E) happened, namely, the horse ate the leaves, and thus the verb appears in the pluperfect. In (20), R is when Enid lingered; E is the other girls' leaving, resulting in the use of the pluperfect, *the other girls had left.*

(19) The first one they met was a horse as thin as a stick, tied to an oak tree. He had eaten the leaves as far as he could reach, for he was famished. (Thompson, 1968, p. 2)

(20) Once in Sibley's Enid lingered by herself after the other girls had left, moving along the aisles like a sleepwalker. (Oates, 1987, p. 41)

The pluperfect is a relative-absolute tense (Comrie, 1985, p. 65). An absolute tense such as the English present or past, or the Spanish and French present, past, and future, locates a situation at, before, or after the present moment (the moment of speech). The meaning of relative tenses, such as the pluperfect, "combines absolute time location of a reference point with relative time location of a situation" (Comrie, 1985, p. 65). In the case of a relative tense, the reference point is at or before the present moment, and the situation is before or after the reference point. With the pluperfect, the reference point (R) is before the time of speaking (S), and the situation or event (E) is before the reference point.[11]

All events or situations that can be encoded by the pluperfect can also be encoded by the simple past, for the reason that all pluperfects are past (but not vice versa). As regards this point, Comrie (1985) raises an interesting question for typology, and an equally interesting question for second language acquisition: "One might then ask, given that any past time point can be referred to by the past, why a pluperfect with its relatively complex meaning should exist in addition in so many languages" (p. 67). The corresponding question for second language acquisition would be to ask why a learner would acquire the pluperfect in addition to the simple past. Comrie (1985) finds the answer in the expression of chronological order. A sequence of events reported in the simple past is generally understood to be in chronological order. If the order of events is not presented in chronological order, "the pluperfect is the ideal mechanism for indicating this" (p. 65). As we saw in Chapter 2 in the study of reverse-order reports, the pluperfect does indeed move into this very environment. In this chapter, I examine emergence from a different perspective and observe early nontargetlike uses of the pluperfect as learners begin to make form-meaning associations.

The Acquisition of Tense-Aspect Morphology

Four general principles have been found in studies of the emergence of verbal morphology. These have been summarized by Klein and colleagues (Klein, 1993, 1994a; Dietrich, 1995; Dietrich et al., 1995) as part of the ESF longitudinal study, but they are to be found in all the studies that investigate the acquisition of verbal morphology. First, the development of temporal expression is slow and gradual. Chapter 2 examined the first two stages of temporal expression, the pragmatic and the lexical, but even within the acquisition of morphology there is a gradual development. However succinctly analysts (or teachers) can describe the tense-aspect system of a language, learners acquire its formal components and form-meaning associations in stages that take time to complete. This is illustrated particularly well by the longitudinal studies, but can also be captured by cross-sectional designs when true beginners are studied.

Second, as part of the slow and gradual acquisition of the tense-aspect system, form often precedes function (Klein, 1993;

Dietrich et al., 1995). In other words, verbal morphology may emerge without a clear meaning; it may offer a formal contrast, but lack semantic or functional contrast with another emergent form. (See also Véronique, 1987.) Early use of verbal morphology is often tentative and represented by very few tokens. Even at later stages, base forms—the default verbal forms used by learners—linger in interlanguage. Longitudinal studies capture the early isolated experimentation with verbal morphology. Cross-sectional studies can also capture the form before meaning sequence if they do not use formal accuracy in obligatory contexts (a measure of forms supplied in obligatory target contexts) as their only measure. Dittmar (1981) identified this as the chief flaw of the morpheme order studies, observing that "the criterion approach" treats a feature of acquisition (in this case tense-aspect) as if the morpheme and its meaning were "indissolubly wedded; or at least, shows no interest in either form or meaning until they reach 80% or 90% appropriate use" (p. 146). Later studies lent quantitative support to Dittmar's observation: An error analysis of composition exams written by advanced learners of English found 7.5 times more errors in the use of tense-aspect morphology than in the form (Bardovi-Harlig & Bofman, 1989). In a subsequent study focusing on tense-aspect use, Bardovi-Harlig (1992a) reported a significant difference in rates of accuracy (form) and use (meaning).

A third general principle is that irregular morphology precedes regular morphology (Dietrich et al., 1995; Klein, 1993). This is supported by the number of languages in crosslinguistic studies of the ESF project. In addition, Rohde's (1996) 6-year-old German learner of English showed a greater number of uses of the irregular past than the regular past. E. Lee (1997) also found that irregular past in English began earlier and included more tokens than regular past in the interlanguage of two Korean-speaking children (10 and 14) in a host environment. Classroom foreign language learners also often show more tokens of irregular verbs than regular ones, as reported by Salaberry (1999a) for learners of English in Uruguay, and for Anglophone learners of French in the United States by Kaplan (1987).

Finally, Bhardwaj et al. (1988) claim that learners tend to avoid considering discontinuous marking such as aux + V-tense inflection and formulate an initial hypothesis that tense relies upon suffixed inflections, as in the case of the use of the past participle for the French passé composé (the V-*e* form), and—as Giacalone and Banfi (1990) argue—the use of the past participle for the Italian passato prossimo. Early stages of the use of progressive are also characterized by V-*ing* in English. In all languages that have been studied, learners appear to begin the acquisition sequence by using the verb and a verbal suffix in the cases where the target form is comprised of an auxiliary and the verb with a verbal suffix. These principles are illustrated in the review that follows.

The next section reviews longitudinal studies of a number of languages that have investigated acquisitional sequences in the development of interlanguage tense-aspect systems. The following section provides an overview of cross-sectional studies that have contributed to the understanding of tense-aspect development. The section also explores issues in research design and analysis that are relevant to interpreting and comparing the findings of longitudinal and cross-sectional studies.

A final observation must be made about the relation of target tense-aspect systems to interlanguage tense-aspect systems: Although in the target languages verbal morphology also encodes, with some variation, grammatical information of person and number in addition to tense and aspect, acquisition studies focus exclusively on tense and aspect.[12] This means that an analyst will code as a good example of the preterite in Spanish, for example, *(yo) bailó* I danced–3rd person (see Hasbún, 1995; Bergström, 1995); in English *he have studied* is a good example of a present perfect. The reason for doing this is that temporal reference and person-number are distinct semantic systems. Moreover, morphology for person is acquired later than tense, at least in L2 English, Spanish (Andersen, 1991), and Italian (Berretta, 1995). Hooper (1980) reports that in child language acquisition, too, tense-mood-aspect emerges before person and person before number markers in the verb. Thus, coding only tokens that show both tense-aspect and person-number agreement as appropriate uses of a given tense-aspect form would result in an analysis that is dependent on the emergence of person-number.

Longitudinal Studies of the Acquisition of Tense-Aspect Morphology

Longitudinal studies observe the use of verbal morphemes and chart the order in which they emerge. Very little interpretation is necessary. Where a learner used a base form during one interview, he may use a preterite form in another interview. More realistically, where a learner used all base forms in one interview, he may use some base forms and some preterite forms in the next interview. Uses of verbal morphology that occur exclusively with a single verb or in a single (idiomatic) phrase, commonly known as formulaic uses, are fairly easy to spot in an extended study; a more limited sample from a learner makes this harder. There is less interpretation regarding the emergence of verbal morphology in a longitudinal study than a cross-sectional study. Within a designated interval, all uses of base forms and morphology are recorded. Intervals are compared for the use of morphology and sequences are constructed.

Andersen (1986a, 1986b, 1989) reports on the acquisition of Spanish by two English-speaking children between the ages of 6 and 14, sampled at ages 6 and 8 for one child and 12 and 14 for the other. The preterite was the first past inflection to appear, followed by the imperfect. It is important to note that the distribution of the verbal morphology was limited to certain semantically related aspectual classes. I will return to the issue of lexical aspect in Chapter 4.

Acquisition of Italian as a second language by adults also shows that the imperfect is the second past form to emerge (Bernini, 1990; Giacalone Ramat, 1995d; Giacalone Ramat & Banfi, 1990). Giacalone Ramat and Banfi observed that "imperfect emerges later, after present, infinitive, and past participle, i.e., after the 'basic microsystem'" (p. 422; see also Berretta, 1995). Learners use a base form before and during the emergence of verbal morphology. Most learners use the third singular of present indicative for the base form. Interestingly, Giacalone Ramat and Banfi noted a difference between learner populations: Learners who live in isolated groups and thus get only poor input may choose infinitives (p. 424). The acquisition of the auxiliary progresses at the same time as the verbal morphology is developing. The auxiliary is often not realized in the first stages of the passato prossimo, and the same holds true for the progressive. The rate of use of the auxiliary in the passato prossimo increases with time, resulting in a gradual change from the use of the past participle alone to the (aux +) past participle that forms the passato prossimo. Giacalone Ramat (1995d) reported an expanded order: present, (aux +) past participle, imperfect, and then future (p. 294).

In Italian, emergence of progressive forms comes after that of other inflections for tense-aspect distinctions. Giacalone Ramat (1997) reported that in the early stages of morphological development there is no explicit marking of the progressive, regardless of the L1 of the learner. The development of the present, past participle, and imperfect all precede the emergence of the progressive forms. Giacalone Ramat has observed that English is an obvious exception to the claim of late acquisition of progressive because "the construction is 'attention catching' for its frequency in discourse" (p. 281).

The sequence of development observed for the French passé composé is very similar to that observed for the Italian passato prossimo (Noyau, Houdaïfa, et al., 1995; Véronique, 1987). Early stages show the alternation between the bare verb, V-Ø, and the V-*e* form (Noyau, Houdaïfa, et al., 1995). Noyau, Houdaïfa, et al. have observed that the V-*e* form may become either an infinitive or a participle. One adult learner in their longitudinal study was able to use Aux + V-*e* (the passé composé), but the learners in the study did not acquire the contrast in grammatical aspect between the passé composé and the imparfait.

In contrast, learners studied by Schlyter (1990) did acquire the contrast. Schlyter compared the acquisition of L2 French by two untutored adult learners (L1 Swedish) with the bilingual (L1) acquisition of French by German-French children. One adult learner was recorded after 9 months residence in France, the other after 11. Schlyter also drew on a larger, unpublished, cross-sectional study of seven adult learners and additional longitudinal data from the two learners and posited an acquisitional order. She posited the following order for French L1 and adult French L2 acquisition (1990, p. 305):

1. one or two basic forms with variable use
2. "passé composé" (in certain cases, not yet entirely productive)
3. *veux* + infinitive or *va* + infinitive (to refer to future)
4. clear cases of "imparfait": first "*était, avait,*" and modals
5. pluperfect, "conditionnel," "subjonctif"

A study of five fifth-grade immersion learners of French and their bilingual and monolingual French fifth-grade counterparts (Harley & Swain, 1978) appears to support Schlyter's (1990) proposed order. The immersion learners favored the passé composé as their past tense form, with only limited use of the imperfect. In contrast to the bilingual and monolingual French comparison groups who used imperfect with a variety of verbs, the immersion learners used the imperfect largely with *être* "be" and *avoir* "have." To illustrate, four out of five of the immersion learners used the imperfect with *être* and *avoir* in 85–92% of all verbs in the imperfect (but only 2–5 different verbs were used in the imperfect by any learner); the remaining learner showed 13 different lexical verbs in the imperfect and only 67% of the imperfect verbs were restricted to *être* and *avoir.* In contrast, the monolingual French group showed more productive use of the imperfect with a variety of verbs; two of the three learners used *être* and *avoir* less than 36% of the time, and one 60%. The bilingual group ranged from 29% for one child to 67% and 77% for the other two bilingual children. The monolingual French children thus seem to be the farthest along with "imperfect spreading," a concept that is taken up in detail in Chapter 4, which refers to the spread of the imperfect from prototypically stative verbs such as *be* and *have* to other verbs. The use of pluperfect, conditional, and subjunctive by all learners is rather limited and suggests the later acquisition reported by Schlyter. Conditionals were used by all the monolingual speakers and by the bilingual speakers, although less often, whereas only one immersion learner attempted the conditional. Two learners in each group attempted the pluperfect; all the monolingual learners and one bilingual learner attempted the subjunctive, but no immersion learners did.

Comajoan's (1998) longitudinal study of Daniel, a tutored learner of Catalan as a foreign language, appears to support the observation that the preterite (*vaig dormir* "I slept") emerges before the imperfect (*dormia* "I was sleeping, I used to sleep").[13] However, as Comajoan (1998) observed, there is very likely a confounding task effect. In the first elicitation task (at week 6 of Catalan study), Daniel used preterite in retelling an episode from a silent film (*Modern Times*), but no imperfect. Imperfect is not used in Daniel's impersonal narratives until the end of the 5th month, and robust use of the imperfect is delayed until the 8th month. However, the conversational data suggest that the preterite and imperfect emerge at the same time with tentative uses of both in the 2nd and 3rd months, with robust use of both in the first part of the 6th month. (There was no elicitation in the 5th month due to winter break). In fact, the number of imperfects used even surpasses the number of preterites in the second half of the 6th month and in the 8th and 9th months in the conversational data. (The importance of discourse is taken up at length in Chapter 5.) Note that both Harley and Swain (1978) and Comajoan (1998) report the number of tokens produced by the learners. This allows a focus to be maintained on the number of emergent forms that are produced rather than on the number that achieve targetlike form or use. This contrasts with the cross-sectional studies that are reviewed in the following section.

Apart from English, the Germanic languages have not received as much attention in the international literature as the

Romance languages. Fortunately, the ESF longitudinal project studied German, Dutch, and Swedish as well as English (Dietrich et al., 1995). Dietrich (1995) reported on the acquisition of German by Turkish and Italian learners. The sequence of morphological development in German is particularly well illustrated by the case of Ayshe, Turkish learner of German, whose first interview showed that she was about to leave the lexical stage of temporal expression (Dietrich, 1995). At her first interview she used the Präsens (the present form), half a dozen Perfekt forms (e.g., *hat gesagt*), and one Präteritum, *war* "was." Six months later she used the Perfekt, and 6 months after that (at 28 months) the Präteritum was on the increase, but restricted to *sein* "to be," *wollen* "to want," and *müssen* "must." At this stage the Präsens was still the default form. By 36 months, the Präsens had receded and Perfekt or Präteritum was used depending on whether a temporal boundary was expressed.[14] In the last stage Plusquamperfekt emerges, expressing anteriority. The Italian learners of German show the same acquisitional sequence as the Turkish learners up through the development of the Präteritum. The Turkish learners, who went to school, all eventually used the Plusquamperfekt; but the Italians, who did not attend language classes, did not.

The acquisition of Dutch by adult learners who speak Turkish and Moroccan Arabic shows that after the present the Perfectum emerges, slowly at first with a few verbs, appearing with *hebben* + past participle, and occasionally with *zijn* + past participle (Klein et al., 1995). The early distribution of the auxiliaries is not targetlike, with learners not taking the verb into account when selecting an auxiliary. A quantitative change was reported for one of the learners in the morphological stage: "bare infinitives disappear, perfect forms become more frequent and slowly take over the role of normal past reference, present tense forms are confined to present and future reference" (Klein et al., 1995, p. 129).

Noyau, Dorriots, et al. (1995) studied the acquisition of Swedish by speakers of Spanish and Finnish. Learners showed use first of base forms, then of the preterite form. The first preterite forms were irregular. A few isolated forms of the perfect emerged. Tense marking was achieved for the preterite first, as opposed to a base form or, in some cases, present; usually present was marked at a later stage. The observed order of emergence was reported as base form, preterite, present, and perfect (*hat* + V-*t*) last (p. 256). Noyau, Dorriots, et al. observed that the perfect involves a different learning task (from that of the present and past), as it is not linked to the observable temporal location of the situation itself and refers to a time interval in which nothing happens except for the consequences of a given situation. The researchers predicted that the Plusqvamperfektum would eventually follow the Perfect.

The full range of stages in the acquisition of English tense-aspect morphology was observed for a learner called Lavinia (L1 Italian) by Klein (1993, 1995). At the beginning of her interviews, after 6 months in the United Kingdom, Lavinia showed emergent use of third person -*s* and the present tense copula. At 7 months she used three irregular past verbs: *said, went,* and *was.* Some cases of V-*ing* come in at the same time. At 8 months she used four tokens of present perfect forms (but these do not contrast with the past) and one future form; at the same time, the V-*ing* forms increased in number. By 11 months her past utterances were marked predominantly by past verbs, but they were still irregulars. At 13 months, she showed her first use of a regular past, and by 16 months there was an increased use of regular past; both the past progressive and the present perfect were observed, and future was often marked by *shall* or *will.* By 17 months a number of correct uses of the progressive were observed, and at 21 months her first clear use of the pluperfect was recorded. Throughout the acquisition process, Lavinia added to her repertoire of adverbials as well.

Whether learners go as far as Lavinia or only as far as acquiring one or two verbal morphemes, the longitudinal studies show gradual emergence of tense-aspect morphology. Corresponding to the lexical stage of development, studies of morphological development note the base form as a starting point. The perfective past emerges as the first past morpheme across languages. In the Romance languages, it is followed by the imperfective past. In the Germanic languages, it is followed by the perfect forms. As the longitudinal studies show, the time involved in following the natural production of individual learners as they reach a targetlike repertoire of tense-aspect morphology can easily be at least 2 to 3 years. An obvious supplement to such time-intensive studies is found in the cross-sectional studies reviewed in the following section.

Cross-Sectional Studies of the Acquisition of Tense-Aspect Morphology

In keeping with other areas of second language acquisition, there are also studies of tense-aspect morpheme acquisition that are cross-sectional in design. The cross-sectional design tends to amplify certain analytical issues which, although present in longitudinal studies, become more salient in cross-sectional designs. Emergence of a form tends to be easier to record in a longitudinal study, although decisions about coding early uses still must be made. (See the longitudinal study in the following section.) Typically, cross-sectional designs have compared accuracy rates across levels of learners, thus introducing a comparison between the target-language and the developing interlanguage. These methodological biases have been identified in much of second language acquisition research (Ellis, 1994; Larsen-Freeman & Long, 1991; and others), and are in no way particular to the study of tense and aspect. However, these differences are important in understanding what different studies reveal about the acquisition process. As a review of cross-sectional studies reveals, the end-state perspective is very much in evidence. Although a focus on formal accuracy subtly guides us back to the perspective of the end-state rather than the acquisition process (Dittmar, 1981; Wode, Bahns, Bedey, & Frank, 1978), an end-state perspective is not an intrinsic characteristic of the cross-sectional design. The design and analysis are independent features of the study. It is possible to score form and meaning separately, thereby capturing learners' attempts at target morphology as they progress (Bardovi-Harlig,

1992a; see also Bergström, 1995). In such a coding scheme, forms such as *tooked* and *bringed* receive no credit for formal accuracy, but they do receive credit for appropriate use in environments where the past is required. On the other hand, formally accurate strings such as *have bought* which are used inappropriately receive credit for form, but not meaning. Such coding allows us to observe that acquisition of form precedes functional use, as in the longitudinal studies (Dietrich et al., 1995).

One difficulty that seems to remain with cross-sectional studies is the lack of availability of true beginners in both FL and SL settings. This is the case in both university FL classrooms in the United States and ESL classrooms, where even low-level learners have had varying degrees of exposure to the target language. This problem is not unique to cross-sectional studies, because previous instruction may contribute to an even greater range among learners than would naturally occur as learners acquire the target language at different rates. Differences among learners are exacerbated when analysts calculate group scores. In longitudinal studies, learners are also often at different levels at the outset of a study, but the tendency to report progress for individual learners minimizes the problem.

Like the longitudinal studies, cross-sectional studies have the potential for demonstrating that the acquisition of tense-aspect morphology as part of a system of temporal expression is often a slow and gradual process. This is captured not only by including an appropriate range of proficiency levels in a cross-sectional study, but also by the design of the elicitation instruments or interviews and the elicitation procedures.

Bailey (1987, 1989) compared the production of simple past and past progressive in four tasks by instructed second language learners of English. Twenty-six learners of ESL of mixed language backgrounds at four levels of proficiency (determined by enrollment in an intensive English program, Levels 2–5 out of five instructional levels) were tested twice in 6 weeks. The first elicitation used an oral picture narration task, an oral "ask about" task in which learners formed questions based on a picture, and an oral

and written personal narrative. The second elicitation used another oral picture narration task, a second oral "ask about" task
in which learners asked questions about a second picture, and an
oral and written story retell task based on a folk tale (a narrative)
that was read twice. Because the "ask about" task was a question-
formation task, I will refer to it in that way in the following
discussion. Learners showed greater frequency of use of simple
past than past progressive on three out of four tasks (picture
narration and oral and written personal stories), but greater use
of past progressive than simple past on the second question-
formation task. Accuracy (meaning formal accuracy, which excluded forms such as *tooked, waked, bringed, was call*, and *was
throw*) was also greater in three out of four tasks, the exception
again being the first question-formation task. Results for the
lowest group (Level 2) at the first elicitation show about the same
rate of production for the past progressive and the simple past in
the picture narration and question-formation tasks and again in
the second elicitation in the question-formation task. The same
level of formal accuracy is found for the question-formation task
in the first elicitation (0% for both simple past and past progressive). Bailey interpreted the greater frequency of use and the
greater accuracy of production of simple past compared to past
progressive as indicating that the simple past is acquired first.

Although Bailey's study varied the tasks in order to eliminate
potential task influence, the fact that learners used more simple
past than past progressive may be a result of the discourse
structure in narrative. In impersonal narrative in particular, there
are typically a greater number of predicates in the foreground (the
main story line) than in the background (supporting information).
(See Chapter 5.) Foregrounded clauses typically correspond to the
simple past. Even if the number of foreground and background
clauses were the same, not every background clause would express
an action reported in the past progressive, because much of the
background is often descriptive. In the question-formation task,
in which the use of past progressive seemed either discoursally or
formally appropriate, or perhaps easier to form, learners used

relatively more past progressives. The task variation suggests alternative interpretations. On the one hand, greater use of the simple past in most of the tasks could indicate greater familiarity and greater comfort in using the simple past, or it could be an artifact of the discourse structure. Alternatively, the use of past progressive in the question-formation task suggests that inversion (*Was he going home?*) may have been easier than *do*-insertion (*Did he go home?*).

Similar issues arise with other studies which compare accuracy or error rates (two sides of the same coin) of the Spanish preterite and imperfect and the French passé composé and imparfait. Kaplan (1987) studied the use of passé composé and imparfait by 16 English-speaking learners of French as a foreign language. The learners were enrolled in 1st- and 2nd-year courses. In 10-minute individual semistructured interviews, 1st-year students showed only six past tense uses (four passé composé and two imparfait); only one passé composé was well-formed, but both attempts at the imparfait were. There were more (but unspecified) uses of both forms by the 2nd-year students with accuracy scores for passé composé exceeding those of imparfait (64% to 29%).[15] Error rates showed greater difficulty with form than use for the passé composé. Kaplan reported higher error rates for distribution for the imparfait, which appear to include non-use of the imparfait, i.e., contexts in which the imperfect was required but the present was used instead. Kaplan reported that "82 percent of all errors in distribution for the imperfect are in fact the result of the learner's supplying a present tense form in an imperfect slot" (p. 54). Non-use of a targeted form is, of course, important information. If learners produce the passé composé, but fail to produce the imparfait, one might conclude that they have not yet acquired it. However, reporting the use of present as an error in the imperfect (see Kaplan, 1987, Table 3-2) obscures the developmental sequence. Passé composé is used first by learners, albeit with some formal irregularities (such as using the wrong auxiliary or regularizing the participle), with apparently less use of imperfect, which comes in later.[16] Although Kaplan summed up the results section of her study by writing "it appears that generally the passé composé is acquired before the imperfect" (p. 54), she was appropriately cautious in interpreting the results, considering discourse structure, input, chunk learning, multiple meanings for the imperfect, and influence of inherent aspect. In spite of the somewhat vague display of the learner production and masking acquisitional sequences in error counts, Kaplan nonetheless advanced the investigation of temporal systems by arguing that rather than investigating order alone (e.g., passé composé before imparfait), understanding of second language acquisition is furthered by considering these forms to be part of a single system.

Van Naerssen (1980) examined the relative order of acquisition of the Spanish present, preterite, and imperfect (among other morphemes, each compared within the appropriate grammatical systems) by 15 college students learning Spanish as a foreign language in the second quarter of their first year. Note that this is neither a longitudinal design nor a cross-sectional design. Data were from oral exams in which learners were told that the emphasis was on quantity produced in a set time. 553 verbs were produced, of which there were 300 obligatory occasions for present, 151 for simple past, and 102 for imperfect. Van Naerssen reported that "there was a significantly higher number of errors for the preterite tense than for the two easier tenses. The imperfect tense appears to be easier than preterite for foreign language learners" (p. 151). Van Naerssen observed that this order contrasts with that of child L1 learners of Spanish. Errors were not defined, nor were actual number uses of preterite or imperfect given.[17]

The results of Hasbún's (1995) cross-sectional study of 80 English-speaking learners of Spanish as a foreign language reflected the order that Andersen (1986a, 1991) reported in his longitudinal study. In a film-retell task, 1st-year university students produced only a single instance of imperfect out of 499 verbs produced. (There were 21 preterite and 435 present forms.) Preterite production continued to be more frequent than imperfect in 2nd-, 3rd-, and 4th-year narratives (155 to 50, 431 to 114, and 545 to 208, respectively). The distribution of these forms is extremely important (see Chapter 4) as is the discourse structure (see Chapter 5), but the initial non-use of imperfect reflects the sequence of emergence in the tense-aspect system.

Salaberry's (1999b) smaller cross-sectional study of 16 learners also at four levels of university Spanish instruction showed the same pattern of use of preterite and imperfect on retell tasks that used the same film used by Hasbún (1995) and a second film. First-semester learners of Spanish showed only a single use of imperfect, compared to 47 uses of preterite out of 150 verbs. Two months later the same group produced 4 imperfects and 75 preterites out of 166 verbs, showing very tentative but emergent use of the imperfect which increased with each subsequent level. Salaberry interpreted this as showing that the preterite is acquired before the imperfect and is used as the default tense in Spanish until the imperfect is established. Note that both Hasbún and Salaberry reported usage rates alone, and did not eliminate forms based on an error analysis, giving a better picture of development than target-focussed accuracy or error rates.

As we look over the stages that have been identified by studies of acquisition of morphology, it is important to remember that although any one stage can be characterized by the emergence or the use of given verbal morphology, learners continue to use base forms, and they may use the target morphology in nontargetlike ways.[18] When Klein et al. (1995) reported that one learner, Mohamed, had the morphology of a native speaker of Dutch, they also cautioned that "we should add that this picture is a bit too perfect: on occasion, Mohamed still uses the bare stem, and there are morphological and also functional mistakes. But they become rarer and rarer, and at the end of the observation period, he is not very far from the language of his local environment" (p. 137). Statements like these keep us focused on the acquisitional process, not on the end state. As tense-aspect morphology emerges in interlanguage, learners have access to additional linguistic devices to express temporality.

As new morphemes enter the interlanguage system, each must have an association between the form and meaning. This does not seem to be immediate, however. Early past morphology (typically a perfective past) may emerge without functional contrast to the base or present form (Dietrich et al., 1995; Schumann, 1987; but see Chapter 4 for a different analysis). Functional contrasts are established as learners make prototypical form-meaning associations. In addition, for each core form-meaning association made, learners also have to learn the contrasts between the form-meaning pairing associated with one morpheme and the others. In the following section, I present a study of acquisition order which explores how learners associate form and meaning in the acquisition of tense-aspect morphology after the acquisition of simple past.

A Study of the Emergence of Tense-Aspect Morphology Related to Past in English

The identification of acquisitional sequences implicitly takes into account form-meaning associations. In this study I investigate the meaning associated with emergent morphology and the way in which core meanings and contrasts are established in the interlanguage tense-aspect system. In this section, I investigate the acquisition of morphology in English that is related to the expression of past. I take my definition of past from the Reichenbachian framework. If we take "E" to represent event time, "S" to represent speech time, and "R" to represent reference time, then tense-aspect forms that encode the expression of past share the semantic feature of E before S, or event time before speech time (Reichenbach, 1947). Tense-aspect forms that share the feature of E before S include the simple past (R, E precede S), the past progressive, which differs from the simple past by grammatical aspect but not by tense and thus shows the same configuration of event, reference, and speech time (i.e., R, E precede S), the present perfect (E precedes S, R), and the pluperfect (E precedes R which precedes S).[19] The acquisition of a targetlike tense-aspect system by learners of English entails the acquisition of both the morphology (i.e., past *-ed,* past progressive *was/were* + V-*ing,* present perfect *have* + V-*en,* and pluperfect *had* + V-*en)* and its semantic and pragmatic features. In addition, learners must come to distinguish the meaning and use of each of the tense-aspect forms from those of their semantically close neighbors.

Method

Participants

The learners in this longitudinal study were introduced briefly in Chapter 2. I give a fuller introduction here. During the course of the two years of data collection, 33 adult learners of English participated in the longitudinal study. The selection of the learners whose language samples were analyzed for the study was based on length of enrollment in the IEP of the Center for English Language Training at Indiana University and the completeness of learner portfolios, including journals. Because the daily journal was of primary importance in the data collection, any learner who did not keep a journal was not included in the final analysis. On the basis of these criteria, 16 learners representing four language backgrounds were selected (5 Arabic, 6 Japanese, 2 Korean, and 3 Spanish). All learners were assigned a language-appropriate pseudonym.

Although the learners began the program at approximately the same level of proficiency as determined by program placement, they showed individual differences in rates of attainment, eventual proficiency, and length of enrollment in the program. The learners who participated in the longitudinal study were by no means a homogeneous group, and for that reason were perhaps all the more representative of the range of learners who form the student body of academically oriented, university-based intensive English programs throughout the United States. The learners ranged in age from 18, having just graduated from high school, to mid-20s, with college (BA) degrees. Three of the 16 learners were women (Hiromi, Ji-An, and Noriko), reflecting the proportion of women to men in the lower-level classes at that time in the program. Even with the requirement that all learners keep a journal, learners varied greatly on their attitudes toward their journals. Some treated it as a friend, writing to it daily in the manner of a diary; some treated it as a means of communicating with the teacher, some as more of an obligation. The journals not only served as a source of communicative language samples, but also provided a source of information about the learners and about their lives while they were learning English. Together with recorded conversational interviews with the learners, they form the basis for the following descriptions of the learners.

Because the learners attended the program at approximately the same time (one group entering in the fall term, the other group in the spring), they knew each other and sometimes wrote about each other. Eduardo and Carlos were friends before arriving at the IEP, funded by the same scholarship program from Venezuela. The musicians also knew each other and once played together in an orchestra at IU, and they went to hear each other perform. Two learners from the United Arab Emirates had not completed a high school diploma (an unusual profile for the IEP) and were studying for a high school equivalency diploma at the same time as they were enrolled in the IEP. Some of the learners oriented exclusively to friends and classmates of the same first language background, others enjoyed meeting other international students and engaging in activities with them, and still others had American roommates and/or friends with whom they socialized or traveled. Some students funded their own study, some had parents who supported them, and others had scholarships from their companies or governments. Two of the students worked during their studies. Only one of the learners was married, some had girlfriends at home who lasted throughout the study, some broke up with girlfriends at home, and others were completely unattached. The three women in the study seemed to have no such attachments. Table 3.2 summarizes the background information for each of the learners. (For brief instructional profiles of the learners, the reader is referred to Chapter 6.)

Data Collection

During the course of the study and the length of enrollment of the learners in the IEP, learners were asked to keep daily journals. They wrote essays, compositions, film-based narratives, and creative pieces in their writing courses. (Only uncorrected first drafts were collected for the study.) They also took program-wide final examinations which included 35-minute compositions. Photocopies of all these were collected for the study and comprise the written corpus. The oral corpus consists of conversational interviews and oral narratives. In any one 7-week term, the learners (and all their classmates) participated in two interviews and one narrative film-retell task, with two narrative retell tasks and one interview in the following term. These meetings took place during the listening-speaking classes in weeks 2, 4, and 6. Written narratives based on the film retell task were written during the writing classes. The one-on-one interviews were conducted by a team of trained interviewers. The interviews ran between 10 and 45 minutes, with a typical session running from 15 to 20 minutes.

This procedure resulted in a sample of 1576 written texts and 175 oral texts that were collected from the learners over the period of the observation. The majority of the written texts come from learners' journal entries (1101 texts); an additional 370 texts are compositions, 73 are essay placement exams, and 32 are elicited narratives based on silent films. The oral texts consist of 102 guided conversational interviews supplemented by 73 elicited narratives based on silent films. Table 3.3 presents an inventory of text types and topics produced by each learner.

In addition to the obvious difference in mode, the written and oral corpora differ in two essential ways. First, the oral texts are constructed by dyads (whereas the written texts are constructed by the learners alone), so that the contributions of the interviewer may influence the production by the learner. Second, the oral samples are more widely spaced in time than the written samples.

Table 3.2

Profile of Learners in Longitudinal Study of English

Learner	L1	Age at Arrival	Months of Study in IEP	Social Contact Outside of Class	General Education	Goals	Language Instruction
Hamad	Arabic	26	16	Hamad had Arabic-speaking and international friends. His cousins also attended the program. He lived in a graduate dorm, then moved to an off-campus apartment. By Level 3 he was helping other learners negotiate school and living arrangements.	Enrolled in a high school equivalency course during language study. Had difficult time in high school at home.	Hamad's goal was to complete an undergraduate major in computer science at a U.S. university.	8 sessions, Levels 1–6. Repeated 4 and 6.
Saleh	Arabic	20	16	Saleh stayed briefly in a dormitory. He shared several apartments with Arabic speakers. He owned several cars, which made him quite mobile.	Attended military high school.	Saleh's goals appear gradually in his journals. Undergraduate major in criminology.	8 sessions, Levels 1–5. Repeated 2, 3, and 4.
Abdullah	Arabic	mid-20s	19.5	Abdullah lived with his wife and young daughter in university married student housing. Socialized exclusively with Arabic speakers. Traveled to Florida with another Arabic-speaking family.	University graduate in library science.	Abdullah's goal was a PhD in library science. Teach at the university in home country. Focused on increasing	10 sessions, Levels 1–6. Repeated 1, 4, 5, and 6.

Table 3.2 (continued)

Profile of Learners in Longitudinal Study of English

Learner	L1	Age at Arrival	Months of Study in IEP	Social Contact Outside of Class	General Education	Goals	Language Instruction
						TOEFL scores through self-study, but made little progress.	
Khaled	Arabic	24	12	Khaled lived in the graduate dorm for 8 months, then moved to a private apartment. Socialized predominantly with Arabic speakers. Khaled had four cousins living in the States and went to visit each during school vacations.	University graduate in history and geography. Worked for a ministry in the government.	Khaled wanted an MA or PhD in public relations. Wanted to help his country be a "first world" country like U.S. and Japan. Intended to return to the ministry after graduation.	6 sessions, Levels 1–6.
Zayed	Arabic	21	12	Zayed lived in a dorm with an American roommate. Spent winter vacation in home country. Went to Florida with friend on spring break.		Zayed hoped to study biomedical engineering in the Midwest.	5 sessions, Levels 2–5. Repeated 3.

Table 3.2 (continued)

Profile of Learners in Longitudinal Study of English

Learner	L1	Age at Arrival	Months of Study in IEP	Social Contact Outside of Class	General Education	Goals	Language Instruction
Toshihiro	Japanese	22	12.5	Toshihiro lived in a graduate dormitory, and later in an apartment, with a roommate from Singapore who helped him with his English. Toshihiro and his roommate traveled together often, taking driving trips to Chicago and Florida, meeting the roommate's English-speaking friends. Socialized with international students, practiced slang in trips to local nightclubs.	Toshihiro was a senior in college when he attended the IEP. His major was domestic and international politics.	Toshihiro wanted to complete college degree after year in IEP. Get a good job, make a lot of money, and get married immediately to his girlfriend.	6 sessions, Levels 1–5. Repeated 3.
Noriko	Japanese	18	16.5	Noriko lived in an undergraduate dormitory with a Japanese roommate, moving to an apartment with another Japanese roommate, then back to the dorm. During the first half of her stay she socialized and traveled with Japanese speakers, then began to socialize with her international classmates. Noriko had	Graduated from a women's high school.	Noriko was admitted to a small private university to major in business. She hoped to work in a trading company after graduation.	9 sessions, Levels 1–5. Repeated 3 once and 5 twice.

Table 3.2 (continued)

Profile of Learners in Longitudinal Study of English

Learner	L1	Age at Arrival	Months of Study in IEP	Social Contact Outside of Class	General Education	Goals	Language Instruction
				an American conversation partner who was learning Japanese.			
Hiromi	Japanese	23	11.5	Hiromi lived in the graduate dorm in a single room. She had many American conversation partners during her stay. She had many international and American friends and had an active social life that she balanced well with her classwork.	Hiromi graduated from a 2-year women's college.	Hiromi hoped for admission to a 4-year American college to study journalism. She wrote that she dreamed of writing stories in English.	5 sessions, Levels 2–6.
Idechi	Japanese	25	10.5	First and foremost Idechi was a musician. He practiced his clarinet 4 hours a day. His social life revolved around music: He went to concerts, the opera, and recitals.	Idechi graduated college and worked as a high school music teacher.	Idechi sought admission to Indiana University's School of Music for a performance diploma. Idechi's goal is to be a professional clarinetist.	5 sessions, Levels 1–5. Idechi attended the IEP half-time from Level 3 to be able to study music.
Satoru	Japanese	20	10.5	Satoru lived in an undergraduate dormitory. He had a con-	Satoru graduated high school. He worked and	Satoru wanted to be a businessman,	6 sessions, Levels 1–5.

Table 3.2 (continued)

Profile of Learners in Longitudinal Study of English

Learner	L1	Age at Arrival	Months of Study in IEP	Social Contact Outside of Class	General Education	Goals	Language Instruction
				versation partner and stayed with an American friend at his parents' home during winter break. Had a range of international friends.	took English classes to prepare to come to the U.S.	perhaps a manager. Viewed school at IU as an international experience.	Repeated Level 3.
Kazuhiro	Japanese	23	12	Kazuhiro lived in a graduate dormitory in a single room.	Kazuhiro graduated from a boys' high school and worked for three years in various jobs before coming to IU.	Kazuhiro wanted to become an international businessman. He wanted to be admitted to undergraduate business school at IU.	5 sessions, Levels 2–6.
Ji-An	Korean	23	7.5	Ji-An lived with her sister, a student of piano at IU's School of Music. She had both Korean and international friends. She had an American conversation partner. She traveled throughout the U.S.	Ji-An graduated from college in Korea with a major in international trade.	Ji-An had hoped to apply to the School of Business at IU, but her mother insisted that she return home when her sister graduated from IU.	4 sessions, Levels 2–5.

Table 3.2 (continued)

Profile of Learners in Longitudinal Study of English

Learner	L1	Age at Arrival	Months of Study in IEP	Social Contact Outside of Class	General Education	Goals	Language Instruction
Sang Wook	Korean	25	7.5	Sang Wook lived in the graduate dormitory, with a summer sublet in an apartment. His sister and brother-in-law lived in a city in a neighboring state. He socialized with a mixed group of international and American students. He wrote that socializing with Koreans was not good for his English.	Sang Wook graduated from college with a degree in civil engineering. He came to the U.S. to earn a graduate degree in business.	Sang Wook's goal was to be a professor in Korea.	3 sessions, Levels 2–4.
Eduardo	Spanish	18	9	Eduardo lived in an undergraduate dormitory in a single room. He was best friends with Carlos. He had an American conversation partner (whom he shared with Carlos) who was studying Spanish. He traveled alone to a neighboring state to have Thanksgiving with an aunt and English-speaking cousins whom he had never met.	Eduardo graduated high school and was a member of the Galileo program for exceptional high-school graduates.	Galileo scholars were expected to seek admission at the undergraduate level to major U.S. universities. Eduardo wanted to study computer science and do research with an international company in his home country.	4 sessions, Levels 1, 2, 4, and 6. Skipped 3 and 5.

Table 3.2 (continued)

Profile of Learners in Longitudinal Study of English

Learner	L1	Age at Arrival	Months of Study in IEP	Social Contact Outside of Class	General Education	Goals	Language Instruction
Carlos	Spanish	18	10.5	Carlos lived in an undergraduate dormitory with an American roommate who helped him with English. He traveled with his roommate to his family home for Thanksgiving. He worked in the dormitory cafeteria as a dishwasher 10 hours per week. Carlos was best friends with Eduardo, with whom he shared a conversation partner. By December tried not to speak any Spanish, but felt isolated and gave it up.	Carlos graduated high school and was a member of the Galileo program for exceptional high-school graduates. Carlos spoke and wrote of his country's history and politics at every opportunity.	Carlos hoped to complete a BA, MA, and PhD in genetic engineering. He applied to three major U.S. universities. He planned to return home to help his country.	5 sessions, Levels 1–3, and 5–6. Skipped Level 4.
Guillermo	Spanish Arabic	early 20s	9	Guillermo lived in a graduate dormitory for the first session, then moved to a house that he shared with three other students, some of whom spoke English. He played in a salsa band in which all but one	Guillermo graduated from the Conservatory of Music and played professionally in the symphony orchestra.	Guillermo came to IU to study percussion with world-famous percussionists. He hoped to play in U.S. orchestras for several	4 sessions, Levels 1–3. Repeated 3.

Table 3.2 (continued)

Profile of Learners in Longitudinal Study of English

Learner	L1	Age at Arrival	Months of Study in IEP	Social Contact Outside of Class	General Education	Goals	Language Instruction
				American spoke Spanish, but he said he needed English for his job in the Percussion Department where he took care of the instruments. He practiced 5 hours daily and invited classmates and teachers to his concerts.		years before returning home. When he was accepted to the School of Music, he realized he needed to study English.	

Table 3.3

Inventory of Written and Oral Texts by 16 Learners
in a Longitudinal Study of English Morphology

Learner	Journals	Written Comps	Exams	Retells	Total	Oral Interviews	Retells	Total
Hamad	51	23	8	0	82	7	5	12
Saleh	66	25	3	1	95	9	6	15
Abdullah	54	24	9	3	90	10	7	17
Khaled	100	26	6	5	137	8	6	14
Zayed	43	23	3	4	73	7	6	13
Toshihiro	70	9	5	0	84	3	1	4
Noriko	129	31	9	3	172	12	5	17
Hiromi	94	31	3	2	130	6	4	10
Idechi	47	7	4	1	59	5	4	9
Satoru	57	40	5	3	105	5	5	10
Kazuhiro	106	18	5	3	132	7	6	13
Ji-An	61	22	3	0	86	4	2	6
Sang Wook	31	14	2	0	47	2	1	3
Carlos	88	36	3	4	131	7	6	13
Eduardo	72	26	3	2	103	6	4	10
Guillermo	32	15	2	1	50	4	5	9
TOTAL	1101	370	73	32	1576	102	73	175

Note. From "Another Piece of the Puzzle: The Emergence of the Present Perfect," by K. Bardovi-Harlig, 1997, *Language Learning, 47,* p. 422. Copyright 1997 by The Language Learning Research Club. Reprinted with permission.

Analysis and Results

The year was divided into 24 half-month periods with the first sampling period of a month running from the 1st to the 15th of the month and the second sampling period from the 16th to the end of the month, and the grid that resulted was used to map the emergence of verbal morphology. Thus, the period of the first 15 days of the 3rd month is indicated as T3.0, and the period from the 16th day to the end of the 3rd month is indicated as T3.5. (Tables 3.4, 3.5, and 3.7 use this convention, as do all the examples in this chapter.) All interlanguage samples are identified by a pseudonym which identifies the learner, time of production, type of sample, and L1 of the learner.

Coding Forms

The oral data were transcribed and the written data were typed. Each of the tense-aspect forms that had been identified for study (past, past progressive, present perfect, and pluperfect) were coded. The accumulated language sample for each learner was analyzed. In the first stage of the analysis, all uses of the targeted verbal morphemes in the learner-texts were identified by use of a computer word-search program. In addition, each text was read by the researcher.[20]

Every verb supplied in past-time contexts was coded for its verbal morphology independently by two experienced coders (the researcher and her assistant) and all adverbials were identified and coded as time, duration, and frequency adverbials (Harkness, 1987). Once the verbs in each sampling period for each learner had been coded, they were sorted into types by a computer sorting program. This analysis distinguished between *tokens* of verbs, counting all the verbs in the learner texts, and *types* of verbs, counting only one instance of each verb form which occurred in the text. Types rather than tokens of verbs were counted; that is, each verb form was counted only once per half-month sampling period regardless of frequency. When multiple forms of the same verb occurred, such as *go, went,* and *have gone,* each form was counted as a single type regardless of the frequency of each of the forms. All negatives were counted as a single type, as were uses of past progressive and passives. Use of types avoids inflation of the rates of appropriate use by multiple occurrences of common verbs like *was* and *went.* Thus, a type analysis provides a conservative view of the acquisition of tense-aspect morphology.[21] Rates of appropriate use of past tense were calculated as the ratio of the number of past tense forms supplied to the number of obligatory environments. All rates are given as percentages (e.g., 16 past tense forms used in 24 obligatory environments would yield an appropriate use rate of 16/24, which, when presented as a percentage, yields a rate of appropriate use of 67%).

Coding the past progressive. A form was coded as progressive if a progressive morpheme was in evidence. "Ø+crying" was coded as a bare progressive, "is crying" as present progressive, "was crying" as past progressive. The focus on the progressive morpheme precluded inclusion of forms such as "something that is happen here" (Eduardo, T6.0), which could also be an emergent progressive but lacks the criterial morphological feature.

Certain forms were excluded from analysis in the oral corpus. Progressive forms such as "they living there" (Eduardo, T3.0) or "mother is coming" (Eduardo, T3.0) which occurred in a phonologically ambiguous environment were excluded because they could also be analyzed as "they live in there" and "mother is come in," respectively. Also excluded from analysis were cases where the progressive and perfect participles are potentially homophonous in the learner's interlanguage pronunciation. For example, although they can be distinguished in the presence of the auxiliary, when auxiliary forms are missing, "seen" and "seeing" sound similar.

The second conjuncts of conjoined predicates such as "I'm sitting here in my apartment and [Ø] *thinking* about the future" (Saleh, T14.5) were not coded because the second predicate is always ambiguous between a bare progressive and a tensed progressive since the auxiliary has been deleted. Second conjuncts in nonreduced clauses such as "I'm sitting here in my apartment and *am thinking* about the future" were always coded. In this manner, 297 past progressives were identified in the written corpus, and 146 in the oral corpus.

Because the past progressive clearly reflects a speaker's viewpoint (C. Smith, 1983), it is difficult to identify appropriate or inappropriate uses of the past progressive (although appropriate uses were coded for the present perfect and the pluperfect). In the written corpus I found only one case where a learner seemed to need to use the past progressive, but did not.

(21) I asked him what he did there [Hiromi, T3.0, creative story, L1]

Overuse of past progressive did not extend to present progressive environments and thus did not cross tense boundaries. There are other ways to analyze the use of the (past) progressive compared to the simple past, and this analysis is taken up in Chapter 4.

Coding the present perfect. Attempts at present perfect were identified by the use of *have/has* (or their corresponding contractions -*'ve* and -*'s*) with a main verb. Thus, *have go, have went,* and *have gone* were all coded as attempts at present perfect. Attempts at the perfect progressive were identified by the use of *have* or *has* and either the presence of -*ing* on the main verb, as in *haven't eating* (Guillermo, T5.0, journal, L1 Spanish), or the presence of *be* and the main verb, as in *has been give* (Guillermo, T5.0, composition, L1 Spanish). Naturally, context is required to distinguish the latter attempts at the perfect progressive from attempts at the perfect passive. If the subject is an agent (as in *My father has been give me his help,* Guillermo, T5.0) rather than a patient or theme (as in *Help has been give to me*), then the attempt was coded as a perfect progressive rather than a perfect passive.

This analysis yielded 502 uses of present perfect in the written samples and 104 uses in the oral samples of the 16 learners. The researcher and a second analyst coded all the uses of present perfect in the environment in which they occurred as appropriate uses or overgeneralizations.[22] Overgeneralizations— uses of present perfect where another tense-aspect form is preferred by native speakers—were identified on the basis of occurrence of present perfect with disallowed adverbials (such as *when*-clauses) and occurrence in chronological sequences and from information provided by context.[23]

Coding the pluperfect. Analogous to the identification of the present perfect, the pluperfect was identified by the use of *had* with a main verb. Thus, *had go, had went,* and *had gone* were all coded as attempts at the pluperfect. The learners produced 192 identifiable uses of pluperfect in the written corpus and 31 in the oral corpus. The researcher and a second analyst coded all the uses of pluperfect in the environment in which they occurred as appropriate uses or overgeneralizations.

At the time of the emergence of the past progressive, present perfect, and pluperfect the rate of appropriate use of the simple past in the written texts and oral texts was also calculated. As explained in Chapter 2, time is a poor predictor of development, and thus the development of the past tense was used as a system-specific means of gauging development and comparing the learners. All past tense uses in the closest half-month interval to the time when learners showed their first use of the targeted forms were analyzed for appropriate use. For learners with very few verb types in the relevant sampling periods, the appropriate use of the simple past was calculated for the closest previous interval, and failing that the closest following interval. In this study, as in the studies reported in Chapter 2, verb types were calculated for the use of the simple past by counting the number of distinct verb forms that occurred in the simple past in past-time contexts for each sampling interval, resulting in type counts. (See Chapter 2 for a fuller discussion.)

The Emergence of Tense-Aspect Morphology

Emergence of the past progressive. The progressive is the first of the formally compound past tenses to emerge in oral and written texts. Its pattern of emergence is somewhat obscured by the fact that the emergence of the past progressive is itself the final stage in a series of stages. Within the progressives the apparent pattern of development is bare progressive (V-*ing*, or what I will call Ø+prog, e.g., *walking, eating*), present progressive (*is walking, am eating*), and past progressive (*was walking, were eating*). In past environments, learners first show use of the bare progressive, present progressive, and finally the past progressive. For most learners, past progressive follows on the heels of present progressive. This is the case for 10 of the learners. There were also cases where present perfect was used in the environment of the past progressive, but never the reverse.

One characteristic of interlanguage is that interlanguage features are not eliminated from the grammar once and for all. They remain and appear—although less frequently—in subsequent samples. For Zayed, bare progressive emerges at the same time past is robust, and he uses bare progressive as late as T8.5. Khaled shows bare progressive as late as 9.5, Abdullah until 14.5, and Noriko until 15.5.

Because the written samples·come from journal entries rather than scheduled interviews, there is greater use in sheer numbers of both the present and past progressive in the written data. Nevertheless, the learners produced a greater absolute number of uses of bare progressive in the oral interviews, in spite of the difference in the sample sizes. Twelve learners (Carlos, Hiromi, Kazuhiro, Guillermo, Ji-An, Zayed, Khaled, Idechi, Toshihiro, Satoru, Hamad, and Abdullah) showed greater use of bare progressive in oral data. Three learners (Eduardo, Noriko, and Saleh) showed greater use of bare progressive in written texts. The remaining learner, Sang Wook, showed only one bare progressive in each condition.

The learners produced a total of 311 tokens of past progressive in the written corpus and 146 tokens in the oral corpus. Table 3.4 shows how and when each learner produced past progressives over the 16-month data collection period. In Table 3.4 the sampling intervals in half-months are displayed across the top, with the individual learners down the left side.[24] The table indicates the number of past progressives produced by the learners. At the first occurrence of the past progressive, the rate of simple past is also provided. The first learner to use the past progressive in his journals was Idechi: At T0.5, Idechi showed a single use of past progressive. At T0.5 he showed 85% appropriate use of past in a sample of 13 verb types. The number of verb types is indicated by the number in parentheses: 85% (13). Because the number of verb types is so small, a second appropriate use rate is presented

Table 3.4

The Emergence of Past Progressive in Oral and Written Texts

Subject	Month 0.5	1	1.5	2	2.5	3	3.5	4	4.5	5	5.5	6	6.5	7	7.5
Carlos Spanish			6 Oral 4 97% (32)		1 Oral 1	5	6	7			2 Oral 1	1 Oral 2		1 Oral 6	
Eduardo Spanish		1 78% (18)			6	Oral 3	Oral 1	4	3 Oral 1	Oral 9	Oral 2		1	4 Oral 15	Oral 10
Noriko Japanese						1 67% (12)		3				1	2	2	3
Hiromi Japanese					1 100% (28)	6 93% (80)	3			1 Oral 1		1			1
Kazuhiro Japanese		85% (13)	72% (25)	2 70% (23)	1						1				
Guillermo Spanish				2 63% (8)	3 88% (24)	Oral 1			1	2	1	2			
Ji-An Korean					96% (25)	1 97% (30)	1	1	1	1			1		
Zayed Arabic				1 Oral 1 68% (25)	3 68% (18)			6			3			4 Oral 4 69% (26)	7
Khaled Arabic		2 68% (19)	2	1 100% (2)	3 68% (18)						1 Oral 2				6

Table 3.4 (continued)

The Emergence of Past Progressive in Oral and Written Texts

Subject	Month 0.5	1	1.5	2	2.5	3	3.5	4	4.5	5	5.5	6	6.5	7	7.5
Idechi Japanese	1 85% (13)	9 83% (30)	3 85% (47)	2			2								
Toshihiro Japanese		1 100% (12)	1 85% (58)	1	5	1		1	2					Oral 7 94% (16)	
Satoru Japanese		1 67% (9)	1 67% (9)		77% (22)	77% (34)					1 93% (14)				
Hamad Arabic						1 72% (18)				1	91% (22)		1 Oral 1		
Abdullah Arabic						3 83% (23)				1		Oral 1	1 Oral 2		
Saleh Arabic			1 20% (5)			1 75% (16)	1	82% (37)	2	1		Oral 1			
Sang Wook Korean					4 (2) 86% (21)	1 86% (36)		2	4 Oral 2	2		Oral 3			

Numeral   Number of uses of past progressive in writing
Oral + numeral   Number of uses of past progressive in oral
%   Percentage of appropriate past tense use in written sample
% + (numeral)   Number of written verb types sampled in half month

Table 3.4 (continued)

The Emergence of Past Progressive in Oral and Written Texts

Learner	8	8.5	9	9.5	10	10.5	11	11.5	12	12.5	13	13.5	14	14.5	15	Total
Carlos Spanish	2 Oral 2	2	4 Oral 5													W 37 O 25
Eduardo Spanish																W 19 O 41
Noriko Japanese	3				.	2	5 Oral 3	1 Oral 1		5	3 Oral 3	2				W 41 O 13
Hiromi Japanese		2	4	4												W 22 O 2
Kazuhiro Japanese	1		2 Oral 2			Oral 2										W 8 O 4
Guillermo Spanish	3	1														W 15 O 3
Ji-An Korean																W 6 O 0
Zayed Arabic	1 Oral 1	2	6 Oral 12	2		7 Oral 1	Oral 1	Oral 2								W 42 O 22
Khaled Arabic	1 Oral 1	1	1	1		Oral 2	Oral 1	1								W 20 O 6

Table 3.4 (continued)

The Emergence of Past Progressive in Oral and Written Texts

Learner	8	8.5	9	9.5	10	10.5	11	11.5	12	12.5	13	13.5	14	14.5	15	Total
Idechi Japanese																W 17 O 2
Toshihiro Japanese						3	2		2							W 8 O 1
Satoru Japanese			2													W 5 O 1
Hamad Arabic			1	1	Oral 1						2					W 7 O 2
Abdullah Arabic				1	4								1	1		W 12 O 3
Saleh Arabic	Oral 1			8 Oral 2	7	2 Oral 1	1			2 Oral 2	6	1 Oral		5 Oral 8	1	W 39 O 16
Sang Wook Korean																W 13 O 5

Note. From "Another Piece of the Puzzle: The Emergence of the Present Perfect," by K. Bardovi-Harlig, 1997, *Language Learning, 47,* pp. 387–389. Copyright 1997 by The Language Learning Research Club. Reprinted with permission.

for T1.0, a period wherein Idechi produced nine past progressives. At T1.0 Idechi produced 30 verb types, with 83% appropriate use of past. Following Idechi's use of past progressive across the row to the right, we see that Idechi's first oral use of past progressive occurred at T7.0 when he used the past progressive seven times. Carlos showed early use of past progressive in both his oral and written samples. At T1.5 Carlos showed six uses of the past progressive in writing and four uses in his oral production. At the same time he showed 97% appropriate use of past in a sample of 32 verb types. The last column in Table 3.4 gives the total number of past progressives produced in writing, indicated by *W*, and in oral production, indicated by *O* (e.g., Carlos produced 37 past progressives in writing and 25 in oral production).

The past progressive was used by one learner (Saleh, L1 Arabic) with as low a rate of appropriate use of past tense as 20% at T1.5. However, it should also be noted that Saleh's language sample was also very small at that time, consisting only of 5 verb types, as Table 3.4 shows. Most other learners showed higher rates of appropriate use of simple past at the first recorded use of past progressive, but many rates were below the 80%–90% level that is often considered to indicate acquisition. This shows that the two forms are developing at the same time.

Guillermo (L1 Spanish) showed two uses of the past progressive with 63% appropriate use of simple past (with 8 verb types). Satoru (L1 Japanese) also showed two uses (at T1.0 and 1.5) with 68% appropriate use, as did Khaled (L1 Arabic) and Zayed (L1 Arabic), although Khaled and Zayed used more verb types. Kazuhiro (L1 Japanese) showed similar rates of appropriate use, 70% with 23 different verbs, when he used his first two recorded past progressives. Other learners showed higher rates of appropriate use of simple past. However, the important thing to notice is that a system with as little as 60%–70% appropriate use of simple past can support the emergence of a second morphological past. Other learners, such as Carlos (L1 Spanish), Hiromi (L1 Japanese), and Ji-An (L1 Korean) showed very high rates of appropriate use of simple past. Notice, too, that the earliest uses are clustered in the earliest periods of observation. To follow a learner's use of the past progressive after emergence, follow the row to the right. Carlos used the past progressive frequently, showing five to seven uses in each sampling period between T5.0 and T7.0. Zayed showed later use of the past progressive: He produced four tokens between T2.0 and T2.5 and sporadic use between T3.0 and T6.5. For Zayed, regular and frequent use of the past progressive began at T7.0 and continued to the end of the observation period. All learners attempted the past progressive, and every learner had attempted spontaneous use of the past progressive by the third month (T3.0). This is quite distinct from the patterns of emergence found in the present perfect and pluperfect.[25]

Unlike the emergence of the present perfect and the pluperfect (to be discussed in the following sections), the emergence of the progressive does not seem to be dependent on the stability of the simple past. The emergence of the past progressive seems only to be dependent on the prior emergence of the present progressive. In this corpus the past progressive rarely appeared before the present progressive. Ten learners first used the present progressive before they attempted the past progressive, and four learners used the present and past progressive in the same 2-week sampling period. Hamad seems to have gone directly from uses of the bare progressive between T.5 and T2.5 to the use of past progressive at T3.0. He used present progressive after at T4.0. Hamad used the least number of tokens of present progressive of the 10 learners, only four tokens in 13 oral and 82 written texts. Zayed showed the past progressive as his first progressive with one each in the oral and written sample at T2.0 followed by the use of the present progressive (2) and the past progressive (3) in writing and bare progressive in the oral sample at T3.0.

Emergence of the present perfect.[26] A total of 502 present perfects were produced by the learners in the written corpus. 457 of the present perfects were simple perfect; 45 were perfect progressive. The production of the present perfect is mapped out in Table 3.5. The number of occurrences of present perfect in the

Table 3.5

Emergence of Present Perfect

Subject	Month 0.5	1	1.5	2	2.5	3	3.5	4	4.5	5	5.5	6	6.5	7	7.5
Kazuhiro Japanese	2 (1) prompt 2	2 87% (15)	1 (0)	3 (2) Oral 1	2	1 Oral 1			1	1 (0)	3 (2)	4 (3)		5 (3)	1 PROG Oral 1
Carlos Spanish		2 83% (6)	2 97% (32)	14 (12) Oral 2	10	8 Oral 5	2			6 Oral 2	8	6 (5) Oral 3	6	27 (26) Oral 19	2 Oral 8
Toshihiro Japanese		1 100% (14)	9 (0) 85% (58)		1 (0) Oral 1	1		1 Oral 1							
Eduardo Spanish		78% (18)	2 85% (33)	6	6	12 Oral 3	5			17 (15) PROG	6	20	6	3	Oral 4
Ji-An Korean				1	2 (1) 96% (25)	3 (2)	2	4 PROG	3 (1) Oral 1	1	4	Oral 2	3		
Hiromi Japanese						2 93% (80)	7 (6)	5 PROG	4	5		Oral 1	1	1	1
Khaled Arabic	Oral 2	68% (19)		1 100% (26)						3				1 PROG 94% (16)	
Noriko Japanese	1 (0) 67% (15)	1 86% (14)			1		1		3 Oral 1		3	2	2	4	2 Oral 1
Hamad Arabic					2 (1) 75% (40)		prompt		Oral 3*		91% (22)	Oral 2			
Idechi Japanese	1 (0) 83% (30)		1 85% (47)							Oral 1	1 (0)			6 (2)	2

Table 3.5 (continued)

Emergence of Present Perfect

Subject	Month 0.5	1	1.5	2	2.5	3	3.5	4	4.5	5	5.5	6	6.5	7	7.5
Zayed Arabic				1 68% (25)	2 68% (18)	2 (0) PROG	2 64% (22)					Oral 1		4 (3)	1 (0) Oral 3
Sang Wook Korean						1 86% (36)	prompt		1						
Satoru Japanese				1* (0) 67% (3)	77% (22)	77% (34)				2 100% (3)	2 93% (14)	3			Oral 1
Guillermo Spanish					88% (24)	Oral 3			1	4 (3) PROG	1	1		6 (5)	4 (2)
Abdullah Arabic						83% (23)	prompt	100% (12)	Oral 1					1	
Saleh Arabic							prompt	82% (37)				2 (0) 81% (26)	1		

Numeral — Number of uses of present perfect in writing
Oral + numeral — Number of uses of present perfect in oral
(Numeral) — Number of appropriate uses of present perfect, if different from number used
% — Percentage of appropriate past tense use in written sample
% + (numeral) — Number of verb types sampled in half month
Prompt — Prompted use of present perfect in writing
PROG — Emergence of perfect progressive
* — Ill-formed present perfect

Table 3.5 (continued)

Emergence of Present Perfect

Subject	8	8.5	9	9.5	10	10.5	11	11.5	12	12.5	13	13.5	14	14.5	15	Total
Kazuhiro Japanese	2	1	1 Oral 3	3	1											W 36 O 6
Carlos Spanish	6 Oral 1	3	9 PROG Oral 2													W111 O 42
Toshihiro Japanese					1 PROG	2										W 16 O 2
Eduardo Spanish																W 83 O 10
Ji-An Korean																W 23 O 3
Hiromi Japanese	1	5	4	5 Oral 1	2											W 43 O 2
Khaled Arabic	1 (0) Oral 1	2	1	3	4			2 (1)								W 18 O 3
Noriko Japanese	7 (6)					7 (4)	6 (5)		4 (3)	3 (3)	1 PROG	1	2	1 Oral 2	5 (4) Oral 1	W 62 O 6
Hamad Arabic				89% (47) Oral 4	1 Oral 1	3 (1)				2 PROG Oral 1	Oral 2		3 (2)		Oral 1	W 12 O 14

Table 3.5 (continued)

Emergence of Present Perfect

Subject	8	8.5	9	9.5	10	10.5	11	11.5	12	12.5	13	13.5	14	14.5	15	Total
Idechi Japanese	1	2	2													W 16 O 1
Zayed Arabic	3 (2)		Oral 2	1 (0)	2		Oral 1									W 18 O 7
Sang Wook Korean																W 2 O 0
Satoru Japanese		1	1	3	1											W 14 O 1
Guillermo Spanish	5 (3) Oral 4	5														W 27 O 3
Abdullah Arabic				4	4							1				W 10 O 1
Saleh Arabic				1	1 Oral 2					1 Oral 1	prompt	1		1	3 (2) PROG	W 11 O 3

Note. From "Another Piece of the Puzzle: The Emergence of the Present Perfect," by K. Bardovi-Harlig, 1997, *Language Learning, 47,* pp. 387–389. Copyright 1997 by The Language Learning Research Club. Reprinted with permission.

written sample is indicated as a numeral. For example, Carlos produced 2 tokens of present perfect at T1.0. At the time of his first use of present perfect, he showed 83% appropriate use of simple past in a written sample of only 6 verb types. Because the number of types was so low, the rate of appropriate use is also provided for the next sampling period, T1.5, where he shows 97% appropriate use of simple past in a sample of 32 verb types. Carlos showed his first oral uses of present perfect at T2.0, indicated by *Oral 2*. At T2.0 Carlos also produced 14 present perfects in writing. Of the 14, 12 were used appropriately. This is indicated as *14 (12)* on the table. Learners occasionally produced ill-formed present perfects; these are indicated by an asterisk (see Satoru at T2.0 and Hamad at T4.5). *Prompt* indicates that a writing prompt was given to learners that contained a token of the present perfect and that the learners used the identical token (and no others) in the written sample. The last column in Table 3.5 gives the total number of present perfects produced in writing and in oral production as well as the number of appropriate uses.

The rate of appropriate use of simple past ranges from 68% (Zayed) to 93% (Hiromi) at the time of first recorded use of present perfect in the sample. The mean group rate for all 16 learners for appropriate use of simple past at the time of emergence of the present perfect is 86%. (Zayed seems to be the exception with 68% at first occurrence at T2.0; Hamad with 75% seems to be closer to the rest of the group.) Fifteen of the 16 learners showed productive use of the present perfect.[27] (Sang Wook showed only two uses.)

The perfect progressive emerges sometime after the simple present perfect. Only 12 of the 16 learners exhibited use of the perfect progressive. These tokens are indicated in Table 3.5 by *PROG*. The time of emergence with respect to the beginning of the study varies across learners, but the relative order is observed across all the learners who use the perfect progressive.

When learner production of present perfect is viewed in terms of the context in which it appears, a use might be appropriate or overgeneralized (uses of the present perfect where another tense-aspect form is preferred). This phase of the analysis focuses exclusively on the written texts because they are constructed solely by the learner.[28] Examining the linguistic contexts in which the perfect is used reveals the form-meaning associations which are the basis of temporal semantics in interlanguage. This is taken up at the conclusion of this chapter.

Eighty-seven percent, or 397 of the 457 uses of present perfect, were appropriate. (Recall that this figure does not include cases of non-use.) This rate is due in part to the prolific and highly appropriate rate of use by two learners, Eduardo and Carlos, as Table 3.5 shows. Subtracting their combined production from the overall sample leaves 216 appropriate uses out of 270 total uses by the other 14 learners. This yields a rate of 80% appropriate use. In the written sample learners had very little difficulty with the form of the present perfect; fewer than 7% of the occurrences were ill-formed (35/502). Because the auxiliary (*have/has*) was required to be present for a string to be considered a present perfect, ill-formed occurrences included cases of *have* + verb-∅, as in *has change* and *have inherit*, or *have* + misformed participle, as in *have wrote* and *have ate*.

Appropriate uses of the present perfect occurred in both present tense texts, as in (22) and (23), and in past-tense texts, as in (24). In the context of the present-tense texts the present relevance of the situation is emphasized, as with the traveling of the father in (22) and the unrealized event of seeing American men greeting by kissing, expressed in the negative *have never seen,* in Example (23). In the context of the past-tense texts, the present-relevance reading is still apparent, with the added reading of the event as having been realized. In (24), *I have been eating puerto-rican food* both characterizes the past week and supports the claim that "today was a beautiful day."

(22) My father is a captin in my family and he works in the [name] Air Lines so he always goes on trips and *has been* many countries. [Ji-An, T5.5, journal, L1 Korean]

(23) For example in my country or in all arapian country use kissing to greet people even if there two men greeting

each other. But that I *have never seen* like this in U.S. [Zayed, T8.5, composition, L1 Arabic]

(24) Today was beautiful day. I did a lot of things like Wednesday I could practice almost everything. Also this week I *have been eating* puertorican food almost everyday too. [Guillermo, T5.5, journal, L1 Spanish]

Approximately two thirds of the present perfects in the sample (292/457 or 64%) occur with no adverbials, as in (22); one third of the occurrences of the present perfect (165/457 or 36%) occur with adverbials, as in (23) and (24). A wide range of adverbials occur with the appropriate uses of the simple present perfect. *For* and *since* are used most frequently (at 18% and 15%, respectively), but together comprise only one third of the adverbials used. Other predictable adverbials, in order of decreasing use, include *never* (as in 23), *already, ever,* and *yet.* Adverbs of frequency indicate the sometimes iterative (or repeated) nature of events described by the present perfect (as in 24, *have been eating everyday*), and the use of *just* indicates "hot news" readings. Like *since* and *for, in* and *during* provide a time frame for the interpretation of the present perfect, as in (25).

(25) It was the hardest exam I have done in my life. [Zayed, T3.5, journal, L1 Arabic]

A total of 45 perfect progressives were produced by the learners (out of the 502 perfect forms). Forty of the 45 occurrences, or 89%, were appropriate uses, which reflects the fact that the appropriate use of (simple) present perfect is established by the time the perfect progressive emerges. A greater proportion of the perfect progressives (62%) occur with adverbials than the simple perfects. The range of the adverbials is also much smaller, with *for* and *since* making up 71% (35.7% each) of the adverbials used. By comparison, the second largest group—the heterogeneous category of frequency adverbs (4/28 or 14%)—is still quite small. Single uses of adverbials make up the remainder.

Examining the use of present perfect in overgeneralizations provides a clue to how learners carve out a form-meaning-use association for the present perfect from their previously established associations of form, meaning, and use for the past and nonpast. The overgeneralizations—uses of the present perfect where another tense-aspect form is preferred—show the features of meaning which learners attempt to convey. The nontargetlike uses show that learners associate present perfect with both past and present time as well as non-sequentiality.

There were 65 identifiable overgeneralizations in the present corpus, 60 in the present perfect and 5 in the perfect progressive. When learners overgeneralized the use of the present perfect, they showed corresponding decreased rates of appropriate use of other tense-aspect inflections in that environment. In the case of Toshihiro, for example, nine uses of present perfect in past-tense contexts depressed his rate of appropriate use for past from 100% appropriate use (on a sample of 14 verb types) at 1.0 to 85% appropriate use of 58 verb types at T1.5, as can be seen in Table 3.5.

Table 3.6 presents the distribution of the overgeneralizations of present perfect according to the environment in which they occur. Most of the overgeneralizations in the corpus are uses of the present perfect in the environment of the simple past. As Table 3.6 shows, 63% or 41 of the 65 overgeneralizations were of this type.

Table 3.6

Distribution of Present Perfect Overgeneralizations

Environment	*n*	%
Simple past	41	63
Pluperfect	15	23
Present	7	11
Ambiguous	2	3
Total	65	100

Note. Present includes simple present and present progressive. From "Another Piece of the Puzzle: The Emergence of the Present Perfect," by K. Bardovi-Harlig, 1997, *Language Learning, 47,* p. 402. Copyright 1997 by the Language Learning Research Club. Adapted with permission.

In (26), the past-tense environment is indicated by the *when*-clause, whereas in (27) it is suggested by the necessary chain of events, namely, that the money had been saved up prior to the purchase of the television.

> (26) I think everyone have ambition. When I was a child I wished if I would be a policeman. It was a drim for me but when I got adult everything *have changed*. [Hamad, T10.5, in-class composition, L1 Arabic]

> (27) . . . After that I went to College mall to buy TV. I want to buy it for quite a long while, but I didn't have mony. So I *have saved* mony. [Kazuhiro, T5.5, journal, L1 Japanese]

> (28) After class, I played base ball in front of Ashton with Kengo, Akihiko and some guys. We have fun it. But our bat was broken off. And our ball was cut. We bought these one yesterday. after baseball, I *have finished* my homework. And I came back Eigenmann [Toshihiro, T1.5, journal, L1 Japanese]

In (28) the learner uses the present perfect in a sequence of events, a use limited to the past given the context established by the learner. The overuses of the present perfect reflect the learner's association of present perfect and past time. However, unlike the use of the simple past with which it is associated, the present perfect cannot be sequenced as the simple past can. This presents some problems in cases like (28) where *I have finished my homework* occurs in the sequence *I played base ball, our bat was broken, our ball was cut, I have finished my homework, and I came back*. Thus, learners must recognize that although past and present perfect may be truth functionally equivalent, they are subject to different discourse constraints.

Cases of overuse also occur in environments associated with the pluperfect, as in (29)–(31). This accounts for 23% of the overgeneralizations.

> (29) I often go to the Union Building with my friends. Sometimes we eat lunch at cafeteria and play billiards game.

We go bowling. I *have never played* billiards because in my country women can't billards. In the U.S. everyone can play billards so my friends teach me and I can play billards. [Ji-An, T4.5, journal, L1 Korean]

(30) Today, I went to the HIPER [sports facility] in the first class. I *haven't been* there [Idechi, T7.0, journal, L1 Japanese]

(31) By the time we reached the Art Museum, the noise from the street *has gone* from us. We contacted our guide, and our outside class began . . . [Carlos, T6.0, journal, L1 Spanish]

In (29) and (30), the learners use the present perfect to report that they have not done something which they have just asserted that they have done. In both cases, the pluperfect is required to express the fact that until recently they had not played billiards or gone to the sports facility, respectively. In (31) the learner reports events out of sequence, which requires the pluperfect given the past orientation of the discourse. (See also Bardovi-Harlig, 1994a.)

The third identifiable area of overuse is in present-tense contexts. This is the least common use in the corpus; only seven cases of overuse of present perfect occurred in the environment of the present tense, accounting for 11% of the overuse. However, examples such as (32) show a learner's association of present perfect with the meaning of the present.

(32) Today, I went to a Thai restlant for eat dinner. I like it and sometimes we *have gone* [go] there. But we always can't understand cantain of the menew. [Idechi, T7.0, journal, L1 Japanese]

The final category of overgeneralization is labelled "ambiguous." There were two uses of the present perfect for which a target could not be determined. Table 3.6 summarizes the distribution of overgeneralizations of the present perfect in the data.

Just under half of the overgeneralizations identified (31/65 or 48%) occur with adverbials. *When*-clauses are the most frequently used adverbial (13/31 or 42%), indicating that disallowed combinations of adverbials and verb tense-aspect are problematic for learners (see (26) and (33)). Like *when*-clauses, other phrases which refer to a specific time are also disallowed, and these occur with 16% of the overgeneralized uses. Together the time adverbials and the *when*-clauses make up 58% of the overuses with adverbials.

(33) When I got there, the class *has already begun.*
[Eduardo, T5.0, journal, L1 Spanish]

(34) In my vacasion I *have done* my homework and made the late Jornals of me. [Zayed, T3.0, journal, L1 Arabic]

(35) Today, I was late in first class. I'm geting lazy because *I've never stdy* anything *in winter vacation* so it's very hard for me. [Noriko, T10.5, journal, L1 Japanese]

In (34) and (35) the learners refer to a specific time, namely a vacation which was completed by the time of the journal entry. (35) uses two adverbials: *never,* which can occur with both present perfect and past, and the specific time adverbial *in winter vacation,* which can occur only with the past when referring to a single particular vacation period. These cases emphasize the need for learners to acquire the co-occurrence restrictions as well as the form and the meaning of the present perfect and the adverbials individually.

Emergence of the pluperfect. The learners produced 192 instances of pluperfect in the written corpus and 31 in the oral corpus, many fewer than the number of tokens of the past progressive or present perfect.[29] The uses of the pluperfect are presented by learner and time in Table 3.7. The conventions of the table are the same as those of Table 3.5, with one addition. Learners produced many more ill-formed uses of the pluperfect than the present perfect, and some of these tokens were both inappropriate and ill-formed. At T1.5, Toshihiro produced two tokens of pluperfect, both of which were ill-formed and inappropriate, indicated by *2* (0).* Other combinations were also found. At T1.0, Kazuhiro

Table 3.7

The Emergence of Pluperfect in Oral and Written Texts

Subject	Month 0.5	1	1.5	2	2.5	3	3.5	4	4.5	5	5.5	6	6.5	7	7.5
Carlos Spanish		4 (0) 83% (6)	2 (0) 97% (32)	9 (7) *1	5 (5)	3 (3)				4 (4), *1	19 (17)	6, *1 Oral 4(3)		3 (2) Oral 2(1)	11 (8)
Eduardo Spanish		3 78% (18)	5 (4)	1 (0)	1	2	1			1 Oral *1(0)	1 Oral 1	1		1	
Kazuhiro Japanese		2 (1*) 85% (13)	1 (0) 72% (25)	2 (1)	2						1 (0)				2 (1)
Hiromi Japanese					1 (0) 100% (28)	3 93% (80)	1*				1	1 PROG	4 Oral 2(1)		3
Noriko Japanese		1 (0) 86% (14)											1 (0)	1 (0)	
Toshihiro Japanese			2* (0) 85% (58)		1* (0)		2* (0)	2* (0)							
Guillermo Spanish					1 (0) 88% (24)					1 (0)		1 (0)			1 (0)
Idechi Japanese		83% (3)	85% (47)	88% (68)		1* 91% (22)	1 (0)								2 (1), *1
Sang Wook Korean								1 (0) 95% (20)	Oral 1 (0) 93% (27)		2	Oral 1 (0)			
Ji-An Korean					96% (25)				Oral 1 (0)	3 (0)	Oral 1 (0)	1			

Table 3.7 (continued)

The Emergence of Pluperfect in Oral and Written Texts

Subject	Month 0.5	1	1.5	2	2.5	3	3.5	4	4.5	5	5.5	6	6.5	7	7.5
Zayed Arabic					84% (19)										81% (63) Oral 1 (0)
Satoru Japanese											2 (0) 100 % (10)	2 (0)	1	1 (0)	
Khaled Arabic														1 (0) 94% (18)	
Hamad Arabic				75% (40)											
Abdullah Arabic															
Saleh Arabic								82% (37)							

Numeral   Number of uses of pluperfect in writing
Oral + numeral Number of uses of pluperfect in oral
(Numeral)   Number of appropriate uses, if different from number used
%   Percentage of appropriate past tense use
% + (numeral)   Number of verb types sampled in half month
PROG   Emergence of pluperfect progressive
*   Ill-formed pluperfect

Table 3.7 (continued)

The Emergence of Pluperfect in Oral and Written Texts

Learner	8	8.5	9	9.5	10	10.5	11	11.5	12	12.5	13	13.5	14	14.5	15	Total
Carlos Spanish	5 (5)		3 (3) Oral 1 (1)	Oral 10 (7)												W 74(60) O 17(13)
Eduardo Spanish																W 17 (14) O 2
Kazuhiro Japanesse		1*	1	Oral 1 (0)												W 12 (7) O 1 (0)
Hiromi Japanese	5 Oral 2	4(3) *PROG	3(2)	3(2)												W 33(29) O 4 (3)
Noriko Japanese	1(0)							Oral 2	1(0)	1					Oral 1*	W 6 (2) O 3
Toshihiro Japanese																W 8 (1) O 0
Guillermo Spanish	1(0)															W 5 (0) O 0
Idechi Japanese			2													W 6 (3) O 0
Sang Wook Korean																W 3 (2) O 1 (0)

Table 3.7 (continued)

The Emergence of Pluperfect in Oral and Written Texts

Learner	8	8.5	9	9.5	10	10.5	11	11.5	12	12.5	13	13.5	14	14.5	15	Total
Ji-An Korean																W 4 (1) O 2 (0)
Zayed Arabic																W 1 O 1 (0)
Saturo Japanese	90% (10)															W 8 (0) O 0
Khaled Arabic	1*		1													W 3 (3) O 0
Hamad Arabic		1(0) 84% (19)		4(1) 85% (46)	1(0)	3							1			W 10 (5) O 0
Abdullah Arabic					1(0) 90% (19)										1	W 2 (1) O 0
Saleh Arabic																W 0 O 0

produced two tokens of pluperfect, one of which was appropriate but ill-formed, indicated as *2(1*)*. The rates of appropriate use of past are once again given at the first occurrence of the targeted tense-aspect form, in this case the pluperfect. However, an appropriate use rate is also given before a pluperfect is produced to show that learners often reach a stable use of simple past some time before the pluperfect emerges.

As is the case with the emergence of the present perfect, the emergence of the pluperfect also requires a stable use of the simple past. The group rate of appropriate use of past tense at emergence of the pluperfect was 89%. The lowest rate of appropriate use of past for any learner who used the pluperfect was 78% with 18 verb types (Eduardo, T1.0), and even this learner showed higher appropriate use of simple past in the following 2-week interval (85% appropriate use with a sample of 33 verb types). All but one learner (Saleh) showed productive use of the pluperfect. As Table 3.7 shows, 11 learners showed fewer than 10 uses of the pluperfect, and 10 learners showed fewer than 8 uses. Of the 192 pluperfects in the written corpus, Carlos produced 74; the group total without Carlos is 118. Carlos was also the most prolific user of the present perfect. The next most frequent user of the pluperfect was Hiromi, who used 33 tokens.

The emergence of the pluperfect seems to start later than any other morphology studied here. Zayed, Satoru, and Khaled showed their first use of the pluperfect between T5.5 and T7.0. Hamad and Abdullah showed emergent use of the pluperfect in T8.5 and T10.0, respectively, and Saleh showed no use in either the oral or written corpus.

The contrast between the simple past and pluperfect is illustrated in Examples (36) and (37), in which the order in which the events occurred is indicated by numbers [1] and [2].

(36) John and I went to her building [2]. She had invited her friends [1]. [Eduardo, T1.0, L1 Spanish]

(37) There were many different shops' bagages [2] maybe
     she had gone shopping many times and different shops
     [1]. [Hiromi, T6.5, L1 Japanese]

Only three learners attempted the pluperfect progressive.
These tokens are indicated on Table 3.7 as *PROG.* Eduardo used
one pluperfect progressive at T3.5 and four others between T5.0
and T7.0, for a total of five tokens. Upon seeing his first snowfall
Eduardo wrote:

(38) I was in front on my window looking at what *I had been
     waiting* for a long time. [Eduardo, T3.5, journal, L1 Spanish]

In (39) and (40) Eduardo supported his use of pluperfect progressive with adverbials, also providing a contrasting adverbial to
support the contrast with the present progressive in (39) and the
present perfect in (40).

(39) I *had been working* on my application before I went back
     to Venezuela, and I am still working on it. [Eduardo, T5.0,
     journal]

(40) Before and since I came here, I *had and have been facing*
     times of challenge. [Eduardo, T5.5, journal]

Hiromi produced three pluperfect progressives. By the time they
appeared, she was already a regular user of the present perfect
and had already shown an instance of the perfect progressive
when she first produced an appropriate use of the pluperfect
progressive at T6.0 (41). In contrast, Sang Wook, who had shown
only a single spontaneous use of the present perfect and one
prompted use, exhibited an inappropriate use of the pluperfect
progressive (42), where the simple past, *didn't find a parking
space,* is suggested by the context.

(41) After dinner one of them visited my room. I *had not been
     locking* [my door] so I said "Come in." [Hiromi, T6.0,
     journal, L1 Japanese]

(42) This morning it was first time my friend and I went to
     class from apartment after moved, My friend and I had

no time because I would be late the first class, so my
friend hurried. but my friend *had not been finding* a
parking space for a long time. When my friend got near
Sycamore Hall at last when my friend drove his car into
a small parking space. [Sang Wook, T4.0, journal, L1
Korean]

Sang Wook showed no other attempt of the pluperfect progressive
and only two attempts at the pluperfect (at T5.5). Interestingly,
Carlos, who showed such enthusiastic use of the present perfect,
showed very late use of the perfect progressive (T9.0) and no use
of the pluperfect progressive in the written or oral corpus.

With the emergence of the pluperfect also comes cases of
overgeneralizations as learners begin to associate the form with
meaning. Early use of the pluperfect is often not targetlike. There
were 62 identifiable overgeneralizations of the pluperfect in the
present corpus. Satoru, Guillermo, and Khaled showed no targetlike use of the pluperfect. The group score, including Carlos,
shows that 32% of the productions of the pluperfect (62/192)
occurred in the environment of another tense-aspect form. Without Carlos's rather high appropriate use (61/74 appropriate uses),
42% of the productions (49/118) were overgeneralizations. Even
with Carlos's apparent mastery of the pluperfect, his early attempts also show the same pattern of overgeneralization before
targetlike form-meaning associations were made. Table 3.7 shows
that in the first three sampling periods in which Carlos used the
pluperfect—T1.0, 1.5, 2.0—he produced 15 tokens of pluperfect.
Only one of the first six attempts was appropriate in use
(T1.0–1.5); seven of the next nine were targetlike (T2.0). Most of
the other learners in the study showed the same pattern for early
use, although many produced fewer than 15 tokens of the pluperfect during the observation period.

The overgeneralizations in the corpus are uses of the pluperfect in the environment of the simple past and the present perfect.
Of the 62 overgeneralizations, 13 were produced by Carlos and
were split evenly between past (6) and present perfect (7). Group

scores that include Carlos show that 35 pluperfects (57%) were used in environments of the simple past, and 27 (43%) appeared in the environment of the present perfect. Group scores without Carlos show an even closer balance: 29 (52%) uses in the environment of simple past and 27 (48%) uses in the environment of the present perfect. (43) and (44)—and also (42)—show uses of the pluperfect in the environment of reference to past intervals.

(43) In the last journal, I *had spoken* about the Galileo Program. I think that you have little idea about it. [Carlos, T2.0, journal, L1 Spanish]

(44) I live in South Korean. Most of Korean people love liberty. The Korean war *had began* in 1950. South and North *had fought*. Many people were dead. It was sad. [Ji-An, T5.0, journal, L1 Korean]

Because the journal to which Carlos referred was written the previous night, it is unlikely that Carlos employed the pluperfect as a remote past. However, that might be the case with Ji-An's use of *had began in 1950*. Bardovi-Harlig (1992a) observed that certain lexical items such as *grandparents* and dates that indicate that an event took place much earlier than the time of speaking/ writing may trigger the use of the pluperfect by learners.

(45) and (46) show uses of the pluperfect in the environment of the present perfect. In both cases, the use of the pluperfect is at odds with the present relevance of the italicized situation to the rest of the context provided by the learner; these contexts strongly suggest the present perfect.

(45) Today, I went to College Mall for buy Christmas presents with June after school. Because My family *had had* a party for long time in Christmas eve, so I have to buy many presents and send to my family in Japan! [Idechi, T3.5, journal, L1 Japanese]

(46) When I was a child I like to spent all my day outside my house, and I like to around with my friends everywhere in the car, but now I am old enough so I have good

experians and everything *had changed.* I feel now if I stay in my house with my family this is my happiness time for me. [Hamad, T8.5, composition, L1 Arabic]

The somewhat later use of pluperfect in comparison to the other tense-aspect morphology emphasizes its nonessential nature for learners (including instructed learners). The pluperfect is only one linguistic device that serves to signal a deviation from chronological order. As was seen in the meaning-oriented approach in Chapter 2, the expression of reverse-order reports—and in fact the concept of anteriority which the pluperfect encodes—can be accomplished by the use of simple past and adverbials.

Order of Emergence

The order of emergence among English verbal morphology which encodes as part of its meaning "Event time precedes Speech time" is the simple past, then past progressive, followed by the present perfect, and finally the pluperfect. The order is most easily observed in the language samples of learners whose verbal morphology was less developed at the outset of the study. For each, the rate of appropriate use of the simple past is a bit higher. The undisputed latest starter is the pluperfect, which shows up later on the calendar. Table 3.8 schematically represents the information in Tables 3.4–3.7.

In Table 3.8, PROG indicates the past progressive, PERF the present perfect, and PLU the pluperfect. In order for learners to receive a marker for a tense-aspect form on the table, a sample had to show three distinct lexical verbs (i.e., types rather than tokens) that were used appropriately. In the case of the pluperfect, some learners did not reach three distinct uses by the end of the observation period, but did attempt some use of the pluperfect. These cases are indicated as *PLU* with a numeral (1 or 2) in parentheses. Thus, learners with limited numbers of pluperfect tokens are distinguished from learners who show no use of the pluperfect. Using the three-token criterion to indicate emergence

Table 3.8

Emergence Sequences in Past-Related Morphology

Subject	Month 0.5	1	1.5	2	2.5	3	3.5	4	4.5	5	5.5	6	6.5	7	7.5
Carlos Spanish			PROG PERF	PLU											
Eduardo Spanish				PERF PLU	PROG										
Noriko Japanese								PROG	PERF						
Hiromi Japanese						PROG PLU	PERF								
Kazuhiro Japanese			PLU	PERF	PROG										PLU
Guillermo Spanish					PROG					PERF					
Ji-An Korean						PERF			PROG			PLU(1)			
Zayed Arabic							PERF	PROG							
Khaled Arabic			PROG											PERF	
Idechi Japanese				PROG										PERF	

Table 3.8 (continued)

Emergence Sequences in Past-Related Morphology

Subject	Month 0.5	1	1.5	2	2.5	3	3.5	4	4.5	5	5.5	6	6.5	7	7.5
Toshihiro Japanese					PROG			PERF							
Satoru Japanese											PROG				
Hamad Arabic													PROG		
Abdullah Arabic						PROG									
Saleh Arabic							PROG								
Sang Wook Korean					PROG		PERF								

Note. PROG = Past Progressive; PERF = Present Perfect; PLU = Pluperfect. Where 3 types were not observed, the number of types appears in parentheses.

Table 3.8 (continued)

Emergence Sequences in Past-Related Morphology

Learner	8	8.5	9	9.5	10	10.5	11	11.5	12	12.5	13	13.5	14	14.5	15
Carlos Spanish															
Eduardo Spanish															
Noriko Japanese										PLU					
Hiromi Japanese															
Kazuhiro Japanese															
Guillermo Spanish															
Ji-An Korean															
Zayed Arabic															
Khaled Arabic															

Table 3.8 (continued)

Emergence Sequences in Past-Related Morphology

Learner	8	8.5	9	9.5	10	10.5	11	11.5	12	12.5	13	13.5	14	14.5	15
Idechi Japanese			PLU												
Toshihiro Japanese						PERF	PLU								
Satoru Japanese		PERF													
Hamad Arabic				PERF									PLU		
Abdullah Arabic				PERF											
Saleh Arabic					PERF							PERF			
Sang Wook Korean															

is a much more conservative measure than the raw number of uses reported in Tables 3.4–3.7, which included all uses of the targeted verbal morphology. By this analysis many fewer learners show "emergence" of a form-meaning association than use of the mere form alone. Recall that some learners attempted very few forms, especially for the pluperfect; counting types rather than tokens further reduces the number of productions reported in this table. Although Tables 3.4–3.7 do not contain information on repeated lexical items, the reader is invited to consider the raw production data in the tables to confirm the emergence orders schematized in Table 3.8.[30]

The past progressive is used at least three distinct times by all 16 learners. As noted earlier, the progressive appears later with the present perfect and the pluperfect than the respective nonprogressive forms. Learners who show the emergence of the present perfect before the past progressive use the past progressive in the following sampling interval, i.e., within two weeks. Kazuhiro's early use of the pluperfect at T1.5 is worth comment because at first glance he appears not to follow the order of emergence just outlined. He used the pluperfect appropriately three times by T2.5 (Table 3.7), followed by a period of non-use in the written and oral samples, and only began what appears to be productive use at T7.5. At T7.5 he continued to fine-tune formal accuracy and form-meaning associations. The two most morphologically advanced learners, Carlos and Eduardo, showed a clustering of the three forms at T1.5 and 2.0 and T2.0 and 2.5, respectively.

The order past→past progressive→present perfect→pluperfect is comparable to that described for Lavinia by Klein (1993, 1995). Lavinia showed emergent use of simple past, V-*ing*, and present perfect, in that order. Pluperfect came in last in Lavinia's interlanguage system, at 22 months (Klein, 1995, pp. 45–46). The relatively few studies of languages other than English that have included the pluperfect in their scope (Dietrich, 1995; Schlyter, 1990; see Table 3.8) have also found that the language-specific pluperfect equivalent appears quite late. The order observed in the present longitudinal study also supports Bailey's (1987, 1989) cross-sectional findings that the simple past precedes the past progressive.

It is important to bear in mind that emergence orders do not suggest that acquisition is in any way complete. Learners in no sense finish with one verbal morpheme before the interlanguage tense-aspect system admits the next. As Klein (1993, 1994a), Dietrich et al. (1995), and their colleagues have observed in their studies of the European learners, learners continue to use base forms even in the more advanced stages of interlanguage. Moreover, in the acquisition of verbal morphology form-meaning associations cannot be said to be truly complete for any given tense-aspect form until the entire system is complete. As the following section will show, emergent uses of one tense-aspect form impinge on the semantic territory of the other tense-aspect forms. Even the acquisition of the core meaning of a form is not sufficient, and learners must struggle to understand the contrast between forms.

Semantics of the Emerging System

As predicted by the linguistic descriptions of the meaning of the present perfect as having features of both the past and the present, overgeneralizations into the environments of both the simple past tense and the present tense are seen in the acquisition of the present perfect. As learners carve out the meaning and use associated with the newly acquired form, they must also reassign part of their understanding of the simple past and present tenses to the present perfect. The process of re-association is reflected in the use of the emergent present perfect.

In the case of overgeneralizations, both the present and past readings of the present perfect are applied to a context in which only one is appropriate. When present perfect is used in an environment for past tense, only the past meaning of the present perfect is relevant; the feature of present relevance is not. The present relevance implied by the use of the present perfect by an

NS is either not integrated into the form-meaning association by the learner (that is, the learner equates the present perfect with its truth functional equivalent, the simple past tense), or the present relevance is not sufficiently apparent to the reader/analyst, resulting in a misunderstanding of the learner's intentions. Although misunderstanding a learner's intentions is a genuine problem in the analysis of any natural corpus, there are also clear cases in which learners use the present perfect in past contexts created by NS interviewers, as in the question "Did you understand the southern accent?" which was answered by the present perfect "I *haven't talked* with them" (when the trip had already been completed; Hamad, T9.5, L1 Arabic) or "Did you do anything during our spring break? The spring vacation we had?" being answered by "I *have stayed* here" (Satoru, T7.5, L1 Japanese). In cases like these, the learner seems to equate the meaning of the past and the present perfect.[31] In those rare cases where the present perfect is used in present-tense contexts, the feature of present relevance of the present perfect is appropriate to the context, but the anterior reading of the present perfect is not. Learners also use the pluperfect in the environment of the present perfect. At 23% of the overgeneralizations, the association of the present perfect with the pluperfect is much less common than the association with the simple past, but it is twice as frequent as the association with the simple present. I will return to this relationship after I discuss the semantics of the pluperfect.

The overgeneralizations of the pluperfect are divided between environments of the past and present perfect. Just over half of the overgeneralizations of the pluperfect occur in place of the past. The semantic association between the simple past and the pluperfect is clear. As Comrie (1985) and Leech (1971) point out, every event that can be encoded by a pluperfect can also be encoded by the past. Thus, all pluperfects are also past. However, the reverse is not true. Not all pasts are pluperfects, and the learners may have difficulty with this relationship. To use an example from Comrie (1985), if "John arrived; Mary had left" is true, then it is also the case that "John arrived" and "Mary left" are both true. However, the pair of sentences, "John arrived; Mary had left" contains information about the ordering of events that the sentences "John arrived" and "Mary left" individually do not. One cannot go from the unconjoined clauses to either "Mary left; John had arrived" or "John arrived; Mary had left" without information about ordering.

The association of the present perfect with the pluperfect suggests that learners recognize the formal similarity of the perfects. (23% of the present perfect overgeneralizations are in the pluperfect environment; about 52% of the overgeneralizations of the pluperfect are in the present perfect environment.) In addition, learners seem to recognize at least one semantic feature common to the pluperfect and present perfect: Both the pluperfect and the present perfect convey non-sequentiality—that is, both are used to encode events or situations which are not reported in chronological order.[32] In (45), repeated here as (47), a learner overused the pluperfect in a present perfect context, with a corresponding underuse of present perfect.

(47) Today, I went to College Mall for buy Christmas presents with June after school. Because My family *had had* a party *for long time* in Christmas eve, so I have to buy many presents and send to my family in Japan! [Idechi, T3.5, journal, L1 Japanese]

(48) When I got there, the class *has already begun.* [Eduardo, T5.0, journal, L1 Spanish]

In (48) another learner showed an overuse of present perfect in a pluperfect context, with a corresponding underuse of the pluperfect. In both examples, the events that the learners have encoded in perfect are reported out of sequence. However, the present orientation of the excerpt in (47) requires the present perfect, whereas the past orientation of (48) requires the pluperfect.

The present perfect and pluperfect might also be viewed by learners as being related to each other through their relation to the simple past. The present perfect and the simple past are truth-functional equivalents of each other, leading to overuse of present perfect for the past (and vice versa; see Bardovi-Harlig, 1997a). The pluperfect is also a past, but the opposite is not true. Thus, the pluperfect and present perfect have different relationships with the past. It may take learners some time to see that the present perfect and pluperfect are distinct from each other and from the past. In addition, learners may assume a closer functional relation of pluperfect and present perfect than warranted semantically because of their formal similarity.[33]

Comparing the differences among the semantic neighbors of present, simple past, pluperfect, and present perfect in a Reichenbach representation of tense-aspect offers another perspective on the relationships between the form-meaning associations that make up the emergent tense-aspect system. Recall that "E" represents event time, "S," speech time, and "R," reference time. The meanings of the tenses and aspects under investigation have the following semantics (Reichenbach, 1947, p. 290) with time moving from left to right:

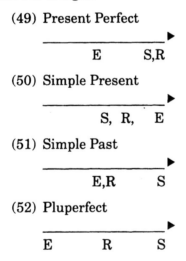

(49) Present Perfect

        E   S,R

(50) Simple Present

        S, R,   E

(51) Simple Past

        E,R   S

(52) Pluperfect

   E   R   S

S, R indicates that speech time and reference time are coincident, as in the present perfect. In the simple present, speech time, event time, and reference time all coincide, as indicated by "S, R, E."

In each case, the present perfect differs from each of the others by one feature. With the simple past, it shares the anterior event time, but not the reference time. With the simple present, it shares coincident reference and speech time, but not event time. With the pluperfect, reference time is again different. For the pluperfect (a relative-absolute tense) the reference time is distinct from event time (as is the case with the present perfect) and is also anterior with respect to speech time; in the case of the present perfect, reference time and speech time are coincident. Thus, in the cases of under- and overgeneralizations with the simple past and the pluperfect, learners must acquire a different reference time for targetlike use, whereas in the case of the associations with the present, an anterior event time must be acquired.

Of all the associations that learners make, the association of the present perfect with the simple past seems to be the strongest, accounting for 63% of the overgeneralizations. In these cases learners apparently draw on the shared feature [+anterior]. However, the shared feature is not a sufficient explanation because the present perfect also shares a feature with the present [+current relevance] and the pluperfect [−sequential]. What the present perfect and the simple past share, which is unique to this pair, is truth value (Inoue, 1979; N. Smith, 1981). Because the present perfect sentence is true in all cases that the simple past sentence is true (i.e., if it is true that *Max has seen the President,* it is also true that *Max saw the President,* and vice versa), and false if the simple past sentence is false, the degree of semantic overlap is greatest for this pair. It is this semantic overlap that makes the association of present perfect with past the strongest and the reason that learners show the greatest overuse of present perfect in past contexts.

These associations do not keep learners from acquiring a targetlike tense-aspect system. They are merely stages through which learners progress. As we can see from the rate of appropriate use of present perfect in the corpus as a whole (at 87% for all learners or 80% adjusting for the most prolific users, Carlos and Eduardo), learners can and do come to distinguish the present perfect semantically from the simple past, as well as from the remainder of the emergent tense-aspect system.

Similar arguments can be made for the relation of the pluperfect to the past, with which it shares semantic features: all pluperfects are also past, but not vice versa. By either Reichenbach's (1947) or Comrie's (1985) account, pluperfect shares more obvious features with the past than with the present perfect, thus making the association between pluperfect and present perfect by learners likely to be at least partially a formal one. However, the formal similarities between the present perfect and the pluperfect lead the learners to inappropriate use of both tense-aspect forms.

We also see that rates of appropriate use for the pluperfect are lower, 68% for the group and 53% without Carlos, the most prolific user of the pluperfect. However, the pluperfect emerges later, and thus there are fewer tokens of it in the corpus. There is no reason to assume that learners who stay in an English-speaking environment would not ultimately be as successful with the pluperfect as they are with the present perfect.

Explaining the Order of Emergence

The present perfect is acquired later than the simple past in L2 as well as in L1, which suggests that attributing late development of the present perfect in L1 acquisition to cognitive development is somewhat suspect. Following von Stutterheim and Klein we assume that "a second language learner—in contrast to a child learning his first language—does not have to acquire the underlying concepts. What he has to acquire is a specific way and a specific means of expressing them" (1987, p. 194).[34]

One alternative factor that has been suggested for the order in L1 acquisition is morphosyntactic complexity (Gathercole, 1986; Johnson, 1985; C. Smith, 1980). Unlike cognitive development, morphosyntactic complexity could be a factor in adult second language acquisition. Although morphosyntactic complexity accounts for the acquisition of the simple past and present perfect, it is a less satisfying explanation if the pluperfect is taken into account, at least for second language acquisition. Morphosyntactically the present perfect and the pluperfect are comparable in complexity, differing only by the formal tense marker on the auxiliary. Nevertheless, pluperfect emerges after the present perfect in the present corpus. Multiple factors such as semantic complexity (C. Smith, 1980), syntactic complexity, frequency of input, and functional load are all likely to contribute to determining the acquisition order (cf. Gathercole, 1986, for L1) and should be investigated further for second language acquisition.

Adult second language acquisition differs from child L1 acquisition in the reported order of acquisition for the perfect progressive. In a study of L1 children, Johnson (1985) found that present perfect and perfect progressive are used by children at the same time. However, there are two differences between Johnson's task and the present one which bear on the interpretation: the task by which the corpus was elicited and criteria by which it was measured. Johnson's child corpus derives from an elicited imitation task. Although Johnson took steps to assure that no learner was solely imitating (by including ungrammatical forms and semantically anomalous uses), the corpus was not spontaneously produced. (See also Gathercole, 1986, and Johnson, 1985, for discussion of the task.)

Johnson (1985) also used a more lenient coding scheme for the imitation tasks completed by L1 English-speaking children. Attempts at the simple present perfect were identified by the use of *have* with a nonprogressive main verb (as done here) or by the use of "a recognizable past participle (including novel forms such as a root verb+*en*) which was distinct from the past tense" (p. 335). The second set was not included in this analysis because without the elicitation task the bare participle often cannot be distinguished from an attempt at the past tense, as in regular participles such as *looked, worried,* or *allowed,* or from a predicate adjective, as in the case of *broken.* Thus, in this corpus only *have* + verb or *have* + ill-formed participle were included as ill-formed attempts. This type represented 27% of the children's attempts at the present perfect in Johnson's corpus. In contrast, in the present study there were very few errors in form in the written corpus (under 7%), but a similar proportion of errors to Johnson's (26%) was found in the oral corpus. Just under half of the total number of present perfects (49%) and the perfect progressives (48%) attempted by the children were grammatical. Gathercole questions Johnson's interpretation of the data as showing acquisition because of the high number of ungrammatical forms. We may find that the acquisition order for child L1 and adult L2 acquisition is not different if oral longitudinal production data are compared for both.

The Influence of the Learners' First Language

There does not seem to be an obvious first language influence in the longitudinal corpus. Although this study was not designed specifically to test L1 influence, learners from four languages are represented. No specific L1 group seems to have a unique profile regarding either number of forms produced or emergent form-meaning associations en route to the target associations. This is true for both the written and oral corpus. In relation to the production of past progressive, for example, Table 3.4 shows that the top producers of past progressive in the written corpus (ranging from 42 to 37 written tokens) were Zayed and Saleh (L1 Arabic), Noriko (L1 Japanese) and Carlos (L1 Spanish). Only the Korean speakers are not represented, but there were only two of them and both had relatively short stays. The remaining learners produced a maximum of 22 and a minimum of 5 tokens of past progressive. Hiromi, Khaled, and Eduardo (L1 Japanese, Arabic, and Spanish, respectively) top the mid-group with 22, 20, and 19 tokens each and Hamad (L1 Arabic), Ji-An (L1 Korean), and Satoru (L1 Japanese) show the lowest production at 7, 6, and 5 tokens.

The distribution of past progressive tokens in the oral sample might be more a reflection of talkativeness than of acquisition, whereas the written format seems to be an equalizer. Two speakers of L1 Spanish, Eduardo and Carlos, show the greatest use, with

Eduardo far ahead with 41 to Carlos's 25. (Note that Eduardo produced far fewer in his written texts—only 19). Two Arabic speakers, Zayed and Saleh, were next with 22 and 16 tokens each, followed by Noriko, a native speaker of Japanese, with 13 tokens. All other learners, equally balanced among the four language groups, produced very few, between 6 and 1, with one learner producing none.

A similar profile is found with regard to the present perfect. Each high producer for any one L1 can be matched by a lower producer from the same group. Table 3.5 shows that two L1 Spanish learners, Carlos and Eduardo, show robust and appropriate use of the present perfect in writing (111 and 83 tokens, respectively). Whereas this might be due in part to the existence of a formally and semantically similar present perfect in South American Spanish, it is necessary to consider that although Guillermo shares a common first language with Carlos and Eduardo, L1 does not seem to confer the same advantage on Guillermo, who produces a respectable 27 tokens. Rate of acquisition and level of attainment must also play a role in determining the difference in uses of present perfect between Carlos and Eduardo on the one hand and Guillermo on the other, and additionally between Carlos and Eduardo and all the other learners. Noriko, Hiromi, and Kazuhiro, all L1 Japanese, produce 62, 43, and 36 tokens respectively, followed by Guillermo (L1 Spanish) with 27 and Ji-An (Korean) with 23. Zayed and Khaled follow (L1 Arabic) with 18 tokens each and the lower range, 16-2, is inhabited by learners of L1 Arabic, Japanese, and Korean.

In addition, the ESF design, which investigated the acquisition of five target languages by learners of two languages each, was set up to answer questions regarding the influence of the first language and of the target languages. However, even in the ESF studies, transfer effects are quite rare. Klein, Dietrich et al. (1995) conclude:

> What is much more striking is the *lack of SL* [source language] *influence* where one would expect it. Some of the source languages have a distinct aspect marking, others do

not. But we have no evidence in our data that this difference plays a systematic role. We must conclude, therefore,
that there is no significant SL influence in the acquisition
of temporality. We cannot exclude that clear transfer exists,
of course; but if so, we have not observed it in the learner
varieties studied in this project. (p. 278; emphasis original)

Although it seems premature to claim that the observed acquisitional sequences are universal, there certainly do seem to be
sequences that are common to the European languages studied in
this chapter. What we can say with certainty is that all of the
learners in the present longitudinal study, regardless of first
language, are equally likely within the same instructional environment to acquire the tense-aspect system of English.

Comparing Meaning-Oriented
and Form-Oriented Approaches

It is instructive to compare the meaning-oriented approach
described in Chapter 2 and the form-oriented approach used here.
As is immediately noticeable, the meaning-oriented approach
casts a broader net than the form-oriented studies. The meaning-
oriented studies include the study of the emergence of morphology
as one stage of the acquisition of temporal expression, and meaning-
oriented studies thus necessarily examine pragmatic and lexical
means of temporal expression as well. However, the differences
are not merely limited to the range of linguistic devices that are
studied. By defining a semantic concept and investigating how it
is expressed, we see the use of morphology as it moves into a
pre-defined semantic environment. Using the metaphor of the
window introduced in Chapter 2, in the meaning-oriented approach, the concept studied becomes the window. Through the
window we see the use of all the forms used to express the concept.
What is not observed in a meaning-oriented approach is other uses
of the form or other meanings. We do not see what is beyond the
frame established by the window.

Consider the emergence of the pluperfect as an example. If we use a characteristic semantic environment of the pluperfect, namely the reverse-order report, it allows us to observe how reverse-order reports are expressed and how the pluperfect eventually takes its place as one of the linguistic devices that encode reverse-order accounts. What we see, then, is how the pluperfect moves into its best defined environment, and how the appropriate use of pluperfect is established in interlanguage. In contrast, using a form-oriented approach requires that we identify an emerging morpheme and track it in all its instantiations in the interlanguage sample. Again taking the pluperfect as an example, we find that early uses of the pluperfect may be nontargetlike. Because in the meaning-oriented approach we follow only the environment of the reverse-order report, we miss the use of the pluperfect in other contexts. Of course, the meaning-oriented approach does reveal the use of other tense-aspect forms to express reverse-order reports, thus illustrating innovative uses of tense-aspect forms by learners (with the exception of the pluperfect).

Another difference between the approaches is that in order to do a meaning-oriented study, a reasonably well-defined semantic concept is necessary, whereas in a form-oriented study the semantics of the interlanguage tense-aspect system are inferred from the distribution of the forms. Because the concept of the past has been widely discussed in the linguistic literature, there is agreement as to what past time is, and thus a concept like "past" is a good candidate for investigation. Similarly, the reverse-order report is easily enough defined. But what of the concepts underlying the English present perfect, a highly contested category? With at least four competing analyses of the present perfect, which one is to be selected? And, even more crucial to carrying out the analysis, how are these concepts to be identified in a language sample? To take one interpretation of the present perfect, how can the notion of present relevance be distinguished from the present?

Such concerns led to my study of the present perfect from a form-oriented approach, rather than setting up a meaning-oriented study in which I would be able to observe the gradual appearance of the present perfect, along with other linguistic devices, in a predefined semantic environment. Areas which are well-suited to the meaning-oriented approach in the expression of temporality are areas that are well-defined. That is not to say that there are cases without controversy in the linguistic literature. However, there are cases for which the core meanings have been defined. Particularly promising as new areas of investigation are the future (with careful delineation where possible between the future and modality; see Moses, 1997, and forthcoming) and conditional expressions (Salsbury, 2000). Both the meaning-oriented and the form-oriented approaches contribute to our understanding of the development of the tense-aspect system. Viewing acquisition through both lenses leads us to a more complete picture.

Chapter Summary

The third main stage of the acquisition of temporal expression is the acquisition of verbal morphology. As seen in this chapter, the morphological stage is comprised of many individual stages. The stages, or acquisitional sequences, are remarkably similar across target languages. To date, little first-language influence has been identified. The emergence of tense-aspect morphology precedes its targetlike use as learners forge form-meaning associations. Examining the tense-aspect systems of learners shows that early relatively simple systems of form-meaning associations are readjusted as new forms enter the system and are assigned meanings. This may cause lower rates of appropriate use in morphology that emerged earlier as learners overuse the emergent morphology in the environments of other tense-aspect forms. However, it is not sufficient for learners to identify only the core meaning of tense-aspect. Learners must also acquire the contrast between different tenses and grammatical aspect, distinguishing the meaning of one form from its semantically close neighbors.

The chapter also compared the meaning-oriented and form-oriented approaches, revealing the different perspectives that they bring to the same corpus. Focusing on the meaning brings attention to how various linguistic devices, including emergent tense-aspect morphology, are used to express a particular concept. Focusing on the form tracks the use of a targeted morpheme in all of the environments in which it occurs. Chapters 4 and 5 continue the examination of form-oriented studies. Both present hypothesis-driven studies that focus our attention more specifically on the patterns of distribution of emergent verbal morphology with regard to lexical aspectual categories and discourse structure.

Notes

[1]The tense-aspect systems of the target languages are more complex synchronically and sociolinguistically than presented here. The grammatical sketches presented in this section make reference only to those tense-aspect forms that have been investigated in acquisition studies and are reviewed in this chapter. For example, Spanish also has a progressive (Comrie, 1976), but I do not discuss it here because it has not been addressed in the L2 tense-aspect acquisition literature. In contrast, the Italian progressive is included because its acquisition in L2 has been studied by Giacalone Ramat (1995c, 1997).

[2]Although the progressive and imperfect are separate grammatical (and morphological) categories, semantically both are imperfective (Comrie, 1985). See the section on the English progressive for a discussion of this.

[3]Also, like French, Dutch has a simple past form *hij werkte* "he worked," but it is seldom used in vernacular Dutch. It seems to be especially rare in the southern Netherlands where the acquisition study was carried out. (See Klein et al., 1995; Kooij, 1987.)

[4]It is perhaps an overstatement to say that the description of every tense-aspect form-meaning association in English (and perhaps other languages) is disputed. (For overviews which emphasize that fact see Binnick, 1991; Comrie, 1976, 1985.) However, in the sketches that follow I attempt to outline what is commonly accepted regarding the meanings of the tense-aspect in question, and provide references for those interested in the arguments surrounding the semantics of the L1 system.

[5]Most theories address the English progressive rather than the past progressive specifically.

[6]Shirai (1998b) argues that the habitual sense is derived from the progressive by semantic extension.

[7]The description of the present perfect given here has been necessarily simplified. For extended theoretical discussions, see Binnick (1991), Comrie (1976), and McCoard (1978), as well as other works cited herein.

[8]The concept of "current relevance" as the defining characteristic of the present perfect is distinct from the Gricean notion of relevance (Grice, 1975). Gricean relevance addresses issues of topical relevance, and contributions which exhibit any tense-aspect morphology may be considered to be germane to the unfolding discourse if cooperatively nominated and accepted by the interlocutors. In contrast, the notion of current relevance is generally understood as being restricted to temporal relevance. All uses of the present perfect could potentially satisfy the requirements of Gricean relevance for the discourse in which they occur, but all pragmatically relevant contributions could not satisfy the semantics of the present perfect.

[9]For an extended discussion of adverbs used with the present perfect, see Matthews (1987) and McCoard (1978).

[10]C. Smith uses the term "viewpoint aspect" to distinguish the viewpoints of English, the simple and the progressive. I am using the term in the spirit of Smith's dichotomy of "situation" and "viewpoint," which distinguishes the character of an event (the situation) from a speaker's reporting of it (the viewpoint).

[11]I gloss over the differences in Comrie's (1985) analysis compared to Reichenbach's (1947).

[12]This is not necessarily the case if a study focuses on formal accuracy in which case tense-aspect may be conflated with person and number. Unless it is explicitly stated, it is sometimes difficult to determine what scoring procedure was used. The longitudinal studies reviewed in the following section all distinguish between tense-aspect and person and number, but some of the cross-sectional studies seem to incorporate them in their focus on achieving the target.

[13]Note that although Catalan distinguishes the perfective and imperfective past morphologically as Spanish, French, and Italian do, the Catalan preterite forms differ radically from those of the other Romance languages because they are formed by using the auxiliary *anar* "to go" followed by an infinitive, which in other Romance languages (e.g., French and Spanish) expresses future meaning (Comajoan, 1998).

[14]Ayshe used the Perfekt when a right boundary was expressed, as in *was haben gesagt?* "What have you said?" and she used the Präteritum when there was no right boundary, as in *sie sprichte ganz anders* "She speaked quite different." I understand the right boundary in Dietrich's (1995) description to be the endpoint in keeping with the Western depiction of the time line as moving from left to right.

[15]Responses were scored for (a) correct form, correct temporal-aspect choice; (b) correct form, incorrect temporal-aspect choice; (c) incorrect form, correct temporal-aspect choice; and (d) incorrect form, incorrect temporal-aspect choice. Only the first, correct form, correct temporal-aspect choice, was counted as "accurate." See Kaplan (1987), Table 3-1.

[16]Kaplan's Table 3-1 divides 1st- and 2nd-year students into semesters, and it appears that 4th-semester students are more accurate than 3rd-semester

students and that passé composé is more accurate than imparfait. No raw scores appear in the paper, so it is difficult to interpret when the forms are produced and in what numbers.

[17]Other error analyses of Spanish preterite and imperfect include L1 Dutch speakers (García & van Putte, 1988) and L1 German, Japanese, Arabic, and French learners of Spanish in a host environment (Fernández, 1997).

[18]Meisel, Clahsen, and Pienemann (1981) make the same observation for other areas of interlanguage grammar.

[19]The pluperfect is also known as "past perfect" in English-language pedagogy. The term "pluperfect" is generally preferred in studies of temporal semantics (cf. Binnick, 1991; Comrie, 1976, 1985; Thelin, 1990). The resulting nonparallel terms, "pluperfect" and "present perfect," stress the semantic differences between the two.

[20]Occurrences of use resulting from an · instructional writing prompt (a statement or question to which learners respond in writing) were eliminated from the sample. There were nine such uses resulting largely from the writing prompt "I *have been* in the United States for [some] months now, and I *have learned* many things." These were identified from the teaching logs that the writing and grammar teachers kept throughout the longitudinal study.

[21]It should be noted, however, that although the use of types provides a more conservative view of the emergence and control of tense-aspect morphology, it does not preserve the integrity of the text. A learner may achieve the feeling of a past-tense text by the use of multiple occurrence of a small number of verbs in past tense, but this effect is not captured in a type-analysis. For this reason, any discourse analysis of tense-aspect must take tokens into account. (See Chapter 5.)

[22]The coding was first done by the researcher, and then checked and entered in summary sheets by the second coder. Disagreements were resolved by discussion.

[23]Undergeneralizations are also revealing but much harder to determine for the present perfect (past progressive or pluperfect) than for the simple past. Undergeneralizations of the present perfect are discussed by Bardovi-Harlig (1997a).

[24]In Table 3.4 and all other longitudinal tables, empty cells indicate no production of the targeted form. The end of the vertical lines indicates the end of the language sample.

[25]The influence of instruction is taken up in Chapter 6.

[26]The section is based on Bardovi-Harlig (1997a).

[27]This is a substantially higher rate than the rate of use cited by Moy (1983). In that study, only 23 learners out of 100 used the present perfect in expository compositions written for a university placement examination. The difference in the number of learners who use the present perfect may be the result of different sampling techniques, longitudinal in the present study and a single sample in Moy's.

[28]See Bardovi-Harlig (1997a) for a discussion of the challenges of interpreting grammatical knowledge in interactional contexts.

[29]Note that the meaning-oriented studies that were presented in Chapter 2 did not analyze all of the texts that had been collected, but rather used a sampling method. The sampling method used in the study of reverse-order reports selected the first three past-oriented texts from each 15-day interval, resulting in a corpus of 430 written texts. (See Table 2.2.)

[30]See also Stanley and Mellow (1998) for a discussion of how to determine developmental sequences.

[31]Shirai (personal communication, November 1999) has pointed out that saying that learners seem to equate the past and present perfect may be too strong.

[32]The pluperfect and present perfect receive quite different semantic accounts in the literature (Comrie, 1976, 1985). However, see Klein (1992) for an argument that the pluperfect and the perfect share a single underlying semantics. See also Salkie (1989) for a different perspective on the relationship of the perfect and the pluperfect.

[33]In addition, the teaching of the present perfect and pluperfect often occurs together, resulting in further pedagogical proximity of the two forms. Teaching effects are discussed in Chapter 6; however, it is important to point out here that even though learners meet the present and pluperfect at the same time in the classroom, there is an obvious delay in the acquisition of the pluperfect, and this is likely to be related to the semantics of the pluperfect in the reverse-order reports discussed in Chapter 2.

[34]Fletcher (1981) and Gathercole (1986) make the argument against a cognitive developmental factor on other grounds exclusively within L1 data.

CHAPTER FOUR

The Aspect Hypothesis

Although the research approaches in Chapters 2 and 3 are distinguished from each other on the basic level of orientation to the data, with Chapter 2 illustrating a meaning-oriented approach and Chapter 3 a form-oriented approach, they are nevertheless similar in that they are both descriptive approaches to the study of temporality in second language acquisition. With the examination of the aspect hypothesis, Chapter 4 introduces a theory-driven inquiry of the acquisition of tense-aspect morphology. Like the studies that described the acquisitional sequences of verbal morphology in Chapter 3, the studies that test the aspect hypothesis are form-oriented. However, like experimental studies in all areas of second language acquisition research, these studies add experimental elicitation techniques to the less-guided data collection found in the studies of Chapters 2 and 3.

Research that tests the aspect hypothesis shows a range of elicitation methods and analyses. Whereas meaning-oriented studies (Chapter 2), acquisitional sequences studies (Chapter 3), and discourse studies (Chapter 5) all work with complete texts generated by learners, the aspect studies show greater diversity in both task and analysis. This stems in part from the broad interest that the aspect hypothesis has generated and the inherent testability of a clearly stated hypothesis. The mix of elicitation tasks also stems from the attempt to quantify the data. The pursuit of generalizability of research results requires large samples and unambiguous cases which often subtly steer research design away from unguided learner production to more controlled tasks. On the whole, the range of elicitation tasks serves to strengthen the support for the aspect hypothesis. In some cases, methods indicate subtle differences in interpretation of the hypothesis itself.

Quantification of results brings additional differences to the discussion as researchers attempt to analyze tense-aspect use by learners. The areas of temporal semantics in linguistics and philosophy, on which the aspect hypothesis draws, offer no model of quantification. Thus, although the linguistic analysis is largely consistent across studies, two main quantitative analyses have developed. As a result of the various design and analytic approaches to the testing of the aspect hypothesis, this chapter includes explicit discussion of both in an attempt to help the reader interpret the results of the studies reviewed here.

This chapter is divided into four main parts. The first part reviews the formulation of the aspect hypothesis for first and second language acquisition and outlines the range of research methods that have been used in L2 research. This section also provides the reader with background on the categories of lexical aspect and reviews the verbal morphology related to grammatical aspect of the target languages discussed in this chapter. The second main section discusses in some detail the larger empirical studies of the aspect hypothesis in second language acquisition. This section also presents a full cross-sectional study of the distribution of verbal morphology in narratives. The third main part of the chapter examines competing quantitative presentations of the data in second language studies. Understanding the differences in analysis is crucial to the evaluation of apparent challenges to the aspect hypothesis discussed in the fourth main part of the chapter.

The Aspect Hypothesis

Like the discourse hypothesis reviewed in Chapter 5, the aspect hypothesis has its roots in theories of temporal semantics. Like the morpheme studies, the aspect hypothesis in SLA research is related to research in child language acquisition (Antinucci & Miller, 1976; Bloom, Lifter, & Hafitz, 1980; Bronckart & Sinclair, 1973; see also Weist, Wysocka, Witkowska-Stadnik, Buczowska, & Konieczna, 1984, for a dissenting view) and in creoles (Bickerton, 1975, 1981; Givón, 1982). (See Andersen, 1989, and Andersen & Shirai, 1996, for a comprehensive review of L1 and pidgin-creole studies.)

The aspect hypothesis is based on a theory of lexical, or inherent, aspect. In contrast to the more widely recognized grammatical aspect, which is typically morphological (such as the simple past and past progressive in English, or the preterite and imperfect in Spanish), inherent aspect is a purely lexical, non-grammatical category (Binnick, 1991). Lexical aspect refers to the inherent temporal makeup of verbs and predicates. Characteristics such as whether a predicate describes an action with inherent duration like *talk* and *sleep,* is punctual like *recognize* and *notice,* has elements of both duration and culmination like *build a house* and *paint a picture,* or describes a state like *want* or *like* are all aspectual qualities. (Aspectual classes are discussed in greater detail shortly.)

Lexical aspect and discourse structure are not unrelated, as shown by work on primary languages (Dowty, 1986; Dry, 1981, 1983; Fleischman, 1985; Hopper, 1979; Hopper & Thompson, 1980) and second languages (Andersen & Shirai, 1994; Bardovi-Harlig, 1994a, 1998; Flashner, 1989; Kumpf, 1984b). However, most studies of second language acquisition, especially the aspect studies, have investigated these functions independently, and I will treat them separately in the present and following chapter for the sake of separating the variables. Chapter 5 will discuss how lexical aspect and discourse are related in second language acquisition.

In Primary Language Acquisition

L1 studies found that children were sensitive to lexical aspect in the morphological encoding of past events. Based on conversational data from longitudinal studies, Antinucci and Miller (1976) reported that seven Italian-speaking children and one English-speaking child (ages 1;6 to 2;5) used the past participle with change of state verbs with clear results (e.g., *venire* "come," *cascare* "fall," *arrivare* "arrive"). (The TL form would be the passato prossimo consisting of an auxiliary and the past participle, which is the past form for non-stative verbs). In contrast, state verbs (e.g., *volere* "want," *sapere* "know") and activity verbs (e.g. *volare* "fly," *caminare* "walk") were not used with the past. Bronckart and Sinclair (1973) reported similar results from an experimental production task in which 74 French-speaking children (ages 2;11 to 8;7) used perfective past forms (passé composé) for actions with clear results and present forms (présent) for inherently durative events. Imperfective past (imparfait) was rarely used. Bronckart and Sinclair concluded that before the age of 6 the aspectual distinction "between the perfective and imperfective events seems to be of more importance than the temporal relation between action and the moment of enunciation [speaking]" (p. 126). From the age of 6 on, when the use of passé composé extends to all actions and imparfait emerges, children use verbal morphology to express "the same temporal relationships as adults" (p. 126). Antinucci and Miller concluded that in Italian and English "the child is able to make reference to and encode past events only when their character is such that they result in a present end-state of some object" (p. 182). Antinucci and Miller hypothesized that the observable end-state allows the encoding of the event in the past. The semantics is not an abstract temporal relation, but a result of the effect of a process on the end-state, and the child's ability to observe it. This interpretation of the distribution of verbal morphology in L1 acquisition is cognitive as well as linguistic (Bloom et al., 1980) because the child's system is said to lack the concept of temporal location, a concept that is necessary for tense.

Weist et al. (1984) interpreted the use of tense to express aspectual rather than deictic relationships as "defective in its normal functions at this phase of development" (i.e., 1;6 to 2;6, p. 348; see also Weist, 1986). They articulated the defective tense hypothesis in three parts: "(a) only telic verbs [verbs with inherent endpoints such as *read a book*] will receive past-tense inflections, (b) tense distinctions will be redundant and only accompany aspectual distinctions, and (c) only references to immediate past situations will be made" (p. 348). In a study of child L1 acquisition of Polish, Weist et al. (1984) demonstrated that Polish children (ages 1;6 to 2;2) make tense distinctions as well as aspectual distinctions. Early acquisition of tense markers in Polish (and other Slavic languages; see Weist et al., 1984) argues that the defective use of verbal morphology by child learners of Italian, English, and French is not a result of cognitive limitations.

However, as Bloom et al. (1980) and later Andersen (1989), Andersen and Shirai (1996), and Shirai and Andersen (1995) have pointed out, a relative interpretation of the defective tense hypothesis is more plausible than an absolute interpretation. Interpreting their study of English-speaking children, Bloom et al. (1980) wrote, "although strongly influenced at the beginning by event-aspect, children are no doubt learning tense relations at the same time; they do not learn tense only after they learn aspect" (p. 407). This was again emphasized by Rispoli and Bloom (1985) in a rebuttal of the position taken by Weist et al. (1984; see also C. Smith & Weist, 1987). Shirai and Andersen (1995) also argued that a relative interpretation is defensible in L1 acquisition: "past inflections are predominately attached to achievement and accomplishment verbs in the early stages (see Bloom & Harner, 1989, and Andersen, 1989)" (p. 746).

In Second Language Acquisition

Formulation of the Aspect Hypothesis

With these exciting and disputed interpretations of L1 research as a background, second language acquisition researchers began a similar line of investigation.[1] With adult learners, the investigation of second language acquisition also afforded the opportunity to test claims of the cognitive-developmental basis for tense-aspect distribution in first language acquisition (Klein, 1986, 1998). The aspect studies in second language acquisition started and flourished at the University of California, Los Angeles (UCLA) with the research of Roger Andersen (1985, 1986a, 1986b) and a very productive group of students who were influenced by his work (including Housen, Huang, Robison, and Shirai) and the earlier pioneering work by Kumpf and Flashner.

What has come to be known simply as the aspect hypothesis in second language acquisition research (Andersen & Shirai, 1994; Bardovi-Harlig, 1994a) has undergone a series of revisions similar to its development in the L1 studies. An early version of the aspect hypothesis (Andersen, 1986a, 1991), called the defective tense hypothesis following Weist et al. (1984), stated that "in beginning stages of language acquisition only *inherent aspectual* distinctions are encoded by verbal morphology, not tense or grammatical aspect" (Andersen, 1991, p. 307; emphasis in the original).

Based on Andersen's work, Robison (1990) proposed the primacy of aspect hypothesis, explaining that "aspect is primary in the sense not that morphemes that denote aspect in the target language are acquired first, but that target language verbal morphemes, independent of their function in the target language are first used by the learner to mark aspect" (p. 316). On the basis of his study, Robison revised his prediction regarding the timing of the association of verbal morphology and lexical aspect, changing from the statement that they "are first used by the learner to mark aspect" to the prediction that "verbal morphology correlates with lexical aspect *at least during some stage* in the development of IL" (1990, p. 330, emphasis added).

However, opposing tense and grammatical aspect to inherent aspect appears to be too strong in second language acquisition as well as in first language acquisition (e.g., Bardovi-Harlig, 1992a; Robison, 1995a; cf. Bloom et al.'s 1980 interpretation above). In the most current formulation of the aspect hypothesis, Andersen and Shirai (1994) have maintained the importance of the initial influence of aspect (cf. Robison, 1990), but have not explicitly set aspectual influence in opposition to encoding tense or grammatical aspect: "First and second language learners will initially be influenced by the inherent semantic aspect of verbs or predicates in the acquisition of tense and aspect markers associated with or/affixed to these verbs" (p. 133).

Results that cannot be interpreted as supporting the defective tense hypothesis (the stronger hypothesis) can be interpreted as supporting the aspect hypothesis for second language acquisition. Take Bardovi-Harlig's (1992a) results as an example. Bardovi-Harlig found that achievements showed more frequent use of simple past than activities or states. As Andersen and Shirai (1996) rightly argued, the results support the aspect hypothesis. And yet, the results also showed some use of tense across categories. Because learners did not appear to use past morphology to mark aspect at the expense of tense (a condition for defective tense use), Bardovi-Harlig stated that it was premature to claim that her results supported the defective tense hypothesis. However, the use of verbal morphology was clearly influenced by lexical aspect, and this is consistent with the less stringent formulation of the aspect hypothesis.

Methods for Studying the Aspect Hypothesis

Studies of individual adult learners carried out in the 1980s provided preliminary support for the aspect hypothesis. Important early studies include those by Kumpf (1984b), Flashner (1989), Robison (1990), and unpublished work by Andersen's students (see Andersen, 1985, 1986a, 1986b, 1986c, and 1991, for a review) as well as Andersen's seminal study of two children (Andersen, 1986a, 1991). However, the studies based on individual learners were viewed with some caution. Meisel (1987) suggested that individual learners may exhibit idiosyncratic interlanguage systems which are not representative of other learners. In his 1987 article, Meisel cautioned that an aspectual system in interlanguage "may well be . . . a very marginal phenomenon, occurring only occasionally, which has received too much attention by researchers who based their expectations on findings in L1 studies or on creole studies" and that it may be a learner-specific characteristic (p. 220). He concluded that "citing isolated examples will not suffice; quantification is indispensable in this case" (p. 220).

Perhaps partly as a result of Meisel's admonition, and no doubt in response to prevailing research designs in other areas of second language acquisition research, studies of second language tense and aspect began to investigate larger groups of learners, incorporate learners from different levels of proficiency, and expand to include tutored as well as untutored learners in an attempt to determine whether early observations were marginal or characteristic of emergent systems. Although some of the case studies and studies with smaller populations were also quantified, quantification of the results was characteristic of the larger studies (discussed in detail in the third part of this chapter.) The combination of the larger studies and the quantification is needed to adequately test the hypotheses that were generated by the smaller studies. The types of data collection techniques have also expanded, and the reporting of the specific linguistic analyses that are employed have been included in greater detail. Data collection techniques have developed to test a wider range of language samples and to assure comparability across learners, as well to handle the increased number of learners that a quantitative approach demands. Better implementation and reporting of linguistic tests for determining aspectual class have led to greater comparability across studies, so that learner production data could be evaluated in the same way by different analysts.

Tutored versus untutored learners. Untutored learners were the subjects of most early research on the aspect hypothesis. Because many researchers pursue what VanPatten (1990) has called the "core of SLA," the features of acquisition that are common to all learners, later researchers began to include classroom learners in tests of the aspect hypothesis. The resulting investigations have demonstrated that the influence of lexical aspectual class extends to instructed learners. The expanded populations include foreign language learners (English: Robison, 1993, 1995a); French: Bardovi-Harlig & Bergström, 1996;

Bergström, 1995; Salaberry, 1998; Spanish: Hasbún, 1995; Ramsay, 1990; Salaberry, 1999b), instructed learners in host environments (English: Bardovi-Harlig & Reynolds, 1995; Japanese: Shirai, 1995; Shirai & Kurono, 1998), and bilingual environments (English in Montreal: Collins, 1997, 1999b).

Elicitation procedures. As the learner populations expanded, so too did the elicitation procedures. Although the primary emphasis was on tasks that would provide comparable samples for all learners, working with tutored learners meant that researchers could introduce written as well as oral tasks. Elicitation tasks have included oral and written personal and impersonal narratives, written cloze passages (Bardovi-Harlig & Reynolds, 1995; Bergström, 1995; Collins, 1997, 1999b), and judgment tasks (Collins, 1999b; Salaberry, 1998; Shirai & Kurono, 1998). Oral personal narratives can be performed by all learners, and obviously are the least influenced by experimental design (although as we saw in Chapter 2, they can be influenced by scaffolding at the earlier stages). Retell tasks have also been used to great advantage. Much work has employed elicited narratives through retelling of silent films (e.g., the well-known *Pear Stories,* Chafe, 1980; the European Science Foundation investigation, Bhardwaj et al., 1988; Dietrich et al., 1995), performed stories (Bardovi-Harlig, 1992b), and picture stories (Bamberg, 1987; Bamberg & Marchman, 1990). (There are differences in narrative structure, and possibly tense-aspect use between personal and impersonal narratives, Noyau, 1984, 1990. This is taken up in some detail in Chapter 5.)

The advantages of the retell tasks are that the sequence of events is known to the researcher independently of the narrative itself and that such narratives can be compared across learners. By providing content to learners and giving less talkative learners a certain amount of information to report, retell tasks may encourage some learners to produce longer samples than they would otherwise. Moreover, the content of stories (in pictures, oral presentations, or film) used for prompted narratives may be manipulated to test specific rules of distribution, by including different actions or states or varying the importance of certain actions.

Many studies have employed silent film as an elicitation procedure. An excerpt entitled "Alone and Hungry" from the silent film *Modern Times* by Charlie Chaplin has been used in a number of studies, although because different researchers chose the film independently, the excerpts vary somewhat. The *Modern Times* excerpt was chosen because there are a series of discrete, easily identifiable action sequences as well as some simultaneous action (ideal for examining the encoding of tense-aspect morphology) and changes of scene (ideal for examining backgrounding). Whereas most excerpts center around the "Alone and Hungry" segment of the film, the ESF excerpt is edited and provides more background information early in the excerpt to explain Chaplin's poverty and subsequent actions (he is newly released from jail and has just been fired from a job). The section excerpt used by Bardovi-Harlig is 8 minutes long and unedited, running from the "Alone and Hungry" title through the imagination sequence, which was not included in the ESF excerpt. (See Bardovi-Harlig, 1995a, 1998, for a description of the segment with titles.) The second excerpt was used broadly by researchers in North America (Bardovi-Harlig, 1995a, 1998; Bardovi-Harlig & Bergström, 1996; Bergström, 1995, 1997; Collins, 1999b; Hasbún, 1995; Liskin-Gasparro, 1997; Salaberry, 1999b, without the imagination sequence). Other films have been used as well, including *The Sorcerer's Apprentice* (Lafford, 1996), *The Pear Story* (Chafe, 1980; Salaberry, 1998), *The Tin Toy, The Thief of Baghdad,* and *The Pink Panther* (Bardovi-Harlig, 1993, 1994b).

The elicitations using film excerpts have varied in subtle but noteworthy ways. With the use of *Modern Times,* the film was viewed twice by the ESL learners in order to reduce anxiety on the part of the learners of having to remember 8 minutes of action (Bardovi-Harlig, 1995a, 1998). Bergström (1995, 1997) and Hasbún (1995) showed the film a single time due to the time constraints of completing the data collection in a single class period. Like the ESF study (Klein & Perdue, 1992), Salaberry (1999b) showed the film a single time to prevent rehearsal on the part of the students. Both Hasbún (1995) and Bergström (1995) attempted to assure the use of past by suggesting frames for the narratives. In the ESF procedure, the researcher left the room to motivate the subsequent retelling of the story to the researcher. Salaberry (1999b) refined the retell process by providing his FL-learners of Spanish with additional motivation for the retelling: The learners reported the events in the film as though they were witnesses for the police, or police officers reporting to supervisors, thus eliminating the need for the framing used by Hasbún and Bergström. Oral and written narratives were collected (in that order) by Bardovi-Harlig (1995a, 1998), oral narratives by Salaberry (1999b), Lafford (1996), and Liskin-Gasparro (1997), and written narratives by Bergström (1995) and Hasbún (1995).

In spite of the combined advantages of the film retell tasks that elicit comparable language samples across learners while maintaining learner control over the construction of the narratives, there are some disadvantages as well. In spite of the fact that retelling a story has the potential of increasing production from learners who would otherwise say very little, there is still noteworthy variation in number of the tokens that learners produce. A second problem is related specifically to the testing of the aspect hypothesis: Certain types of predicates occur more frequently than others. In an effort to solve these problems, language samples have been collected via more directed elicitation tasks such as cloze passages that form complete texts (Bardovi-Harlig, 1992a; Bergström, 1995), short contextualized passages (Bardovi-Harlig & Reynolds, 1995; Collins, 1997, in a replication of Bardovi-Harlig & Reynolds, 1995), and short contextualized passages which form a guided narrative (Collins, 1999a). Cloze passages were used to control for the inherent unevenness in the number of tokens produced in each aspectual class in spontaneous production (Bardovi-Harlig & Reynolds, 1995; Collins, 1999b). Narratives and cloze passages share the feature of providing contexts for learners that are framed in the past. Tasks that ask learners to describe a decontextualized picture with a single sentence (e.g.,

John is opening a window; Quick, 1997) are not proper tests of the aspect hypothesis, but rather are similar to diagnostic tests described in a later section.

The use of cloze passages makes working with larger groups of learners possible. Because the predicate-types in a cloze passage are pre-determined by the researchers, certain ambiguity present in learner production is eliminated, and researchers do not have to classify each predicate produced by each learner for aspectual category. In contrast, free production by learners (whether oral or written) requires analysis of each predicate in learner production, not only for verbal morphology but for aspectual category (discussed shortly in detail). Studies utilizing cloze passages tend to have the largest groups of learners. For example, Bardovi-Harlig and Reynolds (1995) tested 182 ESL learners; Bergström (1995) tested 117 learners of French as a foreign language; and Collins (1997, 1999b) tested 70 learners in a replication study and 108 learners in a follow-up study. (See Table 4.1.) Bergström (1995) and Hasbún (1995) conducted large studies of written narratives with 117 and 80 learners, respectively.

Cross-sectional versus longitudinal design. A key element of design in any study that traces the development of a feature in second language acquisition is how development is to be observed: through a cross-sectional or longitudinal design. Unlike the meaning-oriented studies (Chapter 2) and the acquisitional sequences studies (Chapter 3), which are dominantly longitudinal, the studies of the aspect hypothesis are dominantly cross-sectional. The longitudinal investigations include studies of both children (Andersen, 1986a, 1986b, 1989, 1991; E. Lee, 1997; Rohde, 1996, 1997) and adults (Comajoan, 1998, forthcoming; Housen, 1993, 1994; Shirai & Kurono, 1998). As is typical of longitudinal studies in all areas of second language acquisition, they are case studies of one to four learners, whereas the cross-sectional studies tend to be larger. Instructional settings, such as the universities where many of the aspect studies have been conducted, seem to lend themselves to larger-scale cross-sectional studies because large numbers of learners are available and because the learners are pre-grouped into instructional levels (although only some studies use this means of comparison).

There are also studies that address the aspect hypothesis which are neither cross-sectional nor longitudinal. Studies of a single level of proficiency lack the necessary design feature to be developmental studies and instead describe the relation between lexical aspect and verbal morphology at a single point. Although they provide valuable descriptions, they fall short of providing information on how tense-aspect morphology spreads through interlanguage, which is the main thrust of the aspect hypothesis. (See discussion below of the stages predicted by the aspect hypothesis.)

Speech versus writing. The variable oral and written data collection techniques overlap somewhat with the general types of data collected. For example, cloze passages are written tasks. However, other elicitation tasks can be carried out both in speech and in writing. As discussed in Chapter 2, the opportunity for written production may help some low-level learners produce a more developed sample than they might orally. (This does not always hold at later stages of development, because some learners prefer the oral mode and produce longer, more detailed narratives orally. See Bardovi-Harlig, 1995a.) Studies that collect written narratives also tend to include more learners than studies that collect oral narratives. Oral narratives require transcription, and this factor generally conspires to reduce the number of participants included by researchers (e.g., Robison, 1990, studied one learner; Salaberry, 1999b, studied four learners at each of 4 levels at two points in time; Shirai, 1995, studied three learners), although Robison's (1993, 1995a) study included 26 learners and three native speakers of English. In cases in which small populations are used, it is important to present individual results, as done by Shirai (Shirai, 1995; Shirai & Kurono, 1998). Thus, the desirability of oral data is counterbalanced by the disadvantage of smaller participant groups. As has been argued in SLA research design (Dulay, Burt, & Krashen, 1982; Ellis, 1994; Larsen-Freeman & Long, 1991), small numbers of participants increase the influence of individual variation in group scores in a cross-sectional study, whereas larger samples are thought to be more desirable methodologically.

Proficiency and second language development. In the quest to determine which of the observed patterns in the acquisition of tense and aspect are idiosyncratic and which are common to all learners, researchers have attempted to isolate the influence of level of proficiency. In studies of individuals, level of proficiency and individual variation are difficult to tease apart, whereas in studies of larger groups individual responses are secondary to group scores and level of proficiency is highlighted.[2] In the case of cross-sectional tense-aspect studies learners have been compared in a variety of ways, some quite general and some specifically designed for the study of tense and aspect. Learners have been compared by the characteristics of their interlanguage, such as their stage along the basi-meso-acro-lang continuum (Robison, 1990; Schumann, 1987) and by features of their emergent tense-aspect systems (Bardovi-Harlig, 1998; Bardovi-Harlig & Bergström, 1996; Collins, 1997, 1999b; Robison, 1993, 1995a). Learners have also been compared by their placement in language programs: multitest placement in language programs (Bardovi-Harlig & Reynolds, 1995), placement in university language courses (Bergström, 1995; Hasbún, 1995; Martínez Baztán, 1994; Ramsay, 1990), and placement in university language courses plus screening of scores on discrete tests of Spanish (Salaberry, 1999b). Length of study (Buczowska & Weist, 1991) and length of residence in host country (Shirai, 1995) have also been used to compare learners, as have OPI (oral proficiency interview) ratings (Lafford, 1996; Liskin-Gasparro, 1997). Developing the means by which to compare learners presents a continuing challenge to researchers in all areas of second language acquisition research.

The aspect hypothesis across languages. In addition to the other developments in research design, the range of both target and first languages has grown. This, too, was a necessary step in determining whether the observed effects of lexical aspect on emergent verbal morphology were idiosyncratic or universal.

Early published studies covered a reasonable but still small range of target languages, namely Spanish, French, and English. Andersen's students expanded this range in a series of unpublished studies on both native and nonnative speakers (see Andersen, 1991; Andersen & Shirai, 1994, 1996). The target languages that have been more recently investigated in published studies include multiple studies of Dutch, English, French, Italian, Japanese, and Spanish, with fewer studies of Catalan, Portuguese, and Russian. The range of first languages has also become more diverse, thus providing the opportunity to further investigate the extent of the influence of lexical aspect. A summary of research addressing the aspect hypothesis is presented in Table 4.1.

Grammatical and Lexical Aspect

This section reviews the linguistic concepts employed by the aspect hypothesis. In addition to the grammatical category of tense, two linguistic concepts are central to the investigation of the aspect hypothesis: grammatical aspect and lexical aspect. Grammatical aspect is conveyed morphologically, whereas lexical, or inherent, aspect is part of the inherent semantics of the predicate. The morphological realizations of grammatical aspect were described in Chapter 3 and are therefore only briefly reviewed in the next section. Lexical aspect is described in considerably more detail in the following section.

Grammatical Aspect

Also known as viewpoint aspect, grammatical aspect provides different ways of viewing situations (Comrie, 1976; Dahl, 1985; Leech, 1971; C. Smith, 1983, 1991). C. Smith (1991) compares viewpoint aspect to a camera lens focused on a situation. The lens determines the presentation of a situation just as grammatical aspect does in language. In describing an action such as washing dishes a speaker may say (1a) or (1b).

Table 4.1

Empirical Studies Addressing the Aspect Hypothesis

Target language	Author	L1	N	# Predicates	Instruction	Design	Analysis	Tests	Quantified
Catalan	Comajoan (1998)	English	1	311	CFL, 2 semesters	Longitudinal, conversational interview, & oral story/film retells	Vendler	Yes	Yes
Dutch	Housen (1993, 1994)	English	1	398 (T1) 551 (T2)	DFL, also two 1-month visits to Holland	Longitudinal, 2 samples 1 year apart; guided conversation	Stative / dynamic, durative / punctual	Yes	Yes
English	Kumpf (1984b)	Japanese	1	250	None	Conversational interview	Stative / active	No	Yes
	Flashner (1989)	Russian	3	649	Limited instruction	Personal narratives from spontaneous speech	Perfective / imperfective / irrealis	No	Yes
	Robison (1990)	Spanish	1	553	Contact learner, some instruction	Conversational interview	Stative / dynamic and durative / punctual	Yes	Yes
	Bayley (1991, 1994)	Chinese	20	4,917	10 ESL	Cross-sectional, personal narratives	Perfective / imperfective	Yes (1991)	Yes
	Bardovi-Harlig (1992a)	Mixed	135	945	Intensive ESL	Cross-sectional, cloze passage	Vendler	No	Yes
	Bardovi-Harlig & Reynolds (1995)	Mixed	182	8,554	Intensive ESL	Cross-sectional, short cloze passages	Vendler	Yes	Yes
	Robison (1995)	Spanish	26	3,649	EFL	Cross-sectional, conversational interview	Vendler, punctual activity & punctual state	Yes	Yes

Table 4.1 (continued)

Empirical Studies Addressing the Aspect Hypothesis

Target language	Author	L1	N	# Predicates	Instruction	Design	Analysis	Tests	Quantified
	Bardovi-Harlig & Bergström (1996)	Mixed	20	850	Intensive ESL	Cross-sectional, written narratives (film retell)	Vendler	Yes	Yes
	Rohde (1996)	German	2 children	534	No ESL courses, attended elementary school	Longitudinal, spontaneous speech	Vendler	Yes	Yes
	Collins (1997)	French	70	3,220	ESL	Cross-sectional, short cloze passages	Vendler	Yes	Yes
	E. Lee (1997)	Korean	2 children	1,612	14-year-old, 1 year in Korea; both attended elementary school in U.S.	Longitudinal, spontaneous conversation, story narration, picture description	Vendler	Yes	Yes
	Bardovi-Harlig (1998)	Mixed	37	2,779	Intensive ESL	Cross-sectional written & oral narratives (film retell)	Vendler	Yes	Yes
French	Kaplan (1987)	English	16	Not specified	FFL	Cross-sectional, semi-structured, 10-min interviews	Perfective / imperfective	No	Yes
	Bergström (1995, 1997)	English	117	2,211	FFL	Cross-sectional, written narratives (film retell) & cloze passage	Vendler	Yes	Yes
	Bardovi-Harlig & Bergström (1996)	English	20	650	FFL	Cross-sectional, written narratives (film retell)	Vendler	Yes	Yes

Table 4.1 (continued)

Empirical Studies Addressing the Aspect Hypothesis

Target language	Author	L1	N	# Predicates	Instruction	Design	Analysis	Tests	Quantified
	Salaberry (1998)	English	39	1,200 narrative 1,599 cloze	FFL	Second semester students, multiple choice, written narratives (film retell), & cloze passage	Vendler	Yes	Yes
Italian	Giacalone Ramat & Banfi (1990)	Chinese	4	1,142	Some	Longitudinal, conversational interview	Perfective / imperfective	Not specified	No
	Giacalone Ramat (1995c, 1997)	Mixed	20	148 progressive verbs	4 learners, some instruction; 16, none	4 cross-sectional & 16 longitudinal, conversational interview (oral narratives, film retell, description of picture stories)	Vendler and mental states	Not specified	Some
Japanese	Shirai (1995)	Chinese	3	234	Intensive JSL	Conversational interview at 8 months in Japan	Vendler	Yes	Yes
	Shirai & Kurono (1998)	Mixed	17	939	Intensive JSL	Judgment task at 3, 6, 9 months in Japan	Vendler	Yes	Yes
	Shibata (1998)	Portuguese	1	147 (25 types)	None	Structured conversational interview	Vendler	Yes (Shirai, 1993)	Yes
Portuguese	Leiria (1994), Leiria & Mendes (1995)	Mixed	120	1,125	PSL in university courses	Levels of learners not specified; 218 written narratives (oral retell from formal examination)	6 classes (Moens & Steedman, 1988)	No	Yes

Table 4.1 (continued)

Empirical Studies Addressing the Aspect Hypothesis

Target language	Author	L1	N	# Predicates	Instruction	Design	Analysis	Tests	Quantified
Russian	Leary (1999)	English	40	1,002	RFL university, 1st to 4th year	Cross-sectional, 1st to 4th year university instruction. Film retell task.	Vendler	Not specified	Yes
Spanish	Andersen (1986a)	English	1 child	1,629	None	Longitudinal, 2 years, 2 conversational samples	Vendler	Yes	Yes
	Andersen (1991)	English	2 children	Not specified	None	Longitudinal, 2 years, 2 conversational samples	Vendler	Yes	No
	Ramsay (1990)	English	30	2,130	SFL, some contact	Cross-sectional, oral retell of picture book	States, activities, events	No	Yes
	Martínez Baztán (1994)	Dutch	15	662	SFL	Advanced learners, 2 compositions per learner	Vendler, error analysis	No	Yes
	Hasbún (1995)	English	80	2,713	SFL	Cross-sectional, written narratives (film retell)	Vendler	Yes	Yes
	Lafford (1996)	English	13	387	SFL	Cross-sectional, oral narratives (film retell)	Telic / atelic	No	Yes
	Liskin-Gasparro (1997)	English	8	Not quantified	SFL	Advanced learners, oral narratives (film retell); retrospection	Vendler	No	No
	Salaberry (1997)	English	16	2,054	SFL	Cross-sectional, oral narratives (film retells), grammar test, cloze test, & editing task	Vendler	Yes	Yes

Table 4.1 (continued)

Empirical Studies Addressing the Aspect Hypothesis

Target language	Author	L1	N	# Predicates	Instruction	Design	Analysis	Tests	Quantified
	Salaberry (1999b)	English	20	1,068 T1 986 T2	SFL	Cross-sectional, oral narratives (film retells), 2 samples, 2 months apart	Telics, activities & states	Yes	Yes
	Cadierno (2000)	Danish	10	656 written 1353 oral	8 SFL plus 6–18 months residence in TL countries. 2 SSL in host country	Advanced learners, 1st-year university composition class; oral semi-structured interview; written narratives	Vendler	No	Yes

Note. Vendler stands for Vendler categories, or STA, ACT, ACC, ACH. FL = foreign language; SL = second language; C = Catalan; E = English; F = French; P = Portuguese; R = Russian; S = Spanish. From "From Morpheme Studies to Temporal Semantics: Tense-Aspect Research in SLA," by K. Bardovi-Harlig, 1999, *Studies in Second Language Acquisition, 21*, pp. 354–356. Copyright 1999 by Cambridge University Press. Adapted with permission.

1a. John washed the dishes.

b. John was washing the dishes.

In (1a) and (1b) only the grammatical aspect has changed, not the event itself or the linguistic expression (*wash the dishes*) used to refer to it. Perfective aspect, as in (1a), views a situation in its entirety with its endpoints. Imperfective grammatical aspect, as in (1b), views a situation typically as an interval, excluding endpoints (C. Smith, 1991). Languages differ in the organization of their viewpoint aspect systems.

In English. In English, the progressive is the main imperfective viewpoint. The progressive occurs with dynamic verbs, but does not occur with stative verbs with neutral readings. (For a discussion of states, see the following section on lexical aspect.) Whereas imperfectivity generally includes both habituality and continuousness, the English progressive is defined essentially by continuousness (Comrie, 1976). As discussed in Chapter 3, the progressive has been described as a situation in progress at reference time (Bybee & Dahl, 1989) and as "action-in-progress" by Shirai and Andersen (1995), who described the prototypical progressive using the features [–telic] (not completed) and [+durative]. The contrast between non-progressive and progressive aspect can be found with all tenses in English (e.g., present *John walks to school* and *John is walking to school;* past *John walked to school* and *John was walking to school;* present perfect *John has walked to school* and *John has been walking to school;* and pluperfect *John had walked to school* and *John had been walking to school*).

In other languages. In Romance languages, the main contrast between perfective and imperfective grammatical aspect is expressed in the past tense. In this discussion I include only the Romance languages for which studies in second language acquisition have been conducted: Spanish, French, and Italian. Spanish contrasts the preterite and the imperfect, French the passé composé and the imparfait, and Italian the passato prossimo and the imperfetto. The perfective past, the Spanish preterite, the French passé composé, and the Italian passato prossimo relate the action encoded by the verb as completed. In contrast, the imperfect past, the Spanish imperfect, the French imparfait, and the Italian imperfetto encode habituality or continuousness and view a situation from within. Both the perfective and imperfective pasts occur with all categories of lexical aspect (C. Smith, 1991) discussed in the following section.

Spanish and Italian also have progressives expressed by verbal morphology, a form of *be* and a verb with a progressive inflection: in Spanish *Juan está cantando,* in Italian *Gianni sta cantando* "John is singing" (Comrie, 1976, p. 32). However, the English progressive is broader in meaning than the Spanish or Italian progressives, which can also be expressed by the nonprogressives—Spanish *Juan canta* and Italian *Gianni canta* "John sings/is singing"—without loss of progressive meaning, whereas English must obligatorily use the progressive. French uses a lexical idiom *être en train de* to express the progressive, but this does not belong to grammatical aspect proper. Although the progressive is used in the tests for determining lexical aspect in Spanish and French (see next section), only the Italian progressive has been the subject of investigation within the framework of the aspect hypothesis.

Among the Germanic languages investigated in second language acquisition research, English is the only one that distinguishes the perfective and imperfective grammatical aspects (Comrie, 1976; Klein, 1995). The only non-Indo-European language investigated as a target second language within the framework of the aspect hypothesis is Japanese (Shirai, 1995, 1999; Shirai & Kurono, 1998). Japanese marks nonpast with -*ru* and past with -*ta.* There is an imperfective marker -*te i*- which occurs productively with both past and nonpast. (This is similar to the English progressive.) The imperfect in Japanese marks durative aspect, which has both progressive and resultative readings in specific contexts (Shirai, 1998b). -*Te i*- receives a progressive interpretation with dynamic durative verbs (activities and accomplishments, see next section), as in *Ken-ga utat-te i-ru* "Ken is singing," and a resultative reading with punctual change of state verbs (achievements), as in *Maddo-ga ai-te i-ru* "The window is open" (i.e., the window has been opened and is in a resultative opened state.)

Although grammatical aspect and lexical aspect are two distinct linguistic categories, it is also clear from the preceding discussion that it is almost impossible to exclude one entirely from a discussion of the other. As the descriptions of grammatical aspect show, the distribution and interpretation of grammatical aspect are influenced by lexical aspect.

Lexical Aspect

Lexical aspect, also known as inherent aspect, refers to the inherent semantic properties of the linguistic expression used to refer to a situation. It is important to keep in mind, as C. Smith (1983) reminds us, that the semantic properties belong to the linguistic expressions and not to the real world event itself. Thus, an event such as John's running a marathon could be described variously as *John ran, John ran 26 miles,* or *John ran the Boston marathon.* The linguistic expressions themselves have different properties, although the actual facts of John's running remain unchanged. Just as the actual event remains constant regardless of the way a speaker expresses it, the lexical aspect of a predicate such as JOHN RUN remains unchanged regardless of the grammatical aspect used. Whether the event is reported as *John ran,* viewed externally including endpoints, or *John was running,* viewed internally without endpoints, "run" takes time. In the vocabulary of temporal semantics, it has duration. Inherent semantic properties can be described in various ways. In the sections that follow I review the lexical aspectual categories that have been employed in second language acquisition research. (For fuller discussion of lexical aspect see, for example, Binnick, 1991; Comrie, 1976; Dowty, 1979; Mourelatos, 1981; C. Smith, 1983, 1991.)

Binary categories. Binary categories of lexical aspect contrast predicates in terms of a single feature, such as stative and dynamic, punctual and nonpunctual, or telic and atelic predicates.

The stative-dynamic opposition distinguishes states (such as *seem* and *know*) from all other predicates (for example, *play, read a book, wake up*). The punctual-nonpunctual opposition distinguishes predicates that can be thought of as instantaneous or as a single point (*begin to sing*) from those with duration (*sing a song, sing*). Telic-atelic distinguishes predicates with endpoints (*sing a song*) from those without (*sing*).

With the exception of Andersen (1986a, 1991), most early studies that tested the aspect hypothesis employed binary divisions of inherent aspect (Housen, 1993, 1994; Kaplan, 1987; Robison, 1990). Robison's (1990) study of a very low proficiency adult untutored learner of English showed that punctual verbs were significantly more likely to show past-tense marking than durative verbs (12% vs. 5.1% use of past in past-time contexts) and that durative verbs were more likely to show -*ing* (e.g. "I workin'") than punctual verbs (20.6% vs. 5.1%). Kaplan (1987) showed that college students learning French as a foreign language distinguished events from nonevents in past-time contexts by using the passé composé (functionally a preterite) to mark events and the present to mark nonevents.[3] Likewise, Giacalone Ramat and Banfi (1990) found that the interlanguage of four Chinese learners of Italian used a higher proportion of (aux +) participle (emergent and targetlike forms of the passato prossimo) with telic predicates than atelic predicates.

Bayley's (1994) study of 20 native speakers of Chinese learning English as a second language also showed that the telic-atelic aspectual opposition strongly affects the likelihood that verb forms of all morphological classes will be marked for past tense (see Chapter 1 for a discussion of phonological salience). Telic aspect favors and atelic aspect disfavors past-tense marking, a finding that is constant across proficiency levels and individuals.

A four-way classification of lexical aspect: Vendler categories. Binary aspectual distinctions have the undesirable outcome of grouping dissimilar predicates together. For example, the punctual-nonpunctual opposition distinguishes predicates that can be thought of as instantaneous or as a single point from those with duration, but it also groups states with dynamic predicates in the category of nonpunctual. Thus, a finer-grained analysis is necessary. Such an analysis is found in a classification system traced back to Aristotle and introduced to modern linguistics by the work of philosophers Vendler (1957/1967) and Kenny (1963). (See Binnick, 1991, for the history of the study of aspect.) According to Binnick, the most familiar of the attempts at a definitive Aristotelian classification is the one proposed by Vendler. Vendler proposed a four-way division that distinguishes the aspectual categories of states (STA), activities (ACT), accomplishments (ACC), and achievements (ACH). Although many linguists such as Dowty (1979, 1986) have developed additional tests for the categories, they are often referred to as Vendler categories.

Each of the categories has distinguishing characteristics. States persist over time without change. States are not interruptible. If a state ceases to obtain, then a new state begins (Binnick, 1991). Examples of states include *seem, know, need, want,* and *be* (as in *be tall, big, green*). Activities have inherent duration in that they involve a span of time, like *sleep* and *snow*. They have no specific endpoint, as in *I studied all week*. Examples of activities include *rain, play, walk,* and *talk*. Achievements capture the beginning or the end of an action (Mourelatos, 1981) as in *The race began* or *The game ended,* and can be thought of as reduced to a point (Andersen, 1991). Examples of achievements include *arrive, leave, notice, recognize,* and *fall asleep*. Accomplishments have both an endpoint (like achievements) and inherent duration (like activities). Examples of accomplishments include *build a house* and *paint a painting*. The classes of achievements and accomplishments can be grouped together as telic predicates, known as "events" (Mourelatos, 1981).[4] The classes of statives and activities can be grouped together as atelic predicates. Aspectual categories apply to the verb and its arguments (Dowty, 1979; Freed, 1979; Harlig, 1989) but are most commonly discussed as relating to predicates. Members of an aspectual class are often referred to simply by the label as in "activities" and are often called "activity verbs" as a short form, although everyone agrees that what is meant is "activity predicates."

The Vendler categories can be distinguished by three features (Table 4.2; Andersen, 1991): [± punctual], [± telic], and [± dynamic]. The feature [+ punctual] distinguishes achievements from all other verbs. The feature [+ telic] distinguishes predicates with endpoints (*sing a song*) from those without (*sing*), and so distinguishes achievements and accomplishments from activities and statives. The feature [+ dynamic] distinguishes dynamic predicates (for example, *play, read a book, wake up*) from stative predicates (such as *seem* and *know*).

The literature on lexical aspectual classes has developed diagnostic tests that distinguish the aspectual categories from each other. (See especially Dowty, 1979; Mittwoch, 1991; Vendler, 1957/1967). One such test is the *in + time phrase / for + time phrase* test, which distinguishes activity verbs from accomplishment and achievement verbs. Activity verbs are acceptable with adverbial phrases such as *for ten minutes,* but unacceptable with phrases such as *in ten minutes* (e.g. John slept for an hour/*in an hour). Accomplishment and achievement verbs are acceptable with *in*-phrases, but unacceptable with *for*-phrases (e.g., John built a house in a year/*for a year). It is beyond the scope of this chapter to review the extensive research and debate that has gone into determining appropriate diagnostic tests in the theoretical literature (see Binnick, 1991, for a review; see also Dowty, 1979). Given that the investigation of aspectual categories was first the domain

Table 4.2

Semantic Features of Aspectual Categories

	States	Activities	Accomplishments	Achievements
Punctual	–	–	–	+
Telic	–	–	+	+
Dynamic	–	+	+	+

Note. From "Developmental Sequences: The Emergence of Aspect Marking in Second Language Acquisition," by R. W. Andersen, in T. Huebner and C. A. Ferguson (Eds.), *Crosscurrents in Second Language Acquisition* (p. 311). Copyright 1991 by John Benjamins. Adapted with permission.

of philosophers and only later of linguistics, it is not surprising that tests of the Vendler categories for other languages were devised somewhat later than those for English. The languages investigated included such languages as Spanish (Clements, 1985) and Japanese (Jacobsen, 1982). I will return to the use of diagnostic tests in second language acquisition research shortly.

In contrast to the studies that employed binary aspectual distinctions, Andersen (1986a, 1991) employed the four-way division found in the Vendler categories. Based on his study of the acquisition of Spanish as a second language by two children (Andersen, 1986b), Andersen (1989) posited four stages in the acquisition of perfective past (the preterite): from achievements, to accomplishments, to activities, and finally to states (Table 4.3). Imperfective past appears later than perfective past and spreads in four stages: from states, to activities, to accomplishments, and finally to achievements. Although imperfective past emerges after perfective past, the stages for the two overlap, forming a hypothesized eight stages. Table 4.3 represents the eight stages schematically. The left-hand column numbered 1–8 represents the stages of acquisition of the preterite and imperfect. The verbs written in regular font are base forms (in the case of Spanish these are third person singular present tense forms, as discussed in Chapter 2). Tokens from all lexical aspectual classes first appear in base forms. In stage 2 the preterite form appears, represented in the table by italics. The four stages of acquisition of the preterite (2, 4, 6, and 8) are represented by the double line that begins in the upper right-hand corner of the table with punctual events (achievements) and moves toward the lower left-hand corner, from telic events (accomplishments) to activities to states. The four stages of the spread of the imperfect (stages 3, 4, 5, and 7) are represented by the imperfect forms in square brackets and the single line which moves from states in the upper left-hand corner toward the lower right-hand corner, to activities, to accomplishments, and finally to achievements. When a learner uses grammatical aspect, two forms are entered under the column for the lexical aspectual class at the appropriate stage. Stage 5 represents the first such use,

Table 4.3

Developmental Sequence for Encoding Tense
and Aspect with "Past" Inflections

	STATES "had"	ACTIVITIES "played"	TELIC EVENTS "taught x to y"	PUNCTUAL EVENTS "broke (in two)"
1	tiene	juega	enseña	se parte
2	tiene	juega	enseña	*se partió*
3	[tenía]	juega	enseña	*se partió*
4	[tenía]	[jugaba]	*enseñó*	*se partió*
5	[tenía]	[jugaba]	*enseñó* [enseñaba]	*se partió*
6	[tenía]	[jugaba] *jugó*	*enseñó* [enseñaba]	*se partió*
7	[tenía]	[jugaba] *jugó*	*enseñó* [enseñaba]	*se partió* [se partía]
8	[tenía] *tuvo*	[jugaba] *jugó*	*enseñó* [enseñaba]	*se partió* [se partía]

Note. From "Developmental Sequences: The Emergence of Aspect Marking in Second Language Acquisition," by R. W. Andersen, in T. Huebner & C. A. Ferguson (Eds.), *Crosscurrents in Second Language Acquisition*, p. 314. Copyright 1991 by John Benjamins. Reprinted with permission.

where telic events show both the preterite *enseñó* and the imperfect *enseñaba*. The prototypical form is written above the nonprototypical form (e.g., *tenía* the imperfect is prototypical for the state "have," whereas the preterite *tuvo* is nonprototypical). Andersen's (1991) research was conducted on L2 Spanish, and thus the examples in the table are in Spanish. Nevertheless, researchers have understood the table in a much more abstract way, as Andersen intended, applying the principles of the spread of verbal morphology to a range of other languages.

Examples of the hypothesized stages are found in (2) and (3) below (Bardovi-Harlig & Bergström, 1996). The learner of English uses past with achievements and accomplishments, but base forms with activities. Both states occur with present. The learner of French seems to be farther along according to the hypothesized stages in Table 4.3. She uses passé composé with achievements, accomplishments, and activities. One state occurs with the imparfait, and one in the present. (The spelling has been regularized in the following example.)

2. The police *left* (ACH, past) the man and *caught* (ACH, past) the women. The man *wants* (STA, pres) go to the prison because he *is* very poor (STA, pres) and he *sleep* (ACT, base) on the street every day. After that he *went to the restaurant* (ACC, past) and *took food* (ACC, past) for eating. [Learner E4]

3. Il y *avait* (STA, imparfait) une femme. Elle *a* (STA, present) très faim. Cependant, elle *a essayé* (ACT, passé composé) de voler du pain de l'auto. Une personne *a vu* (ACH, passé composé) ça et *a parlé* (ACT, passé composé) au policier. Le policier *a essayé* (ACT, passé composé) d'arreter ça femme mais Charlie Chaplain *a dit* (ACC, passé composé) au policier qu'il *a volé* (ACH, passé composé) du pain. [Learner F13]

"There was a woman. She is very hungry [literally, has hunger]. However/meanwhile she tried to steal some bread from the car. A person saw this and spoke to the policeman. The policeman tried to arrest this woman, but Charlie Chaplain said to the policeman that he stole the bread."

Many studies have followed Andersen's use of the Vendler categories, and it is the analytic framework in widest use today. Just as the binary categories seem to be insufficient to account for primary language data, they are insufficient for the second language acquisition data. The empirical findings in second language acquisition research reviewed in the next main section show that in interlanguage members of the four lexical aspectual categories behave very differently from each other. Some researchers have divided the aspectual categories even further. In her research on L2 Italian, Giacalone Ramat (1995c, 1997) divided states into mental states (*credere* "believe" and *pensare* "think") and states (*stare* "be"); analyzing L2 English, Robison (1995a) separated punctual activities (which are punctual but atelic, as in *she is jumping*) and punctual states (such as *notice* in *John noticed the scratch in the furniture*).

   Diagnostic tests. A significant result of the theoretical discussions of the categories of lexical aspect was the development of diagnostic tests with which to distinguish predicates. Thus, such diagnostics are available for use in analyzing interlanguage and one does not generally have to rely on semantic definitions to determine aspectual categories. And yet, as noted by Andersen and Shirai (Andersen & Shirai, 1994, 1996; Shirai & Andersen, 1995; see also Robison, 1993, 1995a), early studies in SLA were vague about how predicates were classified into aspectual categories. Studies conducted at UCLA led the way in making explicit the diagnostic tests that were used to divide predicates into aspectual categories. Robison (1990) presented tests for dynamicity and durativity; Robison (1993, 1995a) presented tests that distinguished six aspectual categories. Shirai (1991) included ordered tests that distinguished the four Vendler categories. As a result, a greater number of later studies reported the diagnostic tests they used. (For tests, see Dowty, 1979; Mittwoch, 1991; Vendler, 1957/1967. For use in SLA research see: for English: Bardovi-Harlig & Bergström, 1996; Bardovi-Harlig, 1998; Robison, 1990, 1995a; Shirai, 1991; for French: Bardovi-Harlig & Bergström, 1996; Bergström, 1995, 1997; for Spanish: Hasbún, 1995; and for Japanese: Shirai, 1995). Studies of four target languages—English, French, Spanish, and Japanese—have published the diagnostic tests used on interlanguage samples. I present an example of the tests from each language. Where different diagnostic tests have been used, I have selected tests that identify Vendler categories.

   Shirai (Shirai, 1991; Shirai & Andersen, 1995) used the following ordered tests (based on Dowty, 1979, and others) for English (Shirai & Andersen, 1995, p. 749).

Step 1: State or nonstate
Does it have a habitual interpretation in simple present?

If no⇨ State (e.g., *I love you*)

If yes⇨ Nonstate (e.g., *I eat bread*) ⇨Go to step 2

Step 2: Activity or nonactivity
Does 'X is V-*ing*' entail 'X has V-*ed*' without an iterative/habitual meaning? In other words, if you stop in the middle of V-*ing*, have you done the act of V?

If yes⇨ Activity (e.g., *run*)

If no⇨ Nonactivity (e.g., *run a mile*) ⇨ Go to step 3

Step 3: Accomplishment or achievement
[If test (a) does not work, apply test (b) and possibly (c).]

    (a) If "X V-ed in Y time (e.g., *10 minutes*)," then "X was V-ing during that time."

        If yes⇨ Accomplishment (e.g., *He painted a picture*)

        If no⇨ Achievement (e.g., *He noticed a picture*)

    (b) Is there ambiguity with *almost*?

        If yes⇨ Accomplishment (e.g., *He almost painted a picture* has two readings: he almost started to paint a picture/he almost finished painting a picture)

        If no⇨ Achievement (e.g., *He almost noticed a picture* has only one reading)

    (c) "X will VP in Y time (e.g., *10 minutes*)" = "X will VP after Y time."

        If no⇨ Accomplishment (e.g., *He will paint a picture in an hour* is different from *He will paint a picture after an hour*, because the former can mean that he will spend an hour painting a picture, but the latter does not.)

        If yes⇨ Achievement (e.g., *He will starting singing in two minutes* can only have one reading, which is the same as *He will start singing after two minutes*, with no other reading possible.)

Another well-known test for distinguishing stative and activities from accomplishments and achievements is the test that employs *for* + length of time, for example *for an hour* (Dowty, 1979; see Bardovi-Harlig & Bergström, 1996, and Bardovi-Harlig, 1998, for use in L2 studies.) This test is often used as a pair with *in* + time test that Shirai used in Step 3c because predicates that pass the *in* + time test fail the *for* + time test, and vice versa. Activities and states pass the *for* + time test (e.g., *He ran for an hour*), whereas accomplishments and achievements fail the test (e.g., **He ran a mile for an hour*). Readings with accomplishments may evoke an iterative sense such as running the same mile for an hour, but are typically not the primary reading.

Bergström (1995) used two tests to distinguish four lexical categories in French. The tests are conservative and test aspect, but not thematic roles or agentivity, which interact with aspect: the *être en train de* test (Guenthner, Hoepelmann, & Rohrer, 1978) and the *en x minutes* test (Dowty, 1979; Guenthner et al., 1978; Nef, 1980). As (4) shows, *être en train de* "be in the process of" distinguishes states and achievements (which fail the test) from activities and accomplishments (which pass the test). The test *en x minutes* "in x minutes" distinguishes accomplishments from all other categories, as (5) shows. Both tests potentially result in special effects when applied to achievements. Readings of slow motion, iterativity, or serialization are possible and are indicated by a hatch mark (4e and 5e). These tests were adopted by Salaberry (1998) for a later study of French.

4.   *être en train de*
   a.   STA: **Charlot est en train d'aimer les pommes*
        "**Charlie is in the process of liking apples"
   b.   ACT: *Charlot est en train de manger*
        "Charlie is in the process of eating"
   c.   ACC: *Charlot est en train de manger une pomme*
        "Charlie is in the process of eating an apple"
   d.   ACH: **Charlot est en train d'entrer*
        "**Charlie is in the process of entering"
   e.   ACH: *#La bombe est en train d'éclater*
        "#The bomb is in the process of exploding"

5.   *en x minutes*
   a.   STA: **Charlot aime les pommes en cinq minutes*

    "*Charlie likes apples in five minutes"

  b. ACT: *Charlot dort en cinq minutes*
    "*Charlie sleeps in five minutes"

  c. ACC:*Charlot mange une pommme en cinq minutes*
    "Charlie eats an apple in five minutes"

  d. ACH: *Charlot entre en cinq minutes*
    "*Charlie enters in five minutes"

  e. ACH: #*Les invités arrivent en cinq minutes*
    "#The guests arrive in five minutes"

Hasbún (1995) adopted Clements' (1985) diagnostic tests for Spanish. The first six tests distinguish states from nonstates (dynamic predicates). (Note that (4) involves volitionality which is now currently thought not to be a direct consequence of aspectual class.)

Test of States versus Nonstates

1. Implication *(Juan sabía la lección* 1 *Juan sabe la lección)* "Juan used to know the lesson" 1 "Juan knows the lesson"

2. Progressive *(Juan *está sabiendo / está estudiando la lección* "Juan *is knowing/is studying the lesson"

3. *Obligar / convencer* + S: Only dynamic verbs can be complements of the verbs *obligar,* "force" or *convencer* "persuade." *Juan lo obligó a que *supiera / estudiara la lección* "*Juan forced him to *know/study the lesson"

4. Adverbs of volition: only dynamic verbs take adverbs that describe actions as voluntary such as *conscientemente* "consciously" or *a propósito* "purposely." Juan *sabe/estudia la lección a propósito "Juan knows/is studying the lesson on purpose."

5. Imperative: Only dynamic verbs can be used in the imperative. *!*Sabe la lección! / !Estudia la lección!* "*Know the lesson!/Study the lesson!"

6. *Acabar de* + S test: Only dynamic verbs can be used after *acabar de. Juan acaba de *saber/estudiar la lección* "Juan has just *known/studied the lesson."

An additional two tests distinguish among the dynamic verbs. Activities and accomplishments pass and achievements fail the durativity test in (7). The cessation of activity test in (8) distinguishes accomplishments and achievements (which pass the test) from activities (which fail).

7. Durativity: "X *pasó* Y time *verbando.*" *Juan pasó la tarde escribiendo/escribiendo la carta/*llegando.* "Juan spent the afternoon writing/writing a letter/*arriving."

8. Cessation of activity "X *tardó* Y time *en verbear:*" *Juan tardó dos años en escribir el libro/en llegar/*en leer.* "It took Juan two years to write the book/two hours to get here/*to write."[5]

Salaberry (1999b) distinguished three lexical categories in his study of L2 Spanish: telics (accomplishments and achievements), activities, and states. He adapted two tests for use in Spanish based on the tests Shirai (1991) used for English, listed earlier in this section (Step 1 and Step 2). Applied sequentially, the first distinguishes states from nonstates, the second distinguishes telics (accomplishments and achievements) from atelics by using the entailment test: "if you stop in the middle of doing X have you done X?" (see also Bardovi-Harlig & Bergström, 1996).[6]

Looking ahead to the acquisitional data, it is important to note that, at least in the languages reviewed, statives and achievements typically fail the progressive tests (the use of *-ing* in English, *être en train de* and *en x minutes* in French, and *pasó* Y time *verbando* in Spanish). Accomplishments, like activities, pass the progressive tests. And yet the acquisition data clearly show that accomplishments and achievements pattern similarly in terms of attracting the perfective past, as we shall see in the following main section.

The final set of tests that have been published in the second language acquisition research literature are tests of lexical aspectual categories in Japanese (Shirai, 1993, and refined in 1998b). Like Shirai's tests for English (see earlier), these are ordered (Shirai, 1998b, pp. 307–309).

Tests for inherent aspect for Japanese. Each test is used only on the clauses remaining after the preceding test.

Step 1. State or non-state?
Can it refer to a present state in the simple present tense without having a habitual or vivid-present interpretation?

> If yes⇨ State, e.g., *Tukue no ue ni hon ga aru* (There is a book on the table)
>
> If no⇨ Non-state (e.g., *Boku wa gohon o taberu* (I will eat rice)
>
> Go to step 2

Step 2. Activity or nonactivity? (telic or atelic)
If you stop in the middle of an action, does that entail that you did it?

> If yes⇨ Activity, e.g., *aruku* (walk)
>
> If no⇨ Nonactivity, e.g., *eki made aruku* (walk to the station)
>
> Go to step 3

If it is difficult to distinguish between "punctual verbs denoting a resultative state" and "activity verbs denoting an action in progress," use the following tests (a), (b), (c), and/or (d).

(a) Is it possible to say *X wa Y* (Y = time, e.g., 10 minutes) *V-ta* without iteration involved?

> If yes, activity (e.g., *John wa sanzyuppun hanasita* (John talked for 30 minutes)
>
> If no, resultative state, e.g., **John wa sanzyuppun sinda* (John died for 30 minutes)

(b) Is it possible to say *X wa Y* (Y = place) *de V-teiru*, and if so, is it more natural than to say *X wa Y ni V-teiru*?

> If yes to both questions, activity, e.g., *John wa soko de neteiru* (John is sleeping there).
>
> If no, resultative state (and therefore the verb is an achievement), e.g., **John wa soko ni/?de taoreteiru* (John fell down and is lying there)

(c) Is it possible to say *V-hazimeru* without iteration involved?

> If yes, activity, e.g., *hanasi-hazimeru* (start talking)

If no, resultative state, e.g., **suwari-hazimeru* (start sitting)
(d) Does it have a simultaneous activity reading in the frame
V-nagara?

If yes, activity, e.g., *hanasi nagara* (while talking)

If no, may be resultative state *siri nagara* (although knowing), but not necessarily, since this test also involves "agency."

Step 3. Accomplishment or achievement? (punctual or non-punctual)

If test (a) does not work, apply test (b) and possibly (c).

(a) Does X *wa* Y *de V-ta* (Y+ time, e.g., 10 minutes) entail that X
was involved in V-ing during that time?

If yes⇨ Accomplishment, e.g., *Kare wa zyuppun de itimai no
e kaito* (He painted a picture in ten minutes)

If no⇨ Achievement, e.g., *Kare wa itimai no e ni kizuita* (He
noticed a picture in ten minutes)

(b) Can *V-teiru* have the sense of "action-in-progress"?

If yes⇨ Accomplishment, e.g., *Kare wa oyu o wakasiteiru* (He
is heating the water till it is hot)

If no⇨ Achievement, e.g., *Kare wa sono e ni kizuiteiru* (He
has noticed a picture)

(c) X *wa* Y *de V-daroo* (Y= time, e.g., 10 minutes) = X *wa* Y-*go-ni*
V-daroo

If no⇨ Accomplishment, e.g., *Kare wa itizikan de e o kakudaroo*
(He will paint a picture in an hour) is different from *Kare wa
itizikan go ni e o kakudaroo* (He will paint a picture after an
hour), because the former can mean he will spend an hour
painting a picture, whereas the latter does not.

If yes⇨ Achievement, e.g., *Kare wa nihun de utai hazimeru
daroo* (He will starting singing in two minutes) can only have
one reading, which is the same as *Kare wa nihun go ni utai
hazimeru daroo* (He will start singing after two minutes),
with no other reading possible.

The diagnostic tests used by second language acquisition researchers to classify learner-produced predicates into lexical aspectual categories represent a core of tests regularly used in
analyses of primary languages. The tests typically distinguish two

or more categories from the remaining categories. In the theoretical literature the tests are typically unordered. However, in interlanguage analysis relatively large numbers of predicates must be classified, and Shirai's ordering of the diagnostic tests for English and Japanese (Shirai, 1991, 1993, 1995, 1998b; Shirai & Andersen, 1995) offers an efficient way of analyzing a corpus. There are, of course, predicates that are difficult to classify, especially in interlanguage, but the use and publication of the diagnostic tests promote greater comparability across studies and ultimately facilitates the testing of the aspect hypothesis.

Investigations of the Aspect Hypothesis in Second Language Acquisition

This section reviews the studies of second language acquisition that have been conducted to test the aspect hypothesis. The aspect hypothesis can be broken down into four separate claims (Shirai, 1991, pp. 9–10; see also Andersen & Shirai, 1996), stated in terms of grammatical aspect and its relation to lexical aspect using the Vendler categories reviewed in the previous section:

1. Learners first use (perfective) past marking on achievements and accomplishments, eventually extending use to activities and statives.[7]

2. In languages that encode the perfective/imperfective distinction, imperfective past appears later than perfective past, and imperfect past marking begins with statives, extending next to activities, then to accomplishments, and finally to achievements.

3. In languages that have progressive aspect, progressive marking begins with activities, then extends to accomplishments and achievements.

4. Progressive markings are not incorrectly overextended to statives.

The main effect of the influence of aspectual class is that, when interlanguage verbal morphology emerges, it is in complementary distribution, unlike in the target languages investigated in the same studies, where contrast is possible (Andersen, 1990b, 1994). The predictions are clear: perfective with events, imperfective with states, progressive with activities. It is not until the morphology begins to spread that the system exhibits potentially nativelike contrasts (e.g., see stages 5–8, Andersen, 1991, and Table 4.3; also Andersen 1990b, 1994).

This section is organized around these four claims.[8] See Table 4.1 for a summary listing of studies and characteristics of research design organized by target language. In the review that follows I highlight developmental studies (cross-sectional and longitudinal) when they are available. Only developmental studies are able to test claims made under the aspect hypothesis about the spread of morphology across the verbal system. Studies of learners at a single level may support one or more of the hypothesized associations between lexical category and verbal morphology, but they cannot shed light on changes in the tense-aspect system.

The Spread of Perfective Past

The association of perfective past with events is by far the most robustly attested stage in the distribution of verbal morphology in the interlanguage system, partly because of the dominance of achievements in narrative samples and partly because the perfective past is the first past morpheme acquired and thus easily observed in the interlanguage of learners who have reached the morphological stage of temporal expression. Support for this stage is found in English (Bardovi-Harlig, 1998; Bardovi-Harlig & Bergström, 1996; Bardovi-Harlig & Reynolds, 1995; Collins, 1997; Robison, 1995a; Rohde, 1996, 1997), Catalan (Comajoan, 1998), Dutch (Housen, 1993, 1994), French (Bardovi-Harlig & Bergström, 1996), Italian (Giacalone Ramat, 1995d), Japanese (Shirai, 1995; Shirai & Kurono, 1998), and Spanish (Andersen, 1986a, 1991; Hasbún, 1995).

Hasbún (1995) and Bergström (1995) tested the aspect hypothesis in the interlanguage of tutored foreign language learners using the same film excerpt from *Modern Times* (see also Bardovi-Harlig, 1995a; Bardovi-Harlig & Bergström, 1996). Hasbún found evidence for the hypothesized stages of the acquisition of the preterite in a study of written narratives of 80 learners of Spanish as a foreign language who were enrolled in 1st-, 2nd-, 3rd-, and 4th-year university Spanish courses. In addition, the cross-sectional sample also revealed the emergence of the imperfect in states (in the 3rd year) and its spread to activities (in the 4th year). The evidence for the acquisitional stages posited by Andersen (1986a, 1991) is less robust in the French sample, which drew on written narratives from 117 learners of French as a foreign language enrolled in 1st-, 2nd-, and 3rd-year university courses (Bergström, 1995). Bergström observed fewer stages among her learners: The first-year learners exhibited rather strong use of passé composé with all dynamic verbs (above 55%), suggesting a stative-dynamic opposition. The lack of a base-form stage suggests that the learners of French may have been more advanced than the Spanish learners at the time of data collection.[9]

Robison's (1993, 1995a) study of 26 learners of English at four levels of proficiency attending a Puerto Rican university also convincingly supports the aspect hypothesis. Robison analyzed learner texts collected from oral interviews and found that event predicates showed the highest use of simple past of all the aspectual categories. In addition, the rates of use of simple past tense increased for all lexical aspectual classes with increased proficiency. Whereas many studies have analyzed the distribution of tense-aspect morphology exclusively in past-time contexts (e.g., Bardovi-Harlig & Bergström, 1996; Bayley, 1994; Bergström, 1995; Hasbún, 1995; Salaberry, 1998), Robison examined the distribution of tense-aspect morphology across temporal contexts. Naturally, the narratives elicited by Hasbún (1995) and Bergström (1995) also had nonpast sections, and they were included in the analysis. However, both Hasbún and Bergström attempted to assure the use of past by suggesting frames for the narratives. For the Spanish narratives Hasbún told the learners to begin with *habia una vez* ("once upon a time"). In the French task Bergström provided a written prompt which instructed the learners in English to tell what *happened* in the story. Robison (1995a) included all predicates in the interviews regardless of temporal reference (past, present, future). Whereas other studies traced the distribution of tense-aspect morphology in past-time contexts (as did the child-language studies), Robison provides evidence for the distribution of tense-aspect morphology across temporal contexts, including cases where learners have used past with achievements which denote a present or future event.

Bardovi-Harlig (1998) found a clear progression of past tense use from achievements to accomplishments to activities in the data from the oral narratives. Interestingly, accomplishments and achievements pattern differently in the oral narratives, revealing a use of simple past with achievements that is up to 30% greater than that with accomplishments. This difference is not apparent in the written narratives of the same study in which achievements and accomplishments pattern together as "events" (Mourelatos, 1981) nor in the results reported for the written cloze passages by Bardovi-Harlig and Reynolds (1995). (See also the replication of Bardovi-Harlig & Reynolds, 1995, by Collins, 1997.) The oral data support Andersen's predictions (1986a, 1989, 1991), which posit separate stages of development for achievements and accomplishments.

Rohde (1996, 1997) investigated the acquisition of English in spontaneous conversation by two German-speaking children (ages 6 and 9) over the course of 5 months. Rohde's analysis differs from the others in this section in that he separated the regular and irregular past. He observed, "The results of this study show a distributional bias for both regular and irregular past inflection in the learners' data. In other words, most of the verbs inflected for past tense are achievements" (1996, p. 1129). When the results in raw token scores are converted into percentages indicating which type of verbal morphology is used for each lexical aspectual class (Rohde, 1997), no class exceeds achievements for the simple past inflection.[10]

E. Lee (1997) investigated the acquisition of English by two Korean learners living in the United States, ages 10 and 14. She followed Rohde in separating irregular from regular past. The learners' use of the simple past was dominated by irregular verb forms. Nevertheless, both learners used the irregular past more frequently with telics (achievements and accomplishments) than atelics (activities and states). Both telics and atelics showed increased use of irregular past during the 13-month study. Early use of irregular past for telics began at 30% and rose to a high of 70% for both learners. With atelic predicates, the use of past began at a low rate of frequency and stayed lower longer (under 10% use for 5–6 months). The high reached for irregular past with atelics was 25–30% by 13 months, showing a slow rate of acquisition compared to irregular past with telics.

The findings of Rohde (1996) and E. Lee (1997) are similar to Bayley's (1994) findings. Bayley found that although phonetic constraints determined the likelihood that a verb will be inflected for the past—the more changes in an irregular verb from the base, the more likely that it is to occur in the past given the appropriate past context—the tendency for telic verbs to carry past cuts across phonetic categories. In other words, telic predicates are more likely to occur with past morphology whether they are regular or irregular.

Many fewer studies have been done in non-Indo-European languages such as Japanese. Tutored learners of Japanese as a second language enrolled in an academic intensive Japanese language program provided evidence for an association of the past marker *-ta* in Japanese and achievements (Shirai, 1995). Three learners of Japanese who were native speakers of Chinese were interviewed during their eighth month of residence in Japan. The conversational data showed that achievements dominated the verbs marked for past by *-ta*. Shibata (1998) interviewed a single learner of Japanese whose native language was Brazilian Portuguese. The semi-structured interview yielded 147 verb tokens and 25 verb types. Using raw scores and verb types, Shibata reported that four achievements and five activities were inflected with the past *-ta;* Shibata concluded that activities were as likely as achievements to be inflected for past. However, when Shibata's data are understood in terms of number types inflected relative to the number of types produced, no lexical class shows a higher use of -ta than achievements. The distribution of -ta within lexical categories is as follows: ACH 80% (4/5), ACC 67% (2/3), ACT 46% (5/11), and STA 33% (2/6). As the reader can see, the number of verb types is quite small, and one should be very cautious in interpreting samples of this size, but these results exhibit the patterns that one would expect following the aspect hypothesis. (The issue of analysis is taken up in detail in the section of this chapter entitled "Method of Analysis.")

Studies which employ focused written elicitation tasks in the form of cloze passages also lend support to the claim that lexical aspectual class influences the distribution of verbal morphology in interlanguage. In addition to the narrative retell task, Bergström (1995) employed a second task in the form of a cloze passage of the same *Modern Times* story used for the film retell task. Interestingly, Bergström's learners showed greater support for the aspect hypothesis on the cloze passage than on the written narrative, in that 2nd- and 3rd-year production of passé composé clearly distinguished achievements from accomplishments and activities. This may be related to a broader sampling of predicates in the cloze than in the learner-controlled narratives.

Bardovi-Harlig and Reynolds (1995) used a series of unrelated cloze passages to control for the inherent unevenness in the number of tokens produced in each aspectual class in spontaneous production (Bardovi-Harlig, 1998; Salaberry, 1998). This cross-sectional study of 182 learners at 6 levels of proficiency produced over 8,200 predicates. Learners were given 32 short passages which contained 62 test items and 26 distractors which tested verb forms not under investigation. The passages varied in length from one to five sentences and established time reference through the use of time adverbials or verb tense. Learners were given the base form of the verb and asked to supply the missing word or words in the blank. Sample test items are given in (6).

6. Last night John (*work*) (ACT) _____ very hard.
    He (*write*) _____ two papers (ACC) and (*finish*)
    _____ all of his grammar homework (ACH).

Broken down by lexical aspectual class, the 62 items testing the
use of simple past tense included 14 achievements, 11 accomplishments, 12 activities, and 10 states. (The effect of adverbs of frequency was tested on nine additional activity verbs and six state
verbs.) Vocabulary was restricted to familiar lexical items and was
checked by program teachers for appropriateness. The results
showed that achievements and accomplishments exhibited the
highest rates of use of simple past patterning together, and significantly differently from states and activities. The rates of simple
past increased with proficiency level.

Collins (1997, 1999b) replicated Bardovi-Harlig and
Reynolds' (1995) study with a group of 70 Francophone learners
of English. Collins included learners who showed lower rates of
use of verbal morphology than Bardovi-Harlig and Reynolds did
in order to provide a better view of early stages of the morphological spread. Collins' study also showed that learners used simple
past significantly more frequently with events than activities or
states. In a revised set of cloze passages in which the aspectual
classes were balanced exactly (nine each) and a greater variety of
distractors were used, a second group of Francophones showed the
same pattern. In spite of the differences in the tasks, Bardovi-
Harlig and Reynolds (1995) and Collins (1997, 1999b) reported
essentially the same results as Robison (1995a) for the use of the
simple past.[11]

Support for the first part of the aspect hypothesis dealing
with the emergence and the spread of the perfective past is quite
robust. The use of perfective past with achievements and accomplishments and its spread to activities is observed in both
extended learner production (narratives and conversation, oral
and written) and more focused written data collected from cloze
passages. The spread of the perfective past to states has been more
successfully observed in the cloze passage data than in the less

controlled language samples because researchers have used a variety of lexical statives, whereas learner production is often quite limited (with *be* and *have* the most frequent statives). This also effects the observation of the spread of the imperfect which is discussed in the next section.

The Spread of Imperfective Past

The order of emergence of imperfect after preterite past is well documented in L2 acquisition (Andersen, 1991). Studies on the acquisition of L2 French by children in immersion programs (Harley & Swain, 1978) have shown that French passé composé emerges before the imparfait; similar findings are reported for university students of French (Kaplan, 1987). In Italian, passato prossimo, a compound past tense similar to the French passé composé, emerges before imperfetto "imperfect" in the interlanguage of Italian-Swedish heritage language learners (Wiberg, 1996). The aspect hypothesis predicts the direction of spreading across lexical aspectual categories, beginning with states and spreading to activities, accomplishments, and finally achievements (Table 4.3). Example (7) shows a lower-level learner of French who uses imparfait with statives; the learner in (8) is able to use imparfait with activities as well (Bardovi-Harlig & Bergström, 1996).

7.   Il *a volé* (ACH, passé composé) le pain parce que il *aimait* (STA, imparfait) la belle fille. [Learner F2]
     "He stole the bread because he liked/loved the pretty girl."

8.   Un homme et une femme *s'embrassaient* (ACT, imparfait) [Learner F23]
     "A man and a woman were kissing."

Hasbún (1995) also found evidence for the hypothesized stages of the acquisition of the imperfect in her study of written narratives of 80 learners of Spanish as a foreign language in 1st-through 4th-year university Spanish courses. The cross-sectional sample revealed the emergence of the imperfect in states (in the 3rd year) and its spread to activities (in the 4th year). In the written narratives of 117 learners of French as a foreign language enrolled in 1st- through 3rd-year university courses, Bergström (1995) found that the imperfect emerged with states in the 2nd year and spread to activities in the 3rd year (thus distinguishing activities from other dynamic verbs). Swedish-Italian heritage learners of Italian residing in Sweden also showed a strong association of imperfect with states (Wiberg, 1996).[12] The imperfect begins with states and spreads to activities. One learner in the advanced group (out of 24 learners total) showed use of imperfect with activities as well. A study of advanced Danish learners of Spanish observed what might be the last stages of the spreading of the imperfect to include use with achievements (Cadierno, 2000). Even once the imperfect spreads to accomplishments and achievements (and similarly, the preterite to activities and states), the rates of appropriate use are higher with the prototypical uses (telics with preterite and atelics with imperfect) than the non-prototypical uses.

A study of 20 Dutch teachers of Spanish also suggests that the association of imperfect and states remains strong in the interlanguage of even very advanced nonnative speakers of Spanish (García & van Putte, 1988). Both native speakers and non-native speakers of Spanish read a story by Borges, "El Muerto," that was written exclusively in the present tense. They were asked to supply past tense forms for the story. The use of the preterite and imperfect were compared in the two respondent groups. Although the study was not conducted within the framework of the aspect hypothesis, the item analysis revealed relevant findings. The nonnative speakers supplied the imperfect with statives such as *parecer* "seem," *ser* "be," and *entender* "understand" more often than native speakers, including an instance where native speakers clearly preferred the preterite.

Studies also show that the target-language imperfect is not the first marker of imperfectivity. Kaplan (1987) observed that learners of French used a default present form in the environments of the imperfect before imperfect morphology was acquired. Giacalone Ramat (1995d) also observed the use of the present in learner Italian, stipulating that although the form looks like a present tense form (usually third person singular indicative) it is more properly understood as a default or base form (see also Andersen, 1991). The use of present or base has also been observed with states in English (Bardovi-Harlig & Reynolds, 1995; Robison, 1995a) and Dutch (Housen, 1993, 1994). Housen reported a significant correlation in learner Dutch between present or base and statives and also between present or base and duratives (the latter being dominated by statives, showing statives to be the starting point).[13]

Tokens of states in interlanguage are typically dominated by *be* and *have* and their equivalents. This is the case for both English-speaking immersion children learning French (Harley & Swain, 1978) and English-speaking adults (Bardovi-Harlig & Bergström, 1996), and also for Swedish-speaking adults learning French (Kihlstedt, 1993, 1996; Schlyter, 1990). The number of different stative verbs is often limited to about a half dozen. Such small stative vocabularies means that the higher type/token counts found for investigating the early stages of morphological development of perfective past with achievements do not exist for observing the initial stages of the acquisition of the imperfective past with states. Researchers (and learners) have to make do with little diversity of stative predicates. Limited productive vocabularies may inhibit the spread of imperfect to other lexical classes. This would be an interesting area for future research. Limited spontaneous use of a variety of statives suggests that cloze passages might be useful in eliciting verbal morphology on a range of statives (e.g., Bardovi-Harlig & Reynolds, 1995, for English).

Advanced Danish learners of Spanish who had had both foreign language instruction and 6–18 months contact in a Spanish-speaking country produced higher numbers of tokens of states compared to achievements (Cadierno, 2000). Ten learners produced 740 states in oral conversation compared to 323 achievements, and in the written narratives they produced 287 compared

to 221. (See "Methods of Analysis" to compare the distribution of
states to achievements in other samples.) However, because only
token counts were given and there were no type counts reported,
it is not possible to ascertain what percentage of the states were
ser or *estar* "be" or what degree of lexical diversity was attained
by the advanced learners.

The Spread of Progressive

The spread of progressive has been investigated in Italian,
English, and Japanese. For learners of Italian, Giacalone Ramat
(1995c, 1997) reported that 63% of all progressive tokens occur
with activities and an additional 22% appear with mental states
such as *credere* "believe" and *pensare* "think."[14] Progressive seems
to spread slowly to accomplishments (8%) and achievements (4%).
In cross-sectional studies of English, progressive associates quite
robustly with activities (in written cloze passages, Bardovi-Harlig
& Reynolds, 1995; in written narratives, Bardovi-Harlig &
Bergström, 1996; in written and oral narratives, Bardovi-Harlig,
1998; in oral narratives, Robison 1995a). Interestingly, Robison
(1995a) also found that "the affiliation of progressive marking
with activities strengthens with proficiency level" (p. 356), even as
the association of inflections with tense increased with level.

In the English *Modern Times* narratives collected by Bardovi-
Harlig and Bergström (1996), base forms were the most common
form for activities, but progressive forms (Ø-progressive, present
progressive, and past progressive) proved to be a strong competi-
tor, as in (9) and (10). Note that two of the three progressives are
Ø-progressives (i.e., V+*ing* with no auxiliary).

9. When the bus *was running* (ACT), he *met* her (ACH) in the
   bus. He *stand up* (ACC) for her. When *moving* bus (ACT)
   [when the bus was moving], he *sat on* [ACC] fat woman's
   knee. [Learner E7]

10. Then the girl *crying* (ACT) might be she *was* sad (STA) for
    her setwation [situation] [Learner E16]

Activities are the only category in which progressives were used to a noticeable extent in the first three levels of learners (out of four levels). This suggests that learners initially respond to the durativity of activities in their use of progressive forms by marking lexical aspect redundantly with morphological aspect. The fourth group showed the predicted spread of progressive to accomplishments, with 23.5% of accomplishments showing the use of past progressive.

Shirai's (1995) study of three Chinese learners of Japanese as a second language enrolled in an intensive Japanese program also supports the aspect hypothesis: These learners also showed dominant use of progressive *-te i-* with activities (55% of all uses of *-te i-* occur with activities). In a second study of Japanese, the results of a judgment task administered to 17 tutored Chinese learners of Japanese suggested that "learners found it easier to recognize the correctness of *-te i-* with activity verbs" than with achievements (Shirai & Kurono, 1998, p. 264).

Work that discusses the progressive often discusses tense as well, because the target form of the progressive in many of the languages studied is composed of the progressive participle and a form of *be* or its equivalent, which carries tense. In English, Bardovi-Harlig observed that in past-time contexts the bare progressive emerges first, followed by the present progressive and then the past progressive (Bardovi-Harlig & Bergström, 1996; Bardovi-Harlig & Reynolds, 1995; see also Chapter 3). In this way, tense use becomes increasingly targetlike with progressive even as the association of progressive and activities is maintained or strengthened (Robison, 1995a).

Overgeneralization of Progressive in States

Robison (1990) reported noticeable use of progressive with states by the untutored learner of English he investigated: 22% of all statives (39/176) occurred with progressive. (Calculated another way, 45% of all progressives appeared on statives.) In contrast, none of the three Russian learners of English with limited instruction studied by Flashner (1989, p. 75) used progressive with statives. Neither have tutored learners of English shown the overextension of progressive to states as Robison reported. In oral and written narratives, tutored learners of English show no greater than 3% use of progressive with statives (Bardovi-Harlig, 1998; Bardovi-Harlig & Bergström, 1996; Robison, 1995a). Rohde (1996, 1997) reported only four uses of progressive in the first 3 to 4 months by each of the two untutored child learners of English (the total number of predicates produced is not given).

The progressive has not been investigated widely in languages other than English, with the exception of Italian (Giacalone Ramat, 1997) and Japanese (Shirai, 1995). Giacalone Ramat (1997) also reported very low use of progressive with states by untutored adult learners of Italian. Shirai (1995) found that only 2% of all progressives (*-te i-*) occurred with states in the interlanguage of three tutored Chinese learners of Japanese. Although the use of progressive with states is somewhat higher in cloze passages than in narratives (Bardovi-Harlig & Reynolds, 1995, report a high of 7% and Collins, 1997, 9% in the lower level groups), they do not approximate the higher rate of use by Robison's (1990) learner. Thus it appears that most adult second language learners rarely overextend the use of progressives. Task may influence rates of use, but it is unclear what role instruction plays (cf. Giacalone Ramat's, 1997, untutored learners).

The review of the research shows that several studies of a range of target languages provide evidence in support of one or more of the four claims concerning the effects of lexical aspect proposed by the aspect hypothesis.

Sample Study: The Distribution of Verbal Morphology in
Learner Narratives

In this section I report briefly on a study that tests the aspect hypothesis using oral and written narrative data. This section is based on Bardovi-Harlig (1998). This study addresses the three claims of the aspect hypothesis that pertain to English: the spread of the perfective past, the distribution of the progressive, and the (non)use of the progressive with states.

Method

A cross-sectional sample of oral and written narratives from learners of English as a second language was elicited by means of a film-retell task. An 8-minute excerpt from the silent film *Modern Times* was used because it contained a series of discrete, easily identifiable action sequences (ideal for examining the encoding of serial events and foreground) as well as simultaneous actions and changes of scene (ideal for examining backgrounding).

In the film excerpt, Charlie Chaplin befriends a young woman who has stolen a loaf of bread, and at the same time tries to ensure his return to jail where he has previously found food and shelter. The segment has four distinct foreground episodes (which may be further divided): (on the street) the stealing of the bread by the girl and the events leading to her arrest, (in the cafeteria) Chaplin's eating of two trays of food without paying and the events leading to his arrest, (in the police wagon) the meeting of Chaplin and the young woman, and (on the street) the ensuing escape. The excerpt ends in an imagined sequence which depicts Chaplin and the woman in a blissful domestic scene; at the conclusion of their daydream Chaplin resolves to obtain the house of their dreams. The excerpt has 10 titles: the first one sets the scene, "Alone and hungry," and the remaining nine report the speech of the characters.[15]

Procedure. Learners watched the film excerpt in their Speaking-Listening classes. A member of the interview team provided a brief introduction to the film, including a description of the American Depression and the name of the main actors. The learners watched the film twice and were given the opportunity to ask questions between the viewings. Participants met individually with an interviewer to record the story orally. The interviewers offered minimal back channeling during the retells, supplying vocabulary when asked and replying to comprehension checks by the learners. Following the oral narratives, learners produced written narratives during their composition classes. Learners were given the class period, approximately 45–50 minutes, to produce their written narratives.

Selection of participants. All learners were enrolled in the IEP at the Center for English Language Training at Indiana University. One listening and speaking class from each of the six instructional levels of the IEP was selected to participate in the study. Oral and written samples were collected from 51 learners. A subset of 37 pairs (74 narratives in all) was selected on the basis of three criteria: (a) usable language samples; (b) rate of appropriate use of past tense; and (c) first language. The first step excluded all nonnarrative texts such as movie reviews. The next step grouped learners by overall rate of past tense use. Each narrative was coded for use of a past-tense form in past-time contexts, which included simple past, past progressive, and, more rarely, pluperfect. For the placement of learners into groups, rates of past use were calculated for verb types rather than tokens. Each verb form was counted only once per sample. When multiple forms of the same verb occurred, such as *go, went,* and *have gone,* each form was counted as a single type regardless of the frequency of each of the forms. The use of types ensured that the rates of appropriate use were not inflated by multiple occurrences of common verbs like *was* and *went.* Thus, a type analysis provides a conservative view of the acquisition of tense-aspect morphology. (See Bardovi-Harlig, 1992c, 1994a, for discussion.)

The learners in this study were compared on the basis of their appropriate use of past morphology rather than on the basis of placement in the instructional program by a battery of tests, because learners show a considerable range of appropriate use of tense-aspect when considered individually (Bardovi-Harlig, 1994a, 1997a; see Chapter 3). For example, a study of two intact classes of intermediate learners showed that use of past morphology ranged from 30% to 98% appropriate use in written narratives and 15% to 91% appropriate use in oral narratives (Bardovi-Harlig, 1992b).[16] Moreover, describing interlanguage in terms of the rate of use of verbal morphology facilitates comparison of learners across studies (see Andersen, 1978; Robison, 1990, 1995a; Schumann, 1987). Bardovi-Harlig and Bergström (1996) used this means to compare learners of FL French and SL English where comparing learners by enrollment in different programs would have been meaningless. Although comparing learners in this way does not allow us to answer questions such as "How does an intermediate learner use tense-aspect morphology?" it does allow us to answer other, more finely tuned questions, such as "If a learner uses past morphology in 50% of all past-time contexts s/he creates, how is it distributed?"

Learners were grouped according to the percentage of appropriate use of past in divisions of 10% (10–19%, 20–29%, 30–39%, and so on) and were ranked separately for written and oral texts. Learners were selected to balance as evenly as possible the number of participants and L1 backgrounds in the oral and written groups. This procedure resulted in the selection of 37 narrative pairs, or 74 narratives. The learners were drawn from five L1 backgrounds: Arabic (14), Korean (10), Japanese (6), Spanish (6), and Mandarin (1). There were two idiosyncrasies in the groupings. The five learners who exhibited 13%–33% appropriate use of past in the written narratives were grouped together as W10–30. Group O(ral) 80 had only one learner, who showed over 80% appropriate use in the oral narrative. He was not included with O70 because he showed 89.5% appropriate use and was not grouped with O70 because that group showed a range of only 70.0% to 75.0%.

Analysis and Results

Placing the learners. As outlined briefly above, the first analysis of the narratives scored each verb in a past-time context as "past" or "nonpast." The number of distinct verb forms was scored for the type score, and the number of total verbs used (tokens) was also scored. Direct speech was excluded from both calculations.[17] These calculations were used to identify the participants and to place the learners into groups as outlined.

Aspectual classes. Next, each verb phrase was assigned to one of four aspectual classes according to the tests established for aspectual categories by Vendler (1957/1967), Dowty (1979), and Mittwoch (1991). (See also L2 studies by Bardovi-Harlig & Bergström, 1996; Robison, 1990, 1995a; and Shirai, 1995.) The tests by Dowty were used as the primary determinant of aspectual class, with tests from other sources used in ambiguous cases. All of the tests used by Shirai (1991) were also used (see previous section) with some additions (see Bardovi-Harlig & Bergström, 1996). Verbs which occurred in reports of speech were again excluded.

Verbal morphology. Finally, all verbs were coded for verbal morphology; simple past, past progressive, pluperfect, base, bare progressive, present, present progressive, present perfect, and the rarely used progressive perfects. Uninterpretable morphological forms such as *tooks* and *is stole* were coded as "uninterpretable." Verbs which have the same form for past and base were excluded from the sample (e.g., *hit, put, let;* cf. Bardovi-Harlig, 1992b; Silva-Corvalán, 1983). In the written narratives, misspelled verbs such as *cot/caut* for *caught* or regularized past verbs such as *telled* were counted as past as long as the innovation did not result in an extant verb. It should be noted here that, in contrast to the analysis used to group the learners, this analysis is a token analysis. Although a type analysis controls for multiple uses of a single form in a corpus, it does not respect the integrity of the text and thus cannot be used to analyze the structure of narratives. This was important because a simultaneous analysis of narrative structure was conducted. (See Chapter 5.) Otherwise, a type analysis would have been appropriate.

In the oral narratives, repetition and phonological environment were also taken into account.[18] When a learner repeated a verb exactly, it was counted only once so as not to inflate the number of propositions in the narrative (11).

11.   Then, the police, policeman, *take* him, *take* him to ... [L1 Korean]

In cases where a verb form was not an exact repetition, the ratio of forms was calculated. In (12), for instance, past and base each scored .5; the total number of verbs was 1.

12. while, uh, Charlie Chaplin *go* to, *went* to restaurant [L1 Arabic]

This gives priority to neither the first form that the learner produced nor the corrected form (which is not always "better"), but factors in all forms produced by the learners without inflating the number of propositions.

Finally, phonological environments were considered, following the research on phonetic constraints (Bayley, 1994; Wolfram, 1985). When similarly articulated phonemes are produced sequentially as in the case of the phrase *walked to* [waktu], it is not possible to tell whether the [t] is a realization of the past morpheme or of the following preposition. Thus such tokens traditionally have been eliminated by phonetic constraints studies. Bayley excluded homophonic (same voicing value) stops and interdentals (e.g., *walked through, walked the,* and *entered the*), whereas Wolfram excluded only homorganic stops (*e.g., walked to/down* and *pulled down/to*). The present analysis assumed the most conservative position on the exclusions, combining Bayley's and Wolfram's exclusions. Thus, tokens of nonsyllabic past tense followed by homorganic stops and interdental fricatives were excluded from the sample.

Distribution of Verbal Morphology

Following the procedure outlined above, 1,318 predicates were coded in the written sample and 1,461 in the oral sample. The number of statives includes a large number of tokens of *be.* As Giacalone Ramat (1992) has argued, the copula is a tense carrier (see also Skiba & Dittmar, 1992), meaning that it rarely occurs untensed (or in base form), and that it carries tense morphology earlier than other statives (see also Housen, 1993, 1994). That is certainly true of these data, where *be* accounts for 75.4% of all past-tense use among the statives in the written sample and 88.8% in the oral sample. Because the tensing of the copula is not representative of the tense-aspect marking of other statives (see Bardovi-Harlig & Bergström, 1996; Harley & Swain, 1978), *be* has been eliminated from the analysis in subsequent tables. This has the disadvantage of reducing the number of statives in the corpus, and the advantage of allowing the stative patterns to be viewed more clearly.

These narratives show the patterns that have become familiar to readers from studies that have investigated the aspect hypothesis. Table 4.4 presents the distribution of verbal morphology within the lexical aspectual categories. In the written narratives,

Table 4.4

Distribution of Tense-Aspect Morphology within Aspectual Categories in Written Narratives by Learners of English in Seven Groups

Group	Form	STA %	(n)	ACT %	(n)	ACC %	(n)	ACH %	(n)
Group	Past	0	(0)	9	(2)	31	(10)	32	(24)
10 to 30	Prog	0	(0)	30	(7)	6	(2)	3	(2)
N=5	Pres	14	(1)	4	(1)	3	(1)	1	(1)
	Base	71	(5)	52	(12)	56	(18)	47	(35)
	Other	14	(1)	4	(1)	3	(1)	14	(10)
	Total	100%	(7)	100%	(23)	100%	(32)	100%	(74)
Group 40	Past	0	(0)	30	(7)	55	(12)	48	(25)
N=3	Prog	0	(0)	8	(2)	0	(0)	0	(0)
	Pres	40	(4)	4	(1)	0	(0)	0	(0)
	Base	40	(4)	42	(10)	41	(9)	46	(24)
	Other	20	(2)	17	(4)	5	(1)	6	(3)
	Total	100%	(10)	100%	(24)	100%	(22)	100%	(52)
Group 50	Past	17	(1)	13	(3)	58	(15)	71	(43)
N=3	Prog	0	(0)	33	(8)	4	(1)	2	(1)
	Pres	0	(0)	4	(1)	4	(1)	0	(0)
	Base	83	(5)	46	(11)	31	(8)	26	(16)
	Other	0	(0)	4	(1)	4	(1)	2	(1)
	Total	100%	(6)	100%	(24)	100%	(26)	100%	(61)

Table 4.4 (continued)

Distribution of Tense-Aspect Morphology within Aspectual Categories in Written Narratives by Learners of English in Seven Groups

Group	Form	STA %	STA (n)	ACT %	ACT (n)	ACC %	ACC (n)	ACH %	ACH (n)
Group 60	Past	33	(1)	21	(3)	63	(12)	61	(44)
N=4	Prog	0	(0)	43	(6)	5	(1)	0	(0)
	Pres	0	(0)	0	(0)	0	(0)	0	(0)
	Base	67	(2)	36	(5)	26	(5)	31	(22)
	Other	0	(0)	0	(0)	5	(1)	8	(6)
	Total	100%	(3)	100%	(14)	100%	(19)	100%	(72)
Group 70	Past	31	(4)	37	(25)	74	(29)	85	(160)
N=9	Prog	8	(1)	37	(25)	0	(0)	0	(0)
	Pres	23	(3)	0	(0)	0	(0)	0	(0)
	Base	39	(5)	21	(14)	26	(10)	11	(21)
	Other	0	(0)	6	(4)	0	(0)	4	(8)
	Total	100%	(13)	100%	(68)	100%	(39)	100%	(189)
Group 80	Past	67	(14)	51	(18)	83	(34)	88	(104)
N=7	Prog	5	(1)	34	(12)	5	(2)	3	(3)
	Pres	15	(3)	0	(0)	10	(4)	0	(0)
	Base	15	(3)	11	(4)	2	(1)	8	(9)
	Other	0	(0)	3	(1)	0	(0)	2	(2)
	Total	100%	(21)	100%	(35)	100%	(41)	100%	(118)
Group 90	Past	100	(12)	75	(27)	82	(22)	90	(87)
N=6	Prog	0	(0)	25	(9)	4	(1)	2	(2)
	Pres	0	(0)	0	(0)	11	(3)	0	(0)
	Base	0	(0)	0	(0)	4	(1)	1	(1)
	Other	0	(0)	0	(0)	0	(0)	7	(7)
	Total	100%	(12)	100%	(36)	100%	(27)	100%	(97)

Note. "Prog" includes bare-progessive, present progressive, and past progressive. From "Narrative Structure and Lexical Aspect: Conspiring Factors in Second Language Acquisition of Tense-Aspect Morphology," by K. Bardovi-Harlig, 1998, *Studies in Second Language Acquisition, Vol. 20,* p. 485. Copyright 1998 by Cambridge University Press. Reprinted with permission.

achievements and accomplishments show the highest rate of past-tense inflection in Group 10–30, at just over 30%. Event predicates (i.e., achievements and accomplishments) pattern together and are not distinguished by more than 13% difference in the rate of use in this corpus. This pattern is illustrated in Figure 4.1. Group 40 shows the greatest simple past inflection on the event verbs (accomplishments and achievements) followed by activities, with no past with states. This pattern of high use of simple past with events and lower use with activities persists even at the highest group.

Activities show greater occurrence of the progressive than any other aspectual class. Compared to Group 40, Group 50 shows lower use of simple past with activities, but higher use of progressive. The rates of simple past remain lower than the use of progressive with activities until Group 70 where they are the same, at 36.8%. Activities continue to show increased use of simple

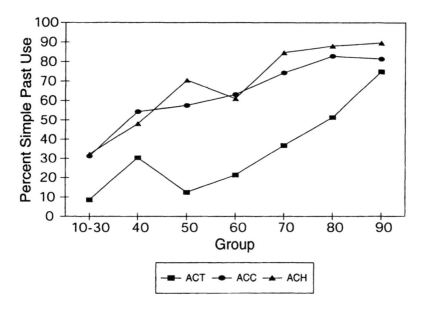

Figure 4.1. The use of simple past within lexical aspectual classes by groups (written narratives). From "Narrative Structure and Lexical Aspect: Conspiring Factors in Second Language Acquisition of Tense-Aspect Morphology," by K. Bardovi-Harlig, 1998, *Studies in Second Language Acquisition, 20*, p. 486. Copyright 1998 by Cambridge University Press. Reprinted with permission.

past in Group 80 (51.4%) and Group 90 (75.0%), where the use of simple past surpasses the use of progressive.

As can be seen in Table 4.4, these learners used very few lexical statives (statives other than *be*).[19] Groups 10–40 used no states in the past and Groups 50 and 60 used only one each. Groups 70–90 showed an increase in the number of states used.

The oral narratives exhibit the same pattern as the written narratives, but—as expected of oral production—the rates of appropriate use for the oral narratives are somewhat lower overall. In the oral data there is a very clear progression of past tense use from achievements to accomplishments to activities (Table 4.5). Of interest in the oral narratives is the fact that accomplishments

Table 4.5

Distribution of Tense-Aspect Morphology within Aspectual Categories in Oral Narratives by Learners of English in Seven Groups

Group	Form	STA %	STA (n)	ACT %	ACT (n)	ACC %	ACC (n)	ACH %	ACH (n)
Group 10	Past	0	(0)	0	(0)	6	(0.5)	6	(1)
N=3	Prog	0	(0)	40	(4)	25	(2)	6	(1)
	Pres	0	(0)	20	(2)	0	(0)	3	(.5)
	Base	0	(0)	30	(3)	44	(3.5)	66	(10.5)
	Other	0	(0)	10	(1)	25	(2)	19	(3)
	Total	0%	(0)	100%	(10)	100%	(8)	100%	(16)
Group 20	Past	11	(1)	4	(2)	16	(7)	43	(38.6)
N=6	Prog	0	(0)	19	(10)	4	(2)	3	(3)
	Pres	11	(1)	12	(6)	0	(0)	3	(3)
	Base	78	(7)	62	(32)	76	(34)	46	(41.5)
	Other	0	(0)	4	(2)	4	(2)	4	(4)
	Total	100%	(9)	100%	(52)	100%	(45)	100%	(90)
Group 30	Past	0	(0)	19	(5.5)	45	(19)	56	(60)
N=6	Prog	0	(0)	22	(6.5)	0	(0)	0	(0)
	Pres	0	(0)	3	(1)	0	(0)	0	(0)
	Base	100	(9)	52	(15)	50	(21)	41	(44)
	Other	0	(0)	3	(1)	5	(2)	3	(3)
	Total	100%	(9)	100%	(29)	100%	(42)	100%	(107)

Table 4.5 (continued)

Distribution of Tense-Aspect Morphology within Aspectual Categories
in Oral Narratives by Learners of English in Seven Groups

Group	Form	STA %	(n)	ACT %	(n)	ACC %	(n)	ACH %	(n)
Group 40	Past	15	(2)	16	(9)	34	(27.5)	62	(88)
N=6	Prog	0	(0)	27	(15)	16	(13)	0	(0)
	Pres	8	(1)	4	(2)	4	(3)	1	(2)
	Base	77	(10)	47	(26)	42	(34.5)	32	(44.5)
	Other	0	(0)	6 ·	(3)	5	(4)	5	(6.5)
	Total	100%	(13)	100%	(55)	100%	(82)	100%	(141)
Group 50	Past	9	(1.5)	22	(4)	37	(16)	67	(73.5)
N=5	Prog	0	(0)	39	(7)	8	(2)	0	(0)
	Pres	0	(0)	0	(0)	0	(0)	0	(.5)
	Base	91	(14.5)	39	(7)	54	(23)	31	(34)
	Other	0	(0)	0	(0)	5	(2)	2	(2)
	Total	100%	(16)	100%	(18)	100%	(43)	100%	(110)
Group 60	Past	42	(5.5)	32	(13)	66	(39)	79	(99)
N=6	Prog	0	(0)	34	(14)	3	(1.5)	0	(0)
	Pres	4	(.5)	2	(1)	6	(3.5)	3	(4)
	Base	54	(7)	32	(13)	24	(14)	18	(22.5)
	Other	0	(0)	0	(0)	2	(1)	0	(.5)
	Total	100%	(13)	100%	(41)	100%	(41)	100%	(126)
Group 70	Past	0	(0)	21	(6)	68	(23)	86	(55)
N=4	Prog	0	(0)	46	(13)	6	(2)	4	(2.5)
	Pres	67	(4)	7	(2)	0	(0)	0	(0)
	Base	33	(2)	25	(7)	24	(8)	7	(6.5)
	Other	0	(0)	0	(0)	3	(1)	0	(0)
	Total	100%	(6)	100%	(28)	100%	(34)	100%	(64)

Note. "Prog" includes bare-progressive, present progressive, and past progressive. From "Narrative Structure and Lexical Aspect: Conspiring Factors in Second Language Acquisition of Tense-Aspect Morphology," by K. Bardovi-Harlig, 1998, *Studies in Second Language Acquisition, Vol. 20,* pp. 487–488. Copyright 1998 by Cambridge University Press. Reprinted with permission.

and achievements pattern differently, revealing a use of simple past with achievements that is up to 30% greater than use with accomplishments (Figure 4.2). This difference is not apparent in the written narratives of the present study (Table 4.4, Figure 4.1) nor in the results reported for the written cloze passages reported by Bardovi-Harlig & Reynolds (1995). The oral data support Andersen's predictions (1986a, 1989, 1991) that posit separate stages of development for achievements (which show use of past first) and accomplishments (whose use with the past follows that of achievements; see Table 4.5). Activities show higher use of past than states by every group except 20 and 60. It is important to note, however, that percentages of use of past must be interpreted with caution, because the number of states other than *be* is quite low. Activities show a higher proportion of progressives than any other category, and this too strengthens with level.

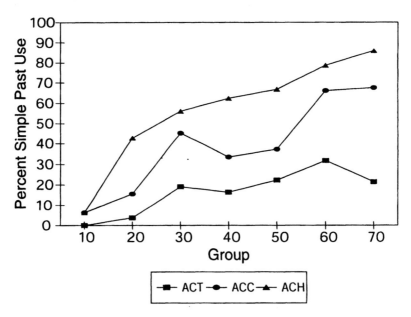

Figure 4.2. The use of simple past within lexical aspectual classes by groups (oral narratives). From "Narrative Structure and Lexical Aspect: Conspiring Factors in Second Language Acquisition of Tense-Aspect Morphology," by K. Bardovi-Harlig, 1998, *Studies in Second Language Acquisition, 20,* p. 486. Copyright 1998 by Cambridge University Press. Reprinted with permission.

Summary

The present study provides support for each of the claims of the aspect hypothesis that applies to English: the spread of the perfective past, the distribution of the progressive, and the nonuse of the progressive with states. The effect of mode seems to be, not unexpectedly, that the rates of use in the written narratives are higher than in the oral narratives. Nevertheless, the overall patterns of use of tense-aspect morphology are the same, with one notable exception: In the present study, the analysis of the oral narratives shows that achievements and accomplishments exhibit different rates of use of past, supporting the four stages of the spread of perfective past hypothesized by Andersen (1991) and represented schematically in Table 4.3. Although the corpus of oral and written narratives examined here differs from the oral conversational data examined by Robison (1995a), the results of both studies are remarkably similar. The initial association of simple past in English with achievements and accomplishments and the association of *-ing* with activities is affected little by genre or mode. Likewise, results based on learner texts (e.g., this study; Bayley, 1994; Robison, 1995a) and cloze passages (Bardovi-Harlig & Reynolds, 1995; Collins, 1997, 1999b) show the same patterns of development.

Assessing the Influence of Lexical Aspect

As I have discussed above, a review of recent studies shows that the aspect hypothesis is widely supported. There are potential counterexamples, however, and these must also be reviewed. Before that, however, I will examine how the distributional evidence has been calculated. Without understanding how the distribution of verbal morphology has been measured and then interpreted, it is very difficult to determine whether there is support for the stages hypothesized by Andersen (1991) or the four hypotheses which constitute the aspect hypothesis. After examining the analyses used by the aspect studies I will examine cases which appear to be problematic for the aspect hypothesis.

Quantitative analysis of larger populations has been one of the clear goals of SLA researchers working in the area of tense-aspect acquisition; larger corpora and quantified data have been employed in order to better establish evidence for claims for the influence of lexical aspect on the distribution of emergent verbal morphology. In the last few years aspect studies have come far enough in satisfying both requirements that there are at least two main types of nonequivalent analyses, each with variants.

Across-Category and Within-Category Analysis

Aspect studies have typically failed to recognize the differences in their quantified analyses. However, explicit articulation is necessary for comparison of studies and assessment of the aspect hypothesis. In fact, the differences in these analyses could lead us to support or reject the aspect hypothesis on the basis of the very same data. Every aspect study aims to determine if verbal morphology shows differential distribution across the aspectual categories. Some studies address the question "Where do various morphemes occur?" and other studies ask "How are each of the lexical aspectual categories marked?"

In Table 4.6, Salaberry (1999b) provides the distribution of all the verbal morphology used by his learners in raw scores. To answer the question "Where does the imperfect occur?" follow the horizontal arrow across the categories. For the learners in SPA123 (a 1st-year Spanish course), 14/42 imperfects appear with telics and 20/42 appear with statives. To answer the question "How are aspectual categories marked?" follow the arrow down the column: 14/190 telics are in the imperfect. Following the arrow down the column for statives shows that 20/91 statives are in the imperfect. Because Table 4.6 uses raw scores and provides information for all the verbal forms used in each category, the reader is able to answer either question.

Table 4.6

Raw-Score Presentation of Distribution of Tense-Aspect Morphology by Learners of Spanish at Four-Levels (Salaberry, 1999b)

Group	Form	Telic	Activities	Stative	Total
SPA 112	Preterite	28	12	7	47
(*n*=4)	Imperfect	0	0	1	1
	Present	55	9	27	91
	Infinitive	10	1	0	11
	Progressive	0	0	0	0
	TOTAL	93	22	35	150
SPA 123	Preterite	150	24	29	203
(*n*=4)	Imperfect	14	8	20	42
	Present	23	5	40	68
	Infinitive	2	1	0	3
	Progressive	1	13	2	16
	TOTAL	190	51	91	332
SPA 203	Preterite	87	7	8	102
(*n*=4)]	Imperfect	4	5	38	47
	Present	9	2	26	37
	Infinitive	1	1	0	2
	Progressive	0	5	1	6
	TOTAL	101	20	73	194
SPA 311	Preterite	164	8	3	175
(*n*=3)	Imperfect	6	6	73	85
	Present	59	14	39	112
	Infinitive	0	0	0	0
	Progressive	7	13	0	20
	TOTAL	236	41	115	392

Note. From "The Development of Past Tense Verbal Morphology in Classroom L2 Spanish," by R. Salaberry, 1999, *Applied Linguistics, Vol. 20*, p. 156. Copyright 1999 by Oxford University Press. Adapted with permission.

As the reader can begin to see from the difference in ratios, the quantitative answers to these questions "Where does verbal morphology occur?" and "How are aspectual categories marked?" can be quite different. The differences in the analyses used in the aspect studies arise at one of three points: when some forms are reported to the exclusion of others, when raw scores are converted into percentages, or when results are plotted on graphs. Each of these steps imposes a specific perspective on the data. Furthermore, the differences in approaches are only relevant to—and in fact only show up in—studies that elicit learner-constructed texts.

It is here that elicitation tasks interact with the quantitative analysis. Communicative texts, whether oral or written, characteristically exhibit an unequal number of tokens in each lexical aspectual category. As an example, consider the distribution of verbs across aspectual categories in the set of narratives from the *Modern Times* retell task just reviewed in the previous section. Approximately half of the predicates in both the oral and written samples are achievements. In the oral sample, for example, there are 666 achievements out of 1,461 predicates. The remaining predicates are almost evenly divided among the categories of statives (246/1,461), activities (235/1,461), and accomplishments (314/1,461). This distribution is quite commonly reported (e.g., Bergström, 1995, 1997; Salaberry, 1998, 1999b). In contrast, elicitation tasks such as cloze passages intentionally balance the number of tokens in each aspectual category (Bardovi-Harlig & Reynolds, 1995; Collins, 1997, 1999b) and thus analysis of cloze data is not affected.

Across-category analysis. I will begin this comparison by examining the studies which ask the question "Where do various morphemes occur?" These studies take the perspective of the particular morpheme under investigation. Studies of this type include Giacalone Ramat (1997, Italian), Housen (1994, Dutch), Rohde (1996, 1997, English), Salaberry (1999b, Spanish), Shirai (1995, Japanese), Shibata (1998, Japanese), Shirai and Kurono (1998, Japanese), and Wiberg (1996, Italian). Rohde (1996) argues that the across-category analysis highlights the verbal inflections used by the learners, whereas "the standard presentation [i.e., the within-category analysis] gives the aspectual categories and shows which inflection occurs on the verbs in that category, thus paying perhaps too much attention to the aspectual categories" (p. 1121).

Two means of presentation are employed in this approach: raw scores and percentages. Raw scores were used by Rohde (1996, 1997) in describing a natural corpus of two child learners over the course of 5 months. Percentages and raw scores were used by Shirai (1995) and Shirai and Kurono (1998); Housen (1994) and Salaberry (1999b) also included both means of presentation. I use the percentage approach to represent the analysis. This approach answers the question "Where do various morphemes occur?" by taking the sum of all the predicates that occur with a given morpheme across aspectual categories. For example, it calculates the percentage of all progressives that are activities. Because this approach calculates distribution across the various aspectual categories, I refer to this approach as the *across-category analysis.*

Table 4.7 illustrates the across-category analysis for three learners at a single time (Shirai & Kurono, 1998, p. 259). The across-category presentation is used to display the percentage of

Table 4.7

Across-Category Analysis of the Distribution of Tense-Aspect Morphology in Conversational Interviews by Three Learners of Japanese (Shirai & Kurono, 1998)

Learner	Form	STA %	STA (n)	ACT %	ACT (n)	ACC %	ACC (n)	ACH %	ACH (n)	Total %	Total (n)
C	-ta	2	(1)	6	(3)	0	(0)	92	(47)	100	(51)
	-tei	0	(0)	62	(13)	10	(2)	29	(6)	101	(21)
T	-ta	3	(1)	19	(6)	6	(2)	72	(23)	100	(32)
	-tei	0	(0)	46	(13)	7	(2)	46	(13)	99	(28)
K	-ta	24	(10)	7	(3)	0	(0)	69	(29)	99	(42)
	-tei	7	(4)	58	(35)	0	(0)	35	(21)	100	(60)
Group	-ta	10	(12)	10	(12)	2	(2)	78	(99)	100	(125)
	-tei	4	(4)	56	(61)	4	(4)	37	(40)	101	(109)

Note. The group scores were calculated from the raw scores in the original article (Table 1). From "The Acquisition of Tense-Aspect Marking in Japanese as a Second Language," by Y. Shirai & A. Kurono, 1998, *Language Learning, Vol. 48,* p. 259. Copyright 1998 by the Language Learning Research Club. Adapted with permission.

all uses of the resultative morpheme -*ta* that occurs with achievements in L2 Japanese. For the group, 78% of all occurrences of -*ta*
occur with achievements. The presentation also shows what percentage of all uses of the progressive-durative morpheme -*tei-*
occurs with activities: 55% of all progressive morphology occurs
with activities. Note that reading across the columns, the totals
add up to 100% (except for rounding). A second example of an
across- category analysis is found in Table 4.8, in which the raw
scores in Table 4.6 are presented in percentages (Salaberry,
1999b). Table 4.8 presents the results of a cross-sectional study.
Recall that for the learners in SPA123, 20/42 imperfects appear
with statives and 14/42 appear with telics. When these are converted into percentages across categories, the analysis shows that
48% of all imperfects occur with statives, and 33% occur with telics.
Each of these studies is interested in answering the question of
where tense-aspect morphology occurs. Now consider studies
which ask how aspectual categories are marked.

    Within-category analysis. The second approach asks the
question, "How are the lexical aspectual categories marked by
learners?" This approach analyzes the morphological use within
each category. For this reason, I call this analysis the within-
category analysis. Tables 4.4 and 4.5 from the study reported in
the previous section illustrate a *within-category analysis.* (See also
Robison, 1995a, Table 2.)

    A within-category analysis calculates the percentage of all
activities that are progressive, for example. Table 4.4 shows that
the percentage of activities that carry progressive in Group 40, 8%,
increases to 33% in Group 50 and to 43% in Group 60. Note that
adding down the columns, the uses of different verbal morphology
add up to 100%; that is, 100% of the activity predicates are
accounted for.

    Robison (1995a) observes that the within-category analysis
has the advantage of not being influenced by the number of tokens
in a category. As Robison rightly observes, the across-category
analysis is sensitive to unbalanced distribution across categories,
whereas the within-category analysis is not. The within-category

Table 4.8

Across-Category Analysis of the Distribution of Tense-Aspect Morphology by Learners of Spanish at Four Levels (Salaberry, 1999b)

Group	Form	Telic %	Activities %	State %	Total %
SPA 112	Preterite	60	26	15	100
(*n*=4)	Imperfect	0	0	100	100
	Present	60	10	30	100
	Infinitive	91	9	0	100
	Progressive	0	0	0	0
SPA 123	Preterite	74	12	14	100
(*n*=4)	Imperfect	33	19	48	100
	Present	34	7	59	100
	Infinitive	67	33	0	100
	Progressive	6	81	13	100
SPA 203	Preterite	85	7	8	100
(*n*=4)	Imperfect	9	11	81	100
	Present	24	5	70	100
	Infinitive	50	50	0	100
	Progressive	0	83	17	100
SPA 311	Preterite	94	5	2	100
(*n*=3)	Imperfect	7	7	86	100
	Present	53	13	35	100
	Infinitive	0	0	0	100
	Progressive	35	65	0	100

Note. From "The Development of Past Tense Verbal Morphology in Classroom L2 Spanish," by R. Salaberry, 1999, *Applied Linguistics, Vol. 20,* p. 164. Copyright 1999 by Oxford University Press. Adapted with permission.

analysis is not sensitive to more frequent production of one lexical aspectual class than another.

An additional difference between the within- and across-category analyses is the inclusion of information concerning the use of base forms by learners. Within-category analysis always includes the use of base forms, whereas across-category analysis often does not (see Salaberry, 1999b, and Table 4.8 for an exception).[20] One reason why across-category analyses often do not include base forms (and other nonfocal or nontargetlike forms) is that across-category analyses have focused on the acquisition of specific morphology, and zero is not the focus of acquisition studies. As a result of this difference in reporting, not all across-category analyses convert well to within-category analyses. Where no base forms are reported, for example, conversion to a within-category analysis would lead to very inflated scores for the use of morphology. As Robison (1995a) and Bardovi-Harlig (1998) show, a significant number of verbs appear in the base form. (See also Chapter 2.) The number of base forms used is also helpful in allowing us to compare learners in different studies.

Reanalysis. To illustrate the differences between the within- and across-category analyses, I will convert one within-category analysis (Bardovi-Harlig, 1998, Table 4.5) to an across-category analysis, and one across-category analysis (Salaberry, 1999b, Table 4.8) to a within-category analysis. Both studies used a *Modern Times* film-retell task and both collected oral narratives.

Beginning with Table 4.5, presented earlier in this chapter, the within-category analysis of the oral narratives produced by learners of English shows that 6% of achievements carry simple past in the language sample of the lowest-level learners (Group 10) in the study. Six percent of accomplishments carry simple past in the same level. No activities occur in the simple past. Look down the columns and notice that 66% of achievements and 44% of accomplishments occur in base forms. In Group 20, 43% of the achievements and 16% of the accomplishments carry the simple past. Only 4% of the activities show use of simple past.

Concentrating only on the distribution of simple past, notice first that the frequency of use of simple past on achievements exceeds the use of past with accomplishments, which in turn exceeds the use of past with activities. Notice too, that the within-category analysis reveals a developmental effect (Figure 4.3a). All the lexical aspectual categories show higher use of simple past as learners use more verbal morphology. By Group 70, 86% of achievements, 68% of accomplishments, and 21% of activities carry the simple past.

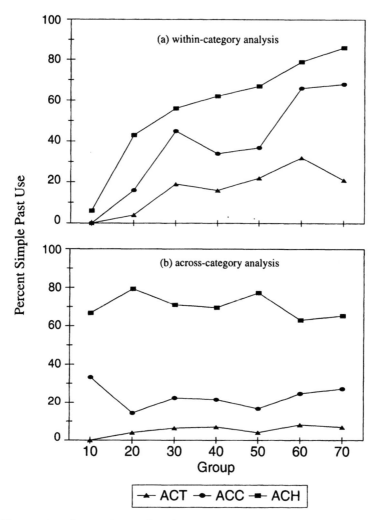

Figure 4.3. Comparison of within- and across-category analyses of the distribution of simple past in oral narratives by learners of English in seven groups. Top panel from "Narrative Structure and Lexical Aspect: Conspiring Factors in Second Language Acquisition of Tense-Aspect Morphology," by K. Bardovi-Harlig, 1998, *Studies in Second Language Acquisition, 20,* p. 486. Copyright 1998 by Cambridge University Press. Reprinted with permission.

Now consider the across-category analysis of the same data in Table 4.9. The across-category analysis answers the question "What percent of past-tense marking occurs on achievements?"

Table 4.9

Across-Category Analysis of the Distribution of Tense-Aspect Morphology in Oral Narratives by Learners of English (Reanalysis of Data in Table 4.5)

Group	Form	STA %	(n)	ACT %	(n)	ACC %	(n)	ACH %	(n)	Total %	(n)
Group 10	Past	0	(0)	0	(0)	33	(.5)	67	(1)	100%	(1.5)
N=3	Prog	0	(0)	57	(4)	29	(2)	14	(1)	100%	(7)
	Pres	0	(0)	80	(2)	0	(0)	20	(.5)	100%	(2.5)
	Base	0	(0)	18	(3)	21	(3.5)	62	(10.5)	100%	(17)
	Other	0	(0)	17	(1)	33	(2)	50	(3)	100%	(6)
Group 20	Past	2	(1)	4	(2)	14	(7)	79	(38.6)	100%	(48.6)
N=6	Prog	0	(0)	67	(10)	13	(2)	20	(3)	100%	(15)
	Pres	10	(1)	60	(6)	0	(0)	30	(3)	100%	(10)
	Base	6	(7)	28	(32)	30	(34)	36	(41.5)	100%	(114.5)
	Other	0	(0)	25	(2)	25	(2)	50	(4)	100%	(8)
Group 30	Past	0	(0)	7	(5.5)	23	(19)	71	(60)	100%	(84.5)
N=6	Prog	0	(0)	100	(6.5)	0	(0)	0	(0)	100%	(6.5)
	Pres	0	(0)	100	(1)	0	(0)	0	(0)	100%	(1)
	Base	10	(9)	17	(15)	24	(21)	49	(44)	100%	(89)
	Other	0	(0)	38	(3)	25	(2)	38	(3)	100%	(8)
Group 40	Past	2	(2)	7	(0)	22	(27.5)	70	(88)	100%	(126.5)
N=6	Prog	0	(0)	54	(15)	46	(13)	0	(0)	100%	(28)
	Pres	13	(1)	25	(2)	38	(3)	25	(2)	100%	(8)
	Base	9	(10)	23	(26)	30	(34.5)	39	(44.5)	100%	(115)
	Other	0	(0)	22	(3)	30	(4)	48	(6.5)	99%	(13.5)
Group 50	Past	2	(2)	4	(4)	17	(16)	77	(73.5)	100%	(95)
N=5	Prog	0	(0)	78	(7)	22	(2)	0	(0)	100%	(9)
	Pres	0	(0)	0	(0)	0	(0)	100	(.5)	100%	(.5)
	Base	19	(14.5)	9	(7)	29	(23)	43	(34)	100%	(78.5)
	Other	0	(0)	0	(0)	50	(2)	50	(2)	100%	(4)
Group 60	Past	4	(5.5)	8	(13)	25	(39)	63	(99)	100%	(156.5)
N=6	Prog	0	(0)	90	(14)	10	(1.5)	0	(0)	100%	(15.5)
	Pres	6	(.5)	11	(1)	39	(3.5)	44	(4)	100%	(9)
	Base	12	(7)	23	(13)	25	(14)	40	(22.5)	100%	(56.5)
	Other	0	(0)	0	(0)	67	(1)	33	(.5)	100%	(15)

Table 4.9 (continued)

Across-Category Analysis of the Distribution of Tense-Aspect Morphology in Oral Narratives by Learners of English (Reanalysis of Data in Table 4.5)

Group	Form	STA %	(n)	ACT %	(n)	ACC %	(n)	ACH %	(n)	Total %	(n)
Group 70	Past	0	(0)	7	(6)	27	(23)	66	(55)	100%	(84)
N=4	Prog	0	(0)	74	(13)	11	(2)	14	(2.5)	100%	(17.5)
	Pres	67	(4)	33	(2)	0	(0)	0	(0)	100%	(6)
	Base	9	(2)	30	(7)	.34	(8)	28	(6.5)	100%	(23.5)
	Other	0	(0)	0	(0)	100	(1)	0	(0)	100%	(1)

Looking again at Group 20, note that 79% of all simple past morphology occurs on achievements, 14% on accomplishments, and 4% on activities. The across-category and within-category analyses are compared in Figure 4.3. Note that in the across-category analysis in Figure 4.3b, achievements and accomplishments show very different distributions. This is due to the fact that achievements outnumber accomplishments by more than two to one. Similarly, accomplishments are much closer to activities than to achievements, in part because the number of tokens of accomplishments and activities produced is closer to each other than either one is to the number of achievements produced. Finally, the across-category analysis shows no increase in the use of past across groups. Achievements garner between 63% and 79% of the uses of simple past at all stages. Without developmental changes, there is no evidence of the spreading of verbal morphology across aspectual categories. Moreover, the most striking contrast comes in the differences between Groups 10 and 40. Where only 6% of achievements and accomplishments are marked by past by Group 10 according to the within-category analysis, 67% of all past occurs on achievements according to the across-category analysis. According to the within-category analysis, Group 40 uses simple past with 62% of all achievements. Thus, the within-category analysis captures the increase in the use of past morphology from Group 10 to Group 40. In contrast, the across-category analysis shows almost no change: In Group 10, 67% of all simple past occurs with achievements; in Group 40, 69% does. The proportion of past morphology across aspectual categories does not change noticeably as the use of verbal morphology increases.

Now consider the reanalysis of an across-category analysis to a within-category analysis, working with the narrative data from Salaberry's (1999b) study of Spanish. (Note that this conversion is possible because information for all of the predicates in the sample is provided.) Focusing on level SPA123 examined previously, the across-category analysis in Table 4.8 showed that 33% of all imperfects occurred with telics and 48% occurred with states. In contrast, the within-category analysis shows that only 7% of telics occur with the imperfect, whereas 22% of the statives occur with the imperfect. Table 4.10 presents a within-category analysis for the data in Tables 4.6 and 4.8. Figure 4.4 compares the representation of the use of the imperfect in the across-category and within-category analyses. Whereas the across-category analysis does not show a developmental effect, the within-category analysis does. The within-category analysis shows that there is very little use of imperfect by learners in the first level (SPA112). The use of imperfect increases in the second level (SPA123) with statives in the lead, activities second, and telics lagging behind, as expected following the aspect hypothesis. The use of imperfect continues to increase robustly in states in levels SPA203 and SPA311.

Note that in the within-category analysis, the use of the imperfect with telics never exceeds the use of imperfect with either activities or states, in contrast to the across-category analysis (see Level SPA123, Figure 4.4b). This is because the analysis is insulated against imbalances in production of tokens in the lexical categories; most notably, it is not sensitive to the fact that there are more telics than any other category. The spread of imperfect is more modest in activities and almost nonexistent in telics, which is not surprising for a group that still makes prototypical associations.

Table 4.10

Within-Category Analysis of the Distribution of Tense-Aspect Morphology by Learners of Spanish at Four Levels (Reanalysis of Data in Table 4.8)

Group	Form	Telic %	Telic (n)	Activities %	Activities (n)	Stative %	Stative (n)
SPA 112	Preterite	30	(28)	55	(12)	20	(7)
(n=4)	Imperfect	0	(0)	0	(0)	3	(1)
	Present	59	(55)	41	(9)	77	(27)
	Infinitive	11	(10)	5	(1)	0	(0)
	Progressive	0	(0)	0	(0)	0	(0)
	TOTAL	100	(93)	101	(22)	100	(35)
SPA 123	Preterite	79	(150)	47	(24)	32	(29)
(n=4)	Imperfect	7	(14)	16	(8)	22	(20)
	Present	12	(123)	10	(5)	44	(40)
	Infinitive	1	(2)	2	(1)	0	(0)
	Progressive	1	(1)	25	(13)	2	(2)
	TOTAL	100	(190)	100	(51)	100	(91)
SPA 203	Preterite	86	(87)	35	(7)	11	(8)
(n=4)	Imperfect	4	(4)	25	(5)	52	(38)
	Present	9	(9)	10	(2)	36	(26)
	Infinitive	1	(1)	5	(1)	0	(0)
	Progressive	0	(0)	25	(5)	1	(1)
	TOTAL	100	101	100	(20)	100	(73)
SPA 311	Preterite	70	(164)	20	(8)	3	(3)
(n=3)	Imperfect	3	(6)	15	(6)	64	(73)
	Present	25	(59)	34	(14)	34	(39)
	Infinitive	0	(0)	0	(0)	0	(0)
	Progressive	3	(7)	1	(1)	0	(0)
	TOTAL	101	(236)	101	(41)	101	(115)

So even though Salaberry (1999b) concludes on the basis of an across-category analysis that "the effect of lexical aspectual class with level of experience in the target language [i.e., course level] is substantiated" (p. 165), the effect of level is even clearer with the within-category analysis, which shows developmental effects.

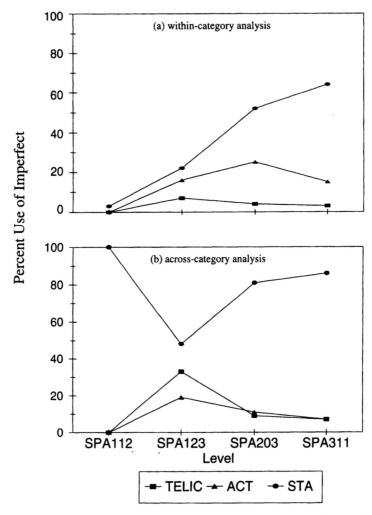

Figure 4.4. Comparison of within- and across-category analyses of the distribution of imperfect in oral narratives by learners of Spanish at four levels. (Based on data from Salaberry, 1998b.)

These comparisons show that the analyses differ in reporting rates of use of morphology in different aspectual categories, in their sensitivity to number of tokens produced, and in their portrayal of developmental effects.

Comparing analyses. Because the analyses are not equivalent, they also show some advantages in specific cases. The across-category analysis was originally used by Shirai (1991) to trace the distribution of verbal morphology relative to lexical aspectual category in the speech of native speakers addressed to child first-language learners. Because the across-category analysis is sensitive to the sheer numbers of tokens produced in a single category, across-category analysis captures the number of tokens of each type that a learner might encounter in the input. Native-speaker competence is not at stake, and one assumes that the native speaker is as able to inflect activities for the simple past as achievements. The across-category analysis captures the frequency with which verbs are encoded for morphology in the input. More input translates into more verbs in a single category.[21]

In contrast, if one's interest in learners is related to competence, an analyst might want to know whether a learner is capable of inflecting activities with the simple past and, if so, the rate at which they do so. This question does not address the actual number of forms in production. Learners may be able to inflect accomplishments with the same regularity as they inflect achievements, but the across-category analysis will never reveal this unless the numbers of achievements and accomplishments are held constant.[22]

Because of the differences in the analyses, they cannot be used interchangeably. When evaluating studies claim to support or not support the aspect hypothesis, it is quite important to take the kind of analysis performed into account, even if the author does not explicitly discuss it.

Challenges to the Aspect Hypothesis

The same things that are required of supporting studies are required of potential counterexamples: a clear distinction between grammatical and lexical aspect, articulation of categories employed and diagnostic tests, quantification of the results, and an indication of which analysis was used. Once the different methods of analyzing the data collected in studies that test the aspect hypothesis are identified, they can be taken into account when evaluating competing claims. The clearest counterexample to any formulation of the aspect hypothesis would be an interlanguage system that exhibits equal distribution of verbal morphology in all categories, that is, states, activities, accomplishments, and achievements. That would involve, for example, the preterite emerging with equal frequency in all categories, and the same for present, imperfect, and progressive as they emerge. Counterevidence would not necessarily involve contrast between morphemes at the earliest stages, because the emergence of verbal morphology is ordered within the tense-aspect system, with default forms preceding past, perfective past preceding imperfective past, and imperfective past preceding future (Giacalone Ramat, 1992). There is no study of which I am aware that presents the type of counterevidence suggested above. Instead, potential counterevidence appears to address the individual predictions of the aspect hypothesis rather than the hypothesis in its entirety.

Counterevidence?

In this section I review studies that have been considered by their authors or by others to constitute counterevidence to the aspect hypothesis. One such example is found in the interlanguage of a single Japanese learner of English who used almost no verbal morphology, except for past on states in the background (Kumpf, 1984b). This case is discussed as a potential counterexample by Bardovi-Harlig (1999b) and Shirai and Kurono (1998). Following the aspect hypothesis, one does not expect the use of past to begin on states. It is important to note, however, that the states consisted largely of tokens of *be* (33/37). Subsequent cross-linguistic research has shown that *be* (like its equivalents in other languages) is a tense carrier; that is, *be* does not occur in the base form and is inflected when other verbs are not.[23] Shirai and Kurono show that the 11 tokens of past verbs in the foreground do favor achievements, consistent with the aspect hypothesis. Bardovi-Harlig

(1999b) and Shirai and Kurono agree that Kumpf's learner—like the learners in Schumann's (1987) study who also showed no correlation of inherent aspect and verbal morphology—may have been at too low a level to show productive use of verbal morphology. In light of the work from the meaning-oriented studies, we see that the learner may not have entered the grammatical stage of temporal expression.

A second study, by Rohde (1996), also presents a challenge to the aspect hypothesis. As discussed earlier, Rohde's study of two children acquiring English shows an uneven distribution of both regular and irregular past inflection with achievements, following the aspect hypothesis. What is not expected, however, is the occurrence of *-ing* with achievements. As Rohde says, "The progressive form does not show a distributional bias, appearing with both activities and achievements" (1996, p. 1129).[24] This constitutes possible counterevidence to the hypothesized spread of *-ing*. The 6-year-old learner shows increasing use of *-ing* with achievements from May to July and in August shows an equal number of verb types with both activities and achievements. However, when the raw token scores (Rohde, 1997) are converted into percentages of verbs in each aspectual category (a within-category analysis), the use of progressive even at its highest neither meets nor exceeds the use of past (regular and irregular combined) with achievements (i.e., 37% progressive to 56% past).[25] Moreover, 91% of the activities with verbal morphology carry progressive, showing a strong distributional bias. The 9-year-old learner shows early use of progressive with achievements, but in each sample the percentage of achievements that shows use of past is greater than the percentage that shows progressive; in contrast, the use of progressive is the dominant morphology for activities.

Rohde (1996) attributed some of the progressive use to the children's uses of *-ing* for future reference, which are targetlike. Future uses are allowed with some volitional achievements in English, such as *he's arriving at noon tomorrow* and *NASA is launching the shuttle Tuesday*. These future uses of *-ing* appear to be quite different from the noncontrasting use of *-ing* in past contexts (to mark activities) that have been reported for other learners. The dual function of the progressive *-ing* in English, as a marker of both continuity and future, is partly responsible for the ambiguity in the coding. Note that this is a language-specific problem that arises because progressive morphology in English can also be used as the future. No such problem arises in French, for example, where there is no morphological progressive.

Rohde's (1996, 1997) data raise an important question for interlanguage analysis: Are future contexts legitimate tests for the aspect hypothesis? Recall that the aspect hypothesis was developed by observing how children refer to the past. The original aspect hypothesis made no claims about how learners mark the future morphologically. Because future contexts were not part of the original formulation of the hypothesis, they might legitimately be excluded from analysis. This problem is worth further investigation.

Robison (1995a) also found an unexpected use of *-ing* with punctual events by the lowest group of six learners in his cross-sectional study (21% of the achievements carried *-ing,* dropping to 3% in the next group). He found, however, that most of the progressive punctual events were tokens of *going to* used in a punctual sense, as in "nine or ten . . . he going to sleep" (p. 357). This use decreases dramatically as learners' level of proficiency increases. In light of the statistically significant results regarding the other effects, including the affiliation of progressive with activities, Robison did not interpret this as a counterexample to the aspect hypothesis.

A third challenge to the aspect hypothesis comes from Salaberry (1999b). In spite of his conclusion that the effect of lexical aspectual class is substantiated by the data, Salaberry interprets the beginning stage of acquisition (see Table 4.8, SPA112 learners) to be a partial rejection of the aspect hypothesis, with support for the aspect hypothesis only in the subsequent stages (p. 165). At the earliest point sampled, by an across-category analysis, 60% of preterite forms are telics, 26% are activities, and 15% are states. The first sampling period for the SPA112 group in the within-category analysis also poses a challenge for the aspect hypothesis, with 30% of telic verbs occurring with the preterite, 55% of activities, and 20% of statives. In the second sampling period, both analyses shows a distribution more in keeping with the predictions of the aspect hypothesis (the rate of preterite with activities goes down), but states remain higher than expected. Following Wiberg (1996), Salaberry suggests that the preterite may function as a default tense marker (see also Liskin-Gasparro, 1996). This bears further investigation, especially by studies focussing on authentic beginners, a population that is very hard to come by among students enrolled in university language courses.[26]

The most important potential challenge to the aspect hypothesis comes from the ESF study (Dietrich et al., 1995). The authors concluded that "in relation to Andersen's 'aspect hypothesis' our results are inconclusive" (p. 271). Because the ESF study is the largest study on temporality and because it employed both longitudinal and cross-linguistic designs, it has a great potential for contributing to the investigation of the influence of lexical aspect on emerging verbal morphology. However, the study is also meaning-oriented, not form-oriented. Although the results of the study significantly advance our knowledge of the acquisition of temporal expression (see Chapter 2), the presentation of the results does not meet the criteria that must be met by tests of the aspect hypothesis, nor should a meaning-oriented study be expected to do so. Without explicit identification of lexical aspectual categories and quantification of the data, results can only be inconclusive. Future work could carry out a formal test of the aspect hypothesis on the ESF corpus.

Do Inflections Mark Tense?

In the study of the influence of lexical aspect on the distribution of what in the target languages are tense-aspect markers, the emergence of tense marking has been overshadowed. Yet several studies address the acquisition of tense.

Robison (1995a) observed that, even though the correlation of morphology with lexical aspectual categories strengthens with level of proficiency, tense also develops:

> The correlation of inflection with tense, PAST with anterior reference and -s with present, increases with proficiency level. While lexical aspect dominates inflectional choices at the lowest proficiency level, the influence of tense becomes at least comparable to that of lexical aspect in the highest proficiency group. (p. 365)

Robison's learners engaged in conversational interviews, but impersonal narratives in English and French showed a similar pattern of higher use of tense with level (Bardovi-Harlig & Bergström, 1996).

Housen (1993, 1994) also investigated the acquisition of tense. After one course in Dutch (of unspecified length) and 4 weeks in Holland, Housen's English-speaking subject used past-tense forms predominantly in past-time contexts, but she used present-tense forms almost equally in present- and past-time contexts. One year, another Dutch-as-a-foreign-language course, and a 5-week stay in Holland later, the learner largely restricted her use of present-tense forms to present-time contexts (Housen, 1993).[27]

By holding aspectual class and grammatical aspect constant, one can observe tense marking as it appears with progressive activities (Bardovi-Harlig, 1992a). The lowest level learners show evidence of bare progressive (verb + -ing) and present progressive, which intermediate learners abandon in favor of the past progressive. The use of past progressive with activities (where NSs supplied the simple past) shows targetlike tense use; however, association of progressive with activities shows continued influence of lexical aspect (Bardovi-Harlig & Reynolds, 1995; Robison, 1995a).

Buczowska and Weist (1991) and Klein (1993, 1994; Dietrich et al., 1995) argue that tense is acquired before grammatical aspect. A comprehension test completed by 60 adult Polish learners of English suggests that learners can more accurately identify contrasts in tense than grammatical aspect (Buczowska & Weist, 1991). These results must be interpreted with caution, however, because the test compared the simple past with the modal future (e.g., *jumped / will jump;* see also Kumpf, 1984a, for a discussion of the effect of instruction on the *will* future), whereas a contrast between past and base or past and present would have more faithfully represented an authentic interlanguage contrast. However, the ESF study relies on natural production data, avoiding the problem of artificial comparisons. In agreement with Buczowska and Weist (1991), Dietrich et al. (1995) conclude "our results clearly contradict the 'grammatical aspect before tense' hypothesis" (p. 270). Consistent with the observation that form precedes function, Klein (1994a) elaborates: "in no case do we observe an early functional use of these forms" (p. 245).

The emergence of tense contrasts in itself does not constitute a problem for the aspect hypothesis. To review, I repeat the current formulation of the aspect hypothesis here: "First and second language learners will initially be influenced by the inherent semantic aspect of verbs or predicates in the acquisition of tense and aspect markers associated with or/affixed to these verbs" (Andersen & Shirai, 1994, p. 133). Robison (1995a) and Bardovi-Harlig (Bardovi-Harlig, 1998; Bardovi-Harlig & Reynolds, 1995) show that tense contrasts are acquired even as the association of past morphology with lexical aspect (simple past with telic predicates, progressive with activities) is maintained. The aspect hypothesis predicts the influence of lexical aspect, but not the exclusion of tense. This becomes even clearer under the prototype hypothesis (Andersen & Shirai, 1994; Shirai & Andersen, 1995), which shows that the "tense-*or*-aspect" question receives a "tense-*and*-aspect" answer when prototypical features of the past and perfective are taken into account. The prototype hypothesis is discussed in Chapter 7.

Chapter Summary

The body of research conducted thus far shows that lexical aspect influences the patterns of distribution of past verbal morphology in initial and later stages of morphological development. Although some methodological and analytical refinements remain to be made, current work shows widespread support from a number of target languages and language backgrounds. Because all natural use of tense-aspect morphology occurs in context, it is also important to investigate the influence of discourse structure on the distribution of emergent morphology. This will be taken up in Chapter 5. In addition, with the support of the aspect hypothesis from a growing number of studies, it is important to consider the sources of the distributional patterns predicted by the aspect hypothesis. Semantic prototypes and discourse structure individually and together have been suggested as explanations for the distribution. Cognitive and input-based explanations have also begun to be explored. These are addressed in Chapter 7.

Notes

[1]Similar investigations of creoles were also conducted (Bickerton, 1975, 1981; Givón, 1982). For a review of tense-aspect studies in pidgin and creole and a discussion of their relation to SLA, see Andersen and Shirai (1996).

[2]Based on his written samples from 89 university students, Andersen (1977, 1978, 1979) has argued that grouping data obscures individual variation.

[3]Kaplan (1987), Giacalone Ramat and Banfi (1990), and Bayley (1994) followed the tradition of using the terms *perfective* and *imperfective* to refer to lexical aspect, whereas following Comrie (1976) I have used those terms exclusively to refer to grammatical aspect. Kaplan also used the terms *event* and *nonevent*, which, although not clearly defined, I have used here. Bayley's use of perfective and imperfective (lexical) aspect is roughly equivalent to the telic-atelic distinction (personal communication, August, 1999) as is Giacalone Ramat and Banfi's (Giacalone Ramat, 1995c), so I have substituted the terms *telic* and *atelic* in the interest of consistency. See Andersen and Shirai (1996, pp. 543–544) for an alternative means of dealing with this issue of terminology.

[4]There are other analyses of lexical aspectual classes which are based on Vendler categories that might be of interest to the reader (e.g. Binnick, 1991; Kenny, 1963; Mittwoch, 1991; Mourelatos, 1981; Quirk et al., 1985).

[5]There is a problem with the last test in that accomplishments and achievements pass the test, but for different reasons. This is perhaps clearer with achievements like *notice* or *recognize*. *It took Juan two hours to notice Mary* can only mean that it was two hours before Juan got around to noticing Mary, whereas for accomplishments an action such as "writing a book" can refer to the whole time interval, i.e., she was writing for a whole year, or it can refer to the amount of time before the action started, i.e., that it took her a year to get around to writing the book. Activities too are eligible for the interpretation that a certain amount of time elapsed before their inception. Dowty (1986) discusses this test (pp. 56–59).

[6]As Hasbún (1995) and Salaberry (1999b) note, Spanish presents an interesting theoretical problem that in L2 research becomes a coding problem. A group of lexical statives have achievement readings if they occur with animate themes and perfective morphology (Clements, 1985).

　　i. *Ella lo conocía desde la infancia.*
She knew [imperfect] him since childhood [STA].
　　ii. *Ella lo conoció esta mañana.*
She met [preterite] him this morning [ACH].

Both authors classify these predicates as states in the learner narratives. The meaning of such predicates remains relatively constant; the preterite forms refer to the inception of the state, rather than to the entire state as the imperfect forms do. See also Bull (1971) and King and Suñer (1999).

[7]Achievements and accomplishments often pattern together as "events" both theoretically (Mourelatos, 1981) and acquisitionally.

[8]For a fuller review of specific studies, see Andersen and Shirai (1994, 1996), Robison (1995a), and Shirai and Andersen (1995); for a review of the larger quantified studies, see Bardovi-Harlig (1998).

[9]Many students in a 1st-year Spanish or French foreign language class have had some exposure to the language in high school, but students often differ in how many classes they have taken previously. Other students have had no exposure to the language. Thus, the 1st-year language classes in a university are both not often composed of true beginners and often made up of learners at relatively different levels. Some of the difference between the students in Hasbún's Spanish study and Bergström's French study may be due to differences in learner populations.

[10]Rohde's (1996, 1997) presentation differs in that counts are provided only for inflected forms (using raw scores). The exclusion of base forms from the report does not change the relative frequency of any morpheme, but also does not show with which aspectual categories learners use no morphology. Rohde also uses type counts, whereas most aspect studies have used token counts. However, token counts can be found in Rohde (1997) in the tables for the individual learners in the *Semantische Analyse* sections.

[11]The results of Collins's study are unique in that the Francophone learners of English show the use of present perfect as an alternative form to the simple past in response to the cloze task (with the highest rate of use being under

25% of the responses). The use of present perfect in the original cloze used by Bardovi-Harlig and Reynolds (1995) was too small to record as an individual category, nor was it reported by Robison (1993, 1995a) in the cross-sectional conversational data. This use of present perfect may be influenced by the formally similar passé composé in French, constituting a case of first language influence. It is also important to note, however, that the first language influence contributed alternative forms, and was not strong enough to override the pervasive acquisitional pattern observed in the interlanguages of learners with other native languages.

[12]Wiberg refers to these learners as "bilinguals" but explains that the learners "range from more or less nativelike to poor" with respect to their use of Italian (1996, p. 1088).

[13]Ideally, present and base should be separated. Collins (1999b) does this successfully by using a task entirely in third person singular.

[14]Progressive with mental states (e.g., *Stavo pensando che è difficile conoscere bene una persona* "I was thinking that it is difficult to know a person well" and *Sto pensando di partire stasera* "I am coming to the idea/thinking of leaving this evening") are grammatical in Italian (Giacalone Ramat, personal communication, August 23, 1998).

[15]In order, the titles are (1) Alone and hungry. (2) "She stole a loaf of bread." (3) "No, she didn't. I did." (4) "It was the girl—not the man." (5) "Remember me—and the bread?" (6) "Now is your chance to escape." (7) "Where do you live?" (8) "No place—anywhere." (9) "Can you imagine us in a little home like that?" (10) "I'll do it! We'll get a home, even if I have to work for it."

[16]Salaberry's (1999b) use of course level plus grammar screening tests is analogous to the placement in the program from which these learners were drawn.

[17]Direct speech was excluded for two reasons. First, two analyses were ultimately performed on the narratives, one for lexical aspect and one for narrative structure. Because it was the intention of the study to compare the analyses on the same texts, both analyses had to conform to the most restrictive analysis. Because direct speech is neither foreground nor background, it must be excluded from the count for a narrative analysis. (See Chapter 5.) Second, excluding speech eliminated the possible influence of the only verbal stimulus in the silent film: Speech was presented as titles and thus could have provided a model for the learners.

[18]For an extended discussion of the coding decisions which are outlined here, see Bardovi-Harlig (1995a).

[19]*Have* and *want* are the most commonly used statives (following *be*, which was eliminated from this analysis).

[20]Rohde (1999) provides the base forms not reported in Rohde (1996, 1997), but they are not integrated into the analysis reported previously.

[21]Some readers will recognize this as a statement of the *distributional bias hypothesis* (Andersen, 1985, 1990a, 1994; Andersen & Shirai, 1996; Robison, 1993, 1995b), the claim that the frequency of tense-aspect morphology is

unevenly distributed across aspectual categories in native speaker speech. The distributional bias hypothesis is discussed in Chapter 7.

[22]An alternative to both analyses is implicational scaling, used by Bayley (1999). For an earlier use of implicational scaling and a discussion, see Andersen (1978). The advantages of this analysis are discussed in Bardovi-Harlig (in press).

[23]Recall that this is why *be* is often excluded from the analysis of statives, as seen in the study reported in this chapter.

[24]Following Andersen (1985, 1990a, 1991), most studies reserve the term *distributional bias* for describing the distribution of inflectional morphology with respect to lexical aspectual categories in the speech of native speakers.

[25]These are calculated on the raw token scores given by Rohde (1997, p. 132). The type counts show slightly less of a difference with achievements (39% progressive to 50% past); however, 92% of the activities with verbal morphology (12/13) are progressives.

[26]Salaberry (1999b) reports that even SPA112 students had an average of 1.75 years of Spanish in high school. This is not at all unusual among 1st-year university foreign (or second) language students.

[27]Housen (1993) separated *zijn* "be," which shows much higher rates of use of target tense markers as tense, from lexical verbs.

CHAPTER FIVE

The Role of Discourse

The Interlanguage Discourse Hypothesis

Chapter 5 completes the investigation of the form-oriented approaches begun in Chapter 3. Like the studies of the aspect hypothesis in Chapter 4, the studies of the discourse hypothesis are hypothesis testing studies. Because studies of the discourse hypothesis must examine learner-produced texts as their database, the studies in Chapter 5, like those in Chapters 2 and 3, rely on learner narratives rather than on more controlled elicitation techniques. In the study of the development of temporality, the narrative is pervasive. As we saw in Chapters 2–4, narratives are used as a carrier or a context for tense-aspect morphology in many types of studies. However, in the studies that have been reviewed so far, the narrative has been more of a backdrop than a focus of study in its own right. Because of its status as a privileged environment for the study of the distribution of tense-aspect morphology, I will begin this discussion of discourse with the narrative.

The first half of this chapter is devoted to the analysis of interlanguage narrative structure and its influence on the distribution of tense-aspect morphology. The chapter begins with a discussion of the discourse hypothesis and an outline of linguistic theories of narrative structure. Next, studies of second language narrative and tense-aspect morphology are reviewed. This is followed by a narrative analysis of the corpus analyzed in Chapter 4 with respect to lexical aspect. In the next section I demonstrate how the influence of narrative structure and lexical aspect combine to produce the observed patterns of development.

The second half of the chapter discusses the relation of tense-aspect distribution and discourse structure more generally. Whereas all types of narratives have generally been grouped together, in the latter half of the chapter the characteristics of personal, impersonal, and personalized narratives are discussed and the influence of tense-aspect distribution is examined. Next, conversation and narrative are compared as vehicles of tense-aspect morphology. The chapter concludes with a discussion of descriptive texts as part of a more general theory of discourse structure and grounding, and as an important environment for further research on tense-aspect development.

In an early study of discourse and tense-aspect morphology in interlanguage, Godfrey (1980) observed that the use of tense morphology could not be fully understood without recourse to discourse. Like many of the studies in second language acquisition of the time, Godfrey focused on errors and avoidance of tense marking, framing the analysis in terms of tense continuity. Subsequent interlanguage discourse analysis followed Hopper (1979), Dahl (1984), and Givón (1982) in their investigations of the distribution of tense-aspect morphology with respect to the structure of the narrative in primary languages. Cross-linguistic investigations have suggested that the distinction between background and foreground is a universal of narrative discourse (Dahl, 1984; Hopper, 1979; Longacre, 1981). Hopper observed that competent (native) users of a language "mark out a main route through the narrative and divert in some way those parts of the narrative that are not strictly relevant to this route" (1979, p. 239). One such marking may be through the use of tense and aspect (Hopper, 1979).[1] In the foreground, Hopper observed, successive events may be marked in the preterite or simple past (1979, p. 239). Dahl observed that in some languages verbs in the foreground may carry no marking, and concluded that "it is always possible to use the least marked indicative form in a narrative [i.e., foreground] past context" (1984, p. 117). An early study by Kumpf (1984b) suggested that a relationship exists between the use of verbal morphology in interlanguage and the grounding of the narrative. Taking interlanguage as natural language which follows linguistic universals (e.g., Flashner, 1989; Kumpf, 1984b), the *interlanguage discourse hypothesis* predicts that "learners use emerging verbal morphology to distinguish foreground from background in narratives" (Bardovi-Harlig, 1994a, p. 43).

Narrative Analysis

In linguistic studies (as opposed to literary studies), a narrative is considered to be a text in which "the speaker relates a series of real or fictive events in the order in which they took place" (Dahl, 1984, p. 116). Narrative discourse is comprised of two parts, the foreground and the background. The foreground relates events belonging to the skeletal structure of the discourse (Hopper, 1979) and consists of clauses which move time forward (Dry, 1981, 1983). The temporal point of reference of any one event in the foreground is understood as following that of the event preceding it. So important is the concept of sequentiality that foreground clauses may be defined by the interpretation of their order: "[I]f a change in the order of the two clauses results in a change in the interpretation of what actually happened, then those two clauses are narrative [i.e., foreground] clauses" (Schiffrin, 1981, p. 47; see also Labov, 1972; Labov & Waletzky, 1967).[2] However, as Dry (1992) shows, the sum of multidisciplinary research on foreground suggests that it is a "cluster concept, commonly manifested as a collection of properties, not all of which need be present to identify any one passage as an instance of foregrounding" (p. 441). (See also Fleischman, 1985; Hopper and Thompson, 1980; Reinhart, 1984; von Stutterheim, 1991.)

Examples (1) and (2) show a sequence of events reported as foreground in narratives by learners of English as a second language. In the examples from the written narratives the learners' spelling has been preserved. The numbers in the square brackets were added and represent the order of the foregrounded events.

(1)   Oral, L1 Japanese
      Foreground   *Background*
      [1] Then she, *stole* the bread.
      [2] And the- she *ran away*,
      [3] and she . . . *hit* the Chaplin . . .
      I: Mm-hm.

                                            S: . . . and uh, different
                                                 woman *saw* the,
                                                 she *stole* the, uh,
                                                 bread . . .
                                            I: Mm-hm.

      [4] . . . and uh, and *cried*,
      [5] and *chased* her,
      [6] and the employer *caught* her,
      [7] and, but Chaplin *said*,
      "I did it, you know, I . . . stole . . . the breads."

(2)   Written, L1 Arabic
      Foreground   *Background*
      [1] she *stol* abroad
      [2] and they *cutch* her
      [3] she *met* charlie

                                            the nice man who *was*
                                            trying to helpe her

      [4] when he *said*
      "she didn't sleel the bread I did that"

The central characteristics of the foreground can be summarized by what Reinhart calls temporal criteria (1984, p. 801):

"Narrativity," or temporal continuity: Only narrative units, i.e., textual units whose order matches the order of the events they report, can serve as foreground.

Punctuality: Units reporting punctual events can serve more easily as foreground than units reporting durative, repetitive, or habitual events.

Completeness: A report of a completed event can serve more easily as foreground than a report of an ongoing event.

The most basic narratives by lower-level learners consist only of foreground. In the pragmatic stage identified by the meaning-oriented approach (Chapter 2), learners rely on chronological order to convey temporality, as in (3) and (4), repeated here from Chapter 2.

(3) *[jāna] [le kase] l'assiette (. . .)*
THERE-IS HE BREAKS THE DISH
"A dish was broken."
"et toi [le kase]"
AND YOU HE BREAK
"The lady asked me whether I had broken it."
"oui madame [e] moi"
YES MADAM IS ME
"I said, 'Yes, Madam I did.'"
"[eskyz] moi [le kase]"
EXCUSE ME HE BREAK
"Excuse me for breaking it."
et après [saje]
AND THEN FINISHED
"It was OK."
[la želete] la poubelle
HE THROW THE DUSTBIN
"The plate was thrown away."
[oral, L2 French, L1 Arabic; Noyau, Houdaïfa, et al., 1995, pp. 158–159]

(4) punjab + I do agriculture farm
before I go + seventy five + in the arab country
afghanistan [. . .]
afghanistan to turkey
to antakia
to syria
to lebanon
after there go to syria
yeah + jordan go india
I work in indian house
[oral, L2 English, L1 Punjabi; Klein, 1995, p. 53]

In the absence of other linguistic devices to convey temporal relations, these learners satisfy Reinhart's first criterion for foregrounding by default.

In addition to chronological order (Reinhart's "narrativity"), Dry (1983) claims that a second textual criterion for evaluating time movement is information value: the information communicated in the foregrounded clause must be new rather than given. In (5), clause (c) is foregrounded, whereas in (6) it is not.

(5) (a) *John gave Mary an apple,* (b) *and she sat down* to take a bite. (c) *She took the bite deliberately,* savoring the taste.

(6) (a) *John gave Mary an apple,* (b) *she sat down* and *took a bite.* (c) She took the bite deliberately, savoring the taste.

In (5) *she took the bite deliberately* presents ordered new information and is foregrounded, whereas in (6) the clause elaborates information already presented in (b). Some work on narrative cites syntax as a determinant of grounding, restricting foreground to main clauses (Labov, 1972; Reinhart, 1984). This contrasts with Dry's semantic analysis, which does not refer to syntax. I have employed Dry's analysis in my work because in early stages of interlanguage development syntactic development is simultaneous with tense-aspect development (Klein & Perdue, 1992).

In contrast to the single function of the foreground, which is to carry the story line, the background has many individual functions which together serve the purpose of supporting the foreground. Although events reported in foreground clauses are understood to be sequential, background events are often out of sequence with respect to the foreground and to other background events. The background does not itself narrate main events, but provides supportive material which elaborates on or evaluates the events in the foreground (Hopper, 1979). For example, a background clause may contribute to the interpretation of an event by revealing a prior event (located before the narrated event on the time line), making a prediction about the outcome of an event (located after the event on the time line), referring to a simultaneous event (located at the same point or interval on the time line; Aksu-Koç & von Stutterheim, 1994), or evaluating an action reported in the foreground (not located on the time line). In the following examples of interlanguage narratives (Bardovi-Harlig, 1995a), the background provides orientation (or scene setting) and evaluation as in (7) and explanation/identification as in (8).

(7)   Oral, L1 Spanish

	Foreground	*Background*
Orientation		And then, in another situation, in another place, there *is* a old lady that *is* really hungry *is* starving—She *is* starving. She *is* starving and so a—a business of bread, loaf of bread, [. .] [. . .] to support it.
Foreground	[1] And she *decided* to hope to take out the the loaf of bread.	
Evaluation		And although this *was* a wrong thing.

(8)   Written, L1 Arabic

	Foreground	*Background*
Scene setting		This movie talk about the man and the women. One day the women *was* too hungre,
Action	[1] so she *stole* a big piece of bread [2] but when she *was* *ranning* [3] she *hit* the man	
Identification		who *is* Charlie Chaplin.
	Although the man	
Identification		who *is* a Baker

[4] he *said* to the policman that there is women
who stole his bread, [5]
so the policman *go* after
the women.

The background also reports events that precede foreground events. In (1) the event described by "different woman saw she stole the bread" is anterior to the event described in clause [3], although it follows it in the linear organization of the narrative. Regardless of its order in the text, it is simultaneous to the event described by clause [1].

In her examination of foreground and background in contemporary English literary narratives, Dry (1981, 1983) reports that foreground clauses are usually in the simple past or historical present. As in the foreground, the simple past is the most prevalent verb form in the background clauses. However, English does not rely primarily on tense or aspect markers to distinguish foreground from background. Instead, other characteristics tend to cluster with tense-aspect to distinguish foreground from background, as shown by Hopper and Thompson (1980), Reinhart (1984), and Fleischman (1985).

Wolfson (1979) and Schiffrin (1981) describe the use of the conversational historical present in spontaneous oral narratives. Schiffrin's detailed analysis of the use of conversational historical present in narratives indicates that native speakers of English switch tense in the foreground. Dahl (1984) and Hopper (1979) agree that time reference is determined more by the narrative context than by tense itself. Schiffrin's analysis shows that even when tense switching occurs, the simple past seems to be the dominant form (69% of the verbs in the foreground were in the past). The phenomenon of tense-switching in the foreground raises interesting issues regarding interpretation of the use of nonpast in interlanguage narrative: namely, the extent to which learner use of nonpast can be interpreted as "historical present" rather than nonuse of past. Equating all learner base forms with historical present clearly meets with counterevidence from distributional patterns. Because historical present does not occur in the background, but many cases of learner base forms do, background base forms are unlikely to represent attempts at historical present. The issue of historical present and tense-switching is unresolved in interlanguage narrative studies and would make for interesting future research.

Studies of L2 Temporality and Narrative Structure

This section reviews studies of second language acquisition that employed a narrative analysis. As was the case with the aspect studies, the first studies were often case studies, whereas more recent studies tended to be larger, often with quantified results; the research methodology developed as additional studies were conducted. Early American and European studies used narrative analysis to account for the distribution of interlanguage verbal morphology (Flashner, 1989; Kumpf, 1984b; Véronique, 1987; von Stutterheim, 1986). Later studies employed the descriptions provided by the earlier studies of narrative as a hypothesis (for English: Bardovi-Harlig, 1992b, 1995a, 1998; for Catalan: Comajoan, 1998; for French: Véronique, 1987; for Spanish: Lafford, 1996). All the studies provide qualitative descriptions of the distribution of interlanguage verbal morphology in terms of narrative structure, and some provide quantitative analyses as well. Oral narratives were collected in all of the studies, and in a few oral and written pairs of the same narratives were collected. Studies that employ narrative theory to analyze the distribution of interlanguage verbal morphology are listed in Table 5.1. When compared to other areas of investigation within L2 temporality, there are fewer narrative studies than either meaning-oriented studies (reviewed in Table 2.1) or form-oriented aspect studies (reviewed in Table 4.1).

Research into interlanguage narratives has shown that grounding influences the distribution of tense-aspect morphology. As in the case of the aspect studies, the early narrative studies

Table 5.1

Studies of Narrative Structure and Distribution of Verbal Morphology

Target language	Author	L1	N	Level	No. of narratives	No. of predicates	Instruction	Design	Quantified
Catalan	Comajoan (1998)	English	1	Beginner	8	311	CFL, 2 semesters	Longitudinal, conversational interview, and oral story and film retells	Yes
Dutch	Housen (1994)	English	1	1 course plus 1 month host stay	Not specified	398 (T1) 551 (T2)	DFL, with two 1-month visits to Holland	Longitudinal, 2 samples 1 year apart; free conversation	Yes
English	Kumpf (1984b)	Japanese	1	Low	Not specified	250	None	Conversational interview, personal narrative	Yes
	Flashner (1989)	Russian	3	1 beginner 1 intermediate 1 advanced	Not specified	649	Limited instruction	Personal narratives from spontaneous speech	Yes
	Bardovi-Harlig (1992b)	Mixed	16	Intermediate	32	1,135	Intensive ESL	Cross-sectional written and oral narratives, story retells	Yes
	Bardovi-Harlig (1995a)	Mixed	37	Beginner-advanced	74	2,779	Intensive ESL	Cross-sectional written and oral narratives, film retells	Yes
	Bardovi-Harlig (1998)	Mixed	37	Beginner-advanced	74	2,779	Intensive ESL	Cross-sectional written and oral narratives, film retells, with aspect	Yes

Table 5.1 (continued)

Studies of Narrative Structure and Distribution of Verbal Morphology

Target language	Author	L1	N	Level	No. of narratives	No. of predicates	Instruction	Design	Quantified
	Housen (1998)	French, Dutch	11	Low to high intermediate	Not specified	550	Primary school English-medium and subject instruction in EFL setting	Conversational interview, personal narratives, film and plan retells, elicited (picture) narratives	Yes
	Tajika (1999)	Japanese	32	360–557 TOEFL	192	3,092 oral 2,704 written	EFL	Six narratives each, oral and written personal, film retell and written passage retell	Yes
French	Trévise (1987)	Spanish	2	Low	3	53	None	Conversational interview, personal narrative	No
	Véronique (1987)	Arabic Berber	5 2	2 low, 3 intermediate, 2 advanced	19	Not specified	None	Cross-sectional, conversational interview, personal narrative	No
	Noyau (1984)	Spanish	2	11–22 and 6–18 months in France	Not specified	Not specified	French for refugees	Longitudinal, conversational interviews, personal and film retell narratives	No
	Noyau (1990)	Spanish	3	About 1 year in France	6	Not specified	Not specified	Two narratives each, approximately 1 year apart; conversational interview, personal narrative	No

Table 5.1 (continued)

Studies of Narrative Structure and Distribution of Verbal Morphology

Target language	Author	L1	N	Level	No. of narratives	No. of predicates	Instruction	Design	Quantified
German	von Stutterheim (1986)	Turkish	10	Cross-sectional	20	Not specified	None	Guided conversations (2 hr), L2 retellings of L1 narrative, translations	Type/token counts
Spanish	Lafford (1996)	English	13	OPI inter-mediate, low, mid, high	15	387	SFL	Cross-sectional, oral narratives, animated-film retell	Yes

Note. FL = foreign language; SL = second language; C = Catalan; D = Dutch; E = English; S = Spanish.

were essentially case studies (Flashner, 1989; Kumpf, 1984b; Trévise, 1987; and later Housen, 1994), and subsequent studies with larger learner populations confirmed and elaborated on the results of the earlier investigations.

Flashner (1989) found that three Russian learners of English distinguished foreground from background in oral narratives by marking the foreground predominantly in simple past, whereas the background verbs occurred predominantly in base forms. Similarly, Housen (1994) reported that an American learner of Dutch with one course of Dutch and 4 weeks of active L2 use in Holland reflected the narrative structure in her use of tense-aspect morphology: Present perfect (with some rare preterite forms) appeared in the foreground, whereas simple present and nonfinite forms occurred in the background. A year later the learner showed the same distribution, although less pronounced. Kumpf's (1984b) Japanese learner of English also showed differential tense-aspect use for grounding in oral interviews, but she used tensed stative verbs in the background, whereas active verbs were marked for habitual and continuous aspect and base forms were used in the foreground. Kumpf's Japanese learner, Tomiko, followed the pattern described by Givón (1982) for Guyanese Creole and Hawaiian Pidgin, and for creole tense-aspect-modality where the morphologically marked members are found in the background.

Early criticism of the discourse hypothesis as represented by Godfrey (1980) and Kumpf (1984b) came from Wolfram (1985, 1989; Wolfram & Hatfield, 1986), who characterized discourse-level analysis as a "somewhat faddish concern" (1985, p. 251). Wolfram attempted to replicate Kumpf's (1984b) findings with a single adult speaker of Vietnamese learning English, but found that the pattern of tense marking did not resemble the distribution described by Kumpf. Note, however, that Flashner (1989) and Housen (1994) also found different patterns of tense-aspect distribution from Kumpf which nonetheless support the discourse hypothesis. As discussed in Chapter 4, Kumpf's learner showed very little use of past beyond *be*. As an alternative to the discourse hypothesis, Wolfram (1985) proposed the phonetic explanation discussed in Chapter 1, claiming that "the empirical facts suggest that the direction of these [discourse-level] studies is premature, and that a number of surface-level constraints must be considered before isolating these higher level constraints" (p. 230). However, as Bayley (1991, 1994) showed, multiple factors can contribute to the distribution of past morphology. In Bayley's study both phonetic constraints and lexical aspect accounted for the distribution of past morphology, although the influence of lexical aspectual class cut across the allomorphs of the past. By the end of this chapter I hope to show that the influence of narrative structure does not exclude other influences on tense-aspect distribution.

Flashner (1989) interpreted the direction of the marking to be an influence of the Russian L1 of her learners. At the time of the Kumpf (1984b) and Flashner studies, the issue was not, as it later became, the direction of morphological marking, but the fact that interlanguage used verbal morphology to distinguish foreground from background. Later studies showed that learners from various backgrounds showed the same pattern as Flashner's (1989) Russian learners. In addition, other L1 Japanese learners of English as a second language (who share the same L1 as Kumpf's learner) were found to exhibit high use of past in the foreground (Bardovi-Harlig, 1992b, 1995a). Recent work on both aspect and narrative analysis has led to a possible reanalysis of the use of tensed statives by Kumpf's learner which takes into account her low level of morphological development and the predominance of *be* among the tensed verbs. (See Chapter 4.)

Véronique (1987) and Bardovi-Harlig (1992b) investigated larger groups of learners. The pattern of morphological marking followed that reported by Flashner (1989), showing greater use of the simple past in the foreground than in the background. In a study of seven untutored Arabic- and Berber-speaking learners of French, Véronique found that the distribution of verbal morphology across background and foreground differed by level, but these findings also showed variation within levels across individuals and within individuals across texts. In the narratives of intermediate learners, emergent verbal morphology—what Véronique called "V + e" (i.e., emergent use of *passé composé* with or without the auxiliary)—tends to cluster in the foreground, with base forms in the background. Bardovi-Harlig's (1992b) study of oral and written narratives from 16 ESL learners from a variety of L1 backgrounds found that 12 learners showed a greater use of past in the foreground than in the background. Nine learners showed both greater use of past in the foreground and greater use of nonpast in the background, and three additional learners showed greater use of past in the foreground than in the background with no appreciable difference in nonpast. The remaining four learners showed discourse-neutral distribution of verbal morphology.

Level of proficiency clearly emerges as a likely factor in determining the distribution of verbal morphology relative to grounding, especially when one takes into account in fact that very low-level learners show no systematic use of tense (Schumann, 1987; Trévise, 1987) and that advanced learners must eventually use past in both foreground and background to reach a targetlike use of tense in narratives.[3] In between the extremes of proficiency, learners seem to show differential use of verbal morphology by grounding. The problem of determining the level of the learners is an issue in narrative studies, just as it is in other studies. When researchers measure proficiency by enrollment in courses (e.g., "intermediate"), this allows too great a difference in tense-aspect use (Bardovi-Harlig, 1992c); measuring learners' use of forms against time of exposure also yields very different profiles for individual learners because learners progress at very different rates (Bardovi-Harlig, 1992c, 1997a; see also Chapter 3). Véronique (1987) compared his learners on communicative and linguistic proficiency at three stages (low, intermediate, and advanced), and he noted that the rating did not necessarily correspond to the number of errors in verbal morphology produced by the learners. Flashner (1989) also compared three learners at low, intermediate, and high proficiency, but did not specify the basis on which proficiency was assigned.

Neither length of narrative nor elaboration of background matches well with general measures of proficiency by course enrollment or percent appropriate use of past tense (Bardovi-Harlig, 1995a).[4] It seems that change in narrative structure or length can best be measured for individual learners against their own production. Although an individual learner may tell longer or more elaborated narratives as time in the target language environment increases, his or her own baseline—his willingness to tell stories, her desire to speak—may be quite different from that of another learner at a comparable stage. That is very likely why cross-sectional studies in which learners are ranked by their conversational ability (e.g., Véronique, 1987) and longitudinal studies in which learners are compared to themselves (e.g., Dietrich et al., 1995) show development in the narrative itself across and within subjects.

As the study in the following section shows, learners' level of proficiency is a factor in the distribution of emergent tense-aspect morphology, as is narrative grounding and lexical aspect. The study begins by isolating the analysis of narrative structure and its effect on tense-aspect morphology. It then combines the investigation of the influence of narrative structure with the investigation of the influence of lexical aspect.

A Cross-Sectional Study of Tense-Aspect in L2 Narratives

In this section, I present the narrative results of the study in Bardovi-Harlig (1998). The analysis has been carried out on the same corpus of narratives (37 pairs of oral and written narratives elicited by means of a *Modern Times* retell task) that was presented in Chapter 4 from the perspective of the aspect hypothesis. After laying out the basic results of the study (for more details see Bardovi-Harlig, 1995a), I synthesize the aspect and narrative approaches and propose how narrative structure may contribute to the spread of perfective morphology to non-prototypical cases.

Analysis

The presentation of the analyses in this section has been simplified where it overlaps with the analysis of the same corpus presented in Chapter 4.

Placement of learners. Learners were grouped according to the percentage of appropriate use of past by divisions of 10% (10–19%, 20–29%, 30–39%, and so on) and were ranked separately for written and oral texts. The first analysis of the narratives scored each verb in a past-time context as "past" or "nonpast" and calculated the number of distinct verb forms for a type score. Direct speech was excluded (see following section). These calculations were used to identify the participants and to place the learners into groups as outlined, balancing as evenly as possible the number of participants and L1 backgrounds in the oral and written groups.

Grounding. The narratives were coded for grounding following published analyses of grounding (Dowty, 1986; Dry, 1981, 1983; Fleischman, 1985; Labov, 1972; Schiffrin, 1981; van Dijk, 1975). Following Dry (1981, 1983) and Dowty's (1986) discussions of sequencing, clauses which moved the narrative time forward were identified as foreground clauses. Determination of grounding was made independently of verbal morphology. Speech was excluded from the analysis, although the verbs which introduce it, if sequenced, were treated as foreground. Excluding quoted speech not only follows established practice for narrative analysis (Dry, 1981, 1983; Labov, 1972; Schiffrin, 1981) but also eliminates a potential external influence on learner production. The only language included in the silent film was the speech of the actors which was presented in the titles. Grounding analysis was performed on all 74 texts by the researcher and a second experienced coder. Interrater reliability on the written narratives was 98.1% (agreement on 1,446/1,474 coding decisions) and on the oral narratives 98.4% (agreement on 1,896/1,927 coding decisions). Disagreements were resolved by discussion.

Verbal morphology. All verbs were coded for verbal morphology (simple past, past progressive, pluperfect, present, present progressive, base, $\emptyset$ + progressive, present perfect, and other less frequently occurring tense-aspect forms). Uninterpretable forms such as *tooks* and *is stole* were coded as "uninterpretable."[5] Verbs which have the same form for past and base were excluded from the sample (e.g., *hit, put, let*; cf. Bardovi-Harlig, 1992c; Silva-Corvalán, 1983). In the written narratives, misspelled verbs such as *cot/caut* for *caught* or regularized past verbs such as *telled* were counted as past as long as the innovation did not result in an extant verb. It should be noted here that, in contrast to the analysis used to group the learners, this analysis is a token analysis. Although a type analysis controls for multiple uses of a single form in a corpus, it does not respect the integrity of the text and thus cannot be used to analyze the structure of narratives.

In the oral narratives, repetition and phonological environment were also taken into account. When a learner repeated a verb exactly, it was counted only once so as not to inflate the number of propositions in the narrative. In cases where the second verb form was not an exact repetition, the ratio of forms was calculated (e.g., in *go* and *went* the past and base each score .5; the total number of verbs is 1.0). Finally, verbs with nonsyllabic past tense followed by homorganic stops (e.g., *walked to/down* and *pulled down/to*) or interdental fricatives (e.g., *walked through / the, entered the*) were excluded from the sample (Bayley, 1994; Wolfram, 1985).

Results: Support for the Discourse Hypothesis

Following the procedure outlined above, 1,318 predicates were coded in the written sample and 1,461 in the oral sample. The distribution of tense-aspect morphology in both the written and oral narratives supports the discourse hypothesis (Figures 5.1 and 5.2). In the written narratives the simple past scores are higher in the foreground than in background for all groups (Table 5.2).[6] Group 50 (i.e., the group with an accuracy rate for the use of past of 50–59%) and those above show robust use of the progressive, but this is restricted to the background. If we understand the

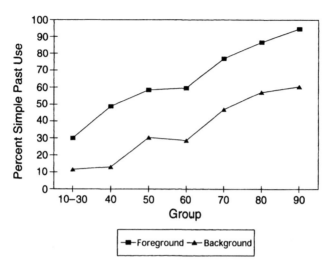

Figure 5.1. The use of simple past by grounding (written narratives). From "Narrative Structure and Lexical Aspect: Conspiring Factors in Second Language Acquisition of Tense-Aspect Morphology," by K. Bardovi-Harlig, 1998, *Studies in Second Language Acquisition, 20,* p. 489. Copyright 1998 by Cambridge University Press. Reprinted with permission.

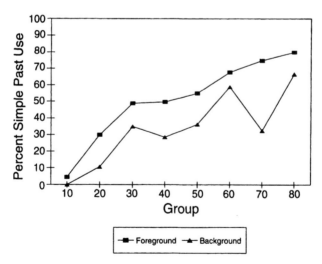

Figure 5.2. The use of simple past by grounding (oral narratives). From "Narrative Structure and Lexical Aspect: Conspiring Factors in Second Language Acquisition of Tense-Aspect Morphology," by K. Bardovi-Harlig, 1998, *Studies in Second Language Acquisition, 20,* p. 489. Copyright 1998 by Cambridge University Press. Reprinted with permission.

Table 5.2

Distribution of Verb Morphology by Grounding in Percent of Verbs
Used (Written Narratives)

Group	Form	Foreground		Background	
		%	(*n*)	%	(*n*)
10 to 30	Past	30	(33)	12	(3)
N=5	Prog	5	(5)	23	(6)
	Pres	3	(3)	4	(1)
	Base	52	(57)	50	(13)
	Other	11	(12)	12	(3)
	Total		(110)		(26)
Group 40	Past	49	(41)	13	(3)
N=3	Prog	1	(1)	4	(1)
	Pres	1	(1)	17	(4)
	Base	44	(37)	52	(12)
	Other	5	(4)	13	(3)
	Total		(84)		(23)
Group 50	Past	59	(55)	30	(7)
N=3	Prog	3	(3)	30	(7)
	Pres	2	(2)	0	(0)
	Base	35	(33)	30	(7)
	Other	1	(1)	9	(2)
	Total		(94)		(23)
Group 60	Past	60	(56)	29	(4)
N=4	Prog	3	(3)	29	(4)
	Pres	0	(0)	0	(0)
	Base	32	(30)	29	(4)
	Other	5	(5)	14	(2)
	Total		(94)		(14)
Group 70	Past	77	(187)	47	(31)
N=9	Prog	3	(7)	29	(19)
	Pres	0	(0)	5	(3)
	Base	17	(40)	15	(10)
	Other	4	(9)	5	(3)
	Total		(243)		(66)

Table 5.2 (continued)

Distribution of Verb Morphology by Grounding in Percent of Verbs Used (Written Narratives)

Group	Form	Foreground %	(n)	Background %	(n)
Group 80	Past	87	(138)	57	(32)
N=7	Prog	4	(7)	27	(15)
	Pres	0	(0)	5	(3)
	Base	8	(12)	9	(5)
	Other	1	(2)	2	(1)
	Total		(159)		(56)
Group 90	Past	95	(122)	61	(26)
N=6	Prog	3	(4)	26	(11)
	Pres	0	(0)	0	(0)
	Base	2	(2)	0	(0)
	Other	1	(1)	14	(6)
	Total		(129)		(43)

Note. Raw scores are given in parentheses. "Prog" includes ∅-progressive, present progressive, and past progressive. From "Narrative Structure and Lexical Aspect: Conspiring Factors in Second Language Acquisition of Tense-Aspect Morphology," by K. Bardovi-Harlig, 1998, *Studies in Second Language Acquisition, 20,* p. 490. Copyright 1998 by Cambridge University Press. Reprinted with permission.

foreground and the background of a narrative as environments in which tense-aspect morphology emerges, we see that the use of simple past emerges first and more strongly in the foreground. Similarly, Table 5.3 shows that the oral narratives also evidence greater use of simple past in the foreground than the background. The use of progressive is restricted to the background.

As an environment for the use of simple past, the background lags behind the foreground. The simple past becomes the dominant tense in the background later than in the foreground, but never reaches the same high level of use because other past-tense forms such as the past progressive and perfect emerge and are used appropriately in the background. (See Bardovi-Harlig, 1995a, for a more detailed discussion.)

Table 5.3

Distribution of Verb Morphology by Grounding in Percent Verbs Used (Oral Narratives)

Group	Form	Foreground		Background	
		%	(*n*)	%	(*n*)
Group 10	Past	5	(1.5)	0	(0)
N=3	Prog	21	(7)	0	(0)
	Pres	8	(2.5)	0	(0)
	Base	52	(17)	0	(0)
	Other	15	(5)	100	(1)
	Total		(33)		(1)
Group 20	Past	30	(43)	11	(5.5)
N=6	Prog	4	(6)	17	(9)
	Pres	4	(6)	8	(4)
	Base	59	(85)	57	(29.5)
	Other	2	(3)	8	(4)
	Total		(143)		(52)
Group 30	Past	48	(69.5)	35	(15)
N=6	Prog	0	(0.5)	14	(6)
	Pres	0	(0)	2	(1)
	Base	48	(69.5)	47	(20)
	Other	4	(5)	2	(1)
	Total		(144.5)		(43)
Group 40	Past	50	(103)	29	(23.5)
N=6	Prog	4	(8)	24	(0)
	Pres	2	(4.5)	4	(3)
	Base	40	(84)	38	(31.5)
	Other	4	(8.5)	5	(4)
	Total		(208)		(82)
Group 50	Past	55	(80.4)	36	(14.7)
N=5	Prog	3	(4)	12	(5)
	Pres	0	(0.5)	0	(0)
	Base	40	(58.6)	49	(19.8)
	Other	2	(3)	3	(1)
	Total		(146.5)		(40.5)

Table 5.3 (continued)

Distribution of Verb Morphology by Grounding in Percent Verbs Used (Oral Narratives)

Group	Form	Foreground %	Foreground (n)	Background %	Background (n)
Group 60	Past	68	(122.7)	59	(33.5)
N=6	Prog	3	(5.5)	18	(10)
	Pres	3	(5.5)	6	(3.5)
	Base	26	(47)	17	(9.5)
	Other	1	(1)	1	(0.5)
	Total		(181.7)		(57)
Group 70	Past	75	(73.3)	32	(11)
N=4	Prog	9	(8.5)	27	(9)
	Pres	0	(0)	18	(6)
	Base	17	(16.2)	21	(7)
	Other	0	(0)	3	(1)
	Total		(98)		(34)
Group 80	Past	80	(8)	67	(4)
N=1	Prog	0	(0)	0	(0)
	Pres	0	(0)	0	(0)
	Base	20	(2)	33	(2)
	Other	0	(0)	0	(0)
	Total		(10)		(6)

Note. Raw scores are given in parentheses. "Prog" includes Ø-progressive, present progressive, and past progressive. From "Narrative Structure and Lexical Aspect: Conspiring Factors in Second Language Acquisition of Tense-Aspect Morphology," by K. Bardovi-Harlig, 1998, *Studies in Second Language Acquisition, 20,* p. 491. Copyright 1998 by Cambridge University Press. Reprinted with permission.

Comparing Theoretical Frameworks

As discussed briefly in Chapter 4, empirical research in SLA has largely treated narrative structure and lexical aspect separately in order to isolate the variables and test their effects. In contrast, temporal semantics has recognized the relation of narrative and lexical aspect for some time (e.g., Dahl, 1984; Dry, 1981, 1983;

Hopper, 1979). Nevertheless, only a few form-oriented interlanguage studies have investigated the distribution of verbal morphology across both lexical aspectual category and grounding (e.g., Housen, 1993, 1994, 1998; Kumpf, 1984b). However, more recently Andersen and Shirai (1994) and Bardovi-Harlig (1998) have emphasized how the two factors interact in second language acquisition. In the title of his 1982 work, Hopper placed tense and aspect "between semantics and pragmatics." The analysis of interlanguage underscores Hopper's observation. In this section the dual influences on tense-aspect morphology are explored.

Chapters 4 and 5 analyzed the corpus of narratives in different frameworks. In Chapter 4, the analysis showed that the distribution of tense-aspect morphology exhibits the patterns predicted by the aspect hypothesis. In Chapter 5 we have seen that the discourse hypothesis also accounts for tense-aspect distribution in narratives. How can apparently competing hypotheses be supported? The answer lies in the fact that although the hypotheses appear to be distinct (one dealing with lexical aspect, the other with narrative structure), both rest on shared features of temporal semantics.[7] This becomes clearer when we consider the temporal criteria for foregrounding which were identified by Reinhart (1984): sequentiality, punctuality, and completeness. Two of the criteria can be related to characteristics of lexical aspectual classes. The criterion of punctuality is the defining feature of achievements, and completeness relates to both achievements and accomplishments (as goal-oriented, telic verbs). Sequentiality—or "narrativity," in Reinhart's terms—is not related to aspectual class directly, but only events which are reported as completed can be sequenced (Dowty, 1986), and what can be sequenced can be foregrounded.

Because of the overlap of features which determine grounding and those which determine lexical aspect, both the aspect hypothesis and the discourse hypothesis can be supported by the same data. However, it is possible to distinguish the hypotheses both theoretically and empirically. In the remainder of this section

I will sketch the means of distinguishing the hypotheses laid out by Bardovi-Harlig (1994a).

Translating the aspect hypothesis and the discourse hypothesis into predictions concerning the distribution of tense-aspect morphology in interlanguage based on acquisitional evidence, we find that the aspect hypothesis predicts that telic (goal-oriented) verbs will carry simple past morphology and the discourse hypothesis predicts that the verbs in the foreground (the main story-line) will carry simple past morphology. When telic verbs (accomplishments and achievements) occur in the foreground, the two hypotheses cannot be distinguished. The use of the simple past in these predicates can be interpreted as support for either hypothesis. Likewise, the hypotheses cannot be distinguished when atelic verbs (states and activities) occur in the background. The lack of simple past-tense inflection can be interpreted as support for either the aspect or the discourse hypothesis.

Predicates 5–7 in (9) give an example of telic verbs in the foreground. Example (9) also contains an example of an atelic verb, an activity, in the background clause "who was trying to help her." The Vendler categories are indicated in square brackets; "NC" indicates that a predicate was not counted (see analysis of verbal morphology). The predicate number of each line is given in the left-hand margin. This shows not only the order of the predicates within the text, but also whether they occurred at the very beginning or the middle of the text.

(9) Written, L1 Arabic

Foreground	*Background*
[5] she *stol* abread [ACH]	
[6] and they *cutch* her [ACH]	
[7] she *met* charlie [ACH]	
	the nice man who *was*
	trying to helpe her [ACT]
[8] when he *said* [ACC]	
"she didn't sleel the bread	
I did that"	

The predictions of the hypotheses do not always coincide, however. Any event that is reported in sequence can be part of the foreground. Thus, atelic verbs can appear in the foreground, as in (10), predicate 12, *he chased her,* and (11), predicate 2, *he ride on the car* and predicate 5, *chaplin follow her.* Similarly, any event which is reported out of sequence to explain, predict, or evaluate, for example, belongs to the background. Consequently, telic verbs may also be found in the background, as in (10) with the verbs *saw* and *stole.* (Note that *saw* and *stole* were simultaneous events in the film, and that they are reported out of sequence in the narrative.)

(10) Oral, L1 Japanese

Foreground	*Background*
[8] Then she, *stole* the bread. [ACH]	
[9] And the- she *ran away,* [ACC]	
[10] and she. . . *hit* the Chaplin. . . [NC]	
I: Mm-hm.	
	S: . . . and uh, different woman *saw* [ACH] the, she *stole* the, uh, bread. . .[ACH]
	I: Mm-hm.
[11] . . . and uh, and *cried,* [ACH]	
[12] and *chased* her, [ACT]	
[13] and the employer *caught* her, [ACH]	
[14] and, but Chaplin *said,* [ACH] "I did it, you know, I . . . stole . . . the breads."	

(11) Written, L1 Korean

Foreground	*Background*
[1] police car *came* to the man [ACC]	

[2] He *ride* on the car [ACT]
[3] He *met* the woman again [ACH]

the woman *was* very sad
[STA]

[4] She *ran away* from the polise
car [ACC]
[5] chaplin *follow* her [ACT]

The hypotheses make different predictions, however, in the following cases: The discourse hypothesis predicts high use of simple past regardless of lexical aspectual class, and the aspect hypothesis predicts low use of simple past in atelic predicates regardless of grounding. Thus, atelic foreground predicates are predicted to have low likelihood of simple past marking by the aspect hypothesis, but high likelihood of past tense use by the discourse hypothesis. Just the reverse is predicted for telic background predicates: They are predicted to show high use of past marking by the aspect hypothesis, but low likelihood by the discourse hypothesis. The test cases, then, are those in which telicity and grounding do *not* coincide. If foreground verbs, regardless of aspectual class, are marked in the simple past tense, and background verbs are not, this will constitute evidence for the discourse hypothesis. If telic verbs, regardless of grounding, are inflected for the simple past while atelic verbs are not, then this will constitute support for the aspect hypothesis.

As Table 5.4 shows, approximately half of the predicates in the sample are achievements. The remaining predicates are almost evenly divided among the categories of statives, activities, and accomplishments. Table 5.4 also shows that the atelic verbs in the foreground are essentially activities. (Compare 150 activities to 12 statives in the written corpus and 127 activities to 23 statives in the oral corpus.)[8] Although Dry (1983) and Hinrichs (1986) convincingly argue that states can occur in the foreground (whereas Reinhart, 1984, argues that they cannot), the fact is that foreground states did not occur frequently in this corpus.

The number of statives includes a large number of tokens of *be.* As discussed in Chapter 4, the copula is a tense carrier, meaning

Table 5.4

Distribution of Verbs by Grounding and Lexical Aspectual Class in Number of Verb Tokens

	# Verbs	STA	ACT	ACC	ACH
		Written			
Total	1,318	226	223	206	663
Background	402	214	73	29	86
Foreground	916	12	150	177	577
		Oral			
Total	1,461	246	235	314	666
Background	482	223	108	47	104
Foreground	979	23	127	267	562

Note. The number of stative verbs includes the uses of *be*. The number of lexical (non-*be*) statives in the written narratives was 72 (63 background, 9 foreground), and in the oral narratives 69 (60 background, 9 foreground). From "Narrative Structure and Lexical Aspect: Conspiring Factors in Second Language Acquisition of Tense-Aspect Morphology," by K. Bardovi-Harlig, 1998, *Studies in Second Language Acquisition, 20,* p. 483. Copyright 1998 by Cambridge University Press. Reprinted with permission.

that it rarely occurs untensed (or in base form) and carries tense morphology earlier than other statives. That is certainly true of these data, where *be* accounts for 75% of all past tense use among the statives in the written sample and 89% in the oral sample. Because the tensing of the copula is not representative of the tense-aspect marking of other statives (see Bardovi-Harlig & Bergström, 1996; Harley & Swain, 1978), *be* has been eliminated from the analysis in subsequent tables. This has the disadvantage of reducing the number of statives in the corpus, and the advantage of allowing the stative patterns to be viewed more clearly.[9]

Empirical Evidence in Support of the Discourse
and Aspect Hypotheses

This section examines the use of tense-aspect morphology with respect to lexical aspectual class and grounding, thus combining the aspect and discourse analyses. In comparing the analyses, recall that the occurrence of different patterns of tense-aspect use within a single lexical aspectual class across narrative categories supports the narrative hypothesis; consistent use of tense-aspect morphology across the grounding distinction supports the aspect hypothesis.

The section is organized by aspectual class. Within each aspectual class, tokens are compared across grounding. The results show that nonpunctual, dynamic predicates show higher use of past inflection in the foreground than in the background, whereas punctual predicates show no difference with respect to grounding. Compared across aspectual categories, both background and foreground predicates show increased use of simple past morphology, moving from the lowest occurrence with activities to accomplishments to the highest use with achievements.

Activities

Beginning with the group scores for the written narratives, Table 5.5 shows that learners use over five times as many past-

Table 5.5

Distribution of Verbal Morphology in Activities by Grounding

Condition	# Verbs	Past		Base		All Prog		Pres		Other	
		%	(n)	%	(n)	%	(n)	%	(n)	%	(n)
Written											
Background	73	10	(7)	14	(10)	67	(49)	1	(1)	8	(6)
Foreground	150	52	(78)	32	(48)	13	(20)	1	(2)	1	(2)
Oral											
Background	108	15	(16)	33	(36)	41	(44)	7	(8)	4	(4)
Foreground	127	20	(25.5)	53	(66.7)	20	(25.5)	5	(6)	3	(3)

Note. Raw scores are given in parentheses. From "Narrative Structure and Lexical Aspect: Conspiring Factors in Second Language Acquisition of Tense-Aspect Morphology," by K. Bardovi-Harlig, 1998, *Studies in Second Language Acquisition, 20,* p. 492. Copyright 1998 by Cambridge University Press. Reprinted with permission.

tense forms in the foreground as in the background. In the oral narratives, where the use of verbal morphology is lower overall, foregrounded activities also show greater past-tense marking than background activities. Moreover, foreground and background activities are differentially inflected for the progressive as well. ("Progressive" includes present progressive, past progressive, and bare progressives.) The progressive is five times more common in the background than in the foreground of the written narratives and twice as common in the oral narratives. Learners recognize the background as the proper environment for the progressive. Verbs that are not inflected for the simple past in the foreground appear almost exclusively in the base form, whereas verbs that are not inflected for the simple past in the background are sometimes inflected for the progressive.

The difference in the rate of inflection is even clearer when we consider the use of the simple past across the groups (Table 5.6). The difference is most striking in the written narratives in Groups 10–70 in which not a single one of the 52 background activities was inflected for the simple past tense, whereas the use of past with activities increases steadily in the foreground (Figure 5.3). Group 80 also shows a noticeable difference (65% past in the foreground and 11% in the background). The gap begins to close in Group 90.

We can conclude that, in the case of activities, simple past is not the only inflection to show differential use across grounding. Activities also show discourse sensitivity in the distribution of base and progressive (Table 5.5).

Accomplishments

Accomplishments show basically the same distribution of simple past as activities, although as Table 5.4 shows, the occurrence of accomplishments favors the foreground. This results in a less well-balanced sample than in the case of activities. Foreground accomplishments show greater use of simple past than background accomplishments, particularly in the written narratives, which contain twice as many simple past inflections, as

Table 5.6

Distribution of Simple Past with Activities by Group

Written

Condition	#Verbs	10–30	40	50	60	70	80	90	Group Mean
Background	73	0 (0/9)	0 (0/6)	0 (0/9)	0 (0/5)	0 (0/23)	11 (1/9)	50 (6/12)	10 (7/73)
Foreground	150	14 (2/14)	41 (7/17)	20 (3/15)	33 (3/9)	56 (25/45)	65 (17/26)	88 (21/24)	52 (78/150)

Oral

Condition	#Verbs	10	20	30	40	50	60	70	80	Group Mean
Background	108	0 (0/1)	4 (1/27)	9 (1/11)	16 (5/31)	29 (2/7)	32 (6/19)	0 (0/11)	100 (1/1)	15 (16/108)
Foreground	127	0 (0/9)	4 (1/25)	25 (4.5/18)	17 (4/24)	18 (2/11)	32 (7/22)	35 (6/17)	100 (1/1)	20 (25.5/127)

Note. Raw scores are given in parentheses. The numerator shows the number of activities inflected for past; the denominator shows the number of activities used. From "Narrative Structure and Lexical Aspect: Conspiring Factors in Second Language Acquisition of Tense-Aspect Morphology," by K. Bardovi-Harlig, 1998, *Studies in Second Language Acquisition, 20*, p. 493. Copyright 1998 by Cambridge University Press. Reprinted with permission.

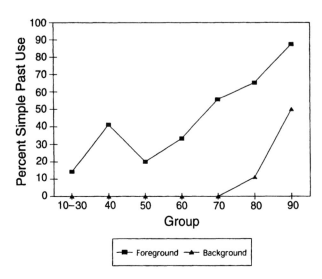

Figure 5.3. The use of simple past with activities by group. From "Narrative Structure and Lexical Aspect: Conspiring Factors in Second Language Acquisition of Tense-Aspect Morphology," by K. Bardovi-Harlig, 1998, *Studies in Second Language Acquisition, 20,* p. 494. Copyright 1998 by Cambridge University Press. Reprinted with permission.

Table 5.7 and Figures 5.4 and 5.5 show. The progressive shows higher use for accomplishments in the background in both written and oral narratives (28% to 4% for written, and 26% to 4% for oral). Learners use the progressive but, as with activities, they use it in the background, not the foreground (Figures 5.6 and 5.7). The pattern of inflection for accomplishments like that for activities reflects sensitivity to grounding. However, the rate of use of past is higher overall for accomplishments than for activities, which also show differential distribution by lexical aspectual category.

It appears, therefore, that for activities and accomplishments, lexical aspectual category is not sufficient to predict use of inflection because both types of predicates are inflected at different rates for different morphemes according to whether they occur in the foreground or the background. Foreground still shows an advantage for simple past tense and background for progressive.

Table 5.7

Distribution of Verbal Morphology in Accomplishments by Grounding

Condition	# Verbs	Past		Base		All Prog		Pres		Other	
		%	(*n*)	%	(*n*)	%	(*n*)	%	(*n*)	%	(*n*)
Written											
Background	29	35	(10)	28	(8)	28	(8)	0	(0)	10	(3)
Foreground	177	70	(124)	25	(44)	4	(6)	1	(2)	1	(1)
Oral											
Background	47	30	(14)	30	(14)	26	(12)	0	(0)	15	(7)
Foreground	267	44	(118)	47	(126)	4	(10)	2	(6)	3	(7)

Note. Raw scores are given in parentheses. From "Narrative Structure and Lexical Aspect: Conspiring Factors in Second Language Acquisition of Tense-Aspect Morphology," by K. Bardovi-Harlig, 1998, *Studies in Second Language Acquisition, 20,* p. 493. Copyright 1998 by Cambridge University Press. Reprinted with permission.

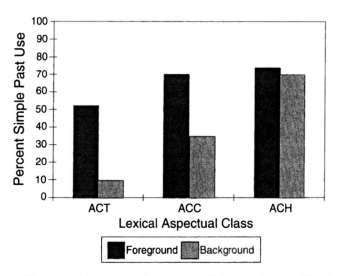

Figure 5.4. The use of simple past by aspectual class and grounding (written narratives). From "Narrative Structure and Lexical Aspect: Conspiring Factors in Second Language Acquisition of Tense-Aspect Morphology," by K. Bardovi-Harlig, 1998, *Studies in Second Language Acquisition, 20,* p. 495. Copyright 1998 by Cambridge University Press. Reprinted with permission.

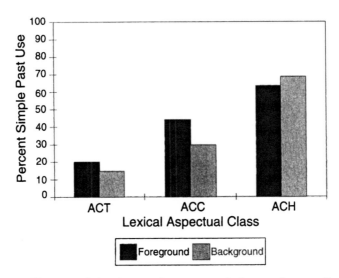

Figure 5.5. The use of simple past by aspectual class and grounding (oral narratives). From "Narrative Structure and Lexical Aspect: Conspiring Factors in Second Language Acquisition of Tense-Aspect Morphology," by K. Bardovi-Harlig, 1998, *Studies in Second Language Acquisition, 20,* p. 495. Copyright 1998 by Cambridge University Press. Reprinted with permission.

Achievements

Achievements show a different pattern from activities and accomplishments. Achievements show remarkably similar rates of inflection for all tense-aspect morphemes in both foreground and background in written and oral narratives (Table 5.8). There is no apparent influence of grounding on achievements in the group scores (Figures 5.6 and 5.7). In fact, considering the use of simple past with achievements cross-sectionally across the groups (as in Table 5.6 for activities) reveals very little evidence for the effect of grounding. As we stated earlier, when a single lexical aspectual class is inflected at the same rate regardless of the grounding, then we can say that the aspect hypothesis shows a better fit with the data than the discourse hypothesis.

I can summarize the results of the preceding analyses as follows: Achievements seem to be inflected for simple past regardless

Table 5.8

Distribution of Verbal Morphology in Achievements by Grounding

Condition	# Verbs	Past		Base		All Prog		Pres		Other	
		%	(n)	%	(n)	%	(n)	%	(n)	%	(n)
Written											
Background	86	70	(60)	14	(12)	5	(4)	0	(0)	12	(10)
Foreground	577	74	(427)	20	(116)	1	(4)	0	(1)	5	(29)
Oral											
Background	103	69	(68)	25	(26)	3	(3)	3	(3)	3	(4)
Foreground	561	64	(356)	32	(178)	1	(4)	1	(7)	3	(18)

Note. Raw scores are given in parentheses. The raw scores are rounded off to the closest whole number. From "Narrative Structure and Lexical Aspect: Conspiring Factors in Second Language Acquisition of Tense-Aspect Morphology," by K. Bardovi-Harlig, 1998, *Studies in Second Language Acquisition, 20,* p. 497. Copyright 1998 by Cambridge University Press. Reprinted with permission.

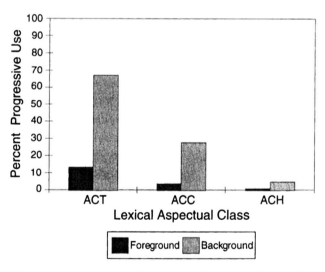

Figure 5.6. The use of progressive by aspectual class and grounding (written narratives). From "Narrative Structure and Lexical Aspect: Conspiring Factors in Second Language Acquisition of Tense-Aspect Morphology," by K. Bardovi-Harlig, 1998, *Studies in Second Language Acquisition, 20,* p. 496. Copyright 1998 by Cambridge University Press. Reprinted with permission.

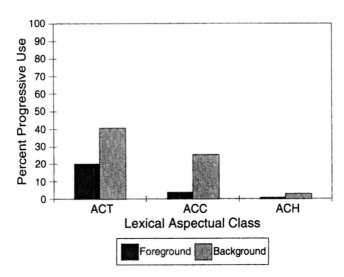

Figure 5.7. The use of progressive by aspectual class and grounding (oral narratives). From "Narrative Structure and Lexical Aspect: Conspiring Factors in Second Language Acquisition of Tense-Aspect Morphology," by K. Bardovi-Harlig, 1998, *Studies in Second Language Acquisition, 20,* p. 496. Copyright 1998 by Cambridge University Press. Reprinted with permission.

of grounding, whereas accomplishments and activities show sensitivity to both grounding and lexical aspect. Although activities and accomplishments show greater past-tense use in the foreground than in the background (sensitivity to discourse), accomplishments show higher use of past than activities (sensitivity to aspectual category). Activities and accomplishments show higher use of pro- gressive in the background than in the foreground (sensitivity to discourse), but activities show greater use of progressive than the other classes do even in the background (sensitivity to aspectual category). Clearly, a description of the distribution of emergent verbal morphology must have recourse to both discourse structure and lexical aspectual category.

Integrating the Analyses

Given the support for both the aspect and the discourse hypotheses in the research literature, it is not entirely surprising that the influence of both aspectual class and narrative structure is so clearly evident in the narratives investigated here. Finding support for both hypotheses in a single corpus suggests that other corpora in the literature would also support both hypotheses; that is, a narrative corpus that provides evidence for the aspect hypothesis would also support the discourse hypothesis, and vice versa.

Using both frameworks of analysis, the data suggest a hierarchy that predicts which verbs in a narrative will be inflected by learners with limited linguistic resources.

- Achievements are the predicates most likely to be inflected for simple past, regardless of grounding.

- Accomplishments are the next most likely type of predicate to carry the simple past. Foreground accomplishments show higher rates of use than background accomplishments.

- Activities are the least likely of all the dynamic verbs to carry simple past, but foreground activities show higher rates of simple past inflection than background activities. Activities also show use of progressive, but this is limited to the background.

What we see here is the influence of both aspectual class and narrative structure. Andersen and Shirai (1994) have identified three principles that determine the affinity of certain tense-aspect morphology for verbs of particular lexical aspectual classes. The *congruence principle* predicts that learners will use tense-aspect morphemes whose meaning is most similar to that of the verb (Andersen, 1993). The *relevance principle* predicts that learners will use morphology which is most relevant to the verb immediately following the verb stem (Bybee, 1985), to which Andersen and Shirai (1994) add that relevant morphology will be acquired first. And finally, learners are also guided by a prototypical meaning for each tense-aspect morpheme and the *one-to-one principle*, which holds that learners expect each new morpheme to have only one meaning and function (Andersen, 1984, 1993). Andersen and Shirai (1994) further observe that

> these principles follow naturally from the speakers' (both learners and nonlearners) need to distinguish reference to the main point/goal of talk from supporting information, within the tradition of research on grounding and the functions of tense-aspect marking in narratives . . .We argue that in ordinary discourse this causes the observed association between past/perfective marking and achievements and accomplishments, progressive marking and activities, and past imperfect marking and states and activities. Achievements and accomplishments typically fill the central role of laying out events in narration and are logical recipients for past/perfective marking. States and activities typically serve supporting roles, and if they receive inflectional marking they tend to be inflected with progressive (for activities) and past imperfectives. (p. 152)

The strong association between aspectual class and discourse function described here by Andersen and Shirai certainly describes this corpus. However, there are also examples of achievements and accomplishments that serve supporting roles (e.g., see (10)) and examples of activities that serve the central role of laying out events (e.g., see (11)). Furthermore, the comparison of foreground and background usage within each of these aspectual classes shows differential use of past, a differential use that cannot be explained by the overlap of aspectual class and narrative structure. To interpret these cases, we return to the features that have been posited for the aspectual classes, the prototypical meaning of the past, and the temporal criteria for grounding.

The prototypical features of the past are [+past], [+telic], [+punctual], and [+result] (Shirai & Andersen, 1995).[10] The lexical aspectual classes are also defined by three features: achievements [+punctual, +telic, +dynamic], accomplishments [−punctual, +telic, +dynamic], activities [−punctual, −telic, +dynamic], and states [−punctual, −telic, −dynamic]. By the relevance principle and the congruence principle, the simple past is attracted to achievements with which it shares the most features (i.e., telic, punctual, and result). The match is somewhat less good between the past accomplishments which are not punctual, and still less between the past and activities, which have no result state because they are atelic. So far, that accords with the interpretation of the aspect hypothesis.

In addition, there are three temporal criteria for the foreground identified by Reinhart (1984) which echo the semantic features that define lexical aspect and prototype past: punctuality, completeness, and sequentiality. When the predicates are used communicatively, specifically in the service of building a narrative, the interaction of features becomes ·more complex because the foreground has its own temporal characteristics; that is, the inherent aspectual features of the predicates interact with the requirements of the grounding. Foreground actions are presented and interpreted as though they were punctual, complete, and necessarily sequential. Thus, by virtue of the fact that it occurs in the foreground, even an activity whose inherent aspectual features are [–punctual, –telic] takes on—as a foreground predicate—the features of punctuality and completeness, thus attracting the simple past. Background activities which are [–punctual, –result] by virtue of their inherent aspect and [–punctual, –complete, –sequential] by virtue of their discourse function do not readily attract the simple past. In contrast, background activities regularly attract the progressive, in keeping with both their inherent aspectual features and their discourse function. Accomplishments in the background, with the overlay of narrative features, also attract the progressive.

Using verbs to construct discourse may be one way in which learners come to expand their interlanguage prototypes and move toward the point-of-view use of tense-aspect which characterizes a native speaker's potential for creative use (what Andersen, 1994, called the native speaker's "advantage"). In cases where achievements and accomplishments are in the foreground, learners can use their prototypical sense of past to assign tense-aspect morphology, but when learners foreground activities, they may be gently nudged into marking activities with the past by the universal pressure to distinguish the foreground from the background. Once a learner's interlanguage accommodates foreground activities with simple past, this may lead to other uses of past activities; similarly, progressive background accomplishments may open the way for other uses of accomplishments in the progressive. This proposed path for expansion is, of course, speculative, and merits further investigation. '

The investigation of states faces two main challenges. First, even given a theory of narrative which allows stative foreground verbs, production of states is essentially limited to the background. So few states occurred in the foreground (35, compared to 437 in the background) that the influence of grounding cannot be tested in the present corpus. Second, states are dominated by the copula. Of the 472 states produced in the combined oral and written corpus, 324 (or 69%) were tokens of *be*. Because the copula is a tense carrier, use of past with *be* cannot be considered representative of tense-aspect use with states. Of the 324 occurrences of *be*, all but one (323) were unambiguously tensed. The productive lexical stative vocabularies of learners also seem to be rather restricted (Bardovi-Harlig & Bergström, 1996; Harley & Swain, 1978), and this further limits our ability to observe how learners mark lexical states. This predominance of *be* has been observed in the interlanguage of other learners as well (e.g., Kumpf, 1984b), and may account for unexpectedly high rates of past-tense use with states, as well as high rates of past in the background, when *be* is not treated separately from lexical statives.

The overextension of progressive to states reported by Andersen and Shirai (1996) for L2 learners (e.g., by Robison, 1990) was observed neither in this corpus nor in the corpus elicited by cloze passages reported by Bardovi-Harlig and Reynolds (1995). This is not particularly worrisome because the nonuse of progressive with states fits the predictions of the aspect hypothesis, and also mirrors the acquisitional patterns of children learning English as a second language (Andersen & Shirai, 1996). However, the lack of agreement from one corpus to another is somewhat puzzling. One possibility is that instruction has influenced the learners who participated in this study as well as the learners studied by Bardovi-Harlig and Reynolds. However, because instruction is unlikely to circumvent stages in an acquisitional sequence (Bardovi-Harlig, 1995b, 1997b; Ellis, 1994; Pienemann, 1989, 1998; and others), I suggest that the tasks themselves may be responsible for the different patterns of use of the progressive. The corpora that show no extension of the progressive to states are elicited and do not draw on a speaker's personal experience in the same way that a personal narrative might. More specifically, in narratives elicited by means of a film retell, learners have little opportunity or need to report habitual (background) activities or states. Such a lack may obviate the learners' perceived need to use the pro- gressive with states to convey such information. The factors of text type and instruction can be tested further with respect to the nonuse of progressive with states.

The results of these studies lead us to conclude that lexical aspect and narrative structure conspire to shape the distribution of tense-aspect morphology in interlanguage. Whereas the basic semantic features of predicates attract verbal morphology with the same features, in actual production these inflected predicates are pressed into the service of communication and may take on features appropriate to the narrative structure, thus going beyond the most basic predicate-level pairing of verbal and morphological features. The understanding that interlanguage temporal systems are shaped by both the semantics of lexical aspect and the pragmatics of discourse provides a point of departure for future research.

Other Discourse Contexts

As we have seen in this chapter, studies of the effect of discourse structure on the distribution of interlanguage verbal morphology have thus far been studies of narrative structure. The reason for this is that, as Bardovi-Harlig (1994a) pointed out, a grounding analysis as presented in narrative theory can only be carried out on narrative texts, or narrative portions of texts. Very few individual studies have investigated a range of texts within a single inquiry in the investigation of temporality, the obvious advantage of narratives for the study of tense and aspect being the presumption of chronological order. In addition, there has been a strong tradition of investigation of the narrative in theoretical linguistics and discourse analysis, resulting in comparable analyses of native-speaker narratives (e.g., Chafe, 1980; Hopper, 1979; Labov, 1972; Schiffrin, 1981).

Within interlanguage narrative study, the function of the background and its expression, and their relation to or influence on tense-aspect use, merit further investigation. The diversity of functions in the background (e.g., explaining, interpreting, evaluating, and predicting) make narrative background much more like other text types because the background lacks the sequentiality which characterizes the foreground. However, the difference between narrative and nonnarrative texts may not represent the analytic dichotomy it appears to at first sight.

Von Stutterheim and Klein (1989) locate narrative structure (and grounding) in a more general approach to main structures and side structures. In a narrative, the foreground answers the question "What happened next?" with unbounded states, habituals, and generics excluded. In contrast, in a description, specific temporal reference is normally excluded, and temporal location on the time axis leads to side structures, "exactly the reverse picture" from that of the narrative (von Stutterheim, 1991, p. 391). What links inquiry into different discourse types, with studies of L2 tense and aspect, is the observation that the dominant temporal relation is determined by the discourse type (von Stutterheim, 1991). Von Stutterheim reports that learners of German are able to negotiate both discourse types by essentially the same means: reliance on the discourse type and the inherent temporal properties of the utterances. In narratives temporal reference is moved forward by bounded events, whereas in descriptions unbounded states imply the maintenance of the temporal frame. Very low-level learners may rely solely on discourse type and temporal adverbials in the absence of verbal morphology, regardless of text type. In descriptive texts, learners of German who have gone beyond the adverbial stage seem to develop a nontargetlike marker of unboundedness, a form of *sein* "be" + infinitive such as *lernen ich bin 5 jahre* "learn I am five years" and *ich bin Deutschland arbeiten,* "I am Germany work." In contrast, in narratives, learners mark boundedness by using the participle as a perfective marker in opposition to the infinitive or present which express unbounded events (e.g., ∅ + *gekommen* "come," a past participle, is bounded, but *kommen* "come," an infinitive, is unbounded; von Stutterheim, 1991, p. 396). Thus, regardless of discourse type, learners use the limited linguistic means at their disposal to distinguish the main structure from side structures.

Noyau (1984, 1990) discussed differences among narrative types. The differences among narrative types may influence the production of tense-aspect morphology. Types of narratives can be divided into impersonal narratives and personal narratives (Noyau, 1984, 1990). Impersonal narratives are fictional and include well-known examples such as the *Pear Stories* elicited by film retell tasks (Chafe, 1980) and "Frog, where are you?" elicited by picture book retells (Bamberg & Marchman, 1990). Personal narratives are told from a speaker's own life experiences; examples include the harassment stories collected by Tannen (1989) and the danger of death stories collected by Labov (1972; Labov & Waletzky, 1967). Noyau argued that personal narratives offer less of a structure than fictional or retell narratives and thus offer greater potential for observing how the learner manages temporal reference outside the bounds of an essentially chronological structure.

According to Noyau (1984, 1990), although a film retell task elicits a narrative that requires the expression of sequences of events, it does not require reference to anterior or future events and thus will yield texts that lack the rich structure of personal narratives, elicited through conversation, in which a speaker may speak of past events, future plans, anterior events, or current states. In support of this argument, Liskin-Gasparro (1997) found that prompted personal narratives of advanced learners of Spanish yielded more background than impersonal narratives. Giacalone Ramat and Banfi (1990) found that learners of Italian used different rates of verb forms in interviews related to personal topics and those related to impersonal topics such as descriptions of illustrated stories, a fairy tale, and retelling a short film. Although film and story retell tasks can elicit rich background (see Bardovi- Harlig 1992b, 1995a), especially with visually rich animation (Lafford, 1996), learners can certainly comply with a researcher's request to "tell what happened" by relating the foreground alone. In any retell task, however, there may be pressure that leads learners to sacrifice background for foreground (Tomlin, 1984). In addition, personal narratives may inherently offer more opportunities for background. Although elicited impersonal narratives show more foreground clauses than background clauses by learners, native speaker personal narratives show greater backgrounding than foregrounding (Schiffrin, 1981), as do personal narratives by learners (Comajoan, 1998; Liskin-Gasparro, 1997; Trévise, 1987). More importantly, Noyau (1984) claims that "the motivation of the speaker for sharing his own experience gives maximal expression of his repertoire" (p. 115). In fact, Trévise (1987) notes that one narrator's explanation in the narrative about how he escaped from Argentina is so important to both the narrator and narrative that it seems hardly less significant than the action. (Of course, the concept of narrative background should not carry the popular and nontechnical notion of being less important informationally; it is simply not chronologically ordered.)

Initial investigations into the variables of text-type and text-structure suggest that there are at least two ways to expand the inquiry into discourse structure, the first being to include nonnarrative texts and the second to include more varied narratives, in terms both of the narrator's relation to the text and of types of texts that allow more backgrounding. Both expansions would allow for the investigation of more varied tense-aspect use. Although I believe that examining grounding in interlanguage descriptive texts following von Stutterheim and Klein (1989) is very promising, I know of no work that has been carried out in that area to date. The examination of such texts should provide a context for the emergence and spread of imperfectives, a process that has not yet been documented to the extent that the acquisition of the perfective past has.

In the following section I investigate three areas of potential inquiry in which there is preliminary work to show what form it might take and to encourage others to go beyond what has been investigated into new areas. For research purposes it is possible to expand types of narratives to include a broader range of expressions, and/or to manipulate the narrative task to induce (desirable) features of personal narratives in more controlled fictional narrative tasks. I present three cases based on Bardovi-Harlig (1999a): a qualitative and quantitative analysis of irrealis text, a qualitative analysis of fictional narratives manipulated to increase the features found in personal narratives, and a quantitative analysis of the difference in fictional and personal narratives.

Realis and Irrealis: The Imaginary in Narrative

This section discusses learners' expression of realis and irrealis. Realis refers to situations that have actually taken place or are actually taking place, whereas irrealis refers to hypothetical situations, including inductive generalizations and future (Comrie, 1985). In a typical narrative of the type we have been discussing in this chapter, the foreground consists of actions that would be represented by realis verbal morphology and lexical expressions. Not all background is hypothetical, naturally, but if a narrative has a portion expressed in irrealis, it would most likely occur in the background. The 8-minute excerpt of *Modern Times* that has been used to elicit narratives includes a dream sequence in which a homeless Charlie and his romantic lead indulge in a daydream about owning a home. In this episode, the poverty of the protagonists is contrasted with the way their lives might be in suburbia; a cute little house provides the backdrop for a scene in which the conveniences of the middle class are exaggerated. This dream sequence provides an excellent opportunity to investigate how learners mark irrealis in narrative compared to their marking of the realis foreground material.

In the film excerpt, the dream sequence is introduced by the title "Can you imagine us in a little home like that?" Although the dream sequence follows the depiction of an episode involving an escape and is therefore ordered linearly in the film, it cannot be interpreted as being on the same time axis as the main narrative— a requirement of foregrounding—because, as Dry (1983) states, "foreground events are presented as actually occurring in the narrative world, as opposed to being merely talked of, expected, or hypothesized" (p. 21), and the time-line here is interrupted by the title "Can you imagine us . . .?"

Of the 37 learners in the cross-sectional study, each of whom produced an oral and written narrative, approximately half of the narratives (18 written narratives and 18 oral narratives) devote one or more finite background clauses to the dream sequence, with 11 written and 9 oral narratives elaborating the imagined scene in three or more clauses (Bardovi-Harlig, 1995a). In contrast to the isolated background clauses, which are interspersed throughout the narrative, the dream sequence presents an extended portion of background text. In general, the use of nonpast in the dream sequence is higher than in the background as a whole for all the learners' written narratives: 52% use of nonpast in the dream sequence contrasts with only 28% use of nonpast in the background as a whole (excluding the dream sequence). The oral narratives show approximately the same use in the dream (49%) as in the background overall (44%).[11]

Some learners distinguish the dream episode chiefly by tense, as in (12). The writer of (12) shows 88% use of past in the background (exclusive of the dream)—reflecting a high level of control of the past—but used nonpast exclusively in the dream. Predicates [14] and [15] provide foreground: [14] They *sat down* green grass [15] and *saw* a family. He continues with background which is part of the realis narration: "They *seemed* to very happy happy. chaplin and the woman *envied* the family." Up to this point in the excerpt the learner has used the simple past, not only for foreground, but also for background. One more narrative clause in [16] introduces the dream sequence and provides a boundary between narration and imagination: [16] and *imagined* future of them. In the dream sequence—which was set off in parentheses by the learner—the learner uses only nonpast forms: "chaplin *is* the woman's husbund" and so on. Line [17] returns the narrative to the realis with the foreground clause: [17] the polise man *came*.

(12) Written 80, Learner 30, L1 Spanish

Foreground	Background
[14] They *sat down* green grass	
[15] and *saw* a family	
	They *seemed* to very happy happy. chaplin and the woman *envied* the family
[16] and *imagined* future of them	
	(chaplin *is* the woman's husbund. It *is* deal. There *are* many food in their home. They *look* like very happy.)
[17] but the polise man *came*.	

Learners mark the dream sequence in other ways as well. For proficient learners, a change in tense (especially to base or present) may be unsatisfactory because the sequence, although imagined, was completed in the film. This raises a conflict between using tense to mark the sequence to distinguish it from the foreground—or even the rest of the background—which suggests the use of nonpast, and reporting the fact that the dream sequence has ended, which suggests the use of the past. For a less proficient learner who only rarely marks tense, a tense contrast cannot be implemented. In (13), a learner delimits the dream sequence from the rest of the narrative by explicitly marking the beginning, *they are to daydream,* and the end, *they wake up.* In the ensuing dream sequence the learner employs seven verbs: five nonpast, one past, and one ambiguous form. (Backchannels have been deleted; [xxxx] indicates an uninterpretable word.)

(13) Oral 40, Learner 11, L1 Arabic

Foreground	*Background*
Then they *are* to daydream,	
	Where he *lives* in this, type of house, beautiful house. And, she *cook* for him . . . The wife *is coming* back from his job. [laughs] [xxxx] The- the girl *put* in the- dinner of rice . . . [xxxxxxx] So, he *took* the, [xxxx], food . . . Then he *call* the cow, to, to squeeze milk, he *get* the milk from. . . . [xxxx]
And they *wake* up from their dream-	

As in (13), 11 out of 18 of the written narratives and 11 out of 18 of the oral narratives explicitly mark the boundaries of the dream at the beginning and the end. The explicit boundary markers occur at all levels, as (14)–(17) show. As was discussed in Chapter 2, the explicit boundary markers are lexical. The boundary markers employed by the learner in (14), which are centered around the lexical *dream,* are rather simple compared to those used by the learner in (16) where the lexical markers are inflected verbs, *imagined* and *realized.* (The number in parentheses is the number of intervening verbs.)

(14) the beginning to dream (2 verbs)
      after the dream [Oral 20, Learner 12, L1 Spanish]

(15) And chaplin saw the little house life (6 verbs)
      they imagined this . . . [Oral 60, Learner 32, L1 Japanese]

(16) they just imagined to live there (2 verbs)

when they realized [Written 90, Learner 35, L1 Korean]

(17) talked to each other about their dream (5 verbs)
However, their happy time did not went so long time
[Written 90, Learner 36, L1 Japanese]

Distinguishing the dream sequence from the rest of the narrative seems to be particularly important when the account of the dream itself contains a narrative sequence. In (18), the learner offers a lengthy account of the dream, using 17 verbs, which is bounded at the beginning with *in the imagine* and at the end with *the imagine over.* In fact, just before the first clause of the embedded foreground clause *he came* (predicate 3), the storyteller cautions the listener a second time that the upcoming sequence is *in imagine.* (Asterisks indicate phonological environments that are excluded from analysis following Bayley, 1994, and Wolfram, 1985.)

(18) Oral 10, Learner 26, L1 Japanese
Um . . . they were in the, in the imagine
[1] the, the, uh, they having, uh . . . they *are having* good time, in the house. [I: Mm-hm.]
[2] They *were doing-* They [laughs] [xxxxxxx] something. Uh, yeah. Uh . . .
[3] and . . . it's in — imagine. He *came,* to- came in the house, and he- he-
[4] *tried* to hug her, but he — how do you say — he . . . [I: Uh, tripped?]
[5] He *tripped* . . . [I: Mm-hm.]
[6] . . . and uh, whoah . . . I think there *was,* dinner time — yeah. And, h-
[7] Chaplin, *pick* — orange? — was some fruit. [I: Mm-hm.]
[8] And, he *was* . . . *eating,* fruit.
[9] And, I think he *didn't* like it.
[10] He *kick* the, orange, outside, yeah. And . . . in the kitchen, uh, they have,

[11] they are h- they are having, they *were having* — dinner, at there, and

[12] uh, Chaplin *realiz-ed* there is no milk . . . [I: Mm-hm.]

[13] And, uh, he **call* the cow. And uh, the cow — I can't ex-
plain, oh. . . .
Um. . . . Anyway, uh . . . uh . . . mm. . . . [laughs] [I:
What did the cow do?]

[14] Uh, well, I am trying to say: Chaplin, uh, *received* milk
. . . [I: Mm-hm.]

[15] . . . from the cow. And, uh, milk was . . . fr- . . . milk *was
fall* in the — glass or something? [I: Mm-hm.] Pot?
[I: In the pitcher.]

[16] And . . . and . . . then, they *are eating* same steak, same
time . . . [I: Mm-hm.]

[17] They *are cutting* their meat.
Seems like, I think that the, imagine over.

Unlike the narrative in (12), in which the learner delimits
the dream by use of nonpast (i.e., present and base), the narrative
in (18) does not use tense alone to mark the sequence. In fact, the
learner shows no use of simple present and only one instance of a
base form; instead, she apparently uses aspect. She shows 46%
use of progressive, more than double her use of progressive elsewhere in the background, at 19% of background verbs. The use of
progressive in the dream is split between past progressive and
present progressive (19% and 27% of all background verbs, respectively). Present progressive occurs nowhere else in the background. Thus, the dream sequence is set off by two markers, high
use of progressive and explicit boundary markers.

At this point, I summarize what can be learned by examining
irrealis text.

• Tense does not spread to all environments. Realis, or deictic,
past—even in fictional narration—appears before irrealis
past. (This is consistent with Andersen & Shirai's acquisitional
sequence, 1996, p. 557, in which the deictic past precedes all
other uses of past.)

- The lexical-before-morphological stage (Dietrich et al., 1995) holds in all areas of verbal morphology and repeats itself as new morphology emerges. That is to say, learners do not "finish" the lexical stage and go to the morphological stage once and for all. Learners may use verbal morphology for other, deictic functions, but use lexical boundaries like "dream" and "wake up" in the background to mark off irrealis sequences.

- Contrast may be one means used by learners to mark verbs in different environments, even if the contrast is not targetlike. Learners who show modest use of base or present in the background for description or evaluation may show increased use of base, present, or even progressive in irrealis sequences.

The third observation leads to a question for further research: Is contrast in interlanguage verbal forms a precursor to using contrast in target verbal forms?

Personal and Impersonal Narratives: The Case of "Personalized" Narratives

As previously discussed, personal narratives may offer more opportunities for background than impersonal narratives. How can the claims about personal narratives be tested while holding content constant? One way to control content is to have learners retell a film narrative both as an impersonal narrator and as a character in the film. The narrative collection project which included the *Modern Times* narratives used six different silent films and wordless film excerpts (Bardovi-Harlig, 1993). One was a computer-animated film, *Tin Toy*. In *Tin Toy*, a baby terrorizes his toys by picking them up, chewing on them, drooling on them, and then smashing them down on the floor. Only the tin toy, a mechanical one-man band, dares to offer himself to the baby to play with.

After ESL learners viewed the film, they were asked first to retell the story. These instructions produced neutral narrations, or third person, "impersonal" narratives. Next, the learners were asked to take the part of one of the protagonists, the heroic mechanical toy and/or the toy-smashing baby. This turned out to be a conceptually difficult task which some participants declined to do. Because of this, the task needs to be modified in some way, most likely by making sure that the protagonists are higher up on the animacy hierarchy (Hill, 1988; Silverstein, 1976) than babies or toys. (Some of the participants told us that babies cannot talk or think.)[12] In spite of the problems with the task, those who did it seemed to have fun with it and, more importantly, they showed noticeable increases in backgrounding in the first person narratives over the third person narratives. In this section, I compare the narratives of two learners, one L1 Arabic learner (Saleh) and one L1 Spanish learner (Carlos) both of whom were in Level 5 of a six-level intensive English program at the time of the elicitation.[13] In (20) and (21), notice that Saleh provides background information which was absent relative to the same reported foreground action in the impersonal narration in (19).

(19) Saleh, L1 Arabic, Impersonal Narration

Foreground	*Background*
[5] the musician man run away from the baby.	
[6] And, uh . . . the, the baby was . . . uh, running after the musician man,	
[7] till the . . . the musician man hide uh, under the couch or something.	
	And there's all of the toys who were /hide/, hiding from the baby
[8] And after that the baby fell down	
[9] and he started to cry. /Nnn/ . . .	
[10] After that the musician. . . .	

Excerpt (20) exhibits the same propositions in foreground clauses [5] and [6], but after predicate 6 the learner adds his feelings about catching the tin toy. Following line 7 he expands on why the toys are hiding, and he reports on what the toys are thinking following predicate 9. In contrast, in the neutral narrative in (19), the learner reports only that the toys were hiding.

(20) Saleh as the Baby

Foreground	*Background*
[5] The musician man just run away from me	
[6] and I follow [him?].	
	And I was so happy. And I was eager to catch it.
[7] Uh, then he just uh, he just hide from me with the . . . other toys	
	which they were, they, they were afraid of me.
[8] And uh, I fall [fell?] down, eh,	
[9] then I started to cry.	
	I was crying, and all of the toys [surprised?]: What's happening?
[10] There is a musician man get out . . .	

In (21) we hear the voice of the Tin Toy who feels sorry for the baby (compare this to predicate [9] in (19) and (20)).

(21) Saleh as the Tin Toy

Foreground	*Background*
[17] and he, he was crying, started to cry.	
	Uh, then uh, his voice was very loud, and I just felt sorry for him

In (22)–(23) we compare the introduction of the baby across narratives. In the narration by the Tin Toy in (23), we are told that the baby is noisy. The loudness of the baby is part of what frightens the toy; thus, we see how the learner personalizes the perspective of this narrator.

(22) Saleh, Impersonal Narration
    [1]   And eh, eh . . . he came to the room
    [2]   and he got play with the toys.

(23) Saleh as the Tin Toy

Foreground	Background
[8] and there is little baby comes.	
	He is noisy.
He came to the . . . to the room,	
[9] and he saw the rings	

    The second learner, Carlos, has rich background throughout his narrations. However, as the neutral narrator, Carlos makes no evaluations in the background. In contrast, evaluations are relatively frequent when the narratives are told in the first person, as we see in (24). (In (24) some of the foreground clauses have been omitted to conserve space.)

(24) Carlos, L1 Spanish, as Tin Toy

Foreground	Background
[3] Wow, he *has already throw* it away. He throw it. He have it throw the toy- those toys.	
	Oh my gosh! It is horrible! But I can't- when uh, it's impossible.
[8] That's uh, that's uh, that baby's walking now	

It is wonderful! He's
walking! Oh, ah!

[12] He- uh, my master *has*
started to cry.

Oh no. This is bad.

[14] Ah, he *has* uh, he *has* uh,
took me- *took* me.

Oh no! Madness, that is
madness!

Carlos not only elaborates the background in the first-person narratives, he changes the time orientation compared to the neutral narration. Carlos has a past-time orientation in his neutral narration (using past and base forms in the foreground and the background). In the first-person narratives, he has a present orientation using present, base, present perfect, and future. In the baby and tin toy narratives, the characters narrate their escapades by talking to themselves, as in (25).

(25) Carlos as the baby
    [5] Ah. Let's run- let's run, no, let's /wo . ./.
    [6] Let's walk.
   [13] Let's move it.

Unlike the impersonal narrative, the first-person narratives also exhibit use of the present progressive and present perfect in the foreground as in (26).

(26) Carlos as Tin Toy
    [7] Ah, but let's take the area under the bed.
    [8] That's uh, that's uh, that baby's walking now
    [9] I *have reach* it. I *have reach* it bed.
  [10] Let's take a breath now
  [11] let's rest and put uh, myself down.
  [12] He- uh, my master *has started* to cry.
  [13] Let's- let's play my- my instruments. [back: Oh no! My goodness!]

[14] Ah, he *has* uh, he *has* uh, *took* me- *took* me. [back: Oh no!]

[15] He *have already throw* me away!

[16] Well, now- I am flying now [back: but I will /fil/- I will fall down.]

In these personalized narratives, we see learners doing what Noyau (1984, 1990) claims that they will do (only) in personal narratives: they look ahead, interpret, evaluate, and give reasons. In addition, in Carlos's narratives we see a range of tense-aspect forms not seen in the impersonal narratives.

We should note that these first-person narratives are not true *personal* narratives, but rather *personalized* narratives. On the other hand, the task retains the advantages of comparability across speakers that is one of the advantages of film retell tasks. The greatest disadvantage of this task is that not every learner was able to narrate from the point of view of another character. The advantages of using the personalized narrative task are that learners who were able to do the task used extended elaborated background compared to the neutral narrator condition. The use of the neutral and personalized narrations provided comparability of story-line across learners and conditions; it also provided the opportunity to observe the use of additional tense-aspect morphology, which, if not the maximal expression of learners' repertoires, was certainly a fuller expression of their repertoires.

Conversational and Elicited Narratives

In the previous section we distinguished between personalized and impersonal narratives collected under experimental conditions. However, elicited narratives and personal narratives are likely to differ by more than one feature. Personal conversational narratives differ from impersonal narratives not only along the dimension of personal and impersonal, but also along the dimension of conversation and monologue. The presence or absence of an active interlocutor converts monologic production into cooperative discourse construction. In this section I compare the quantitative differences between impersonal narratives and personal narratives excerpted from conversational interviews.

These narratives were produced by Daniel, a native speaker of English and an advanced learner of Spanish learning Catalan as a foreign language (Comajoan, 1998). During the course of an academic year, Comajoan elicited and analyzed eight narratives and conducted eight conversational interviews from which the personal narratives were excerpted. He employed two narrative tasks. One was the telling of the story of St. George and the Dragon, which was told to the learner once in Catalan and prompted by the use of illustrations from a picture story book from which all writing was removed. The second task was the retell of the excerpt from *Modern Times*. The narratives were elicited in cycles throughout the year, similar to the ESF study format of repeating tasks within elicitation cycles (Dietrich et al., 1995), although these cycles were shorter. This resulted in four St. George retells and four *Modern Times* retells. These are combined under "Retell Narratives" in Table 5.9. All the conversational narratives are combined as "Conversational Narratives."

Consistent with the impersonal retell data from other studies (Bardovi-Harlig, 1992b, 1995a), the combined retells yield one and a half times more finite foreground clauses than background

Table 5.9

Comparison of Tense-Aspect Inflections in Conversational and Retell Narratives by an Adult Learner of Catalan

| | Conversational Narratives | | | | Retell Narratives | | | |
| | Foreground | | Background | | Foreground | | Background | |
Inflection	%	(n)	%	(n)	%	(n)	%	(n)
Preterite	55	(123)	8	(31)	33	(71)	8	(11)
Imperfect	14	(31)	57	(216)	3	(6)	23	(34)
Base/Present	27	(61)	35	(131)	64	(134)	67	(97)
Pres Perfect	4	(9)	0	(0)	0	(0)	2	(3)
TOTAL	100	(224)	100	(378)	100	(221)	100	(145)

Note. Table based on Tables 10 and 11 of Comajoan (1998).

clauses. In contrast, in the narrative excerpts from the conversational interviews, there are more than one and a half times more finite background clauses than finite foreground clauses. This is consistent with what Schiffrin (1981) reported for (native speaker) personal narratives and what Trévise (1987) found for L2 personal narratives.

Daniel shows greater use of preterite in the foreground of both personal and impersonal narratives and greater use of imperfect in the background of both personal and impersonal narratives. However, the narratives are distinguished by the rates of past use: As shown in Table 5.9, the rates of use of both preterite and imperfect are higher for the conversational narratives, and the difference between the rate of use between foreground and background is also greater in the conversational narratives. Similarly, Giacalone Ramat and Banfi (1990) report different rates of use of verb forms in interviews related to personal experience and non-personal contributions such as descriptions of illustrated stories, a fairy tale, and retelling a short film.

This higher rate of morphology is consistent with Noyau's (1984) observation that the personal narrative offers less inherent structure than fictional narratives and as a result offers greater potential for observing how the learner manages temporal reference. However, in this case, the situation is complicated by the conversational context. The personal narratives in Comajoan's (1998) data differ from the impersonal narratives in two ways: the personal-impersonal dimension and the interactional dimension. The claim that the conversational narratives have less predictable structure—what Noyau calls "less inherent structure"—becomes clearer when we consider that, as Comajoan points out, the conversational narratives, in contrast to the retells, are not monologic.

In Comajoan's (1998) study the interlocutor participates in the conversation with Daniel, often asking questions and taking turns. Thus, we see that the conditions under which the narratives are told are not identical, which serves to further support Noyau's claim. In conversation, the effects of scaffolding (the learner's dependence on the interlocutor to set the scene and provide the morphology) often decreases a learner's use of verbal morphology, as we saw in Chapter 2. On the other hand, the opportunity for imitation (the learner's repetition of forms provided by the interlocutor) may increase a learner's use of verbal morphology (Bardovi-Harlig, 1997b). Thus, in conversation the interviewer contributes to the discourse, not only by adding his or her own turns, but by making the structure less predictable. Because dyadic conversation has a less predictable discourse-temporal structure than of the monologic narrative, verbal morphology assumes a greater burden for making temporal reference, which is evident in the greater use of past-tense morphology.

Although Comajoan's (1998) comparison of fictional retell and conversational narrative rests on 16 texts, it still describes only one learner (and one interlocutor) and should be regarded only as a case study. However, this analysis of the data shows that retells and conversational narratives differ by not one, but two, discourse-based features, and that both must be taken into account.[14]

This section has shown the importance of text structure, relationship of the narrator to the text, and interaction with other interlocutors. We see that interactional features identified by the meaning-oriented studies figure importantly in any text analysis. Although the more advanced learners are not wholly dependent on their interlocutors for scaffolding or on chronological order to convey temporality, these elements continue to figure prominently in discussion of narratives by any speaker.

Chapter Summary

This chapter has demonstrated that discourse is a central influence on the distribution of tense-aspect morphology. Narrative analysis is particularly well developed in the theoretical literature and second language acquisition studies, and its application to interlanguage narratives reveals the role that narrative structure plays in the distribution of tense-aspect morphology in second language acquisition. The influence of lexical aspect interacts with narrative structure, suggesting that the investigation of either one alone provides only a partial picture of interlanguage tense-aspect use. Although the narrative has been the dominant text type in second language acquisition studies of tense-aspect distribution, this chapter has also suggested that an expansion of discourse types to more broadly include nonnarrative texts will provide additional test cases for both the aspect and discourse hypotheses that can only strengthen our understanding of tense-aspect morphology in second language acquisition.

In conclusion, only some studies that derive their data from narratives have fully recognized the role of discourse in L2 tense-aspect use. In order to move the investigation of interlanguage temporality ahead, it is time to take explicit account of the role of text type in L2 tense-aspect distribution. The pursuit of understanding the relation of tense-aspect distribution to discourse structure—in conjunction with other analyses—is an important avenue of research whose value has only been touched on in narrative analysis. Future work must recognize that every analysis of interlanguage use is, or should be, simultaneously an analysis of discourse structure.

Notes

[1]Other markers include word order and voice (Hopper, 1979).

[2]In the literature a distinction is made between *narrative discourse* and *narrative context* (or *narrative clauses*). Narrative discourse encompasses the entire narrative text, or what this chapter simply calls the narrative, whereas the narrative context or clauses refer to the foreground specifically (Dahl, 1984; Labov, 1972; Schiffrin, 1981).

[3]Nonnative contrast in one stage of development may sometimes provide the learners with greater flexibility to mark discourse functions than the stage of development immediately following, as Youssef and James (1999) show for Tobagonian Creole classroom learners of standard English.

[4]Investigating the development of the narratives themselves has been beyond the scope of this field of inquiry. However, a learner's ability to background would influence the number of verbs that can be observed in the background. Changes in narrative structure, I would suggest, can only be observed in the same learner longitudinally because of variables of personality and interest

(or willingness) to tell stories that would affect cross-sectional studies. For a study of developing story-telling skills, see Liskin-Gasparro (1996).

[5]Propositions which require verbs but which lacked them were coded as "no verb" (e.g., *she hungry*) and were counted as either foreground or background as appropriate. These are not discussed further in this chapter because the analysis compares the discourse and aspect hypotheses, and for comparison with the aspect hypothesis only propositions with verbal predicates can be included. See Bardovi-Harlig (1995a) for discussion of the verbless predicates.

[6]In Bardovi-Harlig (1995a), the rates for tense-aspect use in the background were not adjusted for the use of *be*. Thus in Figure 1, p. 273, the use of simple past appears to be equal in both foreground and background at Group 60. However, as we see here in comparison with this analysis, this was due to the use of past with *be*.

[7]As Dry (1992) shows, there are many ways of defining grounding. Temporal criteria may be only one set of features among the cluster of features which define grounding, but they are the most relevant to the present inquiry.

[8]Housen (1998) found even fewer foregrounded atelic clauses and backgrounded telic clauses in the narratives of primary school children learning English.

[9]Because I did not exclude *be* in my earlier analysis of the narratives, Tables 5.2 and 5.3 presented here and Tables 2 and 3 in Bardovi-Harlig (1995a) have different token totals. *Be* also occurred occasionally in the foreground as a change of state verb (analogous to *got* or *became*) and thus the number of foreground tokens may also differ. In addition, due to a difference in research focus, the earlier study examined all propositions in the narratives, including those with no overt verbs (see the "no verb" category), whereas this study included only propositions in which a verb was overtly expressed.

[10]Andersen and Shirai (1994) proposed the features [+unitary], [+punctual], [+result state], and [+past]. I use the more recent formulation here.

[11]The differences between the oral and written narratives in this corpus are discussed in detail in Bardovi-Harlig (1995a, 1998). In the remainder of this section, I focus on their similarities as fictional narratives.

[12]We were not able to identify whether the difficulty with the task was cultural, linguistic, or idiosyncratic.

[13]The reader will recognize Saleh and Carlos as two of the learners from the longitudinal studies reported on in Chapters 2 and 3. Saleh performed his narratives at T14.5 and Carlos at T7.0.

[14]This does not rule out other differences that might exist between personal and impersonal narratives. My claim here is that these features should be taken into account with respect to discourse structure and interaction.

CHAPTER SIX

The Influence of Instruction

I: Has anything changed, do you think that anything's changed for you, uh, because your English uh has really improved?

H: Oh easy, yeah yeah,

I: For . . . example

H: Yeah sure like, for example OK, w-uh the first time we came here, you know I, I know how to speak and to understand the people but, the grammar is very bad with me before and uh I don't know how to use the grammar just I, I talk past and uh mix it with the present [xxxx], so now I I can control I, I mean I can understand if I will talk past or, for the past or the future or the present. This is, yeah I think this is good and uh, but my writing for the spelling is, really is, not good with me. But now I feel, is coming.

[Hamad, T6.0, Interview, L1 Arabic]

This chapter investigates the influence of instruction on the development of interlanguage tense-aspect systems. My interest in instruction in this chapter is not pedagogical but acquisitional; this survey investigates the extent to which different learning environments influence the acquisition of tense and aspect.[1] Van-Patten (1990) has distinguished three areas of investigation in second language acquisition: foreign language, instructed second language, and uninstructed second language. Foreign language learning takes place when learners learn a language that is not commonly spoken in the area in a classroom environment; tutored second language acquisition takes place in a classroom in the host environment; and untutored acquisition occurs in the host environment. Representing the three areas as intersecting circles, VanPatten (1990) places second language acquisition in the intersection, observing that "it is what [a] learner does that is common to all contexts which forms the core of SLA theory" (p. 25). Gass (1989) makes an even stronger claim that second language acquisition, regardless of environment, is essentially the same psycholinguistic process:

> It is difficult to imagine a situation in which the fundamental *processes* involved in learning a non-primary language would depend on the context in which the language is learned ... All learners have the capability of taking information from the input and organizing it within the framework of their current linguistic system and modifying and restructuring that system" (p. 35).

This chapter examines the literature for evidence of the core of SLA and the sequences that may be common to all learners in the acquisition of temporal semantics in a second language.

Instruction has been viewed from at least two perspectives in the second language acquisition research literature. Some studies have taken a local perspective. These target a certain feature of grammar and present it to learners in a controlled environment. Such studies typically ask if an experimental group that received specialized instruction is better off than a control group. This approach compares instructed learners to other instructed learners. Other studies take a broader perspective and compare tutored learners to untutored learners more generally, comparing, for example, sequences, rate of development, or eventual attainment.

Instruction may be viewed as doing at least one of four things. It may provide input that is otherwise unavailable (or not salient); it may provide opportunities for interaction that are otherwise lacking; it may provide form-focused instruction; or, it may enhance a learner's desire to speak or write in a targetlike manner. The studies reviewed in this chapter focus on providing of input and form-focused instruction. Input and form-focused instruction may intersect; form-focused instruction often entails the presentation of input, although enhancing or increasing input does not require focus on form. The instructional units that I will review here may have also promoted the desire on the part of learners to be more targetlike, but this was not investigated directly by the studies.

This chapter is divided into four main sections. The first two sections reflect the local perspective. The first section addresses the question of whether targeted instruction influences learners' development of temporal expression. The studies in this section are experimental and compare a treatment group with an instructed group that did not receive the same treatment. In the second section I present an observational study of the effect of instruction on the interlanguage of tutored learners in the longitudinal study reported on in Chapters 2 and 3. In this study the individual learners are compared to themselves before and after periods of instruction lasting approximately a year. In the third section I compare tutored learners and untutored learners more broadly and discuss the effect that being an instructed language learner has on the development of a learner's system of temporal expression in general. In the final section of the chapter I consider how the instructional variable relates to other known variables in second language acquisition.

Experimental Studies of the Effect of Instruction

In this section I review a small number of the experimental studies of the effect of instruction on the acquisition of tense-aspect. The studies compare instructed learners who received specialized instruction to other instructed learners who did not receive the experimental treatment. The original intent of the studies was to test the efficacy of an experimental form of instruction. However, my purpose in reviewing the studies is to determine whether learners' tense-aspect system responds to instruction. I have selected studies that have employed pedagogical approaches that attempt to help learners make form-meaning associations, consistent with one of the interests of this book. I review five studies: one on French (Harley, 1989), two on Spanish (Cadierno, 1995; Leeman, Artegoitia, Fridman, & Doughty, 1995), and two on English (Bardovi-Harlig & Reynolds, 1993; Doughty & Varela, 1998).[2]

Harley (1989) studied the effect of instruction that targeted the French passé composé and imparfait. The passé composé and imparfait are both past-tense forms; the passé composé represents the perfective past and the imparfait represents the imperfective past. Harley's experiment employed a functional approach that focused on discourse, in which student output focused on both language and content. The experimental approach provided focused L2 input designed to promote perception and comprehension of the form-meaning contrasts between the passé composé and imparfait and to provide opportunities for students to express the functions through thematically related and personalized tasks. Sixth-grade early-immersion students of French received instruction over the course of 8 weeks. Eight theme-based units incorporating rich input and production activities were provided to the teachers, who also attended a training session on the use of the materials. The mean time spent on the units by the 12 teachers was 11.9 hours and the range was 9.3–16.5 hours. A total of 319 students participated in the study; six classes formed the experimental group and another six classes formed the comparison group. Learners were tested by a pretest, an immediate posttest, and a delayed posttest or retention test administered three months after the immediate posttest. The comparison group continued immersion instruction as normal. Sixth-grade learners were selected because they were thought to be familiar with targeted verbal morphology.

Three tasks were used to evaluate interlanguage development: a composition, a cloze passage, and a scripted oral interview. All learners completed the written tasks, and six learners from each school (72 total) completed the oral interviews. The compositions were rated on a scale of 1–5 where 1 indicated a high proportion of errors and 5 indicated no errors. The cloze passage was scored by number of correct items out of a maximum of 38. Learners were provided with the passé composé and imparfait for each item in the cloze passage, and they had to write the appropriate choice in the blank. Because the verbal forms were provided, an answer was scored as either correct or incorrect. In spite of the fact that well-formed tokens of passé composé and imparfait were given for each verb, learners nevertheless supplied their own answers for some questions. No answer, the use of passé composé for imparfait or vice versa, interlanguage forms such as a participle with no auxiliary (a common early manifestation of the passé composé), or an imparfait with an auxiliary were all counted as errors. For oral interviews, an error rate was calculated as the ratio of the number of errors in the imparfait to the number of obligatory contexts for the imparfait. The scoring of the compositions was too general to shed light on the development of the temporal system (and it turned out that this type of global rating showed no effect for instruction). The scoring of the interview is of particular interest because Harley (1989) focused on what she called the "'difficult' questions that required the use of the *imparfait* in association with action verbs" (p. 343)—in other words, the imparfait with nonstative verbs. As we saw in Chapter 4, the use of imparfait with dynamic verbs represents a stage subsequent to the use of the imperfect with states.

Experimental students were significantly superior to the comparison group on the cloze test and the oral interviews on the immediate posttest. However, the comparison groups caught up to the experimental groups in the 3 months between the posttest and retention test. Harley identified methodological issues in the study that made the differences between experimental and control groups less sharp. For instance, several of the comparison immersion classes did have grammar-focused instruction on verbal morphology, contrary to the expressed orientation of the courses. In addition, the students in the experimental courses in which the teachers devoted less time to the experimental lessons than the norm did not show as much progress as learners whose teachers devoted more time to the lessons. However, from the perspective of the acquisition of tense-aspect, we see that the instructional approach designed by Harley did interact with the learners' developing interlanguage tense-aspect system. The effect was also lasting: The experimental groups did not lose ground. The comparison groups also got better, but it took more time and occurred in the time between the posttests; and as noted, the comparison groups also received unplanned grammatical instruction on the passé composé and imparfait. The experimental learners showed a rate advantage of up to 5 months over the comparison group with some grammatical instruction.[3]

Processing instruction seems to have a positive effect on learners' use and recognition of the preterite in Spanish. Processing instruction provides explicit intervention in the processes and strategies used by L2 learners in processing input. Cadierno (1995) compared processing instruction to traditional instruction and to no focused instruction on the past (once again the "no instruction" group were instructed learners). 61 learners in nine classes of a third semester basic university Spanish course participated in the experiment. The processing instruction focused learners' attention on preterite endings as past endings and provided practice in understanding the tense of both present and past sentences. No production was required. The traditional instruction presented the paradigm for regular preterites followed by the paradigm for stem-changing preterites, with appropriate oral practice for both. Both conditions emphasized person and number morphology in the preterite. The students received two consecutive class days of instruction. Instruction in the Spanish program was based in the Natural Approach (Krashen & Terrell, 1983); both the processing instruction and the traditional instruction represented a departure from the Natural Approach and what was experienced by the "no instruction" group.

The elicitation tasks included an interpretation task and a production task (a cloze passage) administered at four different times, a pretest, the first posttest immediately after instruction, a second posttest one week after instruction, and a final posttest one month after instruction. Verbal forms were given 2 points (when the correct preterite form was provided), 1 point (indicating incorrect spelling or incorrect past-tense form, which I assume was number or person), and 0 points (all others). Learners in the processing group showed significant improvement in the interpretation task and maintained their gains in the delayed posttests. There was no significant difference in the traditional or no instruction groups, which were not distinguished from each other. The results of the production task showed that both instructed groups were significantly better than the no instruction group, but not different from each other. Thus, processing instruction helped learners recognize and rely on the preterite in context as an indicator of the past in the absence of adverbials, and both traditional and processing instruction helped learners encode the past.

A study of the effects of a focus-on-form approach on the use of the preterite and imperfect in Spanish in a communicative Spanish classroom was conducted by Leeman et al. (1995). Twenty-two learners completed the experiment. Ten experimental learners received 2 days of focus-on-form instruction while 12 comparison learners continued in their communicatively focused classroom. Both groups received a reading on 20th-century Spanish history with comprehension questions. The focus-on-form group received an enhanced version with the preterite and imperfect underlined and in color in both the text and the questions; they were told to pay attention to how temporal relations were expressed in Spanish. In addition, experimental learners were corrected for nontargetlike use related to the preterite or imperfect. Four tasks comprised the pretest and posttest: a communicative debate related to Spanish history, an in-class essay, a grammaticality judgment task, and a cloze paragraph. The debate, completed by 5 experimental and 10 comparison learners, is discussed here.

Seven categories were coded: (a) preterite instead of imperfect, (b) imperfect instead of preterite, (c) present instead of imperfect, (d) present instead of preterite, (e) historical present, (f) imperfect, and (g) preterite. These were conflated into two categories, nontargetlike (a–d) and targetlike (e–g). The focus-on-form group showed a significant improvement on their accuracy in the debate from pretest to posttest, while the purely communicative group showed no significant change. The focus-on-form group also showed an increased use of past forms in past environments. (This included either preterite or imperfect supplied in any past environment, which was called a suppliance score. This score showed use of past over nonpast.) When the use of preterite and imperfect was analyzed separately, learners in both groups showed higher accuracy and suppliance of preterite than imperfect. Not only did they use the preterite in the environments of the imperfect more than vice versa, but they also used the present more often in imperfect environments, whereas there was almost no use of the present for the preterite. Thus, these instructed learners show the pattern familiar from uninstructed (and other instructed) learners. Namely, they learned preterite before imperfect, and used present as the first marker of imperfect. Interestingly, in spite of the fact that both groups showed increased suppliance and accuracy scores with the imperfect, the focus-on-form group showed decreased accuracy on the preterite due to overgeneralization of the imperfect in preterite environments.

Doughty and Varela (1998) investigated the influence of communicative focus on form in the interlanguage of 34 learners enrolled in a middle-school ESL content-based science class. The learners were in grades 6–8 and ranged in age from 11 to 14 years. The forms that were brought into focus were the simple past and the conditional past, as in *I thought the worm would go under the soil.* Both forms occurred naturally in the context of the science class and the science reports which the students wrote and presented to their classmates. From the research on acquisitional sequences, we would expect *would* to emerge much later than the past. Although Doughty and Varela also noted that *would* is learned later, communicative appropriateness in the context of the science class was the primary concern for the identification of the targeted forms. The instructional tasks were designed to elicit spontaneous and planned production of past and *would*, in both oral and written production. During science labs, class discussion, and individual viewings of the videotape of a student's own science lab presentation to the class, the teacher provided repetition of errors in the past or conditional followed by corrective recasts if there was no uptake by the learner, as shown in (1).

(1) José: I think that the worm will go under the ground.
      Teacher: I think that the worm will go under the ground.
      José: [no response]
      Teacher: I thought that the worm would go under the ground.
      José: I thought that the worm would go under the ground.

No other grammar points were corrected during the experimental period. Six labs were completed by both the experimental and comparison groups. The first lab served as the pretest, the fifth as the posttest, and the sixth as the delayed posttest two months later. Labs 2, 3, and 4 contained focus-on-form instruction along with the science lesson for the experimental group. Each lab took 1 to 2 weeks to complete. The comparison students continued in their science classes with no focus on form. After the posttest, the experimental group received no further focus on form and resumed in the established science-only format of the comparison group.

The oral and written lab reports were coded for suppliance of the past and *would,* appropriate use, and the nature of inappropriate use. These were reported in categories of targetlike use, interlanguage use, and nontargetlike use. Responses in the targetlike category show forms and function used appropriately (past for past, conditional for conditional). The interlanguage category included all attempts at past-time reference whether or not they were accurate in a targetlike sense. This category included the targetlike category plus *toke* for *took, went* for *would go, wode go* for *would go,* and overuse.[4] Nontargetlike use was made up of verbs that showed no evidence of past marking, as in the future used for the past or the past conditional, the present used for past, base forms, or no verb.

The results of the oral reports showed that the 21 learners in the focus-on-form group showed a significant increase and maintained their gains of targetlike forms. They also showed a significant increase and maintained their gains of interlanguage forms (which included targetlike forms). Finally, they showed a significant decrease in the use of nontargetlike forms, and maintained the decrease. In contrast, the 13 learners in the comparison group showed no change in any of the measures. The experimental group also showed gains in the targetlike and interlanguage categories in the written lab reports, but did not maintain their gains in the targetlike category. Slightly lower scores were reported for the interlanguage forms, but the delayed posttest rates of interlanguage scores were still significantly better than the pretest. Similarly, the rate of use of nontargetlike forms decreased between the pretest and the posttest, and although there was a subsequent increase in the number of nontargetlike forms in the delayed posttest, there was still a significant difference between the pretest and delayed posttest. The control group showed an increase in interlanguage forms in the posttest, but this was not maintained by the time of the delayed posttest. Although there is no ready explanation of why the modes were differentially affected, it appears once again that instructional focus in a meaningful context brings learners toward more targetlike use of verbal morphology. Doughty and Varela did not separate the past from the past conditional; it would be interesting, naturally, to examine the scores of these separately.

Bardovi-Harlig and Reynolds (1993, reported in Bardovi-Harlig, 1995b) conducted an instructional experiment employing input enhancement through focused noticing and accompanying production exercises. The instructional unit was based on the results of a cross-sectional study in which 182 learners at six levels of proficiency completed a series of 32 short cloze passages balanced by lexical aspectual category (Bardovi-Harlig & Reynolds, 1995). (See Chapter 4 for sample passage.) The results of the cross-sectional study showed that at all six levels of proficiency learners used the simple past more frequently with event predicates (achievements and accomplishments), with the rates of use of simple past tense increasing for all lexical aspectual classes with increased proficiency. The use of simple past with activities was much lower, and learners favored the past progressive as an alternative to the simple past with activities. The study also investigated the influence of adverbs of frequency on the learners' choice of verbal morphology: Adverbs of frequency encouraged the use of simple present.

The experimental study employed an input flood in the presentation of contextualized use of tense and grammatical aspect in lexical aspectual categories. Written materials were based on an oral narrative from an interview conducted by Larry Massett that aired on the National Public Radio program *All Things Considered* (Massett, 1989). The input flood with focused-noticing exercises (White, 1992) was aimed at two major points: providing text-based evidence that activities occur in the simple past, including tasks in which learners identified the same predicate in simple past and past progressive (e.g., *walked* and *was walking*); and providing evidence for the co-occurrence of simple past with adverbs of frequency. The instruction was elaborated—extensive use was made of natural texts and focused noticing in a 4-hour instructional unit spread over 4 days—but not explicit—no rules were given to the learners (Sharwood Smith, 1981, 1991).[5]

The results of the cross-sectional study reported by Bardovi-Harlig and Reynolds (1995) constituted the comparison for the experimental study. On the basis of the distribution of past in the comparison study, two instructional levels were identified for the experimental instruction: Level 2, which showed 65% appropriate use of simple past with activity predicates, and Level 4, which showed 54% use of simple past with activity predicates. In addition, Levels 2 and 4 were both scheduled for lessons on tense and aspect according to the program syllabus.

Both the cross-sectional comparison learners and the experimental learners received instruction in verb tenses according to the established curriculum of the program (see Azar, 1985, 1989). The experimental learners also received the specialized instruction described earlier, in addition to the established form-oriented instruction. The experimental students were given a pretest, a posttest immediately following the instruction period, and a retention test four weeks after the end of the instruction period. The comparison learners participated only in the single administration of the cross-sectional study on which the experimental study was based. The elicitation task used in the cross-sectional study employed a split-half design and was divided in half for the purposes of the pretest and posttest. Half of the learners received form A for the pretest and half form B. This order was reversed for the posttest. The entire elicitation task (forms A and B combined) served as the delayed posttest. Two teachers at each level and 72 learners in five intact classrooms (three Level 2 classes, two Level 4 classes) participated in the experimental unit.

The results of the pretest showed that the learners in the experimental group were similar to those in the comparison study. With scores lower than or equal to those of the comparison group (e.g., the Level 2 experimental group showed 59% use of past, while the comparison group showed 65% use of past), the experimental group showed no advantage over the comparison group. All of the experimental groups showed improvement at the posttest and the gains were maintained at the delayed posttest. Gains were made in both targeted conditions: Activities without adverbs of frequency showed increased use of simple past and decreased use of past progressive, and activities with adverbs of frequency showed increased use of simple past and decreased use of simple present. The focused instruction also helped other learners move along the developmental sequence. The learners in both levels who used present with activities with adverbs of frequency gave up the use of present and used the past progressive. Although this is not targetlike, these learners did make progress: They recognized that the activities were in past environments, and they joined the acquisitional sequence. (See Chapter 4.) A small group of Level 4 learners showed spurious use of the pluperfect with activities with and without adverbs of frequency on the pretest (the pluperfect had just been introduced in traditional instruction prior to the experimental unit). But they abandoned the pluperfect in favor of the past progressive, a more semantically motivated choice. One month after instruction, the Level 4 learners—and even the Level 2 learners—marked activities with the simple past at rates between those used by Levels 5 and 6 in the comparison group from Bardovi-Harlig and Reynolds (1995). Like the instructed comparison group, who received traditional instruction in Harley's (1989) study, the Level 4 IEP learners who received traditional instruction caught up with the Level 4 experimental learners eventually, by Level 5 or 6, after another 7–14 weeks of instruction and living in the host environment. Thus the experimental instruction increased the rate of acquisition but did not uniquely provide input that led to acquisition; the traditionally instructed learners reached the same rate of appropriate use, just later than the experimental learners.

In evaluating the effect of instruction on tense-aspect acquisition, it is important to note that in at least three of the studies (Bardovi-Harlig & Reynolds, 1995; Leeman et al., 1995; Doughty & Varela, 1998), progress is interpreted to include not merely targetlike use, which represents the endpoint of the acquisitional process, but also advancement along the acquisitional sequence. The acquisitional sequences that are reported for learners who received the experimental instruction are recognizable from the descriptions of tense-aspect studies. We may conclude from these studies that the tense-aspect system is learnable in a classroom setting, but whether this result is due to the increased input or the specific noticing activities cannot be determined. The various instructional approaches employed in the studies reviewed here have one thing in common: contextualized use of verbal morphology that helps learners make the form-meaning association which lies at the heart of morphological development. It is not surprising that the process moves faster in the presence of good input. An additional feature of the studies is the time spent on targeted instruction. Harley's (1989) French teachers spent an average of nearly 12 hours over 8 weeks on the imparfait and passé composé. The teachers in the Bardovi-Harlig and Reynolds study spent an additional 4 hours on the use of simple past, and Varela (Doughty & Varela, 1998) gave learners corrective feedback during three pedagogical labs lasting between 1 and 2 weeks each. Cadierno's (1995) processing and traditional groups received two class days of instruction compared to none. As Klein and his colleagues (Klein, 1993, 1994; Klein et al., 1995) have pointed out, learning takes time, a simple observation about second language acquisition that classroom pressures often cause us to ignore (Bardovi-Harlig, 1997c).

An Observational Study of the Effect of Instruction

Experimental studies, such as those reviewed above, are necessarily of limited duration. Experimental designs that include delayed posttests address the question of whether the immediate effects of instruction are integrated into interlanguage in the long run. Long-term observation of learners is generally determined by a researcher's access to students for follow-up testing and thus delayed posttests are typically conducted within the same instructional term as the teaching unit. To overcome this focus on the short term, in this section I will revisit the acquisitional sequences presented in Chapter 3 in terms of the timing of the instruction received by the learners in the longitudinal study. In this study the individual learners are compared to themselves before and after periods of instruction throughout a period of approximately a year. This provides the opportunity to study long-term effects of instruction, including repeated instruction, on the development of the interlanguage tense-aspect system. Because only 16 learners are involved, the interlanguage tense-aspect systems of the individual learners can be described in some detail.

Method

The Learning Environment

The learners in the longitudinal study were in a mixed learning language environment (Ellis, 1985, 1990). The IEP classes met for 23 hours a week. Students received instruction in listening and speaking, reading, writing, and grammar. Because the learners received instruction in the host environment, all were potentially contact language learners as well as classroom language learners, although they differed individually in their patterns of contact with native speakers and with other nonnative speakers from different first language backgrounds.

According to the teachers' logs, Levels 1, 2, and 4 in the IEP were responsible for the core presentation of tense and aspect in the program at the time of the study. There was no record from any teacher of tense-aspect lessons in Level 3. Level 5 dealt mostly with multiclausal sentences and logical connectors, what is often called grammar for writing.

The textbooks used in Level 2 were Azar (1985) and O'Neill, Kingsbury, Yeadon, and Cornelius (1978). The textbook used in Level 4 was Azar (1989). According to the teaching logs, no supplemental materials were used in this portion of the course. Instruction on tense-aspect in the grammar classes was form-focused. The textbooks by Azar used in the program at the time of observation used time lines and explanations to establish the meanings of the tense-aspect forms and presented decontextualized sentences for manipulation. Level 2 also used *AKL Intermediate* (O'Neill et al., 1978) which, although a grammar book, included a story that was presented in episodes throughout the book. The story contained a range of tense-aspect morphology appropriate to the plot, with an increasing number of forms as more morphology was introduced. The book also contained short contextualized reading passages with comprehension and discussion questions, which targeted the grammar of the chapters in a meaningful way. In addition, it should be noted that the grammar class was only 1 hour of 5 class hours a day, and that learners were exposed to written input containing tense-aspect forms in the reading courses. Students also were assigned readings in the writing classes, but the writing teachers' logs revealed no explicit teaching of tense-aspect.

Data Collection

The primary data, the learners' language production, was collected as described in Chapters 2 and 3. Learner journals formed the largest proportion of the written corpus, supplemented by written narratives, in-class compositions, and program-wide essay examinations. The oral corpus was made up of conversational interviews and oral narratives based on film retells as well as conversations initiated by learners after the more formal tasks were completed. (An inventory of the texts collected can be found in Table 3.2.) In addition to the learner data, the study collected information regarding classroom teaching and the students from the ESL teachers.

Instructional logs. Teaching logs were completed by participating grammar and composition instructors. Instructors became participating instructors when longitudinal subjects were assigned to their classes by the program directors independently of this project. The teaching logs recorded the topic(s) of instruction, classroom activities, type of feedback, homework, and page numbers of lessons in the textbooks, as well as copies of original materials created by the instructors. All instruction, whether related to tense and aspect or not, was recorded, as the instructors were unaware of the specific focus of the investigation. The teaching logs permit the comparison of teaching times and emergence of tense-aspect forms.

Teachers' narratives. The participating teachers were also asked to write short narratives about each of the learners for each 7-week term. Because the teachers were never informed as to which of the learners in their classes were part of the longitudinal study, teachers were asked to write narratives for all the learners in the class. Not all teachers provided the narratives, but sufficient narratives were completed to give a picture of the learners' interactions as students, something the research team could not know independently. Program records also provided evaluations, test scores, grades, and teachers' comments on final placement decisions.

Participants: The Learners as Students

In this section, I reintroduce the learners from the longitudinal study as their teachers and the program viewed them. In these brief profiles of the learners as students, I refer to the program records and to the narratives that I asked the teachers to write about their students. The narratives provide a valuable view of the learners as students, and yet, because the narratives were a burden on the teachers, they are rather sporadic data themselves. The learners often had quite different interactions with the researcher and the interviewers than with their teachers. The individual meetings with native speakers who became very familiar to them gave the learners an opportunity to talk and express themselves entirely without evaluation; in fact, learners were always praised and thanked enthusiastically for their participation.

Table 6.1 lists the learners' enrollment in the Intensive English Program by number of sessions that they attended (first term, second term, and so on) and the course level in which they were enrolled. Half of the learners began to study in the IEP in the spring term (Hamad, Saleh, Abdullah, Toshihiro, Noriko, Hiromi, Ji-An, and Sang Wook) and the second group arrived in the fall (Carlos, Eduardo, Guillermo, Khaled, Zayed, Idechi, Satoru, and Kazuhiro). As in Chapter 3, I use the order of the IEP terms here rather than dates because the learners attended classes at different times. In Table 6.1 the learners are grouped by their first language.

Hamad. Hamad completed eight sessions in the IEP (1–6), repeating Levels 4 and 6, and staying a total of 16.5 months. Hamad was a very eager and forthcoming participant in the

Table 6.1

Academic History for Each Learner in the Intensive English Program (Given in Levels)

Learner	L1	1	2	3	4	5	6	7	8	9
					Term					
Hamad	Arabic	1	2	3	4	4R	5	6	6R	
Saleh	Arabic	1	2	2R	3	3R	4	4R	5	
Abdullah	Arabic	(1) 1R	2	3	4	4R	5	5R	6	6R
Khaled	Arabic	1	2	3	4	5	6			
Zayed	Arabic		2	3	3R	4	5			
Toshihiro	Japanese	1	2	3	3R	4	5			
Noriko	Japanese	1	2	3R	4	4R	5	5R	5R	
Hiromi	Japanese		2	3	4	5	6			
Idechi	Japanese	1	2	3	4	5				
Satoru	Japanese	1	2	3	3R	4				
Kazuhiro	Japanese	1	2	3	4	5	6			
Ji-An	Korean	1	2	3	4					
Sang Wook	Korean		2	3	4					
Carlos	Spanish	1	2	3	5	6				
Eduardo	Spanish	1	2	4	6					
Guillermo	Spanish	1	2	3	3R					

Note. R = Repeat; (1) indicates that Abdullah was enrolled in Level 1 before the longitudinal study began. From "Reverse-Order Reports and the Acquisition of Tense: Beyond the Principle of Chronological Order," by K. Bardovi-Harlig, 1994, *Language Learning, 44,* p. 279. Copyright 1994 by the Language Learning Research Club. Reprinted with permission.

interviews (never missing even one) and in keeping a journal in the early sessions. He passed Levels 1–3 (with grades of Bs and Cs), but was not promoted from Level 4 (earning a grade of C) to Level 5, repeating Level 4 instead with a grade of B–. In the later months his journals entries diminished. Unlike some of the other learners, he did not write about his classes in his journal.

Hamad was described by his Level 2 teacher as a high-average student who participated in class. He enjoyed answering as many questions in class as possible, demonstrated good comprehension, and was friends with many students in class, getting along with everyone. (Hamad, Saleh, Abdullah, Hiromi, and Ji-An were all classmates in Level 2.) His Level 3 writing teacher was less enthusiastic about his work habits and his writing, reporting that he had not turned in any rewrites by the second week. The teacher observed:

> Despite long and detailed lectures, modelling, and hand-outs, he doesn't seem to grasp the concepts of sentences when he writes. He spills ideas onto the page much like he talks, into long, unpunctuated discourses with no paragraph breaks or sentences. I hope he gets the tutor that I have recommended. . . .

In the fourth week of the term she observed that Hamad's feelings were easily hurt and he needed to be encouraged. She identified spelling and run-on sentences as problems, but reflected that his main problem was that he wanted to do everything quickly and that speed did not help his accuracy. At the end of Level 3, Hamad's writing teacher reported a breakthrough:

> Hamad has improved drastically in many ways, although he has to keep a tight rein on his spelling problem. I think he has organization down and he is working on making the technical aspects of his work more polished. He has begun to miss class here and there. I wonder if people really aren't bored at this point?

Hamad showed higher grades in class than his scores on the program-wide final exam and placement test. He scored below grade level on both reading and grammar at the end of Level 2, and in all areas—listening, reading, writing, and grammar—at the end of Level 3. He received a probationary pass to Level 4, and then repeated it. His grades, attendance, and attitude in class all declined in Levels 5 and 6. He confessed to his Level 6 writing teacher that he was tired of studying English and was having difficulty concentrating.

Saleh. Saleh began in Level 1 and stayed for eight sessions. He took levels 1, 2 (repeated), 3 (repeated), 4 (repeated) and 5. In spite of his open conversational style and his enthusiasm as a participant in the longitudinal study, Saleh had a certain amount of difficulty in his classes. His Level 2 grammar teacher identified him as the class clown and many other teachers reported that he made jokes in class. This ultimately was the source of many reprimands by teachers and the director of the IEP. His inclination to joke around in class may be what Saleh referred to in his journal from Level 1: "This teacher She is Mrs. S. She is very nic teacher becuas She is larning me evry day a new something and I am very happe in her class. . . she don't no *any joky* in her class." Three months into the study, Saleh's Level 2 teacher reported that he readily answered questions when called on and occasionally volunteered; he also seemed to be "getting the homework right." By four months into the study, the same teacher reported that Saleh did not seem to take his work seriously. He was asked to repeat Level 2, which he did, beginning a pattern of repeating each course as he took it. Saleh met with the director of the program about his classroom behavior at the outset of Level 2. As a result, Saleh was well prepared for class for that term. Four and a half months into the study, the teacher of his second Level 2 grammar class reported that Saleh told him he was enjoying the session more than the previous one. The teacher observed that "Saleh has been putting effort into the work and I have noticed that his work is slowly improving." In Level 2 his grammar test scores fluctuated between 46% and 76%. His teacher identified tense as an area of difficulty. Saleh apparently felt some pressure to rejoin his original classmates because he spoke to his teacher about skipping to Level 4 (where the others who began with him would have been). The teacher encouraged him to concentrate on his current work. Rejoining his classmates became less of an issue as the class scattered in later levels.

The second Level 2 session seems to have been Saleh's best academic session. After that, teachers lamented his grammar, and more often, his attendance. Thinking that he would go to a program in St. Louis that overlapped with Level 3, he stopped doing his work. He repeated Level 3 in the following session, but started his second attempt at it 3 weeks late, returning from a trip home during summer vacation. The second Level 3 grammar teacher seems more positive about Saleh's antics, reporting that "he requires a lot of attention, but is friendly and likes to joke around." Saleh asked the teacher frequently if he would pass Level 3, but also seemed to be content to do the minimum. The last two weeks in Level 3, about 9 months into the study, were particularly good, and according to the teacher Saleh "has begun to find a certain satisfaction in his increasing abilities in English."

Saleh's classroom progress does not seem to have lasted through Level 4, which he took twice. By the second session of Level 3, his joking around was legendary in the program, and this surfaces again when his Level 4 teacher wrote "I personally find Saleh a good addition to my class. I don't find his jokes and humor distracting at all." This teacher, too, mentioned that Saleh needed to get a tutor, something that does not seem to have happened while Saleh was in the program. Saleh had repeated meetings with the director about his behavior and later, his attendance. Thirteen months into the study, Saleh reported on one such meeting, "Mr. [Director] gave me a hared time when he told me that my teachers aren't happy with me they told him that I'm not behaive in my class and I should be seriose in the class. I'm always seriose in my class but I don't know what does this mean and I couldn't fined any body to understand me."

Saleh seemed to be totally unconcerned with monitoring, which frustrated his teachers somewhat, but made him a very desirable informant because he was enthusiastic and nonhesitant. He was a very skillful storyteller who managed with very few linguistic devices. Because Saleh had a somewhat difficult life in the classroom, he especially enjoyed the interviews. In the interviews, everything he did was acceptable to the research team, and he could be the star of the interaction without any repercussions. After we had talked about 45 minutes one day, I told Saleh that I had to interview his cousin, at which point Saleh replied, "Let him wait! I'm not done talking."

Abdullah. Abdullah attended the IEP for ten sessions, beginning the term before the longitudinal study began to observe learners in Level 1. He joined the study when he repeated Level 1, joining Hamad, Saleh, and Ji-An. He completed Levels 1 (repeated),

2, 3, 4 (repeated), 5 (repeated), and 6 (repeated). Like Saleh, Abdullah had some difficulty as a student, but for not for reasons of behavior. In many ways, Abdullah was a model student according to his teachers. He always wrote in his journals (even if he recycled them from one term to the next, which the teachers had no way of knowing), he completed all the homework, and he studied constantly. As early as Level 2, the teacher observed Abdullah's dependence on prepared answers rather than spontaneous responses. His Level 3 writing teacher's assessment drops with each of three narratives. Four and a half months into the study, his teacher wrote: "A very serious student. He writes strictly formulaic compositions, and does it using his own philosophical thoughts. His compositions are stilted but thorough." Two weeks later, the teacher wrote,

> He's plodding along in his slow-but-sure way. He's making progress that's perceptible, but just barely. He tries hard and that makes an impression. In addition, he uses his journal to write about things he knows or has opinions on . . . He is honestly making an effort to practice.

By the end of the term the teacher observed:

> I think this man has given up. He used to be very serious about his work . . . now he rarely comes to class, and never does the work. I wonder if this has anything to do with the fact that he was denied admission to the school of Library Science?

Abdullah's slow progress began to affect him and at Level 4 he began to repeat all of his courses, as Table 6.1 shows. In Level 5 he began working with an experienced tutor, but in spite of this, his TOEFL score was still below 400 at the end of Level 5 in his 11th month. His Level 5 teacher reported that he was very upset by his score, realizing that it stood between him and admission to graduate school in Library Science. After two sessions in Level 5, Abdullah was promoted to Level 6 on probation. At the same time, however, he was allowed to take a graduate course in Library Science which he very much enjoyed. He also received a grade of *A* on a paper for that course, which he proudly showed to the teachers at the IEP. Taking the library course seemed to improve his outlook regarding his ESL classes. And at midterm of the second attempt at Level 6 after Abdullah had been in the study for 16.5 months, his teacher reported "Abdullah has been at his most lively this session." In spite of the improvement, he did not attend for the rest of the course.

Abdullah's speech was very labored, slow, and difficult to understand. Nevertheless, he attended every interview session. This seemed to be a further indication that Abdullah was doing everything the program suggested that he do in order to improve his English.

Khaled. Khaled completed six levels in the IEP (1–6) with no repeated levels. He stayed at the university for 1 year. He had studied English for about 8 years, beginning at age 12. Khaled was, by all accounts, "the ideal student." In the words of his Level 2 grammar teacher, "he was never absent, worked hard, cheerfully participated and never complained." In Level 1 he was described as a class leader who liked to volunteer answers and explanations about Arab culture, a role that was consistent with his job in his country and his goals for the future. He was described as having a nice sense of humor and a mature nature. He did very well on class work, but throughout told his teachers that he felt writing to be his biggest problem, a concern he reiterated in the interviews, when he confessed that he didn't like writing. His Level 3 teacher described him as enthusiastic about learning and his Level 4 teacher reported that he was a conscientious learner.

Khaled had graduated from the university prior to studying in the IEP. He had a commitment both to education and to independence. Although his father would have supported him during his university studies, he decided to work his way through school instead and secured a job that allowed him the flexibility to study. Khaled's goal was to study public relations at the graduate level, earning an MA or PhD. His studies in the States were supported by a scholarship from his government. He wanted to help his country be with the "first countries" in the world, "like USA and England and Japan."

Zayed. Zayed had studied previously at a commercial language school for approximately 2 months and was placed in Level 2 when he enrolled in the IEP. He stayed for 11 months, completing Levels 2–5, repeating Level 3. Zayed was not entirely happy about his placement into Level 2 in the IEP. The Level 2 teacher reported,

> At the beginning of the session, Zayed voiced disappointment at placing to Level 2. He was a transfer student from [a commercial school] where he had been in Level 4. He soon cheered up, however, and worked steadily throughout the seven weeks. . . . During the midterm evaluations he once again voiced his disappointment at being placed in Level 2. At this time, [one of the directors] explained that [the commercial school] had a nine-level program, while the IEP has a six-level program. This information seemed to satisfy him.

During the first time that Zayed took Level 3, his teacher observed that he was still adjusting to being in Bloomington. He voiced his frustration with the fact that despite his good class grades, he still had to repeat Level 3 as a result of a low TOEFL score. In Level 4 Zayed made friends with a female classmate which the writing teacher thought may have helped his compositions to improve.

At some point prior to enrolling in the program, Zayed traveled to Turkey, and immediately before he went to New York, Niagara Falls, and Washington, D.C. These trips led to interesting stories which he repeated at least once every session in his journals and told once in his interviews. Zayed's repetition of journal entries was not as obvious as Abdullah's, for example, but was noteworthy if only for the fact that learners seem to faithfully copy their original stories without the changes which they could have easily made at their current stages of acquisition.

When he first arrived, Zayed felt that he spoke Arabic too often with his friends, but in later journals he wrote that he thought his English was improving, though he believed he had a long way to go. When he took the TOEFL for the first time, he felt it was the hardest test he had ever taken. He discovered the library during his second session studying English, and he loved studying there. He mentioned at one time that he studied 4–5 hours per night in the library.

Toshihiro. Toshihiro attended the IEP for six sessions, completing Levels 1–5, and repeating Level 3. Two months into the study, Toshihiro was identified by his Level 2 teacher as "the best student in grammar so far." He served as the translator for less advanced students until the teacher separated all the language groups. Toshihiro asked to move up from Level 2 to Level 3 at the end of the first week in Level 2, but the teachers decided that he was appropriately placed and no change was made. He continued to be the strongest student in the grammar class, and took a week off to drive to Florida with his Singaporean roommate. While away, he completed all of his homework during his trip and continued to write in his journal. When he returned the teacher reported that "his attitude improved in that he seems to accept his teachers more now than in the beginning." At this time he began to speak more in class and out of it. The Level 2 teacher felt that Toshihiro attempted to blame the teacher for his own errors, but said that things slowly improved in that area.

Level 3 saw the decline of Toshihiro's academic career as he rarely came to class. At the beginning of the level in the 4th month of the study his writing teacher observed that he worked haphazardly. In the 4th week of the session, 4.5 months into the study, he got into serious trouble for fighting. His teacher's observation of his interest in parties, drinking, and women parallels Toshihiro's own reports in his journals. His Level 3 teacher wrote, "I was really disappointed with his classwork, but in the end, he could write a decent composition. I don't think I had much to do with this anyway. Or maybe we need to revamp our thoughts on the effect of partying on composition skills." He did not pass that session of Level 3 (finishing with an overall C–); he pulled himself together to do very well in the repetition of Level 3 and Level 4, but did not pass Level 5.

According to Toshihiro's journals, much of his time away from class was spent socializing. His personal goals included learning as much slang as he could. He learned and practiced much of this in bars and often tried the slang out in his journals.

Noriko. Noriko completed Levels 1–5, repeating Level 3 once and Level 5 twice. She stayed a total of 17.5 months. Teachers described Noriko as young for her 18 years and very shy. She did very well in her Level 2 grammar tests, but her teacher reported that she had problems with tense and the spelling of irregular verbs (a focus of study for Level 2). Her Level 2 teacher observed that she had to be called on to get her to speak at all. Her Level 3 writing teacher found her to be disengaged during class, often staring off into space. The teacher also found that her ideas were sound and her organization improving, and predicted that Noriko would be a "solid Level 3 by the end of the session." In fact, she repeated Level 3. She seemed to have experienced two major developments in her second session of Level 3. By the 3rd week of class, in the 6th month, she no longer sat by her best friend (another Japanese woman) and began to make friends with and sit by some students from other countries. Two weeks later, the teacher predicted that "[a]side from class work Noriko seems to be approaching the point where her desire to communicate will be strong enough to overcome her shyness about speaking." And in fact, that point came in the 7th month of the study, when the teacher observed

> Noriko is really at a breakthrough point in her communi-cation skills. . . She takes a long time vocalizing her ideas, but when she does, her statements are astute rather than being frivolous examples of the target structure. For exam-ple, when asked what she would do if she had a lot of money, after a long pause she answered, "I would invest in securi-ties," rather than saying she would "buy a car," etc.

The Level 3 teacher was more optimistic than the second Level 4 teacher, who found Noriko to be unreachable and a "slug-gish student." She appeared to be uninterested in the grammar class, to the point where she would not answer even if called on. However, when she showed her teacher an application letter the teacher found it to be surprisingly well-written, but organizationally weak. I was surprised at the sophistication of the language she used, and her expression of ideas. It was proof that perhaps she actually could produce grammatical English on paper, when she needed to and wanted to.

Her Level 5 teacher described her as serious about her studies, but distracted by social interests.

Hiromi. Hiromi began in Level 2 and completed five sessions, Levels 2–6, staying for 11 months. Hiromi was described by her Level 2 teacher as friendly and outgoing and good at written grammar. She did not seem to have problems with oral comprehension but had some problems with speaking. At the end of Level 2 her teacher wrote, "Good worker. She seemed to make a lot of progress as far as listening and speaking over the seven weeks." Hiromi, who hoped to be a journalism major at an American university, liked to write and this was reflected "in the length and creativity of both her classroom work and her journal entries. Both are fun to read, fun to respond to." She improvised on the formulaic formats for essays that were used at the time in Level 3, and responded well to correction. Her teacher observed that "she is usually not afraid to take risks when she writes." At midterm, the teacher assessed her essays as "long and wonderful." Hiromi used her teacher to her advantage by asking for daily attention: "she literally demanded that I should check her journal daily because she is lazy. So I have taken her suggestion, and I am collecting all the journals daily."

In her journals Hiromi wrote that she loved her classes and was learning a lot. When she decided to study journalism at an American university, the TOEFL became important for her and she set a goal of 550. Towards the end of her English studies, she perceived that she had reached a plateau and blamed herself for being lazy and for studying ineffectively while reflecting "I am in the best place to study and get good TOEFL score."

Idechi. Idechi began to study English in Level 1 at the Intensive English Program and stayed for five sessions, advancing each session. During the second session he passed his audition for acceptance into the program leading to the Performance Diploma in the School of Music, a diploma which does not require the level of English proficiency required for academic degrees. By Level 3 (the third 7-week session, at the beginning of the 5th month of his stay), Idechi arranged to study half-time in the IEP. He took English classes in the mornings, practiced in the afternoons, and took orchestra classes every night. He stayed in the IEP through Level 5, a total of 10 months. Of Idechi's attempt to balance English and his clarinet, the Level 1 grammar teacher wrote, "everyday after class, Idechi heads to the practice building for hours of arduous work on his licorice stick. But this doesn't affect his attitude toward learning English."

Idechi liked to joke, although not in the disruptive manner the teachers attributed to Saleh. His jokes included grammar. His teacher reported this story: One day shortly after the grammar teacher had introduced the simple past tense, Idechi and two Arabic-speaking classmates were at the blackboard. Idechi called the teacher over and wrote one of the student's names on the board, A-H-M-E-D. "He underlined the -ed and said 'Ahmed's name is past tense.' Quickly he sketched out 'Ahming' and 'Ahmes,' saying 'Ah yes, present progressive and singular present tense.' Then he did the same with [the other student's] name."

By Level 2, the grammar teacher reported that Idechi would rather play the clarinet than study English. He auditioned for admission to the School of Music at the end of Level 2. When his grammar teacher noted that she had not been receiving his home-work, he began to turn it in. "He seems to be able to make progress in English without giving it his full attention," his Level 2 teacher wrote. The Level 4 teacher described his conversation as "halting" and reported that Idechi read Japanese comics and magazines between English classes.

Satoru. Satoru completed Levels 1–5, repeating Level 3. He stayed for 10 months. He had studied English for 6 years begin-ning in junior high. After graduation he worked a part-time job and studied English to prepare for coming to the United States. Nevertheless, he began the program in Level 1. The Level 1 grammar teacher described Satoru as a very quiet student who got satisfactory grades. He would answer questions in class, but seemed to do a lot of monitoring before he answered. Every teacher described Satoru as very quiet. Satoru became friends with Kazuhiro. He was described as a bit slow in group work and had among the lowest scores for listening comprehension tasks. His teachers suggested that he participate more, but he was not able to do so. His Level 3 writing teacher felt that he was not putting any effort into the composition course, but the Level 4 writing teacher described his essays as "usually well organized with minimal errors." By Level 4, however, Satoru seemed to be participating even less in class, wearing his Walkman between and sometimes at the beginning of classes. He did not attend Level 5 classes, although enrolled, preferring to study in his dorm room for the TOEFL.

In the early journals Satoru wrote about his classes: He found Level 1 to be too easy, but he liked Level 2. He often went to the listening lab and the main library. He perceived that attending IEP classes and doing homework alone were not enough for his English to improve as much as he wished; thus, he studied on his own as well.

Satoru reported wanting to become a businessman, perhaps a manager. He wanted to study business in America after finishing his English studies. He also reported studying English so that he could watch American films. Satoru wrote that he came to the U.S. not only because he thought he could learn English and further his career, but also because he wanted an international experience.

Kazuhiro. Kazuhiro stayed in the IEP for six sessions, taking Levels 1–6, repeating none. He had studied English for 7 years in Japan, beginning in junior high (age 13), but placed in Level 1 when he came to the IEP. Kazuhiro did not say much in class in Level 1, although he did participate well in groups. The teacher reported having trouble understanding what he said. His participation in class increased briefly around the middle of Level 1, but declined again toward the end. The Level 2 teacher identified Kazuhiro's listening and speaking as particularly weak. The Level 3 writing teacher thought that effort was missing in his attempts at classwork. The Level 4 teacher cited severe pronunciation problems, observing that Kazuhiro struggled during grammar class exercises and appeared to be "not especially curious or interested."

He wrote frequently in his journal that his grammar class was easy, but speaking and listening were difficult. He thought Levels 1 and 2 were easy, but reported that Levels 3 and 4 were fast. Kazuhiro took his homework seriously, reporting on it in his journals. He put a lot of emphasis on grammar and generally reported doing the grammar homework before any other assignments. He mostly socialized with other Japanese students, pursuing bowling, tennis, and golf. His best friends in the program were Idechi and another Japanese learner who was not part of the study. By Level 4 he complained that being in class with his friends and other Japanese students caused him to always speak Japanese with them. Kazuhiro wrote several times that he liked the weekly coffee hours that the IEP hosted. The coffee hours provided an hour for the students to socialize with each other and their teachers during school hours. They seem to have been Kazuhiro's main opportunity for practicing English outside of class.

Ji-An. Ji-An attended four sessions of the IEP (Levels 1–4) and stayed 7.5 months. Her Level 2 grammar teacher described Ji-An as a very good student, good at both oral and written work. She sometimes served as a translator for Sang Wook, the other Korean student in this study. The teacher observed that she interacted well with the other students and was not overly shy. He commented that she was "fun to have in class." The Level 3 writing teacher described Ji-An as a "poetic, emotional person. Her early efforts were, to me, the succinct and musical lines of poetry." She was also "a quick study. Models and corrections are only needed one or two times before she puts out an almost flawless product." However, she also was concerned about doing things right, and "takes few risks. If she isn't sure that she can say it correctly, then she doesn't really try." In the middle of the term the teacher described her compositions as "wonderfully 'perfect,' but somewhat limited." At midterm conferences the teacher advised Ji-An to take some risks and try new things. Ji-An reported that she felt that writing was her worst subject and that she wanted more vocabulary, something she also wrote about in her journal. Because of Ji-An's concern about vocabulary, the teacher included vocabulary brainstorming sessions as part of the prewriting activities so all the students would have access to vocabulary they could use for their writing. Ji-An's stay in the program was cut short when her mother recalled her when her sister graduated from IU.

Sang Wook. Sang Wook stayed in the IEP only three sessions, completing Levels 2–4. There are no teacher narratives for Sang Wook. However, the program records show that in Level 2 Sang Wook's program-wide final exam scores surpassed his classroom performance in the areas of listening, reading, and grammar. (This is the opposite of Hamad's performance.) He received marks of highly satisfactory in class, but got excellent marks on the exams, with the exception of writing, where he received a grade of "E" (excellent) in his class, but only "S" (satisfactory) on the program-wide test. His attitudes, participation and work habits were all evaluated as "good" by his teachers. In Level 3 his listening and speaking grades dropped to an "S" because he missed several assignments, but his reading and grammar scores stayed at "S+" and his writing remained excellent. A note on the Level 3 evaluation sheet reported that his writing was creative and imaginative. His attitude in Level 3 was evaluated as fair, participation and work habits as good.

Sang Wook had graduated from the university in Korea with a major in civil engineering. He came to the United States to study business, which he believed was a necessary complement to civil engineering. His ultimate goal was to be a professor in Korea, a theme that he incorporated into several essays. His sister and brother-in-law lived in Cincinnati, where the brother-in-law was in medical school. The brother-in-law encouraged Sang Wook to move to Cincinnati to study, but Sang Wook said that he preferred Bloomington because it was a small town.

Sang Wook socialized with a mixed group of international students and Americans. He reported hosting and attending dinner parties with Peruvians, Japanese, Salvadoreans, Arabs, and Turks as well as Americans. He also wanted to learn Latin dances. He wrote that he did not like to socialize with other Koreans because it was not good for his English.

Carlos. Carlos attended five sessions of the IEP, completing Levels 1, 2, 3, skipping Level 4, and completing Levels 5 and 6. He stayed 10 months. Carlos was a member of the Galileo program for exceptional high-school graduates from Venezuela. (See Chapter 3.) Participants were expected to seek admission at the undergraduate level to major U.S. universities, which was a real difficulty given their level of proficiency in English at the time of application, which was coincident with their intensive English study. For Carlos, the scholarship created opportunity as well as pressure to succeed which is expressed in his journal entries. He was very studious.

Carlos and Eduardo arrived together in the fall first session. The Venezuelan students, which included Carlos and Eduardo, arrived a week late and were placed in classes already in progress. The Level 1 grammar teacher wrote: "For a few days some of the older members were unwilling to speak as much and perhaps resented the fact that most of the Venezuelans were not as orally proficient as most of the class and thus needed more attention."

Carlos's Level 1 teacher described him as "not afraid to attempt communication." As was the case in his early interviews, he would often start to speak in Spanish. He asked a lot of questions and it would sometimes take a while for the teachers to make themselves understood which in turn sometimes irritated his classmates. By mid-September his grammar teacher spoke seriously with him about not speaking in Spanish in class, and he did his best to speak in English. At the end of October the Level 1 teacher described him as "one of the more interesting students I've ever had." The Level 2 grammar teacher described him as "a unique type. If allowed he will blather on for ever, on practically any topic." She also observed that he enjoyed using English.

Another teacher reported that he would follow her back to the office from class happily talking the entire way, although with rather difficult pronunciation. The Level 3 teacher described him as independent. The Level 5 teacher described him as "an extremely serious student." As with the other teachers, the Level 5 teacher reported

> He talks all the time, although his pronunciation is terrible and he is often difficult to understand. He asks a lot of questions in class. The other students are sometimes impatient with him and laugh at him, but he is good-natured about it . . . He reads the newspaper regularly (I think the *New York Times*) . . . He has also been reading something by Hemingway.

Carlos left Level 6 early to start his degree work at another university.

Eduardo. Eduardo was also a member of the Galileo Program. He studied in the IEP for 8.5 months completing four sessions, Levels 1 and 2, 4 and 6. At the beginning of his Level 1 course, his grammar teacher described him as often looking scared in class and not saying much. By the end of his first 6 weeks his teacher wrote,

> Hoorah for Eduardo!! It was interesting to watch Eduardo bloom this session. He developed from a frightened, wide-eyed young man clinging to [another student] for translations to a much more confident user of English. His listening and speaking skills improved dramatically along with a noted improvement on his grammar tests.

He asked the teacher about the present perfect, which was just beginning to emerge in his essays and journals:

> One day he asked me what "He has talked for two hours" means. I don't know where he heard or read that sentence, but he asked, so I answered. He seemed to understand; I also said that he would be getting that in Level 2.

Eduardo learned by leaps and bounds. In Level 2 Eduardo reported that listening was the most difficult for him, but his grammar teacher reported that "by looking at his test scores, nothing seems difficult." She observed that "he asks good questions in class, and has good intuitions when several tenses are possible but one is the best." By 3 months into the study, he had scored 500 on the TOEFL. He skipped Level 3 and then missed several classes in Level 4 to work on his college application statements with the director of students. His Level 4 teacher observed that Eduardo's "personality grew more outgoing as each week went by. He tended to ask a lot of challenging questions (some just for the sake of argument!) and continued to do well both in written work and in oral classwork." Eduardo advanced from Level 4 to Level 6 where his writing teacher described his work as "inventive but not accurate, which seems to be a source of some frustration for him." He received some help with editing from a second writing teacher (who taught the term paper course), but she observed "Eduardo will often defend his own version." He planned to spend the summer in Oklahoma with his aunt's family and to work more on his English before starting the university.

Guillermo. Guillermo's life as a student of ESL was often secondary to his life as a student of music. He studied in the IEP for 9 months, completing Levels 1 and 2 and taking Level 3 twice. He studied English for 6 years in Puerto Rico, but was placed in Level 1 by the placement exam. The Level 1 grammar teacher reported that Guillermo was class leader in spoken work. He often volunteered and enjoyed helping the new Venezuelans when they first came. The teacher observed that his listening did not match his speaking skills. Guillermo was often tired, sleeping as little as 4 hours a day because of his practice schedule. By the end of Level 1, the teacher wrote that Guillermo was a topic for discussion at several Level 1 meetings:

> He never seemed to catch on to the idea that you had to work at learning a language . . . His music is just more important to him than learning English. Perhaps he hasn't made the connection, and believe me we tried to get it through to him, that the music school won't accept you until your TOEFL reaches a certain score. In writing class he would walk out, staying outside for 10 minutes, then

come back, apologize, and turn in an empty piece of paper. In grammar class when we did your cloze exercises [for the experimental teaching discussed in the previous section, Bardovi-Harlig & Reynolds, 1993], he would often turn them in half-finished, saying he didn't understand. Yet he performed reasonably okay on tests and quizzes. I foresee problems for him.

The Level 2 teacher described him as studying English to satisfy the Music School's requirements. He was often impatient in class and he reported to his teacher several times that "his brain was fried." His Level 2 grammar and writing teachers went to hear his concert in mid-November, about two and one half months into the study, and he seemed to put more effort into his grammar class after that.

Results

In this section the acquisitional sequences presented in Chapter 3 are mapped against the instruction received by the learners. As in Chapter 3, the discussion is organized around the emergent tense-aspect morphology: past progressive, present perfect, and pluperfect.

Past Progressive

The first tense-aspect morphology that is introduced pedagogically is the present progressive. Instructional periods were divided into sampling periods using the same system reported for the text samples in Chapter 3. Table 6.2 shows the instructional periods relative to the use of the past progressive in oral and written samples. In Table 6.2 instruction (in shaded blocks) is superimposed on Table 3.4. The shaded areas represent instruction during a particular interval, but should not be construed as filling the whole interval. The darker shading represents present progressive instruction, and the lighter shaded areas represent instruction in the past progressive. The number of written and oral tokens is given, as is the rate of appropriate use of the simple past.[6]

Table 6.2

The Emergence of Past Progressive with Respect to Instruction

Subject	Month 0.5	1	1.5	2	2.5	3	3.5	4	4.5	5	5.5	6	6.5	7	7.5
Idechi Japanese	1 85% (13)	9 83% (30)	3 85% (47)	2			2							Oral 7	
Eduardo Spanish		1 78% (18)	2		6	Oral 3	Oral 1	4	3 Oral 1	Oral 9	Oral 2		1	4 Oral 15	Oral 10
Khaled Arabic		2 68% (19)	2	1 100% (21)	3 68% (18)						1 Oral 2				6
Toshihiro Japanese		1 100% (12)	85% (58)	1	5	1		1	2					94% (16)	
Satoru Japanese		1 67% (9)	1 67% (9)		77% (22)	77% (34)					1 93% (14)				
Carlos Spanish		8	Oral 4 97% (82)		1 Oral 1	5	6	7			2 Oral 1	1 Oral 2		1 Oral 6	
Saleh Arabic			1 20% (5)		1	1 75% (16)	1	2 82% (37)	2	1		Oral 1			
Kazuhiro Japanese		85% (13)	72% (25)	2 70% (20)	1				1	2	1				1
Guillermo Spanish		2	2	58% (8)	3 88% (24)	Oral 1			1	2	1	2			

Table 6.2 (continued)

The Emergence of Past Progressive with Respect to Instruction

Subject	Month 0.5	1	1.5	2	2.5	3	3.5	4	4.5	5	5.5	6	6.5	7	7.5
Zayed Arabic				1 Oral 1 68% (25)	3 68% (18)			6			3			4 Oral 4 69% (26)	7
Hiromi Japanese					1 100% (28)	6 93% (80)	3			1 Oral 1		1			
Sang Wook Korean					4 (2) 86% (21)	1 86% (36)		2	4 Oral 2	2		Oral 3			
Noriko Japanese						1 67% (12)	1	3				1	2	2	3
Ji-An Korean					96% (25)	1 97% (30)	1	1	1	1			1		
Hamad Arabic						1 72% (18)				1	91% (22)		1 Oral 1		
Abdullah Arabic						3 83% (23)				1		Oral 1	1 Oral 2		

Numeral — Number of uses of past progressive in writing
Oral + numeral — Number of uses of past progressive in oral
% — Percentage of appropriate past tense use
% + (numeral) — Number of verb types sampled in half month

Instruction in past progressive
Instruction in present progressive

Table 6.2 (continued)

The Emergence of Past Progressive with Respect to Instruction

Learner	8	8.5	9	9.5	10	10.5	11	11.5	12	12.5	13	13.5	14	14.5	15	Total
Idechi Japanese																W 17 O 2
Eduardo Spanish																W 19 O 41
Khaled Arabic	1 Oral 1	1	1	1		Oral 2	Oral 1	1								W 20 O 6
Toshihiro Japanese						3	2		2							W 8 O 1
Satoru Japanese		2	2						2							W 5 O 1
Carlos Spanish	2 Oral 2	2	4 Oral 5													W 37 O 25
Saleh Arabic	Oral 1			8 Oral 2	7	2 Oral 1	1			2 Oral 2	6	1 Oral		5 Oral 8	1	W 39 O 16
Kazuhiro Japanese	1		2 Oral 2			Oral 2										W 8 O 4
Guillermo Spanish	3	1														W 15 O 3

Table 6.2 (continued)

The Emergence of Past Progressive with Respect to Instruction

Learner	8	8.5	9	9.5	10	10.5	11	11.5	12	12.5	13	13.5	14	14.5	15	Total
Zayed Arabic	1 Oral 1	2	6 Oral 12	2		7 Oral 1	Oral 1	Oral 2								W 44 O 22
Hiromi Japanese		2	4	4												W 22 O 2
Sang Wook Korean																W 13 O 5
Noriko Japanese	3					2	5 Oral 3	1 Oral 1		5	3 Oral 3	2				W 41 O 13
Ji-An Korean																W 6 O 0
Hamad Arabic			1	1	Oral 1						2					W 7 O 2
Abdullah Arabic				1	4								1	1		W 12 O 3

For 14 learners, there were at least some recorded lessons on present progressive in every sampling interval between T0.5 and T2.0. Six learners received instruction in the past progressive early at T1.5 and all the learners received instruction in the past progressive by T2.5. The past progressive is the most targeted of all the tense-aspect forms under investigation (past progressive, present perfect, and pluperfect). The progressive is also the first tense-aspect form to be taught.

The learners can be divided into two groups: those who used the past progressive before instruction and those who used it for the first time after instruction. As Table 6.2 shows, 10 learners (Idechi, Eduardo, Khaled, Toshihiro, Satoru, Carlos, Saleh, Kazuhiro, Guillermo, and Zayed) used the past progressive before the past progressive was formally presented in the grammar classes (represented by the light grey shading). Note, however, that all of the early uses in this corpus occurred during instruction on the present progressive (represented by the dark grey shading). There is variation in timing and frequency within this group of learners. Idechi used the past progressive as early as T0.5, producing 15 written tokens by T2.0; Guillermo and Zayed showed their first uses at T2.0, producing 2 tokens apiece.

The second group of learners (Hiromi, Sang Wook, Noriko, Ji-An, Hamad, and Abdullah) produced no tokens of past progressive in the written or oral corpus until instruction. All learners in this group showed emergence by T3.0, and, as a group, showed higher rates of appropriate use of simple past than the early group. The time of the emergence of the past progressive did not affect the number of tokens that a learner eventually produced in the corpus. In the after-instruction group, Noriko produced 41 written and 13 oral tokens of past progressive, whereas in the before-instruction group Idechi produced only 17 written and 2 oral tokens.

Present Perfect

With one exception, instruction seems to have the same basic effect on the learners regardless of their individual stages of acquisition: to increase the production of the present perfect (Table 6.3).[7] However, the strength of the effect that instruction has, as measured by the quantity of tokens, seems to depend on the learners' acquisitional stages. The learners can be grouped into three main groups: those who show frequent use of the present perfect before instruction, those who show tentative use, and those who show no emergence prior to instruction. In Table 6.3 the learners are arranged from top to bottom by the number of uses of present perfect a learner shows before instruction. The shaded areas represent instruction during a particular interval, but should not be construed as filling the whole interval.

In the first group of learners who frequently use the present perfect, Kazuhiro, Carlos, Toshihiro, and Eduardo show more than 10 uses of present perfect prior to instruction, with Ji-An and Hiromi showing 6 uses. These occur in a rather short span of 1–1.5 months. The next group shows more tentative use of the present perfect, with fewer, more widely-spaced instances per learner. This group (Khaled, Noriko, Hamad, Idechi, Zayed, and Sang Wook) shows between one and three uses prior to instruction. The last group is comprised of three learners (Guillermo, Saleh, and Abdullah) who show no use of present perfect before instruction. Satoru straddles the last two groups because his apparent first use of present perfect is both ill-formed and inappropriately used, and it is thus not clear to which group he belongs.

The learners who have begun to experiment with the present perfect before instruction show the greatest increase in use; that is, instruction seems to encourage more frequent, possibly more confident, use of present perfect, particularly during the periods of instruction. Thus, the learners who show the largest increases are the ones who had greater linguistic resources to begin with. For example, Carlos exhibits increasing use of present perfect in the three periods before instruction, and continues to use the present perfect regularly after instruction begins. Both oral and written use increase dramatically following a unit called "tense review" at T7.0 that contrasted the present perfect and past, perfect progressive and present perfect, and past and pluperfect.

Table 6.3

Emergence of Present Perfect with Respect to Instruction

Subject	Month 0.5	1	1.5	2	2.5	3	3.5	4	4.5	5	5.5	6	6.5	7	7.5
Kazuhiro Japanese	2 (1) prompt 2	2 87% (15)	1 (0)	3 (2) Oral 1	2	1 Oral 1			1	1 (0)	3 (2)	4 (3)		5 (3)	1 PROG Oral 1
Carlos Spanish		2 83% (6)	2 97% (32)	14 (12) Oral 2	10	8 Oral 5	2			6 Oral 2	8	6(5) Oral 3	6	27(26) Oral 19	2 Oral 8
Toshihiro Japanese		1 100% (14)	9 (0) 85% (58)		1 (0) Oral 1	1		1 Oral 1							
Eduardo Spanish		78% (18)	2 85% (33)	6	6	12 Oral 3	5			17 (15) PROG	6	20	6	3	Oral 4
Ji-An Korean				1	2 (1) 96% (25)	3 (2)	2	4 PROG	3 (1) Oral 1	1	4	Oral 2	3		
Hiromi Japanese						2 93% (80)	7 (6)	5 PROG	4	5		Oral 1	1	1	1
Khaled Arabic	Oral 2			1 100% (26)						3				1 PROG 94% (16)	
Noriko Japanese	1 (0) 67% (15)	1 86% (14)			1		1		3 Oral 1		3	2	2	4	2 Oral 1
Hamad Arabic			Oral 1	2 (1) 75% (40)			prompt		Oral 3*		91% (22)	Oral 2			

Table 6.3 (continued)

Emergence of Present Perfect with Respect to Instruction

Subject	Month 0.5	1	1.5	2	2.5	3	3.5	4	4.5	5	5.5	6	6.5	7	7.5
Idechi Japanese		1 (0) 83% (30)	1 85% (47)							Oral 1	1 (0)			6 (2)	2
Zayed Arabic				1 68% (25)	2 68% (18)	2 (0) PROG	2 64% (22)					Oral 1		4 (3)	1 (0) Oral 3
Sang Wook Korean						1 86% (36)	prompt		1						
Satoru Japanese				1* (0)	77% (22)	77% (34)				2	2 93% (14)	3			
Guillermo Spanish					88% (24)	Oral 3			1	4 (3) PROG	1	1		6 (5)	4 (2)
Abdullah Arabic						83% (23)	prompt	100% (12)	Oral 1				1	1	
Saleh Arabic							prompt	82% (37)				2 (0) 81% (26)			

Numeral — Number of uses of present perfect in writing
Oral + numeral — Number of uses of present perfect in oral
(Numeral) — Number of appropriate uses of present perfect
% — Percentage of appropriate past tense use
% + (numeral) — Number of verb types sampled in half month

Prompt — Prompted use of present perfect in writing
PROG — Emergence of perfect progressive
[shaded] — Instruction in present perfect

Table 6.3 (continued)

Emergence of Present Perfect with Respect to Instruction

Subject	Month 8	8.5	9	9.5	10	10.5	11	11.5	12	12.5	13	13.5	14	14.5	15	Total
Kazuhiro Japanese	2	1	1 Oral 3	3	1											W 36 O 6
Carlos Spanish	6 Oral 1	3	9 PROG Oral 2													W 111 O 42
Toshihiro Japanese					1 PROG	2										W 16 O 2
Eduardo Spanish																W 83 O 10
Ji-An Korean																W 23 O 3
Hiromi Japanese	1	5	4	5 Oral 1	2											W 43 O 2
Khaled Arabic	1 (0) Oral 1	2	1	3	4			2 (1)								W 18 O 3
Noriko Japanese	7 (6)	1	2			7 (4)	6 (5)		4 (3)	3 (3)	1 PROG	1	2	1 Oral 2	5 (4) Oral 1	W 62 O 6
Hamad Arabic				1-89% (47) Oral 4	1 Oral 1	3 (1)				2 PROG Oral 1	Oral 2		3 (2)		Oral 1	W 12 O 15

Table 6.3 (continued)

Emergence of Present Perfect with Respect to Instruction

Subject	Month 8	8.5	9	9.5	10	10.5	11	11.5	12	12.5	13	13.5	14	14.5	15	Total
Idechi Japanese	1	2	2													W 16 O 1
Zayed Arabic		3 (2)	Oral 2	1 (0)	2		Oral 1									W 18 O 7
Sang Wook Korean																W 2 O 0
Satoru Japanese		1	1	3	1											W 14 O 1
Guillermo Spanish	5 (3) Oral 4	5														W 27 O 3
Abdullah Arabic				4	4							1				W 10 O 1
Saleh Arabic				1	1 Oral 2					1 Oral 1	prompt	1		1	3 (2) PROG	W 11 O 3

Note. From "Another Piece of the Puzzle: The Emergence of the Present Perfect," by K. Bardovi-Harlig (1997), *Language Learning, 47(3),* 392–394. Copyright 1997 by the Language Learning Research Club. Reprinted with permission.

In an oral task conducted at T7.0, three days after the review lesson, Carlos showed 19 uses of the present perfect, with 20 additional written uses between T7.0 and T10.0. Eduardo similarly increased his production after instruction, most notably at T3.0 and T5.0. Kazuhiro, Hiromi, and Ji-An responded similarly to instruction but with somewhat less dramatic results than Carlos and Eduardo.

Toshihiro shows a different pattern of early use. Although he produced 11 present perfect tokens prior to instruction (which places him in the first group of more robust users), only 1 of the 11 was appropriate. Toshihiro clearly could produce the form of the present perfect but he overgeneralized it to past environments. Instruction seemed to *reduce* Toshihiro's enthusiastic but misplaced use. Perhaps instruction led Toshihiro to retreat from the use of a form whose meaning was not what he thought it was. His use of present perfect after instruction was very sporadic, amounting to fewer attempts in the 9 months following instruction than in the 2 months immediately preceding it. The three recorded uses after instruction, however, were appropriate.

In the second group, some learners do not show an immediate increase in production after the first instructional period, but require repeated instructional periods. Idechi shows increased production after instruction, but not until the third lesson on present perfect at T7.0, after which he shows regular, sustained use. Khaled shows a similar profile to Idechi with increased use in the fourth period of instruction at T5.0, again at T7.0, and afterward, with more than half of his uses occurring after T8.5. Writing prompts, statements or questions to which learners respond in writing and which may be interpreted as non-explicit instruction, also do not seem to have an immediate effect on four of the learners (Hamad, Sang Wook, Saleh, and Abdullah). Learners do not seem to put the present perfect into use by following the model based solely on a prompt. In considering the tentative uses of present perfect by the second group of learners prior to instruction, it is also necessary to note that not all early uses of the present perfect occur in environments in which native speakers would use them. Noriko, Idechi, and Satoru have single initial uses which are inappropriate. Three of the learners, Guillermo, Saleh, and Abdullah, as seen at the bottom of Table 6.3, showed no use of present perfect in the corpus before instruction. However, they did show emergence of present perfect after instruction. Guillermo also showed an increase in use coincident with instruction at T3.0, T5.0 and T7.0, with more regular and sustained use after T7.0.

The second group shows how difficult it is to isolate the effects of instruction. It is much easier to determine that instruction has no effect (see Bardovi-Harlig, 1994b). Repeated instructional periods may also coincide with an accumulation of input received from various other sources during an increasingly long stay in the host environment. An example of this may be seen in Noriko's use of present perfect. The second instructional period at T7.5 is followed by an increase in Noriko's use of the present perfect at T8.0 and sustained use from T10.5 to T15.0. Due to the time lag, however, the effect of instruction cannot be isolated from other factors.

Because the perfect progressive emerges later, the effect of instruction here can be more easily observed. A grammar-focused lesson on the perfect progressive followed the instruction on the present perfect. For 6 of the 12 learners who used the perfect progressive, one or more spontaneous uses are observed during the same interval as the instruction. These learners were Eduardo, Guillermo, Ji-An, Hiromi, Khaled, and Zayed. All but Zayed were identified as frequent users of the perfect progressive in Chapter 3. In contrast, Zayed showed only a single use during the instructional period, with no further use. Kazuhiro exhibited two uses, one well-formed and one not, in the month following instruction. The remaining four learners showed one to two uses in the 2 to 5 months after instruction. For these learners and the four learners who showed no use of the perfect progressive, I would claim that they showed no obvious effect of instruction from the production data available. Even among the five learners who showed fairly robust use of perfect progressive during instruction, three used the perfect progressive during a second or subsequent instructional period.

Thus, the additional input provided by instruction is not in itself sufficient to guarantee the emergence of the perfect progressive, even among learners who already show frequent use of the present perfect.

Pluperfect

Compared to the more robust production of the present perfect during and after instruction, the response to the production of the pluperfect is harder to interpret. As we saw in Chapter 3, the pluperfect is the last of the past reference forms to emerge. There are also fewer tokens produced. As shown in Table 6.4, for the majority of the learners the pluperfect was introduced in the first half of the 3rd or 4th month and was reviewed in the 7th month. Some learners received the original presentation (or the review) more than once or at a very different time because they repeated a level of instruction, as Table 6.1 shows.

As is the case with the present perfect, Carlos and Eduardo show appropriate use of the pluperfect prior to instruction. Despite Carlos's enthusiastic early use of the pluperfect between T1.0 and T3.0, he uses no pluperfects in the recorded oral and written samples in the three sampling periods T3.5 to T4.5, but resumes at T5.0. During that time Carlos also received instruction in past progressive (T2.5–T3.5) and present perfect (T3.0), and his production shows that he was using past progressive during that time. Eduardo shows continued, if modest, use of pluperfect after instruction.

Three learners (Noriko, Toshihiro, Guillermo) had begun to experiment with the pluperfect prior to instruction using between one and three tokens, but none of their attempts was appropriate. In their case, instruction seems to do little to increase either their production or appropriate use. In fact, Toshihiro's production of pluperfect stops after T4.0 and does not resume with the second period of instruction at T6.5. This is nearly the same pattern that he showed with the present perfect: use of tense-aspect morphology in appropriate contexts and retreat following instruction.

Table 6.4

The Emergence of Pluperfect with Respect to Instruction

Subject	Month 0.5	1	1.5	2	2.5	3	3.5	4	4.5	5	5.5	6	6.5	7	7.5
Carlos Spanish		4(0) 83%(6)	2(0) 97%(32)	9(7) *1	5(5)	3(3)				4(4) 1*	19(17)	6, *1 Oral 4(3)		3(2) Oral 2(1)	11(8)
Eduardo Spanish		3 78%(18)	5(4)	1(0)	1	2	1			Oral *1(0)	1 Oral 1	1		1	
Kazuhiro Japanese		2(1*) 85%(13)	1(0) 72%(25)	2(1)	2						1(0)				2(1)
Hiromi Japanese					1(0) 100%(28)	3 93%(80)	1*				1	1 PROG	4 Oral 2(1)		3
Noriko Japanese	67% (15)	1 (0) 86%(14)											1(0)	1(0)	
Toshihiro Japanese			2*(0) 85%(58)		1*(0)		2*(0)	2*(0)							
Guillermo Spanish										1(0)		1(0)			1(0)
Idechi Japanese		83%(3)	85%(47)	88%(68)		1* 91%(22)	1(0)	1(0) 95%(20)							2(1) *1
Sang Wook Korean											2	Oral 1(0)			

Table 6.4 (continued)

The Emergence of Pluperfect with Respect to Instruction

Subject	Month 0.5	1	1.5	2	2.5	3	3.5	4	4.5	5	5.5	6	6.5	7	7.5
Ji-An Korean					96% (25)				Oral 1(0) 93% 27	3(0)	Oral 1(0)	1			
Zayed Arabic					84% (19)						1				81% (63) Oral 1 (0)
Satoru Japanese											2(0) 100% (10)	2(0)	1	1(0)	
Khaled Arabic														1(0) 94% (18)	
Hamad Arabic				75% (40)											
Abdullah Arabic								82% (37)							
Saleh Arabic															

Numeral	Number of uses of pluperfect in writing
% + (numeral)	Number of verb types sampled in half month
(Numeral)	Number of appropriate uses, if different from # used
%	Percentage of appropriate past tense use

Oral + numeral	Number of uses of pluperfect in oral
PROG	Emergence of pluperfect progressive
[shaded]	Instruction in pluperfect

Table 6.4 (continued)

The Emergence of Pluperfect with Respect to Instruction

Learner	Month 8	8.5	9	9.5	10	10.5	11	11.5	12	12.5	13	13.5	14	14.5	15	Total
Carlos Spanish	5(5)		3(3) Oral 1(1)	Oral 10(7)												W 74 (60) O 17 (13)
Eduardo Spanish																W 17 (14) O 2
Kazuhiro Japanese		1*	1	Oral 1(0)												W 12 (7) O 1 (0)
Hiromi Japanese	5 Oral 2	4(3) *PROG	3(2)	3(2)												W 33 (29) O 4 (3)
Noriko Japanese	1(0)							Oral 2	1(0)	1					Oral 1*	W 6 (2) O 3
Toshihiro Japanese																W 8 (1) O 0
Guillermo Spanish	1(0)															W 5 (0) O 0
Idechi Japanese			2													W 6 (3) O 0
Sang Wook Korean																W 3 (2) O 1 (0)

Table 6.4 (continued)

The Emergence of Pluperfect with Respect to Instruction

Learner	Month 8	8.5	9	9.5	10	10.5	11	11.5	12	12.5	13	13.5	14	14.5	15	Total
Ji-An Korean																W 4 (1) O 2 (0)
Zayed Arabic																W 1 O 1 (0)
Satoru Japanese	90%(10)															W 6 (0) O 0
Khaled Arabic	1*		1													W 3 (3) O 0
Hamad Arabic		1(0) 84%(19)		4(1) 85%(46)	1(0)	3							1			W10 (5) O 0
Abdullah Arabic					1(0) 90%(19)										1	W 2 (1) O 0
Saleh Arabic																W 0 O 0

Toshihiro produced no present perfect in the recorded written or oral samples between T4.5 and T9.5, but resumed at T10.0. We might expect that he would eventually attempt the pluperfect again.

Ji-An and Hamad also appear to show the influence of instruction. Ji-An showed no use of the pluperfect before instruction at T4.0, but her first use occurred in the sampling interval immediately following at T4.5. Hamad showed no use of the pluperfect in spite of instruction at T4.0 and T6.0–6.5. At T8.5 his initial use was nontargetlike and overgeneralized, but following instruction at T9.0, he attempted four pluperfects and three targetlike uses at T10.5. Idechi attempted the pluperfect during and after instruction at T7.0. Khaled first used the pluperfect at T7.0 during instruction. Sang Wook produced his first pluperfect during an instructional period and two more 1.5 months after. The remaining seven learners produced no pluperfects, produced so few, or produced them so late after instruction that a reaction to instruction seems unlikely (e.g., Zayed, Satoru, Abdullah).

Even for learners who appear to eventually respond to instruction, the first wave of instruction between T3.0 and T4.0 seems to have had little effect. This includes learners who have high rates of appropriate use of past and have expressed reverse-order reports (see Chapter 2). The learners also received instruction in past progressive and present perfect between T2.5 and T4.0. All learners show emergence of the past progressive by T3.0 and—with the exception of Saleh, Abdullah, and Satoru—have begun to experiment with the present perfect. There is considerable activity in the morphological development of the tense-aspect systems of the learners, but no obvious response to instruction in the pluperfect at T3.0. However, Ji-An begins to experiment with the pluperfect after instruction at T4.0. Noriko and Hiromi, and Khaled and Kazuhiro increase production of the pluperfect during or after instruction at T6.5 and T7.0, respectively.

The Effect of Instruction

As seen in the preceding discussions of learner production relative to instructional periods, it is much more difficult to determine the effect of instruction in an observational inquiry than in an experimental study. The learners in this study were completely in control of their own production both in terms of topic and—at least for the journals—whether or not they produced a language sample. The exclusive use of learner-generated texts raises the issue of a sampling problem. On the one hand, the learner texts that I collected were all communicative examples of learners making meaning. On the other hand, such naturalistic production did not give the learners the opportunity to demonstrate their knowledge through the completion of cloze passages or other more controlled tasks. For example, learners might have been able to demonstrate appropriate use of tense-aspect in the pluperfect had they been given a cloze passage. In the data collection I selected tasks that would yield as communicative a corpus as possible while taking advantage of the writing skills of the instructed learners as well as their oral production.

Extended observation that does not restrict the environment of use for a learner, such as that conducted in the present study, allows observers to see the development of interlanguage as learners incorporate (or do not incorporate) instructionally targeted forms into their interlanguage. Many fewer tokens were produced for the pluperfect than for other verbal morphology. However, one could also point out that learners were able to construct appropriate contexts for the past progressive and present perfect. Perhaps the issue is not the type of samples but the timing of the sample. Because the pluperfect emerges later for most learners, there may have been more opportunities for the learners to produce the pluperfect after the 16-month observation period was over.

Because the teaching of tense-aspect morphology was clustered together (at least for past progressive, present perfect, and the pluperfect), and the emergence of the forms is relatively spread out in comparison, one cannot attribute the order of emergence or frequency of use to the order of instruction. Consider once again Carlos's production during the instruction occurring between T2.5 and T3.5. If we compare Tables 6.2–6.4, we see that Carlos used the simple past and the past progressive between T3.5 and T4.5, but suspended production of the present perfect and pluperfect. In spite of the instructional barrage that he received, Carlos seems to have sorted out his tense-aspect morphology one form-meaning association at a time. We may interpret this in terms of the teachability hypothesis (Pienemann, 1989, 1998). According to the teachability hypothesis, a learner is more likely to integrate a linguistic feature that is targeted by·instruction if the completion of a prior acquisitional stage has increased the potential influence of instruction on interlanguage development, or the instruction has focused on the next stage of acquisition. As Pienemann predicts, Carlos seemed acquisitionally primed for instruction on the past progressive at T2.5–T3.5, and he responded with an increased and steady use of the past progressive. Hiromi also fits the profile outlined by Pienemann. At the time of the first instructional period for the pluperfect (T4.0), she had just begun to use the present perfect, and she showed no use of the pluperfect after instruction. In contrast, by the time of the second period of instruction on the pluperfect (T6.5–7.0), she seems to have satisfied the acquisitionally prior stages, showing use of both the past progressive and the present perfect. She responded to instruction by using a number of tokens of pluperfect in both oral and written production over the next six sampling intervals.

Comparing the learners from the longitudinal study with other learners from the same IEP sheds further light on the issue of teachability. As observed in the longitudinal study, students received instruction in Level 4 that is known as the "tense review." This corresponds to the second concentration of tense-aspect instruction between T6.5 and T7.0. According to the cross-sectional study of learners from the same program (Bardovi-Harlig & Reynolds, 1995), appropriate use rates for simple past drop after instruction in Level 4. This seems to be in response to the introduction or reintroduction of certain tense-aspect forms that learners attempt to use in the elicitation tasks and that cut into the appropriacy rates of the simple past.[8] Two things must be taken into account, however. The drop in appropriate use of past happens only in activities, not in states and not in events. As seen in Chapter 4, activities are the least likely of the dynamic predicates to receive simple past morphology in early stages. Thus they become the most susceptible to restructuring as the learners attempt to make form-meaning associations on the basis of grammar-oriented traditional instruction. Second, consider the length of time involved. According to the cross-sectional study, learners do improve by Level 5. Any apparent losses in appropriate use are shortly regained, and thus, this may be seen as an example of the U-shaped curve (Ellis, 1994; Kellerman, 1985) in L2 acquisition. If we were to evaluate the learners at Level 3 only, we would assume that real progress had been made in the tense-aspect system, but it would be too early for such a claim. A longer perspective is needed with instructed learners if we are to understand the outcome.

It is also important to note that the learners have individual acquisition profiles, especially with respect to rate, in spite of the fact that they are enrolled in the same intensive English program. From the sketches of the longitudinal learners as students, we see that the learners varied greatly in their interactions with the instructional environment. Hiromi, who was described by her teachers as a model student, was morphologically oriented in her temporal expression. Even so, her sustained use of pluperfect appears only after the second period of instruction at T6.5, not after the first at T4.0. On the other hand, Saleh moved slowly, which may be related to the trouble he had as a student. But he approached acquisition on his own terms. Later than most learners, he came to a productive, appropriate, and sustained use of the past progressive and showed even later use of the present perfect. Saleh is likely to have acquired the pluperfect after the observation of the longitudinal study had ended. In contrast, Toshihiro was described by his teacher at T2.0 as "the best student in grammar so far." But what we see from Toshihiro's free production is form without meaning. Being good at grammar early on did not give Toshihiro an advantage in tense-aspect morphology when it came to establishing targetlike form-meaning associations; and, as we saw, Toshihiro retreated after instruction. Such a retreat is not unknown in acquisition (cf. Pienemann, 1989). Abdullah, who had virtually no contact with Americans beyond his teachers and the research team but who studied constantly and was very concerned with grammar, made less progress than the carefree Saleh.

In spite of their individual variations in rate and response to instruction, however, these learners showed virtually the same acquisition orders no matter how spread out or condensed their production. More importantly, all of the learners were well into morphological development, the third stage of temporal expression identified by Klein and colleagues (Klein, 1993, 1994; Dietrich et al., 1995). All the learners made a reliable distinction between past and non-past and most exhibited the acquisition of other tense-aspect morphology. Thus, instruction affected rate, but not route.

To attempt to understand the variable of instruction in light of other variables, we move finally to a comparison of instructed and uninstructed learners in terms of level of attainment at the end of the periods during which they were observed.

A Comparison of Instructed and Uninstructed Learners

To begin the comparison of tutored and untutored learners, this section compares the ESF learners within the same target languages. The ESF reports (Dietrich et al., 1995) present profiles of four (and in one case six) learners of each of the five target languages. The learners represent two different first languages for each target language. The learners were chosen to illustrate a full range of development and thus the presentation often pairs a lower-level (sometimes slower) learner with a higher-level (sometimes faster) learner to cover all the stages of development. The presentation of background information makes it possible to ask the question of whether the instructed learners in the sample are fundamentally different from uninstructed learners of the same language in their acquisition of temporal expression.

Table 6.5 presents a brief profile of each of the longitudinal learners from the ESF study based on the biographical information about the informants in Dietrich et al. (1995) and Bhardwaj et al. (1988). As discussed in Chapter 2, the pragmatic and lexical stages culminate in the basic variety, which all learners attain. Dietrich et al. (1995) identified two potential paths after learners attain the basic variety: Learners may stay at the lexical stage of development and enrich their basic variety through the acquisition of additional lexical items, notably verbs, adverbials, and boundary markers (including *start* and *finish*), or they can enter the morphological stage, the third main stage of development of temporal expression.[9] The elaboration of the basic variety tends to bring immediate increases in communicative effectiveness, whereas the morphological path includes periods of lack of systematic use of verbal morphology prior to the establishment of targetlike form-meaning associations. If a learner reaches only the elaborated basic variety at the end of the observation period, this is listed; otherwise "morphological development" is listed and the morphology used by the learner is given.

There are some clear stars among the ESF learners, most notably Lavinia (L2 English, L1 Italian), Ayshe and Abdullah (L2 German, L1 Turkish), and Mari (L2 Swedish, L1 Finnish). These learners were instructed learners, all of whom lived in the host environment during the study. (There were also other important variables to which I will return shortly.)

Lavinia showed the same progress as the most successful learners in the longitudinal ESL study reported in the previous section. The instructed Turkish learners of German, Abdullah and Ayshe, also acquired a rich repertoire of tense-aspect morphology in contrast to the uninstructed Italian learners, Tino and Angelina. Dietrich (1995) observed that

> No member of the Italian sample acquired the general non-formulaic use of the Präteritum or the complex tense of the Plusquamperfekt, while all the Turkish learners, in

Table 6.5

Profile of Learners from the ESF Longitudinal Study (Dietrich et al., 1995)

Learner	Target Language	L1	Age at Arrival	Months of Study	Social Contact	General Education	Language Instruction	Stage at End of Observation
Lavinia	English	Italian	20	6–36	Worked as a waitress; vocational courses, children, library, book club; worked in garment industry between courses	Not specified; vocational courses in clerical skills in Britain	Husband taught L. some English before arrival; 10 months ESL classes; clerical and English skills course	Morphological development; simple past, present perfect, past progressive, pluperfect
Andrea	English	Italian	36	11–32	Worked as a waiter and barman with other Italians; one English friend, others Italian	Completed scuola media, professional training as electrician	EFL, 4 months 10 hrs/week	Morphological development: use of irregular and some regular past; use of V-0 and V-ing, but no functional contrast
Santo	English	Italian	mid-20s	7–26	Worked in Italian restaurant; had Italian girlfriend	8 years of school	None	Basic variety plus irregular past; use of V-0 and V-ing but no functional contrast
Rudolfo	English	Italian	mid-20s	15–not specified	Worked in Italian restaurant, then coffee-house where English was spoken	High school	None	Basic variety
Madan	English	Punjabi	25	20–48	Worked as press operator; lived with L1 family; little exposure to English	8 years primary school	1 year EFL in primary school; 3 years Hindi; cannot read English	Basic variety and past participle, V-0 and V-ing, no contrast

Table 6.5 (continued)

Profile of Learners from the ESF Longitudinal Study (Dietrich et al., 1995)

Learner	Target Language	L1	Age at Arrival	Months of Study	Social Contact	General Education	Language Instruction	Stage at End of Observation
Ravinder	English	Punjabi	20	13–32	Contacts in English minimal: worked in family businesses	Primary school	2 years EFL in primary school, "rote learning"	Basic variety; rich vocabulary; V-0 and V-ing, no functional contrast
Tino	German	Italian	18	5–34	Waiter in Italian restaurants; positive attitude toward Germany, but wanted to return to Italy and did	Completed school at 16	None	Elaborated basic variety
Casco	German	Italian	18	10–34	Intensive and frequent contact with German; liked speaking German	Primary school, secondary school, 2 years training in hotel management	None	Morphological development: Präsens, Perfekt
Angelina	German	Italian	20	23–49	Very little contact in German	Primary school, 3 years secondary school	None	Basic variety
Abdullah	German	Turkish	16	8–28	Kitchen help in fast food restaurant	8 years school (did not finish)	Instruction in German a couple of hours a week from a social worker	Morphological development; Präsens, Perfekt, Präteritum, Plusquamperfekt, Futur
Ayshe	German	Turkish	16	8–30	Many social contacts, outgoing and talkative; positive attitude; strong	5½ years school in Turkey; went to school in Germany	Type of instruction not specified, but attended school in	Morphological development; Präsens, Perfekt, Präteritum,

Table 6.5 (continued)

Profile of Learners from the ESF Longitudinal Study (Dietrich et al., 1995)

Learner	Target Language	L1	Age at Arrival	Months of Study	Social Contact	General Education	Language Instruction	Stage at End of Observation
					integrative and instrumental motivation	at vocational courses; an attentive and keen pupil	German	Plusquamperfekt, Futur; development of two registers
Ergün	Dutch	Turkish	17	15–33	Factory worker (temporary); access to Dutch NS, played on Dutch/Turkish soccer team	5 years primary school	Language course 2 hrs/week, irregular attendance	Morphological development: present, perfect forms, eliminates present for past and bare infinitives
Mahmut	Dutch	Turkish	19	13–31	1 year unemployed, then worked in meat factory; Turkish friends and relatives	Primary school	None	Elaborated basic variety; adds lexical items, adverbials
Mohamed	Dutch	Moroccan Arabic	19	8–27	Factory worker; lots of contact with NS; Dutch girlfriends	Primary school, 2 years secondary school; trained as motor mechanic	None	Morphological development: Praesens & Perfectum
Fatima	Dutch	Moroccan Arabic	25	14–43	Worked as a cleaning woman	2 years primary school	Migrant training course 2 hrs/week	Basic variety
Zahra	French	Moroccan Arabic	30	14–43	Worked as a cleaning woman; joined husband in clothing workshop	No school in Morocco, received training as a seamstress	20–30 hrs of French (dropped class)	Basic variety, slight tendency toward morphological development, verb forms not yet stabilized

Table 6.5 (continued)

Profile of Learners from the ESF Longitudinal Study (Dietrich et al., 1995)

Learner	Target Language	L1	Age at Arrival	Months of Study	Social Contact	General Education	Language Instruction	Stage at End of Observation
Abdelmalek	French	Moroccan Arabic	19	14–43	Worked as a fisherman and sold clothes in the market; contact with French limited	Some primary education in Morocco, no French at school; spoke some Spanish in Morocco	None	Elaborated basic variety
Berta	French	Spanish	30	12–29	Social life with Chileans; no regular job in France, in 3rd year trained as supermarket cashier	Practically did not read French; not interested in press, radio, TV, except music	None	Elaborated basic variety; emergent verbal morphology; moving toward morphological tense; past-nonpast, periphrastic future.
Alfonso	French	Spanish	31	11–44	Worked in industry and hotel cleaning; most friends were Colombian; had family in Paris; liked meeting people at work and listening to news on TV and read French newspapers	Not specified	Full-time French course for refugees; too difficult, did not get L2 benefit	Elaborated basic variety; emergent verbal morphology; moving toward morphological tense
Nora	Swedish	Spanish	39	18–43	Worked as a cleaner and delivered newspapers	Not specified; took course for immigrants in Spanish at the elementary school level while in Sweden;	Various Swedish courses; Spanish course included a few hours a week on Swedish	Morphological development: present, preterite, and a few tokens of perfect in past contexts

Table 6.5 (continued)

Profile of Learners from the ESF Longitudinal Study (Dietrich et al., 1995)

Learner	Target Language	L1	Age at Arrival	Months of Study	Social Contact	General Education	Language Instruction	Stage at End of Observation
						attended a nursing course once a week		
Fernando	Swedish	Spanish	33	10–35	Unemployed, no Swedish friends; political refugee; balanced attitude toward Sweden	Elementary school; technical course at school for immigrants	Studied Swedish at 2 schools for immigrants; also technical courses	Morphological development: present, preterite, tentative tokens of perfect
Rauni	Swedish	Finnish	29	15–30	Babysitter for Finnish relatives; Finnish friends; married a Swede; positive attitude	6 years elementary school, 1 year public citizen school, 1 year Christian folk college	300 hr course but didn't complete it; husband said course was useless, R. agreed somewhat	Morphological development: present, preterite, emergence of perfect (overgeneralized)
Mari	Swedish	Finnish	22	14–44	Worked as au pair to Finnish family; worked as a cleaner, then textile factory; made Swedish friends at work; married Finn, social life w/Finns; began to read Swedish newspaper at 28 months	6 years elementary school, 2 years vocational training in textiles	600+ hr, but limited ability in speaking, reading, & writing with very limited listening; another 70 hr course, short but effective	Morphological development: present, preterite, perfect, and plusqvamperfektum

contrast, did . . . There is no doubt, on the other hand, about the fact that formal L2 instruction puts the learners' focus more on grammatical structures, written language, and correctness of use than do the interlocutors in everyday communication. (p. 111)

Dietrich also observes that instruction is not the only variable that distinguishes a successful learner like Ayshe from Angelina. (See Table 6.5.) Ayshe had contact every day at school in German, resulting in immersion, where Angelina had none. Ayshe's attitude toward Germans was positive, and she was critical of the Turkish way of life. In contrast, Angelina was indifferent toward German and Germans and negative about emigrant life in Germany. Ayshe and Abdullah were both 16 when they arrived in Germany. Abdullah lived in a dormitory with other Turkish boys and their fathers, but Ayshe went to school and thus had an immersion experience.

The view of multiple factors is echoed in Klein's (1995) interpretation of Lavinia's success:

We should assume that Lavinia's remarkable progress is not so much a direct consequence of the language course she went to but of the general motivation to advance—to take courses of all types, to talk to people, to improve her social status in the host society. (pp. 50–51)

The interpretation that instruction alone is not responsible for success in acquisition is consistent with the findings of the longitudinal ESL study. All learners in that study had virtually the same instruction, and yet the stage of development at the end of the observational period varied by learner. As any teacher knows, instruction itself is not a monolithic variable. (See the review of the experimental literature on the effect of instruction in the first section of this chapter.) Reading down the next to the last right-hand column in Table 6.5, we see that the type of instruction that the ESF learners received varied widely. On the high end, Lavinia (L2 English, L1 Italian) had 10 months of instruction and Mari (L2 Swedish, L1 Finnish) had at least 670 hours; on the low end Ergün and Fatima (L2 Dutch, L1 Turkish) had 2 hours a week. It would therefore be unwise to treat instruction as a binary variable.

Response to instruction also varies. When both Lavinia and Mari were first interviewed after instruction, their L2 production was quite limited, yet both learners became highly successful learners. Ergün and Fatima both had two hours of Dutch per week, but Ergün—with his irregular attendance at what can be described as a minimal language course—went on to exhibit morphological development, whereas Fatima did not. Ergün had access to native speakers of Dutch, but Fatima did not. As Klein (1995) and Dietrich (1995) point out, there are other plausible variables involved in the outcome of acquisition.

It is also important to note that there are learners who enter the morphological stage of development with no instruction (e.g., Casco, L2 German, L1 Italian; Mohamed, L2 Dutch, L1 Turkish; and Berta, L1 Spanish, L2 French). These learners differed from their uninstructed and less successful counterparts by the same features that distinguish the instructed learners from each other: access to the target language which leads to input. Instruction is a form of access to the target language. Because of different approaches, some instruction leads to more input or input that serves acquisition better than others. Even general education may be in some sense boiled down to access to input. Some of the learners could not read in the target language and some may have been unlikely to read. L2 literacy makes available a second rich source of input to learners.

The clearest, perhaps most expected, outcomes are those of the uninstructed learners, who at the end of the 3-year observational period show only the basic variety (Tino, Angelina, L2 German, L1 Italian; Rudolfo, L2 English, L1 Italian; Abdelmalek, L2 French, L1 Arabic) and the very successful tutored learners (Lavinia, Abdullah, Ayshe, and Mari). However, tutored Alfonso and untutored Berta (L2 French, L1 Spanish) end up at the same stage, an elaborated basic variety with emergent verbal morphology; and Ergün and Fatima, with only two hours of instruction, still end up with different outcomes.

Chapter Summary

The studies reviewed in this chapter show that instruction has a positive effect on the acquisition of tense-aspect by adult learners of second languages. The reports of experimental instruction that help learners link form and meaning showed immediate results on the posttests. In contrast, the observational studies showed extended benefits of instruction. The learners in the longitudinal study of ESL learners showed less dramatic immediate effect than the experimental learners. Observation of the learners' stage of development of the simple past and other tense-aspect morphology showed that learners had to have satisfied acquisitional prerequisites in order for instruction to be effective, as Pienemann (1989, 1998) has claimed.

Differences between the experimental studies and the observational longitudinal study may be due to two additional factors: the type of instruction and the type of data collection. The rather traditional form-focused instruction that the longitudinal group received was not as meaning-focused as the instruction in the five experimental studies reviewed. In addition, in some cases, the tasks that tested the learners' progress in the experimental studies were either more form-focused than the texts that compromise the longitudinal ESL corpus or were conducted in the same environment in which instruction had taken place, and thus learners' attention to the use of tense-aspect could have been heightened. Even with these differences—which should be investigated further—both the local and the observational studies suggest that instruction can benefit tense-aspect development. In addition, the ESF study shows the long-term benefits of instruction with respect to eventual attainment. All the tutored learners in the European study entered the morphological stage of development, whereas only some of the untutored learners did.

Aspect studies (Chapter 4) have included three environments in which learners may acquire a second language: uninstructed contact (e.g., Andersen, 1986a, 1986b; Rohde, 1996, 1997; and Andersen's students; see Andersen & Shirai, 1994), instructed second language (e.g., Bardovi-Harlig, 1998; Bardovi-Harlig & Reynolds, 1995; Giacalone Ramat, 1995c, 1997; Giacalone Ramat & Banfi, 1990; Shirai, 1995; Shirai & Kurono, 1998), and foreign language learning (e.g., Bergström, 1995, 1997; Hasbún, 1995; Kaplan, 1987; Leary, 1999). The aspect studies also show essentially the same patterns across environments, emphasizing the similarity among learners and the crucially linguistic nature of the second language acquisition process. Thus, temporal expression provides additional evidence for Gass's (1989) claim that second language acquisition is essentially the same psycholinguistic process regardless of environment. The study of temporal expression also suggests that the acquisitional sequences found in the development of tense-aspect systems may be part of what VanPatten (1990) has called the core of SLA.[10]

There is no doubt that instruction can be a positive influence on the acquisition of a targetlike tense-aspect system. Yet it does not change acquisitional sequences and it does not seem to save steps: Even though tutored learners are plunged into the morphological stage by virtue of instruction, they still exhibit the same pragmatic and lexical stages of temporal expression that have been observed for untutored learners. Tutored learners of English, German, Dutch, Swedish, and French go through the same stages as their untutored counterparts. With respect to sequences within the morphological stage, learners must satisfy the acquisitional prerequisites for a form to appear, even with the help of instruction.

There is also evidence that instruction is only one variable among many, and may be best understood as a component of input. Where other good input is available, learners still enter the morphological stage, even without instruction. Where instructional input, motivation, and input through L2 contact are combined, the outcome seems to be an advanced level of development and, eventually, corresponding targetlike form-meaning associations. However, instruction does not seem to be a privileged variable in any sense. It does not seem to alter acquisition orders, although it very likely increases the rate of acquisition. Even so, the grammars of instructed learners often move more slowly than their teachers would like. Instruction on tense and aspect can be delivered in a relatively short time, whereas learners take much longer to acquire a tense-aspect distinction. Although both instructed and uninstructed learners enter the stage of morphological development, the instructed learners seem to go farther in the same amount of time. We can conclude that this shows that the rate of acquisition is faster, but we should refrain from concluding that their potential eventual attainment is different.

Instruction is perhaps the most cherished variable in second language acquisition. Learners often believe that they can turn themselves over to a teacher who can take over the acquisition process; teachers just as often believe the same thing. However, in order to understand the role of instruction on the development of temporal semantics, we must see that instruction is not a privileged variable. It is just one factor among many, and other variables have as much influence in the instructed environment as they do outside of it. The acquisition of the temporal semantics of a second language remains the same linguistic process with or without instruction.

Notes

[1]Compared to the available research on the influence of instruction on second language acquisition in general, the goal of this chapter is quite modest. For comprehensive surveys and discussions, see, for example, Ellis (1990, 1994), Pienemann (1998), and Skehan (1998); see also Eckman, Highland, Lee, Mileham, and Weber (1995) for individual studies from a range of theoretical perspectives.

[2]Unlike the reviews in the previous chapters, this review is not intended to be exhaustive. I have included studies of three different target languages to provide some breadth, but my main criteria for selection were that the pedagogical approaches focus on helping learners make form-meaning associations within the tense-aspect system, that the description of tense-aspect morphology be consistent with current linguistic descriptions, and that the studies be published so that readers could have access to them for further reference.

[3]It would not be surprising for the comparison group to have caught up eventually with the experimental group even in the absence of the unplanned

grammatical instruction. The instructional units simply provided concentrated positive evidence of how the French passé composé and imparfait function. This same evidence is available in oral and written French. I take this issue up again when I review the instructional study conducted with ESL learners by Bardovi-Harlig and Reynolds (1993).

[4]The interpretation of emergent forms as showing use of past is standard in tense-aspect studies. See Bardovi-Harlig (1992a, 1992b); Bergström (1995); Harley & Swain (1978).

[5]Examples of the instructional materials can be found in Bardovi-Harlig and Reynolds (1995).

[6]In Table 6.2 and all other longitudinal tables, empty cells indicate no production of the targeted form. The end of the vertical lines indicates the end of the language sample.

[7]There seems to be one learner, Toshihiro, who shows fewer uses following instruction. His case is discussed in this section.

[8]Dietrich et al. (1995) observe this throughout with both tutored and untutored learners; the price of progress is morphological instability.

[9]Entering the morphological stage of development does not preclude further adverbial, lexical, or discourse development.

[10]Andersen and Shirai (1994) suggest that the distributional patterns we observe, at least with respect to lexical aspect, may be even more basic than the core of SLA, residing instead in discourse and processing. I will return to this in Chapter 7.

CHAPTER SEVEN

Past, Present, and Future

In this concluding chapter I summarize the research on the acquisition of time talk in second language acquisition, consider explanations, and outline areas where further research would be beneficial. The preceding chapters have explored five different approaches to understanding the emergence and development of temporal expression that emphasize meaning, morphology, lexical aspect, discourse, and instruction—approaches that reflect the present state of the art of second language acquisition research. This chapter concentrates on the future of research in second language temporality as it explores explanations and areas for further investigation.

At first, the many approaches to studying second language temporality may have seemed very different. By the end of the review, we may view their relation more clearly: as a series of nested puzzle boxes. The first box, the most encompassing box, is the meaning-oriented approach. We open the first box to find three main stages of acquisition: the pragmatic, lexical, and morphological. We open the morphological box to find acquisitional sequences among different form-meaning associations, represented by different morphemes. If we open the box of even a single morpheme—the perfective past, for example—we find yet more boxes. The acquisition of the perfective past also exhibits stages as it spreads across lexical aspectual categories and discourse boundaries. Each of the different approaches investigates a slightly different stage of acquisition and has a different scope of inquiry.

Finally, investigations of the role of instruction can be carried out at any stage of acquisition and within any framework.

Because investigations of second language temporal expression are nested in this way, some areas of further research are relevant to them all. Because the investigations are also separate, as the individual boxes are, some areas of further research are relevant only to specific frameworks. Future research in temporal expression in all frameworks would benefit from inclusion of a broader range of target and native languages, learners at a fuller range of proficiency levels, and studies of input and input processing to complement the studies of learner production.

Including a broader range of target languages is consistent with testing the universality of theoretical claims or observations. As readers will have noticed, research in second language temporal expression has been oriented toward European target languages, specifically Germanic and Romance languages. Reports of investigations into languages outside of the Indo-European language family will undoubtedly expand our knowledge of temporal expression and many new research questions will be identified as comparisons across language families are undertaken. A significant contribution in this area is the study by Li and Shirai (forthcoming) of the acquisition of lexical and grammatical aspect in Chinese and Japanese. Specific research questions will lead to the identification of particular target languages for research. For example, the question of how learners cope with verb stem alternations in addition to tense-aspect morphology in a target language may lead to a study of Russian as a target language. Within the framework of the aspect hypothesis, one might ask if learners of languages that have an aspect system but no tense system show advantages in rate or less variation in form-meaning associations than learners of languages like English or Spanish which have tense as well as grammatical aspect. Many questions and orientations lead to the inclusion of more target languages in research on time talk.

The questions that lead to the inclusion of a variety of first languages in learner populations usually involve universality and

L1 influence. No significant L1 effect has been identified in the longitudinal studies of the acquisition of temporal expression. The ESF study, designed to test the effect of first language, was supported in its findings by the longitudinal studies reported here and elsewhere (Bardovi-Harlig, 1994b, 1997a). Comparisons across studies have also revealed little first language influence. Wiberg's (1996) study of Swedish-Italian heritage learners of Italian in Sweden showed no difference when compared to Giacalone Ramat's (1992, 1995d) learners of Italian in Italy from mixed first language backgrounds. Similarly, the Francophone learners of English studied by Collins (1999b) showed the same acquisitional patterns regarding the use of the simple past and progressive within lexical aspectual categories as the mixed background learners studied by Bardovi-Harlig and Reynolds (1995). However, although the Francophone learners showed the same acquisitional sequences as other learners, their first language did seem to influence the use of the present perfect as a minor alternative to the widely used simple past and past progressive. It may thus be in the details rather than in the larger picture that first language influence is found.

Certainly, additional questions based on the research to date can be posed. I offer only a few here: Do Romance learners of other Romance language exhibit advantages (e.g., rate, Andersen, 1983) when compared to learners from other language families? How do learners whose L1 is French (a language that lacks a morphological progressive) accommodate in their interlanguage the morphological progressive of Spanish or Italian (Romance languages that share many features with French, but also have a morphological progressive)? Would these hypothetical French learners of Spanish and Italian differ significantly from native English speakers whose L1 has a progressive (an imperfective form), but no broader imperfect as Romance languages do? Finally, how does acquisition of Catalan by Spanish speakers compare with acquisition of Spanish by Catalan speakers, two languages that have similar semantic categories for the perfective past, but very different forms?

Andersen's (1986c, 1993, 1994) emphasis on collecting native speaker data and learner data of the same type is related to the issue of casting our data collection nets over a broader range of languages. This will become increasingly important as a greater number of genres of learner texts are collected. The goal of collecting native speaker texts is to better understand what features of discourse and tense-aspect distribution all texts share. When learners and native speakers show the same features of discourse, we can assume that explanations for these features would be related to characteristics of human communication and language, rather than to features related solely to second language acquisition.

No matter how carefully researchers of second language acquisition identify their learner-participants, it seems that they always include in their list of recommendations for improvement a broader range of levels of proficiency among the learners (for cross-sectional studies) or a longer period of observation (for longitudinal studies). Crossing the boundaries of research frameworks, we see that researchers who have studied uninstructed learners have been very successful in identifying beginning-level learners, whereas researchers studying instructed learners have relatively greater difficulty in finding true beginners. All areas of research would benefit from investigating the processes by which relatively advanced learners move toward targetlike use of tense-aspect morphology—including, for example, the use of viewpoint aspect in nonprototypical cases—to observe how learners may gain what Andersen (1990b, 1994) has called the native speaker's advantage.

Finally, the integration of studies of input and input processing with studies of production of temporal expression would contribute to a fuller understanding of the acquisition of temporal expression. Both input studies, which determine what input is available to learners, and input processing studies, which determine how learners make use of input that is available to them, may bring us closer to understanding the patterns of acquisition observable through studies of production. Additional areas of investigation that are not production-oriented include recognition or acceptability judgment studies (Collins, 1999b; Shirai & Kurono, 1998) and learner retrospection (J. Lee, 1999; Liskin-Gasparro, 1997). These types of studies may also lead to a better understanding of different levels of learner knowledge. Studies of acceptability and retrospection can be pursued in more than one framework, as Lee's study of comprehension and input processing and Liskin-Gasparro's retrospective study related to a production task show.

In addition to sharing some areas for further research, the various approaches investigating the expression of temporality also share the type of explanations that have been considered. Explanations for acquisitional patterns tend to fall into one or more of three types: explanations that are based on linguistic or cognitive universals, input-driven explanations, and functional explanations. Within those general types, researchers' explanations of specific phenomena depend on the theoretical approaches in which the research was conducted. In the same manner that many research questions are specific to the theoretical framework in which they are conceived, most explanations and areas for further research are located in a specific theoretical framework.

Because the majority of explanations and areas for further research are located in a specific theoretical framework, the organization of this chapter reflects the organization of the book. In each of the next five sections a summary of the body of research is followed by discussions of possible explanations of the findings and directions for future research. The first section reviews the meaning-oriented approach, providing a larger context for the study of the acquisition of temporal expression. The next section considers acquisitional sequences, the first of the form-oriented approaches. The third section addresses the aspect studies. The review of the aspect studies and suggestions for further research leads directly to the fourth section, on the discourse studies, where research in nonnarrative text genres serves to answer questions posed within each of the frameworks. The final section reviews the research on the role of instruction and discusses the potential for further research in each of the theoretical frameworks related to instruction.

Meaning-Oriented Studies

Summary of Findings

Studies conducted within the meaning-oriented approach take into account the range of linguistic devices on which learners draw in temporal expression. The chief finding of the meaning-oriented studies is the identification of three main stages of development in the expression of temporality: the pragmatic, lexical, and morphological stages. All learners pass through the pragmatic stage before moving on to the lexical stage. The features used in each stage tend to be additive: Features such as chronological order (from the pragmatic stage) and the use of adverbials (from the lexical stage) are also present in the linguistic systems of advanced learners and native speakers. These features are not abandoned as learners move to subsequent stages, but their functional load may lessen as other means of temporal expression, most notably tense-aspect morphology, develop.

Explanations

There is a functional explanation for development from the pragmatic stage to the lexical stage. With no explicit means of temporal expression, the pragmatic stage does not afford speakers a range of expression. And since a learner must rely on an interlocutor's help to construct meaning through scaffolding and interpretation, learners at the pragmatic stage tend not to be independent speakers. In addition, development from the pragmatic to the lexical stage could be due to universal characteristics of language or language acquisition. Klein, Dietrich, and Noyau (1995) state that "it seems plausible that the basic variety reflects more or less *universal* properties of language" (p. 269, emphasis in the original). Universal properties, naturally, are easily attainable, which may account for why all adult learners achieve them in interlanguage. According to Klein et al. (1995), these universal properties also mean that the lexical stage shows characteristics that are unique to neither the first language nor the target language.

Whereas all learners apparently achieve the pragmatic and lexical stages of development, fewer learners achieve the morphological stage of development. Because this is the case, explanations other than universals seem more likely. Klein, Dietrich, and Noyau (1995) advance two explanations, one functional and one social. The functional explanation rests on communicative effectiveness. Although learners at the lexical stage produce a basic variety of interlanguage that is much more flexible than the pre-basic variety of the pragmatic stage, their interlanguage nonetheless exhibits some shortcomings, including the lack of fine temporal distinctions and the ambiguity that results from this lack. The social explanation rests on the observation that the basic variety, although communicatively efficient to a point, "stigmatises the learner as an outsider" (1995, p. 272). Klein et al. (1995) conclude that social factors outweigh communicative ones: They report that their observations about development beyond the lexical stage "clearly indicate that the first factor, the subjective need to sound and to be like the social environment, outweighs the other factor, the concrete communicative needs" (p. 273).

A final explanation among those available at this point comes from outside mainstream meaning-oriented studies of production and rests instead on studies of input processing. Research by J. Lee (1998, 1999) and Boatwright (1999) argues that learners rely heavily on adverbials in the input. Lee's study suggests that they may do so to such an extent that verbal morphology may be ignored, at least in the early stages. According to VanPatten (1996), studies of input processing suggest that (a) learners process for meaning before form, (b) learners process content words first, and (c) learners prefer to process lexical items over grammatical items for semantic information. Thus, a processing explanation would suggest that learner production, which prefers lexical means over grammatical means of temporal expression in the early stages, mirrors the features of input that learners make use of in comprehension and processing.

Areas for Further Research

Expanding semantic concepts. One likely direction for further research in the meaning-oriented approach is to investigate additional semantic concepts. Expression of the concept of past has been well (though perhaps not exhaustively) explored, but many other temporal concepts have not been. One concept that should be investigated in depth is the progressive. The progressive has been investigated in Italian by Giacalone Ramat (1995c, 1997). It is worth noting that, although progressive marking has gotten reasonable attention from the form-oriented approaches, no equivalent study has been done from the concept approach. Such a study might begin with the core meaning of action-in-progress (Andersen & Shirai, 1996; Gass & Ard, 1984; Giacalone Ramat, 1997) and ask how learners express the concept of "action-in-progress." Other aspects could also be investigated through the meaning-oriented approach. These include habituality, iterativity, simultaneity, and durativity.

In the literature thus far, investigation of the past has dominated the research. Learners may mark the past first lexically and later morphologically because the past expresses a temporal reference that is displaced from the time of speaking. Recall that the past has a reference time and event time that are coincident and that they precede speech time (E, R → S). Like the past, the future expresses a displaced reference. In the future, the event time and the reference time are coincident, but follow the time of speaking (S → E, R). Because displacement of event time or reference time from speech time requires some type of signal, the emergence of the expression of future will undoubtedly be marked in some way in interlanguage. Investigating the emergence of the expression of future would allow exploration of another significant semantic concept; it would also allow researchers to determine whether the stages of development repeat themselves within the cycle of the acquisition of the expression of each major concept. I will return to this last point after the next section.

Investigating the concept of the future immediately raises the issue of modality. Because expressions of the future encode a speaker's assertion of the likelihood of a future event, all expressions of the future are also expressions of modality. Consider, for example, that in expressions such as *I will go,* the speaker expresses greater certainty than in the expression *I am going to go* (Haegeman, 1989). Of course, the expression of modality extends beyond the future throughout the system. Work in the tense-aspect system in second language acquisition has generally avoided the second element in what is referred to as the "TMA" or "tense-mood-aspect system" (Dahl, 1985; Givón, 1982; Hopper, 1982). However, research into the expression of future will undoubtedly lead to research in modality. The study of modality is already underway on learner Italian (Giacalone Ramat, 1992, 1995a), German (Dittmar & Terborg, 1991; Skiba & Dittmar, 1992), and English (Salsbury, 2000).

Function. From the functional perspective we might ask how interlanguages select among alternative functional equivalents of the same temporal expression. The future, for example, has at least three instantiations in French: the present + adverb, *Je pars demain* "I leave tomorrow," the *going to* construction, *Je vais partir (demain)* "I'm going to leave tomorrow," and the morphological or synthetic future, *Je partirai (demain)* "I will leave tomorrow." In English, there are at least four expressions: the simple present plus adverb "I leave for France tomorrow," the present progressive "I'm leaving tomorrow," the *going to* future "I'm going to leave tomorrow," and the *will* future "I will leave tomorrow." Which one emerges first and what form-meaning associations do these have in interlanguage? Of course, the answers to these questions will very likely be relevant to interpreting the sequences of morphological acquisition identified by the acquisitional sequence studies.

Universality of stages. Another question for further research concerns the universality of the stages that have been observed by the meaning-oriented studies. Does a learner traverse the pragmatic-lexical-grammatical path only once, arriving at the morphological stage, which then satisfies all or most of the need for additional expression of time through the acquisition of additional morphology? Or does a learner go through the cycle again and again (if not all the way through, at least from the lexical stage to the morphological), relying on adverbials to carry the functional load before a new morphological contrast is established? Work by Bardovi-Harlig (1994b) suggests that the second scenario fits the longitudinal data, but additional studies are necessary. A preliminary study by Moses (1997) on the expression of future in French suggested that learners may not always prefer to use the adverb plus verb combination (in this case the present verb and a future adverb) even when it is targetlike. Learners at all stages used the *going to* and morphological future more often than the present verb with an adverb. Moses (forthcoming) includes a longitudinal study to investigate this further.

Acquisitional Sequences

Summary of Findings

Studies of acquisitional sequences investigate the stages of development of different tense-aspect morphemes within the larger picture of morphological development. As we know from the meaning-oriented studies, not all learners arrive at the morphological stage of development. When learners do reach that stage, longitudinal studies of acquisition of the same target language have shown, their interlanguages display remarkable similarity in their acquisitional sequences. In the acquisitional sequence studies, the first temporal morphology reported makes a distinction between past and nonpast in the native system, with the past form being the morpheme that is acquired. The present appears to be a default form.

The target language exerts a much greater influence in the acquisition of morphology than a learner's first language. There is no clear indication of a strong first language effect in longitudinal studies of learners of different first language backgrounds. The acquisitional sequence (which focuses on emergence as used in this book) for Germanic languages (Dietrich et al., 1995) shows the order

Past ➤ Present Perfect ➤ Pluperfect

when the target language (such as English) includes the use of simple past in the input. When the target language does not use a simple past or preterite, the acquisition sequence begins with the present perfect. (The Germanic languages and dialect variation within those languages provide an interesting natural experiment on the effect of input on acquisition.) The acquisition of English, a language that includes the progressive among its past forms, shows the same relative order of past, present perfect, and pluperfect, with the emerging past progressive appearing between the past and the present perfect

Past ➤ Past Progressive ➤ Present Perfect ➤ Pluperfect.

The observed sequences for French (Noyau, Houdaïfa et al., 1995; Véronique, 1987) and Italian (Giacalone Ramat, 1992, 1995d) share the first three stages

Present ➤ (aux +) Past Participle ➤ Imperfect.

More comprehensive sequences have been posited for Italian by Giacalone Ramat (1992, p. 305; 1995d, p. 294), which I have combined here:

Present ➤ (aux +) Past Participle ➤ Imperfect ➤ {Future, Progressive} ➤ Conditional ➤ Subjunctive.

Testing the sequences for generality in Romance languages is a natural area for further investigation.

Explanations

Explanations for the order of acquisition of morphemes have been sought at least since Brown's (1973) landmark study of first language acquisition. Many of the same questions that Brown raised are still with us, as the following brief sketch of explanations shows.

Input. Klein, Dietrich, and Noyau (1995) argue strongly that second language acquisition is "inductive and heavily input oriented" (p. 271). Other researchers take a less comprehensive view of the role of input in second language acquisition. The nature of input has been used to explain certain sequences of acquisition and, when comparing different target languages, the earlier acquisition of a particular form by learners of one target language than by learners of another.

Ease of acquisition may be due to good form-meaning correspondences, where the match of form and meaning is clear (cf. Slobin's operating principles, 1973, 1985). Clear form-meaning associations have been called "iconic" (Giacalone Ramat, 1995b) and "transparent" in the tense-aspect literature (Noyau, Dorriots et al., 1995). Giacalone Ramat (1995b) identifies such a case in Italian when she observes that "a higher degree of iconicity between form and function" in Italian leads learners of Italian to earlier morphological sensitivity than in languages where the match is not as good, such as French, English, and German (p. 132). Giacalone Ramat (1992) cites two facts about Italian as contributing to good morphological input: In Italian, "practically each lexical form bears an indication of grammatical category" (Giacalone Ramat, 1992, p. 303), and word endings are not reduced, even in spoken Italian, which leads to highly salient morphology. A second case of input leading to early acquisition has been identified in Swedish as "transparency" (Noyau, Dorriots et al., 1995, p. 237). In Swedish, tense-aspect morphology is realized as an invariable suffix with no person agreement on the verb. Noyau, Dorriots et al. attribute the early use of tense-aspect morphology in Swedish interlanguage to the transparency of

Swedish morphology. However, they note that "functional differentiation"—the association of form with meaning—takes place much later (Noyau, Dorriots, et al., 1995, p. 237). In other words, it appears that invariance helps morphology get noticed, but may not lead to early form-meaning associations. Also related to the issue of input, Giacalone Ramat (1997) has discussed the early acquisition of progressive in English as compared to Italian, citing the "frequency in discourse and obligatoriness in system" (p. 281) of the English progressive as the cause of its early appearance.

Function. A functional explanation for the early emergence of the past suggests that the past is morphologically marked due to the fact that it displaces the reference time from the time of speaking. In contrast, the present makes no temporal displacement and thus requires no such marker.

Studies of emergence suggest that the present perfect emerges before the pluperfect. An investigation of functional load of the two tense-aspect morphemes might ask whether tense-aspect morphemes with adverbial equivalents are generally slower to develop than morphemes for which no other grammatical and semantic equivalents exist. For example, in English, reverse-order reports, which are the principal use of the pluperfect, can be expressed by the simple past and an adverbial, yielding a combination that not only expresses meaning clearly but is also grammatical. In contrast, the present perfect does not have a functional equivalent. A functional inquiry might extend this line of reasoning to other concepts and morphemes.

A second area where functional load may come into play is in the sequence of acquisition of verbal morphology in Italian, where the progressive appears relatively late. Giacalone Ramat (1997) attributes this to the relatively more marked status of progressive constructions. As discussed above, she attributes the relatively early acquisition of the English progressive to its frequency. However, a second interpretation for the early acquisition of the progressive may also be relevant. The first morphological distinction to emerge is between past and nonpast, and the first past to emerge in all the languages observed so far is the perfective past.

In both Italian and English, as well as Spanish and French, the next morphological contrast is between the perfective past and the imperfective past—keeping in mind that past progressive is one type of imperfect past (Comrie, 1976). English has one morphological imperfect (the progressive), as does French (the imparfait), whereas Italian has two. For English and French the single imperfective available in the target language is acquired after the perfective past in second language acquisition. For languages with two morphological imperfectives, the imperfect and the progressive, some account such as Giacalone Ramat's (1997) markedness account or an account of prototypicality of the imperfective that extends to the imperfect and the progressive is due. In such an account, an appeal to the frequency of the progressive would be unnecessary.

Complexity. Morphosyntactic complexity has been suggested as being responsible for the order of past before present perfect in L1 acquisition (Gathercole, 1986; Johnson, 1985; C. Smith, 1980). Morphosyntactic complexity could also be a factor in adult second language acquisition. Although morphosyntactic complexity accounts for the acquisition of the simple past and present perfect in L1 and L2, it is a less satisfying explanation if the pluperfect is taken into account, at least for second language acquisition. Although both emerge after the simple past, morphosyntactically the present perfect and the pluperfect are equally complex, differing only by the formal tense marker. Nevertheless, pluperfect emerges after the present perfect in the longitudinal study reported in Chapter 3. Thus, complexity does not account for the difference between them, only that between the perfects and the simple past. Many factors—such as semantic complexity (C. Smith, 1980), syntactic complexity, frequency of input, and functional load—are all likely to contribute to determining the acquisition order (cf. Gathercole, 1986, for L1) and should be investigated further by second language acquisition researchers.

Areas for Further Research

In addition to the investigation of complexity just mentioned, the acquisitional sequence studies could be expanded to include a much wider range of tense-aspect morphology. Depth could be added by investigating prototypical and nonprototypical uses of emergent morphology, and breadth could be added by expanding the sequences to include nonpast morphology more generally, moving in this area, as in the meaning-oriented studies, toward investigation of the future and modality. The most natural area of inquiry, I believe, is to expand the inquiry from the tense-aspect system to the tense-mood-aspect system. In this vein, a comparison of target languages with different characteristics is also warranted. For example, languages with uninflected modal auxiliaries, such as English, offer different features for acquisition than languages with inflected modal verbs, such as Spanish. The observation by Noyau, Dorriots, et al. (1995) that invariant morphology in Swedish leads to early use of morphology in Swedish interlanguage but not to early form-meaning association suggests another area for further investigation. This seems to be a natural area of investigation for input processing studies as well as for studies of comparisons of the acquisition of invariant and variable morphology within and across languages.

Aspect Studies

Summary of Findings

The aspect hypothesis has been well supported in the literature. For clarity, it is worth summarizing the evidence individually for each of the four subhypotheses that make up the overarching aspect hypothesis. The hypothesis that is best supported—and most easily observed—is the first, concerning the initial association of perfective past marking with achievements and accomplishments and its extension to activities and states. Data from a range of languages are available, and the research designs include both learner-controlled narratives and experimental tasks. Data regarding the spread of progressive from activities to accomplishments to achievements, and its nonuse with states—the third and fourth hypotheses—largely comes from observing what tense-aspect forms learners use when they do not use past, and there is substantial evidence in this area. However, studies that focus exclusively on the progressive are still relatively rare (see Giacalone Ramat, 1995c, 1997), and developing this line of inquiry in a range of languages would provide a broader database.

Although there is support for the second hypothesis regarding the spread of the imperfective from states to activities to accomplishments and then to achievements, it is not nearly as robust as that for the hypotheses addressing the spread of the perfective past or the progressive. This may be due to the fact that the imperfective is both learned later and more difficult to elicit than the perfective past. This is an area where further research is clearly needed, and one that will require both new techniques in research design and the expansion of the genres of learner texts that are sampled.

Explanations

A number of explanations have been proposed for the observed effects of the aspect hypothesis. Each one points to areas for further research. They include input-based explanations and both linguistic and cognitive universalist explanations.

Input. Anderson (1986b, 1990a, 1990b) has observed that the input available to learners exhibits distributional patterns very similar to those we see in second language production. The question of the influence of input on acquisitional patterns in tense-aspect acquisition was formalized by Andersen (1986b, 1990a, 1990b) as the *distributional bias hypothesis*. Andersen and Shirai (1994) observe that "native speakers in normal interaction with other native speakers tend to use each verb morpheme with a specific class of verbs, also following the aspect hypothesis" (p. 137). Although native speakers differ from learners in that they are able to separate the use of tense-aspect morphology from prototypical uses—this is the native speaker's advantage (Andersen, 1994)—native speakers nevertheless "exhibit in relative quantitative terms the same distributional bias found in more absolute terms in the acquisitional data" (Andersen, 1993, p. 320). This means that native speakers also tend to associate past or perfective morphology with achievements and accomplishments, and progressives with activities.

Cognitive principles and semantic prototypes. Andersen hypothesized that the observed acquisitional sequences are a result of the interaction between the distribution of forms in the input, semantic prototypes, and the *relevance, congruence,* and *one-to-one principles* (Andersen, 1993). Following Andersen and Shirai (1994), the affinity of certain tense-aspect morphology for verbs of particular lexical aspectual classes can be explained by the relevance principle and the congruence principle. The relevance principle states that learners will use morphology that is relevant to the verb, closest to the verb stem (Bybee, 1985), and, moreover, that they will acquire the most relevant morphology first (Andersen & Shirai, 1994). The congruence principle states that learners will use tense-aspect morphemes whose meaning is most similar to that of the verb (Andersen, 1993). The congruence principle has also been called the *redundant marking hypothesis* (Shirai, 1993, 1995; Shirai & Kurono, 1998), and the *principle of selective association* (Giacalone Ramat, 1995d, 1997). Giacalone Ramat's (1995d) formulation of the principle states, "Put together features that are semantically congruent such as telicity, perfectivity, and pastness" (p. 302). Learners are also guided by the one-to-one principle: that learners expect each new morpheme to have only one meaning and function (Andersen, 1984, 1993) and a prototypical meaning for each tense-aspect morpheme (see also Giacalone Ramat, 1997). In a prototype account, learners infer a prototypical meaning for each inflection from the input, such as "'action in progress at that moment' for progressives, 'completed action' for past and perfective marking (and perhaps 'change of state' as a result of the completion), and 'continued existence' for present marking" (Andersen & Shirai, 1994, p. 148). Learners are constrained by the one-to-one principle to associate an inflection first with its prototypical meaning, and by the relevance principle to use the inflection with verbs that most closely share its meaning.

Andersen and Shirai (1994) observed that the three cognitive principles plus the notion of prototypicality would be sufficient to account for tense-aspect distribution in interlanguage, except for the distributional bias hypothesis, which applies to the output of native speakers. Because native speakers and learners show the same distributional tendencies (although those of the learners are much more pronounced and may also be nontargetlike), Andersen and Shirai argued that the same principles, namely relevance and congruence, operate for both learners and native speakers alike. They further argue that *"all* of these principles follow naturally from the speakers' (both learners and nonlearners) need to distinguish reference to the main point/goal of talk from supporting information" (p. 152). This naturally connects the investigation of lexical aspect to discourse, which is taken up in the next main section.

Areas for Further Research

There are numerous areas for further research in the framework of the aspect studies. Although the emergence of the perfective past is well attested, the spread of the imperfective is less well established. Similarly, the spread of the progressive could be studied more intensively in languages that include progressives in their inventory of imperfectives. Any study of progressives will naturally lead to a study of the overgeneralization of progressive, the fourth subhypothesis of the aspect hypothesis. Tasks that elicit tokens of imperfective past will undoubtedly require investigators to elicit a broader range of genres of texts than have been elicited thus far. Descriptions as well as personal narratives that include rich background will not only provide a vehicle for the study of imperfectives, but also inform the discourse studies.

Additional areas of investigation that pertain specifically to aspect studies include the role of input (the distributional bias hypothesis), the role of prototypes and prototype expansions, and the cognitive principles that are the bases for the distribution of tense-aspect morphology in primary as well as second languages.

Distributional bias in the input. Empirical studies of native speaker speech addressed to other native speakers and to first and second language learners support the claim that there is a distributional bias in adult native speaker speech (Andersen & Shirai, 1996; Robison, 1995b), although native speakers are able to use tense-aspect morphology in nonprototypical cases (Andersen, 1993, 1994). However, the question of whether acquisitional sequences are determined solely by input remains.

One way of investigating the input question is to investigate cases in which the input and the learner production do not match. Two such cases have been identified by Huang (1997) and Shirai (1995; Shirai & Kurono, 1998). The first concerns the marking of unitary and repeated events. Huang analyzed interviews of three English native speakers and five Chinese learners of English. She divided dynamic verbs into unitary and repeated event types. With respect to progressive morphology, native speakers and learners showed opposite patterns: Learners showed a strong preference for -*ing* with unitary events and a weaker use with repeated events (73% of tokens of -*ing* occurring with unitary events, 27% with repeated events), whereas native speakers used -*ing* more than twice as frequently with repeated events than with unitary events (31% with unitary events and 69% with repeated events). The differences in distribution suggest that learners do not take their pattern from the target language input alone.

Input that learners of Japanese receive is not transparent with respect to the alignment of verb morphology and aspectual category (Shirai, 1995; Shirai & Kurono, 1998). In Japanese, the durative imperfective marker -*te i-,* which appears with activities to denote progressive, can also be used with achievements to denote resultative states. Thus, -*te i-* can be associated with both achievements and activities, whereas -*ta,* the resultative marker, occurs primarily with achievements. The pattern is found in native-speaker samples in both speech addressed to the learners by an interviewer and a separate conversational corpus of adult native speakers. Thus, neither native speaker speech nor input to learners appears to show a distributional bias. In a sample from a native-speaker interviewer, 54% of all instances of *-ta* occurred with achievements and 33% with states, and 37% of *-te i-* occurred with activities and 59% with achievements. Nevertheless, learners show a bias in their use of morphology: One learner showed 92% use of *-ta* forms with achievements, and 62% of *-te i-* forms with activities. Both Shirai's and Huang's studies suggest that acquisitional patterns may not be determined exclusively by input. It is important to keep in mind, however, that the distinction between input and the cognitive, linguistic, and discursive factors that structure interlanguage temporal systems may be somewhat artificial; Andersen (1993) has suggested that "the native and the learner distributions are both due to the same factors" (p. 320).

Prototypes. I believe that studies of how interlanguage expands prototypes are particularly worthwhile. This is the area in which, along with discourse studies, the study of tense-aspect will tie into other areas of investigation of grammatical and pragmatic development. The research on the aspect hypothesis provides examples of prototypes and extensions of prototypes. The prototype of past [+unitary, +result state, +punctual, +past] is coincident with the prototypes of perfective [+unitary, +result state, +punctual, +past] (Andersen & Shirai, 1994, p. 149). Perfective past associates first with achievements, which share these same features, by virtue of the relevance principle. The spread of the past from achievements to accomplishments, to activities, and finally to states represents an extension of a prototypical association. The spread of the imperfect from states to achievements also represents an extension of a prototype. Both of these sequences in which prototypes are extended are cases where there is a reference to the past. Full targetlike use requires that the use of past morphology extend to other environments as well.

Andersen and Shirai have posited sequences of development for both the past and progressive that take the individual morphemes from their earliest appearance in their prototypical contexts to new contexts that require prototypical extension (Andersen & Shirai, 1996, p. 557; Shirai, 1991, p. 42):

> The spread of the past: Deictic past (achievement ➤ accomplishment ➤ activity ➤ state ➤ habitual or iterative past) ➤ counterfactual or pragmatic softener.

In the development of past, the sequence begins with the deictic past and extends to the realm of pragmatics. The use of tense-aspect forms such as the past and the past progressive as softeners has long been recognized by pragmatic researchers (e.g., House & Kasper, 1981), but had not previously been linked to an investigation of the acquisition of tense-aspect morphology. As in the case of the past, the earliest stages in the hypothesized path of the progressive have been documented (Andersen & Shirai, 1996, p. 557; Shirai, 1991, p. 44; see also Gass & Ard, 1984).

> The spread of the progressive: Process (activity ➤ accomplishment) ➤ iterative ➤ habitual or futurate ➤ stative progressive (➤ pragmatic softener).

Focus on the iterative can be found in the categories of punctual activities and iterative punctuals (Huang, 1997; Robison, 1995a). Recent research on habituals in second language acquisition has been undertaken by Shirai (1999). It should be noted that the past progressive also functions as a pragmatic softener (Bardovi-Harlig & Hartford, 1990; House & Kasper, 1981). I added the last stage of the progressive, "pragmatic softener," to the second path above by analogy to the last stage of past hypothesized by Andersen and Shirai, and on the basis of pragmatic research.

Based on their work on Swedish, Noyau, Dorriots, et al. (1995, p. 256) have proposed a prototype extension for the acquisition of the present, as follows:

> The spread of the present: Present ➤ generic ➤ narrative present.

Prototypes could be identified and extensions of prototypes could be hypothesized for other tense-aspect forms as well, including the imperfective past, present perfect, pluperfect, and future. It is important to note how these functional sequences differ from those proposed by investigations of morphological sequences discussed in the previous section. These refer to the spread of a single morpheme across environments (in keeping with the approach used in the investigation of the aspect hypothesis), whereas the other sequences are concerned with the order of emergence of different morphemes. They are not unrelated, however. For each morpheme investigated in a larger acquisitional sequence, a subsequence exists in which that morpheme spreads across environments.

Discourse Studies

Summary of Findings

Studies that take discourse structure into account have by and large shown that learners distinguish the narrative foreground from the background. Learners accomplish this not only by verbal morphology, but also by relying on the structure of the material within grounding, such as the fact that the foreground will entail sequenced events. There is also interaction between the aspectual categories and tense-aspect morphology. The effect of grounding is especially strong for accomplishments and activities.

Explanation

There has been less research done in this area, and perhaps for this reason fewer explanations have been advanced. Crosslinguistic investigations suggest that the distinction between background and foreground may be a universal of narrative discourse (Hopper, 1979; see also Longacre, 1981). Hopper (1979) observes that competent (native) users of a language "mark out a main route through the narrative and divert in some way those parts of the narrative which are not strictly relevant to this route" (p. 239). Tense-aspect morphology is one way that native speakers and learners mark the main route. Yet even universals must have their explanations. A functional theory of communication would suggest that the purpose of the distinction between foreground and background may be to separate the main point of the text from less important information for the listener.

Areas for Further Research

Such a functional explanation points the way to further research: namely, do learners distinguish the main point of a text from the background in a variety of text types? The work of von Stutterheim and Klein (1989) suggests that the next logical text type to be investigated should be descriptions. Von Stutterheim and Klein (1989) locate narrative structure (and grounding) in a more general approach to main structures and side structures. In a narrative, the foreground answers the question "What happened next?" with unbounded states, habituals, and generics excluded. In contrast, in a description, specific temporal reference is normally excluded, and temporal location on the time axis leads to side structures, "exactly the reverse picture" from the narrative (von Stutterheim, 1991, p. 391). What links inquiry into different discourse types with studies of L2 tense and aspect is the observation that the dominant temporal relation is determined by the discourse type (von Stutterheim, 1991). In narratives, temporal reference is moved forward by bounded events, whereas in descriptions, unbounded states imply the maintenance of the temporal frame. The elicitation of descriptions would allow researchers to test whether learners use tense-aspect morphology to mark main structures regardless of discourse type. As discussed in the review of the aspect hypothesis, this not only provides the opportunity to test additional text types, but also provides contexts for the study of the use and the spread of the imperfective.

The Influence of Instruction

Summary of Findings

Studies of instructed learners who received specialized instruction compared to instructed learners who did not show that instruction that helps learners make form-meaning associations in the tense-aspect system is largely successful. As Harley (1989) pointed out, the longer the amount of time that is spent in establishing form-meaning associations, the more successful the outcome.

Observations of learners in an instructed environment that compare the timing of instruction with spontaneous communicative use of the instructionally targeted forms (discussed in Chapter 6) support Pienemann's (1989, 1998) teachability hypothesis, according to which the effects of instruction on the developing interlanguage are constrained by the learner's current stage of acquisition. However, even learners who apparently satisfy the acquisitional prerequisites for an instructionally targeted form may not immediately integrate that form into productive use.

Comparisons of instructed and uninstructed learners in the second language environment show that in terms of eventual attainment (holding length of stay constant), instructed learners reached the morphological stage of development more often than uninstructed learners did. This is one of the findings of the ESF study, in which all of the instructed learners entered the morphological stage but not all of the uninstructed learners did. Instruction was not the single determining factor, however. Some learners without instruction did acquire tense-aspect morphology, and as Chapters 3 and 6 show, not all instructed learners make the same progress. Thus instruction, it seems, is but one variable among many.

The findings from the studies on instruction are quite consistent with Klein, Dietrich, and Noyau's (1995) conclusion that intensity of interaction in the target language is more important than the length of interaction:

> *Duration of stay is an uninteresting variable.* What matters
> is the intensity, not the length of interaction. Therefore,
> ordering learners according to their duration of stay is
> normally pointless because [it is] too crude a measure for
> what really matters: intensity of interaction. (p. 277)

Interaction can also be understood as availability of input in the instructional setting as well as outside of it. Just as Klein and his colleagues claim that duration of stay is an uninteresting variable so could we claim that, in many instructional settings, length of study is an uninteresting, or uninformative, variable. It is the quality and the intensity of interaction that is of critical importance. Learners can add to or enhance the intensity of interaction in a number of ways whether they are classroom learners or not, and whether they are in the host environment or a foreign language setting.

Explanations

Naturally, the explanation for instructional effects depends on the instructional effects that one sees. When I look at the results from instructional investigations of varying types, I see no other process than second language acquisition itself. In the stages where it overlaps with the acquisition of untutored learners, the stages are the same. However, one advantage of instruction seems to be that the interlanguage of instructed learners often exhibits more stages of development and higher eventual attainment. Input may be more readily available in some instructional environments than others, or than outside the classroom. However, as Gass (1989) argued, the fundamental psycholinguistic process of second language acquisition is the same whether learners enter classrooms or acquire language outside of them. The stage of acquisition of individual learners also interacts with instruction, as Pienemann (1989, 1998) has argued. As Chapter 6 showed, the full range of variables that determine the success of learners in general is also relevant in classroom second language acquisition.

Areas for Further Research

There is no greater experiment on the role of input than the classroom language learning environment. We are at an exciting time in the development of pedagogy and pedagogical theory, which allows researchers and teachers to test the effects of communicative input, negotiated input, and focus on form and input enhancement of various types on the development of tense-aspect systems as well as any other grammatical and conceptual system. Naturally, the influence of instruction can be investigated in any of the theoretical and analytic frameworks discussed in this book. Form-oriented approaches are most naturally linked to instruction, which has tended to put great emphasis on morphology. As we have seen, however, studies that recognize acquisitional sequences are much more likely to see positive effects of instruction than studies whose analyses adopt a targetlike-or-nothing approach. Even so, where a form-oriented approach may show that a learner has made no morphological progress, a concept-oriented approach could show that instructional input allowed learners to make gains in lexical expression of the same concept.

One area for further investigation was suggested in Chapter 4 in the discussion of the imperfective. Bardovi-Harlig and Bergström (1996) hypothesized that one reason that the imperfect may not spread readily is because of the limited stative vocabularies of most learners. A promising area of investigation would be to help learners increase their stative lexicons and observe whether this facilitates the spread of the imperfect. Another promising area of instructional research is processing instruction. The work on processing has already begun to identify a significant step in acquisition, namely, the reliance on adverbs in processing that parallels the early use of adverbials in production. Processing instruction seeks to help students make targetlike form-meaning associations during input processing. Processing instruction has already been studied for the Spanish preterite (Cadierno, 1995), but could be brought to bear on the imperfect as well. Further investigations could follow patterns of development after initial input processing treatments. The concepts of prototypes and distributional bias can also be used to review, modify, or create texts to serve as input to learners (Andersen, 1990a; Bardovi-Harlig, 1997c, 1997d).

Concluding Remarks

Areas of interest for all frameworks include the role of input, universals, and the fuller description of the acquisition of the tense-aspect system. So far, our collective work has described only a part of the tense-aspect system. Clearly, more will be done in the areas of description and explanation. Explanation is by no means the end of the journey. It is interesting to note that what may begin as an explanation may itself become a hypothesis to be tested. In turn, the results from testing a hypothesis may be subject to further explanation which is then tested and explained. The case of the aspect hypothesis seems to be a particularly good example of the cyclic nature of research. Researchers first advanced the aspect hypothesis to explain the distribution of tense-aspect morphology in child L1 and adult L2 acquisition. The explanation—that lexical aspect determined the use of tense-aspect morphology—subsequently became a testable and well-articulated hypothesis. Once evidence for the hypothesis was available, explanations for the relation between lexical aspect and tense-aspect morphology were proposed which included input, prototypes, discourse, the relevance principle, and the one-to-one principle. Each of these explanations can and will be tested further, and new explanations will undoubtedly be offered as we refine our knowledge of tense and aspect acquisition and of second language acquisition processes in general.

This book had three goals: to describe the acquisition of temporal expression, to examine how we study the acquisition of temporal expression in second language, and to consider research methods and analysis as they have been used in the study of second language temporality. The last was the most modest of the goals. The development of temporality is amenable to study through production data. This field of inquiry is dominated by learner-generated texts. There have been some experimental studies done that balance the production of learners among different types of verbs, and these have confirmed the patterns that have been observed in freer learner production. We have seen some noteworthy differences in the analyses that have been conducted in studies, particularly among the analyses conducted in the aspect hypothesis. As in other areas of research, not all studies maintain the same focus of interest. For example, the interest in the (ir)regularity of morphology or phonetic constraints is in sharp focus in only some studies. Coding differs somewhat across studies, but not sufficiently to obscure the major patterns of development.

The second goal, that of examining how we study the acquisition of temporal expression in second language acquisition, led to the discussion of five different research frameworks. The five perspectives cover most of the ways that second language acquisition researchers have looked at language development at large: as form (in both descriptive studies and hypothesis-testing studies), as meaning, as discourse, and as a response to language instruction. The study of the acquisition of temporal expression brings these rather different research frameworks (and agendas) together.

The co-existence of different approaches to the study of acquisition of temporal expression leads to different responses to the goal of describing that acquisition. In a significant way, each approach has its own answer, as I have shown in the preceding chapters. And yet, if we attempt to understand the various frameworks from the perspective of how they are related, we see that they each investigate different stages of the same acquisition process. The meaning-oriented approaches provide an encompassing area of investigation; the investigation narrows as we begin to look exclusively at morphology, and narrows again as we focus on specific morphology and form-meaning associations. Finally, it broadens again as we examine instructional effects in any or all of the stages of development. What links the research that I have reviewed here is the pervasive concern for the association of form and meaning and the development of interlanguage temporal semantics.

I have described the acquisition of temporal expression as we currently understand it. As can be seen from the summary of further research in the combined areas, our knowledge about acquisition is concentrated in the conceptual area of the past. Much remains to be described from all the research perspectives. By presenting the combined findings of researchers in what I consider to be a compelling area of research, it is my intention to encourage even more research in the field. I hope that this book will provide direction for many new research projects.

References

Aksu-Koç, A., & von Stutterheim, C. (1994). Temporal relations in narrative: Simultaneity. In R. A. Berman & D. I. Slobin (Eds.), *Relating events in narrative: A crosslinguistic developmental study* (pp. 393–455). Hillsdale, NJ: Erlbaum.

Andersen, R. W. (1977). The impoverished state of cross-sectional morpheme acquisition/accuracy methodology (or: The leftovers are more nourishing than the main course). *Working papers on bilingualism / Travaux de recherches sur bilinguisme, 14,* 47–82.

Andersen, R. W. (1978). An implicational model for second language research. *Language Learning, 28,* 221–282.

Andersen, R. W. (1979). The relationship between first-language transfer and second-language overgeneralization: Data from the English of Spanish speakers. In R. W. Andersen (Ed.), *The acquisition and use of Spanish and English as first and second languages* (pp. 43–58). Washington, DC: TESOL.

Andersen, R. W. (1983). Transfer to somewhere. In S. M. Gass & L. Selinker (Eds.), *Language transfer in language learning* (pp. 177–201). Rowley, MA: Newbury House.

Andersen, R. W. (1984). The one-to-one principle of interlanguage construction. *Language Learning, 34,* 77–95.

Andersen, R. W. (1985, February). *Interpreting data.* Plenary address presented at the Second Language Research Forum, Los Angeles (UCLA).

Andersen, R. W. (1986a). El desarollo de la morfología verbal en el Español como segundo idioma [The development of verbal morphology in Spanish as a second language]. In J. M. Meisel (Ed.), *Adquisición de lenguaje / Aquisicao da linguagem* [Acquisition of language] (pp. 115–138). Frankfurt: Vervuert.

Andersen, R. W. (1986b). *Interpreting data: Second language acquisition of verbal aspect.* Unpublished manuscript, University of California, Los Angeles.

Andersen, R. W. (1986c, July). *The need for native language comparison data in interpreting second language data.* Forum lecture, TESOL Summer Institute, University of Hawaii.

Andersen, R. W. (1989). La adquisicíon de la morfología verbal [The acquisition of verb morphology]. *Linguística, 1,* 90–142.

Andersen, R. W. (1990a). Models, processes, principles and strategies: Second language acquisition inside and outside the classroom. In B. VanPatten & J. F. Lee (Eds.), *Second language acquisition—Foreign language learning* (pp. 45–78). Clevedon, UK: Multilingual Matters. (Reprinted from *IDEAL, 3,* 111–138.)

Andersen, R. W. (1990b). Verbal virtuosity and speakers' purposes. In H. Burmeister & P. L. Rounds (Eds.), *Variability in second language acquisition: Proceedings of the Tenth Meeting of the Second Language Research Forum* (Vol. 2, pp. 1–24). Eugene: University of Oregon, Department of Linguistics.

Andersen, R. W. (1991). Developmental sequences: The emergence of aspect marking in second language acquisition. In T. Huebner & C. A. Ferguson (Eds.), *Crosscurrents in second language acquisition and linguistic theories* (pp. 305–324). Amsterdam: Benjamins.

Andersen, R. W. (1993). Four operating principles and input distribution as explanations for underdeveloped and mature morphological systems. In K. Hyltenstam and Å. Viberg (Eds.), *Progression & regression in language: Sociocultural, neuropsychological, & linguistic perspectives* (pp. 309–339). Cambridge, UK: Cambridge University Press.

Andersen, R. W. (1994). The insider's advantage. In A. Giacalone Ramat & M. Vedovelli (Eds.), *Italiano: Lingua seconda / lingua straniera* [Italian: Second language/foreign language] (pp. 1–26). Rome: Bulzoni.

Andersen, R. W., & Shirai, Y. (1994). Discourse motivations for some cognitive acquisition principles. *Studies in Second Language Acquisition, 16,* 133–156.

Andersen, R. W., & Shirai, Y. (1996). The primacy of aspect in first and second language acquisition: The pidgin-creole connection. In W. C. Ritchie and T. K. Bhatia (Eds.), *Handbook of second language acquisition* (pp. 527–570). San Diego, CA: Academic Press.

Antinucci, F., & Miller, R. (1976). How children talk about what happened. *Journal of Child Language, 3,* 167–189.

Azar, B. S. (1985). *Fundamentals of English grammar.* Englewood Cliffs, NJ: Prentice-Hall.

Azar, B. S. (1989). *Understanding and using English grammar* (2nd ed.). Englewood Cliffs, NJ: Prentice-Hall.

Bailey, N. (1987). *The importance of meaning over form in second language system building: An unresolved issue.* Unpublished doctoral dissertation, Graduate Center, City University of New York, New York.

Bailey, N. (1989). Discourse conditioned tense variation. In M. R. Eisenstein (Ed.), *The dynamic interlanguage: Empirical studies in second language variation* (pp. 279–296). New York: Plenum.

Bailey, N., Madden, C., & Krashen, S. (1974). Is there a "natural sequence" in adult second language learning? *Language Learning, 21,* 235–243.

Bamberg, M. (1987). *The acquisition of narratives.* Berlin: Mouton.

Bamberg, M., & Marchman, V. (1990). What holds a narrative together? The linguistic encoding of episode boundaries. *Papers in Pragmatics, 4,* 58–121.

Bardovi-Harlig, K. (1992a). The relationship of form and meaning: A cross-sectional study of tense and aspect in the interlanguage of learners of English as a second language. *Applied Psycholinguistics, 13,* 253–278.

Bardovi-Harlig, K. (1992b). The telling of a tale: Discourse structure and tense use in learners' narratives. In L. F. Bouton & Y. Kachru (Eds.), *Pragmatics and language learning* (Vol. 3, pp. 144–161). University of Illinois, Urbana-Champaign: Division of English as an International Language.

Bardovi-Harlig, K. (1992c). The use of adverbials and natural order in the development of temporal expression. *IRAL, 30,* 299–320.

Bardovi-Harlig, K. (1993). *Report to the National Science Foundation* (Grant DBS-8919616).

Bardovi-Harlig, K. (1994a). Anecdote or evidence? Evaluating support for hypotheses concerning the development of tense and aspect. In E. Tarone, S. M. Gass, & A. D. Cohen (Eds.), *Research methodology in second language acquisition* (pp. 41–60). Hillsdale, NJ: Erlbaum.

Bardovi-Harlig, K. (1994b). Reverse-order reports and the acquisition of tense: Beyond the principle of chronological order. *Language Learning, 44,* 243–282.

Bardovi-Harlig, K. (1995a). A narrative perspective on the development of the tense/aspect system in second language acquisition. *Studies in Second Language Acquisition, 17,* 263–291.

Bardovi-Harlig, K. (1995b). The interaction of pedagogy and natural sequences in the acquisition of tense and aspect. In F. R. Eckman, D. Highland, P. W. Lee, J. Mileham, & R. R. Weber (Eds.), *Second language acquisition theory and pedagogy* (pp. 151–168). Mahwah, NJ: Erlbaum.

Bardovi-Harlig, K. (1997a). Another piece of the puzzle: The emergence of the present perfect. *Language Learning, 47,* 375–422.

Bardovi-Harlig, K. (1997b). Assessing grammatical development in interactional contexts. *TESOL Quarterly, 31,* 797–806.

Bardovi-Harlig, K. (1997c). The place of second language acquisition theory in language teacher preparation. In K. Bardovi-Harlig & B. S. Hartford (Eds.), *Beyond methods: Components of language teacher education* (pp. 18–41). New York: McGraw Hill.

Bardovi-Harlig, K. (1997d). Tense and aspect in (con)text. In T. Miller (Ed.), *Functional approaches to written text: Classroom applications* (pp. 186–200). Washington, DC: United States Information Agency. (Reprinted from T. Miller (Ed.), *Grammar and Discourse. The Journal of TESOL France, 3,* 19–33.)

Bardovi-Harlig, K. (1998). Narrative structure and lexical aspect: Conspiring factors in second language acquisition of tense-aspect morphology. *Studies in Second Language Acquisition, 20,* 471–508.

Bardovi-Harlig, K. (1999a). Examining the role of text type in L2 tense-aspect research: Broadening our horizons. In P. Robinson (Ed.), *Proceedings of the Third Pacific Second Language Research Forum* (Vol. 1, pp. 129–138). Tokyo: The Pacific Second Language Research Forum.

Bardovi-Harlig, K. (1999b). From morpheme studies to temporal semantics: Tense-aspect research in SLA. *Studies in Second Language Acquisition, 21,* 341–382.

Bardovi-Harlig, K. (in press). Analyzing aspect. In R. Salaberry & Y. Shirai (Eds.), *Tense-aspect morphology in L2 acquisition.* Amsterdam: Benjamins.

Bardovi-Harlig, K., & Bergström, A. (1996). The acquisition of tense and aspect in SLA and FLL: A study of learner narratives in English (SL) and French (FL). *Canadian Modern Language Review, 52,* 308–330.

Bardovi-Harlig, K., & Bofman, T. (1989). Attainment of syntactic and morphological accuracy by advanced language learners. *Studies in Second Language Acquisition, 11,* 17–34.

Bardovi-Harlig, K., & Hartford, B. S. (1990). Congruence in native and nonnative conversations: Status balance in the academic advising session. *Language Learning, 40,* 467–501.

Bardovi-Harlig, K., & Reynolds, D. W. (1993, April). *Adverbs, aspect, and tense in the development of temporality.* Paper presented at the Twenty-Seventh Annual TESOL Conference, Atlanta, GA.

Bardovi-Harlig, K., & Reynolds, D. W. (1995). The role of lexical aspect in the acquisition of tense and aspect. *TESOL Quarterly, 29,* 107–131.

Bayley, R. J. (1991). *Variation theory and second language learning: Linguistic and social constraints on interlanguage tense marking.* Unpublished doctoral dissertation, Stanford University, Stanford, CA.

Bayley, R. J. (1994). Interlanguage variation and the quantitative paradigm: Past tense marking in Chinese-English. In S. Gass, A. Cohen, & E. Tarone (Eds.), *Research methodology in second language acquisition* (pp. 157–181). Hillsdale, NJ: Erlbaum.

Bayley, R. J. (1999). The primacy of aspect hypothesis revisited: Evidence from language shift. *Southwest Journal of Linguistics, 18*(2), 1–22.

Becker, A., & Carroll, M. (1997). *The acquisition of spatial relations in a second language.* Amsterdam: Benjamins.

Bergström, A. (1995). *The expression of past temporal reference by English-speaking learners of French.* Unpublished doctoral dissertation, Pennsylvania State University, State College, PA.

Bergström, A. (1997). L'influence des distinctions aspectuelles sur l'acquisition des temps en français langue étrangère [The influence of aspectual distinctions on the acquisition of tense in French as a foreign language]. *Acquisition et Interaction en Langue Étrangère, 9,* 52–82.

Bernini, G. (1990). L'acquizisizione dell'imperfetto nell'italiano lingua seconda [The acquisition of the imperfect in Italian as a second language]. In E. Banfi & P. Cordin (Eds.), *Storia dell'italiano e forme dell'italianizzazione* [The history of Italian and forms of Italianization] (pp. 157–180). Rome: Bulzoni.

Berretta, M. (1995). Morphological markedness in L2 acquisition. In R. Simone (Ed.), *Iconicity in language* (pp. 197–233). Amsterdam: Benjamins.

Bhardwaj, M., Dietrich, R., & Noyau, C. (Eds.). (1988). *Temporality.* (Final Report to the European Science Foundation, Volume V.) Nijmegen: Max Planck Institute.

Bhat, D. N. S. (1999). *The prominence of tense, aspect, and mood.* Amsterdam: Benjamins.

Bickerton, D. (1975). *Dynamics of a creole system.* Cambridge, UK: Cambridge University Press.

Bickerton, D. (1981). *Roots of language.* Ann Arbor, MI: Karoma.

Binnick, R. I. (1991). *Time and the verb: A guide to tense and aspect.* New York: Oxford University Press.

Bloom, L., & Harner, L. (1989). On the developmental contour of child language: A reply to Smith & Weist. *Journal of Child Language, 16,* 207–216.

Bloom, L., Lifter, K., & Hafitz, J. (1980). Semantics of verbs and development of verb inflection in child language. *Language, 56,* 386–412.

Boatwright. C. (1999, September). *On-line processing of time reference: Meaning before morphology.* Paper presented at the Second Language Research Forum, Minneapolis, MN.

Brindley, G. (1987). Verb tenses and TESOL. In D. Nunan (Ed.), *Applying second language acquisition research* (pp. 173–204). Adelaide, Australia: NCRC Research Series.

Broeder, P. (1995). Adult language acquisition: The establishment, shift, and maintenance of reference in narratives. In R. A. Geiger (Ed.) *Reference in multidisciplinary perspective: Philosophical object, cognitive subject, intersubjective process* (pp. 584–610). Hildesheim, Germany: Olms.

Bronckart, J.-P., & Sinclair, H. (1973). Time, tense and aspect. *Cognition, 2,* 107–130.

Brown, R. (1973). *A first language.* Cambridge, MA: Harvard University Press.

Buczowska, E., & Weist, R. M. (1991). The effects of formal instruction on the second-language acquisition of temporal location. *Language Learning, 41,* 535–554.

Bull, W. (1971). *Time, tense, and the verb.* Berkeley: University of California Press.

Bybee, J. L. (1985). *Morphology: A study of the relation between meaning and form.* Amsterdam: Benjamins.

Bybee, J. L., & Dahl, Ö. (1989). The creation of tense and aspect systems in the languages of the world. *Studies in Language, 13,* 51–103.

Bybee, J. L., Perkins, R., & Pagliuca, W. (1994). *The evolution of grammar: Tense, aspect, and modality in the languages of the world.* Chicago: The University of Chicago Press.

Cadierno, T. (1995). Formal instruction from a processing perspective: An investigation into the Spanish past tense. *Modern Language Journal, 79,* 179–193.

Cadierno, T. (2000). The acquisition of Spanish aspectual distinctions by Danish language learners. *Spanish Applied Linguistics, 4,* 1–53.

Chafe, W. (Ed.). (1980). *The pear stories.* Norwood, NJ: Ablex.

Clark, E. V. (1971). On the acquisition of the meaning of before and after. *Journal of Verbal Learning and Verbal Behavior, 10,* 266–275.

Clements, J. A. (1985). *Verbal classification and verb class change in Spanish.* Unpublished doctoral dissertation, University of Washington, Seattle.

Collins, L. (1997, October). *The development of tense and aspect.* Paper presented at the Second Language Research Forum, Michigan State University, East Lansing, MI.

Collins, L. (1999a, March). *Achieving new states with a familiar activity: A* Modern Times *accomplishment?* Paper presented at the Annual Meeting of the American Association of Applied Linguistics, Stamford, CT.

Collins, L. (1999b). *Marking time: The acquisition of tense and grammatical aspect by French-speaking learners of English.* Unpublished doctoral dissertation, Concordia University, Montreal, Quebec.

Comajoan, L. (1998, October). *The acquisition of past morphology in Catalan as a foreign language: Interaction of lexical aspect and discourse grounding in the L2 acquisition of past morphology of Catalan.* Paper presented at the Second Language Research Forum, University of Hawai'i, Manoa, HI.

Comajoan, L. (forthcoming). *The acquisition of past temporality and past morphology in Catalan as a foreign language.* Unpublished doctoral dissertation, Indiana University, Bloomington.

Comrie, B. (1976). *Aspect*. Cambridge, UK: Cambridge University Press.

Comrie, B. (1985). *Tense*. Cambridge, UK: Cambridge University Press.

Dahl, Ö. (1984). Temporal distance: Remoteness distinctions in tense-aspect systems. In B. Butterworth, B. Comrie, & Ö. Dahl (Eds.), *Explanations for language universals* (pp. 105–122). Berlin: Mouton.

Dahl, Ö. (1985). *Tense and aspect systems*. Oxford: Basil Blackwell.

de Villiers, J. G., & de Villiers, P. A. (1973). A cross-sectional study of the acquisition of grammatical morphemes. *Journal of Psycholinguistic Research, 2*, 267–278.

Dietrich, R. (1995). The acquisition of German. In R. Dietrich, W. Klein, & C. Noyau (Eds.), *The acquisition of temporality in a second language* (pp. 71–115). Amsterdam: Benjamins.

Dietrich, R., Klein, W., & Noyau, C. (1995). *The acquisition of temporality in a second language*. Amsterdam: Benjamins.

Dittmar, N. (1981). On the verbal organization of L2 tense marking in an elicited translation task by Spanish immigrants in Germany. *Studies in Second Language Acquisition, 3*, 136–164.

Dittmar, N., & Terborg, H. (1991). Modality and second language learning. In T. Huebner & C. A. Ferguson (Eds.), *Crosscurrents in second language acquisition and linguistic theories* (pp. 347–384). Amsterdam: Benjamins.

Doughty, C., & Varela, E. (1998). Communicative focus on form. In C. Doughty & J. Williams (Eds.), *Focus on form in classroom second language acquisition* (pp. 114–138). Cambridge: Cambridge University Press.

Douglas, D., & Selinker, L. (1994). Research methodology in context-based second language research. In E. E. Tarone, S. M. Gass, & A. D. Cohen (Eds.), *Research methodology in second language acquisition* (pp. 119–131). Hillsdale, NJ: Erlbaum.

Dowty, D. (1979). *Word meaning and Montague grammar*. Dordrecht: Reidel.

Dowty, D. (1986). The effects of aspectual class on the aspectual structure of discourse: Semantics or pragmatics? *Linguistics and Philosophy, 9*, 37–61.

Dry, H. (1981). Sentence aspect and the movement of narrative time. *Text, 1*, 233–240.

Dry, H. (1983). The movement of narrative time. *Journal of Literary Semantics, 12*, 19–53.

Dry, H. (1992). Foregrounding: An assessment. In S. J. J. Hwang & W. R. Merrifield (Eds.), *Language in context: Essays for Robert E. Longacre* (pp. 435–450). Arlington, TX: The Summer Institute of Linguistics and the University of Texas at Arlington.

Dulay, H., & Burt, M. (1973). Should we teach children syntax? *Language Learning, 23*, 245–258.

Dulay, H., & Burt, M. (1974). Natural sequence in child second language acquisition. *Language Learning, 24*, 37–53.

Dulay, H., Burt, M., & Krashen, S. (1982). *Language two.* Oxford: Oxford University Press.

Eckman, F. R., Highland, D., Lee, P. W., Mileham, J., & Weber, R. R. (Eds.). (1995). *Second language acquisition theory and pedagogy.* Mahwah, NJ: Erlbaum.

Ellis, R. (1985). *Understanding second language acquisition.* Oxford: Oxford University Press.

Ellis, R. (1987). Interlanguage variability in narrative discourse: Style shifting in the use of past tense. *Studies in Second Language Acquisition, 9,* 1–20.

Ellis, R. (1990). *Instructed second language acquisition.* Oxford: Blackwell.

Ellis, R. (1994). *The study of second language acquisition.* Oxford: Oxford University Press.

Erickson, F., & Shultz, J. (1982). *The counselor as gatekeeper.* New York: Academic Press.

Fernández, S. (1997). *Interlengua y análisis de errores en el aprendiazaje del español como lengua extranjera* [Interlanguage and error analysis in the acquisition of Spanish as a foreign language]. Madrid: Edelsa.

Flashner, V. E. (1989). Transfer of aspect in the English oral narratives of native Russian speakers. In H. Dechert & M. Raupach (Eds.), *Transfer in language production* (pp. 71–97). Norwood, NJ: Ablex.

Fleischman, S. (1985). Discourse functions of tense-aspect oppositions in narrative: Toward a theory of grounding. *Linguistics, 23,* 851–882.

Fletcher, P. (1981). Description and explanation in the acquisition of verb forms. *Journal of Child Language, 8,* 93–108.

Freed, A. F. (1979). *The semantics of English aspectual complementation.* Dordrecht: Reidel.

García, E. C., & van Putte, F. C. M. (1988). The value of contrast: Contrasting the value of strategies. *IRAL, 26,* 263–280.

Gass, S. M. (1989). Second and foreign language learning: Same, different, or none of the above? In B. VanPatten & J. F. Lee (Eds.), *Second language acquisition / Foreign language learning* (pp. 34–44). Clevedon, UK: Multilingual Matters.

Gass, S. M., & Ard, J. (1984). Second language acquisition and the ontology of language universals. In W. E. Rutherford (Ed.), *Language universals and second language acquisition* (pp. 33–68). Amsterdam: Benjamins.

Gathercole, V. C. (1986). The acquisition of the present perfect: Explaining differences in the speech of Scottish and American children. *Journal of Child Language, 13,* 537–560.

Giacalone Ramat, A. (1990). Sulla rilevanza per la teoria linguistica dei dati di acquisizione de lingue seconde. L'organizzazione temporale nel discorso [The relevance of second language acquisition for linguistic theory: The temporal structuring of discourse]. In E. Banfi & P. Cordin (Eds.), *Storia dell'Italiano e forme dell'italianizzazione* [The history of Italian and forms of Italianization] (pp. 123–140). Rome: Bulzoni.

Giacalone Ramat, A. (1992). Grammaticalization processes in the area of temporal and modal relations. *Studies in Second Language Acquisition, 14,* 297–322.

Giacalone Ramat, A. (1995a). Function and form of modality in learner Italian. In A. Giacalone Ramat & G. Crocco Galèas (Eds.), *From pragmatics to syntax: Modality in second language acquisition* (pp. 269–293). Tübingen: Narr.

Giacalone Ramat, A. (1995b). Iconicity in grammaticalization processes. In R. Simone (Ed.), *Iconicity in language* (pp. 119–139). Amsterdam: Benjamins.

Giacalone Ramat, A. (1995c). L'expression de l'aspect progressif en italien seconde langue et le rôle des propriétés sémantiques des verbes [The expression of progressive aspect in Italian as a second language and the role of semantic properties of verbs]. *Acquisition et interaction en langue étrangère, 5,* 47–78.

Giacalone Ramat, A. (1995d). Tense and aspect in learner Italian. In P. M. Bertinetto, V. Bianchi, Ö. Dahl, & M. Squartini (Eds.), *Temporal reference: Aspect and actionality: Vol. 2. Typological perspectives* (pp. 289–309). Turin, Italy: Rosenberg & Sellier.

Giacalone Ramat, A. (1997). Progressive periphrases, markedness, and second-language data. In S. Eliasson & E. H. Jahr (Eds.), *Language and its ecology* (pp. 261–285). Berlin: Mouton.

Giacalone Ramat, A., & Banfi, E. (1990). The acquisition of temporality: A second language perspective. *Folia Linguistica, 24* (3–4), 405–428.

Giacalone Ramat, A., & Bernini, G. (Eds.). (1990). *La temporalità nell'acquisizione di lingue seconde* [Temporality in the acquisition of a second language]. Milan: Franco Angeli.

Givón, T. (1982). Tense-aspect modality: The creole prototype and beyond. In P. Hopper (Ed.), *Tense-aspect: Between semantics and pragmatics* (pp. 115–163). Amsterdam: Benjamins.

Givón, T. (1984). *Syntax: A functional typological introduction* (Vol. 1). Amsterdam: Benjamins.

Godfrey, D. L. (1980). A discourse analysis of tense in adult ESL monologues. In D. Larsen-Freeman (Ed.), *Discourse analysis in second language research* (pp. 92–110). Rowley, MA: Newbury House.

Grice, H. P. (1975). Logic and conversation. In P. Cole & J. Morgan (Eds.), *Syntax and semantics: Speech acts* (pp. 41–58). New York: Academic Press.

Guenthner, F., Hoepelmann, J., & Rohrer, C. (1978). *Papers on tense, aspect and verb classification*. Tübingen: Narr.

Guiora, A. Z. (1983). Language and concept formation: A cross-lingual analysis. *Behavior Science Research, 18,* 228–256.

Haegeman, L. (1989). *Be going to* and *will:* A pragmatic account. *Journal of Linguistics, 25,* 291–317.

Hakuta, K. (1974). A preliminary report on the development of grammatical morphemes in a Japanese girl learning English as a second language. *Working Papers on Bilingualism, 3,* 18–43.

Halliday, M. A. K., & Hasan, R. (1976). *Cohesion in English*. London: Longman.

Harkness, J. (1987). Time adverbials in English and reference time. In A. Schopf (Ed.), *Essays on tensing in English: Vol I: Reference time, tense and adverbs* (pp. 71–110). Tübingen: Niemeyer.

Harley, B. (1989). Functional grammar in French immersion: A classroom experiment. *Applied Linguistics, 10,* 331–359.

Harley, B., & Swain, M. (1978). An analysis of the verb system used by young learners of French. *Interlanguage Studies Bulletin, 3,* 35–79.

Harlig, J. (1989). *The interaction of verbal aspect and noun phrase determination in Hungarian*. Unpublished dissertation, University of Chicago.

Hasbún, L. (1995). *The role of lexical aspect in the acquisition of tense and grammatical aspect in Spanish as a foreign language*. Unpublished doctoral dissertation, Indiana University, Bloomington.

Hatch, E., & Wagner-Gough, J. (1975). The importance of input data in second language acquisition studies. *Language Learning, 25,* 297–308.

Haugen, E. (1987). Danish, Norwegian and Swedish. In B. Comrie (Ed.), *The world's major languages* (pp. 157–179). New York: Oxford University Press.

Hawkins, J. A. (1987). German. In B. Comrie (Ed.), *The world's major languages* (pp. 110–138). New York: Oxford University Press.

Hill, J. H. (1988). *Language, culture, and world view*. In F. J. Newmeyer (Ed.), *Linguistics: The Cambridge survey: Vol 4. Language: The socio-cultural context* (pp. 14–36). Cambridge: Cambridge University Press.

Hinrichs, E. (1986). Temporal anaphora in discourses of English. *Linguistics and Philosophy, 9,* 63–82.

Hooper, J. (1980). Child morphology and morphonemic change. In J. Fisiack (Ed.), *Historical morphology* (pp. 157–187). Berlin: De Gruyter.

Hopper, P. J. (1979). Aspect and foregrounding in discourse. In T. Givón (Ed.), *Syntax and semantics: Discourse and syntax* (pp. 213–241). New York: Academic Press.

Hopper, P. J. (1982). Aspect between discourse and grammar: An introductory essay for the volume. In P. Hopper (Ed.), *Tense-aspect: Between semantics and pragmatics* (pp. 3–18). Amsterdam: Benjamins.

Hopper, P. J., & Thompson, S. A. (1980). Transitivity in grammar and discourse. *Language, 56,* 251–299.

House, J., & Kasper, G. (1981). Politeness markers in English and German. In F. Coulmas (Ed.), *Conversational routine: Explorations in standardized communication situations and prepatterned speech* (pp. 157–185). The Hague: Mouton.

Housen, A. (1993). L2 acquisition of verb morphology: A case study. In B. Kettemann & W. Wieden (Eds.), *Current issues in European second language acquisition research.* Tübingen: Narr.

Housen, A. (1994). Tense and aspect in second language acquisition: The Dutch interlanguage of a native speaker of English. In C. Vet and C. Vetters (Eds.), *Tense and aspect in discourse* (pp. 257–291). New York: Mouton.

Housen, A. (1997/8). Inherent semantics versus discourse-pragmatics in the L2-development of tense-aspect. In L. Diàz & C. Pérez (Eds.), *Views on the acquisition and use of a second language* (pp. 229–312). Barcelona: U. Pompéu Fàbra.

Housen, A. (1998). Facteurs semantico-conceptuels et discursivo-fonctionnels dans le developpement des systemes temporo-aspectuels: Aperçu de l'acquisition de l'anglais comme langue etrangere [Semantic-conceptual and discursive-functional factors in the development of temporal aspectual systems: Overview of the acquisition of English as a foreign language]. In S. Vogeleer, A. Borillo, C. Vetters, & M. Vuillaume (Eds.), *Temps et discours* (pp. 257–279). Leuven, Belgium: Peeters.

Housen, A. (1999, March). No time for coherence at this juncture: Some conditions on semantic pacesetting in the second language acquisition of temporal morphology. In Y. Shirai & R. Salaberry (Chairs), *Description and explanation in L2-acquisition of tense-aspect morphology: Complementary perspectives.* Colloquium conducted at the meeting of the American Association of Applied Linguistics, Stamford, CT.

Huang, C. C. (1997, March). *Semantics of verbs and the use of tense-aspect morphology by L2 learners of English.* Paper presented to the American Association of Applied Linguistics, Orlando, FL.

Inoue, K. (1979). An analysis of the English present perfect. *Linguistics, 17,* 561–589.

Jacobsen, W. M. (1982). Vendler's verb classes and the aspectual character of Japanese *te iru. Proceedings of the Eighth Annual Meetings of the Berkeley Linguistics Society* (pp. 373–383). Berkeley: Berkeley Linguistics Society.

Jespersen, O. (1924). *The philosophy of grammar.* New York: Norton. [Reprinted 1965.]

Johnson, C. (1985). The emergence of present perfect verbs forms: Semantic influences on selective imitation. *Journal of Child Language, 12,* 325–352.

Kaplan, M. A. (1987). Developmental patterns of past tense acquisition among foreign language learners of French. In B. VanPatten, T. R. Dvorak, & J. F. Lee (Eds.), *Foreign language learning: A research perspective* (pp. 52–60). Cambridge, MA: Newbury House.

Kellerman, E. (1985). If at first you do succeed. . . . In S. M. Gass & C. Madden (Eds.), *Talking to learn* (pp. 345–353). Cambridge, MA: Newbury House.

Kenny, A. (1963). *Action, emotion, and will.* London: Routledge and Kegan Paul.

Kihlstedt, M. (1993). A longitudinal study of two university students' use of verb forms and functions in the French interlanguage. In B. Hammarberg (Ed.), *Problem, process, product in language learning* (pp. 87–104). Stockholm: Institute of Linguistics, Stockholm University.

Kihlstedt, M. (1996). *La référence au passé dans le dialogue: Étude de l'acquisition de la temporalité chez des apprenants dirs avancés de français* [Reference to the past in dialogue: A study of the acquisition of temporality in advanced learners of French]. Stockholm: Department of French and Italian, Stockholm University.

Kim, N-K. (1987). *Korean.* In B. Comrie (Ed.), *The world's major languages* (pp. 139–156). New York: Oxford University Press.

King, L. D., & Suñer, M. (1999). *Gramática española: Análisis y práctica.* New York: McGraw-Hill.

Klein, W. (1986). *Second language acquisition.* (Rev. ed., Bohuslaw Jankowski, Trans.) Cambridge, UK: Cambridge University Press. (Original work published 1984)

Klein, W. (1991). SLA theory: Prolegomena to a theory of language acquisition and implications for theoretical linguistics. In T. Huebner & C. A. Ferguson (Eds.), *Crosscurrents in second language acquisition and linguistic theories* (pp. 169–194). Amsterdam: Benjamins.

Klein, W. (1992). The present perfect puzzle. *Language, 68,* 525–552.

Klein, W. (1993). The acquisition of temporality. In C. Perdue (Ed.), *Adult language acquisition: Cross-linguistic perspectives: Vol. 2. The results* (pp. 73–118). Cambridge, UK: Cambridge University Press.

Klein, W. (1994a). Learning how to express temporality in a second language. In A. Giacalone Ramat & M. Vedovelli (Eds.), *Italiano: Lingua seconda / lingua straniera* [Italian: Second language/foreign language] (pp. 227–248). Rome: Bulzoni.

Klein, W. (1994b). *Time in language.* New York: Routledge.

Klein, W. (1995). The acquisition of English. In R. Dietrich, W. Klein, & C. Noyau (Eds.), *The acquisition of temporality in a second language* (pp. 31–70). Amsterdam: Benjamins.

Klein, W. (1998). The contribution of second language research. *Language Learning, 48,* 527–550.

Klein, W., Coenen, J., van Helvert, K., & Hendriks, H. (1995). The acquisition of Dutch. In R. Dietrich, W. Klein, & C. Noyau (Eds.), *The acquisition of temporality in a second language* (pp. 71–143). Amsterdam: Benjamins.

Klein, W., Dietrich, R., & Noyau, C. (1995). Conclusions. In R. Dietrich, W. Klein, & C. Noyau (Eds.), *The acquisition of temporality in a second language* (pp. 261–280). Amsterdam: Benjamins.

Klein, W., & Perdue, C. (Eds.). (1992). *Utterance structure: Developing grammars again.* Amsterdam: Benjamins.

Klein, W. (with Dietrich, R., & Noyau, C.). (1993). The acquisition of temporality. In C. Perdue (Ed.), *Adult language acquisition: Cross-linguistic perspectives: Vol. 2: The results* (pp. 73–116). Cambridge: Cambridge University Press.

Kooij, J. G. (1987). *Dutch.* In B. Comrie (Ed.), *The world's major languages* (pp. 139–156). New York: Oxford University Press.

Krashen, S. D. (1977). Some issues related to the monitor model. In H. Brown, C. Yorio, & R. Crymes (Eds.), *On TESOL '77.* Washington, DC: TESOL.

Krashen, S. D. (1985). *The input hypothesis.* London: Longman.

Krashen S. D., & Terrell, T. (1983). *The natural approach.* Oxford: Pergamon.

Kumpf, L. (1984a). Comments on the paper by Gass and Ard. In W. E. Rutherford (Ed.), *Language universals and second language acquisition* (pp. 69–72). Amsterdam: Benjamins.

Kumpf, L. (1984b). Temporal systems and universality in interlanguage: A case study. In F. Eckman, L. Bell, & D. Nelson (Eds.), *Universals of second language acquisition* (pp. 132–143). Rowley, MA: Newbury House.

Labov, W. (1972). *Language in the inner city.* Philadelphia: University of Pennsylvania Press.

Labov, W., & Waletzky, J. (1967). Narrative analysis: Oral versions of personal experience. In J. Helm (Ed.), *Essays on the verbal and visual arts* (pp. 12–44). Seattle: University of Washington Press.

Lafford, B. A. (1996, October). *The development of tense/aspect relations in L2 Spanish narratives: Evidence to test competing theories.* Paper presented at the Second Language Research Forum, Tucson, AZ.

Larsen-Freeman, D. (1975). *The acquisition of grammatical morphemes by adult learners of English as a second language.* Unpublished doctoral dissertation, University of Michigan, Ann Arbor.

Larsen-Freeman, D., & Long, M. H. (1991). *An Introduction to Second Language Acquisition Research.* London: Longman.

Leary, A. (1999, September). *Acquiring Russian tense-aspect: Opaque input for learners.* Paper presented at the Second Language Research Forum, Minneapolis, MN.

Lee, E. J. (1997). *Acquisition of tense and aspect by two Korean speakers of English: A longitudinal study.* Unpublished master's thesis, University of Hawai'i, Manoa.

Lee, J. F. (1998). The relationship of verb morphology to second language reading comprehension and input processing. *Modern Language Journal, 82,* 33–48.

Lee, J. F. (1999). On levels of processing and levels of comprehension. In J. Gútierrez-Rexach & F. Martínez-Gil, *Advances in Hispanic linguistics* (pp. 42–59). Somerville, MA: Cascadilla Press.

Lee, J. F., Cadierno, T., Glass, W. R., & VanPatten, B. (1997). The effects of lexical and grammatical cues on processing past temporal reference in second language input. *Applied Language Learning, 8,* 1–23.

Leech, G. N. (1971). *Meaning and the English verb.* Harlow, Essex: Longman.

Leeman, J., Artegoitia, I., Fridman, B., & Doughty, C. (1995). Integrating attention to form with meaning: Focus on form in content-based Spanish instruction. In R. Schmidt (Ed.), *Attention and awareness in foreign language learning* (pp. 217–258). (Technical Report 9). Honolulu, HI: Second Language Teaching and Curriculum Center, University of Hawai'i at Manoa.

Leiria, I. (1994). Aquisição do aspecto verbal por falantes nao-nativos de Portuguêse-Europeu: O exemplo dos pretéritos perfeito e imperferfeito [Acquisition of verbal aspect by nonnative speakers of European Portuguese: An example of perfect and imperfect past]. *Revista Internacional de Língua Portuguesa, 11,* 74–112.

Leiria, I., & Mendes, A. Q. (1995). Acquisition of tense and aspect in European Portuguese (L1 and L2). In I. S. Faria & M. J. Freitas (Eds.), *Studies on the acquisition of Portuguese* (pp. 97–113). Lisbon: Edições Colibri–Associação Portuguesa de Linguística.

Li, C., & Thompson, S. (1987). Chinese. In B. Comrie (Ed.), *The world's major languages* (pp. 811–833). New York: Oxford University Press.

Li, P., & Shirai, Y. (forthcoming). *The acquisition of lexical and grammatical aspect.* Berlin: De Gruyter.

Liskin-Gasparro, J. (1996). Narrative strategies: A case study of developing storytelling skills by a learner of Spanish. *Modern Language Journal, 80,* 271–286.

Liskin-Gasparro, J. (1997, March). *Acquisition of tense and aspect in Spanish: Exploring learners' perceptions.* Paper presented to the American Association of Applied Linguistics, Orlando, FL.

Longacre, R. (1981). A spectrum and profile approach to discourse analysis. *Text, 1,* 337–359.

Long, M., & Sato, C. J. (1984). Methodological issues in interlanguage studies: An interactionist perspective. In A. Davies, C. Criper, & A. P. R. Howatt (Eds.), *Interlanguage* (pp. 253–279). Edinburgh: Edinburgh University Press.

Lyons, J. (1977). *Semantics* (Vol. 2). Cambridge: Cambridge University Press.

Martínez Baztán, A. (1994). Análisis transversal del uso de los tiempos indefinido/imperfecto por estudiantes holandeses de Español L2 [A cross-sectional analysis of the use of preterite and imperfect tense in Spanish L2 by Dutch students]. In P. J. Slagter (Ed.), *Aproximaciones a cuestiones de adquisición y aprendizaje del Español como lengua extranjera o lengua segunda* [Approaches to questions about the acquisition and learning of Spanish as a foreign or second language] (pp. 31–48). Amsterdam: Rodopi.

Massett, L. (1989, October, 6). *Michael Kerwin* [Radio transcript]. NPR: All Things Considered.

Matthews, R. (1987). Present perfect tenses: Towards an integrated functional account. In A. Schopf (Ed.), *Essays on tensing in English* (pp. 111–176). Tübingen: Niemeyer.

McCawley, J. D. (1971). Tense and time reference in English. In C. J. Filmore and T. C. Langdoen (Eds.), *Studies in linguistic semantics* (pp. 96–113). New York: Holt, Rinehart and Winston.

McCawley, J. D. (1982). *Thirty million theories of grammar.* Chicago: The University of Chicago Press.

McCoard, R. W. (1978). *The English perfect: Tense-choice and pragmatic inferences.* Amsterdam: North Holland.

Meisel, J. M. (1980). Linguistic simplification: A study of immigrant workers' speech and foreigner talk. In S. W. Felix (Ed.), *Second language development* (pp. 13–40). Tübingen: Narr.

Meisel, J. M. (1987). Reference to past events and actions in the development of natural language acquisition. In C. W. Pfaff (Ed.), *First and second language acquisition processes* (pp. 206–224). Cambridge, MA: Newbury House.

Meisel, J. M., Clahsen, H., & Pienemann, M. (1981). On determining developmental stages in natural second language acquisition. *Studies in Second Language Acquisition, 3,* 109–135.

Mittwoch, A. (1991). In deference to Vendler's achievements. *Belgian Journal of Linguistics, 6,* 71–85.

Moens, E., & Steedman, M. (1988). Temporal ontology and temporal reference. *Computational Linguistics, 14*(2), 15–28.

Moses, J. G. (1997, October). *Looking into the future: The expression of future events in French as a foreign language.* Paper presented at the Second Language Research Forum, Michigan State University, East Lansing, MI.

Moses, J. G. (forthcoming). *The expression of futurity by English-speaking learners of French.* Unpublished doctoral dissertation, Indiana University, Bloomington.

Mourelatos, A. (1981). Events, processes, states. In P. Tedeschi & A. Zaenen (Eds.), *Syntax and semantics: Tense and aspect* (pp. 191–212). New York: Academic Press.

Moy, R. H. (1983). The perfect aspect as a state of being. *Language and Communication, 2,* 249–350.

Musumeci, D. (1989). *The ability of second language learners to assign tense at the sentence level.* Unpublished doctoral dissertation, The University of Illinois at Urbana-Champaign.

Nef, F. (1980). Les verbes aspectuels du francais: Remarques sémantiques et esquisse d'un traitement formel [The aspectual verbs of French: Semantic remarks on the semantics and an outline of a formal treatment]. *Semantikos, 14,* 11–46.

Nehls, D. (1988). On the development of the grammatical category of aspect in English. In J. Klegraf & D. Nehls (Eds.), *Essays on the English language and applied linguistics on the occasion of Gerhard Nickel's 60th birthday* (pp. 173–198). Heidelberg: Julius Groos.

Nguyen, D.-H. (1987). Vietnamese. In B. Comrie (Ed.), *The world's major languages* (pp. 777–796). New York: Oxford University Press.

Noor, H. H. (1993). The acquisition of temporal conjunctions by Saudi Arabian learners of English. *International Journal of Applied Linguistics, 3,* 101–124.

Noyau, C. (1984). The development of means for temporality in French by adult Spanish-speakers: Linguistic devices and communicative capacities. In G. Extra and M. Mittner (Eds.), *Studies in second language acquisition by adult immigrants: Proceedings of the ESF/AILA symposium held on the 9th of August 1984 in Brussels* (pp. 113–137). Tilburg, Netherlands: Tilburg University, Department of Language and Literature.

Noyau, C. (1990). The development of means for temporality in the unguided acquisition of L2: Cross-linguistic perspectives. In H. W. Dechert (Ed.), *Current trends in European second language acquisition research* (pp. 143–170). Clevedon, UK: Multilingual Matters.

Noyau, C., Dorriots, B., Sjöström, S., & Voionmaa, K. (1995). The acquisition of Swedish. In R. Dietrich, W. Klein, & C. Noyau (Eds.), *The acquisition of temporality in a second language* (pp. 211–259). Amsterdam: Benjamins.

Noyau, C., Houdaïfa, E., Vasseur, M., & Véronique, D. (1995). The acquisition of French. In R. Dietrich, W. Klein, & C. Noyau (Eds.), *The acquisition of temporality in a second language* (pp. 145–209). Amsterdam: Benjamins.

Oates, J. C. (1987). *You must remember this.* New York: E. P. Dutton.

O'Neill, R., Kingsbury, R., Yeadon, T., & Cornelius, E. T., Jr. (1978). *AKL: Intermediate.* New York: Longman.

Pica, T. (1984). Methods of morpheme quantification: Their effect on the interpretation of interlanguage data. *Studies in Second Language Acquisition, 6,* 69–78.

Pienemann, M. (1989). Is language teachable? Psycholinguistic experiments and hypotheses. *Applied Linguistics, 10,* 52–79.

Pienemann, M. (1998). *Language processing and second language development: Processability theory.* Amsterdam: Benjamins.

Quick, D. (1997). *L1 influence and primacy of aspect in adult second language acquisition.* Unpublished master's thesis, University of Pittsburgh, Pittsburgh, PA.

Quirk, R., Greenbaum, S., Leech, G., & Svartvik, J. (1985). *A comprehensive grammar of the English language.* London: Longman.

Ramsay, V. (1990). *Developmental stages in the acquisition of the perfective and the imperfective aspects by classroom L2 learners of Spanish.* Unpublished doctoral dissertation, University of Oregon, Eugene.

Reichenbach, H. (1947). *Elements of symbolic logic.* Berkeley: University of California.

Reinhart, T. (1984). Principles of gestalt perception in the temporal organization of narrative texts. *Linguistics, 22,* 779–809.

Rispoli, M., & Bloom, L. (1985). Incomplete and continuing: Theoretical issues in the acquisition of tense and aspect. *Journal of Child Language, 12,* 471–474.

Robison, R. E. (1990). The primacy of aspect: Aspectual marking in English interlanguage. *Studies in Second Language Acquisition, 12,* 315–330.

Robison, R. E. (1993). *Aspectual marking in English interlanguage: A cross-sectional study.* Unpublished doctoral dissertation, University of California, Los Angeles.

Robison, R. E. (1995a). The aspect hypothesis revisited: A cross-sectional study of tense and aspect marking in interlanguage. *Applied Linguistics, 16,* 344–370.

Robison, R. E. (1995b). Verb inflections in native-speaker speech: Do they mean what we think? In H. Pishwa & K. Maroldt (Eds.), *The development of morphological systematicity* (pp. 199–224). Tübingen: Gunter Narr.

Rohde, A. (1996). The aspect hypothesis and emergence of tense distinction in naturalistic L2 acquisition. *Linguistics, 34,* 1115–1138.

Rohde, A. (1997). *Verbflexion und Verbsemantik im natürlichen L2-Erwerb* [Verbal inflection and verbal semantics in natural L2 acquisition]. Tübingen: Narr.

Rohde, A. (1999, March). The aspect hypothesis in naturalistic L2 acquisition: What uninflected and non-targetlike verbs forms in early interlanguage tell us. In Y. Shirai & R. Salaberry (Chairs), *Description and explanation in L2 acquisition of tense-aspect morphology*. Colloquium conducted at the annual meeting of the American Association of Applied Linguistics, Stamford, CT.

Rosansky, E. (1976). Methods and morphemes in second language acquisition. *Language Learning, 26,* 409–425.

Salaberry, R. (1997). *The development of Spanish past tense aspect among classroom learners.* Unpublished doctoral dissertation, Cornell University, Ithaca, NY.

Salaberry, R. (1998). The development of aspectual distinctions in academic L2 French. *Canadian Modern Language Review, 54,* 508–542.

Salaberry, R. (1999a). The development of English past tense morphology among classroom learners. In P. Robinson (Ed.), *Proceedings of the Third Pacific Second Language Research Forum* (Vol. 1, pp. 139–149). Tokyo: The Pacific Second Language Research Forum.

Salaberry, R. (1999b). The development of past tense verbal morphology in classroom L2 Spanish. *Applied Linguistics, 20,* 151–178.

Salkie, R. (1989). Perfect and pluperfect: What is the relationship? *Journal of Linguistics, 25,* 1–34.

Salsbury, T. (1997). *The grammaticalization of hypotheticals.* Unpublished manuscript for the Seminar in Second Language Acquisition at Indiana University, Bloomington.

Salsbury, T. (2000). *The acquisitional grammaticalization of unreal conditionals and modality in L2 English: A longitudinal perspective.* Unpublished doctoral dissertation, Indiana University, Bloomington.

Sanz, C., & Fernández, M. (1992). L2 learners' processing of temporal cues in Spanish. *MIT Working Papers in Linguistics, 16,* 155–168.

Sato, C. J. (1984). Phonological processes in second language acquisition: Another look at interlanguage syllable structure. *Language Learning, 34,* 42–57.

Sato, C. J. (1986). Conversation and interlanguage development: Rethinking the connection. In R. Day (Ed.), *Talking to learn* (pp. 23–45). Rowley, MA: Newbury House.

Sato, C. J. (1990). *The syntax of conversation in interlanguage development.* Tübingen: Narr.

Schiffrin, D. (1981). Tense variation in narrative. *Language, 57,* 45–62.

Schlyter, S. (1990). The acquisition of French temporal morphemes in adults and in bilingual children. In G. Bernini & A. Giacalone Ramat (Eds.), *La temporalità nell'acquisizione di lingue seconde* (pp. 293–308). Milan: Franco Angeli.

Schopf, A. (1984). *Das Verzeitungssystem des Englischen und seine Textfunktion* [The temporal system of English and its text-function]. Tübingen: Max Niemeyer.

Schopf, A. (Ed.). (1987). *Essays on tensing in English*. Tübingen: Max Niemeyer.

Schumann, J. (1987). The expression of temporality in basilang speech. *Studies in Second Language Acquisition, 9*, 21–41.

Selinker, L., & Douglas, D. (1985). Wrestling with "context" in interlanguage theory. *Applied Linguistics, 6*, 190–204.

Selinker, L., & Douglas, D. (1988). Using discourse domains in creating interlanguage: Context, theory, and research methodology. In J. Klegraf & D. Nehls (Eds.), *Essays on the English language and applied linguistics on the occasion of Gerhard Nickel's 60th birthday* (pp. 357–379). Heidelberg: Julius Groos.

Sharwood Smith, M. (1981). Consciousness raising and the second language learner. *Applied Linguistics, 2*, 159–68.

Sharwood Smith, M. (1991). Speaking to many minds: On the relevance of different types of language information for the L2 learner. *Second Language Research, 7*, 118–132.

Shibata, M. (1998). The use of tense-aspect markers in a Brazilian worker's Japanese. *Annual Report of The Institute of Regional Study, The University of Okinawa, 11*, 45–63.

Shirai, Y. (1991). *Primacy of aspect in language acquisition: Simplified input and prototype*. Unpublished doctoral dissertation, University of California, Los Angeles.

Shirai, Y. (1993). Inherent aspect and the acquisition of tense-aspect morphology in Japanese. In H. Nakojima & Y. Otsu (Eds.), *Argument structure: Its syntax and acquisition* (pp. 185–211). Tokyo: Kaitakusha.

Shirai, Y. (1995). Tense-aspect marking by L2 learners of Japanese. In D. MacLaughlin & S. McEwen (Eds.), *Proceedings of 19th Annual Boston University Conference in Language Development* (Vol. 2, pp. 575–586). Somerville, MA: Cascadilla Press.

Shirai, Y. (1998a). The emergence of tense-aspect morphology in Japanese: Universal predisposition? *First Language, 18*, 281–309.

Shirai, Y. (1998b). Where the progressive and the resultative meet: Imperfective aspect in Japanese, Chinese, Korean and English. *Studies in Language, 22*, 661–692.

Shirai, Y. (1999). The prototype hypothesis of tense-aspect acquisition. In P. Robinson (Ed.), *Proceedings of the Third Pacific Second Language Research Forum* (Vol. 1, pp. 151–164). Tokyo: The Pacific Second Language Research Forum.

Shirai, Y., & Andersen, R. W. (1995). The acquisition of tense-aspect morphology. *Language, 71*, 743–762.

Shirai, Y., & Kurono, A. (1998). The acquisition of tense-aspect marking in Japanese as a second language. *Language Learning, 48,* 245–279.

Silva-Corvalán, C. (1983). Tense and aspect in oral Spanish narrative. *Language, 59,* 760–780.

Silverstein, M. (1976). Hierarchy of features and ergativity. In R. M. W. Dixon (Ed.), *Grammatical categories in Australian languages* (pp. 112–177). Canberra: Australia Institute of Aboriginal Studies.

Skehan, P. (1998). *A cognitive approach to language learning.* Oxford: Oxford University Press.

Skiba, R., & Dittmar, N. (1992). Pragmatic, semantic, and syntactic constraints and grammaticalization: A longitudinal perspective. *Studies in Second Language Acquisition, 14,* 323–349.

Slobin, D. I. (1973). Cognitive prerequisites for the development grammar. In C. A. Ferguson & D. I. Slobin (Eds.), *Studies of child language development* (pp. 175–208). New York: Holt, Rinehart and Winston.

Slobin, D. I. (1985). Cross-linguistic evidence for the language-making capacity. In D. I. Slobin (Ed.), *The cross-linguistic study of language acquisition* (Vol. 2, pp.1157–1256). Hillsdale, NJ: Erlbaum.

Slobin, D. (1993). Adult language acquisition: A view from child language study. In C. Perdue (Ed.), *Adult language acquisition: Cross-linguistic perspectives: Results* (Vol. 1, pp. 73–116). Cambridge, U.K.: Cambridge University Press.

Smith, C. S. (1978). The syntax and interpretation of temporal expression in English. *Linguistics and Philosophy, 2,* 43–99.

Smith, C. S. (1980). The acquisition of time talk: Relations between child and adult grammars. *Journal of Child Language, 7,* 263–278.

Smith, C. S. (1983). A theory of aspectual class. *Language, 59,* 479–501.

Smith, C. S. (1986). A speaker-based approach to aspect. *Linguistics and Philosophy, 9,* 97–115.

Smith, C. S. (1991). *The parameter of aspect.* Dordrecht: Kluwer.

Smith, C. S., & Weist, R. M. (1987). On the temporal contour of child language: A reply to Rispoli & Bloom. *Journal of Child Language, 14,* 387–392.

Smith, M. C. (1992). *Red square.* New York: Random House.

Smith, N. V. (1981). Grammaticality, time, and tense. *Philosophical Transactions, Royal Society of London, B 295,* 253–265.

Stanley, K., & Mellow, D. (1998, October). *Overgeneralization and underapplication in past time expression.* Paper presented at the Second Language Research Forum, Honolulu, HI.

Starren, M., & van Hout, R. (1996). Temporality in learner discourse: What temporal adverbials can and what they cannot express. *Zeitschrift für Literaturwissenschaft und Linguistik, 104,* 35–50.

Suh, K. (1992). *A discourse-analysis of the English tense-aspect-modality system.* Unpublished doctoral dissertation, University of California, Los Angeles.

Tajika, H. (1999). *Variable patterns of tense / aspect marking in interlanguage.* Unpublished doctoral dissertation, University of Minnesota, Minneapolis.

Tannen, D. (1989). *Talking voices: Repetition, dialogue, and imagery in conversational discourse.* (Studies in Interactional Sociolinguistics 6.) Cambridge: Cambridge University Press.

Thelin, N. B. (1990). Verbal aspect in discourse: On the state of the art. In N. B. Thelin (Ed.), *Verbal aspect in discourse* (pp. 3–88). Amsterdam: Benjamins.

Thomas, M. (1994). Assessment of L2 proficiency in second language acquisition research. *Language Learning, 44,* 307–336.

Thompson, S. A. (1968). *One hundred favorite folktales.* Bloomington, IN: Indiana University Press.

Thompson, S. A. (1987). "Subordination" and narrative event structure. In R. Tomlin (Ed.), *Coherence and grounding in discourse* (pp. 435–454). Amsterdam: Benjamins.

Thompson, S. A., & Longacre, R. E. (1985). Adverbial clauses. In T. Shopen (Ed.), *Language typology and syntactic description* (pp. 171–234). Cambridge: Cambridge University Press.

Tomlin, R. S. (1984). The treatment of foreground-background in the on-line descriptive discourse of second language learners. *Studies in Second Language Acquisition, 6,* 115–142.

Trévise, A. (1987). Toward an analysis of the (inter)language activity of referring to time in narratives. In C. W. Pfaff (Ed.), *First and second language acquisition processes* (pp. 225–251). Cambridge, MA: Newbury House.

Trévise, A., & Porquier, R. (1986). Second language acquisition by adult immigrants: Exemplified methodology. *Studies in Second Language Acquisition, 8,* 265–275.

van Dijk, T. A. (1975). Action, action description, and narrative. *New Literary History, 6,* 273–294.

van Holk, A. G. F. (1990). Aspect in textual deep structure. In N. B. Thelin (Ed.), *Verbal aspect in discourse* (pp. 367–382). Amsterdam: John Benjamins.

Van Naerssen, M. (1980). In S. D. Krashen & R. C. Scarcella (Eds.), *Research in second language acquisition* (pp. 146–154). Rowley, MA: Newbury House.

VanPatten, B. (1984). Processing strategies and morpheme acquisition. In F. R. Eckman, L. H. Bell, & D. Nelson (Eds.), *Universals of second language acquisition* (pp. 88–98). Rowley, MA: Newbury House.

VanPatten, B. (1990). Theory and research in second language acquisition and foreign language learning: On producers and consumers. In B. VanPatten & J. F. Lee (Eds.), *Second language acquisition/Foreign language learning* (pp. 17–26). Clevedon, UK: Multilingual Matters.

VanPatten, B. (1996). *Input processing and grammar instruction: Theory and research.* Norwood, NJ: Ablex.

Vendler, Z. (1967). Verbs and times. In Z. Vendler (Ed.), *Linguistics and philosophy* (pp. 97–121). Ithaca, NY: Cornell University Press. (Reprinted from *Philosophical Review,* 1957, *66,* 143–160)

Véronique, D. (1987). Reference to past events and actions in narratives in L2: Insights from North African Learners' French. In C. W. Pfaff (Ed.), *First and second language acquisition processes* (pp. 252–272). Cambridge, MA: Newbury House.

von Stutterheim, C. (1986). *Temporalität in der Zweitsprache: Eine Untersuchung zum Erwerb des Deutschen durch Türkische Gasterbeiter* [Temporality in second language: A study of the acquisition of German by Turkish guestworkers]. Berlin: De Gruyter.

von Stutterheim, C. (1991). Narrative and description: Temporal reference in second language acquisition. In T. Huebner & C. A. Ferguson (Eds.), *Crosscurrents in second language acquisition and linguistic theories* (pp. 385–403). Amsterdam: Benjamins.

von Stutterheim, C., & Klein, W. (1987). A concept-oriented approach to second language studies. In C. W. Pfaff (Ed.), *First and second language acquisition processes* (pp. 191–205). Cambridge, MA: Newbury House.

von Stutterheim, C., & Klein, W. (1989). Referential movement in descriptive and narrative discourse. In R. Dietrich & C. F. Graumann (Eds.), *Language processing in social context* (pp. 39–76). Amsterdam: Elsevier.

Weist, R. M. (1986). Tense and aspect. In P. Fletcher & M. Garman (Eds.), *Language acquisition: Studies in first language development* (pp. 356–374). Cambridge: Cambridge University Press.

Weist, R. M., Kaczmarek, A., & Wysocka, J. (1993). The function of aspectual configurations in the conversational and narrative discourse of Finnish, Polish, and American children. *Papers and Studies in Contrastive Linguistics, 27,* 79–106.

Weist, R. M., Wysocka, H., & Lyytinen, P. (1991). A cross-linguistic perspective on the development of temporal systems. *Journal of Child Language, 18,* 67–92.

Weist, R. M., Wysocka, H., Witkowska-Stadnik, K., Buczowska, E., & Konieczna, E. (1984). The defective tense hypothesis: On the emergence of tense and aspect in child Polish. *Journal of Child Language, 11,* 347–374.

White, L. (1992). On triggering data in L2 acquisition: A reply to Schwartz and Gubala-Ryzak. *Second Language Research, 8,* 120–137.

Wiberg, E. (1996). Reference to past events in bilingual Italian-Swedish children of school age. *Linguistics, 34,* 1087–1114.

Wode, H. (1981). *Learning a second language: An integrated view of language acquisition.* Tübingen: Narr.

Wode, H., Bahns, J., Bedey, H., & Frank, W. (1978). Developmental sequence: An alternative approach to morpheme order. *Language Learning, 15,* 37–57.

Wolfram, W. (1984). Unmarked tense in American Indian English. *American Speech, 59,* 31–50.

Wolfram, W. (1985). Variability in tense marking: A case for the obvious. *Language Learning, 35,* 229–253.

Wolfram, W. (1989). Systematic variability in second-language tense marking. In M. R. Eisenstein (Ed.), *The dynamic interlanguage: Empirical studies in second language variation* (pp. 187–197). New York: Plenum.

Wolfram, W., & Hatfield, D. (1986). Interlanguage fads and linguistics reality: The case of tense marking. In D. Tannen & J. Alatis (Eds.), *GURT '85 languages and linguistics: The interdependence of theory, data, and application* (pp. 17–34). Washington, DC: Georgetown University Press.

Wolfson, N. (1979). The conversational historical present alternation. *Language, 55,* 168–182.

Young, R. (1988). Variation and the interlanguage hypothesis. *Studies in Second Language Acquisition, 10,* 281–302.

Youssef, V., & James, W. (1999). Grounding via tense-aspect in Tobagonian Creole: Discourse strategies across a creole continuum. *Linguistics, 37,* 597–624.

INDEX

A

Abdullah (participant in IEP studies), **130 table 3.2, 356 table 6.1,** 359–61
  tense-aspect morphology emergence studies, 143, **144–47 table 3.4, 150–53 table 3.5, 161–164 table 3.7,** 165, **171 table 3.8;** on adverbials and acquisition of the simple past, 52–53, **54 table 2.3,** 57, 61; on adverbials and reverse-order-reports, 69, **80–83 table 2.7;** observational study of effects of instruction, **373–77 table 6.2,** 378, 379, **380–83 table 6.3,** 385, **387 table 6.4,** 395
accomplishments (ACC), 215–20, 300, 312–16, 428–29
  diagnostic tests for in terms of aspectual categories, 221–26, 273n5
  grounding, 301–4, **304 table 5.4,** 430; distribution of verbal morphology, 306, 308–9, **309 fig. 5.4, 309 table 5.7, 310 fig. 5.5, 311 fig. 5.6,** 312, **312 fig. 5.7**
  patterned together with achievements as events, 215, 231, 273n7 (*see also* events)
  verb forms used to mark, 227–28, **245–46 table 4.4,** 246–51, **248–49 table 4.5,** 258–61, 265, 349; imperfective past, 234–37; by learners of Japanese, **255 table 4.7;** by learners of Spanish, **253 table 4.6,** 254; perfective past, 228–34, 423; the progressive, 237–38, 424
accuracy orders of English past tense, 94–95; Ellis's study of, 5, 8–9
achievements (ACH), 197, 215–20, 300, 312–16, 428–29

diagnostic tests for in terms of aspectual categories, 221–26, 273nn5, 6
  grounding, 301–4, **304 table 5.4;** distribution of verbal morphology, **309 fig 5.4,** 310–12, **310 fig. 5.5, 311 table 5.8**
  patterned together with accomplishments as events, 215, 231, 273n7 (*see also* events)
  verb forms used to mark, 227–28, **245–46 table 4.4,** 246–51, **248–49 table 4.5,** 258–61, 349; by German-speaking child learners of English, 267–68, 275n25; imperfective past, 234–37; in Japanese, **255 table 4.7,** 427–28; by learners of Spanish, 252–54, **253 table 4.6;** perfective past, 228–34, 423; the progressive, 237–38, 268, 424
acquisitional sequences, **12 fig. 1.1,** 13, 94–95, 254–55, 418–23; as an area for further research, 405, 413, 422–23; morpheme order studies, 4–6, 20n2
action-in-progress: as area for further meaning-oriented research, 416; English progressive described as a, 211; as a feature of the past progressive, 104
activities (ACT), 215–20, 238, 270, 312–16
  diagnostic tests for in terms of aspectual categories, 222–26, 273n5
  grounding, 302–4, **304 table 5.4,** 430; distribution of verbal morphology, 305–6, **305 table 5.5, 307 table 5.6, 308 fig. 5.3, 309 fig. 5.4, 310 fig. 5.5, 311 fig. 5.6,** 312, **312 fig. 5.7**
  and statives grouped together as atelic predicates, 215, 231

oral reports, use in investigation of instruction effect in an ESL middle-
school content-based science class,
347–48

oral tasks

picture narration, use in study of ESL
students' use of simple past and
past progressive, 121–23

use as elicitation procedures for aspect hypothesis studies, 199–202,
203–4, **206–10 table 4.1,** 262–64;
IEP study, 239–40, 243–44,
248–49 table 4.5, 248–51,
258–62; on the perfective past,
229–30; on the progressive,
237–39

use in meaning-oriented studies, **29
table 2.1**

order of mention contrast, 25 (*see also*
chronological order)

outsider, stigmatizing of language
learner as an, 91n12

overgeneralizations/overuse

of past tenses, 175–80, 176; in IEP
studies, 141, 157–60, **157 table
3.6,** 167–69, 384

of the progressive, 227, 238–39,
316–17, 426

P

passato prossimo, in Italian, 96, 113, 115,
214, 234; contrast with the imperfetto to distinguish between perfective and imperfective
grammatical aspect, 211–12; use
by children, 194

passé composé, in French, 11, 96, 101,
234, 273n11, 291

acquisition of: targeted in early-immersion class, 342–44, 406n3; use
of Vendler categories to study,
218–19

contrast with the imparfait, 17,
211–12

use by French-speaking children, and
sensitivity to lexical aspect, 194

use by learners, 113, 115–16, 123–24,
188n16; to mark events, 214, 229,
232

past-in-the-past. *See* pluperfect

past participle, in French and Italian:
preceded by an auxiliary to form
the compound past, 101–2, 115,
419; use with change of state
verbs, by children, 194

past perfect. *See* pluperfect

past progressive, in English, 17, 92n16,
102, 113, 126, 429

place in acquisitional sequence, 175,
419

production of by ESL students,
121–23

semantics of, 104–6

tense-aspect morphology related to
and aspect hypothesis study, 241,
243

use by Italian-speaking learner, 119

use in IEP studies, 94, 126–27,
142–49, **144–47 table 3.4,** 169,
170–73 table 3.8, 174, 182–83; for
activities in film retell task,
237–38; on adverbials, 52; coding,
139, 140–41, 169; observational
study of effects of instruction,
373–78, **374–77 table 6.2,**
392–93, 394; on reverse-order reports, 77

past tense (preterite) forms, 6–10, 114,
314–15, 337n10, 422, 428–30 (*see
also individual forms*); distinction
between nonpast and as first temporal morphology reported in acquisitional studies, 419, 422;
possible function as a default
tense marker, 269

past tense (preterite) forms, in English,
266–67, 419 (*see also individual
forms*)

irregular, 4–7, 20n2, 112, 230–31,
273n10

study of emergence of tense-aspect
morphology related to, 126–84,
241; analysis and results, 138–84;
method, 127–38

past tense (preterite) forms, in Germanic
languages, 102–4, 419 (*see also
past tense forms, in English*); in
Dutch, 118–19; in German, 46,
102–3, 118, 396, 402; in Swedish,
103–4

From Minnie,
with Love

So Fair a House
Prelude to Mutiny
The Devil's Wind
The So Beloved
Surgeon James's Journal, 1812
Katherine Fry's Book
Adventurers of the Mayflower
The Silver Swan

From Minnie, with Love

THE LETTERS OF A VICTORIAN LADY 1849–1861

Edited by

JANE VANSITTART

Peter Davies: London

Peter Davies Limited
15 Queen Street, Mayfair, London W1X 8BE

LONDON   MELBOURNE   TORONTO
JOHANNESBURG   AUCKLAND

© 1974 by Jane Vansittart
First published 1974
432 18000 1

*The author wishes to thank Miss M. Bethel for her
immaculate redrawing of sketches which appeared
in the letters but which were not reproducible.*

Printed and bound in Great Britain by
Morrison & Gibb Limited, London and Edinburgh

This book is for

Miss Dorothy Scobell Wood of Newquay,
Minnie's granddaughter and the owner
of these letters,

with my thanks and love

CONTENTS

ILLUSTRATIONS

Photographs

Line Drawings

The Early Years

Minnie Wood's letters lay forgotten in a trunk in store in London for many years. They must have been put away at the time of the death in 1881 of Minnie's mother, Mrs Blane, to whom they were addressed. Minnie's granddaughter, Miss Scobell Wood, with her father, discovered the letters years ago, and again they were put away until recently, when Miss Wood realized their interest and allowed them to be edited for this book, more than a hundred years after they were written.

The pages are faded and yellow; some are in envelopes, others just folded and addressed. The letters are all on very thin paper, and many have the writing running in two directions, presenting a difficult criss-cross puzzle, even though the writing is well formed. To read them is to find Minnie herself and to become curious to know more about her.

Maria Lydia Blane, always known as Minnie, was born in March 1835, and grew up in the sheltered atmosphere of the home of a well-to-do family in Slough. Her father was born in 1788 of an Ayrshire family, his uncle being physician to the Prince Regent. Mr Blane served in the Civil Service, was Superintendent of Police in Mauritius, Inspector of Customs, held various appointments in England, and finally became Deputy Governor of the Australian Agricultural Company. In 1834 he married Mary Broughton, granddaughter of the fourth Baronet, Sir Thomas Broughton, a direct descendant of Dorothy Vernon of Haddon Hall, and aunt of the famous novelist, Rhoda Broughton.

Minnie, their eldest child, was devoted to her young sister, Cecilia (Cissy), and to her three brothers, Archie, William and Robert.

The family lived at Salt Hill, Slough, during Minnie's school-days at Miss Grigg's select seminary for young ladies at No. 1

Lipson Terrace, a small crescent situated on the side of the hill overlooking Plymouth Sound.

Minnie's early letters written from this school show her lively mind and her devotion to her family, in particular to her father whom she adored, and who undoubtedly fondly spoiled her.

When Minnie was fourteen she became very ill with a severe attack of diphtheria. During her convalescence and isolation at school she wrote several letters to 'Dearest Mama' and 'My dear Papa'. The following are extracts. . . .

Lipson Terrace,
Plymouth
17th February, 1849

Dearest Mama,

How grateful I ought to feel that I am again allowed to take up a pen and write even a few lines to my dear parents.

The Doctor has just been and was exceedingly kind to me. My throat is quite relieved. I now do nothing but eat and sleep all day. For my breakfast I eat bread with the raspberry jam you bought. Then I am beautified and my Doctor appears. After that I have my lunch – an egg and a glass of Port Wine. About two hours afterwards I have my dinner, consisting of a mutton chop, rice pudding and again Port Wine. Then I sleep till teatime when I stuff at buttered toast and coffee, and then sleep till supper, when I again stuff at sponge cakes and Port Wine. Then I settle for the night.

What do you think of my day? Are you shocked at it?

A few days later she wrote to:

Dear Papa,

It is now your turn to have a few lines from Miss Minnie. I am much stronger than I was only a very little time ago, and am taking powders three times a day to purify the blood. My throat has been terribly bad, but the ulcers are now healing admirably. I am having the holes left by them burnt with caustic, as well as my knee which has a sore place, as have other limbs. I have got on my clothes at last, and it now feels quite natural, although I must own that my stays for the first few days felt like a strait-jacket.

I have been highly amused by the constant popping of my bottles of bitter ale which is supposed to be good for me. The boys will say it is nothing for me but drink, drink, drink!

Next Thursday is my birthday, and I shall be entitled to ask for a holiday, though I shall not yet be able to join my companions, still being in quarantine.

There was a dreadful fire in Plymouth a few nights ago. A large brewery was burnt to the ground, and the Mayor, who lives on this terrace, was called up at three o'clock in the morning. The men who came to call him frightened Miss Grigg very much by ringing at her front door bell instead of the Mayor's.

Recently the girls took a walk to see the new Plymouth Prison. The wall is nineteen feet high, and there are two condemned cells at each end of the building.

My brave little sister, Cissy, had the courage to have her teeth pulled out by one of the young ladies instead of going to the dentist. The upper ones were first taken and then an under one. The new teeth are now coming up I hear.

Miss Grigg desires her very kind love to you and dear Mama, but being much engaged she is not able to write.

I am sure I never wrote such a long letter in my life, and I hope you will think it worthy of an answer, for the shortest line is received with pleasure.

I must now conclude, and with love and kisses to all in which Cissy unites, believe me, your very affectionate daughter,

Maria Lydia Blane

A short and indignant letter which speaks for itself was addressed to:

My dear Papa,

Who dared to be so impertinent as to send me a Valentine?

I received one with an ugly man carrying a hunk of bread in a basket and underneath the words –

> 'Be not crusty but kindly come
> And let us feast on love's soft crumb.
> Like rolls and butter let us join
> Upon this day of Valentine.'

It is crudely coloured over the print. Really, Papa, who could have sent it? One of the boys? Kindly find out.

To go to a less annoying subject, Willie tells me he went to Hengler's Royal Circus at Windsor. He was much pleased with the horses and the dancing on the tight rope. The clown drove four cats in a little carriage round the circus, and seems to have done a great many funny things. I wish I could have seen it too. Willie also tells me that they are getting on with the railroad very quickly, and have begun the bridge across the road at Slough. I should like to travel on it soon.

Pray thank Mama again for the lovely birthday cake she has sent me. . . .

In March she wrote again that 'I am so happy to say I am nearly convalescent, although my tongue is still much swollen. I have just finished my fifth bottle of Port Wine. Am I a toper?

I had a most delightful drive on Friday to Devonport to have my hair cut, and, as it comes off very badly, I have had a very short cut. What a nuisance I have been to everyone. I have however been good I am told, but young Miss Gilby was so troublesome when she was ill that Miss Grigg could do nothing with her, and she was sent to her grandmother's. It appears that when at home her nurse used to give in to her in every way, and when ordered to take any nasty medicine this nurse threw it away, and made the Mama believe the child had taken it! Was that not shocking?

The first day young Miss Gilby was here she looked at Miss Grigg and said, 'I do not think your young ladies are clever, and I do not see that you are any cleverer than they are.' You can fancy what a pert little thing she is, and I do not wish to have the pleasure of knowing her.

Now I must bid adieu to you, with love to you all,

I remain, my dear Papa, your affectionate daughter,

Minnie

On 12 June 1849 Minnie wrote a joint letter to her parents:

It is with pleasure that I inform you that the vacation will commence on the 19th inst. Should the progress I have made in my education prove satisfactory to you, I shall have much pleasure at our meeting. I have been kept by illness from my lessons but trust that recently, under Miss Grigg's care, I have made sufficient progress to show you I have not been idle.

May we travel by ourselves? I assure you Cissy and I are experienced travellers, and I am quite steady. We shall have other pupils with us most of the way to Salt Hill.

Last night we went to the opera in Plymouth to see *La Somnambula*. Dear Miss Grigg took eleven of us which was a great undertaking. We enjoyed ourselves very much and arrived well before the press. There was a short overture before the curtain was drawn up. Signora Montenegro acted the part of the Somnambuliste. The music was splendid and the acting admirable, but the part I liked best was when she walked across the bridge and the planks gave way under her!

A few days ago we had a delightful picnic. The weather was very favourable as we drove to Saltram House and found a beautiful shaded bit of grass in the park, where gooseberry tarts, veal patties, etc., were dispatched very quickly. Miss Grigg made a kind speech in which she wished us and our parents health and happiness. We followed with our words, and did not forget to drink to your healths, and please tell the boys they were not forgotten.

After our meal we went up to the house, a very splendid pile, and were allowed to go through eight rooms, some hung with red velvet, some with blue silk. There were many pictures, many done by the Countess of Morley herself, mostly before she was married. There is a bust of the Earl by Nollekens on a splendid Buhl table which originally belonged to Sarah, Duchess of Marlborough, and again given by her daughter, the Duchess of Montague, to the grandfather of the present Earl. The portrait I most admired was of Mrs Greenwood by Sir Joshua Reynolds.

As we returned through the fields we roused a brace of partridge and a pheasant, and saw several young hares. It was a most delightful outing.

On the fourth of June Uncle and Aunt Broughton took us to see the Breakwater Lighthouse. The bell that they ring in foggy weather was sounded so that we could hear it. It has three different tones and can be heard for more than two miles. Everything is kept so very clean and tidy in the house, and the bunks looked so delightfully cool I should have liked to have lain on them on such a hot day. We saw several porpoises and they are aptly named 'sea pigs'.

Do not worry about our journey to Slough, as Miss Arabella Rose is going to London to join her parents and will be with us. It will be very pleasant, do you not think?

Cissy unites with me in love to all kind friends and to your own dear selves, believe me, your affectionate

Maria Lydia Blane

In August of that year Minnie and her sister were back at school and Minnie writes to her Dearest Papa:

It is your turn to have a letter from your little girl, and I must try to make it amusing or you will never take the trouble to answer it. We are not yet all arrived for the start of the new term. The French Governess arrived this morning by the steamer from London. She should have reached Plymouth yesterday but the sea was so rough they were obliged to put in at some place for shelter. They only reached here early this morning.

We have been out in the garden this morning playing, and if it is still fine we are going for a scrambling walk this afternoon over hedges and ditches, which we like very much.

We wage war against the wasp nation daily. They invade our schoolroom and there must be a nest nearby. . . .

In April 1850, after her fifteenth birthday, Minnie wrote:

My dearest darling Papa,

I must thank you for all your good wishes which were expressed in Mama's letter. Although you did not write to me I give you my full pardon, knowing how much you are engaged with Water and Milk Company.

I had a delightful day. We acted a tableau in four parts, which I copied out of *Punch* in the holidays. It is about a policeman falling in love with a nursery maid, and Emma Ley took the part of the clock, in a large cloak and a fringe hanging over her face. You would have killed yourself with laughing had you seen it.

I have been a martyr to the toothache. It is the same tooth that the dentist told me I should suffer from in about a year, which it almost exactly is. It is very decayed. My cheek and gum have been exceedingly swollen and have given me much pain, but thanks to Miss Grigg's kind care and keeping me in bed for a day, it is now quite well.

We have had complete April weather. Last evening we took our first walk after tea, but were caught in a heavy shower near the small village of Compton. It is quite delightful to see the trees and hedges budding forth.

It is little more than two months to the holidays and then we shall see all your dear faces again. I think time passes so very quickly while we are at school. I must now bid you adieu as the young ladies are settling to reading and working and I shall be wanted to help.

With our united love, I remain your fondly attached child,

Maria Lydia Blane

In August of the same year, the young ladies had another outing with 'dear Miss Grigg', who seems to have been very ready to take her flock to see what was going on in Plymouth.

My dear Papa,

The Plymouth Regatta which takes place on two days began on Monday. Miss Grigg took us all to the Hoe to see it. There were so many yachts about that we could not at first see which were racing, but eventually we picked them out, their white sails heeling in the brisk wind. It was a lovely day, and the Sound was looking beautiful. There was a tremendous number of people on the Hoe.

We went to look at the prizes which consisted of silver tankards, a wine cooler, breadbasket, ink stand and money.

The ball took place last night at the Royal Hotel; would that I had been old enough to attend. The opera *La Somnambula* was again performed at the theatre, but that I have seen. On each night fireworks were let off from the Botanical Gardens and we watched them from our windows.

On Monday night Miss Grigg was so kind as to let us go into a field and we heard the band play several things, amongst which was a chorus which the soldiers sang, which sounded very pretty. Tomorrow there is to be a concert given by Miss Newcombe at the theatre, assisted by Madam Soutag, 'La Blanche Pardour' and several other accomplished singers. Oh, how I should like to go!

This letter continues with many inquiries for friends at home, comments on her brothers' progress, descriptions of the flower paintings which she and Cissy were very keen 'to do very nicely', and ends, as usual, with the sisters' united love and the almost inevitable 'kind compliments from Miss Grigg'.

The Griggs were a well-known Plymouth scholastic family. In 1844 Nathaniel Batt Grigg had a school in Caroline Place, and in 1864 Miss Emma Grigg is recorded in the Plymouth Directory as having a ladies' school at 4 Alton Place, just above where the Library stands today on North Hill.

In the summer of 1850 Mr Blane was appointed Deputy Governor of the Australian Agricultural Company. At short notice and considerable inconvenience to himself, he left for Australia on 5 October in the ship *Tartar* with Captain Rudge.

Just before his departure, Mr Blane and his wife were painted by Kilburn, and his small portrait shows him to be a handsome, kindly man, seeming younger than his sixty years. The portrait of Mrs Blane cannot be found.

The sorrowful parting cast a gloom over the whole family and Minnie wept bitterly. She wrote frequently to her father, but those letters have not survived.

Minnie had left school when the tragic news came of her father's death in Booral, near Newcastle, New South Wales, on 6 November 1852. It was months after the event that the news reached the family, and soon after Mrs Blane moved from Slough to 8 Pultney Street, Bath; a smaller house and garden, more suitable to a widow in reduced circumstances with two marriageable daughters.

Mr Blane had been well liked and respected by the people with whom he had worked, as is shown by letters and extracts from newspaper obituary notices which were treasured by Mrs Blane and clearly marked in her handwriting: 'Not to be destroyed'. A memorial was placed in Stroud church at the expense of the Agricultural Company which extols his virtues in flowery terms.

The family settled themselves in Bath and Minnie, being a buoyant soul, recovered from her deep grief before the rest of them. Bath, with its pleasant social life, its genteel company and many entertainments was greatly to her liking. Once the long period of mourning was over, the two girls often set off in their carriage, chaperoned by 'dear Mama', for balls, concerts and parties.

The sisters looked charming in their sprigged muslin with full flounced skirts. Each wore a flowered bonnet and carried an ivory-handled parasol. They attended balls in the Assembly Rooms, carefully chaperoned, dressed in white or pastel coloured gowns, their hair parted in the middle and gathered into a knot on the nape of the neck, their eager faces framed in carefully curled ringlets.

Minnie's fine features and delicate complexion caught everyone's attention as she entered a ball-room, holding herself well, her lively eyes seeking her friends. She was excellent company, and sometimes 'dear Mama', watching with some concern her animation and quick repartee, felt obliged to give her daughter a quiet word for decorum; but Minnie took little notice.

When Minnie was twenty years old she accompanied her mother and Cissy, as usual, to morning service in Bathwick Church. She wore her best bonnet, her mittens, and a paisley shawl round her plump shoulders; and she greeted her friends with her gay smile. She was aware that a handsome officer was seated in the pew behind the Blanes' seat, and she wished that she could turn round to have a closer look at the scarlet uniform, gold braid and luxuriant whiskers she had glimpsed as she moved into her pew.

The long sermon over, the Blanes went down the aisle to the door, the officer well ahead of them. On reaching the porch they found that it was raining heavily outside and, to Minnie's surprise, the handsome captain rushed forward and gallantly offered Mrs Blane his umbrella. In a flutter Mrs Blane accepted, and Captain Archibald Wood shepherded her and the two girls out to the road under as much shelter as one umbrella could afford.

He accompanied them to the door of 8 Pultney Street, but with the conventions of the day he went no farther than their doorstep, no formal introductions having been made. Mrs Blane noticed Minnie's excitement, her heightened colour, and the fact that nothing but Captain Wood was discussed throughout the afternoon, with a sharp eye kept on the window in case he should pass down the street.

Captain Wood was a handsome, soldierly man, fair, with full moustache and whiskers. He had a somewhat delicate air, his skin pale from the bouts of fever which had sent him home on leave from India to the healing waters of Bath, and into lodgings only a few doors from No. 8.

Nothing of his attractive appearance missed Minnie's sparkling eyes, nor did she fail to observe his aristocratic mien, the result of a lengthy pedigree which stretched back through military fore-bears to the original Manchester fustian and silk merchants of Queen Anne's reign, and so to the Earl of Dumfries attainted for his part in the ill-fated 1745 rebellion. Another ancestor was the daughter of Mr Tyers who founded the Vauxhall Gardens. Archie's father had been a colonel in the East India Company's army, and Archie had followed in his footsteps to join the Bengal Native Infantry. At only twenty years of age he had gained medals and distinction in several Indian campaigns and now, after the gruelling Multan war, he had returned to England, aged thirty-seven, with the intention of finding new health and a suitable wife.

He wasted no time. He lent his umbrella and on the following Tuesday a letter was sent 'from Captain Wood at No. 2 Pultney Street to Mrs Blane at No. 8'. It read: 'Captain Wood's compliments to Mrs Blane and he solicits the honour of calling upon her this afternoon if convenient'.

Within a few weeks Minnie heard one of her friends say: 'I expect you will soon be marrying that handsome and fascinating officer'.

It seemed a most suitable match, but one wonders whether Mr Blane, had he been alive, would not have inquired and seen more deeply into Archie's character. However, Mrs Blane saw no more than the well-mannered and brave officer who flattered and delighted her and completely enchanted her radiant elder daughter.

Up to the time that Minnie met Archie, she had little idea of life in the East India Company's army, or of what the force consisted. She had undoubtedly heard of the tragedy of the Black Hole of Calcutta in 1756, when 123 out of 146 died of suffocation, crammed into a tiny room in the fort by the victorious Indian ruler of Bengal. She had heard of the subsequent victories of Clive, and of the growth of the Company's army from that time. In 1856 it was the ambition of many British young men to go to India, after training at Addiscombe, near Croydon, as officers of that military body.

The East India Company, under a board of twenty-four in

London and an appointed Governor-General in Calcutta, levied taxes, collected revenue, and administered justice over enormous areas of the country. Its army consisted of Indian mercenaries, sepoys, under British officers; also a few wholly European regiments which never left India, as well as regiments hired from the Crown which did foreign service in India.

Minnie had no idea of the discomforts and dangers of army life in a cruel climate, nor of the immense distances to be traversed; and no doubt Archie did not stress those facts. He talked of the balls, the racing, the carriage-driving and the lovely mountain resorts, not of cholera, heat and isolation.

Minnie's general idea of a Company army officer was culled from romantically delicate-looking lieutenants and captains she had met while they were on leave from India after long service, wounds and severe fevers: men who came home starved for the company of white women, smart young gentlemen in scarlet uniform with charming manners. Her proof of this idea was Captain Archibald Wood himself.

Mrs Blane saw Archie in the same light, heightened by the memory of her husband's opinion that the great organization of the Company's army was in India not for conquest and empire, but because it kept law and order and brought enlightenment to a backward people. Whether he added that it was also there because it seemed the best and only way to make the most money for the Company's shareholders by enforcing peace is unlikely.

The *Bath Journal* of 31 May 1856 records:

'On May 22nd at Bathwick Church, by the Reverend Charles Wools, assisted by the Reverend John Polehampton, Archibald Wood, Esq., Captain, of the 14th Bengal Native Infantry, son of the late Colonel William Henville Wood of the same service, to Maria Lydia, eldest daughter of the late Archibald William Blane, Esq., formerly Governor of the Australian Agricultural Company, Member of Council and Collector of Customs of Mauritius.'

No description of the wedding survives; but there is a photograph of a lost portrait of Minnie in her wedding dress. She is wearing a flounced crinoline printed with flowers, with lace at the edges of the wide sleeves, and the rings on her fingers are carefully displayed. Her tranquil face is framed by a charming flowered bonnet. It is a pensive portrait: Minnie's mind is full of dreams and ideals, and she is very conscious of the dignity of her new status.

The huge trousseau was ready for the final packing; and Minnie owned all her life a small book setting forth the extensive outfit which was considered necessary for anyone going to live in far-off India. The following are a few extracts from the hundreds of entries:

Outfit for a Lady by an Anglo-Indian:
One dozen cotton chemises, one dozen thick
Six vests of flannel
Six white petticoats, long for evening wear, flounced with
    bodices, six shorter with bodices
Six white flannel petticoats, two red flannel petticoats, two
    crochet either red, or red and white
Two pairs of corsets with extra cases to wash
One dozen pairs of cotton drawers, one dozen thicker
Twelve pairs of white thread stockings, not open work
Twelve pairs of stockings, coloured to match your dresses
Six pairs spun silk, black, and six pairs warm coloured
Four pairs of long black mittens, four pairs of white ditto
One dozen kid gloves, six pairs dogskin for riding, one dozen
    pairs thread or silk for matching dresses

Dresses
Two plain white washing, two afternoon regular costumes
One black silk with two skirts and two bodices
One cloth costume, one ulster dress, waterproof
Two evening dresses, with bodies and slips
One lace ditto ball dress
One dinner dress full toilette, one dinner dress demi toilette
Total twelve dresses, beside four wrappers

Also plain white washing linen or calico for morning wear

Uncrushable net, gauze or lace for evening wear with silk slips, made body and skirt in one, to wear under dresses

One good black silk made with square and high body

Afternoon dresses, silk cashmere or tussore

One or two tea gowns of some patterned material now fashionable, not expensive and exceedingly comfortable. They should not be made tight, but skirts and bodies half fitting and separate

Vary your white dresses by different coloured bows and bands

Hats to match your dresses and jackets. Do not take out velvet as there are insects which revel in these.

A soft hat for travelling, a shady hat, and one black bonnet, but bonnets are little worn in India as they are no protection against the sun

A riding hat, a pith hat, an extra waterproof cloak, a handsome opera cloak

A loose hood lined with flannel for night travelling or on board ship

A black parasol edged with lace, and another

Two umbrellas, one of a large size for which your tailor will make you a washing cover

A stick, for you may get lame and need it, and a stout riding whip

Boots and shoes, and be sure to take an easy fit as your feet will swell in India

Neat button boots, with moderately high heels, not those now fashionable with very small, high, brass-tipped heels you see ladies hobbling along on, suffering pain and discomfort

Boots for out of doors, so your feet will not get bitten by sand flies, mosquitoes, etc., four thin pairs, two thick

Riding boots, six pairs of house shoes, four pairs of best evening shoes

Two pairs of walking boots, one pair of tennis shoes

Be sure to shake any pair of boots or shoes before putting them on, in case scorpions, centipedes and other insects may be in them.

There follows a lengthy list of household linen, curtains, muslin, lace and crash for ornamental antimacassars and mantelpiece boards, together with yards of 'furniture lace which makes very pretty fringes for brackets and the like'.

The outfit for gentlemen is an even longer list, culminating in the provision of such varied articles as Eno's fruit salts, Pears soap, a good gun, a revolver, opera glasses, deck chair, a map of India, sealing wax and a case of saddlery.

Other items were:

Three dozen long cloth shirts, linen fronted with linen wrist bands
One dozen flannel shirts
One dozen merino drawers
Four dozen pairs of cotton socks, unbleached, one dozen spun silk for evening
Four dozen white ties, four pairs of braces
Four white morning suits, American drill
Twelve white waistcoats
One good black dress suit for evening wear, and an extra pair of trousers
One frock coat, one waterproof, one dust, one medium overcoat
Two strong shooting suits, one tall hat for dress occasions
Two deerstalkers, two soft wideawakes, one solar topee
Two pairs thick shooting boots, one pair thigh fishing boots.
Four pairs walking boots or shoes, two pairs tennis shoes
Two pairs dress shoes and two pairs of slippers
Ample provision of gloves, riding, driving, ordinary and evening (kid)
White and black silk ties for evening and coloured silk scarves for morning wear
It is advisable to take quinine, chlorodyne, aperient pills, mustard leaves and Jamaica ginger (Oxley's essence)

A small box fitted with plated spoons and forks will be useful, as in camp silver is soon stolen by the natives.

The mind boggles at the amount of luggage to be taken on board the cramped quarters of a sailing ship, particularly as it often included all the cabin furniture and a piano.

From 23 May 1856, Minnie's letters to her mother, with a few from Archie Wood, give an intimate picture of the life of a Victorian couple travelling to and in India.

Life was never easy for Minnie; but her first letter, written while she was on her honeymoon in Torquay, reflects those halcyon days with not the slightest shadow upon them.

The Honeymoon and the Arrangements
for the Voyage to India

During the first days of her honeymoon Minnie wrote to her mother from a hotel in Torquay, the notepaper headed by a charming print of Torquay showing the harbour, the hills, houses and the Public Library on the sea-front.

24 May, 1856

My dearest Mama,

I intended yesterday to have sent you a few lines to show that I was in the land of the living, but I find that excepting looking at each other all day there is nothing particular to write about. We like this place very much and though the weather has not been in our favour, we have been enabled to take several nice drives and see the lions of this place.

My maid, Jane, is a perfect treasure, and takes care of everything for us. Indeed, I do not know what I should do without her.

We are both enjoying good health and wonderful appetites, and extraordinary spirits, in fact we are as happy as possible. Archie is almost too kind to me and I think, without any humbug, is fonder of me every day. We are going to drive to Newton today to see Miss Ley. She tells me Miss Trevor has run off with a married man who has already two wives living. She met her in Exeter, dressed most magnificently. The man has nothing but £600 which he obtained by selling out of the army, so she has been and gone and done it!

Archie unites in best love to all, and hopes you will no longer call him Captain Wood, and with my love and kisses, ever believe me, your affectionate child,

Minnie Wood

By the beginning of June Minnie and Archie were in rooms at 8 The Esplanade, Plymouth. This arrangement enabled Archie to be in touch with the army and the barracks near by, the time for the arrival of his orders to return to India being very close.

My dearest Mama,

We arrived here yesterday afternoon after a very hot, dusty coach journey, and have taken apartments at this address. Fancy our travelling from Torquay with Nicholas Kendall. He and Archie are quite thick, and the former has put down his name at the Club and offered me the use of his wife's horse while she is in Guernsey. He is most kind and has taken quite a fancy to my husband. Mrs Wellington and her husband were here, and embarked this evening for Cork with the Militia which is ordered home. We watched them sail out of the harbour in the evening.

Archie's Colonel White is in London and has not yet been able to settle the exact date of troops starting for India, but he has promised accommodation to Archie at the first opportunity.

Today is intensely warm and breathless, an almost scorching heat, so please will you send me my brown muslin with flounces, my straw bonnet, and the blue silk which I bought before I was married.

Will you tell me how much bread Jane ought to have a week and how I am to manage about her, as I am to find her everything. Archie is going to London by sea from here to Southampton, as it is a cheaper route than by train or by coach. . . .

On 11 June Archie wrote to Mrs Blane himself:

My dear Mrs Blane,

Our plans are now settled so I hasten to inform you. Monday next, the 16th (D.V.), Minnie will be with you at Bath by train at 3 o'clock. I go to London via Southampton by steamer, to take our passage to India, for the sooner I arrive there and receive my pay, the better for me. If I cannot secure a Detachment of Troops within thirty days from today, I propose sailing from England in

July, in one of the best passenger ships, with a comfortable cabin for my wife.

I shall now leave my wife with you for a few days, my dear Mrs Blane, until I secure apartments in London, and make all comfortable for her reception, and we will, as soon as all arrangements are completed, come to pay you a farewell visit at Bath.

Minnie has hinted to me about a Grand Archery Meeting and Ball, which she and her sister, Cissy, would like to attend. By the by, talking of sister, Cissy, would you kindly allow her to accompany Minnie to town when she will join me there?

I am charmed with Devonshire and should like to settle in some part of it when I become Colonel Wood commanding a regiment in England with my £1200 a year for life, which I may expect (if I am spared so long) in fifteen years hence.

Plymouth is very pretty and we have a charming view of the Sound from our drawing and bed rooms. The climate is not bracing enough for me, in fact it is decidedly relaxing. As we are just going out sightseeing I must away.

Believe me, dear Mrs Blane, with respect, yours affectionately,

A. O. Wood

With that letter was enclosed a short one from Minnie:

My dear Mama,

Many thanks for the box and its contents which arrived quite safely.

We are most comfortable and many people have called on us.

I am having to be very strict with Jane, who has given me some trouble lately. She is rather skittish and will not eat cold meat (good honest sweet lamb) or brown bread, which foods we both like. She desired me to ask you if you have the handkerchief and piece of red velvet Mary Anne had of hers, and which you took away from the former.

Archie unites in best love and will tell you what his plans are as soon as Colonel White has arranged something. . . .

Three days later she wrote to 'Dear Mama' again:

I hasten to inform you that our plan of leaving on Friday still holds good as it is really the best we can think of, seeing that Archie must be in London *now*, so he can fix something about our voyage. Unless he is on the spot, bothering Colonel White, nothing will be done. Then again, I want to see about my outfit, for if we sail in July it will be a tremendous hurry to have my things completed.

Yesterday and today have been awful, the wind blowing hurricanes and raining tremendously. Had it been fine yesterday, Archie would have dined in the Mess but he remained at home and Miss Baker dined with us.

I shall start for Bath by express train on Monday, and should the weather still be unfavourable for Archie to go to Southampton by sea, he will accompany me as far as Bath, and then go on to London, by train, of course.

There is no record of their visit to Bath and the next letter comes from Minnie to her mother from 13 Holles Street, Cavendish Square, London on 25 June:

Our journey yesterday, though a very hot one was pleasant and we reached Paddington in safety, where we found Archie waiting for us.

We are very comfortable in our apartments, and it is quiet, which is fortunate as the very stones of London are alive with people.

Yesterday Archie, Colonel White and myself spent the day at the East India Docks looking at vessels bound for Calcutta. The *Blenheim* in which we intended to have sailed we found quite full, every cabin having been taken a month or two before. Indeed the difficulty we had to procure accommodation was very great, as there are now so many passengers going out. However, we have taken our passage in the *Southampton* which sails from Gravesend on the 20th July, consequently everything must be on

Minnie Wood at the time of her marriage in 1856, wearing
one of her best day dresses of brown silk trimmed with lace
and a crimson bow. Note the wedding ring.

Captain Archibald Wood. Captain in the 73rd Native Infantry
in the scarlet and gold glory of full regimentals at the time of
his marriage.

board at Gravesend on that date. We shall embark at Portsmouth about the 27th, thus avoiding the Straits of Dover of which I have a great horror. As time is so short I think it would be better that I should procure my under outfit here at Mrs Haggar's, and also my boxes. It will be on the spot, and I can leave out those things I do not require, and indeed, look over her estimate.

Colonel White is a nice sort of person and has the whole management of the ship's outfit. He desires me to say it is useless taking a piano out to India, unless it has been prepared for the Tropics, as it goes to pieces in the first hot wind.

By the by, no money has yet been received by him for Archie. He went to Denton's yesterday about it, and they appeared quite callous as to whether we got it or not. Something must be done, as we have to procure our cabin furniture. They, Denton, wanted me to sign papers but I refused without asking you first what I am to do.

There is to be a grand affair when the Guards enter London. We hope to have a good view as Archie's tailor lives in St James's Street. Tonight we are going to the Princess Theatre, and the ball on the 2nd to which we are going will be a very grand affair. That is why I want my wedding dress, as it is customary for a bride to wear it at the first big party she attends.

Hoping to have a reply soon as no time can be lost, believe me, ever your affectionate daughter,

Minnie Blane

['Blane' is here furiously crossed out, and 'Wood' substituted with several exclamation marks.]

To Mrs Blane from 13 Holles Street, Cavendish Square, 4 July:

My dearest Mama,

I fully intended to have written to you yesterday but was engaged all day with Colonel White and Archie, so had not one moment to spare, as we also dined at the Watsons', afterwards went to the Marshalls', both very pleasant parties. Old General Hewetson was there, sporting a grand false, I guess, moustache and whiskers, black as jet! Young Cissy went with us to the ball and enjoyed herself and danced much. We met many Anglo-Indians, very nice people generally, but a few terrible snobs.

Tuesday we spent the afternoon at Kensal Green seeing about poor dear Papa's grave. It will, when properly finished, be handsome, but at present the crosses and crowns have the appearance of being half melted, and the garden very, very weedy. I like the design extremely and it only wants a few flowers to make it nice.

Today I have been engaged all day with Messrs Denton and Engstrom. I enclose you an account of the money I received and the papers we signed. Mr Engstrom told me that he could not say when the next dividends pay, but he hopes soon.

Please will you have my chemises made of cambric. It will be impossible to wear those I have at present, only in the cold weather.

We are so much obliged to you for the wine, and the couch and the lamp are most acceptable. We are gathering in as fast as we can, as we intend coming to Bath as soon as our things are on board by the 15th. Will you see us off from Portsmouth?

I want to give my brothers some little thing in remembrance of me before I sail. Can you assist me in saying what will be the best?

My brother and sister in law, Mr and Mrs William Wood, dined here this evening. She is expecting an addition to her family soon.

My wedding dress was greatly admired at the ball.

I am very tired so pray excuse me writing more. We are going to the Crystal Palace tomorrow.

My best love to all, in which Cissy and Archie unite,

> Ever your affectionately attached daughter,
> Minnie Wood
> (Finished on Thursday night, 11 o'clock)

A day or two later she again wrote:

I have just returned, dear Mama, from a very wet drive. We have searched everywhere for Tomkinson's Piano Forte Warehouse, and he is nowhere to be found. On inquiry we were told that he gave up business two or three years ago. Therefore I think the piano will not have time to be properly done, but we can have it made right in Calcutta. So if you still think of giving it to us, we shall be only too happy to have it, and beg you to forward it as soon as convenient to Colonel White's, 6 Haymarket, who is fitting up our cabins for us.

The gloves I have secured must be packed in flannel by Colonel White's man, who is accustomed to it.

I wish I might have those two crayon drawings of you and poor Papa that used to hang in the sitting room. Could not you and the boys have your portraits done for me to take with me so far away? Archie and I have had ours taken, and I hope you will like them.

On Saturday week we hope to be in Bath, and all our things on board. Thank you for everything you have procured for us.

Give my best love to the boys and tell them I am longing to see them and have some fun. In haste, believe me, etc., etc. . . .

Minnie and Archie paid their farewell visit to Bath at the end of July. It was a bitter-sweet occasion, for Minnie was haunted by the impending parting, yet delighted with the company of the three brothers, Archie, William and Robert, aged sixteen, thirteen and twelve respectively, and of Cissy, now nearly twenty. It was a gay and rather noisy household, and Mrs Blane bore up bravely, at least in public.

The entire family, with several friends, came to Bath station to see the travellers off, forming a tearful group. Handkerchiefs waved, top hats were flourished, shrill voices mingled with the deeper shouts of farewell, and Minnie, supported by Archie, leaned from the first-class carriage window, tears streaming down her face as the train pulled out of the station, the engine puffing noisily and trailing a cloud of sooty smoke.

The next letter comes from Minnie at the Quebec Hotel, Portsmouth on Friday, 25 July:

My dearest Mama,

On our arrival here today at 2 o'clock we found much to our annoyance that our vessel was not arrived, and that we are not to embark until tomorrow afternoon, consequently we are obliged to put up at this hotel with our fellow passengers who are in the same predicament as ourselves.

However, Captain Roe of the *Southampton* is lodging here also and has just sent word that all passengers are to embark after breakfast tomorrow morning, so we shall at last be settled, only I do hope the wind will go down or I shall be in an awful funk. Fancy having to venture in a boat in such rough weather!

Your sandwiches were most delicious. We became perfectly ravenous in the train after leaving Reading, and found them most acceptable.

Thanks, dear Mama, for your very kind letter. I felt very miserable at leaving you all, but I do hope we shall be spared to meet again. Archie is very, very kind to me, and more especially at this time when I am leaving dear old England and all my dear ones.

Mr Ryder, a brother officer of Archie's, dined with us and took us out after to see the lions of the place. Portsmouth is very much in the style of Plymouth only there are numbers of nice walks round the town, and a fine sea view from Southsea Common.

I hope our telegraph message of our safe arrival reached you safely. Please send my kind love to everyone who waved to us so vigorously this morning. I do hope you are feeling better now and the boys not worrying you.

I will write tomorrow from the vessel and give it to the pilot. God bless you all.

Saturday morning at 9 o'clock.

We are to embark in an hour, dear Mama, and I have only just time to say I have sent off Cissy's stockings, and a number of London Journals.

Goodbye. Archie will write by the pilot, but as it is a calm day with hardly a breath of wind, perhaps we shall not sail till tomorrow. Goodbye.

Your very affectionate, Minnie

The last letter in this period comes from Archie Wood to his mother-in-law, written at sea on 26 July on the ship *Southampton*, in a flowing hand and with much underlining.

My dear Mrs Blane,

We are fairly off and bidding adieu to the cliffs of dear England. We embarked today about 12 o'clock, came on board, and my wife was *very active and busy in* arranging our cabin. There is a good stiff breeze and we are progressing rapidly. I do not know when the pilot will leave us, but I commence this note in anticipation.

We dined at 4 p.m., some twenty three passengers at table, and now all is comfortably settled in our cabin.

Minnie is *most kind and considerate in* leaving her home and friends to travel with me over the wide sea. She is *very dear* to me, and I will do my utmost to make her lot happy and contented.

Sunday morning. My wife is very sick. She will I hope soon get better. I have escaped as yet, but alas! my time must come as I am a bad sailor.

About the overland dates for letters. The 20th via Southampton, the 27th via Marseilles, are two of the dates I know, in every month. White and Company of Haymarket will be happy to give you every information if you will write to them. Why not send your first overland letter to us by them? Address it to 'Captain A. O. Wood, 14th Regiment B.N.I., Calcutta, care of White and Co., to be forwarded'. This will save you trouble.

I know not when the pilot will leave us so think it better to close with these few lines.

Many thanks for your kind and affectionate farewell letter to my darling Minnie.

God bless you, dear Mrs Blane, and believe me,
Your affectionate and obliged,
A. O. Wood

P.S. I will have a letter ready to be despatched by the first home-
ward bound vessel we may speak to.
Our affectionate love to all the dear ones at home with you.
A. O. W.

Minnie's Voyage to India and the Sailing Ship *Southampton* 1856

Minnie and Archie took great pains to draw plans of the passenger accommodation of the *Southampton*, no doubt for the benefit of Minnie's brothers as well as her mother.

The ship was new, under sail, with eighteen passenger cabins which all had to be furnished by the passengers themselves. There was a dining-room but no other accommodation. The cabins were the living-quarters, unless it was good enough weather to be on certain parts of the deck.

The ship carried much cargo and a menagerie of animals, hens, possibly a cow which did not survive long, and a pack of hounds and several horses, most of which were the captain's commercial venture.

It was cold and draughty, or intensely hot and airless. Water was short and the food mediocre, yet in spite of seasickness, early pregnancy, overcrowding and discomforts, Minnie managed to keep a diary which eventually found its way to Bath.

Minnie's diary, written on board the *Southampton* from Portsmouth en route for India, and addressed to her mother:

At sea, on board the *Southampton* (Captain Roe), off Start Point

29 July, 1856

The Pilot left us today, dearest Mama, and I am thankful to say I am so much better that I went on deck last night and sat there some time. We are still in sight of dear England, which is most tantalizing. I am still feeling giddy and sickish from my severe attack which came on Saturday, and made me very weak and miserable. Today I touched food for the first time as I have been in bed with the Doctor attending me during the last thirty-six hours. What would I not give to put my foot on land for *one* hour! I hate this voyage. At night you can hardly sleep for the awful noises made by the sails being shifted and the sailors singing, though it had an extraordinary effect to hear them in the dead of night shouting in chorus as they heave the sails up.

My dear Archie is wonderfully well and so kind and attentive to me. During my sickness he was always by me, ready to assist me in any way, putting towels to my poor head dipped in cold water, and doing all in his power to ease my suffering. My ayah too is so gentle in her manner that I quite like her to be near me. We manage to get on very well by dint of a few words Archie taught me, one of which, 'mut' (don't), figures immensely with me.

My dear Archie had the most narrow escape the day we came on board of being killed. The boom of the cutter which took us to this vessel gave way and fell on his head. Luckily for him he had his tall hat on, or it *must* have killed him. Indeed, I did not dare turn round to look at him.

Our fellow passengers are awfully scrubby. A Mrs Goldsworthy and her daughter, with Lieutenants Tomkinson and Evans, are the only people worth speaking to. The former has been in our cabin today listening to our music, and seems a very nice young fellow.

The wind is most unfavourable and we are making very little way. I quite long for this voyage to be over. Had I known half what I should have to go through it would have taken me a longer time to make up my mind to come on board. Tell Cissy never to undertake such a thing. *It is horrible!*

Sunday, 3 August

I have been unable to continue this letter having been again ill during the last *four* days, the vessel pitching and rolling awfully. Today however it has been very fine and warm, enabling us to have a Service on deck. I cannot describe how impressive it was.

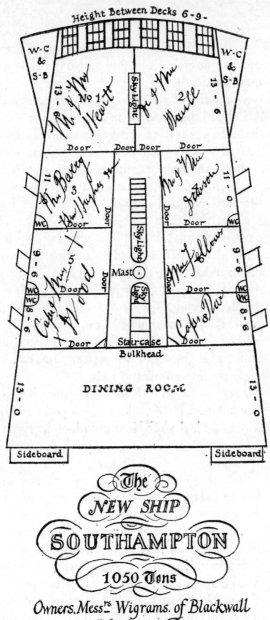

Height Between Decks 6-9-

| W·C & S·B | | 13 - 6 | | Mr & Mrs Newitt No 1 Skylight | Mr & Mrs Mauell 2 LL | | 13 - 6 | | W·C & S·B |

Door   Door Door   Door

Mr Bavey 3 — Mr Hughes —   Mr & Mrs Jetison   11 - 0

Mr Fellows

Caps May 5 — Mr Wood   Mast   Skylight   Skylight

Caps Slaw

Door   Staircase   Door
Bulkhead

DINING ROOM

13 - 0   13 - 0

Sideboard   Sideboard

The
NEW SHIP
SOUTHAMPTON
1050 Tons
Owners. Messrs Wigrams. of Blackwall
Robert Roe
Commander

The passengers sat on the poop, whilst the Captain read prayers at the capstan, and the crew sat behind on bars placed on buckets, dressed in their Sunday best.

We are now entering a warmer climate and are passing Cape Ortegal. We hope to pass Madeira in a week's time. I am so sick of this life, indeed were it not for the two Lieutenants we should be very dull. Archie and young Tomkinson play at quoits every day, whilst I mark, and of an evening a fiddler enlivens the crew whilst they exhibit their hornpipes, etc., and the midshipmen 'Sling the Monkey', which I must tell you is played by placing someone in a seat fixed like a swing, and the others beat the unfortunate creature's fundamental base with both cords. Archie got six the other day and could hardly sit down for two days.

Last night, the 2nd August, there was a *whale* outside our cabin window, but unfortunately I was in the arms of Somnus and never heard him spouting. The greatest nuisance on board is a pack of foxhounds who invariably begin to howl just as one is falling asleep. And the *babies*! The little horrors never stop crying, morning, noon and night. They are perfect pests, and I for one would willingly pitch them overboard!

Goodnight, dearest Mother, I am with you all often in my dreams, and only wish myself back amongst you all, this voyage is so nasty. I would I had your pictures to look at every day.

Another week has gone and still we are making very little head way, having today, the fifteenth on board, only just passed Madeira, which, as the wind was foul, we could not get a glimpse of. This is a disappointment to most of us, as we are dying to see a wee bit of land. The weather is lovely, and so warm that I have commenced thin clothing. Indeed, the Captain is beginning to despair of ever getting a favourable wind, as the present breeze is wafting us towards the African coast. I am now a good sailor, and generally spend my days on deck, as it is so much more pleasant than in our cabin, comfortable as it is. Often the sailors amuse us of an evening by dressing up and dancing for the amusement of the crew.

Several porpoises have shown themselves, and we hope to see the flying fish in a day or two. We have spoken several vessels but none homeward bound. Indeed, the Captain told us yesterday that he feared we would meet none at this season, as they generally take a more westerly direction. However, I shall continue writing in hopes of meeting one which will take mail home to dear England.

We thought of my dear brother, Archie, yesterday, and I drank his health. Tell him, please, with my love, I hope he will take care of himself and not be going beyond his strength.

The vessel rolled awfully one day last week and I was thrown down in my chair, and there was a tremendous scrimmage among the china and glass in the Cuddy. Indeed, for dinner we were obliged to have green baize boards placed at intervals on the tables to prevent dishes, etc., from rolling off.

11 August
Another day passed, thank goodness. A breeze is getting up which I hope will take us past the Canaries. The Captain is getting quite savage at our ill luck, and I fear we shall not reach Calcutta till the middle of November. Oh, horror! How shall we survive till then?

12 August
Today after dinner the welcome cry of 'land' was heard, which occasioned a general rush. It is the island of Palma, the Canaries, and I assure you it made me quite miserable not to be on it. It is quite ridiculous the joy one feels at being near terra firma.

13 August
During the night a porpoise was caught, which the men are now enjoying for dinner. It is such an ugly creature. We are getting on splendidly at last, and made 280 knots since yesterday at noon. I only hope it may continue.

14 August
The vessel is rolling and pitching awfully. I am now a capital sailor and it does not inconvenience me in the least, though my

hand is shaky with the movement and I cannot write properly. The tumbling and knocking one gets is trying, but also rather amusing! The weather is *very* warm now.

14 August

The vessel is still unsteady, but there is very little wind today. I have seen an immense number of flying fish, and the phosphorus occasioned by the marine insects at night has a very pretty effect, as the light follows in the track of the vessel. We are alone in this wild waste of waters, nothing in sight, and the heat unbearable. We are now in the Tropics, and every day makes an immense difference in the temperature.

15 August

No wind. Making about 120 knots a day, awfully slow work. The thermometer in the coolest place is 82 degrees, and increasing daily until we reach the Line, which will not be for a fortnight.

Archie is getting disgusted at the heat and the voyage and wishes he had gone overland. No white trousers or light clothing can he find, beside other misfortunes.

16 August

I am melting. In the evening two of the soldiers in charge of the Government horses quarrelled and one stabbed the other with a knife. In consequence there was a grand row, an inquiry was held, which ended in nothing, as it appears it was that fellow 'Fiend Jealousy' which caused the row, and the wound was unintentional. However it was a little change from our daily routine as it afforded excitement – to the females a fright, and a topic of conversation to the males.

Sunday, 17 August

No prayers as all hands are busy. No breeze. The vessel is scarcely moving, everyone looking disgusted with the intense heat. Archie has come out such a Swell in Mr Evans's white trousers and Mr Tomkinson's light coat, and looks comparatively happy.

Monday, 18 August

I have been in bed all day with the most fearful headache occasioned by the heat, which is something beyond description. India, I hear, is cold by comparison, for we are off the most unhealthy part of Africa. As to wearing in bed anything beyond a gown, the idea is preposterous, as yesterday, though lying in a through draught, you would have thought I was in a vapour bath from the perspiration running down me. My ayah never stops fanning me and keeping the flies off me whilst I sleep, for these latter are now a regular *plague*. I am sure, dear Cissy would never survive this heat. Tell her those three days in London were *cold* to what this is.

This evening a shark made his appearance at the stern, upon which a hook was immediately thrown out, baited with pork. The brute bit in a few minutes but the hook, not being strong enough, broke and the fish escaped. We are in a dead calm, making about *one* knot an hour. We are now 17.8 North 21.39 West – that is approximately 300 miles off Dakar in West Africa.

I have never told you, dear Mama, how we spend our days. At half past eight we breakfast, then till luncheon at 12 o'clock I either work or write to you. After that I go on deck until dinner at half past three. By the time that is finished it is cool enough to proceed on to the poop, where those who prefer it take Tea at six and remain there until Wine and Biscuits at nine, and soon after retire to bed, though not to sleep, as the heat, dogs yelling, babies squalling and sails shifting, prevents anyone from closing an eye with comfort all night.

I enclose you an invitation we received last night. The midshipmen are such jolly little fellows, we intend accepting their kind invite. Here is the letter:

'The Midshipmen of the ship *Southampton* request the pleasure of Captain and Mrs Wood's company to Tea on Wednesday evening, the 20th inst., at 6 o'clock.

Ship *Southampton*, Monday evening'

It is surprising gentlemen should like to place their sons on these merchant vessels, but we have several on board.

I have just seen a dolphin. Unless you see them you can have no conception of what a pretty appearance they have in the water, as they change colour every five minutes.

We are enjoying this fine weather, but unfortunately we are scarcely moving. Captain Roe says he has never made before so bad a passage, but as yet the winds have all been contrary. We sighted two vessels today, August 20th, none homeward bound, and as we shall soon have passed their track, I fear, dear Mama, you will not hear anything of us until we reach India, when I shall send off all my letters en masse, trusting you will find patience to read them.

1 September

Most memorable day for me, for at half past eleven we crossed the Line. Splendid weather and a nice breeze. In the evening Neptune's Secretary came on board to inquire if there were any of his children on board, and as there are many who require shaving, I expect we shall have great fun. Neptune and his wife are to be on board tomorrow at half past nine to witness the ceremony. The Secretary disappeared in a fire barrel, which, however, was put out through the violence of the waves. However, all the passengers had their letters given to them and I enclose the one to the Captain.

'To the Captain of the *Southampton*
Sir,

As I hear your ship is about my territories, I have sent you my Secretary to see if you have any of my children aboard that has never had the pleasure of crossing Neptune's territories before. I shall pay you a visit myself tomorrow to go through my daily occupation of shaving.

I am, Sir, your obedient servant,
John Allister McGriggor,
Odlum Dodlum Who'

2 September

Beautiful bright morning. All hands busy preparing for the Sea King's arrival. One sail has been so placed as to receive an immense quantity of salt water in which the poor victims are to be dipped after the operation. The drawing [not extant] will explain better than I can the procession round the deck, which was too ludicrous. One of the guns was dismounted and the carriage used as the Triumphal Car, but the scene which ensued when the creatures were shaved was rich. The person was placed blindfold on a spar in such a position that he could be tossed backwards into the bath where a bear was supposed to be waiting to smother him, and I assure you the growlings which issued from the depths of that water were enough to daunt the most courageous. On one side was Neptune's Doctor, on the other the Barber. The latter asked the question 'What is your name?' and if the person answered a tar brush covered with everything that is horrible and dirty – tar, pitch, old fat and tallow – was thrust into his mouth whilst the Doctor stuffed pills very much more disgusting at the same time. On the whole it was a little change for us all, for boardship life is very monotonous. After it was all over the ladies made a small subscription for the sailors, who also had an extra allowance of grog.

Here endeth the doings of the Line.

Our Captain is the most good-tempered man, for he has had a good deal to try him and has borne it bravely. Most of the hounds on board and four splendid horses belong to him, as he is taking them out on spec., as these animals fetch an immense price in India. Unfortunately, poor man, one very fine horse has died, worth 160 guineas, and three dogs, £30, which makes a great loss to him. We like him and the old Doctor very much.

Fancy, we are within a few hundred miles of Rio Janeiro on the coast of South America. We cannot get the proper winds. The fates seem determined to keep us out at sea until the end of November. The very idea is enough to drive one mad, one gets so tired of the stupid sameness, and there are such little tattling mischief makings going on amongst some of the ladies that it is quite disagreeable. One's thoughts are not even safe. As to anyone of my acquaintance ever coming out *alone*, I would never advise them to do so, as I have now had good opportunity of seeing what takes place on board. One lady accuses two others of being Half Castes, another tells the Doctor of the vessel 'he is not worth his salt', a most elegant phrase, which of course makes a row on board, and everyone looks cross and suspicious at each other for a few days. When a woman is without protection her conduct is scrutinized and she is miserable from the remarks made unless she keeps entirely to herself, which is no doubt the best plan, though rather dull work. I believe my conduct at first astonished the 'natives', but as my husband finds no fault with me I don't much care, as he, dear old fellow, won't allow anything to be said about me, my fault being *talking* and making myself agreeable! Hurrah! Mrs Heath is the greatest scandalmonger I ever met, but Mrs de la Tour put me on my guard against her. She tried to be mighty friendly with me at first, but thank goodness I showed her the cold shoulder when I found out what her real character was.

18 September
Bravo! Wind making us at last turn our backs on America and we are making very good runs. The Captain says we shall double the Cape in ten days, I hope sooner, and reach Calcutta six weeks from Saturday next, the 26th. It has quite set up my spirits as I do not find I am a bit better for the voyage.

Sunday night about three o'clock, I was awoke by a most fearful thump against the side of the ship. For a moment I thought it must be the mainmast given way. One gentleman went up on deck thinking we had struck against an island, but however it proved to be a sea which had risen and dashed against the side, as the wind had been rising, and the sea mountains high, giving some evidence of us being in the vicinity of the Cape. You may suppose how beside myself I was with fright when in a few moments a tremendous knocking came at our door, and we found the Carpenter and a Midshipman with a dark lantern come to put in our dead lights. Oh, Mama! I thought of you and Cissy, what a state of mind you would have been in and sincerely do I wish myself in my home at this moment.

Sunday, 5 October
Hurrah! Five weeks more we hope. Bitterly cold, raw weather,

snow falling, and we are off our course, steering S.S.W. instead of N.E. Yesterday we saw whales near us, but not so close as to harpoon them, such huge black monsters, throwing the water from their nostrils into the air. In the evening there was a 'Quadrille' party in the steerage, but I did not attend. We have witnessed, during this week, a very *severe gale*. The *Southampton* proved herself seaworthy and she rode well through it, and sustained no injury. We shipped a little water in our cabin. The waves towered over the poop, and over fell and nearly washed overboard some of the passengers and the First Mate. The rolling was frightful, indeed, as to walking it was impossible. As the boats which are hung by the poop were continually under water, this will give you some idea of our position if you know the whereabouts of the boats. The scene was grand in the extreme, but as usual I have been suffering all this week from violent sea-sickness which prevented my seeing more than the small aperture in the dead light would permit. I try very hard to become a good sailor, but alas! my efforts are in vain. Indeed, poor Archie is quite angry with himself at times for having brought me so long a voyage, as I suffer so much, but he did it for the best so we must not complain, though I confess it makes me low spirited and miserable to be so constantly sick. My poor inside has been so strained that for some days my stomach rejected everything, but I am now much better, though rather pulled down by my late attack.

One of our sailors died on Thursday night and was buried between seven and eight next morning. No ladies were present, but I heard the bell tolling for Service, which sounded awfully solemn at such an hour. With the exception of one man meeting with an accident, we have been most fortunate as regards illness, not one person having been seriously ill.

On Friday last I gave a *Tea Fight* and *Soirée Musicale* in my room, No. 7 Cabin Street, *Southampton Roe* (!!!), on the occasion of my recovery. Great fun we had too. I invited Mesdames Dawson, Bowhill, Fellowes and Miss Palmer. Archie did waiter, and, as the Cuddy servants will do anything for me, I coaxed a nice plum cake, some gingerbreads and biscuits out of the Steward, and thanks to the tea which you gave me, we all fared very well and enjoyed it thoroughly. The tea we have on board is beastly, to say the least of it, for I have never touched it but twice since I came on board, as it quite upsets me. This is a great privation to me as you know I am a regular old 'Tea Sitter', and willingly would I drink some of the rubbish which I used to make at home of an evening, and which called down such denunciations (Archie suggests 'wiggings') on my devoted head! Comprenez-vous, ma chère Mère?

Tell Cissy she must never come a long voyage, for she would starve if she were with us. Fancy, we have lived every day during the last three weeks on pork. I have taken such a disgust to it I cannot touch it. This has been our dinner every day – *Pork*, boiled, roasted, fried, chops, curry (with so much garlic in it, it is quite uneatable), and one leg of mutton, half raw. The feeding is the only thing we have to complain of. At breakfast there is never enough, the butter is salted to such a degree that large lumps of salt stick in one's mouth, consequently I never touch it and eat dry toast and bread. Though we have five weeks more on board all the lump sugar is gone, and the eggs all went bad and were thrown overboard weeks ago, and though there is dessert on the table every day, I cannot touch a thing, as biscuits, figs and ratafias are *alive*. This is all fact, but all ship's stores of that kind are the same. I cannot tell you how sick it made me one day, on cutting open a fig, to see three or four large white maggots lying comfortably inside!

It is all very well to talk of going to India, but I believe few would undertake the voyage did they know the disagreeables attendant upon it. All my romantic ideas are fled, that is certain, and I really am not trying to prejudice you against it, for I make the best I can of it. Dear Archie does his best to make me comfortable, though at times, my dear Mama, I do sincerely wish myself amongst you, for I think my sickness has made me nervous and weak. I feel so upset at times.

Dear Archie has not found the cold agree with him, indeed he suffers more than ever from dyspepsia and shivering fits which make me very anxious. The cold in these parts is most intense, as it comes straight from the Antarctic regions. I never leave my cabin unless to walk on deck, it is so bitter, and I have my meals here. Archie looks like an unfledged bird without its feathers! Such a guy with three or four coats on, each shorter than the other, and, as he can't get his legs warm, he thrusts them through the armholes of his coat! He is thinner and skinnier than ever. We were all weighed the other day. He is 10 stone 6 pounds and I am 10 stone 10 pounds. He has been sitting by me whilst I write and now he desires me to bid you goodnight, as he is going to hide himself between the blankets till dinner time.

How I am longing to see the de la Tours in Calcutta and to hear all about you. I suppose you are ruralizing in the Highlands. Tell Cissy I wish she would marry some rich young Laird with a nice place, so that when we return like burnt up pieces of parchment, she might ask her poor old brother and sister to stay with her and recruit their failing health.

Now I have finished my say for the day, so adieu and au revoir.

Sunday, 26 October
Since I last wrote, dear Mama, we have made great progress, though it has been made slowly. We are, thank goodness, in the Tropics again and hope to reach the Line by Wednesday night, the 30th October. We are at 11.49 lat. and 86.10 E long., that is roughly 2,500 miles south of Calcutta, having made a run since yesterday of 235 miles, and I only hope and trust good luck may attend us for we have made a very bad passage. We are all dying of ennui, and I shall bless my stars the day I turn my back on the *Southampton* and her passengers, who are, with but three exceptions, the most extraordinary set I ever met. I and Archie have not escaped the venom of their tongues, but I soon settled the business by telling the lady in the case to mind her own affairs, beside giving her a bit of my mind in true Broughton style, for my blood was up and I never felt so thoroughly incensed in my life. It has ended in our cutting the whole family of Goldsworthys dead, and not admitting a soul but Mesdames Bowhill and Dawson in to our cabin. This is decidedly their loss, not ours, as fortunately we do not have the full force of the tropical sun on *our* cabin of an afternoon!

During the last fortnight we have been waiting for the South East Trades to carry us up to the Line, and on Monday the wind freshened so much that the Captain thought we had caught it. However, after giving us one good run and tumbling us about mightily, it left us, to his great astonishment, in a dead calm for four days. But after some patience, we had it again on Saturday, yesterday, and are now, we hope, in a fair way to reach Calcutta by the 8th November, fifteen weeks from the day we left Portsmouth, 105 days!

Oh, hurry! I can hardly realize the idea of being on land, though today, just before prayers, the trunk of a tree torn up by the roots passed us, a sure index of us being near something green.

Of course, every day the heat is growing more intense. Archie is alive again. I, however, suffer more from headaches. Today, poor fellow, he is suffering from a sprain in his shoulder, brought on last night by joining the midshipmen at 'High Cockolorum, Jig, Jig, Jig', a kind of leap-frog played by boys – intellectual, is it not? You cannot imagine what a man's mind comes to after several weeks at sea. A child might do anything with them.

Last Monday you would have pitied us had you seen Archie on the sofa, me in bed, as sick as we could be. Oh dear, it was miserable work, and the poor ayah helping us both. What I should have done without her I cannot imagine as I am so weak at times from retching, in fact my eye at this moment is most horrid to look at, as the exertions of all last week have caused an effusion of blood in the left eye, which now presents a most horrible appearance. However, I hope to have it all well by the 8th.

Tuesday is to be the last luggage day, is it not glorious! I am now thinking of beginning my packing so that I may have the three days in the river all to myself to enjoy the novelty of the scenery. A lottery has been got up amongst the married people at 10/– each, to see which day we shall reach our destination. The tickets were drawn on Friday. Mine is the 12th November, Archie the 13th, but I hope to be settled in Mr Wood's house before then.

My Hindustanee is rapidly improving, and if I had only some nice little book to learn the names from, I should get on splendidly.

I am sure if Cissy saw my legs now she would not believe they were the same. They are so much thinner, indeed were it not for *substantial* reasons (which will be apparent in April!) I should be much thinner than when I was on land. The longing I have for green vegetables is *dreadful*, and a wee bit of fish, but I suppose it will all come in good time.

Today we sighted a brig. We exchanged signals. She was the *Abel Tasman*, a Dutchman bound for Liverpool from Benloeken in the Island of Sumatra.

Of course, my friends in England must not think I have forgotten them by not writing to them, but it is impossible to write more when one is on board ship, and you must please give my love to *all* of them.

1 November
Today we have passed the Line and hope soon to be at the Sand Heads. We find the heat very oppressive now as there is very little wind, and the sun straight over our heads.

4 November
Dr Bowhill has just been here and desires me to say the mutton has now all gone bad. I like him so much, and whenever I feel ill, he attends me as he is an Army man, and I do not quite like trusting entirely to our ship's Surgeon, who, though always willing to do anything he can for the passengers, is rather too rough in his treatment of ladies.

Our Captain is in great distress. Last night some evil-disposed person, or persons, thought proper to amuse themselves by cutting ropes, which, if it continues, may be of serious consequence, as it will delay us. However, the watch is to be doubled tonight and every precaution taken to prevent its reoccurrence.

5 November
A fine day, everyone looking happy at the prospect of soon landing and being safe, for actually ropes were cut last night, notwithstanding the Captain's watchfulness, and there is not a clue to the persons, but it appears the crew are getting dis-

contented. This evening two men were seen ascending the main rigging without permission, whilst their comrades were amusing themselves with Guy Fawkes. One has been placed in irons on suspicion as well as insubordination, so I hope we are all right, though I must confess it makes me feel rather nervous as these parts are very subject to squalls which come on suddenly, and would prove very dangerous were we unable to have the sails taken in.

8 November
Instead of being in Calcutta today, we are, and have been, in a dead calm in this disgusting bay for nearly a week, with not a breath of wind to carry off the effects of this sun, which is now almost unbearable. I cannot find words to express the intense heat we have here. I am feeling quite knocked up by it, nothing to amuse us, and the gentlemen, without exception, all getting grumpy and cross at the length of our voyage. The only events which have amused them have been catching sharks, and a Court of Inquiry as to who has been the delinquent in the late rope question. Some of the principal ropes sustaining the foremast have been attempted, but without success, but nothing has been discovered by the Inquiry, only that so much fuss has been made by Captain Roe it may have the effect of stopping it.

Monday, 9 November
At four this morning a breeze sprang up, and if it continues we may hope to see the Pilot at the end of this week.

13 November
Bravo! Bravissimo!!Hurrah!!!Yoicks!!!! (This last is Archie's suggestion.) We are only a hundred and fifty miles from the Pilot, whom we may hope to have on board tomorrow night, and that within a few hours of our having been in this vessel *sixteen weeks*, a hundred and twelve days from leaving Portsmouth. It has been an unfortunately long voyage, and the very idea of being once more on land is almost too much for me. It is almost worth while to take a voyage to feel the pleasure of

anticipating the novelties awaiting one. Since tiffin we have seen several date and coconut trees drifting past us. Really, dearest Mama, I am feeling so perfectly crazy that I believe I shall require a strait-jacket before reaching Calcutta. Poor dear sober Archie is quite shocked at this ebullition of my spirits, but nature must have its way. Oh, Gemini! Oh, Jupiter! How very jolly!!

16 November
Still no Pilot as the wind is right in our teeth. However, we hope this week will see us safe and our journey over.

Monday, 17 November
Hurrah! At eleven o'clock last night we had the pleasure of seeing our Pilot come on board. We sighted the Pilot brig in the afternoon, and at nine we signalled our wants by lime lights. The effect on the vessel was really beautiful, as it was quite dark and everything was thrown into bold relief.

18 November
We have been all day stationary waiting for a steamer to tow us up the river. We hope to send this by the Mails on Friday.

19 November
Today the coconut trees on Sanger Island made their appearance in sight on board. Then everyone rushed on deck at the sight of land, and as the steamer which we procured this morning is towing us fast, we shall anchor tonight at Kedgeree where I shall post a short note to you to catch the steamer *Briston* in case we do not reach Calcutta in time. Today a native boat came alongside with a number of natives nearly naked. I laughed immoderately at their strange appearance with nothing but a wee white bandage round their waists.

20 November
We anchored last night, and, oh, the excitement which came over us all at the sight of the Dawk [dak] Boat coming with letters. I hoped our agents would have had the gumption to send

ours down, but alas! I must exercise my patience for twenty four hours longer. However, we heard from William Wood in Calcutta, who, I am sorry to say, cannot receive us, as his house is full.

This morning at five o'clock I was awoke by Archie who told me there was a dingee with fruit coming under our ports. So up I jumped. We bought four coconuts, one pineapple, one dozen eggs and a bunch of plantains, and one shaddock or grapefruit, for which we paid the sum of two and a half rupees. This is a perfect godsend, as our provisions are gone, and we are dying for a change.

21 November

More fruit and fish, and the scenery is getting more beautiful. The dates, coconuts and bananas are lovely, and rice has the appearance of corn in the distance, and the trees are lovely today. I saw a dead body on the bank of the river being devoured by Pariah dogs, a horrible sight.

Today at three o'clock we are to land at Calcutta. Yes, absolutely set foot once more on terra firma. It is delightful to think of, and of your letters which I hope to have this evening.

We have been passing several pretty bungalows, and while I write we are passing Budge Budge, an indigo factory. I must now go on deck, and shall close this on shore tonight.

So ends my voyage to India, and this account of our long voyage which I send to you, dearest Mama, with my fondest love.

Minnie Wood

On 19 November Minnie also wrote a letter to her mother, which she sent off, with one from Archie, from the river. The diary of the voyage was kept to be sent from Calcutta, as the post from Kedgeree Point in the Hoogly river was reputed to be somewhat unreliable.

To Mrs Blane from Minnie and Archie in the *Southampton*, off Kedgeree Point:

19 November 1856

My own dearest Mama,

I am sure you will be most delighted to hear that we have at last arrived within a few miles of our destination, after a very, very long and tedious voyage of *sixteen weeks and three days*.

I have kept a journal of the few events which may interest you, and which have happened during our long imprisonment, but I will not send it now, as I hear the postage from this place is a very great risk, and we shall not, I fear, be in Calcutta until the mail has left. I was unwilling to lose even the chance of your receiving these few lines, which, if it arrives safely, all the better. But you will receive a long yarn from me with full particulars by the mail which leaves early in December.

We are both well, but worn out with the tedious passage, which throughout has been attended by ill luck. Our provisions would have been all gone had we not arrived just in the nick of time, but I will not add more on this subject as you will hear from me soon again.

We are dying to get all your letters, indeed, dear Mama, you cannot imagine how mad I am at the prospect of again seeing land, and hearing how all our dear friends at home are.

Our Pilot came on board on Monday evening at eleven o'clock. Such a pretty sight, the floating light brig coming alongside, and the picturesque-looking lascars in their turbans with the moon shining brightly on them. Really, it had a very pretty effect.

Now, darling Mama, as Archie intends adding his note, I will bid you goodbye, with my most affectionate love and kisses to all my dear home circle, ever your fondly attached and loving daughter,

Minnie Wood

Archie continues:

My dear Mrs Blane,

Thank God we have almost arrived after a dreadful tedious long voyage of 116 days. I am very anxious to arrive at Calcutta for my dear wife's sake, who requires a thorough change of air and diet, poor girl. She has bravely faced all the *disagreeables* and *discomforts* of a long sea voyage, the want of good, nourishing food, vegetables, etc., and daily *land* exercise. She is looking bonnie and well nevertheless. I am, and have been, most anxious about her for the past *three months*, for she is about to become a mother. Please God if all goes well she may expect her confinement in April. You and the dear ones with you will, I know, rejoice to hear this glad tiding. She yearns to taste vegetables, especially peas, which she will in two or three days at Calcutta.

We are being towed by a steamer, and the vessel will anchor for good the day after tomorrow.

I propose posting this at a Post Office on our way up the river, as we hear the Overland Mail leaves Calcutta before our expected arrival there. There will be a risk in dispatching this way, but we feel you must be very anxious to hear some tidings of us, as 'tis nearly four months since we left Portsmouth. I will conclude this hurried letter as time is precious, and we will both write on our arrival at Calcutta. Indeed, Minnie has a wonderful long letter of thirty-six sheets all ready, written for you. 'Twill astonish you of our doings and sayings on board the *Southampton*.

God bless you all, and with our united love and best wishes, ever believe me,

Yours affectionately,
A. O. Wood

India

After the long voyage Minnie and Archie reached India tired, unwell, and somewhat disillusioned with each other. No background could have been more trying to a newly-wed couple than the cramped quarters of a sailing ship in extremes of climate, and the bad food, poor ventilation, and the unavoidable propinquity of people with whom they had little in common.

It was Minnie's first experience of a life very different from the conventional sheltered one of Bath, and she had faced it with considerable courage, a certain amount of petulance, and the shocked realization that married life, travel, and even Archie himself, were not quite what she had expected.

Her first glimpse of India was the low, vague line of the Sunderbunds – the Ganges delta – which, as the ship sailed nearer, revealed deadly swamps with palms and tangled mangroves rooted in the sticky mud. It was a jungle shunned by man but teeming with wild life: birds, monkeys, snakes and crocodiles, all dominated by numerous tigers, those fierce kings of the jungle.

As they went up the forty miles to Calcutta, the scene changed. Tributaries ran into the channel, sometimes bearing the swollen carcass of an animal. Minnie gazed at these byways, half fascinated, half repelled, wondering where they led, or whether they were no more than a backwater, ending in a smelly, stagnant pond.

For mile after mile luxuriant jungle clothed the banks, later broken by native villages with fishing boats moored beside them, or a neat clearing where a European indigo planter had his bungalow and factory.

Minnie was delighted when the ship passed Garden Reach, an area outside the city comprising big, two-storeyed houses with deep verandahs, flower-beds, trees and acres of well-kept lawns:

47

the homes of rich European merchants and officials, and a few aristocratic Indians. To Minnie these villas meant the India she expected. The pleasant effect was heightened by the sight of British children running about the lawns with their ayahs, and pet dogs barking round them: a scene so reminiscent of English life.

As the ship rounded the final curve, a forest of masts became visible against the hot, metallic sky, and behind them the magnificent outline of towers and minarets which had earned Calcutta the name of 'city of palaces', a name that lost its aptness when the squalor below them was seen.

Minnie's attention was riveted on the scene immediately around her, for the harbour was complete confusion, crammed as it was with boats: narrow 'flats' towing strings of barges, fishing-boats, clipper ships, men-of-war, and a thousand small craft bent on their own concerns, regardless of others. The noise was indescribable: yelling boatmen, the pilot bawling at craft blundering in his way, the sweating crew's bare feet thudding on the hot deck, and the rattle of the chain as the anchor sank beneath the surface and the ship was still at last.

Minnie looked up at the green heights of Fort William, where a patrol of scarlet-coated European soldiers paced the ramparts, then turned her eyes to the dock side, where British people – women in crinolines, men in top hats – stood calling to their friends on board. Among the crush of white-clad coolies, bullock carts, camel carts, and barrows of every description, stood a few London-built landaus gleaming in the sun, the well-groomed horses held by a smart syce.

When all the greetings and farewells had been said, it was delightful for Minnie and Archie to sink back on to the soft seats of Henry Wood's stylish carriage and be driven to his cool garden house for the night.

How secure, how gracious, and how permanent that European influence seemed.

Even though Minnie was tired, not very well and pregnant, she still managed to begin a letter to 'dearest Mama' that very night.

My dearest Mama,

We disembarked today and I must tell you with what joy I left that nasty old vessel. I can hardly yet realize my being once more in a house.

The approach to Calcutta by Garden Reach, Bishop's College and the Botanical Gardens, is truly the most beautiful. Private houses are situated on the banks of the river with large gardens attached. Henry Wood met us and has given us asylum for the present at his Garden House, so I do not await the night mail. I cannot tell you how you enjoy the quiet of an Indian house. None of the servants ever wear shoes, and their uniform is a white turban, a kind of waistcoat, and a long cloth girt round their middles. Their legs, I believe, are quite naked.

The punkah is most refreshingly constantly waving over one, for it is very warm – indeed I find muslin almost too hot – and a servant pulls it all the time. Last night I slept for the first time on Indian soil under a mosquito curtain in a room about the size of our drawing-room at Salt Hill. The two beds have four poles at three foot distance from them, and on these are placed the curtains, so that the bed and appendages are quite as large as a moderate sized room. This is no exaggeration, and is too delightful, after our cramped cabin. Then the bath and dressing rooms which are attached to each bedroom – oh, they are glorious!

The mosquitos swarm around, but then so do the Bearers who, before we went to bed, swept all the mosquitos off the inside of the curtains, but nevertheless just as I was going to sleep I heard 'buzz, buzz' close to my ear and found that one of the wretched creatures had got in by hook or by crook, though luckily he did not bother me any more. His devastations were all directed on poor Archie, who this morning has been in a great state of irritation, but bites and all, he has gone to report himself at Fort William near the harbour, as his regular pay will then commence from today. We hear our regiment has left Multan, which is a great comfort as I see by the paper there has been great sickness amongst the soldiers, upwards of six hundred in hospital.

Our new station is near the hills, Jhelum, a most delightful place I am told.

Dear Mama, I am almost heartbroken. *No letters* from any of my family. I sent this morning both to Gillanders and Co. and also to the Post Office, and nothing is waiting for me.

Why is this?

Surely you have not forgotten poor me? Never send anything to Colonel White. *He is a blackguard. I hate him.* I expect you have sent them to him and he has laid them aside and forgotten them, just as our Wedding Cards were. Neither the Woods nor the Younges living here have received the latter. It is shameful. Archie, I trust, is now having his eyes opened and will now take his affairs out of his hands.

Oh, dear Mama, *write.* Surely you or Cissy will write to me. If you only knew how fearfully disappointed I am at not hearing from any of you. It was the only thing which kept up my spirits during the long and tedious voyage. However, I must not write more or I shall miss the mail.

God bless you all. Our most affectionate love and kisses,

Your fond and loving daughter,

Minnie Wood

Between 22 November and 9 December some letters are missing, which is not surprising considering the complicated route taken by mail for England. The Suez Canal was not yet open, and the letters went by sea in a sailing vessel or a paddle-wheel steamer to Suez, thence over the desert by carriage to Port Said, and on by sea to Marseilles, over France and the Channel, then at last to the addressee who had been waiting for an answer to his last letter for anything up to eight months.

Possibly Minnie wrote no letters during that first breathtaking two weeks in India. The contrast between the elegance of Mr Wood's quiet house and the teeming, noisy streets must have astonished her, with their kaleidoscopic whirl of half-clad men, the whining beggars, the wild and dirty fakirs, and mules, horses, oxen and camels. She enjoyed driving out in her host's carriage, either into the country, or in the social parade round the Maidan in front of the magnificent Government House, a white palace modelled on Kedleston Hall in Derbyshire. How English the parade of carriages appeared, with pretty women bowing to their friends, and dashing young men riding thoroughbreds or driving fast buggies, doffing their tall hats to acquaintances.

Minnie saw no further than this conventional surface, and it is unlikely that Archie, intent on his affairs, would have noticed the unrest that was stirring.

Minnie's next letter was written on 9 December 1856:

Yesterday's mail, my dearest Mama, brought me your No. 3 letter with Cissy's enclosed, only just after receiving Nos. 1 and 2, which through great carelessness of Gillander and Co. had been mislaid. A thousand thanks from us both for them all, and as we feel sure that the same pleasure must attend the arrival of Overland Steamers in England as they do here, you may rely in us never missing any mail if possible.

We are now preparing for our long journey up country, and indeed I shall be very, very happy to get settled comfortably in my new house before my little one arrives, for I begin to feel much fatigued with this dreadful packing.

Archie is not as well as he should be. This climate does not agree with either of us, it is so hot, and the mosquitos worry one so dreadfully, that we shall be glad for some rest. We have left Henry Wood's and are staying at an hotel which we find dreadfully expensive, but we are obliged to stay here in order to see Mrs Roberts, Archie's sister, who is to pass through here en route for England with her three children. She has just had a premature confinement and is in a very precarious state.

I do not like Calcutta at all – the smells are awful, indeed I do not see one redeeming quality in the place. The country round is very pretty, but the Indians and their habits are disgusting. It is nothing uncommon to see a man stark naked begging, as do boys who run by the side of our carriage.

The letter continues in Archie's handwriting:

I believe India is a very good country for a poor man. The
tailor's bills are not expensive I assure you, my dear Mama.
Minnie will like it better when we get up to the headquarters of
the regiment. Once we get into our cosy house with all our
comforts about us, I hope my wife will like India.

I do not like Calcutta. No – the country, green fields, cultivation and shooting for me. The mosquitos here are dreadful.
Minnie has been severely bit by them. I quite long to leave this
'city of palaces'.

My dear sister has just arrived here, very ill, poor girl. Please
God to spare her. She will arrive in England about next spring,
when I hope you will see her. She will go to Bath to visit you,
and you will hear all about us from her. You will like her, I
know.

I am very anxious to arrive in Jhelum for Minnie's sake. She
is in good health, barring the *exciting* circumstances attending her
present state. She will be confined about April, and I want her
to get over her long journey and be comfortably housed before
the great event.

Minnie continues:

Dearest Mama, I attend strictly to all your advice, and I never
leave off my stays. We have been staying for three days with
Mr and Mrs Cockburne, very nice people in the Civil Service.
He is a son of Lord Cockburne. We hope about the 10th or 11th
to go to Dum Dum, a few miles north of this town, to an officer
and his wife previous to starting up country. Their name is
Sherwell.

We were much grieved to hear of dear Archie's illness. I hope
my dear brother will take care of himself after two attacks.

Thanks, dear Mama, for the parcel received from the *Blenheim*,
and also for that sent by young Jenner. He called when we were
out, but we hope to have him to dinner some day.

Archie and I drive out at four o'clock into the country. In the

Mrs Blane, Minnie Wood's mother, in about 1857. Probably one of the photographs sent out to Minnie in India at her request.

A letter from Minnie written on her honeymoon. (*See* page 17)

course of one of our rambles we came upon a very beautiful house belonging to a Baboo, an Indian gentleman. We walked the grounds for some time and were charmed with everything.

The Indian scenery, particularly where coconuts, plantains and pines abound, is very beautiful. The natives are very slow, indeed they would rather we ran over them than move out of the way of the horse. The women are frightful, and carry their children across their hips, but they all have very fine eyes.

Buckingham Palace sinks into insignificance by the side of Government House. It is a magnificent structure formed like a star. Lord and Lady Canning are absent at present so there are no balls going on, but on Tuesday there is to be one at the Lieutenant Governor's to which we could have gone, but as I cannot dance, and my dresses are all packed up, it is not worth having all the trouble of unpacking for nothing. I screamed with laughter the other day for trying on some of my dresses I wore in England. They came as far as my hips, and no further! So I really am in distress for warm dresses for going up country.

Dear Mama, I assure you I will be as economical as I can for dear Archie's sake, but our expenses for travelling here are awful. Our luggage alone going up to the Regiment will cost 300 rupees, or £30, and our expenses by Government dak, that is the cost of travelling, will be 700 rupees. However, we shall do our best.

We drove down to meet the last steamer, hoping to meet the de la Tours, but we were disappointed, and I fear we shall not see them as we shall have left Calcutta, I hope, before Christmas.

Archie has just gone out with his sister, but begs me to say he has a letter in course of construction to you, which his sister's arrival has put out of his head, as he had not seen her for five years. She is a very nice person. She has had thirteen children in fifteen years, and now a bad miscarriage! There is a nice prospect for me!

God bless and preserve you, my dearest Mama, and that we may meet again is the fervent prayer of your fondly attached and loving child,

Minnie Wood

To travel from Calcutta to Lahore was a formidable undertaking. There were 1,300 miles to be traversed, and several ways of doing it. The most pleasant and leisurely was to hire a boat and go up to Hoogli river from Calcutta to join the main stream of the Ganges after ten days, and proceed slowly up river. It was an idyllic form of travel for anyone not in a hurry. The comfortable two-storeyed boat with an awning on the top deck had fourteen oars and a steersman to propel it; and it towed a smaller boat where the servants lived, the cooking was done, and the hens cackled. Each night they tied up to the bank, having made twenty miles during the day, probably less. Sometimes they sailed but mostly rowed to the monotonous chant of the crew, which could be heard half a mile away. The country was flat, in places cultivated, often with jungle to the water's edge. Drifts of balsam flowers, white and pink, grew everywhere. Sometimes the boat was towed through shallow water, the men pushing their way through tangles of daturas, the great trumpet flowers scenting the air with a heady sweetness.

One could also travel up the Ganges by public paddle-steamer, or go by railway to Ranigunge, 120 miles from Calcutta, where the line ended. The train chugged along at a maximum speed of twenty-five miles an hour, emitting smoke and soot, and without any facilities for passengers, except a stop at Burdwan for tiffin. From Ranigunge one continued up country by Government dak gharry, a box-like vehicle in which one could jolt to the frontier.

Unfortunately for Minnie this was her route, as Archie had to reach his regiment north of Lahore quickly. Tired and dirty they left the train, a turmoil of coolies round them, and thankfully reached the squalid hotel where they spent the night.

Next morning they were awoken before dawn by the uproar in the yard below their window. A jumble of ark-like carriages were being loaded with luggage by the light of flickering torches. Horses were forced between the shafts with shouts, blows and the maximum of disturbance. Minnie was indignant about the ill-treatment of the scrawny animals, as they were lashed and kicked into their places. In the glare of the torches and the first scarlet streaks of dawn it seemed to her like a vista of hell itself.

When the trunks had been strapped on the roof and a servant was perched on top of them, Minnie entered the gharry with some trepidation. It was as comfortable as any box-like vehicle without springs could be, with a small cupboard containing lemonade and other comforts. Attached to the roof was a sagging net into which went Minnie's bonnet and wraps. There were boards which could be laid over the well of the conveyance, with a mattress to be spread over them for night travel; and the green wooden slats at the window let in some air.

With a storm of abuse from the driver and the merciless lash of his whip, the horses went galloping up the Grand Trunk road, the gharry jerking and lurching until every bone in Minnie's body ached. After five or six miles they drew up, and fresh horses were harnessed with all the former uproar.

Archie rode much of the way beside the gharry, but if travelling at night, he joined Minnie in her already cramped quarters. Sometimes rivers were crossed on creaking, unsteady bridges of boats; but often streams had to be forded, Minnie being carried by a servant in case the water came into the bottom of the carriage.

Lord Dalhousie, when Governor-General, had pressed forward with the building of the Grand Trunk road, which would eventually stretch from Calcutta to the extreme north of India. For as far as it went it was reasonably good, shaded by trees on both sides for most of the way, such bumps, gullies and potholes as there were being taken for granted. Once off the road it was a bumpy trip over rutted tracks, the vehicles taking detours whenever the going became too rough.

At intervals they stopped for the night in an uncomfortable dak bungalow, occasionally with friends. Frequently they travelled right through the night, which, if cooler, gave no rest and less sleep.

Minnie was now six months pregnant, holding faithfully to her promise to her mother to wear always her thick and boned stays. She was new to it all, this sharp contrast to her sheltered life in England, but she survived the journey without disaster.

Archie writes next:

My dear Mrs Blane,

My wife will have informed you of our safe arrival here from Calcutta, a distance of some 1,300 miles, in safety, thank God.

We are still residing with my brother-in-law, Arthur Roberts, the Commissioner of Lahore on a salary of £3,000 a year, a splendid appointment, but a very responsible and onerous one. His duties are very numerous, in fact his time is much occupied from four in the morning until sunset. He likes his work and is most zealous.

You will, I know, be much pleased with his wife, my youngest sister, who has left her husband to reside in England to look after her children, eight in number. The eldest boy, about fifteen, is at Harrow, and is to come out to India in the army, his father having obtained a cavalry cadetship for him. My sister will reside in town on her first arrival, afterwards at Harrow to be near her eldest boy. She will also be at Ravensbourne Park, Lewisham, her mother-in-law's residence, a very pretty spot, and a good house and garden.

The climate here is delightful. We burn fires day and night, and I am glad to sit down in the house with closed doors. Rain has fallen in abundance since our arrival here upwards of three weeks, but now the weather is delightful, clear and sparkling with hoar frosts at night.

We leave here tomorrow and march with Arthur Roberts who is going to visit his division or district. We accompany him as far as Wizierabad, then leave him, and proceed on to Jhelum, our destination which is only some forty miles off. This town is on the river Jhelum and stands quite high, therefore has an agreeable climate, and it is within two hundred miles of the famous, or infamous, Khyber Pass.

I am very anxious to arrive there and get comfortably housed on account of Minnie, who is very well, I am thankful to say. She travels in a palanquin up to Jhelum, a sort of bed carried by four bearers, who run barefoot and frequently change places with accompanying relief men. Arthur Roberts kindly bought a carriage partly on her account. We have been driving about Lahore in it visiting people, and Minnie wanted to have driven in it on our march, but I have persuaded her not to, but to go quietly in her palanquin. The roads are bad on account of the heavy rain and she would have been shaken in the carriage. She will only have to move from her bed into the palanquin, and eight men, four and four, will carry her smoothly on the road every morning into her tent, when she will perform her toilet and have breakfast.

The only objection will be the early rising fag to leave her bed by 6 a.m., put on her dressing gown, partake of some coffee and toast, and pop into her litter, which is very comfortable, I assure you. She can sleep for three hours, a distance of ten miles, if she likes, when she will arrive at the new camp at a comfortable, large tent, with a stove in it, and prepare for a good breakfast.

She will have the whole day to herself in tents, and proceed on the following morning as usual. I shall ride on horseback by her side sometimes, but she will have an armed horseman always by her side as an A.D.C. and for protection.

We did not like Calcutta. 'Twas very expensive and uncomfortable and the mosquitos were as big as *cats*! Dear Minnie was nearly devoured by them. She suffered terribly, poor girl, and her arms and legs (excuse me for saying so) were covered with bites.

We went out to Dum Dum, the Indian Woolwich, and stayed with some charming old friends of mine, most hospitable hosts. We much enjoyed our visit, Minnie escaping from her dread enemies, the mosquitos. We attended a good Ball given by the Artillery Officers in their splendid Mess House, and Minnie walked through a quadrille.

Our luggage is becoming alarmingly extensive, the weight of which is now 36 maunds, or 2,880 pounds! This, of course, includes household furniture, cooking apparatus, etc., etc. We shall require four large carts with 4 or 5 bullocks in each!

We are gradually getting our servants, and have acquired a cook, two table attendants, watchmen, washerman and woman, a tailor, a waiting woman for my wife, and a Sirdar bearer for myself. We have no horses nor conveyance of any kind, can't afford it. Our English baggage has all arrived safely, nothing broken, and all Minnie's pretty millinery and outfit arrived *dry*, nothing injured, except our prints which were slightly wet, but nothing to speak of. We ought to be thankful, for little Mrs Paske, General Jervis's daughter, had all her outfit, millinery, etc., quite spoilt. Their loss amounted to some 8,000 rupees (£800), as the rain got into the packages and ruined them.

Considering the distance our baggage came, 1,300 miles, the rivers and small streams crossed over, bad roads, etc., we were lucky. I was afraid our plate chest had been robbed, for the outer case was stoved in, but we only lost a broken bottle in the cruet stand, which we cannot get replaced in India.

And now I must say goodbye as 'tis Sunday, and we are going to dress for church. When I am settled with my regiment I will write you every month regularly. My affectionate love to dear Cissy, who I trust is in good health, and not dancing too much at Bath. My kind regards to Archie and his brother, and with every kind wish from myself,

Believe me to remain, dear Mrs Blane,

Your very affectionate,

Archie Wood

Minnie is busy writing to her sister. God bless you all.

On the journey from Calcutta to Lahore there were signs of the growing unrest which, though still underground, was slowly building up to explosion point. Neither Minnie nor Archie noticed anything, for their minds were bent on their own discomforts and fatigue, but once in Lahore in the Punjab, and staying with Arthur Roberts, the Commissioner, they heard much discussion on the situation.

Lord Dalhousie, Governor-General of India, was a man regarded more with awe than with affection when he left Calcutta in February 1857, and was succeeded by Lord Canning, a man of warmth and great administrative powers.

Before he left England, Canning had told the East India Company's Board that he saw in the Indian sky a cloud 'at present no larger than a man's hand, but one which could grow and overwhelm the country'. He knew and admitted that there was unrest.

Dalhousie would not see the danger, and pressed on with the policy of total annexation of native states which, if there were no direct heir, must pass to British rule, revenue and all. He would not heed the advice of men such as Henry Lawrence, Colonel Sleeman and many others who had been in India for years, who understood the point of view of Indians, spoke their language, respected and liked them. Dalhousie, backed by the Board in distant England, annexed the small states of Satara, Nagpur and Jhansi, and then the far bigger one of Oude.

The kingdom of Oude was a large tract of land roughly 300 miles by 200, lying on the Ganges plain approximately equidistant from Calcutta and Lahore. It was a fertile and rich land, with its own king, royal family and aristocracy; and it was the main recruiting ground for the native regiments, officered by Europeans, an army made up by generations – father and son – of loyal sepoys, whose proud regiments had given little trouble for many years.

The king of Oude and the chief families were oppressive and corrupt, and the state was overrun with bandits and rogues of all kinds. Many natives and the wiser Europeans knew that British administration would clean up the country and establish law and order; and they held that the revenue, which would be large when various grafts were stopped, should be used for the good of Oude and its people. Many in Oude were for this policy, knowing that it would bring peace, employment, security, and the chance to live unharried by a cruel king, rapacious troops and lawless landowners.

Dalhousie did not see it like that. He wished to add the whole state, its thousands of square miles and thousands of good rupees, to Britain.

This was done, thus sowing the seed of a terrible harvest. The royal family, good members and bad, were exiled, and Oude lost its status as an ancient country to become no more than a small patch of red on the map of the British Empire.

Dalhousie appointed a new commissioner for Oude, a man with little tact and a flaming temper, quite incapable of reconciling the dissatisfied population with its new status, or even of keeping peace with his own staff.

The king's disbanded army was scattered all over the country, without employment and bent on trouble. The members of the royal family were treated without the respect to which they were accustomed. Opium was heavily taxed, leaving the poorer classes without the drug they depended on; and within the Lucknow Residency there was discord and disagreement.

Lord Canning, who arrived in India early in 1856, realized how dangerous was the situation in Oude, with trouble brewing in the very heart of the Company's army there. He immediately sent for Henry Lawrence from his post in Rajputana where Dalhousie had put him out of the main stream of events. Canning appointed him commissioner in Lucknow. He knew that Lawrence, that wisest of men, had a profound understanding of Indians, from the lowest 'untouchable' to the king himself; that he had great tact, years of experience, and a genuine liking for the people, who in turn had a deep affection and respect for him. Dalhousie had virtually exiled him, jealous of the affection in which he was held and of the influence he had over most of northern India. Now Canning sent for him, hoping that his authority would quiet the situation; but both knew that perhaps it was already too late to stave off disaster.

To add to this there were other more widespread circumstances. There was a resurgence of the fear of attack from the north by the Russians. There were persistent rumours, spread by agitators, that native troops would be forced to 'cross the black water', that is, cross the seas to other countries, which would break their rigid caste system, and render them outcasts, that most awful fate any Hindu could face. There was no real basis for this rumour, but it was known that British forces had been diminished by the losses in the recent Crimean War. The activities of well-meaning Christian missionaries gave added strength to the agitators' tales that all sepoys were to be forcibly converted. Furthermore, the story was spread that the new Enfield cartridges were greased with cow fat, anathema to any Hindu, and those used by Mahommedans with pig fat, both materials regarded as unclean and defiling to followers of either religion.

The banished king of Oude was living in a palatial house on Garden Reach, and it was suspected that he was up to his eyes in rebellious plotting, for there were many mysterious comings and goings from his house.

Minnie and Archie on their journey saw men along the dusty road who unknown to them were bent on spreading sedition against the British; and they looked with disgust on some nearly naked, ash-strewn fakir, a holy man, unaware that after dark he would gather men around him to rake up the old prophecy that a hundred years after the battle of Plassey in 1757, the East India Company's raj (rule) would be destroyed. Mysterious chapatties, flat dry cakes, were being passed from hand to hand over the vast length of India; but if the complaisant British heard of this they dismissed it as some strange religious practice, only a few recognizing it as a sign of unrest, stemming from some organized headquarters – a kind of fiery cross.

Once in Mr Roberts's comfortable house in Lahore, Minnie and Archie heard talk of all this but paid little attention to it, being more interested in their own difficult journey, and in the fate of their four bullock carts ambling up the hot plains of India with their baggage.

In any case the average officer of a native regiment was convinced of the loyalty of his sepoys, and the more senior the officer the deeper his conviction. Should any man voice his doubts he was likely to be called a panicmonger, or even a coward.

From Lahore to Jhelum

The Woods' stay in Lahore was short. Mr Roberts was due to go on tour of his district, travelling with a considerable train of followers. Camping was not a simple matter of a couple of tents, but a caravanserai almost like a complete village, with horses, mules, elephants and crowds of servants, each bound by the rigid caste system to do only the one appointed task, be it house servant, grass cutter for the animals, coolie for baggage and the pitching of the tents, syce for the horses, messenger for running back to Lahore or on ahead to some place they were approaching, and a dozen other varieties of jobs. There were also native clerks and several junior Europeans on the commissioner's staff, as well as wives and fellow travellers heading in the same direction.

The tents for use on the hot plains were elaborate. The camp for each night was an orderly group of tents, the commissioner's the tallest of all, some 18ft high and 20ft or more square. It had an outer brown shell, and an inner lining, often of bright chintz, several feet apart from the outer canvas, thus providing an insulating air space against the heat. The tents were usually divided into sleeping- and living-quarters; and meals were served with ceremony on good china and plate, though not silver, as that disappeared too quickly with light-fingered people who liked to melt it down.

At night the lights of the camp illuminated the servants' figures as they squatted on their heels or moved about; and horses, camels, oxen and possibly a herd of goats were grouped under trees. The whole scene was lit by the glow of fires that were kept blazing all night to ward off wild animals, particularly the tigers that frequented the jungle.

It must have been a fascinating scene, with the ceaseless chatter
and rustle of monkeys in the trees, the strange cries of birds, the
endless variety of trees and creepers, and the occasional snarling
roar of a hunting leopard or tiger.

This was just the camping outfit of a commissioner on a
comparatively short route of a few hundred miles. When the
Governor-General went on one of his stately progresses from
Calcutta to Simla, at least 1,200 miles, the 'tail' of the camp
stretched for miles and numbered thousands of men and beasts,
with an impressive escort of troops. The party had to encompass
everything which would make up a self-supporting, fair-sized town,
with farriers, tailors, clerks, merchants, bakers, butchers, etc., and
as the Governor was out to impress the native princes, the tents
were palatial, and even boasted glass doors.

Such a progress would take the best part of two years, but
Mr Roberts's journey was to last only a few weeks. As he was
going north-west, in the direction of Jhelum, Minnie and Archie
accompanied him as far as Wizierabad, some sixty miles on the
route to Jhelum, then only forty miles distant.

The idyllic journey through almost roadless country to
Wizierabad must have delighted Minnie, but she set down no
description of it, her mind full of the distressing news from Bath.

She wrote:

From our Camp at Wizierabad,
sixty miles from Lahore
20 February 1857

It was only two days ago, my dearest Mother, that I learnt the
sad intelligence of my poor dear brother, Archie's death. I need
hardly tell you how much shocked I was by it, having heard
nothing of the poor fellow's illness, and yesterday's post brought
me dear Cissy's long letter from London dated only three days
previous to his death, describing all she had been doing, and not
a word said of his being even poorly. I am looking forward with
much anxiety to your next letters to hear all particulars. How

much I would have given to have been with you. Here, out as we are at present in the jungle with Mr Roberts, I can hardly realize the loss I have had, and the sad fact that he has been dead many weeks without my being able to know or mourn his loss.

When I left home last July I felt persuaded I should never see him again, but now that the blow has come I feel it more than I can tell from being so far away from you all. Would that I had seen his last moments, but that being denied me, I shall trust to you for recounting all concerning him. Was he able to remember me, or send me some message, and have you a bit of his hair for me?

[These lines are badly blotted with Minnie's tears.]

My poor dear boy, how he must have suffered. My heart nearly broke at reading Uncle Montgomery's letter about him. Please, dearest Mama, send me out pictures, it would be the greatest boon for me.

My dear husband has felt for me in my distress. I am now not very strong and feel anything very much, but he is kindness itself. He was shocked on opening his letter and finding it contained such bad news, and hardly liked to break it to me, but I saw there was something wrong, and would not be satisfied until I knew. Please tell me all about poor dear Archie's funeral, which I hear is to take place in Kensal Green. Little did I think when I visited it previous to leaving England that Papa's grave would so soon be opened. . . . [Several words here are illegible because blotted with tears.] But no doubt it is all for some good purpose, though now I do not see it.

Dear Mama, I wish I could comfort you, and I want some myself, for this has been our first loss amongst your children. I cannot write more, I am so miserable.

God bless you all, my dearest Mama,
Your fondly attached daughter,
Minnie Wood

The next letter is from Archie, written at the same camp at Wizierabad on Sunday, 22 February:

My dear Mrs Blane,

Mr Montgomery's kind letter shocked us greatly. Fortunately it was marked private, which enabled me to keep the sad tidings from my dear wife for a short time. I broke the melancholy news gradually to her, for in her present delicate state I was afraid of a sudden shock. Had she opened the letter for me, or had wished to read the contents with me, it might have been injurious to her. Thank God she is as well as can be expected. She is near her confinement. I think she will be a mother (D.V.) in about a month hence. Dear girl, she often talks to me about the approaching happy event, and hopes it will be a boy, not a girl. She has been amusing herself with getting all the necessary little creature comforts for the wee baby that is to be. As for the Christian names of the babe, they are something wonderful! I know not where the godpapas are to come from. However, there will be lots of time when the little precious is born.

Accept our united love and best wishes, and may God in his infinite Goodness watch over and protect you in your present severe affliction.

Believe me, my dear Mrs Blane, very affectionately yours,

A. O. Wood

Minnie's next letter is written to her sister and shows a curious detachment from the sorrow of her brother's death. The time lapse, the distance, the novelty of her surroundings and the imminence of her baby's arrival account for much, yet it seems out of character.

Camp Gugerat, 22 February, 1857

My dearest Cissy,

Many thanks for your long, interesting letter, which reached me on the 19th. It had been dancing all over India, to Calcutta, Meerut, Jhelum, Lahore, and finally arrived safely at our camp which was then pitched at Moorrudkee.

Tonight Archie and I go to Jhelum, I in my Palkee, and he on a small pony carriage which he has got for me. My ayah and her children in an ekka, or native cart, and our two Kitmaghars also, and we hope to reach Jhelum tomorrow morning by 7 o'clock, where a Mr Donald Macnabb, the Assistant Commissioner, has kindly given us the use of his house until we are suited with our own, which must be done quickly, as the 14th Regiment marched from Multan on the ninth of this month, and will be in Jhelum in the course of ten days. I cannot express how inconvenient it is not being able to get things as in England. I have sent upwards of 300 miles to Umballa for some more muslin, as there is not such a thing as a shop or Box-wallah to be had anywhere in these parts, and my figure has now become so changed that I cannot tell how I shall get on.

Dearest Mama, I have felt so for you during this sad trial. How very lonely you must feel now. I quite regret being out here, for as I am now placed I never have a moment quiet, constantly something fresh to interest one, particularly in the Punjab. For instance, last evening we started about half past four in the carriage, Arthur Roberts driving, and, as he is Chief Commissioner, we were attended by eight Sowers or mounted police, two Sirdars, or native noblemen, magnificently attired, and numerous others for an escort. In this manner we crossed the famous Chenab river. The sun was just setting and the reflection of his rays in the snow clad summits of the Himalayas was a sight I shall never forget.

This was not all, for we are now camped on the very field of Gugerat, which yesterday eight years ago (1849) was the scene of so sanguinary a battle between the Sikhs and the Anglo-Indian army under General Gough. It is strange that we should arrive here on the anniversary of that event.

Whilst you are enjoying mild, wet weather, we are suffering from intense heat, which I think has been in part caused by the shock of an earthquake which has been felt about here, as it has come in quite suddenly.

I have superintended the vaccination of a number of native children at each place we have stopped. We have a native doctor with us for that purpose, and I must say that judging by the hundreds I have seen done, it appears to be thoroughly appreciated, as smallpox is one of the worst diseases amongst natives.

I am looking forward to making everything comfortable in our new house. Everything is ready for the baby (which I think may come sooner than I imagined), except the Doctor and nurse, and the latter is most difficult to get.

My dear Cissy, do write to me often, and send me many of your pictures. Do please make me a pair of baby's shoes similar to the pattern Mama had in red cashmere, but let it be some cool colour.

God bless you, my darling Cissy. How I wish I was near you all,

Ever your fondly attached sister,

Minnie

Jhelum was a small military station strategically placed on the Jhelum river. There was nothing there but the cantonments which consisted of the native infantry lines, two magazines and a parade ground. A central dusty road ran through the middle of the station with the officers' mess and the colonel's house on one side of it, near to the edge of the cliff above the river, where no doubt the maximum of breeze could be felt in the hot weather. There was a church which looked somewhat Georgian, and a few houses for married officers, round which the gardens showed colour and many pot plants for at least part of the year.

The native town was a little away from the military settlement, and was no more than a maze of shabby houses and huts, with a cramped bazaar. Near by were some gardens where a few vegetables were produced.

The river ran between low rocky cliffs, at times a shallow stream, at others a raging torrent capable of rising many feet in a few hours, swollen by the rains or by melting snows from the mountains. It was crossed by a bridge of boats moored side by side, with planks laid across them forming an unsteady road for men, cattle and vehicles, with a rickety fence on both sides. There were no shops, no amenities, and it was a treeless dreary part of the country.

It did not take Minnie long to sum it up after her arrival at the end of February. The first three weeks were occupied in moving into her house, and this next letter of Minnie's to her mother again shows the uncertainty of the mails and the length of time in transit.

Jhelum, 1 March

Your letter, my dearest Mama, through Colonel Gerrard, reached us a few days ago, and as I was already aware of poor dear Archie's death, through Uncle Montgomery's letter, my husband did not conceal it, but gave it to me at once to read. How my heart ached for you, dear Mama, as I saw how blotted the words were with your tears. Poor, poor fellow, to be carried off at last so suddenly. God grant that we may meet again in Heaven. I quite long to receive the bust of my poor brother. Could you not have that already taken of dear Papa copied, for as stereotypes they are so much life like.

Today we have entered our own house, a capital one, with a good garden, and rented besides, which is a great piece of good fortune, everyone here being anxious to sell. I quite dread housekeeping as I have no power over the servants, being unable to speak to them. I have to get my husband to translate the accounts every morning when my Khansahmah and Bearer bring them, and this he does not like, poor boy. He is quite disgusted with me for not being able to make custard, jellies, etc. I suppose it will all come in good time, but he is so absurd expecting me to be able to do everything as well as those who have been out here for years.

I have a very nice storeroom which I christened the other day by putting three pots of preserve in it, and that is all I can think of, as you cannot as in England go out to shops. There is no such thing here, and everything is frightfully dear. I intend trying to draw a picture of my house, and sending it to you. It is far preferable to those in Cantonments, as we are so private, having no houses to overlook us.

The 14th Regiment marched in on Saturday last, the 7th. I went down to meet them with Archie, who joined his comrades. He is in high feather having just had two companies, the

Grenadiers and the 1st, given to him. He is very busy fidgeting about as usual.

I am thankful I have secured the services of a most excellent nurse for my approaching confinement. She is the wife of our Quartermaster Sergeant Benaham, and bears a very excellent character. Our great comfort is that she drinks neither wine, beer nor spirits of any kind. So many of these women do so to excess.

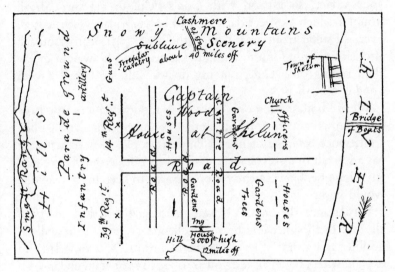

I have seen her and like her appearance very much. She is young, but has good certificates, and the ladies of the Regiment all recommend her as an industrious, hard-working little woman. I feel quite comfortable on that score now. She says I may expect my illness at the end of this month, so that is a comfort. I will be sure and have everything well aired, as you say. Indeed the sun is beginning to get so warm that everything feels warm to the touch.

Oh! I have *just* received a letter of yours written on January 11th. It has been all over India and is No. 5. No. 4 has never reached me. I suppose it may turn up one day. I am so grieved to hear of my letter being lost, as I put down every event that occurred on board ship likely to interest you. Let us hope it may yet turn up. I wish to goodness I had sent it via Marseilles instead of by the *Southampton*. In future I shall never send letters by sea, via the Cape.

You will be glad to hear that up to this time I wear my stays always. I do not think I have had them off one week the whole time. Now, of an evening, I am obliged to take them off, or I feel very uncomfortable, even though they are loose. I take a walk every morning, and have been most particular in attending to all your advice, so I trust, with God's help, to get through all troubles which I expect daily. I shall be very glad when it is all over as I suffer from great pain in the lower part of my stomach after sitting only for a few minutes, caused by the weight of the child resting on a bone, but my doctor tells me I shall have a good confinement.

We are both getting on very well in money matters. We have only the servants that are absolutely necessary, but there is such a difference between them and English people. Each department has a servant of a special caste which does not permit them to do anything else. Consequently it obliges one to keep more than one would wish.

For instance, the ayah. A Mussulmanee ayah will dress and keep all your clothes nice and be an excellent servant, but she will do nothing more, not attend to your bathroom (ask some lady to explain what I refer to), and you are obliged to have an under-ayah who will do nothing else. These women are much cheaper and more useful than any other caste, but the other servants will take *nothing at all* from their hands, which is a horrid nuisance. Bearers and other castes will not go near a table or put anything on it which has beef on it, as it is the animal they worship. I assure you, dear Mama, it requires a most excellent temper to stand all their nonsense.

Actually the other day I desired my table servant to bring me the drawing-room lamp to clean, as I take charge of them. He refused, saying that he would lose caste to touch it. Fool! I got so angry, and after a hard battle got my way, but really they are enough to drive one mad!

12 March

I have, I grieve to say, lost this mail, but after writing the other day I became so sick I was obliged to lie down, and even now I shall not be able to write much at a time, as sitting up hurts me so.

General Reed from Peshawar is expected here soon to inspect the troops. Consequently everyone is hard worked. By six in the morning every officer has to be on the Parade Ground. Then after that is over, they proceed to the Mess House where Sword Exercise detains them till nine. Again at five o'clock they have another Parade.

I have managed to procure some mourning, viz. a best bonnet and dress with a crepe mantle, also some black ribbon to trim my bonnet, and a white dressing-gown, as in the hot season people never stir out, and it is almost an impossibility to wear anything at all. However, I have been most fortunate in disposing of a great number of my things, and when you send me out a box, please have any dresses made large, as then my old tailor can alter them, and I dare say my dear Cissy will make up any little things for me that are new and like she wears.

Dearest Mama, I cannot go on any further as I am feeling qualmish, but I will post this to be certain of the next mail, and commence another to dear Cissy, which I may still be able to send by the same steamer going to Suez.

My dearest husband joins me in most affectionate love to you both, and with many kisses, dear Mama, believe me,

Your affectionately attached daughter,

Minnie

I cannot procure a black envelope anywhere, so pray excuse this one.

Archie added a postscript:

Jhelum

We have arrived here in safety after a long, tedious journey. We ought to be thankful to Almighty God for His protection and guidance through many dangers and difficulties over the vast extent of country we have traversed, over the sea and dry land. He has indeed watched over us in times of danger. I do not think you heard how we were nearly lost coming up the river to Calcutta. A steamer was taking us in tow and the anchor slipped, and had we run upon it the *Southampton* must have been ripped up and sunk.

All our baggage has arrived here in safety and now the post closes this morning, so I will conclude this short letter and write you a long one next mail.

Believe me, my dear Mrs Blane,
Very affectionately yours,
A. O. Wood

Jhelum, 23 March

My dearest Mama,

I dispatched my last letter to you, my dearest Mama, two days ago, but as I hope to be unable to write by next mail day, I shall scribble a little every day, and then my husband can send it for me.

Last week we had nothing but noise and racket, sometimes lasting night and day, barring all one's efforts to sleep. It has been the great festival of the Hoolies, a Hindu festival in honour of Krishna and Gopis (milkmaids), which always takes place near the Vernal equinox. Everyone looks the greatest guys, as the grand aim is to throw as much red powder over one another as they can. Then they cook as much food as they can in the night, and eat till they almost burst! The Sepoys of our two companys came up to make their salaams and presented us with some powder in a paper, and were much pleased by my taking a handful and throwing it in their faces. I like these native soldiers much, they are so respectful and nice in their manners.

My dear old husband appears a great favourite amongst the men, who were delighted to see him back. They were all up here on Friday to receive their pay. The Native Officer and Pay Sergeant made their bows to me, such fine men, tall and well made, so different from the dirty, puny natives of Bengal. We have an orderly always in attendance, a most useful appendage to our household, as he runs with any messages we may require.

On Saturday, whilst driving, I suddenly fainted! Fancy *me* being guilty of such a thing. The gallant Captain was in a dreadful fright, and sent off for Dr Kilkelly thinking I was near my confinement. He came, but found me all right again, but weak. Mrs Knatchbull was with me immediately, and she has promised to be with me in my illness, so do not be frightened should you receive a letter from her, as I shall ask her to give you a full description, as I am sure you will like to know how I get on.

General Reed arrived here yesterday, Friday, and was received with a salute of thirteen guns. He is, I hear, a very particular man about parades, etc.

Every one of us is disappointed with Jhelum. The heat is dreadful. We are quite melted, and night and day are the same, as there is no refreshing breeze of an evening as in Bengal. There is a *hot* wind often accompanied by dust storms. Every door is shut at nine in the morning and not opened until after sunset, but still there is no relief, but a feeling of suffocation which is quite horrible. All who have been at Multan say that at this time of year there it is quite cool and delightful. True, we have a good view of the hills, but the very circumstance of having them all round keeps this place very warm. Residents give a very different account of the climate here than we were told. They say six months of the year are unbearable. So much for other people's notions of cool weather!

Next month spiders come into season, with stings enough to kill one, and would not Cissy scream if she saw the *wasps* of these parts! Everything of that kind is so large out here, that I run the moment I see one, and my storeroom is a magnificent place for the latter.

Today the Artillery were received by General Reed. I did not go as I hardly slept all night for the restlessness of Master Wood. Poor me, it troubles me dreadfully, and I can hardly sit, particularly after eating anything.

My husband often goes out fishing, but usually catches nothing.

It is lucky for us that we do not depend on the produce of his rod, for I fear we should soon starve.

The people in our regiment are very sociable. I like the ladies very much. Often we send over our dinner to the Smiths who live close by, and dine with them. It makes a pleasant change. Our new medical man, Doctor Cole, has just joined. I hear his appearance is not as prepossessing as our late Doctor Kilkelly's.

24 March

At six this morning the 14th were reviewed by General Reed, and every officer caught it. The 14th are beginning to feel shaky as they have not practised for such a time, but I believe they will come off with flying colours. The Quartermaster of the 39th is sent to drill for not knowing sword exercise. Hurrah! For I dislike him so much. He is such a lout and wears his jacket three inches too short, consequently one has a good view of his undergarments!

Poor Hubby has been stewing at his sword exercise and saluting all this morning, wretched him. I have been personating lately the 'Flag of England' and showing all due respect, as the Captain marches in solemn grandeur round and round the dining table!

Today I have strawberries for the first time. They, with the roses, are just coming into season.

25 March

This morning I was up at half past four, dressed, made an excellent chota hazaree (little breakfast – see how I am learning the language!), and off with the Knatchbulls to see the 14th reviewed. The General was delighted. No fault found and everything went off splendidly. I enclose a copy of what appeared in the Order Book when brought round to the officers. Is it not gratifying! I am quite delighted about it, as so many officers of the 39th kept chaffing me and asking if I had come to see Captain Wood reprimanded. One in particular, the wretch, kept bothering me until I told him that 'had I been on the ground yesterday I then should have said "Yes", as I was perfectly aware how much satisfaction the Officers and Men of the 39th had given the General'!

Oh, it is so hot! I am sitting in nothing but a chemise and a white dressing gown, and yet I am in an awful state of perspiration.

Mrs Benaham, the midwife, was with me today, and after examining me said she thought I should be confined about the 29th. Strange if the event should take place on dear Papa's birthday.

26 March

The 14th gave a dinner tonight to the 39th, so as Archie was at Mess, I dined with Mrs Knatchbull. It is still very warm.

Sunday, 27 March

I did not go to church but remained quietly at home. Everyone is disgusted with the Chaplain, Mr Thomas, as he quite forgot himself at the Mess dinner and was extremely overcome with wine. This is a man who brings in religion on every occasion, and has given much annoyance to people by his constant interference with them and their families.

29 March

Hurrah! Dear Mama, your February 25th letter came this morning. I am so glad you are all well, but you must indeed cheer up. No, there is no chance of my having my little one yet, though I make the bed nearly every day in hopes it may act as a charm but nothing appears to have effect.

Let me again assure you that I have attended strictly to all the advice you have given me, and will not fail to do so when confined. Out here everything is so differently conducted than in England. We have no rain or damp of any kind (would to gracious we had, for I am quite ill from the heat), and fires are never thought of. The only thing that is done is that the Punkah is stopped at the moment the child is born.

As regards servants, my life has been worried out by ayahs. I have had no less than four since my arrival in Jhelum, and I am not yet suited. They are a thousand times worse than English servants. You, I am sure, would never stand them. They perfectly spoil one's temper, for they are such fools, without a gleam of sense, and yet to do without them is impossible. They live in the compound in mud houses which are free, but that is all. You do not feed them or have anything to do with them, only allow one hour and a half each day for their Khana or dinner, which is the only meal they ever partake, and as to touching anything from off our table, that is unheard of. They generally have the same thing, rice or lentils, over and over again through the year.

1 April

I dined yesterday with the Smiths, Archie being at Mess as it was Band night, and our new Bandmaster, Herr Ludwig, wants a great deal of encouragement. My husband was out quail shooting this morning, but shot nothing. On his return home his horse stumbled and fell with him, luckily without hurting him more than a strain in the leg.

2 April

I must post this today, but alas, without any domestic occurrence being recorded. I was over this morning with the Knatchbulls, and to my disgust found little Mrs Hickey ill with her first pains. It has been a regular race between us, but she will beat me, as she expects her baby tonight. I sat with her a long time this morning, making her laugh and forget her troubles. Poor little woman, her husband is obliged to leave her tomorrow to join his Regiment at Multan, and she will follow as soon as her strength will permit.

I have seen Doctor Cole, and dislike his appearance extremely. He is the sort of man who takes no interest whatever in his patients, never gives an opinion, or prescribes without being well *pumped*.

Thanks, dearest Mama, for all the trouble you are taking about any little money belonging to me. Remember, please, to keep whatever falls to me towards the liquidation of my £20 debt to you. We neither of us want it. Also for your offer of sending me anything I require through Mr Armstrong. We have had no letters from him, but I believe he proposes coming out in the spring of 1858.

Now, my dearest Mama, I must fain bid you adieu, and send this off. By the by, you marked your letter wrong. It should have been No. 7, not 6, as I have two of that number.

With our united best love to you and dear Cissy, and the boys, believe me, ever your very affectionately attached child,

Minnie Wood

I enclose a copy of the General's most flattering account of dear Archie's Company.

'Colonel Gerrard has the most sincere pleasure in conveying to the 14th Regiment the following observations made by the Inspecting Officer, General Reed, with reference to the general behaviour and appearance of the men at yesterday's and this morning's drill.

'Major General Reed, C.B., begs that his best thanks be offered to the European Officers, Native Officers, Staff Sergeants and Non Commissioned Officers and Sepoys of the 14th Regiment Native Infantry for their united exertions which combined to assure the success attained at the late inspection. The Major General observed with entire satisfaction the cleanly appearance of the accoutrements, and was exceedingly pleased with the steadiness of the men throughout the evolutions performed this morning. The only instance in which he could point out an error, was that he considered the Light Infantry was performed too steadily.

'Colonel Gerrard cannot withhold thanks which he owes to the Regiment for conduct so creditable, and he trusts that each ensuing inspection may draw forth remarks equally gratifying.'

Dearest Mama, is that not pleasing!

Jhelum, 15 May

My dearest Mama,

As my husband is writing I cannot resist adding a few lines just to tell you how myself and darling Baby are getting on, and to give a description of your grandchild.

Well, to begin with, myself. I was taken ill between two and three of the morning of the 1st, but as my dear Archie had to attend Muster I did not say a word. I waited until he was gone when I called my Nurse, who slept in the adjoining room, and who then prepared the bed, made me comfortable, and sent for Mrs Harry Smith, who was with me the whole time. Dear Mama, I had much for which to be grateful. My pains were very long and severe, and this, with the aid of an injection, hastened the birth of my child, who entered this world at twenty minutes past four, fully eight hours sooner than my Doctor expected. Indeed he was not present.

Baby was born and Nurse in the act of cutting the navel string when he returned. I cannot describe my feelings when I first heard my dear Sonny cry. Dear little pet, he is a very healthy looking child. A round face like mine, but the head and hair ridiculously like his Papa's. His eyes will, I think, be blue.

My Doctor is not the most agreeable man for a confinement. He sits like a piece of stone and does nothing to encourage me, *in fact I hate him*! He is so rough in his treatment, indeed he hurt me much more in 'taking pains' than in all my labour, and as soon as Baby was safe on another bed, he bandaged me up as tight as possible, and in about five minutes took the afterbirth from me, and never gave it time to act by itself.

How I wish my son could be seen by you and Cissy. How she would love her nephew. Of course I nurse him, but am sorry to say I have suffered from a sore nipple, and the horrible agony I endured when the poor boy was brought to me was frightful. Now I am ordered to feed him with arrowroot every other time as I am so weak. I am taking quinine three times a day, and plenty of beer, as I suffer from fainting fits.

My Baby is asleep by my side as I write, looking so nice. We both went out on Tuesday in the little carriage for the first time. The weather is still terribly hot, punkah going day and night. The sun rises now at a quarter past five and sets about quarter to seven, an awful long day as we cannot venture out except at four in the morning, or seven at night, and our dinner is not commenced until past eight.

Oh, I hate this country! I am sure it would kill you, this dreadful heat, no wind to cool one, only a hot, dusty blast. It seems to take the very skin off one's face.

I am so tired, I must give up writing. My very best congratulations on your birthday, dearest Mama. May you be spared many years is the sincere wish of your fondly attached child,

Minnie Wood

Tucked into this same envelope was a scrap of paper written hastily by Archie, probably without Minnie's knowledge. The words read like a distant roll of thunder.

15 May 1857

My dear Mrs Blane,

Minnie and our dear boy are both well, thank God.

Bad news from India. Several regiments in open mutiny. Delhi has been attacked, several British Officers murdered. A large force, including European soldiers, are coming here to Jhelum. Our officers have confidence in our Sepoys. The 14th is loyal, so you need have no fear from my regiment. May God preserve us all.

Archie Wood

The Mutiny, 1857

Archie's short note gives merely a hint of the appalling tragedy which had happened in Meerut on 10 May, and in Delhi on the following day. Minnie, so deeply occupied with her own affairs, knew nothing of the troubles as yet. Neither she nor her husband had the faintest qualm for the loyalty of their regiment, the 14th. How could they after Colonel Gerrard's glowing report?

Isolated as Jhelum was, news came through quickly on the telegraph, and more slowly by detailed letters and newspapers which took several days to reach the town. By 15 May they knew that a telegraph message had come through from Meerut to Agra on 10 May which read: 'The cavalry has risen setting fire to their own lines and several officers' houses, besides having killed every European they could find and. . . .' The message ended there unfinished, whether because of the murder of the sender or the cutting of the wires was unknown.

Archie knew that at the end of April the elderly colonel at Meerut had made an example of eighty men who had refused, without violence and on religious grounds, to use the cartridges issued, believing them to be greased with animal fat. The colonel had heaped every indignity upon them, sentencing them to ten years' hard labour, and keeping them standing in the blazing sun while their irons were put on. Their brother sepoys were forced to watch until the prisoners were marched off in their clanking chains to jail. Some officers visited the men, offering to do what they could for their wretched wives and families, but it was too late for any sign of mercy to save the day.

The affair was discussed all over India, but few British attached much importance to it. It was said that it was only another little incident like that in Barrackpore in March, and several others; perhaps it had been too severely dealt with, but even so it would teach those natives a lesson.

So went the general trend of opinion.

For the next two weeks the native regiments seethed with fury, augmented by agitators, and on 10 May the rage and discontent boiled over. Joined by the rabble of Meerut, they stormed the prison and freed their comrades. They sacked and burnt their cantonments, murdering their officers as they went.

Two miles away in the European cantonments, the British dithered. The colonel was not to be found, and protocol forbade that anyone else should give orders. By the time the troops got moving and went down to the native lines these had been reduced to ashes, and not a mutineer was in sight. The British did some mopping up, presuming that the fuss was over, and then, seeing smoke rising from their cantonments, they tore back to find the mutineers had evaded them and attacked, leaving a shambles of dead and dying, burning buildings, and all the ghastly aftermath of unchecked violence: violence that had met no resistance in the undefended settlement, save for the heroism of a solitary man, the succour of a faithful Indian servant, or the useless sacrifice of a woman for her screaming children.

The greatest military station in India did nothing, stunned by the tragedy. Due to the system of army promotion by seniority only, those who were in command were old and indecisive, and they took no action.

The mutineers, their ranks swelled by every ruffian in the district, marched the thirty-odd miles to Delhi unpursued, and stormed into the unalerted city at dawn to continue their terrible work.

A mile or so out of Delhi, in the barracks on the Ridge, the British would not believe that the uproar in the city was caused by mutineers from Meerut; and by the time they moved with such sepoys as had not yet deserted, the city was in the hands of the mob.

For some time the soldiers on the Ridge looked towards Meerut for the help they were sure would come, and meanwhile not a European soul was left alive in Delhi.

At Meerut the incompetent commanders of the remaining troops determined not to split their forces, and were deaf to the appeals of younger and more able officers, who knew that instant retribution for the mutineers was the only way to halt the terrible tide of rebellion. Nor was the restless fury of the ranks heeded; and while the fires flickered out and the dead were buried, not a soldier was allowed to go to the aid of those in Delhi or to wreak the vengeance which, at that stage, might yet have halted the uprising.

By the strange grapevine that covered India, the news spread rapidly. Information went quickly by telegraph, and later by more detailed letters and newspaper articles. Minnie and Archie were undoubtedly perturbed, but to them it was still other people's disaster and could never happen to them. Archie was convinced that his native regiment would be loyal to the end, but as more details filtered through, they began to realize the appalling danger to all British and even to themselves.

By 30 May the 39th Native Infantry had been moved from Jhelum, three native regiments being considered too much of a risk on one small station. Some women wished to go to Lahore as a safer place, but it rapidly became too dangerous to travel.

Archie's letters show clearly the lightning progress of the rising which enveloped place after place, taking a terrible toll of life and property, sweeping over India, as the saying was, 'like the Devil's wind'. They also reveal the state of mind he was in: a man without the stability and the moral fibre to face the situation calmly. Not one of the bravest, but can one altogether blame him?

Poor Minnie. The contrast from peaceful England to this holocaust was shattering; and the courage with which she relates the facts is astonishing in a young girl of only twenty-two, with a baby at her breast, unaccustomed to everything around her, and facing violence on an unimaginable scale. She writes:

Jhelum, 17 May

My own darling Mama,

By the same mail as this letter will be received in England the dreadful intelligence of the horrible massacre at Delhi, Meerut, etc., and the fearful state the country is in from these brutes of

Sepoys. Our lives are not now worth much, for although our regiment, thank God, are faithful as far as we can tell, still no one is certain from one hour to another whether we shall not be murdered by the natives.

You can have no idea, dearest Mama, of the state of mined one is in from one day to another. My dear husband looks ten years older from the anxiety he suffers on my and darling Sonny's account. Poor fellow, he hardly sleeps at night. At the least sound he is up, revolver in hand, for we have that loaded by our bedside, and his sword hung at the foot.

Our kind friend, Mr Frazer, was killed at his desk, and Mr Jennings, the Chaplain, with his daughter, a very sweet girl of twenty, were speared as they were returning from church in their buggy, poor things. Although we only met en route here, still we took a mutual fancy to each other. I have felt dreadfully shocked at her untimely end.

Two of our fellow passengers on the ship have been murdered at Meerut, Mr and Mrs Dawson, I believe, slowly burnt to death in one of the houses the mutineers fired, and would not allow them to escape from.

Is this not enough to appal officers who have been toiling here for years, treating the natives kindly, and then this is the return they get. It is abominable.

Nothing is thought of or spoken of now but these mutineers. Our little station is becoming desolate, the 39th Native Infantry having left last week, as it was not considered advisable to have three native regiments on this same station, and no Europeans.

My darling child is quite well and looking so pretty, dear wee thing. Oh, I wish you could see him. His lungs are the thing which I consider too powerful!

The letter continues from this point in Archie's handwriting:

30 May
The mutiny, I regret to say, is spread from Barrackpore, which is but fifteen miles from Calcutta, up to our Frontier station, Peshawar. About twenty five Sepoy regiments have been false

to our Government. The 9th Native Infantry have joined the mutineers at Delhi, and they have *murdered their European officers!!!* They, the mutineers, have butchered every white man, woman and child in the city. The last accounts are most heart-rending. More than fifty women and children, Christians, who took refuge for safety in the King's Palace there, have all been murdered. Such revolting atrocities, etc., have never been heard of before.

Minnie here continues her letter, crossing the fresh lines over her earlier ones:

> Our hot season, dearest Mama, has commenced with a vengeance, which makes everything worse. We can open no door or window between nine in the morning and seven at night, in an effort to keep the house bearably cool. The Thermantidote is going all the time, a most ingenious contraption of fans, etc., which blows a little air about, but it is stifling.
> The mail is leaving. I hope it reaches you.
> My love and many kisses,
> Your fondly attached child,
> Minnie Wood

27 May

My dear Mrs Blane,
I have been spared to write to you, my dear mother-in-law, since my last letter. The whole country from Calcutta to Peshawar is up in arms, and no European is safe for an hour together. The Sepoys of more than thirty regiments are in open mutiny. Some of the rebel regiments have murdered several of their European officers. Delhi has been sacked, every European murdered in cold blood. Several British officers, their wives and children have been butchered at Meerut where there are even European troops.

All the principal large Military stations in the North West Provinces between Delhi and Jhelum have been in open mutiny. Churches have been burnt down, also barracks, hospitals and officers' houses. They have broken open Treasuries, in fact the mutineers have placed the Government in open defiance.

At Meerut British officers with their wives have been cut down returning from church in broad daylight. We have lost several friends with whom we formed friendships on our journey – Mr Simon Frazer, the Commissioner of Delhi, whose guests we were when passing through there, was killed in his own house. The Reverend Mr Jennings and his daughter, the Chaplain at Delhi, both brutally murdered. The officers of the 54th, all killed except one who escaped. At Meerut the rebels fired the officers' quarters and shot them down as they came out for safety.

The Commander-in-Chief, General Anson, is collecting a large force entirely of Europeans to march on Delhi for its relief. Sepoy regiments have refused to march there, in fact the whole country is in a terrible uproar.

My regiment, the 14th, is quite loyal, but the Government cannot trust any of her Sepoy regiments, none after the diabolical conduct of some of them. The British officers have lost confidence in their men, so how can duty be carried on for the future?

If my life should be spared through this terrible crisis (which is very doubtful), I shall endeavour to reach England with my wife and baby. I cannot risk their lives longer in this land of murder and bloodshed. I assure you since we received intelligence of the Delhi massacre I have not known what sleep is. I am on the qui vive day and night. My revolver and sword are beside me in our bedroom at night. I do not like leaving my wife and baby in the house alone for a minute. We know not whether our servants can be trusted. The least noise at night, I am off my bed with pistol in hand.

I dare not sleep.

We have not a European soldier here, the whole of us British are quite at the mercy of the Sepoys, and of the natives here. We British officers go about day and night un-armed. We must not, we cannot, show an atom of fear, and we have to show that we have confidence in our men.

Our property is worth 5,000 rupees, but I could not get that money for it at this present unsettled time. Nevertheless, I will do my utmost to get away from India. Minnie and her precious baby should live in safety.

I shall endeavour to exchange into a European regiment. The Government will have to disband some thirty Sepoy regiments and raise a great many European ones. My regiment, the 14th, is behaving steadily. It will rebound immensely to their credit, and to the credit of the officers, if they come unscathed and loyal through this ordeal. But my confidence, so strong for seventeen years, in the Sepoys is nearly gone.

Communication between the Punjab and Calcutta is now open again. The mutineers fired the bridge of boats at Delhi and cut the wire of the telegraph lines. 'Tis working now again, I am thankful to say. The Commander-in-Chief, General Anson, is popular though his movements are slow. We require an energetic Chief at the head of our army to strike immediately a severe and decisive blow. Delay is dangerous, more especially as the King of Delhi is against us. He will be punished and lose his pension. Several loyal Rajahs are marching on Delhi to its relief, and they are men we can trust.

Will you please send me the *Times* newspaper accounting the Delhi massacre and the mutinous state of this country? I am anxious to see what the Queen's Ministers will say to all this.

I fancy when it is all over India will be governed by the Queen and her Ministers, and there will be no India House and East India Company in power any longer.

Alas! News has just arrived of the death of General Anson at Kurnal, near Delhi, of cholera, which is rife in the army. What now?

The army is expected to march on Delhi by the 31st, and today is the 29th. Let us hope our European troops will soon have their revenge for the blood of our countrymen, and that they will give no quarter.

My regiment is now the only one here, and God grant it may remain loyal and true to its colours, which are nearly one hundred years old. We have no other Europeans in the town, and the Civil Treasury and the bridge of boats are entrusted to the regiment. If they revolted what could we do, seven British officers against eight hundred Sepoys? They could fire this station and destroy all the European women and children in ten minutes. Is this not fearful!

To say I am not alarmed would be a falsehood. I have placed my beloved wife and sweet babe in God's hands, and have fervently prayed to Him to save them, and to restore them to you if I fall.

We officers go about as usual without arms, but we do wear our swords as usual when on duty. As you know I am armed in the house, and my revolver might save our lives as there are five bullets in it. What I fear is, that should they fire our house, then escape would be impossible.

The rest of the letter is written on the inner flap of the envelope:

Adieu, our affectionate love to dear Cissy. This is her birthday and we wish her many happy returns of the day.
Believe me, affectionately yours,
Archie Wood

This somewhat panicky letter from Archie can have done nothing to reassure or comfort poor Mrs Blane in Bath, but Minnie's next letter shows a commendable calm and acceptance of events.

2 June, from Jhelum

My dearest Mama,

We are, thank God, still alive and quiet in our little station, but the fearful accounts which reach us daily of the atrocities committed by these barbarians keep us in a state of the greatest anxiety.

My beloved husband is away on Treasure escort, that is travelling with the money that is used for paying the troops, a hazardous duty in these days. Poor fellow, he feels much at leaving me and my babe at such a time of trouble. Our Colonel and his wife, the Gerrards, are most kind and wished me to stay with them during his absence, but I do not like leaving our house to servants at this time, so I just spend each day with them and come back for the night.

The Colonel has allowed me a guard of Sepoys to be constantly on our premises so now I have no fear of anything being stolen, as I do not think the men of the 14th would allow any ill to befall any of us. At present all is going on well, and we hope to hear of the reduction of Delhi in the next day or two.

I have just been told that our corps marched off from Jullundur with all their arms, and last evening at Peshawar 150 mutineers were blown away by artillery. This is the kind of punishment due to such brutes for they are nothing else.

We have not yet had your letters by the steamer of April 29th. These wretches have stopped all traffic so the letters are detained in Agra until the road is cleared. This is yet another trial, as one longs to hear from one's relatives.

I am suffering from terrible boils and can wear neither shoes nor stockings, and little Sonny has caught them from me. Nevertheless he is thriving nicely, and becomes more precious to us each day. I wish sincerely he was safe with you instead of out here. How you would love his sweet little face, and he has such pretty attitudes that I sit for hours looking at him.

It is now next day, June 3rd, and I have just arrived at the Colonel's and heard the startling intelligence that Goolab Singh in Kashmir has collected 10,000 men and is coming down on Jhelum. Consequently all the ladies and children are to be packed off to Rawalpindi, and we are to have everything in readiness to start at a moment's notice. Dearest Mama, I am almost beside myself. My husband away, and I have to superintend everything, and that while I cannot speak fluently, and while I am not at all well, and with my little one to take care of.

Pray for us all, dearest Mama. God knows if we shall be spared by these wretches. If we had the money we, baby and I, would be in England in a very short time, for Archie says he will take us home as soon as he can. Several of our officers' wives are going home sharp, as they do not like being exposed to monsters, and yet we hear the roads are not safe to travel on. Oh, what is the best to do?

How are you all? I have just received a parcel containing papers and a London Journal. They started from Bath on the 30th March, that is over two months ago, which is not too bad.

I cannot write more as the mail is going out. I trust my news will be better next time.

With my most fond love and many kisses,

Ever your most affectionate child,

Minnie Wood

P.S. I am off tomorrow night at ten o'clock as the Chief Commissioner has telegraphed to say all ladies must leave immediately, or they will run great risks. Consequently I am very busy. I shall travel in my little carriage drawn by bearers, three camels with luggage, and two Banghy budars, that is a pole carried on the shoulders of the bearers with goods attached to it. What servants will agree to go with me I shall take, but no furniture, not even a chair. Shall we lose all our belongings?

Jhelum again! 18 June

My last letter to you, my darling Mama, was written when on the point of leaving for Rawalpindi. Well, thanks be, I am back again after only a few days to please some old croaker here, who advised the ladies should be sent away he said, just to hasten us, that he was sure the 14th would mutiny. I shall advise him to pay the expenses of our trip, for it has amounted to 200 rupees. I could cry to think of our having thrown away so much just to please him. Heaven knows we have enough to do with our money without scampering about this wretched country in the hottest month of the year, under a broiling sun, for a pack of rumours. It really is abominable.

Well, now for our travels. I and my baby and ayah, and the Sirdar bearer, started at 8 o'clock in our little carriage drawn by twelve bearers, and five men to carry my traps on the evening of the 10th June. We travelled all night, as the heat is too intense in the daytime. The road was frightful, up and down hills all the way, in some places almost perpendicular, and in other places on the brink of the most horrible precipices with only a foot or two between yourself and destruction. But these bearers are as sure footed as mules, and really I was not much alarmed.

By six next morning I was within ten miles of my darling husband who was encamped at a place called Googir Bhan, where I was also to halt at the bungalow for travellers until the evening.

Imagine my horror on arriving at this place where my relay of bearers ought to have been waiting, to find not a single man to take me on to Googir. I was in a pretty fix, for the men who were with me refused to take me a step further. This nearly set my brain on fire, and I had the prospect of spending many hours waiting if no one came to my assistance, which was not likely, seeing I was miles in the jungle from any human being.

However, after remaining one hour and a half, persuading these black brutes to take me on, and after promising to give them baksheesh (a present), they dragged me on, but had it not been that dear Archie sent out fresh men to meet me, I think I should never have arrived.

Oh, the delight of a cup of tea when I reached his tent! I was feeling dreadfully knocked up with the heat, which I can assure you was something frightful, the thermometer being at 120 in the tent, and my dear baby suffering from a bowel complaint as well as the heat. You people in England have no conception what an Indian summer is, and fancy our having to leave our comfortable house with Punkahs, tatties and a Thermandidote, all able to battle with hot winds and dust storms. I did not remain with Archie but went on to 'Pindi where a Mr and Mrs Brown kindly took me and mine in until our movements were decided.

Later I took half a house with our Doctor Cole's wife, and of course in *three days time* I was ordered back to Jhelum again! And here we are, safe and sound, thank God, and our regiment is behaving admirably. I sincerely hope nothing may go wrong here, but we cannot now say what a day may bring forth.

It has been discovered that letters were sent to every regiment from Calcutta to Peshawar desiring that on the 1st of June they should rise en masse and murder every European in this country. How we have been preserved I know not. Matters are getting worse and worse. Three more massacres have just taken place, one at Bareilly, Saharanpore, and Morabad in Rohilkand, and we have just received intelligence that Lucknow, the capital of Oude is burned to the ground. Mr and Mrs Martin are there, also the Reverend Polehampton, who officiated at our wedding. I really dread looking at the papers. The atrocities are awful at Delhi and Meerut, poor little infants and children were thrown into the air and received back on spears, and ladies first had their clothes set on fire, their breasts cut off and then hewed in pieces. Can anything be more dreadful, more revolting?

I feel very sad when I see my pretty little baby to think of what his fate might be.

Here Archie's writing begins

Yes, my dear Mrs Blane, we Christians in India that will survive this gigantic mutiny and be so fortunate as to reach England in safety will indeed, and ought to be, most thankful to Almighty God for his aid and protection. I verily believe this has been, and is, a religious panic amongst our soldiery, for the mutineers cruelly and barbarously murder women and babies. The last massacre was at Saharanpore on a Sunday, where they murdered all the European Officers, wives, etc., in church! Is this not most barbarous!

The whole of India is now up. Sepoy regiments from Calcutta to Pershawar are in open mutiny and no regiment is safe. My own regiment is loyal, but what faith can we British officers now place in our Sepoys after all the atrocities that other Sepoy regiments have committed?

I often feel ill from over anxiety about my beloved wife and babe. Sleepless nights. I wake up suddenly and imagine I hear that our pretty little cantonment is fired, and any noise makes me grasp my pistol expecting these blood-thirsty mutineers are approaching our house. Were I alone I should not care what becomes of me, but my darling wife and sweet babe, to think what they might suffer at the hands of these butchers! I should like to send my wife and child to England as soon as possible and to leave this cursed land.

India and the Bengal Army will require at least 30 European

regiments to keep the country quiet, and I shall endeavour to get exchanged into one of them. I suspect the Queen will hereafter govern India, so adieu to the old Gentlemen of Leadenhall Street and the Court of Directors who will be shut up.

This unexpected mutiny in this country will indeed startle Her Majesty's Ministers, and indeed the whole of Europe. If England does not send out troops quickly and *overland*, we shall be having the Russians and French landing on our shoes. India is a *gem* worth keeping.

Get a commission for your son Willie in Her Majesty's Army, and let him come out to India if he wishes, for there will be a great reform in the army out here, and not before it was needed. There are too many old men in high places, the promotion by seniority does nothing to counteract this stultifying method.

Minnie is behaving like a soldier's wife. She does not fear much. 'Tis impossible not to think about the danger we are in. We may be murdered any day, perhaps by our own regiment. 'Tis very hard, for we are all alone here, not a European soldier with us, only the Sepoy regiments protecting cantonments, the town, and the bridge of boats. We cannot trust any Sepoy after the brutal and sudden attacks on officers. We hear that one regiment supposed to be loyal asked their officers to send for their wives and children from the hills, as they, the Sepoys, would protect them all. The following Sunday the men of that very regiment murdered all their officers and their families, and every Christian native in church. How truly dreadful, so how can one trust anyone?

The Civil authorities here anticipated danger, so all ladies, children and Sergeants' wives were ordered to leave Jhelum for Rawalpindi some 70 miles towards Peshawar and the frontier. I had left the headquarters of my regiment previous to this order on Detachment duty with 200 Sepoys and the Treasure. I was the first British officer that escorted the Treasure since the mutiny broke out. *I ought to be rewarded for it.* I can tell you I never expected to reach Rawalpindi alive. Imagine one British officer alone with 200 Sepoys escorting Treasure! My brother officers took leave of me with sadness, I thought. I had only a minute's notice, and I was off, leaving my darling wife and babe all alone. I know not how I parted with Minnie. I felt heart broken, but at the same time I did not allow duty to be interfered with by private family feelings. No. I took leave of her and our sweet babe, and I confess a tear fell on my babe's little face, for I feared it might be my last look.

However, the men behaved admirably. I expected an attack one night from a party of Goolab Singh's soldiers, and I took precautions, loaded every musket, and formed a little camp round my treasure (the money). The heat was intense during the day, the thermometer about 120 or 130.

I was thanked by the General and Sir John Lawrence for this duty.

I know not when officers will be allowed to visit England. You will, I know, always give your daughter and grandson a home.

I should like to get £1,500 from my regiment and my commission and return to get some appointment in England.

Goodbye and affectionate love to dear Cissy. I am most affectionately to yourself, ever
Your affectionate son and daughter,
Archie and Minnie

By the beginning of July over fifty places had felt the fury of the mutineers in varying degrees of severity. Cantonments and houses were looted and burnt, men, women and children were murdered; and heroic efforts were made to stem the bloody tide. Delicate British women and their children had fled into the jungle for refuge, their crinolines discarded, their skirts torn up for bandages. There were cases of superb loyalty by native servants, cases of black treachery, and murder on a scale never dreamed of by sane men, as blood lust and crowd hysteria went out of all control.

Many British perished in the jungle; some got through after nightmare journeys to reach the safety of a fort such as Agra. Cawnpore had fallen with appalling loss of life, and Lucknow, with its 1,600 defenders and some 600 civilians, largely women and children, was holding out against tremendous odds, thanks to the forethought and preparation of its brilliant commander, Sir Henry Lawrence.

British regiments were slogging up in the heat from the south, making forced marches, decimated by cholera and heat stroke, their progress too slow for any immediate assistance to be given to those in such desperate need of help. Sepoys in regiment after regiment mutinied, or at least deserted, and still the officers of the 14th Native Infantry in Jhelum had some confidence in their men.

A letter came to hand at this time from Dr Kirk in Gwalior which shows the blind trust – or blind eyes – which the British had even after the outbreak at Meerut.

He writes:

On the 10th May three corps at Meerut became mutinous, killed most of their officers, and rushed over to Delhi where they took the place. The regiments there joined the mutineers and all was at an end. Our European soldiers were rushed from various points, and will meet the insurgents today, when they will catch it, and not one will escape. Some of our Gwalior troops leave this morning to intercept the escape of the mutineers, who are already fighting among themselves, and summary justice has been dealt out to many who have been caught.

The occupation of Oude is, I believe, the cause of this trouble. There was much black villainy carried on there over the poorer people, which is now prohibited, and thousands of scoundrels there would now do anything to injure us, and have the old system restored.

This outburst, once over, they will be done for for ever. At Agra and here we are *perfectly* safe, and a few weeks hence will find those wretches totally defeated.

Dr Kirk's complacency was unfounded as a later letter shows; the story of the Jhelum rebellion is told in Archie's next letter:

Jhelum, 12 July 1857

My dear Mrs Blane,

My regiment is *no more*. It *mutinied* on the 7th inst. A detachment of European Infantry and Artillery with three guns were sent here to disarm it. My wife, babe and self have *escaped*! The Almighty saved us.

I was on duty as Captain of the week, and did not attend the parade on that dreadful morning. About half an hour after gunfire at daybreak, I received a note from the Commanding Officer, Colonel Gerrard, to take my wife and infant to Major Brown's, the Commissioner, as there was danger. I was in bed, my wife fast asleep. I awoke her, got her up, but before she was out of our bedroom we heard shots fired. The carriage had to be got ready. We had barely time to put on our clothes. My wife and babe got in the carriage, and I drove, aye, galloped the horses furiously through the centre of cantonments, the battle going on at our left, and we arrived at the Commissioner's house in safety.

The regiment refused to give up its arms and fired upon the European officers on parade. The Colonel told them that the Horse Artillery had come during the night, and were in front to disarm them. He begged them to lay down their arms, but no, the whole regiment commenced loading their muskets, fired at their officers and at the Artillery in front, then rushed from the parade ground to their lines. Then the battle commenced.

It raged from daybreak until dark, for sixteen hours. I joined the officers of the regiment as soon as my wife and babe were in safety. I took the ladies of the regiment, the wife of the Colonel, of the Doctor, and my Minnie and sweet babe, in all three ladies and six children, from Major Brown's house to a village a mile further on, away from the scene of the strife, and soon after I left them to take my share of the dangers. I did not see Minnie until the following morning.

It was a terrible day. We were exposed to bullets and the blazing sun for fourteen hours. I know not how I escaped. I picked up five balls which fell around me. I was the whole day under fire. The British regiment which had arrived made the most determined resistance. They disputed every inch of ground in our lines, also in the empty lines of the 39th regiment, then the mutineers fled over to a village near our house, where they made a desperate stand.

There the bullets fell thick and a great many of our Horse Artillery fell. The fire was so destructive that we were obliged to leave a Howitzer and our poor wounded and dead. I was close to the Artillery with a body of Irregular Horse, and seeing many horses and men falling around me, I retired to the left flank towards the river, out of musket range.

The battle raged for sixteen hours. We had twenty five Europeans killed and some sixty five wounded, several since dead – one British officer killed, Captain Spring, H.M.'s 24th Foot. Lieutenant Streatfeild, 24th Foot, had his leg amputated. Lieutenant Chichester and Colonel Ellice were wounded.

The Colonel knew the regiment was to be disbanded and the troops coming, but did not tell me of it. Had he done so I would have picked up some valuables and removed my wife and infant *in safety* and good time to Major Brown's about three miles away. As it was we might have been killed during that last-minute headlong drive through Jhelum cantonments.

We killed some 150 mutineers of the regiment in our lines. We have blown away from guns, and shot by musketry about fifty six. Some 150 are coming in as deserters, seized by the Rajah Goolab Singh of Cashmere.

The regiment made a most obstinate stand. They would not come out into the open to fight us, but were hidden behind walls and in Guard Houses. It was a terrible day, and I am most thankful to have escaped, for I was under fire the whole day, and was in my saddle for twenty-four hours with no food.

Minnie and baby are both well considering the great heat. I have already lost some £50 by this horrid mutiny, for no officers have been paid since the outbreak, and when we shall be paid I know not.

God bless you all. No more time to write as the mail goes off soon, but I will tell you more of these terrible days in my next.

Yours affectionately,
A. O. Wood

Jhelum, July

My dear Mrs Blane,

I can now tell you more about these terrible days. I send you a rough sketch of the Jhelum cantonments, and further particulars of the battle with the mutineers of my regiment. You will see in my drawing below that my house is quite isolated on the left flank, and that I had to drive my wife and infant to Major Brown's house through the entire length of the cantonment, about a mile in length and with 600 mutineers with their muskets loaded and in open rebellion 200 yards off the road. The complete journey was about two and a half miles long.

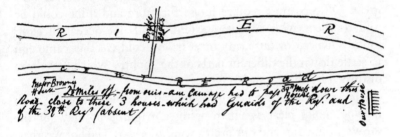

Our carriage had to pass down the Centre Road close to those houses which had guards of the regiment. As I was driving, our Artillery guns, which were then in position, opened out on to our lines. Some cannon balls came tearing through near us, and went into the river, and we might have been killed by any of them. I look upon the escape of my family and myself as most providential.

As you can see, my dear Mrs Blane, your daughter and the infant had the most narrow escape. Had I known my regiment was going to be disarmed on the 7th of July, I might have endeavoured to have driven out of the cantonments, and the chances are that our party would have been murdered, for we hear now that the 14th mutineers had pickets out on the high road on the lookout for the European detachment, and they would have attempted to kill every European residing in cantonments, and would have certainly stopped every carriage coming out. We hear that the rising was premature, as it was planned for the regiment to rise on the 15th July, when they intended to murder every one of us, children and all.

I want to get my wife and child out of this country. Jhelum is favourable to travellers as in five days a boat could get down the river to Multan, from where steamers go down to Kurrachee on the sea coast, thence Bombay is only four days' steam away, and there a ship to Europe. I could remit £100 a year to her from my pay and pay her travelling expenses out of what I could sell, some £300.

Jhelum will eventually become a *large* military station. A European regiment will certainly be located here, perhaps two. The climate is pretty good, and the advantage of the river very great. Officers must require house furniture and mine could be sold to them with advantage. This could not occur till eight months hence, for our army must have a cold weather campaign to settle down the different parts of the country which have been disturbed by these murderers.

The cold season up here is delightful for seven months, with bracing, cold, clear weather, with a magnificent view of the snowy mountains and our pretty winding river. The hot weather, as you know, is very trying.

We hear glad tidings of the arrival in Calcutta of some twelve European regiments, who are being pushed up country to the relief of Delhi and the other stations. You will read with horror of the heart-rending savage murders and atrocities committed on Europeans all over India. Some unheard of barbarous acts as burning children in closed boxes, cutting into mince meat a father, and forcing the pieces down the throats of his children. Is this not terrible, and we hear on *good authority* that it is so.

Many stations through central India have been destroyed, cantonments burnt, and all Christians put to the sword or worse. All the public records have been destroyed. Cawnpore is entirely ruined, and Sir Hugh Wheeler, the General commanding the Division, killed with nearly every officer there. We hear there was treachery. The force finally gave itself up as it could do no more. An influential native swore on the Holy Ganges, the most binding of Hindoo oaths, to protect their lives, and those of the wretched women and children, if the officer in charge would trust him. This he did.

The unfortunate sufferers were put into boats according to the wording of the Treaty, so as to go down river to safety, but, when they had reached the middle of the stream, the fiend gave a prearranged signal, and guns which had been laid for the purpose were opened upon the frail thatched boats from the Cawnpore bank. They sank, they blazed, and as our helpless countrymen tried to escape by wading or swimming to the opposite bank, they found that arrangements had been made for their reception. They were cut to pieces by Cavalry ready for that purpose.

Retribution must come, aye, that day will dawn soon when the murderers will not escape us Englishmen, and then there will be such bloodshed in this land as will never be forgotten. Our women and children must be avenged, as well as our brave men.

To return to the events of July 7th. It is only as time goes by that one gets a complete picture of that dreadful day.

The mutineers assembled at our Regimental Main Guard, and they fought desperately from behind walls and in houses and huts, never in the open. Our European men had to go right to the walls of this Main Guard which was loopholed, and so faced a murderous fire. Colonel Ellice had his horse killed under him, and he himself was dangerously wounded through the neck and legs.

It was a hard day's work for all of us, but especially for the European detachment who had marched up here all the previous night, and then fought all day without food or rest. We had no more than 200 men in the battle, and only half a troop of Horse Artillery with but three guns.

I often had to turn my face on either side to escape being hit straight in the face. I was acting A.D.C. and was in my saddle for 26 hours.

Once I was ordered to charge a part of the village on the right, with a detachment of Irregular Cavalry, when lo! a sharp rattle of musketry came into us and caused some empty saddles, and I was left alone and potted at as well! But they bolted out of range. I was laughing so I forgot I was too near the enemy for safety, until the bullets made my charger plunge violently, and then bolt away towards the Horse Artillery on the left. Not one of the 14th officers were killed, though Captain Fullerton's charger was wounded. How the Colonel, the Adjutant, and young Gurning escaped I know not, as they were fired at murderously on the Parade Ground by the mutineers.

I enclose, dear Mrs Blane, an eye-witness account of the affair in Jhelum, which I think is a better account than my disjointed attempt. There is an excellent map of the field of battle at the end of it.

My dearest Mrs Blane, that we may all meet again is my constant prayer.

Your affectionate,
A. O. Wood

A Short Account of the Mutiny at Jhelum by an Eye-witness

At daybreak on 7 July 1857, the 14th were ordered to parade and did so; then the Colonel informed them as a precautionary measure their arms were to be taken from them. He was answered by the discharge of musketry, and the officers made the best of their way towards a small force of Europeans who were then entering the cantonments, having marched all night to reach us.

Some Cavalry with this force, on hearing the fire, charged the Native Infantry and pursued them into their lines. The Artillery then unlimbered and fired grape into the lines, but with little effect as the distance was great and all the mutinous Sepoys behind mud walls. Over 200 Europeans then came up and entered the lines at the east end. The Sepoys disputed every inch of ground and fought obstinately and well.

Then the Quarter Guard was taken in charge by Colonel Ellice with a few Europeans. On entering he received a ball in his neck, and one in his left leg which killed his horse. Shortly after this the Artillery blew up the magazine, when the mutineers vacated their lines and made for the village of Seels, where they again made a stand, and a determined one. Here our guns went close up, but, having continued to pour in heavy fire all day, expended all their ammunition. The fire from the enemy was heavy, and as our horses were quite unable to move, we had to abandon one gun, which the mutineers seized and which we afterwards recovered.

The mutineers fought till nightfall, when our men were withdrawn from the village, and at daylight it was discovered that the enemy had vacated it. They were pursued and followed up, and driven across the river at a spot which, being in the Cashmere Rajah's territory, we could not enter, but made the wretches over to him. There were originally about 600 men of this 14th Regiment, but it is supposed now that not more than 120 or 130 are in existence.

The official account of Jhelum's mutiny, as recorded by Kaye and Mallison in their *History of the Indian Mutiny*, differs in several ways from that of Archie and the 'eye-witness'.

Sir John Lawrence, brother of Sir Henry, was Chief Commissioner of the Punjab, and held the district comparatively quiet. He regarded the loyalty of the 14th Native Infantry at Jhelum with less complacency than did Archie and Colonel Gerrard, so he sent troops to disarm the 14th, with orders that it was to be done under strict secrecy and as a complete surprise.

However, Colonel Gerrard thought that he knew his troops better than did a Civil Commissioner, and he made plans of his own. It was no surprise to the sepoys when British Infantry, Artillery and Horse were seen approaching the morning parade. The sepoys loaded their muskets and, disregarding their officers' frantic commands, broke ranks and took up a strong position in the Quarter Guard and their own barracks.

The battle was on.

The sepoys had the cover of walls, and loopholes for their rifles to take a deadly harvest; but the British made a fierce attack and eventually the mutineers were driven back to a nearby village.

The British rested for the worst of the heat of the day, and attacked again at four o'clock. The insurgents were well entrenched in the village, and the troops found themselves cramped and caught in the narrow streets. They had to retreat, leaving a gun which was turned on to their rear-guard. Nothing more could be done that night except count the casualties, which numbered twenty-five killed and over sixty wounded, and 150 corpses of mutineers lay about the cantonment and the village.

An attack was planned for the morning, but when dawn broke the mutineers had disappeared.

The commissioner, ever outspoken, was furious, and commented that British Horse, Foot and Artillery had been beaten by a regiment of disorganized sepoys because his plan had not been adhered to. Had the 14th been quietly surrounded they could have been disarmed without trouble.

This account does not altogether tally with that of the 'eye-witness', nor with Archie's somewhat melodramatic letter to Mrs Blane; but it is interesting to note that Colonel Gerrard had given his officers no information about the approaching troops, no doubt trusting to his own plans and his conviction that his regiment would never revolt.

Minnie's next letter gives more details from a different angle:

Jhelum, 22 July

My dearest Mama,

We are the only people left in this station now besides Doctor Cole and his wife, and I know not from one day to another what will become of us. Arthur Roberts, kind as usual, is anxious that I and my dear baby shall reside with him at Lahore, but my husband could not accompany me, so it is out of the question, as I have not the nerve to travel alone at night in these dreadful days. Yet, dear Mama, we have much, very much, to be thankful for in having escaped in the late outbreak here. It was miraculous.

I was nursing my sweet son in bed when the firing commenced, and had only time to slip on the skirt of a muslin dress, the body of another, and rush barefooted into the carriage. Oh, Mama, you can little know how fearful it is to feel at any moment you may be murdered in the most cruel and bloody manner. I thought of you all at home, and prayed we might meet in Heaven, for I never expected to live, and indeed it was only through the mercy of God we were permitted to survive.

Even as our little carriage *flew* through cantonments, the guns of the Artillery under Lieutenant Cooke opened out, and *boom* they went, carrying death at every sound. It was awful. I shall never recover from the terror, aye, worse than terror I endured that dreadful morning. It was worse than any battle, everyone says. We ladies were all sent to the Deputy Commissioner's house in the Civil lines, and then to a village a mile further on, where we had to remain until twelve in the boiling sun. I was almost naked, for I was obliged to take off my chemise to put on baby, who was dreadfully wet, and I had no napkins, in fact *nothing* with me. It has been dreadful work. Even now matters look anything but cheerful, and until Delhi falls things will be no better.

Every day we hear of some fresh mutiny or massacre. It certainly is a most fearful time for us all. The Punjabis and Sikhs are staunch, if there is such a thing among blacks. Strange that the very people against whom we fought only a few years back are those to whom we now look for protection. We have a guard of Sikhs always, fine strong young men, more like us in their habits, drinking spirits, etc., and eating meat. Indeed, they found a bottle of *Eau de Cologne* and drank it! I like them and their appearance is frank and open.

You can't think how miserable and deserted this station is. I can hardly believe that in the space of a few hours it could become so changed. The day I returned it resembled a charnel house, and the stench was awful, as many bodies were still lying about the lines, and in this great heat decay is rapid.

I do not think there can be many of our mutinous men left. Numbers are being shot, and blown away from the guns whenever they are brought in. A terrible death, if instantaneous, but one that the Sepoy on religious grounds dreads more than any other. It is an awful thing to hear the volleys of musketry, and to know that human life is being taken.

The other day twenty men were blown from guns here in the lines. They are tied by threes with their backs to the mouth of the cannon, and then the word is given. Unfortunately we were taking our drive that evening and came upon them all on their way to the lines. It certainly sent a shiver of horror through me when I thought of them being so fearfully deprived of life, but they deserve it richly, for they have taken others' lives, and had I not escaped that morning from my house, they would have killed me.

I have a cannon ball which fell at Archie's feet the day of the battle.

I know you will be sorry to hear that since my confinement I have been very unwell, indeed at one time it was proposed to send me to the Hills for a change, but I am thankful to say I have managed to do without that, as it would have put us to great expense. It has been 'piles', but now I hope I have got over the worst, but the agony I have endured during the last three months has been intense.

Thank you for all the papers you send, and I have just today received Cissy's letter of June 1st. I should so much like to bring my dear baby to England. You, dearest Mama, can easily imagine what a dreadful fear I have, for after all the atrocities committed on women and infants, my mind is never quiet. Just at the least sound I am on the alert, and this state of anxiety is very trying, besides which my dear husband knows not from one moment to another where he will be ordered, for orders and counter-orders are continually coming in. He is supposed to be here now until after the trial of a hundred of our men who have been caught in Goolab Singh territory, that is Cashmere. They are expected daily, of course only to meet the same dreadful fate as their companions.

I send by this mail some more scraps of newspapers, which you will find interesting, one written by Mr Roberts. You would be so charmed with him. I should like very much to be with him in Lahore as I would be taken good care of, but it is utterly impossible that baby and I should travel.

One has to put up with so much now from one's servants.

They are most insolent, and think nothing of telling you that soon we shall all be in the service of the King of Delhi. One of our kitmaghars left us saying he was going to enter the service of his King where he would get much better pay. I doubt it, and he may well be caught and treated as a Sepoy.

Please will you send me in your next letter five yards of two or three kinds of lace to trim my little boy's caps with, as in the winter he will wear them. Also could you give me some idea of what warm dresses are made of for children of his age, and some paper patterns as my Dirzee is a very good workman and can make anything. Should you have any braid patterns for little dresses I should be much obliged if you would let me have some, and a pattern of children's leggings. I cannot procure a thing here as all shops are closed.

It is most awfully warm here, though we are rejoicing that the weather is cooler, the thermometer at only 98!

Now I must mention the other subject which is worrying me, in fact on top of the mutiny and its horrors, it is almost the last straw that could break me.

The matter of Archie's debts. I was quite innocent that such a debt existed until a letter arrived from one of the securities begging that he would pay. The facts have caused much unpleasantness between us. That my husband has acted wrongly I freely admit, and when he first proposed asking your assistance I would not hear of it, knowing how hard pressed you are for money since the death of poor dear Papa. I have been really angry with him, and he had no business to bring things out from England knowing how badly off he was, and then expect others to pay his debts for him.

By a letter we have just received from William Wood, his brother, we have heard that you have taken the matter of this Bombay debt in hand, and that everything is to be settled by the 10th of this month. I need hardly tell you how immeasurably grateful I am to you for doing this and overlooking Archie's conduct. It has been a sore subject between us for weeks. I know his character well now, and for all our sakes you must *insist* that the measures he proposes by which to repay you will be carried out. This I beg you to do, otherwise he will spend all his pay.

I have been most careful of all money I have had given to me, and managed to save about 120 rupees (£12), but alas these mutineers have carried it all off, as they have so much else from our house, and I feel quite disheartened at this, my first effort, to be economical. We have lost upwards of 300 rupees in these troubles, and this is a very large sum to lose in these days when we are not stationary two days together, and in our present financial circumstances, and with no pay coming to us at all.

God bless you, my dearest Mama. I wonder whether I shall ever see England and you all again. I must close this as it is time for my evening drive. Archie intends writing to you by this mail. Ever with my fondest and best love, and a kiss from my little baby who is a very great crower.

Your fondly attached daughter,

Minnie Wood

P.S. Baby has dark eyes like you and the boys. He has a dear little face and is just beginning to take great notice, and laughs and crows with us, bless him!

No letters survive from Minnie written during the next month, which is not surprising, considering the state of India at that time. It is unlikely that anything she wrote ever left the country, as communications were chaotic, with marauding bands looting and attacking everywhere and everything.

Delhi was still under siege, the British battering at the walls, awaiting stronger reinforcements. Sir Henry Lawrence had been killed by a stray shell in Lucknow, depriving the British of one of their finest soldiers, and of a far-seeing man, years ahead of his time who, had he been spared, might have done much to rebuild peace in India on a surer foundation than was finally done. Lucknow was still under siege, and General Havelock's advancing column still far off. But in spite of the continuing trouble, the tide had begun to turn; and as the British rallied from the first shock and troops poured into India from wherever they could be obtained – from Persia, Ceylon, England and even intercepted on their way to China – the end of the uprising could be hoped for before long.

It all took time. Transport was slow, the Suez Canal not yet open, communications most unreliable and the climate at its most furnace-like, with the country later in the grip of the wet monsoon. In previous years the British had never fought at that time of year. In 1857 they were forced to do so.

Communications were very difficult: places only a few miles apart were cut off from each other, scant items of news getting through only by runners travelling secretly through the night Rumours flew, often without a grain of truth in them, but some letters showed the facts with accuracy and calm.

A letter written by Mrs Kirk, wife of the so-optimistic doctor at Gwalior, a place, as Lucknow, some 500 miles to the south of Jhelum, is an example of incredible courage against peril and tragedy. She tells her story very simply, without any heroics. The letter is dated 19 June:

You must know for a fortnight previous many things occurred to create distrust in the minds of all, but the Commanding officers, who were supposed to know best, would not allow that there was any danger to apprehend. On that very day, the unhappy 14th June, my dearest Kirk had asked one of them if arrangements had been made for the safety of the ladies in case of an outbreak. The answer he got was, 'Such a thing need not be thought of. There are always a few discontented men in any regiment, but what of that?' Another answered him that he was certain he had some men so faithful in his battery they would tell him if there was danger at hand. Both of these poor officers were shot on their parade ground that day by their own men, as well as two other officers, all men of kind dispositions and against whom there was not a single grievance.

Brigadier Ramsay and several others escaped, their houses being on the banks of the river, which they crossed to safety, but even so met difficulty and danger.

We, unfortunately, lived further back, and no sooner than the alarm was given that the troops had mutinied, than the roads were closed against us by parties of armed men in all directions. We had not left our own house in minutes when a servant was told if he entered it to get our things he would be shot.

Such was the state of things at 10 o'clock that night, and after remaining in the garden some time we concealed ourselves in an outhouse, where we were discovered in the morning, when, after plundering all the houses and then setting fire to them, they searched the grounds for Europeans.

The instant I found we were detected I walked boldly out with my little Aleck, poor mite but four years of age, in the hope they would not discover my beloved husband. They pulled me towards them and demanded my rings, bruising my arms. I said, 'Let me go and I will give them to you.' Even my wedding ring was taken from me.

At this moment to my horror my dearest Kirk rushed out before at least twenty-five armed ruffians with but a walking stick in his hand. A volley was fired on him by those cowards, and he fell, never to rise again. Poor fellow, it was an instant death, not a moan or symptom of pain was evident, thank God.

This most awful scene took place close to my side. I begged of them to shoot me too. 'No,' a wretch replied, 'we have killed you already,' pointing to my darling on the ground. I dared not touch him fearing they would ill-use his precious body if I did. I stood transfixed to the spot, and would not have left it regardless of the consequences, but for poor little Aleck who stood screaming at my side.

I was then taken to a hut where three other ladies were. Three more joined afterwards. They, the rebels, surrounded the place, insulted us with their language but did not touch our persons. Some men were better than others, and defended us as well as they could, and put us all into one carriage with a few Sepoys to see us safe out of the station. On the fourth day we reached Agra after encountering all manner of hardship and peril.

I was in too great grief to care for evils of that nature. I had no happiness to look for at the end of the journey. The world had lost all interest to me, and I lived, but that was all.

On the road I had fever, and also on my arrival here, Agra, but I have not wanted for kind friends and the very best of attention.

Victorian women are often referred to as weak, silly and given to vapours. In fact they were one of the toughest generations ever, and in India they showed the most incredible endurance, bravery and devotion.

One would have liked to hear Minnie's comments on this account, but no letter exists.

In the midst of all this drama the problem of Archie's debts looms larger, adding another worry to her already heavy load, as she tells in her next letter:

Jhelum, 24 August

Dearest Mama,

Yesterday we received the joint letters of yourself and Cissy written on July 7th. Our mutiny took place on that date. Little did you think as you were writing that at that time we did not know from one moment to the next, what would happen to us.

I am not surprised to hear of the non-arrival of our letters, but we have never missed writing by every mail. Perhaps they will turn up one day. Letters are taking twenty days from Bombay to here, which is almost as long as coming from England to Bombay overland. And now the rains being at their height, the roads are sometimes impassable, which makes more delay.

I have had a terrible abscess in my right ear. I had hardly recovered from that when I was attacked by the regular Indian complaint, fever and ague. After the three alternate days it left me, but so weak that I fainted from the exertion of moving from one room to another. I am obliged to take heaps of quinine to prevent another attack, which of course flies to my ear and sends me nearly crazy with pain. Doctor Cole is a perfect fool and knows nothing of his profession, and he is the only so called medical man here.

This is very distressing as dear Sonny is far from well. His two upper front teeth are beginning to teaze him, and I have no one to whom I can go for advice. I wish I could get letters from you sooner, as it would be such a comfort to hear what you suggest, and I feel so very nervous about my darling.

Oh, Mama, he has such beautiful eyes, jet black, and makes the most charming little noises as he struggles to speak in his own way. Our night's rest is far from peaceful. The little man makes a dreadful noise, and cries and cries, and nothing will do but walking up and down the room with him until we are utterly tired. He generally sleeps on his stomach, and kicks and amuses himself by the hour in that position.

He has this very moment been brought to me by Ruggio, the ayah, and is lying on the sofa by me, crowing and amusing himself, and looking so sweet, whilst the ayah takes him for a little ride round the room on the sofa, which for a wonder out here has castors. He has an immense liking for his toes, which he is now trying to put into his mouth. Oh, how I wish you could see him!

Now, dear Mama, let me assure you that we have had a lesson about debts which will never be forgotten, indeed I have suffered more than I can express on this subject. Now I have a child I have much to think about. Now he is no expense, but, oh, how we are ever to educate him and bring him up, I do not know. Had it not been for this mutiny we should have done very well indeed, but, alas, not only have we lost a large sum of money, looted on that dreadful day, but our pay is *all stopped* for three months! How do they expect us to live and not to be forced to borrow money?

I have been fortunate enough to dispose of an outfit at a good price (things that are now too small for me), but in *one* hour every rupee we had went, carried off by those brutes. I cannot remember if I told you that our drawers and boxes were forced open by the villains' bayonets, and then ransacked for money. All was carried off.

It is hard on one now, but I trust there is a brighter future for us. We will not fail to send you the money. I think it will be better to send you 200 rupees at a time. I promise faithfully to attend to all you have said, indeed I know the necessity of it.

You and Cissy both appear to look upon these mutinies in a very cool manner. You people in dear, quiet England, have no conception of what it is like to be out here, in hourly dread of meeting some cruel death. The accounts we hear get worse daily. At Jhansi the gentlemen were tied in a row, and their heads taken off. The ladies and children were then obliged to see them taken up by the legs and torn asunder, and after, the ladies and children were all barbarously murdered. It makes my blood boil to hear of such atrocities. Surely you and Cissy must now realize what a precarious position we are in. It is all very fine sitting quietly in one's drawing room reading about these Indian mutinies in the *Times*, and quite another thing living out here in the midst of it. Every sound one hears drains the blood out of one, and holds one for two or three minutes enduring terror indescribable. I assure you I cannot endure to hear the guns go off, it makes me so awfully nervous. I have no power over myself, and tremble as if I had ague.

Dear Mama, I cannot write more now. Our most affectionate love to you all, and a very wet kiss from darling little Cecil to dear Grandmother and Aunt Cissy.

Ever your fondly attached child,

Minnie Wood

The next existing letter is written on 16 September in Lahore, where it was quiet, the quick action of the Chief Commissioner in May having saved further trouble by disarming the Sepoys and seizing the fort. The mutiny was rumbling on in outbreaks in other places but the tension in the Punjab was lessening, enabling Minnie to travel to Mr Roberts's house to obtain medical advice, which she sorely needed.

The final assault on Delhi had started and news was coming through of desperate attacks, big losses and the tragic death of General Nicholson, one of the best soldiers ever in India. Lucknow was still besieged and Havelock's column was approaching the battered Residency.

Lahore, 16 September

Only a few lines, my dearest Mama, to tell how I am getting on. My dear little baby is very unwell from fever, but I sincerely trust he may soon get over it. The Doctor here assures me there is no cause for alarm as this month is the most unhealthy of all, being the end of the rains. Every servant of Mr Roberts's has it, and my ayah has just told me she has it. I do not know what to do, as my under-ayah took herself off on the day of the mutiny and has never come back. I find it most difficult to get another like her, for she was one who did not possess what is the greatest nuisance to us in this country, namely husband and children, and consequently she slept in the house at night.

I can hardly move for boils, and you cannot imagine, dear Mama, how much I have suffered through the carelessness of Doctor Cole and the ignorance of the nurse at baby's birth. I have endured agony every day for months. You will understand what I mean when I say what I told was piles was not, but was one ulcer after the other, so dreadful that at times I could not move my legs and had to be carried from my bed. This has been going on for months and at last, in despair, I came down here to Lahore for advice. You can suppose that this has weakened me very much, and it was all caused by my ignorant nurse who pressed so hard upon me just as baby made his appearance, that she injured me to this terrible extent. My new Doctor here knows what he is about, which Doctor Cole did not, and is treating the ulcers with caustic every morning.

Dearest Archie has just sent on your last letter from Jhelum. I need hardly tell you again how distressed I am about the debt, but I am so comforted now you are able to assist us.

Mr de la Tour will do nothing for us and refused point blank to give me the £20 you told him to give me if I required it in Calcutta, and it now takes longer for a letter from here to reach Calcutta than it would to get to England, the country being very disturbed and communication having been cut off. I think we had better go to Australia, where dear Papa had interests, when my husband is able to get his purse [pay]. It will pay the Parsee his debt and leave us enough for our passage there – I can see

nothing else to do. Dear kind Arthur Roberts would assist us if
he could, but he has a wife and eight children in England, which
is a heavy expense, and in his position as Commissioner he is
obliged to keep a certain number of servants and to live in a good
style.

I have to have two ayahs, dearest Mama. Until my baby was
born I had but one, but now I am obliged to keep another as all
his napkins and soiled clothes have to be washed by her before
the Dhobie will touch them, as he would lose caste by touching
anything dirty. This is a dreadful, tiresome country. I enclose a
list of the servants we keep, perhaps large to you, but essential
out here. The punkah coolies are an expense as they must work
day and night, but I hope in another ten days it will be cool
enough to require them no longer.

The news is still terrible. Lucknow besieged and Delhi still in
the hands of the rebels. I trust most sincerely that this mail or the
next will carry the news of the fall of Delhi. They are fighting
desperately hard there, and on this issue depends our lives. It is
well known that if Delhi does not fall completely into our
possession soon, the Hill tribes will rise, and then we shall be
threatened and shall have to run for it. Where?

Goodbye, my dearest Mama. With my most fervent prayer
that we may meet again on earth, believe me, with much love,
Your fondly attached daughter,
Minnie Wood

Archie writes the next letter from Jhelum. He is clearly feeling
the strain of the Mutiny, the separation from Minnie, and the
weight of the debt into which he has run himself. He had chronic
dysentery, and like everyone at that time, was treated for it with
doses of opium. This probably accounts for the weakness in his
character which is more and more apparent from this time.

Jhelum, 30 September

My dear Mrs Blane,
I have received your two letters. The last distressed me greatly,

especially after having been informed that the Bombay debt was to have been settled, and I had informed my two securities of the good news. I had made arrangements to send you a remittance of the interest agreeable to your instructions, but alas! after all this delay, the money has not been advanced to the Bombay Parsee, and interest has mounted since May last when I first wrote to England on the subject. I *cannot* possibly raise so large a sum in this country. As to Mr de la Tour being written to, it would be lost time, for he even refused to advance us the £20 which you kindly placed at our disposal when in Calcutta. So you see, my dear kind Mrs Blane, there is no assistance to be had from him.

Thus I had to procure money elsewhere. 'Tis a most distressing and unfortunate business, and the interest runs up. I know not how to raise the money. I place us entirely in your hands, and do for mercy's sake assist us. I promise faithfully to remit to your bankers quarterly the sum of money you shall name as interest, say £80 a year. If you will not settle this Bombay debt I shall be *ruined*, and lose my prospects in the army. My next promotion, as long as I can transfer into a European regiment, should be worth £3,500, that is, I could sell out of that regiment for that sum. The officers junior to me would gladly pay that for the step up. I entreat you to pay this money for us.

This terrible mutiny alone is most distressing to bear, but this debt hanging round my neck is *more* than I can bear. I pray to God to give me strength to bear up against this calamity. I have placed all in His hands, for my heart is sore afflicted now.

My beloved wife and infant are away from me too. I hear from her daily, but I see her not, and our little boy, who is sick, the joy of my heart, is torn from me, but I do not repine. No. I pray daily to the Almighty to bless and protect them. I have given them both to Him, with fervent prayer to spare their lives and to deliver them from the hands of murderers.

They are at Lahore with Arthur Roberts. It was considered dangerous to have ladies here, and besides Minnie did not like our Doctor Cole and wanted advice for herself and baby. Our little boy kept on suffering and was looking ill and quite yellow, and Doctor Cole kept saying there was nothing the matter with him. He is ignorant, careless, and indifferent.

The new Doctor in Lahore says Sonny's spleen is affected but, thank God, he is much better, also my darling wife. She has suffered terribly from the effects of a bad nurse. How I wish she and her wee son were in England with you all. Minnie talks of joining the Australian Agricultural Company, in which dear Mr Blane was so much interested. I sincerely hope, for your sake, that the new venture there will be favourable for you and your family, and that plenty of gold will be found on the estate. Would that we were there.

We so often talk of dear Bath and the happy days passed there. I frequently think of the dear boy we left at home who was so soon taken from you, poor boy. I see his handsome face before me now with his beautiful black eyes. His departure was indeed very sudden. I was dreadfully shocked when I read Doctor Montgomery's letter. You did all which a kind, indulgent, fond and beloved Mother could do for our dear departed brother, poor lad. God bless and preserve him for ever for Jesus Christ's sake, for are we not led to believe that our prayers for blessing and protection to the Almighty through the mediation of His Son, our Lord and Saviour, He will not refuse us. This is a great consolation to us poor sinners.

Now for news of this terrible mutiny. Delhi was stormed on the 14th of this month, September, and was in our immediate possession on the 21st. The King is our prisoner and two of his sons and one grandson have been killed. A young officer, Lieutenant Hodson of the 1st European Fusiliers, is the fortunate man who took the King prisoner. He is sure to receive honours. I enclose seven cuttings from newspapers. They are interesting and authentic. We have lost many brave officers and men, ten officers killed and some 50 wounded, many since dead.

One fine, promising young officer has fallen at Delhi, Brigadier General John Nicholson mortally wounded, in front leading his storming party against a gate. He was the right man in the right place. Only eighteen years in the army and he commanded old Colonels! This supersession caused much bickering and jealousy in the army, but promotion by merit is long overdue, instead of by seniority.

This fine young soldier took a liking to your nephew, Captain Seymour Blane of the 52nd Regiment, and he put him on his personal staff. Colonel Nicholson has been honourably mentioned in the General's dispatches of the battle of Najafgarh on 25 August last, which took place near Delhi when the enemy attempted to cut off our siege train, but the gallant Nicholson and his force interrupted them and gained a glorious victory over the mutineers. Seymour Blane may get honours. I hope so. Arthur Roberts saw him in the field and liked him much.

The mail between Multan and Lahore has been robbed and we have subsequently not received any letters from England by the last overland of 10 August. Minnie wrote to you from Lahore but I fear that mail was robbed.

I have just received my daily letter from her. She writes, 'Baby boy is much better and the moment he sees me he puts out his little arms for me to take him'.

God bless and protect them both and spare them from sudden death. I feel very anxious about them, for there are four disarmed and mutinous regiments at Lahore, bent on mischief if they could, but they are well watched. They have guns trained on them and European Infantry and Sikhs around them.

And now, my dear Mrs Blane, I must say goodbye. I trust you will kindly assist me, for is not my wife and child all to me? Do, for mercy's sake, liberate us from the dreadful Bombay debt, and we will bless and thank you for ever. We will remit the portion of your interest, which will reduce the sum quarterly. Minnie is very anxious and unhappy about this.

Give dear Cissy my affectionate love and I will write to her soon.

Believe me, your obliged and affectionate,

A. O. Wood

The enclosed cuttings will show you that all that Minnie and I have told you is true.

From the Commissioner's Office, Lahore, 21 September 1857: 'The capture of the city of Delhi, of the Palace, and the Fort

A typical cantonment of Minnie's day showing bungalows and the church with a strong Georgian influence in the design.

An officer learning the language with his teacher (Monshee). Archie Wood's efforts under a similar aegis were not very successful.

The bridge of boats at Jhelum with the barracks and officers' quarters on the cliff above the river. (*See* page 67)

Travelling in palkis, normally carried by four men with the reserves in the background. (*See* page 57)

of Selimguth was completed yesterday. All honour to the noble army, which, under command of Major General Wilson, has effected this important conquest, by which the widespread of the rebellion of the mutinous Bengal Army has received a complete defeat in Upper India. Neither the devastation of that terrible scourge cholera, nor the deadly stroke of an Indian summer's sun, which have so grievously thinned the ranks of our small army, has abated the ardour of our troops. Nor have the harassing and incessant duties of the camp, the ever recurring combats with a highly trained, mutinous army, who outnumbered us by thousands, their stubborn and desperate resistance on the 14th – none of this abated the ardour of our troops, their persevering energy and indomitable courage, which takes no denial and will brook nothing short of success.'

Another cutting reads:

'The news from Delhi is that the King was taken prisoner yesterday by a party of sowars under Lieutenant Hodson, near the Kootub where four guns were also found. No sign of a mutineer is now to be seen at Delhi. They abandoned their camp outside the Ajmere Gate, leaving all sick and wounded who could not walk, their drums and instruments, clothing, bedding, cooking pots, etc., etc.

'Cholera has shown itself in the town. Dead bodies and carcases are being removed, and the stench in some places is unbearable.

'Later reports bring the news that Lieutenant Hodson has returned from Hoomayon's Tomb, near Delhi, and reports having killed the King's two sons and his grandson. A quantity of the King's attendants, his personal elephants, carriages and horses, have been taken.'

Another report gives news of beleaguered Lucknow:

'The siege began on 1 July, after several mutinies. Vast preparations for the defence of the Residency, whence all were gathered for protection, were made by Sir Henry Lawrence, the Chief Commissioner of Oude and the Brigadier General. Sir Henry Lawrence was tragically killed by a stray shot which entered his room in the Residency on 4 July, but he had planned well and the Residency continued to hold out against a desperate siege.

'All is well at Lucknow up to the 2nd instant, and European reinforcements are advancing from Allahabad to join General Havelock and enable him to proceed in force to the relief of Lucknow. The garrison has been most galled by the fire from a house near the Residency, from which two heavy guns had done damage to the defences. The house was successfully mined, and about 200 of the enemy destroyed by the explosion. A sally was then made and one of the guns spiked.'

In this letter also, dear Mrs Blane, please find a plan of our house in Jhelum. This house was sacked, looted and spoiled by the Mutineers on 7 July. We have no compensation.

My affectionate love,

Archie Wood

Lahore, 2 October

Only a few lines, my beloved Mother, to tell you how I and my boy are. Baby, bless him, is quite well and was five months old yesterday. He is very strong, the Doctor says, for his age. Indeed I am proud of my son and wish you could see him in one of your white dresses, but, oh dear, what a wet boy. I declare he has a spring inside him!

Poor me, I am ailing again from my old pain, and the Doctor tells me that unless I am well in a few days he must give me chloroform and operate on me, as my health will suffer from the wear and tear of the pain I suffer every day. God grant that I may recover my health soon, for I feel quite disheartened. I look as well as usual, but no one can tell what agony I endure in private.

I do not know what is happening to the mails, Several tribes rose between Multan and Lahore and the mails have been plundered. It is most distressing as one's only comfort is to hear from dear England. These beasts take them so near to their destination, it is so infuriating.

You in England cannot conceive what we have gone through in the last months. Even now one never feels safe. Last night Arthur Roberts intercepted a letter between two Mahommedans, both Government servants, the one here being the Sheriff of the Court, begging him to raise an insurrection to slay all Feringhees (English) and establish the true faith. It went on to say that Delhi had not fallen, and that it was only a big lie to deceive them. The letter was red hot treason throughout. You can see, dear Mama, that one never can feel safe with such letters flying about, even from good places in the Government.

Dearest Mama, my fondest love and kisses, and to dear Cissy,
Your fondly attached child,
Minnie Wood

Lahore, 11 Oct.

My dearest Mama,
I have received the missing letters of the last three mails! Most

truly grateful was I to get them as I had not heard from you for so long.

Dearest Mama, I indeed feel for you as I know the anxiety under which you are suffering must be painful, though we may now look on the worst as being past, but there is no doubt that our position will remain precarious until fresh troops are dispersed all over India. We who are left without regiments are most anxious to know what will become of us. Everything is in the greatest state of confusion, and even the wisest heads think that many months must elapse before we shall be in quietude. Our officers are sent hither and thither. Our Colonel is now posted to a new regiment at Peshawar, where two of our Subalterns were sent to join the Foot Artillery. We shall never again be together as a regiment. And still the disturbances which delayed your letters are not quelled, for as one tribe is defeated another rises.

The last few days has brought the news of the relief of Lucknow. General Havelock arrived there on 25 September, but the siege continues and it may be many weeks before the whole place is free of these wicked mutineers. Food may be short and many more brave men fall before the Residency is entirely relieved. I fear that many horrors must have happened in that place, but none to equal the frightful atrocities of Cawnpore. An officer writing from that place says:

'We found arranged in rows in a barrack fifty pairs of men's feet in their shoes, 30 women's cut off just above the ankle, and numberless children's feet and hands lying about.'

Oh, Mama! can you imagine human beings being guilty of such things? I am unspeakably grateful to the Almighty for having spared us from such barbarities.

Alas, I am still a sufferer from my old pain, and though last Monday I underwent an operation under chloroform, I still am a martyr to this dreadful pain. Doctor Smith assures me, however, that I am getting better, but it will be a long time before all is healed. I have Blue Stone applied every morning. To think that neglect and ignorance by Doctor Cole and that nurse have been the cause of my distress! It is very hard that an officer's wife is obliged to employ the medical man of her regiment, whether he is competent or not.

Archie intends handing up that man Cole for his neglect of duty, and preciously glad I shall be if he is turned out of the Service. My dear husband is here, having obtained a few days' leave in order to be present when the operation was performed. Poor fellow, he is quite wretched about me, and only our Cecil, who is such a sweet pet and so interesting now, seems to divert him.

He is so strong that sometimes I can hardly hold him. He throws himself back with such violence, and, oh, has he not a naughty little temper! It is astonishing how he manages to make such a noise, and at night Papa rushes off in disgust at his son's screams, and takes refuge in a room where he can finish his night's rest undisturbed. Ayah and I struggle ineffectually to quiet him, and in the middle of the scolding the little darling looks up and gives such a sweet smile one cannot admonish him further!

He is to be christened directly Arthur Roberts comes in from camp. We shall call him Archibald Cecil. I am hoping to find someone who will take photographs so that I can send you a likeness of my boy.

The cold weather is setting in and I am busy getting baby his warm clothing. I have today begun wearing my flannels. Though the mornings and evenings are very cold, we have not yet given up the punkah during the day, for when it is still it is very hot.

I have been braiding a blue flannel dress for baby, and a nice little Cashmere jacket to wear over his low dresses when out of doors. I cannot procure a felt hat for the Mannie, and they are so soft and warm. I have, however, trimmed a straw hat with red ribbon and put a feather in it. You can't think how jolly he looks when he goes for drives.

I really am glad that my dear brother, Willie, is not of a proper age to come out here. I should have been dreadfully anxious were he out in this vile country.

You ask me if the Colonel's wife accompanied me to Rawalpindi. She offered to but did not in the end. I have nothing to thank her for. She has a vile temper and Archie could have had her up for defamation of character had not things been so disturbed, which would have been very awkward for her husband. Once offended she never forgives, and her tongue cannot say bad things enough of one. My only excuse for her is that she has not been in England for twenty-five years, and does not know how better to conduct herself.

Do you remember all the nice muslin dresses you gave me, unmade? They were all stolen on that terrible 7 July. Next year, dear Mama, I shall ask you to send me more muslin. The washerwomen destroy everything by beating it violently, so that those nice, cheap dresses from England are just the thing. As long as they are pretty and clean I do not mind if they are inexpensive.

This is my baby's day. At six in the morning he is taken out for a walk, and on his return arrowroot is given. He is bathed at half past eight and then I nurse him. He then sleeps for about three hours and then sago is given, and at two o'clock he now has a little chicken broth and jelly. Does he not enjoy that, and how he smacks his lips! I nurse him again when I go to bed, and again in the night, for his gums are now so hot that he gets very thirsty.

I have often been obliged to use soap, as you mention, as his bowels are often very troublesome, but I prefer a little cotton wool dipped in oil, it is softer and more soothing.

Dearest Mama, I have written a very long letter, I hope you can read it. Pray do not cross your letter to me. Your last were almost unreadable as they had had all sorts of misfortunes before reaching us. They were still wet, and had had a soaking on the way.

My dear husband joins me in most affectionate love and kisses, and my darling Sonny sends a kiss to you all.

My own dear Mother,
Your fondly attached and loving child,
Minnie Wood

Lahore, 2 November

My dearest Mama,
I really was so distressed to think you should be so deceived

about the different stations in the Punjab. People who never have been in India seem to make statements without foundation. I can assure you that neither Rawalpindi nor Lahore have strong forts. 'Pindi is nothing but a military station, and I should be sorry to place myself in the Lahore Fort, as it is most insecure.

I am living in Annakalli, the civil station of Lahore, which is distant from Mean Mur, the cantonments, about five miles. The disarmed Sepoys are between us, and should they ever attempt a rush over this way, we are ordered to make for the Fort. A somewhat faint hope.

Dearest Archie came down here to be present at my operation and the very day he was to return to Jhelum ague and fever came on so violently that we were obliged to send for our Doctor. On his appearance he immediately ordered thirty-six leeches over the sides and twelve on the temples. It appears that he was suffering from congestion of the liver, poor fellow. He had a severe attack and is now on Medical Certificates to remain here for two months, as the Doctor will not allow him to return to Jhelum at present. This illness took place in Mean Mur where we had gone to spend a day with the Cookes, and of course we could not return. We remained for a week in barracks next door to them, where we ladies in Cantonments are permitted to live, and wherein I certainly should not like it as a permanency, as it is much like a *piggery*! Sleeping, eating and the bathroom also in this small room, not so large as our morning room at home.

Christmas is drawing near and I wish I could feel as charitable as you do. It sickens me to hear people talk of Merry Christmas and showing mercy towards wretches who have been guilty of every foul deed. The Sepoys in Mean Mur are actually paraded morning and evening in uniform by some person's orders (nobody seems to know whose), for fear they should forget their drill. I should say the sooner they forget it the better.

As to that old sinner, the King of Delhi, he is actually allowed the same show of royalty he had when in Delhi. It is disgraceful. You people in England are not inclined to have justice done on these brutes, and disregard the opinions of those out here in high positions who know the situation. I have heard newly arrived officers say that they are soldiers, not hangmen. Had they known my feelings and the happenings of July 7th they would not speak of 'insulting the men's dignity'. No punishment is too great for those inhuman monsters. When I think of the pretty, elegant girls and their charming mothers, and the brave men I met in Cawnpore coming up here and their terrible fates, it makes me wish to shoot every Indian I see.

It is sad on Sunday mornings in church to see the number of people in mourning and so many young widows amongst them.

Arthur Roberts came in a few days ago from his tour of the Frontier. He was at Groggra where he went to set things to rights. The tribes who have risen are the most wild, uncivilized beings you can imagine, subsisting on lizards, frogs and filthiness of every description. They are immensely wealthy in cattle, and until their pride and arrogance is subdued, they will never be quiet. However, herds of the animals are being constantly taken from them, so I hope the mail route between here and Multan will soon be safer. Our letters go down the Indus for the overland mail.

I am so grateful to you for thinking of my darling Cecil. It is impossible to procure anything for him here. A common little straw hat costs 8 rupees, that is 16 shillings, and that untrimmed. Nearly all my dresses, made and unmade, were taken by the mutineers, and also all my skirts, leaving me only the bodies. That nice warm dress with flounces, checked, has gone, and the only bonnet I have left is the one I had on when my picture was taken, the horse hair with the feathers. I am in great need of a straw bonnet, as they are the most useful things out here. My little straw hat has become quite rotten. I suppose the heat has done that. I cannot wear tight bodices, as when nursing it is worrying. I have a loose jacket of black cloth which does with any skirt.

Mrs Routh of our regiment is on her way to England with her little boy. She has taken a bag from me with things for you, dear Mama. It contains my books, which will get eaten by insects out here, my malachite ornaments we bought at Torquay, a pot of Mangoe Chutney of my own making, a pot of green chilli in vinegar, also curry powder, a chinelle [chenille] cushion, a pen case, envelope case and other things all made at Wizierabad, and a paper cutter of steel with a Persian inscription, and last but not least a cannon ball which I found in my dressing room. These, dear Mama, will soon be ornamenting your drawing room.

Please, dear Mama, do not write so closely, and do not cross your lines. It takes away half the pleasure of receiving letters when you have such difficulty in reading them, and they frequently arrive soaking wet.

I had a letter from a friend now in Delhi, and she says her husband with his men is now engaged in digging for loot. He has been most successful, having in two days dug up clothes, jewellery, articles of every description, and two lacs, that is £1,600 in gold mohurs.

I fear several of your letters and most of the *Illustrated London*'s have been lost for ever.

Dearest Mama, I must close to catch the post. God bless you. With most affectionate love and kisses from all,

Your fond child,

Minnie Wood

Lahore, 20 November

My dearest Mama,

Plague take the mails! No letter from you to answer and the mail from here closes at five today.

Baby's *first tooth* came through *last night*! Poor little fellow, he was very unwell, sick constantly and fever hanging about him. I gave him some castor oil in the morning but as he still continued ill I sent for Doctor Smith, who gave him fever powders, and he will be here again in the morning. The tooth is in front in the lower jaw. He seems very stout and healthy, and this cold weather is setting him up beautifully.

I am in a regular fix what to do. Archie wishes to return to Jhelum, as he does not wish to lose the appointment he has there, as it may be an opening for something better. I have a great objection to going back as we have no medical man there, and

I should be very nervous of having my poor baby teething and no one to consult.

Oh, this dreadful India! I hate it and an officer's life is a miserable one. I cannot let poor Archie live by himself, and if I did go and anything happened to little Cecil I should never forgive myself.

The little man was vaccinated the other day, but it did not take effect. Children are not brought, as in England, from whom vaccine can be obtained, but in the cold season it is sent down from the hills, and I am sure loses its power.

I am sitting in Arthur Roberts's room, by a roasting fire and am in a flannel dress, for the cold here when it does come beats an English winter hollow. It is very jolly though, for I can get a good walk now, and come in with my hands and feet quite dead. Such a change from the heat of a few weeks ago.

Our late Commanding Officer, Colonel Gerrard, was, I am grieved to say, killed in an engagement with the Judpore Legion on Tuesday last. Poor Mrs Gerrard is left a widow with six children. He was a good, kind old gentleman, and did not deserve to meet his end by the hands of these ruffians.

How grateful I am that my husband is with me, whilst so many poor creatures are grieving for theirs. When shall we have an end to these wars? Even travellers are not safe, for a few days ago a young officer of the 81st was brutally murdered by some blacks whilst proceeding down the Sutleg River en route to England. So many bad characters are roaming at large, and it will be years before there is quietness and order throughout this vast Empire.

I have been most fortunate in procuring an excellent English nurse from the 8th. Her husband was killed at Delhi, and her one child is going home to his relations, so she will have no encumbrances. Mrs Collins is a steady young woman, and thoroughly understands children, having had six of her own. My ayah is about to increase her family, her fifteenth child. This is the worst of Indian females, they are always having babies. You would be astounded to see the herds of little black, naked children running about the servants' quarters, their huts that is. How they all manage to live is a perfect miracle to me.

By the bye, I forgot to tell you the great bit of news. Baby was christened a few days after I dispatched my last letter. Mrs Cooke stood for Cissy, and Lieutenant Cooke is one of the Godfathers and Arthur the other. Baby was so good and struggled to get hold of Doctor Carshore's red band the whole time, and kept crowing, laughing and moving, to the utter consternation of everyone. And Mama, he ended by 'peeing' the clergyman and someone else took hold of him! He is the most awful boy for this, and nearly every moment he wets someone, laughing the whole time, and looking so cocky!

I have just invested in a small stool with a hole in it (comprenez-vous?), and he looks a regular little monkey perched on it. This is a great amusement to his Father, who takes great delight in placing him on it and carrying him round the room.

I am dying to know what our new Commander in Chief, General Wilson, will do with the Company's officers, such as Archie. I wish they would raise new regiments and officer them from the Native regiments which have mutinied.

If you see Colonel Birch in Bath pray remember me to him, and tell him that poor Richard Beecher committed suicide the other day at Barrackpore. He lost his wife and baby in August and it affected his mind so much that he took his own life.

If you can get paper like this to write on, pray use it, dear Mama, as it is stronger than yours. Whenever you have any nice embroidery patterns, or braid ditto, please send them in a letter, as light things can be sent that way, such as sewing silk, a little at a time, you know.

I am in great want of a worsted needle, none are to be had here, in fact we can get hardly anything as the Lahore merchants have not been able to procure fresh goods for some time owing to the disturbances.

Should baby continue to keep well I shall go into camp next week with Arthur Roberts. It is a delightful life, all but having to get up so early. Cissy would enjoy it as she could ride ten miles every morning. I am grateful to say I continue quite well. Doctor Smith has cured me, and my pain has gone and all my boils. In fact, 'Jack's himself again'!

Dearest Mama, I hope you get my letters regularly. I often feel quite unwilling to send them off for fear they should come to an untimely end. Dear Mama, I fear this letter is not very interesting, but it is such a mercy to live in comparative peace! My fondest love to Cissy, who I hope you will never allow to set foot in this horrid country, and to the boys, and with every prayer and wish that you may be spared to us many years,

Your fondly attached child,

Minnie Wood

Lahore, 3 December

I have written such a long letter to Cissy, my dearest Mama, that this must be a short one. Baby at this moment is sitting on my knee trying to eat my penwiper! Little pet, he is such a fine, healthy little chap and good looking, but such a temper of his own! I am obliged to be very firm with him, or he would soon be spoiled. The moment he gets displeased he throws himself back and stretches so stiffly that no one can bend him. He will be a difficult young man to bring up. I have just commenced a little frock for him from your pattern, and also a pair of shoes in blue flannel. Please, dear Mama, get me some shoes and socks for him, and two pairs of the former in black for me. Indeed anything you can put into a box will be most acceptable out here. I cannot procure boy's elastic belts, could you get me some as they look so nice. Anything you send, wrap in coarse Housemaid's Cotton, as it preserves all nicely.

Also, *please* send me your picture, I want it more than anything else. I have placed the feathers you kindly gave me in a box which Mr Roberts is shortly sending home. I cannot use them out here as it is impossible to get them curled or dressed.

I have never known till now what it is to be in want of money. I do think it *very* hard that all officers' pay is stopped for three months. It is most distressing, as one's servants are grumpy at not being paid regularly, and are continually asking for money, and I am obliged to say 'I have none to give'.

All the money I had saved, as you know, went on the day of

the mutiny, together with our pay for June which had just been issued. So we have nothing to go on with, and of course have had to borrow money, which will be repaid *whenever* we are paid, but the interest mounts up.

I made out a list the other day, and I find we have lost things upwards of 600 rupees. Of course, our loss is small compared to others. Our house was not burned, which was a miracle, but we feel it none the less, and what with this and the debt I feel so disheartened. Now our movements are all unsettled, and everything is so expensive. Even our food is rising, and sometimes I am quite done for and have a good cry, which sometimes does one good.

In one of the boxes on the way to you are my husband's Light Infantry wings. They have never been worn, and if you will kindly dispose of them for him he will be greatly obliged. They ought to fetch a good price as they are gold.

I do not think my dear husband will be able to return to Jhelum in any case. He suffers so much from his liver that he may have to go to the hills on Sick Certificate, which will mean more expense we can ill afford.

Do not let Cissy marry anyone who has not plenty of the needful. One cannot live on nothing in this world.

My best love to you all, in which Archie joins,

Your fondly attached child,
Minnie Wood

In Camp, Wizierabad
Dak Bungalow, 19 December

My dearest Mama,

I can only write a few lines by this mail, as I fear I have already lost it, having left Lahore last Sunday evening with all our traps en route to Old Jhelum, bother take the place! However, I do not want to miss any opportunity for writing to say we are quite well and dear baby awfully jolly.

We are at Wizierabad which we reached this morning. Arthur has lent us a cottage tent, and it is most comfortable. The caravanserai consists of four tents, camels, servants, and this marches every night to the new camping ground, and we follow in the morning. I and baby travel in a doolie, a sort of bed carried by four men, and Archie is on his Cashmere pony, which was given by that poor Captain Barnett who was the first officer killed in the assault on Delhi.

The weather is so exquisite that this is a delightful way of travelling. In my last letter I think I told you of poor Mrs Smith having become a widow, her husband having cut his throat on the 20th May. He was a nephew of Sir Harry Smith, the victor of the battle of Aliwal in the Sikh war of eleven years ago. There is strong madness in that family. Mrs Smith and her little boy are now in Bombay in great distress, for when the contents of the will were forwarded from England to Captain Fullerton, President of the Committee of Adjustment, it was discovered that he had left the whole of his property, real and personal, to his brothers and sisters, and his wife and baby are beggars. There is nothing but her pension, which, as he was only a lieutenant, is very small. Poor thing, it is very sad.

My husband is out shooting. He is not at all well, and his side gives him much pain. We are now almost crazy about our table attendants. They are so impertinent and give me so much trouble that I declare I feel inclined to kill them all, the beasts! Oh, Mama, you would go out of your mind if you had these devils to deal with. The Mahommedans have been the cause of all our miseries in India, and unfortunately our servants are mostly of that creed.

As to ever liking this country, that is quite out of the question. One feels quite differently now, even I who have been so short a time here, now begin to see the creatures one has to deal with. I think they are a nasty, stinking, dirty race and nothing more can be said of them.

I am afraid my last letter may have been interrupted, and you may never receive it. I shall write again soon.

Our most affectionate love to you all,

Your affectionate child,

Minne Wood

By the beginning of January 1858 the situation in India had changed a great deal. The worst of the uprising was over, and some further small rebellions were put down, but the fight for Lucknow was far from won, though Delhi had been captured. Sir John Lawrence in September had directed all the strength of the army on that city, which was really the heart of the insurrection, and after desperate fighting the devastated town was in British hands, the mutineers flying for their lives.

At Lucknow General Havelock had entered the Residency and reinforced it, but had done nothing to ease the food shortage, or finally lift the siege. The battle was to go on for several months yet, while General Colin Campbell fought desperately for the last victory which would quieten the whole district.

The hot weather was over, and Minnie's health improved. Archie was with her in Lahore, but had to return to Jhelum if he were to keep his job there. This put Minnie in the difficult position of so many army wives of having to choose between going with her husband and risking her own and the baby's health, or staying in the safety of Lahore with medical attention at hand, and leaving her husband by himself in Jhelum.

Their financial state was bad. The officers had not received any pay for three months, the powers that be in the Paymaster's office apparently thinking that they could exist without cash, thus pushing many of them more and more into the hands of money-lenders and gathering crippling interest as the weeks went by.

Archie's future – and that of many British officers of native regiments of the East India Company's army – was uncertain. The number of sepoys was to be greatly reduced and kept well below the numbers of British troops, thus ensuring the impossibility of any future rising. The new régime of government by the Queen and the end of the rule of the East India Company meant that all troops now found themselves in the Queen's service, no longer sure of serving in India only. The question was: when regiments were disbanded, what would become of their British officers?

There was an astonishing outbreak of violent demands for merciless retribution to be dealt out to all mutineers: voiced not only in India, but also in the British press. Others realized that reconciliation was the only road to lasting peace, and after the first frenzy, imprisonment was a more usual sentence than execution for all but convicted murderers.

The reasons put forward for the causes of the Mutiny were many and contradictory: too many missionaries or too few; too rapid modernization or too slow; too much interference with native customs or insufficient; too much contact with Indians or not enough. The army was blamed, the Company was blamed, and Indians were vilified wholesale, whether loyal or not. A hundred different ideas were argued endlessly.

Everything was unsettled and uncertain, and there was little to counteract the reaction to months of tragedy and strain.

By this time Archie was in a highly nervous state, his health undermined by incessant dysentery treated with opium, which if it eased the pain certainly did him no good mentally. The worry of debt wore him down, and there was no peace in the house as neither he nor Minnie seemed able to cope with native servants. Relations between the two of them were strained and tempers were frayed: no wonder Minnie's buoyant spirits were sinking.

However, she, Archie and the baby, proceeded up to Jhelum with Arthur Roberts, camping as they went, a method of travel which Minnie always enjoyed and which seemed to have done Archie some good, as he was able to go shooting, somewhat to Minnie's disgust.

Once back at Jhelum the money troubles again came to the fore, putting the events of the diminishing mutiny rather into the background.

Archie's letter of 6 January 1858 gives an insight into the methods of army pay and the cost of living at that time. The underlining in his letters and the note of hysteria point to his state of mind; but, unattractive as it is, can one condemn him too hardly for his instability?

Jhelum, 1 January 1858
Here is the first day of a New Year upon us, my darling Mama.

Accept our very best wishes on this auspicious event, and our sincere prayer that we may all be spared to meet again in dear England. Oh! How unspeakably happy I should be could I but know my next New Year's Day would be spent in England, but I must not even think of such pleasure for many, many years to come.

I suppose the boys are home for their vacations. The dear old things! I would give everything I possess (which is not much by the bye) to have one little peep at you all. Dear Mama, it is very dreadful being so far away from you, and no circumstances will ever reconcile me to this country.

My darling little pet is eight months old today, such a funny little sweet face, and always laughing and crowing. I should go mad if I had not him to amuse me. He has only two teeth, but that is quite enough to cause me much pain by the little rascal sometimes biting me. Of course I always give him a sharp tap when he does, and then as if to say 'Dear Mama, please don't' he places his little 'pud' across my mouth for me to kiss.

We arrived in this place the day before Christmas Day, after a very pleasant march from Lahore, but our Christmas dinner was very dull. We drank your healths, all, and I was selfish enough to wish you were here to have a taste of our good Indian Mulligatawny Soup and Curry. Oh, do not ever let Cissy come out here.

I found on my arrival here your letter to my dear husband about the debt. He is dreadfully cut up about it, for it appears he quite forgot having once insured his life. However, we will pay off the interest as you propose. You know we are receiving 137 rupees a month in addition to Archie's regimental pay, but not one anna of our latter pay have we seen since July. The Colonel Campbell, who is our Deputy Paymaster, is *a beast*, and has refused to give Archie his full pay as Captain, as he says he is drawing Consolidated Salary from the Civil Department. I enclose a copy of what Sir John Lawrence says in reply to a letter from Archie on the subject.

I propose sending the Parsee in Bombay the 137 rupees a month as long as we get it, and should the Levy continue, which

Archie is in charge of with extra pay, then I shall send 100 rupees a month. This will soon diminish the debt at 1,644 rupees or £164 a year in the first place, and in the second at 1,200 rupees or £120 a year.

Oh, dear Mama, this will be a great thing off my mind, and the first instalment will go to Bombay this month. Whenever any moneys falls to me in England, pray send it to this man, for by working at both ends the debt will be sooner done.

I am so grieved that my letters do not reach you regularly, as I write by every mail. I have got baby's Christening Certificate safely in my dressing case. Your letters have all arrived here, but I have not had a single *Illustrated London News* since July. The arrival of the overland mail of Nov. 26th is just telegraphed. I hope I get your letter before having to dispatch this.

My husband is out on his boat on the river duck shooting. He has been most successful lately, and we often have a fine duck for dinner.

Goodbye for today, dear Mama, for I am tired.

2 January

Hurrah! Your letter of 26th November arrived this morning with the welcome intelligence about the debt. Dear Mama, I cannot tell you how unspeakably grateful I am to you, as now the former part of this letter is cancelled, and instead of sending the instalments to Bombay I will send them to you, *dear* Mama, and I shall hope that the Levy with its extra pay will continue for some time.

Did you not receive my letter containing an account of our losses and on the robbing of our house? All my table linen, house linen, unmade dresses and six skirts of summer muslin, all went, leaving me the perfectly useless bodies. Almost all of the numerous stock of shorts that Archie brought round the Cape with him also went, besides a large cask containing all my most useful things, dish covers, china, so much else amounting to between £20 and £25. This last was destroyed between Allahabad and Cawnpore on its way up here. There is no redress.

I hope you have not forgotten to send me pictures of you all, I so long to have them.

Your fondly attached child,

Minnie Wood

From Archie at Jhelum to Mrs Blane:

6 Jan, 1858

My dear Mrs Blane,

I have so much to talk to you about that I am perplexed how to commence. First of all let me thank you most heartily for the arrangement you have so kindly made about the unfortunate Bombay debt. *In return* for your extreme kindness, etc., I propose giving up my Staff pay of 137 rupees and remitting you the same monthly. I have already commenced from yesterday, when I sent 137 rupees or £13.14.0 to a bank at Lahore, and shall receive a Bill on London, which I will make payable to yourself. Should I be fortunate enough to receive more pay, I will make it over to you. In fact my wife receives all my pay, and we are becoming very economical I assure you.

I enclose for your perusal our Monthly Expenditure, and particulars of my pay, past and present.

My pay I received during 1857 up to the day of the Jhelum mutiny on July 7th.

Captain's pay per month	415 rupees 6 annas
2 Companies	100 rupees
	515 rupees 6 annas

Deductions

Monthly instalment of my dona- tion to the Military Fund 720 rupees or £72	60
On my Marriage Subscription to Military Fund	20
Ditto Orphan Fund	10

Deductions—contd.

Male Child from 1st May, our
Cecil, God bless him   1
                                               ——
                                               91 rupees

Regimental Institutions
Monthly Subscriptions to Mess   5
Book Club   5
Band   6
Repairs of Arms and Accoutre-
  ments   10
Two Writers (clerks)   10
Church   4
                                               ——
                                40 rupees   Total *131 rupees*

Pay	515 rupees
Deductions	131 rupees
	——
Total	384 rupees

Our monthly expenses
Servants   100
House rent   80
Table expenses   50
Mess bill including beer, wine,
  etc., oilman's stores, etc.   100
Dresses for Baby and making up
  clothes for ourselves   20
Miscellaneous, punkahs, chicks (for
  the doors), carpet, etc.   20
Firewood for kitchen and house   10
Nurse for attending Minnie dur-
  ing her confinement   80
Her Beer, etc. (Beer is 1 rupee a
  bottle)   30   Total *490 rupees*

Servants

I will try and explain to you this *Expensive item*. During the hot season, 7 months of the year, we require many more to pull the punkahs, and water the tatties, etc. The latter are the reed blinds which are hung in doorways, etc., and kept sprinkled with water to try to afford a little cool air. Four punkah coolies are *absolutely* necessary to be in attendance *day and night* at our house. *You* cannot imagine what the *heat* is during the *hot months*. These four men each receive four rupees, which makes *additional 16 rupees* for *servants*.

As long as I receive this Staff pay I will remit you £13.14s. monthly. I cannot assure you enough how earnest I am to remit as much as I can to England.

Indian living is totally different to what you have been accustomed to, that it is quite impossible for us to attempt to give you particulars, but we have commenced this year with a *determination* to economize, and *please God* we will do so.

I command the Jhelum Levy, a body of 300 men, and I am likely to hold on to it for some time, and it may lead to something better, but I must not be too sanguine.

I shall never forget your extreme kindness to us about this sad, sad, Bombay debt.

From here on in this letter Archie's writing becomes untidy and his words extravagant. One must remember that he was a sick man, taking large doses of opium – the recognized treatment of that day – to ease his stomach. How much this undermined his weak character and increased his instability one can only guess, but it is obvious that he was very close to what today would be termed a nervous breakdown.

His letter continues:

Let us now speak on other subjects.

This terrible, gigantic rebellion is fast being crushed (thanks be to God) in this country. Get the map of Hindustan before you, and I will inform you of the doings of our noble Commander in Chief, Sir Colin Campbell, and our brave army. Look for

Futtygurh or Ferukhabad. Sir Colin is there with a large Force, about to march a movable column into Rohilound to occupy Bareilly, Maradabad, etc., our former Military Stations, and the Garden of India.

There has been *very hard fighting* at Lucknow and Cawnpore. The officer commanding there, General Windham of Crimea notoriety (the Redan Hero), has got into a scrape with our brave Chief, Sir Colin. He allowed the Gwalior Contingent and a very large body of the rebels to take him by surprise and capture nearly all his baggage. The Advance Camp of our Army, with the exception of H.M.'s 82nd Regiment, fell into the hands of the enemy. 11,000 Enfield Cartridges, the Mess Plate of some four Queen's Regiments, Paymaster's chests, and immense quantities of baggage of both officers and men fell into the hands of the Philistines, who dislodged our men, but whom we could not in return dislodge. H.M.'s 64th behaved most gloriously, they immortalized themselves. (Oh, how my blood tingles in my veins!) Four brave heroes gave their lives for their country; Colonel Wilson, Captains Wright, McCrea and Morphy were cut down by the enemy's guns, and Major Stirling was also shot. Captain McKinnon and Lieutenant Gordon were left on the field wounded, and the former is said to have been hanged by the mutineers on the gallows on which we used to execute the Rebels. The other man was bound hands and feet to a cartwheel and whilst thus helpless, progged with bayonets and otherwise ignominiously treated. How heart-rending and brutal to narrate! Poor fellows, but they will be *revenged*.

A brother officer of mine, Macdowel, writes from Cawnpore:

'We came back from Lucknow just in time to see Cawnpore in flames, our troops having been well beaten, and being in possession of nothing but the entrenched camp. We polished off the Gwalior Contingent the other day, and we had a splendid run after them down the Calpee Road, following them beyond the 14th milestone, and taking seventeen guns and mortars which they absconded as we came up.'

Brave Mac! Would that I had been with you, you lucky fellow!

The London Mail of December 10th just in. The box you have

kindly sent my wife will not come to hand for a long period as the Government require the Indus river steamers up to Multan for troops and war stores, ammunitions, etc.

Tomorrow is your Willie's birthday. We will drink his health, but not in a bumper of champagne, for we have none, no such luxury for us soldiers in India in these hard times.

Upon my life, I do not care about wine. I would much rather sit with my wife and baby boy (oh, he is such a beauty! God bless our little one) at my quiet home than all the fashionable champagne dinner parties.

Speaking of our Boy, you would love him. He has beautiful black eyes, silken eyelashes, soft features, and is as fair as the *lily*. Dear Grandmama would cherish her Baby Boy, and would imprint burning kisses on his little lips, and he would cling to her bosom. He is all that is lovely on earth to us and bitter would be the blow were evil to happen to our dear little blossom.

I hope it may please God to spare us all, and *you* to fold our *Blossom* in your bosom, to gaze on his beautiful countenance, and *Bless* our offspring, your *daughter's* child, and our *first born*.

God bless you, dear Mrs Blane. I feel very sad tonight, happy recollections of dear England are forcing themselves upon me, and of you and your family, and my having robbed you of your dear Minnie, your first born. But we *are happy* – ask her – in this distant land, away from all those we love and who love us. God bless you, dear Mrs Blane and believe me ever,

Yours affectionately,
A. O. Wood

To Mrs Blane from Archie in Jhelum:

21 January

My dear Mrs Blane,

I have much pleasure in sending you a cheque on London for £13.7.10d No. 2871 dated Lahore 18th January, 1858, signed T. Bailey, Manager, payable to myself and on the Agra and U.S. Bank, 27 Cannon Street, London.

I trust it may please God to spare us to remit regularly. My pay is still in *arrears three months*! By order of the Government on account of this terrible mutiny, which has caused many brave men sleepless nights and great anxiety of mind. I have only just received my pay for July, August, September and October, all in a heap.

We keep only just as many servants as are really necessary, and we have no conveyance. I have a pony for Duty matters. My wife keeps her Accounts *daily*. We pay ready money for Bazaar expenses. Minnie has her Store Room and serves out what species, etc., are required for the Cook Room, such as rice, sugar, flour, spices, even food for my charger, which is a Cashmere pony, a *gift* by a very old friend, Captain Barnet, killed at Delhi. The keep of a horse in the country is about three rupees, six shillings a month!!

Minnie buys poultry, thirty four chickens for two rupees or four shillings. Is this not cheap! I send one of my own Levy people, not a servant, about six to eight miles off amongst the country villages and I am able to buy poultry thus cheaply.

Minnie has just been making *marmalade*, and it cost her for oranges, sugar, jam pots, 4 rupees for twelve pots, and very good it is, I assure you, and will save us many rupees.

We are living in a splendid house on the banks of the River Jhelum. The owner, Lieutenant Warrand, Engineers, *lost an arm* at Delhi. Such a fine, handsome fellow. He only asks us half rent, 40 rupees, £4 a month.

I like Jhelum, and only wish my present appointment would turn into something better, say a Captain of Police on *800 rupees* a month. If so I would remit you half.

I am very fortunate being in the Punjab, in this quiet and safe part of the country, instead of getting hard blows down below at Cawnpore and Lucknow. Poor fellows, how they have roughed it, with the brave Havelock, Campbell, Outram and others.

Now I can tell you that I offered my services to Sir James Outram as an extra A.D.C. or Orderly Officer, but I have never had a reply to my application, perhaps forunately for me. Had I been at Lucknow and not been killed, you would have heard of me by now as *Major Wood*! Brevit Rank is the ambition of every officer. It was for that reason I volunteered. Captain Chamier on General Outram's staff is a very intimate friend of mine, and I thought he would get me with Sir James. Perhaps it was all for the best that I did not succeed.

As to new regiments for the Bengal Army, who can tell? I hope to be posted to a European one. We *must* have a *large* force of *White Men* and our Army cannot serve a *double* Government. No, let us abolish the Board of Control, the East India Company. We can do without Mr Vernon Smith. Either let the *Queen* rule India, and let us become a Royal Army, or the East India Company rule India with the Premier or First Lord of the Treasury as President. We cannot serve two masters.

I hope we shall soon hear what Lord Palmerston intends doing, and is he not becoming an old *Grumpy*!

I intend sending in a Compensation Bill to the Government for loss of our property on the day of the Mutiny, and it amounts to nearly 1,000 rupees. We lost the following:

My wearing apparel, my wife's ditto, etc., etc., etc.	200 rupees
Pieces of silk, muslin, etc.	250
Household property, beds, linen, etc., etc.	88
	538
Cash in hand of my pay	180
Beer and wine stolen by H.M.'s 24th Regiment	80
Miscellaneous property from my house	115
	375

Total 913 rupees (£91)

I *may* get this sum from the Government.

Now let me give you some of the prices we have to pay. A bottle of vinegar is 3 rupees, small bottle of salad oil 4 rupees, tea 6/s a pound, 6 pieces of Windsor soap 5/s, small case sardines 4/s, small mustard 4/s, Worcester sauce, Lee and Perrins sauce, 3/s, sago 3/s a pound, arrowroot ditto, bottled beer 2/s a bottle, and it holds but two small tumblers. Pint beer bottles are 14/s a dozen, and English ham (a luxury we have never had) is 33 rupees a pound or £3.6s.! So you see, dear Mrs Blane, how dear everything is.

And now goodbye, and God bless you, my dear Mrs Blane. This is the sincere wish of both of us, and our united fond, affectionate love to yourself, dear Cissy and the boys, believe me, ever your affectionate,

A. O. Wood

Jhelum, 9 Feb, 1858

My dearest Mama,

I have been much disappointed in these last few days at receiving no mail. I feel there must be some cause for the delay.

We are all well, thank God. Little Cecil has one eye tooth, which looks strange – the only one in his top jaw. He tries very hard to crawl and is a great favourite with everyone.

The weather still continues most beautifully cool, though we have had an immense deal of rain accompanied by thunder and lightning.

Archie Wood has been laid up with lumbago, though I say it is gout, caught while out duck shooting. However, that was no sooner cured than he must needs go out twelve miles from here with a Captain Marquis, H.M.'s 12th, in search of Aurial, a wild sheep with magnificent horns. He has not yet returned, but I expect him for breakfast tomorrow. He sent me in last night by a servant a hare, a corial and a ravine deer, which promises to make good Venison Pasty.

I hope the draft arrived safely and also the second one, so I hope, dear Mama, that you will give us credit for something. I am doing my best to get quite clear of debt, for until that happens I shall never be able to return to England, and this hope is all that keeps my spirits up. Never let Cissy marry a man who owes one penny –

What I have gone through this last year! The restless nights, thinking and trying to devise means to pay off the debts. Oh,

Mama, I have so much to thank you for. I don't know how to express myself, but indeed I am deeply grateful to you.

What I hinted to you about myself is, I am afraid, *too true*. As far as I can tell I have been in the family way since the middle of November according to your method of calculation. I am *not* glad at this. One is quite enough, particularly in these sad times.

I have procured some pretty ivory crochet needles for you from Delhi, and a brooch and a pair of bracelets for Cissy. I have had a beautiful piano lent me, so I practise every day.

Now, dear Mama, I will close this. With fondest love and a kiss to you and dear Cissy.

Ever your fondly attached child,
Minnie Wood

From Archie to Mrs Blane on 11 February:

My dear Mrs Blane,

Here is a *Duplicate* of the *Bill* I sent you overland. I have just returned from shooting and we killed two wild sheep (Corial) and four deer.

Good news from this country. One more struggle at Lucknow then *all* will be over. The Chiefs in Oude wish to make terms with Government. Lord Canning is at Cawnpore or Allahabad, and this looks as if this terrible revolt is nearly over. Sir Colin Campbell has gone down to Cawnpore again to meet the Governor General.

We are all well, thank God, and your Grandson is cutting teeth beautifully. How you and Aunt Cissy would love him could you see and caress him.

Ever your affectionate,
A. O. Wood

Jhelum, 10 March

My darling Mama,

I fear you must have imagined all kinds of evil by not hearing from me for some time. The fact was that my poor Sonny's eyes became very sore, and of a morning when he woke the poor child's lids were glued together, and not until warm milk and water had been applied by me for half an hour with a sponge, could we open them. I was in a great fright as Ophthalmia up here in the Punjab is a most *horrible* disease. I immediately made a circuit of our servants' huts, and to my horror found that my Indian woman's children had Ophthalmia in the worst of forms, brought on by dirt and filthiness of every description. The woman had undoubtedly been wiping their eyes with her chuddah (shawl) and then instead of using Cecil's handkerchiefs, used her filthy chuddah to wipe his darling little peepers. He is better now, but the upset put the mail out of my mind.

I gave a dinner party on my birthday and Charles Hunter came – you remember him? – looking very well, and a beard and thick whiskers had improved him vastly.

Another evening we went down to Colonel Rennie's, and he permitted the Band to play for us. We had such a jolly time, Mrs Cole and I being the only ladies. Two officers, including Mr Hunter, imitated ladies, and the latter put on my skeletons, the frame of my new crinoline, and Doctor Corbett serenaded him, 'blew him up' as he called it, with my lute. The scene was rich and never since I have been in India have I laughed so much. Indeed I could not sleep for stomach ache brought on by laughing!

Mama, you tell me to get a straw bonnet from Calcutta. Dear Mama, I have paid *25 rupees* for a plain straw with the ribbon just crossed in top curtain, and *no* inside flowers. I wish you would get some lady who knows India to put you up to all the things which to us are of such importance. You have no idea of the prices and the shortages. It is a fact when I tell you I cannot go out as I have no shoes or boots to put on, nothing left but bronze kid, which would be highly ridiculous to wear here.

Thank you for the worsted needles. Pray tell Cissy she never tells me anything about the fashions, how to trim a bonnet, or make my muslin dresses and jackets.

The new Postal arrangements are abominable. Some have

turned up posted in England eighteen months ago. The last letter of yours was marked 21, the second marked by you thus.

My fondest love, dearest Mama,

Your fondly attached child,

Minnie Wood

By the end of February 1858 the violence of the Mutiny was virtually over, though pockets of trouble still continued, largely in Oude. The fight for Lucknow was bitter and costly, but at the end of March the city was taken and the Residency siege at last lifted. Communications were better and it was comparatively safe to move about in the quiet areas. The chief rebels were being chased and caught, and the fury aroused by the ghastly slaughter of women and children at Cawnpore was dying down; but the rising left a bitterness which survives in the minds of both Indians and British to this day.

Minnie, deep in her own troubles, makes very little comment on all this. As so often happens when one is in the midst of history in the making, she was not taking very much notice of it.

Between the last letter and the next one that survives, affairs in the Woods' household had taken a turn for the worse. Two drafts of money failed to reach Mrs Blane, causing trouble; and a period of disillusionment had begun for Minnie as she realized Archie's inability to cope with money affairs, and his state of mind, no doubt due to his ill-health and the treatment given for it.

Jhelum, 9 April 1858

Dearest Mama,

Your letters make me *very* sad, dearest Mother. I only wish I could see you to tell you all I want to. You shall *always* have whatever extra pay we have, and even if we have only our Captain's pay, you shall have 50 rupees a month. We have received no Staff pay for March, which accounts for your not getting the draft, but I send 50 rupees for February's pay, the rest having been cut.

It is indeed a great drawback that Archie is so *totally ignorant* on money matters. He has for so many years been accustomed to his Mess, and to spend *double* what he has, that I really wish I had never been married. I find it most difficult to keep things straightened. With this Bombay debt always hanging over me, and the constant worry about money, I am quite ill.

I hope by now you have received Archie's letter and the draft, and you will then see that he *has* written to you. I confess I was extremely angry with him, for not only you, but all his correspondents suffer from his neglect, and I have to keep up his correspondence, which comes very hard on me, as I have more to do in the day than *his* writing.

I fear the last box you sent has gone for ever, as there had been a great robbery on the Grand Trunk road between Allahabad and Cawnpore.

We have just seen [read about] the death of one of our own officers at Lucknow. He was killed the very day before the place fell.

Archie is still suffering very much from Dyspepsia, and nothing seems to relieve him. His appetite is gone, and the little he eats disagrees with him. Dr Cole declares that the hot season will make him much worse, so I have made up my mind that we must leave Jhelum and go to Murree in the Hills. In any case we should have to go there in June or July, as my confinement will take place in the latter part of July.

Yes, alas, I am again in this very unenviable position, and after what I underwent last year from bad management of nurse and doctor, I do not care to what expense I am put so long as I get good attendance.

I am delighted with the pictures you have sent me of the family, and am now hunting for frames for them. They arrived yesterday in good condition, and I cannot describe to you how something like them cheers one in one's troubles and banishment. A thousand thanks for them and for your good wishes. I would give all I have not to have come to this vile country, and it is hard to think that many years must elapse before I can meet you again. We could not find enough money for the journey. I hope to goodness Cissy will never marry a soldier, for it is a very different life from what we both imagined.

Cecil is great fun now as he tries so hard to talk. He walks holding on to things and tries to climb everywhere. The moment he has done something he should not, or has 'peed' himself which he knows is wrong, he squats on the floor, screws up his nose and says 'Bum Bum'. He is so sweet, and puts his arms round my neck and kisses me so prettily. What should I do without him?

I am so glad Mrs Smith has reached England and is going to stay with you. She was with me when baby was born and is one of my greatest friends. You will like her very much.

Ever your fond child,
Minnie Wood

The next letter is in a happier vein, and comes from the Hill Station of Murree on 4 May:

Dearest Mama,

I fear you may be anxious at not hearing from me, but on the last mail day I was on my travels to this delightful place where my dear husband has been ordered for a change of air, the Medical Board at 'Pindi having decided that unless he escaped this hot weather in the plains he would be most seriously ill.

You cannot conceive what a change has taken place in the poor fellow. He is awfully low about himself, fancies all sorts of things bad, that he makes me quite miserable.

Oh, Mama, if only you could see these lovely hills! Our house is on the top of the highest hill here, seven thousand feet up from those horrid plains. Oh, the deliciousness of having no hot weather, no punkahs, no tatties to endure. It is a truly English climate, our doors and windows all day open, no mosquitos or other luxuries of this delightful country.

We are obliged to keep a Jampan, or sedan chair on poles, in which I am carried by four men called Jampanees, as the hills are quite beyond one's legs, unless one be a hillman.

From our verandah we have a view of the whole of Murree,

and of the snowy range, and at the back Rawalpindi, forty miles off, and down to the plains where the poor wretches are now stewing in all the miseries of a hot season.

I took three days from Jhelum to Murree travelling at night in my Palkee, a hundred miles or more. Archie left me on the 14th April in order to appear before the Board, and then proceeded on to Murree to procure a house. Everything is exorbitantly dear. The house we are in is small and comfortable, but not an atom of furniture in it. For this we have to pay £90 for the season. It is a high rent but we could not live in two rooms and a bath room which was £70. However, all is going on well. Archie does not drink beer and walks a great deal, so please God, I trust he may soon get well again.

For February and March and 14 days in April we have not received *one shilling*, as there is some *squabbalation* going on with the Civil Auditor on the subject. We shall be sure to get something, and whatever it is, however small, it will be sent to England to you. In the meanwhile I have put 50 rupees in the Bank here out of our *Pay* for March. Out of Feb's Pay we could not put in, as we had to pay so much for travelling expenses. Arthur Roberts has advised me to send it straight to you, not via William Wood, my brother-in-law, as he understands nothing of Indian concerns, has never been out here, and meddles with what he does not understand. Please, dear Mama, will you attend to *our* directions and not to Mr Wood's, who knows nothing beyond his stool in Somerset House.

I am in a dreadful state for clothes. What I have I cannot wear, as I am so large, but it seems useless writing to you on this subject. Neither you nor Cissy understand what it is to be without things, and to be unable to purchase them out here. Others are getting boxes from home of all they need, but I seem to be left to fish for what I want. What I can get here I shall ruin myself if I buy. You have never been out of England so I suppose it is impossible for you to understand how difficult this vile country is. People here have sisters who keep them constantly supplied with what they need, and you may tell Cissy to keep her ball dresses, her flowers, and her letters too,

Travelling in a dooly on a mountain. Minnie used this form of transport and remarked on one occasion that there was only a foot or two between herself and destruction, but the bearers were sure-footed 'and really I was not much alarmed'.

A typical dinner party for a well-to-do family. Note candles encased in glass to protect the flame from the draught of the flapping punkah.

After the dinner, the ball – waltzing in costumes which appear to have no relevance to the climate. A punkah coolie seems to have taken the wrong turning.

I do not want them now. I suppose out of sight she forgets me.

The post will be going out soon, so believe me, with love, dear Mama,

Your affectionate child,
Minnie Wood

Tell Cissy she never answers my questions nor tells me how she does her hair and all the things I long to hear. I had to buy a cotton dress the other day and it cost 10 rupees. *Ruination.* I have asked you not to send parcels by Calcutta, they never arrive as the route is unsafe. I have told you to send things by *Indian Parcel Post*, that is by the arrangement between the P and O Shipping Company and the Indian Post Office. I have mentioned this before, but repeat it now in case you did not understand – or take notice. At the rate of one shilling per pound, parcels can be sent anywhere in India from England. Send them to the Company's office in London, and from there forward to India, thus requiring two wrappers, one addressed to the Company, the inner one to the destination in India. Goods sent this way are much cheaper than if purchased in Bombay or Calcutta, costing more than treble the value of articles purchased in England. The Calcutta route is unsafe, but the Bombay and the Indus route is much better. Please, dear Mama, send things this way, and pay no attention to what you are told in England.

M.W.

From Archie in Murree on 20 June 1858:

My dear Mrs Blane,

I regret we shall not now be able to remit you £13 monthly, as I have been driven up to the Hills by ill health, and unfortunately only receive my Captain's pay of 384 rupees, approximately £38, and no other allowances.

My leave on medical certificate will expire on the 15th October when I hope to receive a Staff appointment either at Rawalpindi or in the Punjab. What ever my emoluments will be, you shall receive them all.

This is a very expensive place of residence. Our house rent is £90 for a 5½ month season. Provisions are very dear. Meat, bread, vegetables, etc., are much more expensive than on the Plains. All most exorbitant.

I have written to Colonel Clark the owner of our house telling him we can only afford to pay him £10 a month. In winter no visitors remain here, as it is too cold, three to five feet of snow being on the ground.

My wife is pretty well considering her confinement is only five weeks hence. Our boy, Cecil, is very well, thank God, and our nurse, Mrs Loveridge, takes great care of him. He rides his pony every day and I had a nice little saddle made for him. Dear little Blessing, how we wish Grandmama could see him. We dote upon him almost too much, and we pray that God will be pleased to spare him to see you in England.

Now goodbye. My affectionate love to you and Cissy,

A. O. Wood

The Abbey, Murree Hills, 20 June

My dearest Mama,

I am busy getting my baby things in order for the 'little stranger' whose arrival I expect in the first week in August. I suffer dreadfully from cramp in my stomach, and whether I intend having a *Brace* or whether it is a girl, I do not know, but I am much larger than when I was carrying Cecil. I have an excellent, kind Doctor, a Dr Tuson, and a clever nurse, so I hope, please God, to get over my troubles easily this time, but I am dreading it most thoroughly.

Cecil has become a little scamp during the last three weeks. He trots about by himself, and is always in mischief. He has splendid lungs but can only say 'Mum, Mum', and I wish you could have seen him yesterday thumping round my room with my shoes on. It was the richest thing in the world!

Of course, your box has never arrived. The mutineers attacked the bullock carts and destroyed an immense amount of property. I have to thank Mr Wood for this loss, as he insisted on sending it from Calcutta. I beg and entreat you not to listen to other people but to do what we, who are on the spot, know is best. William Wood is an *ass*.

I cannot write more, dearest Mama, as I cannot sit up for long. Our united love, ever your fondly attached child,

Minnie Wood

Colonel and Mrs Muter are arriving here shortly. I hear they are delightfully agreeable people. He led the skirmishes of the 4th column at the assault of Delhi and assumed command of them at the fall of Colonel Reid. A very gallant officer.

From Murree:

My dear Mrs Blane,

On the 17th August my wife was safely delivered of a male child. She had a very easy confinement, no pains to speak of. About 2 a.m. she was restless and in pain and I begged her to walk about our bedroom. She drank some tea and tried not to think about her approaching troubles. At four I asked the nurse if I should send for the Doctor but she said no, as the baby would not come for another five hours. However, I left the room, roused the servants to prepare hot water, and then wrote a note and dispatched it by messengers to call Doctor Tuson. They had no sooner departed when the ayah came hastily into my sitting room to say Minnie had given birth! A fine child was born exactly at day break. I then dispatched another messenger to the Doctor saying 'Child born, both doing well'. The nurse will receive 80 rupees for her twenty day visit.

I am doing Duty here with the European Convalescent Depot, but receive no extra pay. Colonel Muter has arrived, but Minnie does not like his wife.

God bless you and all dear to us,
Believe me, affectionately yours,

A. O. Wood

For the next two years few letters have survived, and it is probable that few letters were written. Minnie had ill-health and Archie's illness increased. Doubtless the treatment with opium did much to undermine his already weak character, as well as his failing strength. Minnie, despite her troubles and her growing disillusionment with her husband, made great efforts to remain cheerful, and her courage in the face of so many misfortunes, the lack of money being perhaps the worst of them all, is commendable.

She wrote to her mother in October 1858:

Dearest Mama,

I got over my confinement most wonderfully, though I have been ill on and off ever since. I had a bad flooding after Baby's birth which weakened me greatly, and I am at this moment in bed suffering great pain due to the Doctor ordering me cold baths. Leeches and hot fomentations are applied to my stomach but the pain is the same. Indeed I am very miserable. I have a return of the illness I had last year, and Doctor Tuson tells me I now have inward piles and has ordered me enemas four times a day, first of all warm water and sweet oil, and then one of opium and other strange things. I am not what I was, and I find the least excitement too much for me, and the Doctor has forbidden me to go anywhere.

My husband is far from well. Ever since he has been up here he has had diarrhoea and he is looking terribly thin. He has applied twice to Sir John Lawrence for an appointment, but was refused. He has applied to the Governor General, the Commander in Chief, Sir John Lawrence, the Adjutant General, General Mansfield, etc., etc., and all without success. The poor fellow is very downhearted. I do grieve for him for he has tried very hard to get something better than this appointment with the Convalescent Depot up here. Were we not so hard up, and with the money to remit to you each month, we should jump at staying here, for we should have a year up here, escaping the hot weather, and the dear children would benefit by that so much. I suppose it is all for the best but I do feel so very, very sad at times.

Mr Roberts, though so closely related to us, will not ask Sir John for anything for Archie. He has begged him to speak for him, and I have written and entreated him to do something for us, but he is obstinate on the point, and I cannot ask him any more. He knows our affairs and that we are responsible to send you £120 a year, yet he will do nothing. So much for relations. Dearest Mama, we have promised you to do our utmost. Can we do more than this?

Now to more pleasant things. Just fancy that long lost box has arrived! I cannot thank you sufficiently for all the beautiful things you have sent. My petticoats I like very much and the dresses are lovely, and there is a woman here who can make them up. The shoes are much too small for Cecil after all this time, but will come in for dear Baby. He is a big boy with lots of light hair very like me, they say. His brother pats and kisses him and calls him 'Baba'. It is a pretty sight to see our two blessings together.

Mama, you should not say you have nothing to live for. Do you not wish to see your grandsons? The Deputy Commissioner of Jhelum has just left for England, and has your address. He will come and see you and tell you all about us. Take heart, dear Mama.

Lady Lawrence left India last January, but I had the pleasure of knowing her in Lahore, and thought her a most charming person. Sir John goes home in January.

I have just received your letter containing the views of Bath. Archie and I will look at them a thousand times a day. I can picture you in dear old Pultney Street. It is such a pleasure. If I could get Home I should be perfectly mad with delight. I must hope that we may soon see brighter days, but at present it is very cloudy.

It is very cold now and the hills in Cashmere are covered with snow, such a grand sight.

I was very pleased at being asked to help with Miss Charlotte Smith's wedding. I went up and helped her and her sister with things, and decorated the Cake Favour Baskets and the table. In fact I flatter myself that everything would have been vile without me! However, I went to dress her, and then in the church I was taken with one of my horrible attacks of hysterics and was obliged to come home. The fact was I was awfully excited, and then thought of my own wedding and you, and then I commenced crying and could not control myself.

Dear Mama, my love and kisses,

Minnie Wood

10 October

Dear Mrs Blane,

Minnie has been a great invalid since the birth of our baby boy. She has been suffering acutely from rheumatism in her joints. I think it was brought on by her taking cold baths on doctor's orders, who recommended them to strengthen her. But alas, it injured her health. She was confined to her room for days, but the last three she has been able to go out in her Jonpon during the warmest part of the day. The weather is now most charming, hoar frosts in the morning, and clear, dry, sparkling weather.

I regret to say I have not been able to procure staff employment in the Punjab. I am greatly distressed in mind, and worried to death over money.

I am your affectionate son-in-law,

Archie Wood

10 October

My darling Mama,

I have been laid up with acute rheumatism in all my joints, and have been in bed, unable to turn, but now thank God, I am able to move about again. I could not nurse dear baby, but now I am able to once more.

We had baby christened the other day, Percy Arthur Everest. Had we known in time we would have obeyed your wishes and called him Archibald. I was too unwell to have any party, but Mr Roberts lent me a large tent called a Shamianah, and we had breakfast for twenty people, a jolly party, and afterwards archery.

I am very busy making winter clothes. The snow is frightful here, and we have to lay in stores for the winter months, as often people have to be dug out. We must change our house and go lower down for we would be perished up here. More expense.

The officers gave a Pic Nic on Wednesday last and it poured cats and dogs all day!

We have seen a comet for the last three weeks. It is a most brilliant sight on a clear night, and Cecil cries for it!

I am much obliged to Cissy for her hints on trimmings, but I cannot conceive where I am to get them in this country! There is no Jolly's to walk into here as in Bath.

Cecil now rides nicely on his pony, and our baby is a monster, little darling. He sleeps all day and roars all night. He was born with a rupture in his private parts, but the Doctor tied them up tight with his napkin, and he has got all right I am happy to say.

The Muters are living here now, quite nice but Mrs is very prim, wears awfully shabby, old-fashioned clothes, and her back looks as if it had a poker down it. She never pronounces her 'r's', and talks of 'Webels' and 'Wifles', which nearly kills me with laughter. Nevertheless, she is a kind-hearted body and her husband is a brick, delightful, tall and good looking, and the last man to have chosen such a wife I should think!

I must close to catch the mail,
Your affectionate child,
Minnie Wood

Minnie's next letter is not written until the end of January 1859:

Rawal Pindi

My dearest Mama,

I have not written since the end of November, for I was laid up in Murree without the use of my arms or legs. This new attack was worse than any I had endured before. My joints were swollen to a frightful extent, and leeches were applied and the Galvanic Battery and all without success, and I was then sent down here by the Doctor. Both children got ill on arrival, Cecil with congestion of the liver, and baby with croup, the first time he has ever ailed. They are both getting on now, thank God.

To add to my troubles my ayah suddenly left, and my European nurse got drunk, so I was left with one new, perfectly useless ayah to take care of the children night and day, my arms being at that time unable to hold anything. My milk nearly left me, and the Doctor advised a wet nurse, but this I would not listen to and by perseverance I managed to get on somehow. I cannot get a decent ayah, thanks to the last one's lies – she went about telling people I had flogged her!!! I was forced to take another English servant but shall dismiss her when I can get a good ayah.

My dear husband came down on the 5th January, and immediately fell ill with Bronchitis and is only now recovering from it.

Altogether I have had a most trying time of it and I am only thankful that I was well enough to deal with it all.

I cannot write to either of my brothers or Cissy this mail, but give them, please, my very best love, and thank dear Cissy for her charming letters, and ask her to tell me how she has her own dresses made, and how her bonnets are trimmed, for I long to wear the same as she does.

I am expecting my piano up from Jhelum every day. It has been lying there packed up ever since the Mutiny. It will be such a treat to have it again.

I have been reading the Life of Henry Polehampton who died in the Mutiny, and was at our wedding. It is very interesting but not so much as 'A Lady's Diary of the Siege of Lucknow' written by the other chaplain's wife there, Mrs Harris.

I went to a Ball on the 31st December given by the officers of the 4th Punjab Infantry. Very jolly, but myself and two other ladies *only* danced Waltzes and Polkas, etc. There were ten ladies present and thirty gentlemen. This is often the case at Indian parties. It is very tiring work as when a lady dances she is expected to dance *everything*, and the consequence was I went through nineteen dances and only stopped because my shoe cut me so much.

All my shoes are too small now for one's feet swell so in this country. When I go out I am now wearing a pair of Archie's shoes, Oxfords I think they are called. I hope there are some for me in the box, and also a pair of stays.

If a mail passes without one from me do not be anxious. You say you have missed six, so some must be lost. I do not spin you a yarn, and I have never missed more than three, and that was not on purpose.

Your fondly attached child,

Minnie Wood

Sunday, 6 February
Rawal Pindi

Dearest Mama,

We have just had prayers at home as the day is too wet to venture out. The rains have swollen the nullahs and prevented the arrival of your letters for some time.

Thank goodness the Rebellion is at last over, though that horrid Nana and the Begum are still at large. The General Orders say that ladies and their families may now reside in Oude. Our kind friends Mr and Mrs Montgomery are coming up from Oude this month as he is appointed successor to Sir John Lawrence as Lieutenant Governor of the Punjab. I hope that Archie may have some chance of a better appointment. I shall use my powers as a diplomatist to the best of my ability. I was often at their house in Lahore and got on very well with them.

10 February

You see I cannot finish my epistles without interruptions. I no sooner get started before a heap of visitors are announced. First the officers of the 18th Cavalry just arrived here, a Major Byres and a Mr Hand, the latter a very handsome fellow, and done up within an *inch* of his life, in such a magnificent uniform, all blue and gold. Some of the toggery of these regiments is really very fine.

The 7th Fusiliers are coming here which will be jolly, but they will have no ladies with them. The other day the officers gave a tiffin in the Mess Tent on the Parade Ground. Had the weather been warmer it would have been much better, as it was I sat shivering next to the Brigadier's wife, not daring to move.

Cecil went with me and was the amusement of the whole tent, laughing and talking with everyone. He is not a bit shy and wore the Tuscan hat with the feather, and the green merino pelisse you sent him, and you cannot think how proud I was of my son! When I talk to him of you he says, 'Dear Danmama' and Cissy is 'Aulity Cissy'.

I have just received from Jhelum my poor little piano. It was in wonderful preservation and tune after all these months, and I was congratulating myself on it being free from insects which destroy most pianos out here, when the bandmaster of H.M.'s 70th, Mr Deitrich, opened it. *Oh, horror!!!* It was one mass of fluffy cottony insects who had eaten the red cloth on the notes and commenced on the green baize. However, it was able to be cleaned, and except for great vibration it is in very good order.

We are looking forward to a trip round the district with Mr Roberts. I think camp life is a very jolly one.

Bye bye for the present. I am nearly asleep.

14 February

I dined out last night with Major Cox, our new Commander. He is a Bath man. Do you know of him? Archie and Arthur Roberts and a few others were there, a very jolly evening I assure you.

I am going to try to get a Baby Jumper. My little Percy is such a fidget that I think he will be delighted with it.

I should be so happy if you would send me portraits of all of you. Mr Roberts is constantly having pictures of his family sent to him. Could you not do so too? Perhaps you could all be done on Stereoscopes and then send them with the Glasses to me, that would be delightful.

My love to you all, your affectionate child,

Minnie Wood

In Camp, 18 miles from Rawal Pindi
Camp Chireigh, 16 February, 1859

My dearest Mama,

We left Rawal Pindi yesterday to join Arthur Roberts in camp as he is out on his district, and the doctor recommended a change of air for all of us. Archie rode and I and my children went in my doolie. We started about eight in the morning, and reached the ground between two and three in the afternoon. I was quite done up and the children had been very troublesome, and Master Cecil had thought proper to upset a bottle of rhubarb, which made me awfully sick.

We are now quite out in the jungles, in a magnificent tent of three rooms and a verandah all round, with a large store, and as comfortable as possible. Our party is Mr Roberts, Captain and Mrs Cracroft, the Deputy Commissioner, and Mr Harding our Jhelum friend and Assistant Commissioner, all as jolly as they can be. The children look very well, and will, I have no doubt, benefit by the change.

We were objects of great interest to the Punjabees, and whenever we stopped to change the bearers crowds of women and naked children surrounded us, and could not without some difficulty be induced to leave us. Baby and Cecil were the chief attraction, White Babas having never before penetrated into these wilds. The day was very sultry and we were glad when the tents made their appearance. I shall make this a Journal day by day.

Thursday, 17 February
Dear Baby is six months old today, bless him.

Here we are after a most fatiguing march of eleven miles, pitched in a valley between high mountains. This place is 600 feet higher than from where we started this morning. The road was awful, but the scenery wild in the extreme and very pretty. Tomorrow's road will be worse, but I have made up my mind to brave it.

I am in an awful rage as I have a perfect fool of an ayah and a jackass of a bearer who drive me wild by their stupidity. I literally have to do everything for children *and husband*, pack up the beds, arrange the clothes and tent, wash and dress the children, and not a soul to assist me. It is too much for me and I was so tired when all the work was finished I was obliged to go to bed.

Saturday, 19 February

We halted all day yesterday as there was a heap of work to be done by the Civil folks. I was able to get things in order, if only that wretched ayah will not muddle them all up again.

We arrived here, Kuhouta, at three in the afternoon, having left Nurare at gunfire this morning. I was nine hours going nine and a half miles. I was tired as I walked much of the distance, though the Chicks were carried, as there were no roads today, nothing but a tortuous mountain path, which was merely trodden by goats. Mercy! When I was carried the bumps made my poor B.T.M. very sore! How my poor doolie escaped being broken I do not know. I had coolies in front cutting down shrubs, clearing away stones, in fact making a way for me. We went clean over two mountains, in many places along nothing but huge precipices, into which the least trip on the part of the bearers would have thrown us. I was very nervous but Cissy would have enjoyed it, as the Cracrofts did as they rode the distance. But I cannot ride so it is no use my lamenting.

We have now descended into the plains and the camp is pitched at the foot of a long, low range. I walked there with Archie and Arthur, and after a lot of scrambling succeeded in getting to the top. We were well paid for our trouble, for the view was magnificent, the Himalayas, and Pass into Cashmere, lay in front of us, a mass of snow, and at our feet the Ling river wound its way between huge rocks. In the far off distance stood the mountains of Rawal Pindi, backed by range on range of hills, altogether forming one of the prettiest scenes I have ever seen in India.

The sky now threatens rains, but I trust we shall be fortunate and avoid it, for it is miserable work under canvas in the wet.

Sunday, 20 February

It has been drizzling all day, and I fear we are for it. Mr Roberts proposes marching into 'Pindi tomorrow if it is fine. I shall be very sorry, for it is so jolly out here.

We had service twice today in Arthur's tent. Mr Harding read prayers and Arthur a sermon. Two Native Christians and the Cracrofts were our congregation. The children are awfully tiresome, they cry the moment I leave them and they cannot endure the ayah. Nor can I.

Monday, 21 February

Oh, such weather! Down came the rain this morning, pelting, just after the Cracrofts had struck their tents and marched. Poor things, I hope they liked it! Here we are, boxed up, everything damp and dirty, and the poor children as cross as two sticks. Archie too, as he has been done out of his shooting.

Poor little Cecil has nettlerash. I have given him a dose of Magnesia and fomented the rash, and I hope tomorrow he will be better.

Tuesday, 22 February

A most fearful storm in the night. I thought the tents would be blown away, and the rain poured down. No chance of stirring this evening.

Your letter arrived this morning written on the 17th January. What a pity you did not take the opportunity to go to Cannes. Dear Mama, I am sure the change would have done you good. You should not, dear Mama, write so despondently.

I am much better than I was, though my complaint comes on by fits and starts. I have to thank you very much for thinking of me, and I am sure the instrument you are sending me will do me good.

Will you send me patterns on paper of a cloak. My Cashmere tailor embroiders beautifully and I want to send you and Cissy something, only I must have a good pattern. He will work waistcoats for the boys very well too. I have a loose jacket which I find very useful. Please will you tell me how you fasten flannel petticoats? I fasten them on to little stays, and I don't know where to put buttons for the little trousers I make.

Friday, 25 February
Dearest Mama, we have just arrived in 'Pindi after a very long journey. We left Koohooters this morning at day break, breakfasted half way in tents at Seala, and came on in the afternoon, and reached 'Pindi at six o'clock in the evening. Archie leaves me on Sunday for Murree, and does not come down again, but prepares a house for my reception. The season promises to be a gay one.

The post is going, dearest Mama, so goodbye,
Ever your fondly attached child,
Minnie Wood

Murree, 9 April

My darling Mama,
A box has arrived for which I cannot thank you enough. Oh, the beautiful things you have sent! My bonnets are the admiration of everyone, for I must tell you that when an English box is received out here, all the ladies in the Station flock to one's house to see the contents. Consequently I have been besieged by all my friends, and they all declare they never saw any display greater than the one you have sent.

The lilac bonnet is my favourite, and as to my baby's hat, it is a bijou. He wears it of an evening with the pretty blue dress and looks a little angel in it. Dear Cecil, however, broke the dog and the railway before he had them two hours. I like my brown dress very much, but am a little afraid it will not wear long in this damp climate.

Unfortunately all the shoes and boots are too tight across the toes for me. I will send you my measurements in my next letter. My silk dress is a real beauty, the jacket beautifully made and conveniently too loose for me. I like everything so much I could write for an hour about it.

The heat in 'Pindi increased so much that I came up here on the

5th instant. We are in a different house from last year, as the roof of that was bad. This is called 'Nutwood' and is in a very nice situation.

Every house is taken for this season, and I fancy we shall have a gay one. General Sir Sidney Cotton is here now with his adopted daughter. He is a very fine, soldier-like old man, but not at all popular on account of his strictness to rules, etc.

Archie is suffering very much from his old complaint, dysentery. No climate seems to suit him out here.

Mr Montgomery and his wife will be up here soon, and won't I be nice to him on Archie's behalf! We have a beast of a man commanding the Depot now, such a *Funk Stick*. He is a Major General and such an old woman. I hate him.

Mr Roberts has just been appointed as Officiating Financial Commissioner of the Punjab on pay of £350 a month. This is an immense promotion for him. His son has just arrived in Calcutta. Oh Mama, get Willie to study for the Engineers. There is no pay or service like it, and it is the crack service out here.

Ever your affectionate child,

Minnie Wood

Murree, 25 May

My dearest Mama,

We are all as jolly as possible up here. The Lieutenant Governor and his wife commenced a series of dinners which enliven the place. We were there last night, eighteen persons to dinner and everything so nice. Sir Robert and Lady Montgomery are most charming people. There is talk of getting up a ball, but as most of the ladies are in an interesting condition, I fear it will be a failure, for with the exception of the two Miss Smiths and myself, no one else will be dancing.

So Cissy is not thinking of getting married. She had better take care as she is twenty-two in a few days and could be an old maid!

The Native Regiments such as the Bengal Horse Artillery have been treated most shamefully. Everything is for the Queen's

Regiments. What will become of us all? All sorts of reports are circulating, some that we shall be sent to England to join our new regiments. I only wish this could come true. It would be glorious. Anything to get out of this vile hole.

The dear children are so well. Everyone says I should get the prize if there was a baby show. Baby is so big for his age. He is growing out of his white satin and now wears his white felt, and one of those handsomely worked drawers and jacket, dress and sash the same as his brother's, and scarlet shoes. Cecil wears his Tuscan hat and he rides on his pony every morning and evening.

Dear Mama, how ought I to wash Honiton lace? Also how do I clean a Tuscan or a straw hat? In this country one must do these things oneself. Please send me some sleeve patterns in coloured silver paper. You can get them at the milliner's.

I send you some correspondence of my husband's. You will see that there is about £150 which cannot be accounted for. I also wish you please to get from Archie's tailor, Wells, in St James's Street, the whole of his account, as a sum of £200 was paid to him before we left England, and he has never sent in the receipt for that amount.

A kiss from all of us to you and Cissy,

Your fondly attached child,

Minnie Wood

Murree, 10 September

My dearest Mama,

You will think us horrible correspondents, but I have nothing that would interest you to write about. The children and I are all well and baby is the most mischievous piece of goods I have ever seen, he requires half a dozen people to watch him.

Archie is *not* well, but studying hard for the examination on November 19th, the day Government has appointed for all the officers who have not yet passed the prescribed examination.

I cannot tell you how pleased I am that he does at last see the necessity for getting more pay, for I shall feel then that my anxious days are over when we can get enough to save and to send you as much as will make up for all the time you have had nothing. Oh, how jolly it will be to know we are able to save money to pay our fare home. Neither you nor Cissy can fully understand the yearning we poor exiles feel for England and everything connected with it, or how treasured everything is that comes from it.

There are plenty of balls going on but we never go to anything but dinners and musical parties. We are happy at home with our children and we really do not care for going out.

We had a very delightful musical party at Lady Montgomery's on the 17th, baby's birthday. Two of the ladies sang as well as any I have heard in an Opera. It was a great treat. My husband sang three times. We need some new songs badly. It is quite delightful to meet with really nice gentlefolk, for out here the most extraordinary characters are met with. Among the 'ladies' here two have been *actresses*, and one, the wife of a Captain, a bar maid from a small inn near Plymouth! Really, society is very recherché!!

Archie is with his Munchee, his native teacher, or he would join me in affectionate love to you all.

Your attached child,
Minnie Wood

Murree, November 1859

Dearest Mama,

Just a short note which is coming home with this little parcel, which consists of a baby's dress and my wedding sleeves, which were eaten by a bullock the other day in the compound. Can you get them mended for me? Can the appliqué sleeves be put on muslin or something stronger than this net, which is so frail?

We are all in such a mess packing the camels, sending off servants, etc., and all the other miseries attending the removal to Peshawar in this hole.

Your fond daughter,
Minnie Wood

Peshawar, 26 November

My dearest Mama,

Here we are up in Peshawar on the Frontier, with the celebrated Khyber Pass just in front of us. I have certainly seen India from one end to the other.

I must tell you about our affairs. Archie without my knowledge telegraphed to the Assistant Adjutant General for the appointment of Barrack Master in this Division, on an *increase* of salary of about 300 rupees a month. He got it, and three days after Government cut it down to 120 a month, which was not sufficient pay for us to incur such expenses as moving our goods, chattels and selves to Peshawar. He therefore threw it up, and General Sydney Cotton appointed him at once to do duty with the renewed 33rd Native Infantry up here, on the *wonderful pay of 60* rupees a month extra. It is disgusting, and to be with natives again as well!

Of course, this has interrupted Archie's studies, but he will not, *I hope*, give up the effort. I do not know what is going to become of us if we do not get more pay. The expense of moving in this country with servants, baggage, cattle, etc., is enormous, and we are frightfully out of pocket.

My husband has been ill with dysentery and diarrhoea. He cannot shake it off, and the Doctors here seem to think it is chronic. Sea air is the only thing which might do him good, so we may have to leave and go down to Kurrachee by boat. This complaint is very serious. It seems fated that we are never to be happy and comfortable in this country. I wish to heaven he had passed his exam for that is the only means I can see of us ever having enough money to come home, and leave this accursed country.

I have nothing to tell you except that I am sick of the world. It is such a misery that life is a burden to me. Forgive my writing more now.

Your affectionate daughter,

Minnie Wood

On 1 November 1858, the proclamation was made public which ended the East India Company's rule, and brought India under the direct rule of the Queen, the British Government and as part of the British Empire. Queen Victoria and the Prince Consort had interested themselves in every detail, the Queen determined to show her personal concern, and her benevolence to British and Indians alike.

This proclamation was read in all the chief towns and was the official end of the Mutiny, though in fact it was another six months before there was complete peace in Oude and Central India.

It ran, to quote some short extracts:

'Victoria, by the Grace of God, of the United Kingdom, etc., etc., Queen . . . whereas for divers weighty reasons . . . we have resolved to take upon ourselves the Government of India, heretofore administered in trust for us by the Honourable East India Company . . . we do hereby confirm in their several offices, civil and military, all those now employed in the service of the Honourable East India Company . . . we do hereby announce to the Native Princes of India that all treaties made under the Honourable East India Company will be scrupulously maintained, and we look for the like observance on their part . . . we declare that none be favoured, nor molested by reason of their religious faith . . . and that all shall enjoy equal protection of the law . . . and we strictly charge that they abstain from all interference with the worship of any of our subjects. . . . It is our further wish that our subjects of whatever race or creed be freely admitted to offices in our service . . . and we will see that due regard be paid to ancient rights, usages and customs of India . . . we do deeply lament the evils and misery brought upon India by ambitious men . . . who deceived their countrymen and led them into open rebellion. . . . When internal tranquillity is restored it is our earnest desire to stimulate the peaceful industry of India . . . to promote . . . public improvement . . . to administer Government for the benefit of all . . . and may the God of all Power grant unto us . . . strength to carry out these our wishes for the good of our people.'

The East India Company was made the scapegoat for the Mutiny, though it was the Board of Directors in England and their representative, Lord Dalhousie, who had pressed for annexation and other acts which were at the bottom of the discontent. They had not listened to men, long in the Company's service, who had warned them of the dangers. The Company's rule was over, according to the prophecy which had said that it would last for a hundred years. It fell, but with a revered name, and with regrets for the passing of its era. It had done much: it had built canals, roads and railways, brought up to date communications and cultivation, perhaps too quickly, but with enormous benefits to the country. Mistakes had been made, wrong policies followed, and wise men's counsel ignored, but the East India Company had brought justice and progress, and on the whole it deserved its adjective 'Honourable'.

From this time all Minnie's worries come to the surface. She had been hiding many troubles in her letters to her mother up to this, but from now on she makes plain the incessant upheaval in her household, Archie's incapability of coping with life, and the nagging anxiety over money.

Archie was taken very ill and Minnie's next letter tells the course of events:

January 1860 at Mr Gore Ouseley's house in Shanpore

My dearest Mama,

By the end of the next three months I hope to be in England, as Captain Wood has been so ill from dysentery that his doctors ordered him away at once to England for two years on Medical Certificate. I shall not enlarge on this subject as I consider it *his* business to inform you of his affairs.

I regret to say that he is so insufferably lazy he never writes to anyone, attends to his affairs, nor does anything like other men. Consequently everything with us and ours goes to the bad. Why?

Because there is no one to put matters straight. I do as much as I can but it is impossible for me to do everything. I firmly believe there is no other lady in India who has to do what I have, in fact, were I not blessed with a strong constitution I could not go on as I am doing, for it is wearing both to mind and body.

Captain Wood is so frightfully fussy and fidgety that nothing ever goes with us as with other people. We are always in a state of confusion, and of changing mind, that it is a miserable existence.

Here we are on our way to England, no affairs settled before leaving the country, nothing thought of, nothing paid for. It really is the most lamentable thing when the Master of a family is *so ignorant* of business as is Captain Wood.

I am most anxious to get to England as soon as practicable, for I am expecting another confinement in April, and I am already quite done up with two children. All I know is, once let me see the shores of England, and not all the husbands in the universe will get me to leave again. I have endured too much worry and misery since I married to induce me to come out again.

I wish to know most *particularly* if you ever told my husband that I had £500 a year of my own. He is constantly at me about it, and I consider his conduct most unkind upon this subject. If I applied to the lawyer when I arrive would he allow me to have so much for me and my children's use? We cannot live on Captain Wood's pay, viz. £191 per annum and Income Tax besides.

I trust, however, that Captain Wood will exert himself to procure some employment.

The children are well but they will go to no one except me, not even their father, so I am constantly washing and dressing them which is very tiring.

We hope to get to Kurrachee about the 1st of February. I then intend to do my utmost about a box that is missing. I cannot get Captain Wood to move in the affair. He is so negligent, and all he says is, 'It's gone, and what is the good of making a fuss about it?' He makes me feel vicious.

God bless you all,
Your fondly attached child,
Minnie Wood

From Archie Wood at Shanpore, January 1860

My dear Mrs Blane,

I regret to inform you that in consequence of continued ill health, I have been compelled to appear before a Medical Board at Peshawar, who have recommended me to return to England, and we are now en route to Kurrachee and Bombay.

My pay will be so small in England, I wish to procure employment to increase my income, and I would willingly accept an *Adjutantcy of Militia*. This would give me, with my Queen's pay of Captain, 10/6 a day, about £400 a year. Have you any County interest, either in Cheshire or Lancashire?

The Regimental Staff of the Militia is permanently kept up, and the Adjutant always paid. Could you use your interest with the Broughton family or the Earl of Derby to procure me this in England, if possible, or even in Scotland or Ireland?

I am much reduced by prolonged sickness, and I feel very weak. My complaint, dysentery, is chronic, and I have suffered from it for over two years. I take medicine and diet myself most strictly, but, alas! with all precautions I am still a martyr to it. What with this and severe dyspepsia, at times I am quite helpless, confined to my room for hours, and unable to walk or take any exercise.

The fact is that my health was injured on the day of the Jhelum mutiny. The great exposure I underwent fighting the whole day, for twelve consecutive hours, under a burning sun and an incessant fire of musketry. As Orderly Officer to the late Colonel Gerrard, I was more exposed than any officer in carrying orders to and fro. I sometimes had to gallop thro' large numbers of mutineers, incessantly exposed to their bullets, and being bare headed for a very considerable time, having lost my helmet.

This, and the great anxiety I felt for my wife and infant, whom I had left at a village within sight of the battle field, was too much for me. The excitement of the fight kept me up, but I felt it afterwards, and it tells upon me now.

Our boy, Cecil, caused much anxiety last year for he suffered from congestion of the liver and severe dyspepsia. We are anxious to get him home quickly.

My wife is well, thank God, but worried with the care of our two boys. We could not afford to bring our nurse with us. Minnie has to do everything for them as they will not allow a black servant to dress them, and when it is necessary to separate the Baby from her he cries most pitifully.

We travel down the river Jhelum to the Indus in country boats covered over with grass and brush wood. One boat we live in, and the other is our cooking boat, which contains our servants and goats, which are an indispensable necessity, owing to the demand for milk for our little ones. At sunset we stop for the night, and anchor at a secure bank, where the boatmen and servants cook and eat their victuals. We sleep in the boat and leave again at sunrise. Our progress daily is about forty miles.

My gun usually provides our table. Our fare is very homely, one day wild fowl, another a domestic fowl made into cutlets. We have only one dish, and our little ones feed with us. I usually bag two or three geese or ducks daily from the banks of the river. Sometimes we have a stew, another day curry, and plenty of chapatties, or flour cakes, and our beverage is the river water filtered and tea.

I am not feeling well today. I will write you again soon, probably from Multan. In the meantime accept our best love and believe me, most sincerely yours,

A. O. Wood

At Mr Ouseley's house, Shanpore, 12 January 1860:

My dearest Mama,

My last letter was also dated from this place and informed you of our being en route to England. Since that was dispatched Archie has been so seriously ill with a violent attack of dysentery which will detain us here for some long time before he is fit for a long journey. This means that it is too late in the season for me to travel with my third child due in April, so we are obliged to give up the idea of seeing England for some time.

I need not say that the disappointment is very, *very* bitter, but it is unavoidable.

Archie's attack threatened for some time to be very serious indeed, and he lost much blood and was greatly weakened. We are in the jungle here and Mr Gore Ouseley, with whom we are staying, sent off an express messenger to Jhelum for immediate medical aid. For upwards of two days the poor fellow was enduring the most awful agony, and not until blisters had been applied to the pit of his stomach, and other remedies and much opium had been tried, did he experience any relief. As long as he is in this country he will never enjoy good health, and yet how can we leave it, and where is the money to come from?

He now intends to commute his leave to Europe and to visit Simla in the hills this hot season. Yet another change of plans.

Troubles never come singly, and so the two boys were taken ill with bronchitis and fever, and I have been up night and day for the last weeks attending to all three invalids. Had it not been for the kindness and consideration of our host, who assisted me in every way, I must have knocked up. The fatigue has been so great, and I have no servants of my own to help me, and only an old fool of an ayah who I picked up on the road here.

I am quite unsettled as to what is best to be done. If Archie continues to suffer from severe dysentery we must, nolens volens, get out of this country by hook or by crook, but where the means are to come from after these useless journeys I do not know. I must hope for the best.

Had I but had a faint idea of Indian life with a penniless and helpless officer, nothing would have induced me to marry and come out here, and now we are without hope of getting home until we are old and worn out.

Mr Ouseley is one of the nicest and most unselfish men I have ever met. I shall never forget his kindness to two total strangers. His personal appearance is not prepossessing, but he is so good hearted. He is just thirty and draws £150 a month. There is a mighty difference in being a Civilian and an Army man. He is very fond of the children and takes such care of them when I am busy or too tired. Archie does, and can do, nothing.

Dearest Mama, I have bothered you sufficiently, so I will shut up shop.

Ever, dearest Mama, your very affectionately attached child,

Minnie Wood

The next letter is from Simla, written on 1 April:

My own dearest Mama,

Your picture is in front of me, and at last I have something which reminds me of home, and most delighted was I when I opened the letter containing the stereotypes.

We are settled, I hope, for some time in these delightful Simla Hills. It is the oldest Sanatorium in India and far preferable to Murree.

The truth must out. We have not the means to go to England, and should Archie not regain his health and we are finally forced to go to England or the Cape, we shall be forced to borrow *more* money, a thing which I hope will never happen.

It was preposterous thinking of going to England when we did. It would have ended in our utter ruin for our expenses would have been about £300 for travelling, and we could not live on £190 a year. His illness at Shanpore perhaps was sent to give me time to think. I could not conscientiously encourage Archie in such a scheme. It would be madness to leave India without some ready money to hand.

It makes me very unhappy that Archie cannot send you what we promised. Our family is increasing and this incurs much expense. I am very low spirited.

Yes, Mama, as you say I am much changed, and feel sometimes that it would be a relief to die and so have no more troubles. This, I know, is wicked. Oh, if only you were here for me to talk to!

Arthur Roberts is now a Judicial Commissioner for the Punjab. Soon he will be Governor General of the Punjab, I am sure. He considers that when a man has power his relations should be the last people he helps. I begged and prayed him to use his influence to procure Archie some appointment until he had passed his examination. He would not even *speak* for us. All he says is, 'My good girl, have patience. Let Archie study and then perhaps something can be done. Go to Simla and live quietly on 200 rupees a month.' All very well for him to say when he is living on *3,500 rupees* a month. It makes me so angry.

Next mail, dear Mama, I hope will bring you the news of another grandchild. It is expected about the 15th. I have suffered much this time from the weight and have had to wear bandages, as walking was sometimes agony on the bone. I had a false alarm the day before yesterday, brought on I fancy by an overdose of castor oil.

This is to be a gay season I am told, and Lord and Lady Canning will be here on the 10th, and the Commander in Chief soon after.

I hope most heartily that my brother Willie will take the opportunity of coming out here in the Artillery. It is a noble service, and I should be proud to have him in it, and besides it is such handsome pay. I am tired of sitting so will close.

Your fondly attached child,

Minnie Wood

Three days later Archie wrote:

Simla, 4 April

My dear Mrs Blane,

My wife presented me with a *son, number three*, this morning at seven o'clock!

Mother and Babe are *doing well*. Minnie had a *good time* of it, and the babe was born before the Doctor arrived. She has a *strong constitution* and a *good appetite* and is a *wonderful woman*. Baby is small with dark hair and *gigantic* feet like his mother's!

He has blue eyes and is very pretty, in fact there is not such another babe in India.

My health is a *little* better, I am thankful to say, but I am obliged to take *great care* of myself in the way of *diet*.

Accept our sincere thanks for your kind offer to receive our boys in England. We do not wish to part with them until we bring them home ourselves. Nevertheless, should it be necessary for *their health* to send them home, we will not hesitate to send them to you, as you are the *one* we know would cherish and love them.

16 April
Twelve days have now elapsed since my dear wife's *confinement*, and she is wonderfully well and strong. God has been most *merciful* and *good* to us, but it was most trying to me to see her suffer so. The *nurse assured me all was well*, but I humbled myself on bended knee and *prayed fervently* to the Almighty to spare my wife to me. I offered up the beautiful prayer in your book by Jenks for *women in travail*, and behold, the Lord heard the prayer of the husband (*however imperfect*) and the babe was born during my prayer, and Minnie *rejoiced*!

Dear Mrs Blane, I am so thankful.

My *pecuniary affairs* worry me *greatly*. I am often greatly *distressed* in mind and body. You have indeed been *most liberal* to me and I most deeply regret that I have been the cause of so much *anxiety* to you.

I hope your son Willie will pass for *Artillery or Engineers*. Do not let him come out in the Infantry, as this branch of the Army since the Mutiny has gone to the devil. None but officers in Lord Clyde's pet regiments such as the 79th and 93rd Highlanders get *any appointments*. I assure you that Willie would better himself in England by being a *Civil Engineer* than coming out here in the Infantry. I speak from experience.

Our united love,
Yours affectionately,
Archie Wood

Simla, 16 April

My dearest Mama,

Here I am, thank God, up again and able to sit in the drawing room, feeling, of course, weak, but otherwise well. My dear Baby is the picture of health and getting quite fat, which I am glad of as he was very skinny when born. I have a first rate nurse, who is also my Doctor, as the man who calls himself that name is most negligent. I am so glad it is a boy, I have no fancy for girls. I wish you could see my three darlings round me. Cecil not yet three years old, Percy nearly two, and my new darling.

    Dearest Mama,
     My fondest love, your attached child,
        Minnie Wood

P.S. I am sad that it seems that many of my letters have not reached you. There have been several instances of native servants taking off the stamps from letters in order to sell them, and destroying the letters. You cannot conceive the dodges these black people get up to.

Poor Minnie. Her letters have traced her progress from being a cheerful schoolgirl, a sociable young woman, and a happy wife on a honeymoon during which she found that 'excepting looking at each other all day there is very little to write about'. They have recounted her trials of travel, illness and frequent childbirth, the terrors of the Mutiny, as well as some gay and happy moments; and they have revealed her disillusionment with Archie, who, despite the excuses one can make for him, was undoubtedly a pompous, selfish and ineffectual creature. She had said very little to his detriment in her letters to her mother, but now, in 1860, and after the birth of her third child in three years, she lets the truth come out.

Her life must have been insufferable. She was living in army circles in which social occasions, dress and the mode of behaviour meant so much. Her grinding poverty and perpetual embarrassments over money must have been a terrible trial and shame. It is obvious that Mrs Blane, living in the security of Bath, did not fully understand the circumstances, and this was another sorrow for Minnie.

Even in her worst moments Minnie still showed courage; and though she is at last driven to pour out her griefs to her mother, in the same paragraph she is able to hope that brighter days will come.

Simla, 4 June, 1860

My dearest Mama,

I need hardly say that your last two letters about our debts have distressed me beyond measure. I see exactly the position we are in, and I can do nothing. The price of everything has increased enormously.

Captain Wood is now very busy with his Hindustanee and goes up for his examination on the 10th July. Heaven knows what we shall do if he does not pass and so get a better appointment. Our affairs are now in that mess that unless he gets more pay he will have to sell out of the army. He is so frightfully negligent about his money matters, and allows everything to go on year after year without attending to them, and now I find out that we are in a most precarious position.

Do not think, dear Mama, I am telling this for the sake of worrying you, but it is a relief to me to unburden my mind. Rarely do I lie down at night that my thoughts and anxieties are too much for me. If only I could run away from it all.

I blush for the negligent way in which my husband goes on, yet if I broach the subject of our affairs he gets into dreadful passions, tells me he is sick of me and I am to leave the room as he will not be dictated to, and many other things which make my heart break.

Oh, dear Mama, it is no good hiding it from you any more that we are much in debt, not from extravagance, but from allowing bills to stand over month after month, year after year, and Archie just tossing them aside, and saying they may write again. The interest then rises frightfully. I have not the slightest influence now. I have begged him to write you the truth, but he will not. I am quite despairing, and were it not for my children I would not remain here another day. My husband's temper is so changed, and the least difference of opinion makes him so furious that I find the best way is to leave him to himself, for the epithets that are used to me are most awful. Would that I had listened to your advice and not married in such a hurry.

After you, who are so particular in business matters, it astonishes me to see a man so perfectly blinded to the position he is now in, constantly being hauled up before the Civil Court to pay bills. It makes me wretched to see how he is going on. He is lazy and apathetic, never joining with other men, but just moping at home and sleeping. He has no ambition.

> Goodbye and God bless you, dearest Mama,
> Your ever affectionate daughter,
> Minnie Wood

Very few letters survive during the next year. Those that do are full of worry and heartbreak for poor Minnie. She makes great efforts to look on the bright side, and to comfort herself with her children, but things go from bad to worse.

In August 1860, Minnie writes:

I am in great distress for my head ayah is leaving me, all because her husband, who is Sirdar to Captain Wood, was found fault with for not having the Captain's clothes aired. That woman is invaluable to me. What shall I do?

Captain Wood has been ill again and not allowed to take anything except Port Wine and water. This wine is 48 rupees a dozen, or £4.16s.

Captain Wood has failed his examination but will take it again. I am sorry as he did work hard recently. He does almost nothing and I cannot stir him up, indeed his health is now so bad and he is so weakened from his complaint that I consider it cruel to do so. He is most irritable. Indeed, were it not for my boys my heart would break.

You will be quite tired reading this stupid letter, but I go out nowhere and have no happy news.

Cecil sends his love to 'Ganmama',

Your affectionate child,

Minnie Wood

29 August

My dearest Mama,

God knows I wish from the bottom of my heart that I had never married. Captain Wood never thinks of consequences, and everything is done on the spur of the moment. My temper is quite soured from the intense worry I have, and of course Captain Wood's is the same, as these are the fruits of our marriage.

Our house is one continuous scene of noise, servants being scolded by Captain Wood, children crying, indeed I do not wonder at all at people who, when badly in debt, put an end to themselves.

I get no allowance from Captain Wood and there is a scene each time I or the children need new clothes, as we do frequently in this climate where things wear out so quickly.

Surely, Mama, there must be a little money from the six shares Papa left me in Australia? This would prevent some unpleasantness for me.

My clothes are worn out and my bonnets are dirty. You would not like me to go out looking dirty, but my husband will pay for nothing.

I feel so much at being debarred from joining in amusements with other people. On the 1st of September we are to dine at the Bishop's, an invitation we could not refuse.

Captain Wood tells everyone that he married me because he thought I was an heiress. I do not like it. If I reason with him I am told I am 'a mad woman', and as to discussing our affairs that is out of the question, for he flies into a rage and slams the door in my face.

My heart is full and ready to burst, my dearest Mama, and there is no one to talk to but you. My darling children are my only comfort out here.

Your fondly attached child,

Minnie Wood

A letter written in October 1860 is the last to survive. No doubt there were later ones which either got lost, or, through the typically Victorian habit of hiding family scandals, were destroyed by Mrs Blane. This letter throws light on the final break-up of poor Minnie's first marriage.

Simla, 10 October

My dearest Mama,

Your letter about Cissy's marriage came today. I so hope that when she is Mrs Dawn she will not find out at the end of four years that her husband is not all that she thought him to be. I hope and trust she may be as happy as she is now to the end. Mr Dawn seems to be a gentlemanly and nice man, and they have more means to start with than I had.

The rest of this letter must be entirely on business matters. The time has come when I must know my exact position, and all the points which were made in my marriage settlement. I took no interest then, but now I must know.

In the first place I do not understand what you wrote in this last letter of yours to me. You say, 'I have given Cissy £50 a year, like I gave you, but not the principal.'

Am I to understand that my money has been touched by Captain Wood to pay his debts? I hope and trust this is not the case, for if it exists, it should be entirely in my power to use for the benefit of myself and my children, for whom Captain Wood can do nothing. I have my darling children to think of and shrink from believing that Captain Wood has been using the money I did not know I had.

Captain Wood allows me no regular allowance and the consequence is whenever I buy anything there is an awful row. Bills flood in, he has not the money to pay, the trades people are abused, and it all ends up in the Civil Courts. We can hardly keep a servant, and there is constant bickering and fighting in our home.

Yet Captain Wood has the most sanguine expectations and wrote on my last letter to you that he would shortly be sending you £100! Sooner or later a crisis must come, and then what?

I pray my husband may pass his exam, for then we might see our way. Otherwise it will be only misery, and perhaps prison before us, and that is the truth.

Dear Mama, this letter is not enlivening, but to you alone can I pour out my griefs. I cannot much longer endure this anxiety. If only we could take the children home, but we have not the means.

I need warm stockings for the winter. I am so afraid of getting that terrible rheumatism again.

So Napoleon has had an attempt made to assassinate him! These French are always up to something.

Now, dearest Mama, do not fail to tell me what I have asked. Perhaps brighter days are in store for us, and also dear Willie will be with me soon, and that gives me so much hope and happiness to contemplate.

Your fondly attached child,
Minnie Wood

Minnie was busy with preparations for her brother's coming when letters arrived telling of his landing in Bombay and his progress up country to join her.

Then a letter came from a Captain Attley in Meerut with the news that her beloved Willie had died of cholera on the previous day, just after his arrival there.

The captain had written: 'Your poor brother was attended by two doctors, and was kindly watched and nursed by three brother officers. The progress of the disease was so rapid that he was unable to leave any directions, or even avail himself of the services of a clergyman. He was taken ill in the evening, and died in the early hours of the next morning. He was buried that evening, followed by all his brother officers to the grave which is bricked inside and out. Any memorial you wish can be erected over it. I enclose a lock of hair in this letter. . . .'

Minnie was heartbroken; and the next thing we know is the startling fact that she had left India, without her precious children, and was on her way to England.

Epilogue

What was the final cause of Minnie's sudden departure in October 1861 we shall never know. It must have been something desperate, as it is quite out of character for her to leave her three sons behind as she did.

Did life with Archie become totally unbearable? Was her brother's death the last straw? Did the fact that she was carrying her fourth child break her nerve? Had Mrs Blane sent her the money for her fare? Or did she, as she had wished in a letter of June 1860, at last 'run away from it all'?

All we know is that when these letters were discovered in a long-forgotten box by her son, Cecil, in 1916, he was unable to read Minnie's final letter from India without tears, and destroyed it by fire so that no one else 'should see her terrible depth of misery'.

By 16 November Minnie was at Suez in the P and O vessel S.S. *Nemesis*, where her daughter Ada was born.

Dr Cresswell, M.R.C.S., L.S.A. wrote to Mrs Blane to tell her that 'Mrs Wood was unable to continue her voyage as she had been delivered of a daughter on the 2nd of November 1861. Everything proceeded favourably until the 12th, when she overtaxed her strength by packing boxes, etc. Fainting and high fever followed, necessitating perfect quiet and rendering her quite incapable of moving. This serious indisposition is now putting on a favourable appearance, and all the symptoms are ameliorated. Be assured, dear Madam, that all that skill, good nursing and careful attention will do, will be done for her, and I sincerely trust that she will be able to proceed on the Mail after this, viz. in about a fortnight. I will write more fully by the earliest opportunity.'

On 25 November Dr Cresswell wrote again that Minnie's

183

progress was good. He says: 'I will, dear Madam, accompany her across the desert in the carriage used for the purpose of reaching Port Said, and see her on to the ship there. When the canal is made, travel will be much less fatiguing.'

Minnie went to her mother in Bath, and about eighteen months later Archie returned to England with the three boys. Very soon after their arrival the boys were with Mrs Blane and Minnie in Bath. They were brought up there, becoming deeply devoted to both their mother and grandmother, and they all did well in life. Cecil was the father of Miss Scobell Wood, the owner of these intriguing letters.

Archie returned to India and became a lieutenant-colonel. He divorced Minnie in 1874, and married a widow with a down-trodden daughter. He retired to Sydenham where he died in 1895, aged seventy-six.

For Minnie, her later years were her happiest. In 1874 she married Colonel Vyvyan of the 7th Bengal Native Infantry, and it was a very happy marriage. They returned to India until Colonel Vyvyan retired in 1887, then settled in Naples with Minnie's daughter, Ada. Two years later in 1889 Minnie died.

An extract from Colonel Vyvyan's letter to Seymour, Minnie's youngest son, shall be her epitaph:

Your dear mother passed away at 2 a.m., the 28th of January. By her sweet, calm face, lit up by a smile, I know that her last moments must have been those of peace. She was very beautiful in death.

Note

The originals of these letters are on long loan to the India Office Library, where they lie beside a unique collection of personal records of lives and an Empire long vanished.

INDEX

Anson, General, Commander-in-Chief, 86

Bath, assembly rooms, 9; Blane residence at 8 Pultney Street, 9
Bathwick Church, 10
Blane, Archibald, father of Minnie, birth in 1788, Civil Service career, marriage, residence in Slough, 1; with Water and Milk Company, 7; Deputy Governor of Australian Agricultural Commission, death in Australia, memorial to, 9; grave at Kensal Green, 22, 64
Blane, Archibald, brother of Minnie, 1839-57, at Salt Hill, 1; death of, 63
Blane, Cecilia (Cissy), sister of Minnie, at school, 1-8; at Bath, 9-10; in London, 22; marriage in 1860, 180
Blane, Mrs Magdalene, née Broughton, mother of Minnie, her descent, marriage, children, 1; husband's death, move to Bath, 9; as grandmother, 184
Blane, Maria Lydia (Minnie), 1835-89, early letters, 1-8; father's death, move to Bath, 9; meets Archibald Wood, 10-11; marriage, 12; see Wood, Maria Lydia
Blane, Robert, brother of Minnie, 1844-1918, at Salt Hill, 1; at Bath, 23
Blane, Seymour, 52nd Regiment at Delhi, 116
Blane, William, brother of Minnie, 1843-61, at Salt Hill, 1; career, 174, 175; arrival in India, death from cholera, 181-2

Broughton, Mr and Mrs, uncle and aunt of Minnie, visit to Breakwater Lighthouse, 6

Calcutta, description of, Henry Wood's Garden House, 47-49; Government House, 53; journey from Calcutta to Lahore, 54-5
Campbell, Sir Colin, Commander-in-Chief during Indian Mutiny, 137
Canning, Lord, Governor-General of India, 58; his policy, 59, 60
Carshore, Doctor, 127
Cockburne, Mr and Mrs, 52
Cole, Doctor, 102, 109, 114-15, 120
Cracroft, Mr and Mrs, 159, 160, 161
Cresswell, Doctor, 183-4

Dalhousie, Lord, Governor-General of India, 55, 58-9
Dawn, Captain William, 1st Dragoon Guards, married to Cissy Blane in 1860, 180
Delhi, rising, 81; assault on, 111; recapture of, 115
Dum Dum, 52, 57

East India Company, The, 11-12, 58-61; official end of, 167-8

Gerrard, Colonel, 87, 95, 101-2, 126, 170
Grigg, Miss Emma, 1-8
Gugerat, 66

Hengler's Royal Circus, 4
Hewetson, General, 22

186